KANT'S ETHICAL THOUGHT

This is a major new study of Kant's ethics that will transform the way students and scholars approach the subject in the future.

Allen Wood argues that Kant's ethical vision is grounded in the idea of the dignity of the rational nature of every human being. Undergoing both natural competitiveness and social antagonism, the human species, according to Kant, develops the rational capacity to struggle against its impulses, toward a human community in which the ends of all are to harmonize and coincide.

The distinctive features of the book are twofold. First, it focuses for the first time on the central role played in Kant's ethical theory by the value of rational nature as an end in itself. Second, it shows the importance of Kant's systematic theory of human nature and history and its implications for the structure, formulation, and application of Kant's moral principles.

This comprehensive study will be of critical importance to students of moral philosophy, the history of ideas, political theory, and religious studies.

Allen W. Wood is Professor of Philosophy at Yale University.

MODERN EUROPEAN PHILOSOPHY

General Editor

Robert B. Pippin, *University of Chicago*

Advisory Board

Gary Gutting, *University of Notre Dame*
Rolf-Peter Horstmann, *Humboldt University, Berlin*
Mark Sacks, *University of Essex*

This series contains a range of high-quality books on philosophers, topics, and schools of thought prominent in the Kantian and post-Kantian European tradition. It is nonsectarian in approach and methodology, and includes both introductory and more specialized treatments of these thinkers and topics. Authors are encouraged to interpret the boundaries of the modern European tradition in a broad way and in primarily philosophical rather than historical terms.

Some Recent Titles:

Frederick A. Olafson: *What Is a Human Being?*
Stanley Rosen: *The Mask of Enlightenment: Nietzsche's Zarathustra*
Robert C. Scharff: *Comte after Positivism*
F. C. T. Moore: *Bergson: Thinking Backwards*
Charles Larmore: *The Morals of Modernity*
Robert B. Pippin: *Idealism as Modernism*
Daniel W. Conway: *Nietzsche's Dangerous Game*
John P. McCormick: *Carl Schmitt's Critique of Liberalism*
Frederick A. Olafson: *Heidegger and the Ground of Ethics*
Günter Zöller: *Fichte's Transcendental Philosophy*
Warren Breckman: *Marx, the Young Hegelians, and the Origins of Radical Social Theory*
William Blattner: *Heidegger's Temporal Idealism*
Charles Griswold: *Adam Smith and the Virtues of Enlightenment*
Gary Gutting: *Pragmatic Liberalism and the Critique of Modernity*

KANT'S ETHICAL THOUGHT

ALLEN W. WOOD
Yale University

CAMBRIDGE UNIVERSITY PRESS
Cambridge, New York, Melbourne, Madrid, Cape Town, Singapore, São Paulo

Cambridge University Press
The Edinburgh Building, Cambridge CB2 2RU, UK

Published in the United States of America by Cambridge University Press, New York

www.cambridge.org
Information on this title: www.cambridge.org/9780521640565

First published 1999

A catalogue record for this publication is available from the British Library

Library of Congress Cataloguing in Publication data
Wood, Allen W.
Kant's ethical thought / Allen W. Wood.
p.   cm. – (Modern European philosophy)
ISBN 0-521-64056-3 (hc.). – ISBN 0-521-64836-X (pbk.)
1. Kant, Immanuel, 1724–1804 – Contributions in ethics.   I. Title.
II. Series.
B2799.E8W59   1999
170'.92 – dc21   98-32168
                                                                         CIP

ISBN-13 978-0-521-64056-5 hardback
ISBN-10 0-521-64056-3 hardback

ISBN-13 978-0-521-64836-3 paperback
ISBN-10 0-521-64836-X paperback

Transferred to digital printing 2006

To the memory of my parents

Alleen Blumberg Wood
April 18, 1906–July 28, 1986

Forrest E. Wood
July 2, 1909–February 4, 1998

CONTENTS

Preface   *page* xiii

Abbreviations   xvii
   Citations   xvii
   Formulas and propositions   xx
   Table of duties of virtue   xxiv

Introduction   1
  1 An Enlightenment moralist   1
  2 Human equality   5
  3 Morality and human nature   8
  4 Kant's ethical writings   11
  5 The structure of this book   13

I   METAPHYSICAL FOUNDATIONS

1 Common rational moral cognition   17
  1 Grounding ethical theory   17
  2 The good will   21
  3 Acting from duty   26
  4 Moral worth and maxims   40
  5 Respect for law   42

2 Rational will and imperatives   50
  1 The will   50
  2 *A priori* practical principles   55
  3 Hypothetical imperatives   60
  4 Assertoric imperatives   65
  5 Categorical imperatives   70

3   The formula of universal law   76
    1 Objective practical principles   76
    2 The derivation of FUL and FLN   78
    3 Applying FLN: suicide   82
    4 False promises and converted deposits   87
    5 Rusting talents   90
    6 Refusing to help   91
    7 The problems with FUL   97
    8 Exceptional behavior and self-preference   107

4   The formula of humanity as end in itself   111
    1 Ends and determining grounds of the will   111
    2 Ends in themselves and existent ends   114
    3 Humanity and personality   118
    4 Things and persons   122
    5 Kant's derivation of FH   124
    6 The equal worth of all rational beings   132
    7 Applying FH   139
    8 The structure of arguments from FH   150

5   The formula of autonomy and the realm of ends   156
    1 The ground of obligation   156
    2 FA as a moral principle   163
    3 The realm of ends   165
    4 Freedom and the moral law   171
    5 Formulating the moral law   182

II   ANTHROPOLOGICAL APPLICATIONS

6   The study of human nature   193
    1 Practical anthropology   193
    2 The difficulty of self-knowledge   196
    3 Pragmatic anthropology   202
    4 Human history as a natural phenomenon   207
    5 Natural teleology   215

7   The history of human nature   226
    1 Herder vs. Kant   226
    2 Historical conjectures   233
    3 The first free choice   235
    4 The origin of morality   238
    5 Kant's historical materialism   244

8   Human inclinations and affections   250
    1 Natural desire   250
    2 Natural passions   253
    3 Social passions   259
    4 Desire and deception   265
    5 Sympathy, love, and charity   269
    6 Friendship   275

9   The historical vocation of morality   283
    1 The radical evil in human nature   283
    2 Nature and culture   291
    3 Reason, communication, and enlightenment   300
    4 The ethical community   309

    Conclusion   321
    1 The final form of Kant's ethical theory   321
    2 The sphere of right   322
    3 Ethics as a system of duties   323
    4 Ethics as a system of ends   325
    5 Ethics as virtue   329
    6 What is Kantian ethics about?   333

Notes   337
Index   419

PREFACE

The ideas for this book were already taking shape in the 1980s, while I was at work on *Hegel's Ethical Thought*.[1] There I tried to present Hegel's critique of Kant in a way that was accurate and fair to both philosophers, but as the work progressed I became increasingly aware how difficult this would be. I realized from the beginning that Hegel's criticisms of the Kantian principle of morality do not entirely succeed because, like most of Kant's readers, Hegel attended exclusively to the Formula of Universal Law, ignoring the other formulations, which are more adequate statements of the principle.[2] I also began to see that on the deeper issues that separate the two philosophers, Kant's position is grounded on a distinctive theory of human nature and history, whose importance for Kant's ethics has seldom been appreciated. In some ways this theory anticipates Hegel's own philosophy of history, but it also provides a compelling explanation for Kant's notorious view that natural inclinations are a "counterweight" to moral reason (G 4:405) rather than being (as Hegel thinks) an expression of reason. I decided to write a book on Kant's ethical thought when I realized that along with the overemphasis on the Formula of Universal Law, the neglect of Kant's empirical theory of human nature and history is responsible for most of the misunderstandings of Kant's ethical thought that prevail among its supporters as well as its critics.

The picture of Kantian ethics that emerges is, I think, not only a more accurate historical portrait but a deeper and more engaging ethical view than that with which Kant is usually credited. While I do mount my own criticisms of Kant's ethical theory in some of its details, I argue that many familiar objections to it are based on serious misunderstandings of Kant's position. Here I chiefly criticize the overemphasis on the Formula of Universal Law, when it is taken as the definitive expression of the principle grounding Kant's ethical theory and as most authentically characterizing its conception of moral reasoning.[3] Under this heading I also place the common charges that Kantian ethics is unconcerned with the empirical realities of psychology, society, and history, that it sees no value in the affective side of our nature, and that it is individualistic both in its conception of moral agency and in its moral conclusions. In all these cases, I think the truth is exactly the reverse. At other points I try to show Kant's detractors that even where they may continue to reject some Kantian doctrines even after they have properly understood them, these doctrines are nevertheless far more thoughtful and well-grounded than they realize. Under this rubric I place Kant's theses that ethics must be founded on an *a priori* principle of reason, that natural inclinations generally require rational constraint, which only the motive of duty is adequate to provide, that our natural desire for happiness is more a foe than an ally of morality, and that feelings such as love and sympathy, though beautiful and amiable, are unworthy of moral esteem.

These aims are carried out by emphasizing some crucial features of Kant's theory whose centrality is not fully appreciated or whose very presence is often barely recognized. At the top of that list is Kant's conception of human dignity: the absolute, hence equal, worth of all rational beings. The list also includes the following: a theory of the historical development of human culture, including economic forms, social relationships, customary morality, and the political state; a shrewd, penetrating analysis of the psychological and social meaning of familiar human dispositions, inclinations, and passions; and the indispensable importance for the moral life of free rational communication, the intimacy of friendship, a community of shared collective ends, and an enlightened, progressive organized religion.

In the past twenty years, my interest has been drawn back to Kant's ethical thought also by my experience of the present age. Our time (the twentieth century, and especially its last two decades) has been, and still is, a disillusioning time in which to live. The social, political, and intellectual climate of my country (and therefore of the globe over which it tyrannizes) has grown blinder, nastier, more irrational. The always dominant economic and political structures have become increasingly wealthy, powerful, arrogant, ambitious, greedy, and shortsighted. As life becomes harder and more hopeless for those excluded from these structures, large numbers of people turn back to old enthusiasms and superstitions, which are usually the pretext for outgrown passions and

old hatreds. Ancient and parochial forms of community reassert themselves because the only order presenting itself as new and rational is
devoid of any genuine community, since it holds people together only
by entangling them in a confused nexus of unbridled power and self-
interest. Progressive social movements, whose vocation has been to build
a free community grounded on the rational dignity of all human beings, must now use their whole strength and courage merely to survive
in a world grown hostile to them. The job of intellectuals is to oppose
unreason, speak truth to power, and think the way toward a genuine
community. Some, as always, choose instead to apologize for the rationally indefensible; but too many others in our age are caught up in
the fashionable mood of irony, absurdity, and self-destruction because
they have lost confidence in the mind's authority over human life and
its power to find better ways for people to live.

At such a time it is not difficult to see some truth in Kant's somber
account of the evil in human nature. It even becomes easier to sympathize with his stern, moralistic insistence that people must subject their
ways of thinking to rational criticism and reform their ways of acting
through a fundamental change of heart. Still more than that, however,
the age needs Kant's sober, principled hope for a more rational, cosmopolitan future. In other words, we need to recapture an authentically Enlightenment conception of the human condition, especially an
interpretation of that conception that makes clear the Enlightenment's
still unrealized radical potential.

My first attempt to deal with the themes of this book was a paper written in 1989.[4] Work on the book itself began in 1992, while I was living
in Bonn. During the next six years, while the book was being written, this
work spawned ten more papers dealing with themes in Kant's ethics,
political philosophy, and philosophy of history. Three of them have been
at least partly incorporated into the present book.[5] The other seven
were originally conceived as parts of it but were eventually excluded in
order to keep the book's size within reasonable limits.[6] For like reasons
of economy in exposition, a number of important discussions have also
been relegated to the endnotes. Despite their length and their exile to
the back of the book, I urge readers not to neglect them entirely.

My research in Bonn was supported by the National Endowment for
the Humanities. There I was affiliated with Philosophisches Seminar A,
Rheinisch-Friedrich-Wilhelms-Universität, Bonn. I want to thank its
Director, Professor Hans-Michael Baumgartner, and two of its academic
administrators, Eduard Gerresheim and Thomas Zwenger, for their

help and cooperation. Philosophisches Seminar B and its Director, Professor Ludger Honnefelder, were also generously supportive. Particularly useful in my work for this book was the opportunity to speak on and discuss Kant a number of times in Germany and Austria. I would like to thank Dieter Schönecker, Rudolf Teuwsen, and Ingrid Rissom for helping me prepare lectures in presentable German.

Paul Guyer, Thaddeus Metz, Onora O'Neill, and Jerome B. Schneewind served as official commentators on papers I gave on themes in Kant's ethics; their remarks led to improvements in this book. Andrews Reath and Dieter Schönecker gave me helpful comments on a draft of Part I, and Brian Jacobs on a draft of Chapter 6. My wife Rega Wood was supportive and helpful in many ways, and my son Stephen Wood saved me more than once from computer glitches. Kelly Sorensen helped with proofreading.

There have also been countless discussions with colleagues and students at Cornell and Yale Universities, participants and questioners at conferences I have attended, and lectures I have given in North America, the European Union, the island of Taiwan, and the region where Kant lived. There are literally dozens of passages where I could name the individual whose challenging question or objection they try to address. Without the input of those people the present book, whatever its actual merits and defects, would have been much poorer. In some conspicuous cases I have thanked particular individuals in endnotes. I tried to prepare a list of all the people to whom I owe this sort of gratitude, but gave up when it ballooned to over a hundred names and I knew it was still not complete. I would like to think that many of those individuals will one day cross paths with this book. When they do, I hope they will recognize their questions or objections. Whether or not they find my responses satisfying, I hope they will at least know that they have my gratitude and that they will accept my apology for not thanking them by name. Beyond expressing gratitude to individuals, I also offer the thought that the generally high level and the cooperative spirit of all these discussions shows that Kant studies in our time is a field of conspicuous scholarly and philosophical excellence, of whose collective achievements all who labor in it may be justly proud.

ABBREVIATIONS

Citations:

Ak   *Immanuel Kants Schriften*. Ausgabe der königlich preussischen Akademie der Wissenschaften (Berlin: W. de Gruyter, 1902–). Unless otherwise footnoted, writings of Immanuel Kant will be cited by volume:page number in this edition.

Ca   *Cambridge Edition of the Writings of Immanuel Kant* (New York: Cambridge University Press, 1992–). Most English translations now include Ak pagination, and all writings of Kant available in English are (or presently will be) available in this edition with marginal Ak volume:page citations. Specific works will be cited using the following system of abbreviations (works not abbreviated below will be cited simply as Ak volume: page):

AN   *Allgemeine Naturgeschichte und Theorie des Himmels* (1755), Ak 1
Universal natural history and theory of the heavens, Ca Natural Science

BM   *Bestimmung des Begriffs einer Menschenrace*, Ak 8
Determination of the concept of a race of human beings, Ca Anthropology, History and Education

BS   *Beobachtungen über das Gefühl des Schönen und Erhabenen* (1764), Ak 2
Observations on the feeling of the beautiful and sublime, Ca Anthropology, History and Education

D   Inaugural Dissertation: *De mundi sensibilis atque intelligibilis forma et principiis* (1770), Ak 2
On the form and principles of the sensible and the intelligible world, Ca Theoretical Philosophy before 1781

DG   *Untersuchung über die Deutlichkeit der Grundsätze der natürlichen Theologie und der Moral* (1764), Ak 2
Inquiry concerning the distinctness of the principles of natural theology and morality, Ca Theoretical Philosophy before 1781

ED   *Das Ende aller Dinge* (1794), Ak 8
The end of all things, Ca Religion and Rational Theology

EF   *Zum ewigen Frieden: Ein philosophischer Entwurf* (1795), Ak 8
Toward perpetual peace: A philosophical project, Ca Practical Philosophy

G   *Grundlegung zur Metaphysik der Sitten* (1785), Ak 4
Groundwork of the metaphysics of morals, Ca Practical Philosophy

I   *Idee zu einer allgemeinen Geschichte in weltbürgerlicher Absicht* (1784), Ak 8
Idea toward a universal history with a cosmopolitan aim, Ca Anthropology, History and Education

KrV   *Kritik der reinen Vernunft* (1781, 1787). Cited by A/B pagination.
Critique of pure reason, Ca Critique of Pure Reason

KpV   *Kritik der praktischen Vernunft* (1788), Ak 5
Critique of practical reason, Ca Practical Philosophy

KU   *Kritik der Urteilskraft* (1790), Ak 5
Critique of the power of judgment, Ca Aesthetics and Teleology

MA   *Mutmaßlicher Anfang der Menschengeschichte* (1786), Ak 8
Conjectural beginning of human history, Ca Anthropology, History and Education

MS   *Metaphysik der Sitten* (1797–1798), Ak 6
Metaphysics of morals, Ca Practical Philosophy

O   *Was heißt: Sich im Denken orientieren?* (1786), Ak 8
What does it mean to orient oneself in thinking? Ca Religion and Rational Theology

R   *Religion innerhalb der Grenzen der bloßen Vernunft* (1793–1794), Ak 6
Religion within the boundaries of mere reason, Ca Religion and Rational Theology
When followed by a four-digit number and a citation to Ak, "R" abbreviates "Reflexion" from Kant's *handschriftliche Nachlaß* (or handwritten literary remains).

RH   *Recensionen von J. G. Herders Ideen zur Philosophie der Geschichte der Menschheit*, Ak 8
Reviews of J. G. Herder's Ideas toward the philosophy of the history of humanity, Ca Anthropology, History, and Education

RM   *Von den verschiedenen Racen der Menschen*, Ak 2.
       The different races of human beings, Ca Anthropology History
       and Education

SF   *Streit der Fakultäten* (1798), Ak 7
       Conflict of the faculties, Ca Religion and Rational Theology

TP   *Über den Gemeinspruch: Das mag in der Theorie richtig sein, taugt
       aber nicht für die Praxis* (1793), Ak 8
       *On the common saying: That may be correct in theory but it is of no
       use in practice*, Ca Practical Philosophy

UE   *Über eine Entdeckung, nach der alle neue Kritik der reinen Ver-
       nunft durch eine ältere enbehrlich gemacht werden soll* (1790),
       Ak 8
       *On a discovery according to which every new critique of pure rea-
       son is made dispensable by an older one*, Ca Theoretical Philos-
       ophy after 1781

VA   *Anthropologie in pragmatischer Hinsicht* (1798), Ak 7
       Anthropology from a pragmatic standpoint, Ca Anthropology,
       History and Education
       Vorlesungen über Anthropologie, Ak 25
       Lectures on anthropology, Ca Lectures on Anthropology

VE   *Vorlesungen über Ethik*, Ak 27
       Lectures on ethics, Ca Lectures on Ethics

VL   *Vorlesungen über Logik*, Ak 9, 24
       Lectures on logic, Ca Lectures on Logic

VP   *Pädagogik*, Ak 9
       Lectures on pedagogy, Ca Anthropology, History and Education

VPG   *Physische Geographie*, Ak 9.
       Lectures on physical geography, Ca Writings on Natural Science

VpR   *Vorlesungen über die philosophische Religionslehre*, Ak 28
       Lectures on the philosophical doctrine of religion, Ca Religion and
       Rational Theology

WA   *Beantwortung der Frage: Was ist Aufklärung?* (1784), Ak 8
       An answer to the question: What is enlightenment? Ca Practical
       Philosophy

Rousseau Writings of Jean-Jacques Rousseau will be cited by En-
       glish title and by volume:page in Jean-Jacques Rousseau,
       Oeuvres complètes (Paris: Bibliothèque de la Pléiade,
       1962–).

Herder Writings of Johann Gottfried Herder will be cited by volume:
       page in *Herders Sämmtliche Werke*, ed., B. Suphan (Berlin:
       Weidmann, 1881–1913).

Formulas and propositions:

Formulas of the moral law   Kant formulates the moral law in three principal ways. The first and third of these have variants which are intended
to bring the law "closer to intuition" and make it easier to apply. These
five principal formulations of the moral law will be abbreviated as follows.

FIRST FORMULA:

FUL   *The Formula of Universal Law.* "Act only in accordance with
            that maxim through which you can at the same time will
            that it become a universal law" (G 4:421; cf. 4:402);

with its variant,

FLN   *The Formula of the Law of Nature.* "Act as if the maxim of your
            action were to become by your will a universal law of nature"
            (G 4:421; cf. 4:436).

SECOND FORMULA:

FH   *The Formula of Humanity as End in Itself.* "*So act that you use hu-
            manity, whether in your own person or that of another, always at the
            same time as an end, never merely as a means*" (G 4:429; cf. 4:436).

THIRD FORMULA:

FA   *The Formula of Autonomy:* ". . . the idea of the will of every ra-
            tional being as a will giving universal law" (G 4:431; cf.
            4:432); or "Choose only in such a way that the maxims of
            your choice are also included as universal law in the same
            volition" (G 4:439; cf. 4:432, 434, 438);

with its variant,

FRE   *The Formula of the Realm of Ends:* "Act in accordance with the
            maxims of a universally legislative member of a merely pos-
            sible realm of ends" (G 4:439; cf. 4:432, 437, 438).

Following is a preliminary form of FUL:

CI   Adopt only maxims that conform to universal law as such
            (cf. G 4:421).

In Chapter 3, I argue that unlike FUL and FLN, CI actually follows from
the mere concept of a good will and a categorical imperative.

A "universal formula of the categorical imperative" (G 4:436–437)
(which I argue is to be read as a version of FA, not of FUL) is given in
all Kant's major ethical works:

FG   "Act in accordance with a maxim that can at the same time make itself a universal law" (G 4:437).

FK   "So act that the maxim of your action could always at the same time hold (*gelten*) as a principle of universal legislation" (KpV 5:30).

FM   "Act upon a maxim that can also hold as a universal law" (MS 6:225).

In addition, Kant's theory of right is grounded on the following principle:

R   *Principle of Right:* "Any action is right if it can coexist with everyone's freedom according to a universal law, or if on its maxim the freedom of choice of each can coexist with everyone's freedom in accordance with a universal law" (MS 6:230).

Deduction of the moral law

Kant's deduction of the moral law is treated in Chapter 5 § 4. It is based on the "Reciprocity Thesis," a mutual entailment between the following two propositions:

F   The rational will is free.

M   The moral law is unconditionally valid for the rational will.

Thus the Reciprocity Thesis is: F↔M. I interpret Kant as arguing that F is a necessary presupposition of rational judgment. Then using F together with half of the Reciprocity Thesis, namely,

F→M   If the rational will is free, then the moral law is unconditionally valid for it

he infers that M.

Nonmoral principles of reason

In Chapter 2, I also formulate three nonmoral *a priori* principles of reason:

EI   *The Imperative of Ends:* If you set an end Z (and as long as you retain Z as an end), then if possible perform some set of actions which will foreseeably result in the attainment of Z, and refrain from any action which would preclude the attainment of Z.

HI   *The Hypothetical Imperative.* If you set an end Z, perform what-
            ever actions are indispensably necessary means to the at-
            tainment of Z which lie in your power (cf. G 4:414–417).

PI   *The Pragmatic (or Prudential) Imperative:* Form an idea for your-
            self of the greatest achievable sum of your empirical satisfac-
            tion (under the name 'happiness') and make happiness your
            end, preferring it over any limited empirical satisfaction.

Maxims

The following maxims are discussed in Chapter 3 (some occasionally
later):

M1   "From self-love I make it my principle to shorten my life
            when by longer duration it threatens more ill than agree-
            ableness" (G 4:422).

M2   "When I believe myself to be in need of money, I will bor-
            row money and promise to repay it, although I know I will
            never do so" (G 4:422).

Md   "I will increase my property by every safe means" (KpV 5:27;
            cf. TP 8:286–287).

M3   I will neglect the development of my talents and instead de-
            vote my life entirely to idleness and pleasure (cf. G 4:422–
            423).

M4   I will do nothing to harm others or deprive them of what is
            rightfully theirs, but I will refuse to help them or participate
            in their aims unless the assistance they need from me is one
            I owe them by strict right (cf. G 4:423).

Mv   "I will not tolerate any unavenged insult" (KpV 5:19).

Mk   I will kill other human beings whenever that is a safe and ef-
            fective way of promoting my own self-interest.

Ma   "I will buy a clockwork train, but never sell one."

Mb   "In order to avoid crowded tennis courts, I will play on Sun-
            day mornings (when my neighbors are in church and the
            courts are free)."

Mb'   I will make use of what others may be expected to do in or-
            der to secure advantages for myself.

Mc   "When the Dow-Jones average reaches the next thousand, I
            will sell all my stocks."

Teleological judgment

Kant's theory of teleological judgment is based on the following *principle of natural teleology*:

NT: *An organized product of nature is one in which everything is an end and reciprocally also a means"* (KU 5:376). This involves the assumption: "Nothing in such a being is in vain (*umsonst*)" (KU 5:376, 379, 437). "Regarding [living beings], reason must assume as a necessary principle that no organ, no faculty, nothing superfluous, or disproportionate to its use, hence nothing purposeless is to be encountered, but rather that everything is to be judged as precisely suitable to its function" (KrV B425).

NT grounds various maxims of teleological judgment, including the following:

NT1   If F is a feeling whose naturally purposive function is to bring about P, then it would be self-contradictory to suppose a system of nature one of whose laws is that under certain circumstances F systematically produces the contrary of P (cf. G 4:422).

NT2   "In the natural constitution of an organized being, . . . we assume as a principle that there will be found in it no instrument for some end other than what is also most appropriate to that end and best adapted to it" (G 4:395, cf. 4:398).

NT3   "Nature arranges things so that eventually all the natural predispositions of an organism are fully developed" (I 8:18).

DUTIES OF VIRTUE

The complete taxonomy of duties of virtue (Conclusion, § 3) is represented in the following table:

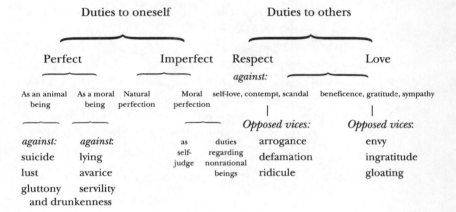

Duties to oneself					Duties to others	
Perfect		Imperfect		Respect		Love
				against:		
As an animal being	As a moral being	Natural perfection	Moral perfection	self-love, contempt, scandal		beneficence, gratitude, sympathy
				Opposed vices:		*Opposed vices:*
against:	*against:*		as self-judge	arrogance		envy
suicide	lying		duties regarding nonrational beings	defamation		ingratitude
lust	avarice			ridicule		gloating
gluttony and drunkenness	servility					

INTRODUCTION

1. An Enlightenment moralist

Kant's ethical thought is perhaps both the finest and the most characteristic product of the Enlightenment (*Aufklärung, éclaircissement*). This was an intellectual movement, and to some extent also a social and political movement. In its original form it accompanied, reflected, and contributed to the European bourgeoisie's growing economic, social, and political power and influence. But the Enlightenment was never committed to the interests of a single social class, nation, or segment of humanity. The Enlightenment still exists today, since many people throughout the world still struggle for the expansion of liberty in human thought and action, equality in the social, political, and economic spheres, and tolerance regarding religious and cultural diversity. The thoughts of the movement's eighteenth-century founders are still the driving forces behind most of these struggles, at least to the degree that they occur in cultures influenced by European thought.

The Enlightenment was never a monolithic movement. Its underlying principles have always been subject to change, reinterpretation, and continuing dispute. Any attempt to define it is both a theoretical exercise and a part of an ongoing praxis that aims at supporting, opposing, or transforming the movement itself. The struggle over the identity of the Enlightenment had already begun in Kant's time. From the beginning, its conservative enemies have held it responsible for what they perceive as the moral chaos and spiritual decline of modern society. Enemies arising from within its own ranks attempted to use its own values against it, just as today self-styled critics of 'modernity' undertake to deconstruct Enlightenment thinking as part of their attempts to reconfigure intellectual and social options and alliances. If we read eighteenth-century Enlightenment thinkers with sensibilities trained under the influence of such opponents, we are apt to blame those thinkers for not being already what they, more than anything else, have made us to be.

Because the Enlightenment still influences the course of things, Kant's ethical thought is the (direct or indirect) source of much that is now standard in normative theories in ethics, political philosophy, and public policy. Many think of Kant's ethical theory (in John Rawls's apt words) "not as a morality of austere command but an ethic of mutual respect and self-esteem."[1] Kantian ethics is grounded on the dignity of rational nature. It requires not only respect for individual rights and the equal worth of human beings, but also the idea of a cosmopolitan community in which the ends of all rational beings must form a unity to be pursued collectively.

For the same reason, however, Kant's ethical thought is also a focus of controversy, often an object of strong aversion. Many regard it as a metaphysical system of mindless rule-following, grounded on an ineffable moral command. For them, to be a "Kantian" about any ethical issue is to be irrationally inflexible about it and irresponsibly heedless of the consequences of one's actions.

The detractors find support for their views in some of Kant's moral opinions about particular topics, some of which seem to them excessively strict to the point of inhumanity. Kant infamously maintains that it is wrong to lie even to a would-be murderer in order to protect his intended victim (MS 6:429–431; Ak 8:425–430). He maintains that suicide violates a strict duty to oneself because "to annihilate the subject of morality in one's own person is to root out the existence of morality itself from the world, as far as one can" (MS 6:423). For the crime of murder Kant thinks the punishment of death is so strictly required that "even if a civil society were to be dissolved by the consent of all its members . . . , the last murderer remaining in prison would first have to be executed, so that . . . blood guilt does not cling to the people" (MS 6:333).

Kant's views about sex are repugnant to nearly everyone today (just as they were to many in his own time). He thinks sexual intercourse is "a degradation of humanity" because it is an act in which "people make themselves into an object of enjoyment, and hence into a thing" (VE 27: 346). He regards sex as permissible only within marriage, and even there it is in itself "a merely animal union" (MS 6:425). "Unnatural" sexual practices, such as masturbation, "are still viler than suicide" and turn a human being into "a loathesome object," lower than a beast (VE 27: 347, MS 6:425). "Paederasty" (like rape) should be punished with castration, while "bestiality" deserves permanent expulsion from human society (MS 6:363).[2]

Nor can any enlightened person today approve Kant's opinions about race and gender. Kant distinguishes four races: (1) White, (2) "Yellow Indian," (3) Negro, and (4) "copper-red American." He ranks the characteristics of these respective races in descending order as regards their inborn talent for perfecting human nature, and conjectures that henceforth human progress is to be expected solely from the white race (VPG 9:316, VA 25:1187–1188; cf. BM 8:93–94).[3] Kant thinks that although women are rational beings, they are not suited by temperament or intellectual endowment to be treated as full adults in the public sphere.[4]

Kant holds that it is always unjust to rebel against the existing government or depose a head of state, no matter how unjust the rulers themselves might be. One must, on the contrary, obey all the commands of the authorities (except when they command us to do something that it is in itself wrong, such as bear false witness against an innocent person) (TP 8:297–303, MS 6:317–323, 370–372; cf. KpV 5:30, 155–156). Kant's views may often strike us as politically conservative in other ways, too. For example, while advocating representative political institutions (such as did not exist at all in his own nation) Kant accepts the property and occupational restrictions on political participation that prevailed where there were such institutions. These restrictions relegate all wage laborers, servants, and peasants (and, of course, all women) to the status of "passive citizens": they have civil rights, but take no part in the legislation or government of civil society (MS 6:314–315; cf. TP 8:295).[5]

To Kant's detractors, such views are only what we should expect from a theory that accords moral worth only to actions done from duty, treats our entire emotional nature as worthless, and places moral principles ahead of human happiness at every turn. Kant's high-minded talk about duty and personality is an empty formalism that can easily become a pretext for any sort of tyranny or manipulation.[6] Kant's admiration for "good will" is an unhealthy individualism focusing on the agent's inner intentions rather than their social setting. Those who see Kant this way regard it as entirely suitable to the inhumanity of his ethical doctrine that he locates his good will entirely outside nature, in an unknowable noumenal world.

To correct such utterly erroneous images of Kant's ethical thought, we must begin by asking why we should study the history of ethics at all. Our chief purpose is one that belongs squarely within the Enlightenment tradition: to improve our understanding of ethical issues so that we may justify, criticize, and correct our opinions about them. For this we need knowledge of the historical roots of these issues, and of the theories that address them. A critical understanding of the history of ethics is indispensable for our ethical thinking.

To read historical philosophers critically is to read them with intellectual sympathy, but it is never to treat them as oracles whose pronouncements on any subject we should accept blindly on trust. The point is not piously to admire their wisdom and virtue, which, since they are human and bound by the limitations of their age, are always far from perfect. Such piety teaches us nothing, and that approach only sets us up for unedifying disillusionment. The point is instead to further our own philosophical thinking, by understanding the history of the issues we now face. We often learn most from past philosophers when we come to understand why we think their opinions should be rejected.

We need to respect the unity of a philosopher's thought because we can learn most from a set of doctrines by seeing how some depend on others in ways that are not obvious. But respecting the unity of Kant's thought is not only compatible with but even requires distinguishing the teachings that are central to it from those that are peripheral, and separating the conclusions that actually follow from his principles from the conclusions he may have drawn but do not follow. Such respect is utterly incompatible with treating a philosopher's thought as a monolith, or using Kant's deplorable views about race and gender as some sort of hidden key to the "real meaning" of his principle that all beings are possessed of equal dignity.

The sole measure of what might deserve to be called Kant's "greatness" is how far it is possible for us to learn about *philosophy* from studying his writings (whatever might be the final mix of our agreement and disagreement with what they say). It is a sad form of intellectual bigotry to treat our first, emotional reaction to a philosopher's isolated opinions as if it were a reliable gauge of that potential. When we let that reaction shape an invidious image whose main function is to keep us at a distance, we succeed only in depriving ourselves of whatever we might have learned by studying Kant.

"Enlightenment," as Kant understood it, is a gradual process through which not only individuals but even an entire public attains maturity and increases its self-understanding through critical reflection and open communication. If this is what enlightenment is, then it would speak badly for the Enlightenment if two hundred years later the movement's heirs had not been able to make some important corrections in Kant's own beliefs about morality, society, and politics. It would speak well both for the movement and for Kant's principles if such corrections followed a trajectory marked out by those principles. And in fact they do. Kant's views about gender and race offend us not merely because we now see them as false (for not all errors of past ages are *morally offensive* to us), but rather because we see them as demeaning to the *human dignity* of women and nonwhites. Likewise, we object to a morality of stern duty and rigid rules because we think moral rules are grounded on the values human beings place on themselves, their feelings and desires, and their capacity to direct their own lives. The most influential philosophical articulation of these values is Kant's theory of moral autonomy, grounded on the dignity of humanity as an end in itself.

A proper understanding of Kant's ethical thought also requires the correction of errors about it which are still unfortunately common even among Kant's sympathizers. These include not only its supposed "individualism" and its alleged unconcern with the history and social context of morality, but also the exaggerated emphasis usually placed on the Formula of Universal Law in expounding Kant's approach to moral reasoning. We shall see in the early chapters of this book that this formula is only a stepping stone on the argumentative path leading to a more adequate, concrete, and systematic formulation of the principle in the Second Section of the *Groundwork*.[7]

2. Human equality

We have found it easy to be offended by some of the opinions expressed in Kant's writings. On other subjects, however, Kant expressed far more creditable opinions having a far more direct and demonstrable affinity with his basic principles. A frequently quoted passage from Kant's early reflections acknowledges the influence of Jean-Jacques Rousseau in shaping his moral outlook:

> I am an inquirer by inclination. I feel a consuming thirst for knowledge, the unrest which goes with the desire to progress in it, and satisfaction at every advance in it. There was a time when I believed this constituted the honor of humanity, and I despised the people, who know nothing. Rousseau set me right about this. This blinding prejudice disappeared. I learned to honor human beings, and I would find myself more useless than the common laborer if I did not believe that this attitude of mine can give worth to all others in establishing the rights of humanity. (Ak 20:44)

People tend to judge themselves better than others on various grounds: birth, wealth, honor, power, or (in Kant's case) learning.

These judgments, Kant holds, whatever their basis, are never more than false opinions based on self-conceited illusions. "The opinion of inequality makes people unequal. Only the teaching of M. R[ousseau] can bring it about that even the most learned philosopher with his knowledge holds himself, uprightly and without the help of religion, no better than the common human being" (Ak 20:176).

Kant's commitment to the equal worth of all human beings pervades his ethical thought. For this reason alone, by no reasonable standard could he be considered conservative in relation to the issues of his day. Certainly not in *politics*; living under an absolute monarchy, he openly subscribed to republicanism, calling a republican constitution the only one consistent with the idea of right (EF 8:349–350). Nor in *religion*, where his defense of liberty and toleration and his support of the Enlightenment earned him a royal reproof and a stern command not to teach or write on religious topics unless he altered his opinions (SF 7:6). Nor in *education*, where he was an early supporter of the liberalizing innovations of the Philanthropin academy (Ak 2:445–452). What looks like conservatism is often only an expression of Kant's conviction that the human race still has very far to go on the path toward a free and cosmopolitan realm of ends. Our social life is thoroughly corrupt and in need of radical reform, but even our grip on the institutions that promote progress is still so precarious that it may put all our hopes at risk if we call too much into question all at once.

Kant's egalitarianism shows itself in his conviction that the republican form of government is the only one that accords with the idea of right because it respects the freedom, equality, and independence of its citizens (EF 8:349–351; cf. TP 8:290–296, MS 6:311–318). Living under a government that was never more than a harsh military despotism, Kant was a consistent and impassioned defender of freedom of belief and expression (WA 8:35–42, KrV A738–757/B 766–785, O 8:143–146). Kant's essay *Toward perpetual peace* was the first, and is still the most significant, attempt by a major figure in the history of philosophy to articulate principles aimed at achieving a condition of just and permanent peace between nations, and ending the arms race which (he believed) poses the greatest lasting danger to the moral, political, and material progress of the human species. Despite his principled opposition to civil insurrection, and his pessimistic assessment of the practical prospects of the French Revolution, he continued to feel (and express) a "wishful participation that borders closely on enthusiasm" for the *ideals* of the Revolution, even after the terrifying deeds of the revolutionaries had turned many younger enthusiasts against these ideals (SF 7:85).

Another notable consequence of Kant's egalitarian principles is that he conspicuously declines to infer from the racialist beliefs we noted earlier that there is any difference in the *human rights* possessed by different peoples. His attitude toward European colonialism is therefore one of strong and unqualified disapproval. European nations, he says, invade and conquer non-Europeans as though the inhabitants of other parts of the earth had no claim on their land and even no rights as human beings (EF 8:357–359; MS 6:352–353; see also Chapter 9 § 2.4). Though he thinks Europeans more civilized than other peoples, Kant regards their civilization itself as directly unfitting them for their gratuitously self-appointed task of civilizing others. Perhaps the best testimony on this point comes from nineteenth- and early twentieth-century critics, who accused Kant of failing adequately to appreciate the diversity of races and cultures, and consequently the incapacity of non-European peoples to relate to Europeans on equal terms.[8]

Kant agrees with Rousseau that the social inequalities of honor, power, and wealth are fundamentally unjust, even when they result from transactions consistent with principles of right. Hence he agrees that the "civil equality" of citizens required for a legitimate form of government is consistent with large disparities of wealth (TP 8:291). Nevertheless this inequality constitutes a "general injustice" throughout society. Because this injustice arises not from individual acts of wrong but from the entire social system, those who benefit from it generally turn a blind eye toward it, and ascribe to their own merit whatever pitiful steps they may take to remedy it.

> In accordance with [benevolence], people are merciful to others and show beneficence to them after they have earlier taken from them, even though they are conscious of no injustice to anyone. But one can participate in the general injustice, even if one does no injustice according to the civil laws and institutions. Now if one shows beneficence to a wretch, then one has not given him anything gratuitously, but has given him only what one had earlier helped to take from him through the general injustice. For if no one took more of the goods of life than another, then there would be no rich and no poor. Accordingly, even acts of generosity are acts of duty and indebtedness, which arise from the rights of others. (VE 27:416)

> In our present condition, when general injustice is firmly entrenched, the natural rights of the lowly cease. They are therefore only debtors, the superior owe them nothing. Therefore, these superiors are called 'gracious lords'. But he who needs nothing from them but justice can hold them to their debts and does not need to be submissive. (Ak 20:140–141)

The general injustice prevailing in society produces a systematic deception in regard to people's benevolent feelings. It leads them perni-
ciously to exaggerate the moral importance of feelings of sympathy and
generosity, which permits them systematically to misinterpret as voluntary beneficence what they really owe the poor by right:

> Many people take pleasure in doing good actions but consequently do
> not want to stand under obligations toward others. If one only comes to
> them submissively, they will do everything: they do not want to subject
> themselves to the rights of people, but to view them simply as objects of
> magnanimity. It is not all one under what title I get something. What
> properly belongs to me must not be accorded to me merely as something
> I beg for. (Ak 19:145)

The last two passages I have quoted belong to some of Kant's earliest
reflections on morality, when the influence of Rousseau's ethical writings was both strong and fresh. Kant retained these convictions to the
end of his life, however, and expressed them even in his final ethical
work, the *Metaphysics of morals*, written nearly thirty-five years later:

> Having the resources to practice such beneficence as depends on the
> goods of fortune is, for the most part, a result of certain human beings
> being favored through the injustice of the government, which introduces
> an inequality of wealth that makes others need their beneficence. Under
> such circumstances, does a rich man's help to the needy, on which he so
> readily prides himself as something meritorious, really deserve to be
> called beneficence at all? (MS 6:454)

3. Morality and human nature

The passages just quoted assert that all human beings are equal and
ought to treat one another as such. They also contain another message,
perhaps less obvious but just as important for Kant's ethical thought,
not about how human beings ought to treat one another but about how
they *in fact* tend to treat one another and *why*. Though people are of
equal worth, this equality is something they are disposed to deny – as
Kant himself admits he did when he thought his learning constituted
"the honor of humanity" and made him better than the ignorant; or as
the "gracious lords" do when they think their noble birth or wealth
entitles them to look down on those who lack these privileges. The
deepest theme of the preceding passages is therefore not that people
are equal, but that people's equal worth must be vindicated against a

powerful propensity in human nature to claim for oneself an imagined worth greater than that of others.

It was also from Rousseau that Kant derived the idea that human beings in the social condition inevitably acquire the illusion of inequality. For Rousseau this deception is the ugly secret of all "civilization," raising troubling questions about the trajectory of human history. If the progress of culture only makes us more unequal, deceptive, and evil, does it make sense to want to improve the human lot in history? Can we believe in a purposiveness in the natural history of our species or a divine providence cooperating with our rational efforts to improve ourselves and our condition? (This set of problems about ourselves as rational, social, and historical beings preoccupied the greatest thinkers of the eighteenth century; it might be called "Mandeville's dilemma."[9])

In the mid-1760s, Kant apparently decided that Rousseau also had satisfactory answers to these questions: "Rousseau was the first who discovered, beneath the manifoldness of the forms assumed by the human being, his deeply hidden nature and the concealed law according to which destiny is justified by his observations. . . . According to Newton and Rousseau, God is justified" (Ak 20:58–59). Throughout his life Kant struggled with Rousseau's conception of human nature, attempting to provide an interpretation of it that justifies both the quest for a natural purposiveness in history and a faith in providence as governing that history. Kant's ethical thought can be properly appreciated only when it is seen in relation to this problematic.

The composition of Kant's first mature ethical work, the *Groundwork of the metaphysics of morals* (1785), coincides with his study of an alternative interpretation of Rousseau developed by Johann Gottfried Herder (who had been Kant's own student in the 1760s while he was discovering the social thought of Rousseau). It was in this context that Kant wrote his first two important essays on the philosophy of history: *Idea toward a universal history with a cosmopolitan aim* (1784) and *Conjectural beginning of human history* (1786). Kant's continuing interest in the philosophy of history is displayed in a number of later works, including the *Critique of the power of judgment* (1790), the essay on theory and practice (1793), *Religion within the boundaries of mere reason* (1794), *Toward perpetual peace* (1795), the *Conflict of the faculties* (1798), and *Anthropology from a pragmatic standpoint* (1798).

The fact that Kant's empirical conception of our human nature and his philosophy of history play a significant role in his ethical thought often comes as a surprise to those who know his ethical theory only through the standard images, interpretations, and caricatures of it. Many of these are based on misinterpretations of Kant's important claim that the *fundamental moral principle* must be *a priori* and owe nothing to empirical anthropology (G 4:387–389). This claim is taken to mean that Kant's ethical thought attaches no importance to the empirical nature of human beings or the social and historical situatedness of moral thinking. Thus Bernard Williams contends that Kant "rejects any biological, historical, or psychological theory of morality."[10] Alasdair MacIntyre comments that Kant's only conception of the human nature to which moral principles are applied involves merely "the physiological and non-rational side of man."[11] Richard Rorty declares that it is Kant's hope to "derive solutions to moral dilemmas from the analysis of moral concepts."[12] And Philippa Foot remarks that Kant holds "that an abstract idea of practical reason applicable to rational beings as such could take us all the way to [something like] our own moral code."[13]

But of course as a self-conscious representative of the Enlightenment, Kant never meant to deny the essential place in ethics of an empirical study of human nature.[14] He is just as quick to criticize other moralists for ignoring human nature as others have been to criticize him:

> One can, indeed, certainly consider practical philosophy even without anthropology, or without knowledge of the agent, only then it is merely speculative, or an idea; so the human being must at least be studied suitably. [Otherwise, moral philosophy becomes] tautologous repetitions of rules that everyone knows already, [which] strikes us as very tedious . . . , and pulpit orations on the subject are very empty, if the preacher does not simultaneously attend to humanity. (VE 27:244)

We can see immediately that Kantian ethics is very much concerned with empirical human nature as soon as we consider the *reasons* Kant gives for stressing the very point that the supreme principle of morality must be grasped as *a priori* and independent of the empirical nature of human beings. He declares it to be "of the greatest practical importance" to present the moral law unmixed with anthropological considerations (G 4:411). "Morals themselves are liable to all kinds of corruption" if we do not grasp "the moral law in all its purity" (G 4:390). Philosophical theories of virtue can accomplish much good in the world, but only if their teachers separate the pure moral law from everything empirical (G 4:410n). This is because pure respect for the law is the only motive which can subject our inclinations to reason (G 4:410).

Only the *a priori* motive of duty is capable of producing good actions *reliably* (G 4:390, 411).

These are not claims about the epistemic status of the moral law. They are assertions about the effects on human conduct (human nature being what it is) of *presenting* the claims of morality in one way or the other. They amount to the claim that none of our empirical desires is naturally in harmony with the demands of morality, and further, that neither education nor habituation is capable of creating a dependable accord between reason and inclination. Taken together they amount to a highly controversial *empirical* thesis about human nature: our nature does not permit of an *inclination* to do what morality demands of us, or a *liking* to do what duty demands, and therefore that such impossible states are not suitable objects of moral admiration or striving; the thought of them serves only the ends of sentimental self-delusion and enthusiastic self-conceit (KpV 5:81–89).

Kant's critics often call attention to the deep distrust of human nature exhibited in his insistence on the opposition of reason and inclination and his reservation of moral esteem only to actions motivated by duty.[15] (Even in Kant's own time, his ethical views were criticized on these grounds, by men such as Garve, Rehberg, and Schiller.[16]) But the critics display shortsightedness when they condescend to this feature of Kant's ethical thought (as by making snide references to his personality quirks or pietistic upbringing). They overlook the fact that Kant's interpretation of the *a priori* moral principle itself, as well as his conception of its application to the human will, depends on some quite distinctive views about human nature and history. In Part II of this book we will see that these views are worked out in his writings with a good deal of theoretical sophistication and constitute a vital component of his ethical outlook.[17]

4. Kant's ethical writings

Kant did not begin as a moral philosopher. He was first drawn to philosophy in the 1740s through his interest in the natural sciences. Kant's earliest published reflections on moral philosophy, in the early 1760s, are governed less by his substantive moral convictions than by concerns about the grounding of knowledge and the architectonic structure of a system of philosophy. His earliest piece of writing to address the role of morality in such a system is the *Inquiry concerning the distinctness of the principles of natural theology and morality* (written in 1762, published in

1764). Here he draws a distinction between actions that are necessary for an end (and whose goodness is therefore demonstrable by reference to that end) and actions that are immediately necessary in themselves (and whose goodness is therefore indemonstrable). Only the latter, he says, are truly *obligatory* (DG 2:298–300). As he does in his lectures of the same period, Kant toys with the moral sense theory of Francis Hutcheson as a way of making intelligible the idea of this unconditional moral necessity. About 1765, Kant begins to project his own system of moral philosophy under the name "metaphysics of morals." This is evidently conceived as a decisive *rejection* of moral sense theory in favor of a theory grounding morality in rational concepts. Yet Kant does not begin to work seriously on this project until several years after he revolutionizes theoretical philosophy in the *Critique of pure reason* (1781).

When we consider the course of Kant's career as a philosopher, however, we cannot help noticing his increasing interest in moral questions, the rising importance of the practical (or moral) standpoint within his conception of philosophy as a whole. Nothing is more characteristic of Kant's critical system than the thesis that the metaphysical questions with which human reason is most profoundly concerned – questions about the existence of God, freedom of the will, and immortality of the soul – cannot be answered by theoretical or speculative reason, but can be addressed only from a practical (or moral) point of view. Kant's chief enterprise in the last half of the 1780s was working out the fundamentals of a practical philosophy (in the *Groundwork* and the *Critique of practical reason*) and bridging what he saw as a serious gulf between theoretical and practical philosophy (in the *Critique of the power of judgment*). Kant's chief works in the 1790s all deal with the application of practical philosophy to human life – to religion, as in *Religion within the boundaries of mere reason* (1793–1794) and to politics and international relations, and the human race's vocation in history as in the essay on theory and practice (1793) and *Toward perpetual peace* (1795) – culminating in the completion (finally) of the *Metaphysics of morals* (1797–1798). Kant's mature thought is at least as much a moral outlook on the world as it is a position on questions of epistemology, natural science or speculative metaphysics.

Despite its brevity, the *Groundwork* is one of the greatest and most influential achievements in the history of philosophy. Nevertheless, it must be said that a disproportionate amount of scholarly attention has been paid to it. For Kant intends this little book not as a complete exposition of his ethical theory but only as an attempt to identify and secure the fundamental principle on which a system of ethics might be based. Nor does acquaintance with the *Critique of practical reason* do much to correct the one-sided impressions created by the *Groundwork*, for it, too, is conceived as a foundational work, a critical propaedeutic to ethical theory, and not a statement of Kant's ethical theory itself. The foundational works will mislead us unless we attend to the *Metaphysics of morals*. At the same time, the system of duties presented in that work will be even harder to understand unless we already appreciate the foundation on which it rests. Kant's other writings on ethics, politics, and religion, which also make important contributions to our understanding of his ethical thought, are equally dependent on the foundational writings but are also important for the proper interpretation of them. Since Kant's empirical theory of human nature (his "anthropology" and philosophy of history) are just as crucial for an understanding of his ethical thought as his conception of the *a priori* foundations of morality, both the foundational writings and the resulting system of duties in the *Metaphysics of morals* must also take them into account.

The proper way to treat Kant's ethical thought would be to begin with (1) an exposition of its foundations in the *Groundwork*, supplemented by the *Critique of practical reason*, but also using the *Metaphysics of morals* and other writings as a clue to their interpretation. Then (2) we must try to understand Kant's theory of human nature and its consequences for the application of the foundational principles. Only then are we in a position to provide (3) a systematic exposition of the *Metaphysics of morals* as the definitive form of Kant's practical philosophy. That was the plan I intended to follow in writing this book, but it eventually became evident that the entire plan is too ambitious for any single book. Therefore, although I will make significant reference to the *Metaphysics of morals* in the course of the book and provide a brief exposition of it in the Conclusion, the full execution of stage (3) of the plan must be deferred to a future occasion.

5. The structure of this book

The first three chapters will deal with themes far more familiar in the Kantian literature than the last six. What I say about these themes is intended to gain a hearing for the later parts of the book by showing that many of the controversies that have surrounded the more familiar themes are of less significance for Kantian ethics than is usually appreciated.

Part I will deal with the metaphysical foundations of Kant's ethical theory. It will be structured as an exposition of the *Groundwork*. Chapter 1 will consider Kant's famous appeal to common rational moral cognition in the First Section of the *Groundwork*. Chapter 2 will take up the Second Section's philosophical account of the will and rational imperatives. Chapters 3–5 will be devoted (one each) to Kant's three main formulations of the supreme principle of morality. Chapter 5 includes Kant's grounding of the moral law in the practical presupposition of freedom and Kant's final conception of the moral law in the *Groundwork*, as a system constituted by all three formulas.

Part II turns to Kant's application of the moral principle to human nature. Chapter 6 discusses Kant's conception of "anthropology," the study of human nature, tracing his method to its basis in his theory of teleological judgment. Chapter 7 expounds Kant's theory of history, contrasting it with the views of Herder and showing how it anticipates later views, especially the historical materialism of Marx. Chapter 8 explores Kant's theory of natural feeling and desire, the social basis of human passions, and Kant's reasons for mistrusting sociable inclinations as moral motives. The chapter ends by treating a badly neglected topic: Kant's theory of friendship. Chapter 9 discusses Kant's account of our moral destiny in history.

The Conclusion uses the contents of the nine chapters to indicate certain notable features of the ethical theory with which Kant presents us in the *Metaphysics of morals*. After briefly expounding the theory behind Kant's system of duties, the Conclusion focuses attention on two themes Kantian ethics has often been thought to neglect or mishandle: namely, moral *ends* and moral *virtues*.

Kant's ethical thought is one of the few products of the history of philosophy that exercises such a strong and continuing influence on us that replacing commonly accepted ideas about it with more accurate and less oversimplified ones might help to transform our conception of our own history and of ourselves as heirs of the Enlightenment. The aspiration of this book is to contribute in some small way to that revolution.

I

METAPHYSICAL FOUNDATIONS

COMMON RATIONAL
MORAL COGNITION

1. Grounding ethical theory

1.1. Formulating the principle of morality   Kant's project in the *Ground-work* is simple enough: "the search for and establishment of the s*upreme principle of morality*" (G 4:392). But the project's execution is subtle and complex. The First Section carries out the search by appealing to moral common sense ("common rational moral cognition") to motivate a more rigorous account of the commitments of common sense ("philosophic moral cognition") (G 4:392–393). The Second Section makes a new start, bypassing "popular moral philosophy" and employing a philosophical theory of the will to lay the ground for a "metaphysics of morals" (G 4:392, 406). The "supreme principle of morality" is formulated only provisionally in the First Section, as the Formula of Universal Law (FUL). The parallel search in the Second Section has more definitive results: a *system* of three formulas (two of which are provided with a variant form):[1]

FIRST FORMULA:

FUL   *The Formula of Universal Law.* "Act only in accordance with that maxim through which you can at the same time will that it become a universal law" (G 4:421; cf. 4:402)

with its variant,

FLN   *The Formula of the Law of Nature.* "Act as if the maxim of your action were to become by your will a *universal law of nature*" (G 4:421; cf. 4:436).

SECOND FORMULA:

> **FH**   *The Formula of Humanity as End in Itself.* "So act that you use humanity, whether in your own person or that of another, always at the same time as an end, never merely as a means" (G 4:429; cf. 4:436).

THIRD FORMULA:

> **FA**   *The Formula of Autonomy:* ". . . the idea of the will of every rational being as a will giving universal law" (G 4:431; cf. 4:432) or "Choose only in such a way that the maxims of your choice are also included as universal law in the same volition" (G 4:440; cf. 4:432, 434, 438)

with its variant,

> **FRE**   *The Formula of the Realm of Ends:* "Act according to the maxims of a universally legislative member of a merely potential realm of ends" (G 4:439; cf. 4:433, 437, 438).

The three formulas are claimed to be reciprocally equivalent and to represent one and the same principle from different sides (G 4:436–437). We will look at this systematic interconnection at the end of Part I (Chapter 5, § 5).

1.2. The argument of the Groundwork   The second task of the *Groundwork,* "establishing" the principle, has already begun in the First and Second Sections. It takes the form of a conditional claim whose antecedent is to be discharged in the Third Section. The First Section argues that if morality, as conceived according to certain alleged propositions of moral common sense, is not merely a high-flown figment of our imagination, then moral motivation and the moral principle must be of a certain kind (G 4:394, 401–403). The Second Section argues for an analogous hypothetical proposition in terms drawn not from "common rational cognition" but from a philosophical theory of the will. This theory enables the principle to be specified in much greater detail (G 4:419, 425, 429, 439). Kant therefore says that in the first two sections he has been proceeding "analytically," which means (in scholastic-Aristotelian terms) moving from "what is more evident to us" toward the "first principle" (G 4:445). Then the Third Section "establishes" the principle using the final formulation arrived at in the Second Section (namely, FA). Here Kant argues ("synthetically") that the law in this formulation is valid for the human will if and only if it is free, and that from a practical standpoint freedom must be presupposed as a property of the will (G 4:447–448).

Along with finding and establishing the supreme principle of morality, the *Groundwork* has at least two other collateral aims that are dictated by its strategy. First, Kant realizes that some of the claims he attributes to moral common sense are at odds with traditional moral theories and moral teachings. Among these teachings are (i) that morality must be grounded on an end to be achieved through action (G 4:400), (ii) that happiness is the highest good grounding all moral principles (G 4:393), and (iii) that qualities such as self-control and courage are moral virtues deserving unconditional esteem (G 4:394). Kant's strategy in the *Groundwork* requires him to argue that these traditional teachings are not only false but actually at odds with "common rational moral cognition." Second, if Kant is to establish moral philosophy as a "metaphysics of morals," he must argue that the supreme principle of morality is an *a priori* principle. He begins to do this even in the Preface (G 4:387–390). Because he appeals at the outset to "common rational cognition" Kant must also claim that moral common sense is committed to the moral principle's having this epistemic status. Once we see how much Kant is taking on right at the beginning of the *Groundwork*, we should be less surprised that many of his claims in the First Section do not immediately command universal assent. However, the excessive ambitions of the First Section, instead of offering us a pretext for dismissing Kant's entire theory, should rather create in us a heightened expectancy regarding the philosophical arguments that are meant to vindicate Kant's claims in the Second Section. (These arguments will be examined in Chapters 2–5.)

1.3. The starting point Kant's point of departure in the First Section is *gemeine sittliche Vernunfterkenntnis*, that is, "common moral cognition through reason." I have referred earlier to "moral common sense," but Kant's term does not refer to common sense beliefs *about* morality. As Stephen Engstrom has pointed out, it does not refer fundamentally to any kind of *reflective* knowledge at all, such as might have "morality" as its object. Instead, it refers to an everyday unreflective awareness of the rational standards Kant thinks anyone must use in moral deliberation and judgment.[2] "Common rational moral cognition" is prephilosophical in its origin and therefore subject not only to philosophical explication, but also to rigorous philosophical criticism, correction, rejection, or vindication.

To be a moral agent at all, you must be capable of recognizing both what morality demands of you and acknowledging the value of complying with those demands. "There is, accordingly, no need of science or philosophy in order to know what one has to do to be honest and good, and even wise and virtuous" (G 4:404). To put it another way, Kant thinks we must attribute to anyone who is to be held morally responsible at all (even to the person with an utterly evil will) all the *cognitive* capacities that are needed to have a good will.[3]

The *Groundwork* could thus be said to begin with the idea of a good will in a twofold sense.

First, the idea of such a will, and the value it possesses, is the basis of the *scheme of values* Kant lays out in its opening pages for the purpose of expounding his theory from a commonsense standpoint. (We should not assume, however, as too many of the *Groundwork*'s readers do, that the concept of the good will plays such a fundamental role in Kant's developed philosophical theory of moral duties. In fact it does not. Concepts such as "categorical imperative," "end in itself," "autonomy of the will," and "duty of virtue" or "end which is the same time a duty" are all far more important to Kant's ethical theory than the concept of a good will.)

Second, beginning from the standpoint of common rational moral cognition consists in beginning with *only that knowledge which* all moral agents necessarily possess, and which therefore *constitutes the cognitive precondition for having a good will.* (It is questionable whether this is enough knowledge to yield Kant's main conclusions unless it is supplemented by independent philosophical arguments. This is the main reason why we should lower our expectations for the First Section and raise our expectations for the Second.)

The aim of the First Section is to develop this practical knowledge into a kind of theoretical knowledge. Kant thinks this enterprise is very much in the interest of morality itself. For common rational moral cognition in its unreflective form is a species of innocence, which, though possessed of special charms that make us yearn for it after we have lost it, is incapable of guarding itself against evil. It will be easily seduced unless we take the affirmative step of abandoning it for the protection of a reflective theory (G 4:404–405).

2. The good will

2.1. The unlimited good "It is impossible to think of anything at all in the world, or indeed even beyond it, that could be considered good without limitation except a *good will*" (G 4:393). Kant proposes to elicit our assent to this arresting proposition by considering the good will alongside some other categories of good things. First he considers "gifts of nature," the more or less permanent features of a person belonging to her natural endowments: "talents of mind" (understanding, wit, judgment) and "qualities of temperament" (courage, resoluteness, perseverance in one's plans). These are "undoubtedly good and desirable in many respects, but they can also be extremely evil and harmful" if they are made use of by a bad will (G 4:393).

He makes an analogous claim about "gifts of fortune." This category includes all the contingently possessed goods we strive after and compete for: power, wealth, and honor (the good opinion of others). It also encompasses everything we regard as constituting our personal self-interest: health and that all-round contentment with our condition called "happiness." All these are good, Kant says, but only when combined with a good will. For all these gifts of fortune can "easily lead to courage and thereby often to presumption" (*Mut und hiedurch öfters auch Übermut*); presumption, at least, is a bad quality (morally as well as prudentially) unless accompanied by a good will that restrains its evil influence. Happiness, Kant says, is something we cannot approve as good unless its possessor has become *worthy* of it through having a good will (G 4:393).

Notice that Kant's *first* reason for excluding happiness from the class of things that are unqualifiedly good is *not* that we may not deserve to be happy. It is instead that *happiness itself* (along with every other species of good fortune) is likely to have a *corrupting influence* on us, given the innate propensities of human nature. Kantian anthropology holds that when people enjoy good fortune (when they become richer, more powerful, or more famous than their neighbors) they have an innate propensity to infer that they *deserve* to be better off, and this arrogant delusion frequently contributes both to prudential unwisdom and to moral evil.

Of course the qualified goods do not result in evil if a good will corrects their influence, and some qualities of temperament (such as moderation in affects and passions, self-control, calm reflection) are actually conducive to a good will. For this reason we may easily confuse them with "the inner worth of the person" and come to esteem them unconditionally. Kant thinks the ancients mistakenly did this when they put courage and temperance (along with wisdom and justice) on their list of the four cardinal virtues (G 4:394). Yet courage and self-control remain distinct from the unqualified goodness of a good will. They can be combined with a bad will, and in that case *they themselves* become bad, and make a bad will even worse: "The coolness of a villain makes him not only far more dangerous but also immediately more abominable in our eyes" (G 4:394).

Kant's assertions call into question the worth of things that were traditionally regarded as unqualified goods, either as virtues (courage and temperance) or as the final end of all rational action (happiness). Of course, when courage was treated as a virtue in traditional ethical theories, it was typically held to belong only to those who had *good ends*. Such considerations also led to the view that the virtues are connected (so that they support or produce one another in a sort of homeostatic psychological system) or even identical (so that the words and concepts standing for them, though not synonymous, are necessarily coreferential). Presumably the classical ethical theorist who held such views would be in a position to say that *true* courage or self-control is present only in a person who has what Kant would call a 'good will'. Happiness, when taken to be the final end of life, was also not restricted in its content to a person's *state* but was either identified with, or at least included in (as its dominant component), what Kant would call the "inner worth" of the person herself (which is constituted by having a good will).

The real point of controversy here is Kant's implicit view that the good will is wholly distinct from other goods – natural talents of mind and qualities of temperament, health, or happiness. Can the good will be treated as something that might exist apart from (or even in opposition to) any or all of these other goods? Kant's real challenge to the tradition is his attempt to conceive of *human nature* in such a way that such an opposition is not only conceivable but even constitutes the central issue of the moral life.

We could also ask the question this way: Is the good will something that emerges spontaneously, even prior to reflection, from the dispositions and feelings of any healthy person? Or does it instead have to be conceived of as the will of a reflective person who must struggle with unruly desires in order to do the right thing? In the latter case, it will attain its most distinctive and heroic form *only* under adverse conditions, when separated from and even set in opposition to the other things traditionally considered good.

Kant acknowledges the appeal of the idea that the best will is one that naturally and spontaneously does the right thing (G 4:404–405). By comparison to the innocent charm of that sort of will, the reflective will which must discipline itself may seem, even at its best, a will whose goodness is rendered tarnished and impure, perhaps even sophistical and pharisaical, by its need for reflection and internal struggle. We will not recognize the strength of Kant's position until we see why he thinks that for mature human beings in a historically developed condition, the charms of innocence are invariably illusory, and the state of mind that values them is never very far from evil. When we attribute to ourselves a will that is good spontaneously, innocently, and without thoughtful effort – or even wish sentimentally that we might have such a will – we indulge in a piece of self-serving self-flattery whose function in our psychological economy is to rationalize some of the more common forms of moral corruption (KpV 5:82–89).

2.2. *Limited goods*   The principal claims that Kant seems to be making in the first three paragraphs of the First Section are these:

(α) A good will is always good, good unconditionally, and never in any respect bad.

(β) All other goods (gifts of nature, gifts of fortune) are good only conditionally, and are worthless (or even bad) when the pertinent conditions are not fulfilled.

(γ) The goodness of any good other than a good will depends on its being combined (in the right way) with a good will; any such good becomes bad when combined (in the relevant way) with a bad will. (The combinations in question appear to be chiefly of the means-end type.)

(α) does not say that everything that accompanies a good will is good, or that a good will cannot be combined with anything bad. A good will is unfortunately sometimes found in combination with defects of mind or bad qualities of temperament, and then it can fail to achieve the good it wills "owing to the special disfavor of fortune, or the niggardly provision of a stepmotherly nature" (G 4:394).[4]

Kant ascribes to moral common sense the position that neither the bad results of a good will nor the defects of mind and temperament responsible for these results are to be attributed to the good will itself. These bad things take nothing away from its goodness, just as the good results of a good will (when it has good results) add nothing to its unlimited goodness. Instead, they merely attach to the good will a distinct, conditioned, and qualified good, which does nothing to alter its inner (unconditioned and unqualified) goodness. The good consequences of a good will are at most like the fancy setting of a jewel, which may make it more convenient to handle or serve to inform non-experts that it is a genuine precious stone rather than a paste imitation. But like the true gem apart from such a setting (or even placed in a cheap or ugly setting), the good will, whatever its results, "would still shine by itself as something that has its full worth in itself" (G 4:394).

(β) tells us that we must say just the opposite about the qualified goods of nature or fortune. Traditional moral theories, even if they did not maintain the identity or connectedness of the virtues, might want to say of courage or self-control, when found in separation from other virtues, that it is at least in itself a good quality, and that the person is good *to the extent that* she has it. According to Kant, however, this is *not* the verdict of common rational moral cognition. Courage, intelligence, or calm deliberation, when put in the service of villainy, become something bad and even make the villain more abominable than he would have otherwise been. It is the same with the happiness a villain may derive from his villainy: "The uninterrupted prosperity of a being graced with no feature of a pure and good will" is something of which a "rational impartial spectator" cannot approve (G 4:393). Nor would Kant permit the explanation of this judgment often advanced by eudaemonistic consequentialists, that we disapprove of the bad person's happiness because it must have been achieved at the expense of a greater happiness of others. On the contrary, Kant thinks that our impartial moral judgment is that the happiness of a wicked person would be bad in itself, even if it subtracted nothing from the happiness of others.

(γ) tells us that the happiness of a person with a bad will is bad, just as the happiness of a person with a good will is good. Presumably, Kant ascribes to common rational moral cognition parallel judgments about other gifts of nature or fortune. It is good in itself (not merely circumstantially) that people of good will should have intelligence, courage, self-control, power, riches, honor, and health; and bad in itself that people of bad will should have them – though he would doubtless want to qualify this claim to the extent that these qualities are thought of as conducing to a good will and hence tending to diminish the bad will's badness. (But note one asymmetry between the good and bad wills: The goodness of the good will can be neither augmented nor diminished by combination with other things, while the bad will itself becomes even more abominable when combined with other qualities or objects it has turned from good to bad.)

(α)–(γ) stress the *unconditioned* goodness of the good will, in contrast to the *conditioned* goodness of the gifts of nature and fortune. From what Kant says elsewhere, there is no doubt that he believes that the good will's goodness stands in this conditioning relation to the goodness of other goods (KpV 5:108; KU 5:450; R 6:36, VA 7:277). In this particular passage, however, the word Kant uses to describe the good will's goodness is not "unconditioned" (*unbedingt*) but "without limitation" (*ohne Einschränkung*). He says of the other goods that they are good only "in some respects" or "for some purposes" (*in mancher Absicht*). This suggests that, alongside the conditioning relation between the good will and other goods, Kant is claiming that the good will is good unlimitedly, good in every respect, but other goods are good only in a limited way, good in some respects, so that in other ways they are not good at all and may even be bad.

Kant might defend this further claim on the basis of the conditioning relation: If talents of mind, qualities of temperament, and gifts of fortune can be combined with a bad will and are bad when so combined, then the fact that they *can* exist in this combination is already a limitation on their goodness. With respect to gifts of fortune, however, we have already seen one further reason for thinking them bad in some ways, namely, that they make for courage and even presumption unless their influence is corrected by a good will (G 4:493). Though he does not say so, Kant might argue that the same corrupting influence can also belong to gifts of nature, for some of these "seem to constitute part of the inner worth of a person" (G 4:394). If we stress "seem" here, we have reason to worry that even these apparently benign gifts of nature may lead us (presumptuously) to think more highly of ourselves than we should.

Some of these claims clearly go well beyond anything Kant can pretend to draw solely from common rational moral cognition. They involve Kant's theory of human nature, and specifically his thesis (whose basis we will examine in Part II) that human beings in the social condition have tendencies to competitiveness, self-conceit, and self-deception, which combine in the radical propensity to evil in human nature. Moreover, Kant's sharp separation of the good will from other qualities in a person, and the absolutely fundamental value he places on good will as the sole determinant of the value of all other things, are theses in moral philosophy. It is not clear that one would need to be even implicitly cognizant of these theses in order to be a moral agent at all.

Kant seems to have realized this himself, since he immediately considers the objection that the idea that mere willing has supreme value in the absence of any utility might seem like a high-flown fantasy (G 4:394). His response to the worry is to argue, on the basis of his methodological principles of natural teleology, that the purpose of rationality in human beings cannot be to insure their happiness or welfare, since the use of reason seems to be largely superfluous, even counterproductive, to this end (G 4:395). This suggests that reason, our highest faculty, is present in us for some other end, and Kant thinks this harmonizes well with the idea that the good will is the supreme good, since reason is required for such a will (G 4:395–396). This argument is not an appeal to common rational moral cognition, but is driven by fairly deep theoretical considerations underlying Kant's teleological conception of human nature. In the context of the First Section of the *Groundwork*, it surely counts as an acknowledgment on Kant's part that "common rational moral cognition" will support the claims of his ethical theory only if it is supplemented or even corrected by philosophical arguments.

3. Acting from duty

Kant's next task is to tell us what the good will is by "developing" (or explicating) its concept. He proposes to do this by considering the related concept of *duty*, which, he says, "contains that of a good will, though under certain subjective limitations and hindrances, which, however, far from hiding it and making it unrecognizable, rather raise it up by contrast and allow it to shine forth the more brightly" (G 4:397). The ensuing discussion is famous and controversial. It is also both confusing and misleading. Consequently, some of Kant's central contentions in it are widely misunderstood.

To begin with, the principal thought expressed in the passage just quoted is one readers of the *Groundwork* tend to overlook. This is that the concept of duty "contains" that of a good will, but adds other conditions to it, so that the concept of a good will must be *broader* in its extension than the concept of a will which acts from duty. Thus MacIntyre misinterprets Kant when he says that "the good will's only motive is to do its duty for the sake of doing its duty. Whatever it intends to do it intends because it is its duty."[5] This is obviously false when we consider the divine will, which is good but never requires self-constraint and hence cannot act from duty (cf. G 4:414, KpV 5:20, MS 6:379–380, VpR

28:1075–1076). We will see that MacIntyre's claim is also false for the good will in finite and imperfect beings like ourselves. In short, here Kant intends to direct our attention only to *certain special cases* of the good will (in which it must overcome "subjective limitations and hindrances"). He does this because he thinks that the good will's unlimited worth "shines forth more brightly" to common rational cognition under these adverse conditions. He needs to direct attention to these special (even atypical) cases of the good will because only in them does it become clear that the good will is different from such things as a fortunate temperament, and possessed of an essentially higher value.

3.1. In conformity with duty/from duty Kant distinguishes actions that are "in conformity with duty" (*pflichtmäßig*) from those done "from duty" (*aus Pflicht*) (G 4:397–398). An action conforms to duty if it complies with what duty requires, whatever might be our motives for doing it. Only acts done *from duty*, Kant says, have true "moral worth" or "moral content." Here the terms "moral worth" and "moral content" do not refer to just any sort of value morality might attach to actions, but designate only that special degree of worth that most conspicuously elicits *esteem* (*Hochschätzung*) from common rational cognition. Hence if an action lacks "moral worth" in this sense, it by no means follows that it is *worthless* from the moral point of view. Obviously all actions that conform to duty are valued from the moral standpoint or they would not be commanded as duties. "Moral worth" refers to a special degree of value that goes beyond such mere moral *approval*, and elicits from common rational moral cognition an *esteem*, a recognition of the unconditional worth it reserves solely for the good will.

But the good will does not always act from duty, nor do all acts of the good will have this special moral worth. Even with the best conceivable will, it would clearly be impossible for a human being to act from duty on every occasion. Many of our actions do not involve duties at all; even the best possible will could not act from duty where no duty applies.[6] Even where duty is at stake, Kant does not hold that we have to act from duty in order to avoid blame. He holds that we have only an imperfect, wide, or meritorious duty to *strive* to make duty alone a *sufficient* incentive of our actions, that is, to will in such a way that the motive of duty wins out over contrary incentives when necessary (MS 6:393). But we can not only have a good will but even can achieve moral merit and deserve esteem in cases where that striving is not perfectly successful.

Kant discusses acting from duty through the discussion of four examples. The first is that of the shopkeeper who has no immediate inclination to deal fairly with inexperienced customers (which is his duty), but conforms his actions to this duty out of self-interest, in order to avoid a bad reputation (G 4:397). The other three involve a comparison between two situations in which an agent performs actions required by duty (preserving one's life, acting beneficently toward those who need our help, promoting one's happiness in order to avoid temptations to transgress duty). In each case, Kant wants us to compare our reactions (engaging common rational moral cognition) to those actions when they are performed from an immediate inclination (of self-preservation, sympathy, and self-love, respectively) with our reaction to the same action when these empirical incentives are removed, and they are performed solely from duty.

All the examples of acting from duty involve cases in which the incentive of duty must overcome opposing incentives, or (in the example of beneficence) must at least move us to act without any cooperating ones. That is, they are cases in which a person acts according to duty in the absence of any incentive other than duty, perhaps even in the face of strong incentives of inclination to act contrary to duty. Hence if Kant held (as the above quotation from MacIntyre would suggest) that a good will is present only where one acts from duty, then he would be committed to saying that we can have a good will *only* when there are no nonmoral incentives to do our duty. Perhaps he would even have to say that we have a good will only when we actually resist incentives that tempt us *not* to do our duty. If we further attribute to Kant the view that we should always *strive* to have a good will (and hence strive to satisfy the necessary conditions for having one),[7] then the thesis that one has a good will only when one acts from duty would commit Kant to hold that we should strive to avoid having nonmoral incentives to do our duty, perhaps even that we must strive instead to have contra-moral incentives.

This *reductio ad absurdum* of Kant's supposed position seems to be the source of Schiller's well-known satire:

Scruples of Conscience

I like to serve my friends, but unfortunately I do it by inclination
And so often I am bothered by the thought that I am not virtuous.

Decision

There is no other way but this! You must seek to despise them
And do with repugnance what duty bids you.[8]

But is the absurd conclusion derived from Kant's actual contentions or from alien assumptions that are gratuitously added to them, grossly distorting his position? Needless to say, Kant does not advocate that we cultivate hatred of our friends or other contra-moral desires in order to give ourselves opportunities to resist them. (That would make about as much sense as putting your loved ones in needless danger so as to give yourself the opportunity to display your courage by rescuing them.) On the contrary, Kant says (unsurprisingly) that we have a duty to cultivate love, sympathy, and other inclinations that make our duties easier to do (MS 6:402, 456–457). The highest praise he can think to give to the Christian religion is that it cultivates feelings of love in people in such a way as to promote their observance of moral duty (ED 8:338–339).

Kant clearly does not conceive of actions done from duty as done "with repugnance." Acts done in this spirit, he says, always involve a "hidden *hatred* of the [moral] law" and are therefore the very reverse of acts done with a good will (R 6:24 note). He thinks of acts done from duty as done *willingly*, with a *desire* to do them, and hence with a feeling of pleasure accompanying the representation of their end. For him, the difference is whether the desire arises from freedom, from reason recognizing the action as practically necessary, or from an inclination that contingently coincides with duty (MS 6:211–213). Thus he thinks that acts done from duty are easily distinguished from the shopkeeper's honest action, where a rational incentive (of prudence) might have to overcome an immediate inclination to transgress duty. He says acts done from duty are *harder* to distinguish from actions to which we also have an immediate inclination. Presumably this is because both actions are done with a direct desire to do them. The motive of duty is not, like the shopkeeper's motive of calculated prudence, something that prompts us to do an action we do not value for itself but only do reluctantly for the sake of its consequences. On the contrary, to act from duty is to recognize the inherent moral value of the act, and that recognition gives rise to a direct desire to perform the action for its own sake. Kant's view that all duty implies self-constraint, hence reluctance, is based on his distinctive theory of human nature, according to which our direct rational desire to do the morally right thing systematically meets with a counterweight in the form of our natural inclinations. In his foundational writings on ethics, Kant often conceals the complex motivation for these views beneath the utterly unpersuasive argument that the needs of any finite being must constitute a resistance to moral

reason. His real line of thinking, which dominates his writings on anthropology and history, will be explored in Part II of this book.

It would be equally absurd to suppose that Kant is committed to saying that we must, all things considered, prefer the situation where
someone acts from duty to the situation where she acts in conformity
to duty but from some other incentive. Clearly it is better for everyone
if the merchant's honest actions also serve his interests, if we are inclined to preserve our lives and promote our happiness, and if the man
of philanthropic temperament is inclined toward acts of generosity.
But because Kant thinks the good will most conspicuously exhibits the
distinctive moral worth for which we esteem it when it is faced with ad-
versity (G 4:398–399), he expects common rational cognition to show
maximal esteem for the good will when it is placed in unhappy circumstances (which, of course, every well-disposed person would try to
avoid).

3.2. Approval/esteem   The shopkeeper's honest action is described as
one "in conformity with duty but to which human beings have no *inclination* immediately and which they still perform because they are impelled to do so through another inclination." He continues: "For in this
case it is easy to distinguish whether an action in conformity with duty
is done from duty or from a self-seeking aim. It is much more difficult
to note this distinction when an action conforms with duty and the
subject has besides an immediate inclination to it" (G 4:397).

These remarks do not strike us as unclear or ambiguous, and yet we
can begin to see that they are difficult, or even seriously misleading, if
we ask what Kant means in the last sentence by "this distinction." The
first and most natural thought might be that it is the distinction, apparently just referred to, between a dutiful action done from duty and
one done from self-interest. But there are several reasons for rejecting
that interpretation. In the *Groundwork* we soon find out that Kant thinks
it is *never* easy (indeed, never even possible with certainty) to distinguish
duty from self-love when we examine our inner motivation (G 4:407).
Moreover, in the three examples that follow, the theme is not the opposition of duty to self-seeking but only the need for duty to move us
when there is no inclination (whether selfish or unselfish) capable of
getting us to do our duty. (The man tempted to suicide is moved by de-
jection and despair, not by selfishness; the podagrist tempted to violate
his diet is moved by an inclination that directly opposes his self-interest;
the formerly sympathetic person does not need to overcome selfishness

but only an insensibility to the sufferings of others into which his own misfortunes have plunged him.)

The next thought may be that the distinction is one between acting from duty and acting from inclination in cases where inclination and duty both provide us with incentives to the same action. We suppose Kant to be saying that in such cases it is hard to distinguish the "real motive," to decide whether the action is done from duty or from an immediate inclination. That thought misleads us into concluding that Kant's discussion of acting from duty must turn on his theory of "motivational overdetermination." But it turns out that nothing in Kant's ensuing discussion turns on "motivational overdetermination." The issues he is raising have nothing to do with the *psychological causality* of actions in cases where the very same action might have, or might have had, more than one distinguishable cause or motive. On the contrary, Kant assumes throughout that acting *from duty* is possible only where rational self-constraint is required, hence where there is no incentive other than duty. In the three examples of acting from duty, he simply stipulates that there is no motive of inclination for performing the dutiful action.

"This distinction," I suggest, turns out to be a distinction not between motives or actions but between two different reactions we (in applying common rational moral cognition) may have to dutiful actions or two different attitudes we may take toward the agent. The difference in our reactions of course presupposes a difference in the actions, but it is the former difference rather than the latter which most interests Kant. When we consider the care most people take for self-preservation or their (permissible) promotion of their own happiness, we *approve* of these actions because they conform to duty (or at least we do not disapprove of them). But Kant contends that we do not ascribe any "moral worth" or "moral content" to these dutiful actions, simply because they are prompted by an immediate inclination (G 4:397–399). In the case of beneficent actions done from sympathetic inclinations or acts promoting the common interest done from an inclination to honor (i.e., a desire for the good opinion of others), our approval goes as far as thinking the action worthy of "praise and encouragement" (G 4:398). But when we compare all these cases of dutiful acts prompted by immediate inclination with the same acts done in the absence of any inclination, hence merely from duty, Kant thinks we will take a different attitude, that of "esteem" (*Hochschätzung*). Esteem is what rational moral cognition has for that special worth of character, which cannot be the product of a fortunate temperament or of inclinations that happily coincide with duty. It is rather reserved solely for the good will. Not all acts proceeding from a good will, however, elicit this attitude, but only those that display "moral worth" – that worth an act has when all other incentives have been taken away besides duty, and the agent performs the act solely from duty.

Kant thinks we approve the shopkeeper's honest dealing with inexperienced customers, even though it is prompted by no immediate desire but only by a self-interested concern with his reputation. But we obviously do not *esteem* the shopkeeper for merely following prudent calculations. The difference between mere approval and esteem is harder for us to notice when a beneficent action is done from sympathy. For here we find in the agent an immediate willingness to do a morally good action, and we deem this praiseworthy. But Kant thinks we can notice a difference in our reaction if we compare the beneficent action done from a sympathetic inclination with a similar act done from duty. For in the latter case the agent's good will is not supported by any comfortable natural feeling or desire. The dutiful action is done solely because the agent's *willing* is good, and the agent must even rise above all natural feelings and inclinations in order to do what duty requires.

Kant's thought experiment is directed chiefly against moral sense theories, such as Hutcheson's or Hume's, which identify the moral motive with a natural feeling, such as sympathy. Kant thinks that such theories appeal to us only insofar as we do not clearly distinguish mere moral approval (including "praise and encouragement") from esteem. Common rational moral cognition, he contends, approves what is done from sympathy, but esteems only the supreme and unconditioned worth of a good will when it is displayed in acts having moral content and moral worth. These acts are done solely from that sublime rational respect for moral value, which has no need of natural feelings like sympathy. It even acts, when necessary, contrary to all such feelings.

Kant expects the experiment to elicit the right responses from his readers because he thinks that these responses accord with common rational moral cognition in every rational being – even in those who subscribe to erroneous philosophical theories. Probably Kant underestimates the extent to which his own interpretation of his examples, and hence his responses to them, are driven by his theoretical commitments. Consequently, he also underestimates the extent to which readers influenced by alternative theories of morality or moral psychology are apt to interpret the examples in ways that are uncharitable to his theory, and thus respond to them in ways he does not expect. We must keep this point in mind as we explore further the issues raised by Kant's attempt to shed light on the special value of the good will by developing the concept of acting from duty.

3.3. Motivational "overdetermination"   A sympathetic reader of the *Groundwork* will want to avoid the invidious caricature of Kant's position represented by Schiller's satire and ascribe to Kant the view that it is possible to have a good will even when one has nonmoral incentives (such as self-interest or sympathy) for doing one's duty. There are basically two ways we can do this: (a) We can deny that a will can be good only when it acts from duty, or (b) we can assert that it is possible to act from duty even where there are no temptations to act contrary to duty and nonmoral incentives to act in conformity with duty. Above I have suggested compelling reasons why we should choose (a), but many of Kant's readers tend to opt for (b). This tendency requires explanation, and also that we show why (b) is the worse interpretive option.

Option (b) may owe some of its attraction to the idea (which we have seen to be false) that Kant considers actions morally worthless unless they have what (in this one isolated passage of the *Groundwork*) he calls "moral worth" or "moral content." For that would lead us to want to extend "moral worth" to many more actions, including many dutiful actions that are "overdetermined." However, I think the main reason for choosing (b) is that it may seem plausible, quite apart from Kant's assertions, to think that a person can be *motivated by duty* even in cases where there is no temptation to violate duty and there are even nonmoral incentives to perform the dutiful action. As Marcia Baron points out, this thought is especially tempting if we assume a standard empiricist theory of action, according to which actions always are the causal results of desires, impulses or passions. "The motive of duty" is then seen as one of these, tugging at us along with other inclinations and producing actions by something like a parallelogram of psychic forces. Baron is also right in thinking that such a theory of action is entirely alien to Kant's view of agency.[9]

Since option (a) holds that a will conforming to rational principles is to be evaluated as good even when it does not act from duty, it does not require us to worry about how we should evaluate cases of "motivational overdetermination" in order to understand Kant's concept of the good will. Option (b) does require us to ask what Kant thinks of cases in which an action is prompted both by duty and nonmoral incentives. Does he think that even in these cases we can "act from duty"?

Is it possible to act partly from duty and partly from other incentives? If so, how are such actions to be evaluated regarding the goodness of will they display? I take it to be a point in favor of option (a) (both exegetically and philosophically) that Kant never even hints at an answer to such questions. He puts forward *no* theory of motivational overdetermination, not in the *Groundwork* and not anywhere else.

The proponents of option (b) may not be ready to concede this point, though. First, it might be pointed out that Kant does regard "impurity of will," the need for nonmoral incentives in order to do one's duty, and the failure of the moral law alone to be the all-sufficient incentive, as one of the three degrees of radical evil in human nature (R 6:30). But this says only that we are less than morally perfect as long as we need nonmoral incentives to do our duty. It says exactly nothing about how we are to judge particular cases in which the incentive of duty is present alongside other incentives. Specifically, it does not commit Kant to saying that a will is not good if the action lacks "moral worth" because other incentives are present.

Second, Kant says that we must strive to see that no nonmoral incentive gets mixed into the "determination of duty" (TP 8:279). This might be read as saying that we act badly if we ever let nonmoral incentives move us to do our duty. But it says no such thing. To say that we must not let nonmoral incentives mix into "the determination of duty" is to say that we must not let them corrupt our judgment about what our duties are. The danger here is not that we may "do the right deed for the wrong reason," but that nonmoral incentives may lead us to deceive ourselves about which deeds are the right ones (as when we see an action as right just because it is easy, pleasant, or advantageous).

A third objection might appeal to Kant's remark that it is "hazardous to let any other incentive (such as that of advantage) so much as cooperate alongside the moral law" (KpV 5:72). Kant says that this is *hazardous*, but not that such cooperation would by itself compromise the will's goodness. It is "hazardous," presumably, because (as we have just seen) nonmoral incentives may corrupt the "determination of duty." When the hazard of self-deception is one to which we do not succumb, our will is no less good just because considerations other than duty motivate what we do.

Perhaps yet a fourth objection could be drawn from Kant's insistence that we have a *duty* to strive after a disposition that does duty from duty or makes the moral law alone a sufficient incentive to action (MS 6:387, 392). This is entirely consistent, however, with holding that this disposition need not come into play unless duty opposes other incentives, which threaten our conformity to duty. The duty to act from duty, moreover, is only a wide, imperfect, or meritorious duty.[10] We act meritoriously whenever we act from the motive of duty (in the face of competing incentives to act contrary to duty). But we do nothing *wrong* or contrary to duty by acting in conformity to duty from other incentives. The worth of the good will shines forth more brightly in the former case, but the latter will may be equally good.

We may be disposed to think that motivational overdetermination must be an issue here because some motives seem bad or discreditable even when the actions they incite conform to duty.[11] Surely Kant would not praise or encourage actions performed from those bad motives, even if the actions conform to duty. If it is my duty to tell the truth about you, I may still do it from a vicious motive, such as envy or malice. Here my act of truth-telling deserves praise and encouragement because it is in conformity to duty, but my motivation is blamable because it involves a vicious end (one that is contrary to duty because opposed to the obligatory end of the happiness of others) (MS 6:387–388). But from this point nothing follows about how we are to evaluate cases of motivational overdetermination.

No doubt there are interesting psychological and ethical questions and controversies about what might happen when more than one incentive favors a given course of action and about how we should morally evaluate the various possibilities (once we have sorted them out).[12] The First Section of the *Groundwork* has provided philosophers with the opportunity for many interesting reflections on this fascinating topic. It is too bad that such reflections are wholly irrelevant to Kant's discussion and only mislead us about what Kant is saying there.

3.4. Duty and love   When it is correctly understood, Kant's claim that moral worth is found only in actions done from duty is much more commonsensical and less controversial than it is often taken to be.[13]

But Kant's discussion of the good will as acting from duty contains still one more stumbling block, which is probably the most difficult of all. In the course of his attempt to elicit our esteem for the will that acts from duty, Kant asserts that when a man sympathetically constituted performs beneficent acts from sympathy, these acts have no moral worth; but when the same man's sympathetic temperament has been clouded over by his own sorrows and he acts beneficently solely from duty, then his action for the first time has moral worth. There is probably nothing in Kant's ethical writings (not even the outrageous and unenlightened opinions listed in Introduction, § 1) that has gained him more hostility than his attempt to elicit people's agreement to that judgment. Sidgwick puts it very well:

> We recognize that benefits that spring from affection and are lovingly bestowed are more acceptable to the recipients than those conferred without affection, in the taste of which there is admittedly something harsh and dry: hence, in a certain way, the affection, if practical and steady, seems a higher excellence than the mere beneficent disposition of the will, as resulting in more excellent acts.[14]

Because sympathy is a mode of perception of others' needs as well as a motive of action, help given from duty may actually be less responsive to the whole range of our needs. It will, it seems, be in any case grudging and therefore damaging to our self-esteem in ways it would not if the help came from someone who enjoyed helping us. So we rightly think that beneficence from love is not only more amiable, but even more genuinely beneficent, than beneficence solely from duty. Perhaps we even think that beneficent actions performed from cold, dry duty could not be genuine beneficence at all.

The Kantian answer to this line of objection must be complex, for it depends both on what Kant thinks it is to act from duty and what he thinks it is to act from love or sympathy. Misunderstandings of the judgment to which Kant solicits our assent are only one source of these objections. The second source is a set of assumptions about the psychology of love and sympathy that are deeply at odds with Kant's anthropological theory. Kant denies moral worth to acts done from love and sympathy because he thinks that when we understand the role of those feelings in human life, we will see that moralists who hold them in unconditional esteem are sadly mistaken. We will discuss the first source of the objections right now and will address the second source only much later, in Chapter 8, § 5.

Kant's example is one in which a man of warm temperament has been rendered unsympathetic by the burden of his own sorrows. He nevertheless "tears himself out of this deadly insensibility and does the action without any inclination, simply from duty" (G 4:398). Unfortunately, Kant's description of this case is often mistaken for a general account of what his theory takes the "motive of duty" to be. But there are good reasons for thinking that he intends to be describing an *atypical* case. As we have seen, Kant thinks of actions done from duty as *difficult to distinguish* from actions done from an immediate inclination. Presumably, this is because both are actions we *want to do*. Kant is taking for granted that the desire arising from the thought of duty is typically mixed with other empirical motives, such as sympathy. Here he is trying to construct a case in which an action from duty can (for once) be clearly distinguished from an act done from any immediate inclination.

Unlike Kant's other examples of acting from duty, the example of beneficence is not one in which there is an *opposing* incentive, for the man is supposed to have a good will, which could not be reconciled with having a positive desire *not to help* others who are in need. His sorrows have rendered him *insensible* to their need, but the motive of duty *lifts him out* of this insensibility, making him *want* to help them.[15] Because the man who acts from duty *wants* to help, it is an invidious caricature to represent him as giving help *grudgingly*. In general, actions done from duty are actions to which we must constrain ourselves, but since the constraint arises internally, from a rational *volition* to do them in response to a self-given law, they are also necessarily actions we *want* to do. When we act "from duty" (in Kant's sense of this phrase), we do the dutiful action because rational incentives matter more to us than the opposing incentives of inclination, and therefore we want to do them despite the cost to us this involves. A *grudging* action is one we do under *external* constraint, which we would not want to do apart from this constraint. Hence actions done "from duty" are *never* done grudgingly, even in cases where we have self-interested incentives for not doing them. (The whole point of an ethics of autonomy is to reject the conception of moral duties as an onerous set of external constraints imposed by parents, society, God, or other external authorities.)

What we are told about the motive of duty in Section Two of the *Groundwork* helps further to correct the unappealing conception of this example that Kant's readers often form. For there Kant identifies the "motive" (*Bewegungsgrund*) proper to morality with the dignity of humanity as an end in itself (G 4:427–428). This means that the sorrowful man who acts from duty is not moved simply by the annoying thought "it is my duty to help" but rather acts out of a recognition that those he helps are beings whose worth as ends in themselves gives him a *reason* to help them. He may not care for them out of *sympathy*, but he does care for them as beings who have *dignity*. In other words, he helps them not merely because he *feels like* helping but because he rationally recognizes them as beings whose objective worth *makes a claim* on him. That recognition should make him more and not less sensitive both to their needs as a whole and to the dangers his helping may present to their self-respect.

We get a different (though not inconsistent) supplement to what Kant says about this example in the *Groundwork* if we look at his account in the *Metaphysics of morals* of the mind's receptiveness to duty through feeling. Kant lists four feelings that "lie at the ground of morality as *subjective* conditions of receptiveness to the concept of duty" (MS 6:399). It cannot be a duty to have these feelings, because they are presuppositions of moral agency. It is only "by virtue of them that [one] can be put under obligation. Consciousness of them is not of empirical origin; it can instead follow only from consciousness of a moral law, as the effect this has on the mind" (MS 6:399).

These feelings include (a) "moral feeling," which is "the susceptibility to feel pleasure or displeasure merely from being aware that our actions are consistent with or contrary to the law of duty," (b) "conscience," which is the susceptibility to moral feeling directed at *oneself*, according to one's judgment on whether one has followed the moral law, (c) "love of human beings" or "philanthropy" (*Menschenliebe*), and (d) "respect" (MS 6:399).

Because he highlights it in his foundational works, *respect* is the feeling associated in people's minds with Kantian ethics (see § 6.4). For our present purposes, however, "love of human beings" is the feeling that should draw our attention. In the *Metaphysics of morals*, as in the *Groundwork*, Kant distinguishes "pathological love," or love as a matter of feeling, from "practical love," which is a rational disposition to unselfish beneficence in response to a command of duty (MS 6:401, G 4:399). In both texts Kant also emphasizes the point that only practical love can be commanded as a duty; pathological love cannot. When we read this in the *Groundwork*, we tend to interpret him as saying that only practical love is relevant to morality, while pathological love is entirely nonmoral in content. We therefore think Kant would deny moral worth to actions motivated by any form of love as feeling. But the *Metaphysics of morals* directly contradicts that interpretation.

Philanthropic love is not an inclination, since "inclination" refers to *empirical* desire (MS 6:212, VA 7: 251, 265). Like respect, it is a feeling produced directly by pure reason acting on our sensibility; it constitutes the sensible side of motivation of the will by pure reason. Love of human beings cannot be practical love, since practical love is not a feeling, and it can be commanded by duty, but the love of which Kant is speaking here both is a feeling and cannot be a duty.[16] The reason it cannot be a duty is not that love as feeling is necessarily *irrelevant* to morality, but on the contrary because philanthropic love *is an indispensable ground of morality,* susceptibility to which is a condition of our being put under moral obligation at all. Kant underscores the point that the love of which he is speaking here is *felt* love by noting that "love is a matter of *feeling"* and hence practical love, which is a rational disposition rather than a feeling, is only "very inappropriately" called love at all (MS 6:401).

Kant's discussion of philanthropic love in the *Metaphysics of morals* forces us to revise conclusions we are likely to form based on his much better known discussion of beneficence in the First Section of the *Groundwork.* Although Kant describes the sorrowful man who acts beneficently from duty as "tearing himself out of his deadly insensibility" and acting "without any inclination," it is *not* his view that beneficent actions done from duty are done in the absence of feelings of love for those to whom one is beneficent. From the *Groundwork's* account itself, of course, we might have reasoned that "tearing himself out of deadly insensibility" is the exact opposite of *remaining in* that unfeeling state. Hence we ought to have inferred that the man who acts beneficently from duty is *not* devoid of loving feelings for those he helps. What the *Groundwork* does not tell us, though (but the *Metaphysics of morals* does), is that the very possibility of the man's having a duty to be beneficent presupposes his rational predisposition to *feelings of love* for them.

If the *Groundwork* is to be read in a way that is consistent with the *Metaphysics of morals,* then we *cannot* suppose that the sorrowful man feels no love for those he helps. His "tearing himself out of deadly insensibility" must consist in opening himself to the philanthropic love for them to which his rational nature makes him susceptible. His beneficent acts are performed "without inclination" only in the sense that the desire (the love) from which he acts is not *empirical* desire but an immediate *a priori* effect of the moral law on the mind. Perhaps a reader of the *Groundwork* could not be blamed for not reaching this interpretation based on that text alone. What that shows is that the *Groundwork* needs to be read in light of the *Metaphysics of morals* if it is to be properly understood.

Why didn't Kant say in the *Groundwork* that the sorrowful man, in acting beneficently from duty, is also acting out of love? (He would have certainly made fewer enemies among his readers if he had told them this.) Perhaps he should have, but he nevertheless had a good reason for not doing so. Philanthropy is not the only kind of love we feel for others. We can love people for other perfections besides the dignity of their rational nature, which gives us our basic *moral* reason to love them. Other forms of love are grounded on empirical inclinations and have nothing to do with morality or moral motivation. Presumably, there is no way to tell which sort of love we are feeling just by feeling it. This is one reason why actions done from duty are difficult to distinguish from those done from an immediate inclination, hence why Kant must devise *atypical* cases in his attempt to distinguish common rational moral cognition's esteem for beneficent action done from duty from its lesser evaluation of beneficent actions motivated by sympathy or other inclinations arising from a fortunate temperament.

4. Moral worth and maxims

4.1. Moral worth is not in the end   After presenting his examples of actions done from duty, Kant puts forward three propositions. The first he never states explicitly, but it is usually formulated as follows:

1. An action has moral worth only when it is done from duty.

This is followed by two propositions that are explicitly stated. The second is:

2. "An action from duty has its moral worth *not in the end* to be attained by it but in the maxim in accordance with which it is decided upon, and therefore does not depend upon the realization of the object of the action but merely upon the *principle of volition* in accordance with which the action is done without regard for any object of the faculty of desire" (G 4:399–400).

There are two points here, one negative and one positive. The negative point says about an action with moral worth what was earlier said about the good will: Its unqualified and unconditioned value, the worth for which we esteem it, is not derived from or dependent on what it accomplishes.[17] The positive point tells us where the moral worth of the action is located: in the "maxim" or "principle of volition."

Suppose I loan you a book on the condition that you promise to return it by next Monday noon. On Monday morning, thinking of your duty to keep the promise, you get in your car, drive to my house, and hand me the book, even though it has been inconvenient for you. Here the actions of coming to my house and handing me the book fulfill your duty to keep your promise, and they are performed from duty. The end, or object, of these actions is to get the book back into my possession. If I need the book at Monday noon, then I, too, will desire that end, which contributes to my happiness. Hence I will value your actions as means to it. But when someone (either I or anyone else) *esteems* your actions as having moral worth (because they were done from duty), they are not *thereby* valuing them as a means to my happiness (or to any other end). They are instead valuing your actions because they constitute the keeping of a promise (the fulfillment of a duty), and because you have chosen (meritoriously) to keep the promise even at the cost of some inconvenience to yourself. To put it in more Kantian language, your "maxim" or "principle of volition" was to keep your promise, and your action is to be esteemed because you chose to follow this maxim from the motive of duty, even in the face of contrary (nonmoral) incentives. Of course, it is still true that your action had an end (getting the book in my hands by Monday noon). But Kant thinks that common rational moral cognition supports his claim that our esteem for the action is based not on the value of this end, but solely on the fact that you chose to observe the maxim or principle of volition that promises are to be kept and did so from the motive of duty.

4.2. *Consequentialism and the value of virtue*   Consequentialists sometimes think they can accommodate this point every bit as well as Kant can. They point out that there is no inconsistency in holding these two propositions at the same time:

(i) The good will or virtuous action is valued for its own sake.
(ii) The criterion for a good will or virtuous action (what makes a will good and an action virtuous) is its good consequences.

The consequentialists are right that there is no inconsistency between these two propositions, but wrong in thinking that this solves their problem. The problem is that they owe us an account both of the value in itself which, according to (i), belongs to virtuous action or the good will. They also owe us an account of the consequentialist criterion in (ii) which is consistent with the account of the goodness of volition and action given in (i). Kant's second proposition in effect declares that there can be no satisfactory consequentialist accounts of these two matters.

Perhaps Kant underestimates the inventiveness of consequentialists, but scrutiny of one famous consequentialist account of these matters would seem to bear him out. John Stuart Mill says that virtue is originally valued for the sake of the happiness it produces, but then subsequently, by a process of habitual association, we come to value it for itself (just as money is valued first for the sake of the things it can purchase, but then by association with these it comes to be valued for its own sake).[18] Even if we accept this as a *psychological* explanation of the way people come to value virtue for its own sake, it still provides no satisfactory account of the *value* ascribed to virtue. On the contrary, it encourages the suspicion that like money, virtue really has *no value at all* considered in itself, but is valued *rationally* only when it is valued as a means. On Mill's account it apparently comes to be valued for its own sake only through an *irrational* process of psychological conditioning (which, as rational agents, we might decide we had better unlearn). Even if (begging all sorts of questions in favor of utilitarianism) we hold it to be a good thing to encourage this particular irrationality in people for the sake of its instrumental value in promoting the general happiness, we still have no satisfactory account of the *value for its own sake* that virtue is supposed to have. Mill even seems to be giving us an *error theory* of valuing virtue for its own sake.

Things become even tougher for the consequentialist if we accept Kant's proposition that the value of the good will is the sole unlimited and unconditioned good and the condition of the goodness of whatever else is good, for this entails that the value of the good will's consequences is conditional on the value of the good will itself. (The value of someone's happiness, for example, is conditional on their being worthy of happiness through the possession of a good will.) That clearly undermines the properly consequentialist proposition (ii), since it no longer makes sense to use good consequences as a criterion for determining when a will is good if the goodness of the will must be determined independently of the goodness of its consequences. And it must if it is to serve as the ground for their goodness.

That is really what is at stake in Kant's second proposition. As Kant later puts it, no material principle, presupposing an object of practical reason, can ever serve as a practical law (KpV 5:21–22); the very concept of the good, as an object of practical reason, must be derived from the moral law; the concept of the good, as such an object, can never serve as the ground of the law (KpV 5:57–58).

5. Respect for law

5.1. Duty as practical necessitation   What remains obscure at this point is the nature of the unlimited value that is being attributed to the good will (or to the maxims of actions done from duty). Kant's setting aside the value of all objects and consequences of actions seems only to make it harder to provide an account of this value. Perhaps some may think it even makes it impossible. Why is the maxim of keeping one's promises, and the disposition to act on this maxim from duty even in the face of contrary inclinations, something worthy of esteem considered merely in itself, and apart from the value of the ends or consequences of such action?

Kant's real answer to this question is not drawn merely from moral common sense and therefore is not provided anywhere in the First Section of the *Groundwork*. (We will get part of the account in Chapter 2, § 5.2, but more of it in Chapters 4 and 5, since it depends on conceptions developed in association with FH and FA.) Nevertheless, he tries to address the question as best he can at this point, by stating a third proposition he attributes to common rational moral cognition:

3. "*Duty is the necessity of an action from respect for law*" (G 4:400).

Kant says that this proposition "is a consequence of the two preceding" (G 4:400), but he cannot mean that it is logically entailed by them, for it plainly is not. In fact, at the beginning of the next paragraph he seems to be inferring (2) from (3) (G 4:401). More likely he means merely that (3) is a consistent extension of (1) and (2) or lies a bit farther along the same path of thinking down which he has been directing us with (1) and (2). Proposition (3) may be seen as "putting together" the *subjective* side of the good will, brought out in (1) through the idea of acting from duty, with the *objective* side brought out in (2) as the principle of the will that legislates to it *a priori* and is distinct from all material incentives of the will. This synthesis results in the idea of the practical necessity of an action performed purely from respect for law.[19]

Looking at (3) as a development and synthesis of (1) and (2) may also help us to get beyond Kant's rather opaque formulation of the proposition. It should not be taken as any sort of general description of what we have a duty to do, but rather as further specification of what it means to *act* from duty or of what motivates us when we act from duty in the face of contrary inclinations. The point Kant stresses is that action from duty involves "necessity"; duty is something we feel we must do, as opposed to something we do because we want to do it (on the basis of some antecedent desire) or something about which we can weigh whether or not to do it by consulting different desires and weighing them against each other.

5.2. Perfect and imperfect duty   There is a danger at this point of quite a serious misunderstanding of Kant's position. He does not mean to say that duties are constituted by inflexible, inviolable moral rules, nor does he think that when duty is in question we may never consult our inclinations concerning what to do. Kant distinguishes between "narrow" or "strict" ("owed" or "unexceptionable") duties and "wide" (or "meritorious") duties (see also Conclusion, § 3). The former alone involve *actions* (or omissions) that are strictly *required*, so that any failure to do them (or refrain) would be morally *wrong* and worthy of reproach. Wide duties are duties to set *ends*. We are required to have these ends, but it is left up to us what and how much we do in pursuit of them.[20] The particular actions we take toward them are meritorious, while any particular failure to act represents only a lack of merit rather than a piece of wrongdoing (MS 6:227). From the standpoint of ends we are required to have, actions are wrong (or a violation of narrow duty) only if they are inconsistent with having the required end, for instance, by presupposing ends which are directly contrary to the required ones. With respect to wide duties, there is a "latitude" (*Spielraum*) concerning not only which actions we perform in fulfillment of them but even how much we must do (MS 6:390). From Kant's account of the closely related distinction between "perfect" and "imperfect" duties, it is clear that within this latitude our inclinations are fully entitled to play a role in determining what we do. Perfect duties, namely, are defined as those which "admit no exception in favor of inclination," whereas imperfect duties do allow us to take inclinations into account (G 4:421).

The "necessity" of duty, which applies equally to narrow and wide or to perfect and imperfect duties, consists solely in the fact that duty involves rational *constraint* on our actions. In the case of ethical duties, this is "internal" constraint through the free power of our own reason. External constraint (through self-interested incentives such as reward and punishment) applies only to *juridical* duties, those which admit of enforcement by a state authority; in the case of ethical duties, only inward or *self*-constraint is intended, and any other sort would involve a violation of the agent's rights. Constraint applies even to wide (or imperfect) duties, such as the duty to help others in need. For here, too, the action, when done from duty, has the character of an action we want to perform because it falls under a law of reason rather than because we have an antecedent inclination to do it.

5.3. Innocence and goodness   This aspect of constraint is probably why Kant's readers are tempted to oppose actions done from "duty" to those done from "love," and to question the esteem Kant has for the former in contrast to the latter. Kant would say, I think, that the contrast they really have in mind here is one between moral *goodness* (which always involves constraint) and *innocence* (a spontaneous and wholly pre-rational impulse to do good – that is, to do what proper rational reflection would tell us should be done).

But he denies that innocence can be relied upon because it does not last and is easily seduced (G 4:404–405). He thinks that when we who have lost innocence pretend to find in our own spontaneous feelings something either more reliable or more estimable than the self-constraint of reason, this enthusiasm involves a dangerous self-deception closely allied to moral corruption. What the sentimentalist's reflective endorsement of our spontaneous sentiments expresses is not the spontaneous love of goodness he pretends to find in himself but instead the mendacious arrogance of representing himself as too good to need rational constraint in order to do his duty (KpV 5:82–86). In Part II we will look at Kant's reasons for thinking that the human will can never securely achieve the superior state to which he pretends.

The point is not merely that constrained goodness is the only sort available to us. It is also that when common rational cognition compares innocence with goodness through self-constraint, it finds on reflection that the latter alone is worthy of its true esteem. Looked at in this way, Kant's example of the man of philanthropic temperament is a story about lost innocence.[21] The man is first depicted as acting beneficently from motives of sympathy. He takes spontaneous (innocent) satisfaction in the happiness of others insofar as it is his own work. We are then to imagine his sympathy clouded over by his own sorrows and misfortunes, so that he can no longer help others merely from sympathy. Now if he is to be beneficent at all, he must "tear himself out of deadly insensibility" and *make himself* care about others through the rational thought that they have an objective *claim* on his concern. We have seen earlier that this help provided from duty does not preclude his having feelings for them, even love for them; but his concern, and even his love, can now be the result only of rational self-constraint, not of innocent feelings. They are reflective actions, actions on good principles rather than on amiable impulses.

Clearly, in his sorrowful state this benevolence on principle is supposed to be the only sort of benevolence possible for this man. We have seen that Kant does not think he could reasonably have *chosen* his present condition in preference to his earlier one, since not only was it happier for him, but it involved a benevolence to others that was easy and entirely free from inner conflict. Yet Kant is supposing that his readers are reflective beings (possessing common rational moral cognition). He hopes they can attain to the rational judgment that the man's beneficence is of greater worth now than it was earlier, precisely because it is the outcome of a struggle and is the man's own work rather than a gift he receives innocently from nature. For precisely through his loss of innocence, he has become able for the first time to give his actions "the worth of character, which is moral and incomparably the highest, namely, that he is beneficent not from inclination but from duty" (G 4: 398–399).

5.4. *The feeling of respect*   Acting from duty involves the feeling of *respect*. Kant distinguishes that feeling from all empirical desire or inclination (G 4:400). Respect is "merely an effect and not an activity of a will" (G 4:400). In other words, it results from our submitting our will to a principle or law, rather than from the process of already desiring something and then determining how to get it. I have respect only for "what is connected with my will merely as ground and never as effect" (G 4: 400). This is because respect refers us to a reason for action which is always distinct from (and prior to) any object of desire that is to result from the action. Respect is not a feeling "*received* by means of influence," but rather "*self-wrought* by means of a rational concept" (G 4:401).

We respect something not because we (antecedently) *want* to respect it, but because we are aware of reasons why we *have to* respect it. Our rational response to these reasons is what makes us want to show respect for it. Respect is basic to Kantian ethics because it is the feeling that corresponds to rational self-constraint. This kind of constraint does not involve feeling unfree or imposed on. We are not confronted by something external that *forces* us to act respectfully contrary to our rational judgment about the worth of the object (that would not be respect, but intimidation). The sense of constraint here is the feeling that we *have to* respect it, and consequently *want* to respect it, even if we antecedently didn't want to and even if respecting it involves the frustration of some of our inclinations.

Respect is a feeling of which metaethical antirealists can consistently give only deflationary accounts or error theories. For it is our fundamental experience of *objective value*.[22] Respect is directed at something whose worth we recognize by reason from within ourselves, and we recognize that worth as essentially greater than the worth of any object of inclination (whether of desire or aversion). Thus as Kant tells us later

in the *Groundwork*, the respect we have for the moral law, or for humanity as end in itself, is virtually an equivalent expression for the esteem we
have for the good will (G 4:436).

Respect is a complex and even a problematic feeling, because it goes
with a loss of innocence and involves an ambivalent mixture of contrasting attitudes, principally toward oneself. Kant tells us that respect
strikes down our self-conceit, because it presents something to us (the
dignity of the law or the worth of rational nature as an end in itself),
which absolutely requires our recognition without ingratiating itself to
us by flattering our self-preference or appealing to our inclinations. Yet
it does this only through the awe and wonderment we feel at the dignity of our sublime vocation as rational beings which we must strive to
live up to (KpV 5:73, 161–162; KU 5:245, R 6:49).

The *innocent* will *can* respect nothing, because it lacks the self-
reflection presupposed by both self-esteem and self-conceit. It *does not
need* to respect anything because its inclinations, which are in a natural
(if fragile) harmony with the good, do not yet need to be checked by
reason. The innocent will needs no law. Its goodness may be adequately
accounted for by a theory of moral feeling, such as we find in Hutcheson and Hume, which grounds everything on natural feelings of sympathy, approval, and disapproval. But the supreme goodness of the will,
which acts from duty and which we *esteem* precisely because it is good despite its loss of innocence – this cannot be understood except through
the concept of a law we obey simply as rational beings and toward which
we have the more complex, problematic, and wholly self-generated feeling of *respect*. "Hence nothing other than the *representation of the law* in
itself, *which can of course occur only in a rational being*, insofar as it and not
the hoped for effect is the determining ground of the will, can constitute the pre-eminent good we call moral" (G 4:401).

5.5. The first formulation of the law   Kant now asks *what law it is* for which
we have this respect. His answer is: "Since I have deprived the will of
every impulse that could arise for it from obeying some law, nothing is
left but the universal lawfulness of actions in general, which alone is to
serve the will as a principle, that is, *I ought never to act except in such a way
that I could will that my maxim should be a universal law*" (G 4:402). It is
through this argument that Kant introduces the first formulation of the
supreme principle of morality, usually called the Formula of Universal
Law (FUL).

We saw in the previous section that Kant's acute analysis of what is involved in acting from duty, taken together with his views about the nature of the good will and its fundamental status among values, poses serious problems for any ethical theory that would ground moral values in the value of ends or consequences. But it is one thing to create such problems and another for Kant to attempt to infer the content of a supreme principle of morality solely from his analysis of moral motivation. Nevertheless, Kant is anxious to arrive at a formulation of the moral law, even on the slim basis of the value claims he has argued for thus far. His impatience leads him into fallacious arguments and has occasioned a lot of misunderstanding of his ethical theory.

First, he infers that since he has claimed that respect for law must not involve any impulse for an object that might be attained by obeying the law, the law itself cannot command anything but universal lawfulness. However, the property of being free from material impulses has been claimed to be a property not of the moral law but only of the motive we have for obeying it. We have been given no reason for thinking that the latter property entails anything at all about the former.

Second, the sole property ascribed to the law on the basis of this inference seems to be utter vacuity: The content of the law is described as "nothing but the universal lawfulness of actions in general." There are any number of ways in which we might take this description. We cannot decide what interpretation to place on it by appealing to its derivation, since that (as we have just seen) is based on fallacious reasoning (or at least it is an argument with a large gap remaining to be filled). It would be highly uncharitable to interpret Kant as saying that we are bound by any universal law anyone might propose, since that would lead to absurdity and even contradictions (since people could propose mutually contradictory laws). A more natural interpretation, that we are to obey whatever *valid* universal laws there are, would be innocuous, but it would leave us totally uninformed about the content of these laws.[23]

When he infers from "the conformity of actions as such to universal law" to FUL, Kant once again reasons fallaciously. (We will run into similar problems with Kant's derivation of FUL in the Second Section.) FUL goes well beyond the idea of mere conformity to universal law, no matter how it is interpreted, since it introduces the further idea that the test of whether a maxim conforms to universal law is whether *I could will the maxim to be a universal law*. No reason has been suggested why the test of conformity to universal law should be what *I* can or do will.

Of course, once we are familiar with the later argument of the *Groundwork*, we recognize this as an introduction of the Kantian idea of autonomy (which was also hinted at in the footnote discussing respect at G 4:401). That idea, however, is grounded on philosophical arguments we cannot evaluate at this point because we will not even get to them until well into the Second Section. Here Kant is supposed to be appealing only to ordinary rational moral cognition, which is obviously insufficient to get him what he wants.

The First Section does all it really needs to do, however, if it shows readers how they may interpret their everyday moral attitudes in the new ways that Kant's philosophical theory will eventually require. For the strategy of the *Groundwork* does not require complete argumentative success in the First Section. In the Second Section, namely, Kant undertakes an entirely new search for the moral law, this time on *philosophical* grounds. Because independent arguments for Kant's reinterpretation of our moral attitudes will be presented in the Second Section, readers who stubbornly resist it should not think they yet have any decisive objection to Kant's theory.

RATIONAL WILL AND IMPERATIVES

1. The will

1.1. The faculty of desire   In the Second Section of the *Groundwork*, Kant undertakes a properly *philosophical* search for the principle of morality. "Everything in nature," he says, "works in accordance with laws. Only a rational being has the capacity to act *in accordance with the representation of laws*" – a capacity Kant characterizes as *will* and directly equates with "practical reason" (G 4:412). Behind these claims lies a theory of the will that Kant tended to take for granted but soon found it necessary to explain a bit more fully in response to bewildered critics (KpV 5:9; cf. MS 6:211–214).

Kant divides the mind's powers into three basic ones: the faculty of cognition, feeling (of pleasure and displeasure), and the faculty of desire (KU 5:198). These powers typically work together. It is especially true in the case of the faculty of desire that it operates only in concert with both cognition and feeling. Kant defines the faculty of desire (*Begehrungsvermögen*) as the capacity to produce an object (or state of affairs) by means of a representation (*Vorstellung*) of that object (KpV 5:9, MS 6:211). To *desire* an object (or state of affairs) is to have a *representation* of it accompanied by a feeling of *pleasure*. (*Aversion* is a representation accompanied by a feeling of displeasure.) Desire may or may not involve an awareness of our capacity to produce the object. Where this awareness is lacking, desire is called 'wish' (VA 7:251). In the case of empirical desire, the feeling of pleasure comes about through the way the representation of the object affects our susceptibility to feeling, and the feeling is called an 'impulse' (*Antrieb*) (MS 6:213). When such a sensuous desire becomes habitual, it is called an 'inclination' (*Neigung*) (MS 6:212; VA 7:251).

1.2. Ends and maxims Everything said so far about the faculty of desire applies equally to rational beings and to brute animals. Kant holds that in the brutes, impulses operate mechanically to produce behavior predetermined by instinct. Brutes are not only "pathologically affected" by impulses, but "pathologically necessitated" by them (KrV A534/B562). This means that a brute cannot resist impulses, or decide whether to satisfy a desire, or even deliberate about how to satisfy it. Brutes do not subject their behavior to self-direction or (therefore) to norms of any kind; they are not agents because they have no conception of themselves as agents (VA 7:127).

The fundamental normative act for Kant is *setting an end*, which is therefore the prerogative solely of rational nature, and it is an act of freedom (G 4:437). Setting ends means submitting to the self-discipline of performing those actions (called 'means') which are judged suitable to achieve the end.[1] The teleology in a brute's behavior is never consciously self-imposed, but is always the result of mechanisms hard-wired into the brute's instinctive behavioral repertoire (including learned associations grounded on instincts). Even the idea of an "end" with respect to the behavior of brutes is the product of our reflective theorizing about the observable arrangement of mechanical causes of what the brute does.[2]

A faculty of desire that responds mechanically to impulses is called a "brute power of choice" (*tierische Willkür* or *arbitrium brutum*). Kant contrasts this with the human power of choice, which is "sensitive" (affected by sensuous impulses) but also "free" (a *freie Willkür* or *arbitrium liberum*) (KrV A534/B562). Only a free power of choice is a will (*Wille*). It follows that although brutes have a kind of 'choice' (*Willkür*), they have no will (*Wille*). Not only do rational beings have the capacity to resist impulses, but even when the rational faculty of desire acts on sensuous impulses, it is never determined by them mechanically, as a brute power of choice *always* is.[3]

Will is the capacity to act on the *representation* of laws or on principles (G 4:412). In the case of a will (or *free* power of choice), an empirical impulse does not act directly or mechanically as the cause of action but serves instead only as an incentive (*Triebfeder*) to the adoption of a *principle* and the setting of an *end*. "An incentive can determine the will to an action *only insofar as the individual has taken it up into his maxim* (has made it into a general rule, according to which he will conduct himself)" (R 6:24). (This crucial Kantian idea has been emphasized by Henry Allison under the name "the Incorporation Thesis."[4]) The Incorporation

Thesis says that in the case of a will, desires produce actions only by the way they are incorporated into maxims or practical principles that serve the agent as subjectively adopted norms. Every maxim, Kant insists, involves an end, which serves as its "matter" (G 4:436, KpV 5:21). Conversely, the setting of an end always involves the implicit adoption of some general rule serving as the basis for a choice of means.

The Incorporation Thesis says that desire is involved in "volition" mainly through being incorporated into a maxim. But it does not say that volitional agency consists merely in the adoption of maxims. Cases of weakness of will, for example, often involve an exercise of volitional agency in which someone fails to act according to a maxim, but not necessarily by adopting a contrary maxim. In such a case, desires do not merely push us around as a stick moves a stone; they have an impact on the way we act (or fail to act) on maxims. The most Kant needs (or wants) to claim along this line is that to be a volitional agent one must have the capacity to adopt maxims, and to respond to desires by incorporating (or refusing to incorporate) them into maxims. Nor is the claim that when people perform actions they act on maxims (or subjective normative principles) the same as saying that they must formulate these principles consciously.

Kant understands inclination as habitual desire, and he understands habit as operating unreflectively (MS 6:479). Which norms we decide a person really accepts depends in part on their verbal profession and conscious intentions and in part on their actual behavior; when there is sufficient conflict between these two factors, it is unclear or indeterminate what norm they adopt. Since Kantian maxims are subjectively normative principles, this point applies to them.

Nor does the Incorporation Thesis imply that people's actions are predictable or that they follow some sort of rigid (proverbially "Prussian") regularity. A person might act on a general principle only once and then abandon it, or might keep it as a subjective norm but simply neglect from then on ever to act on it. The Incorporation Thesis is just as applicable to people who act capriciously and unreflectively as to those who follow the same course throughout their lives and can tell you beforehand what they will do. Kant's theory of action, as interpreted through the Incorporation Thesis, does not deny that feeling plays an essential role in motivating actions (by providing incentives for the adoption of maxims). Kant also allows that there are cases where we act from "affects," or sudden rushes of feeling that overpower us, although they do not deprive us of free agency (see Chapter 8, §1).

(When we fail to act rightly through the influence of affects, we are to blame not for acting on bad maxims but rather for failing to act on good ones.)

The point of the Incorporation Thesis is to claim that impulses or desires determine action chiefly by serving as incentives for the adoption of maxims. To put the point negatively, the Incorporation Thesis denies that desires (simply as such, even when combined with beliefs) can ever suffice to explain actions. To be a rational agent is to see oneself as standing over against one's desires and to regard them as possible *grounds* for making or modifying choices.[5] In the face of a new desire, I can modify my existing ends, perhaps choosing to pursue them to a more limited extent than before, or by adopting different means to them. Or I can choose simply to resist a desire and not satisfy it at all. Of course this is not to say that the desire will simply go away, nor is it to deny that we sometimes act on desires whose influence on our actions we refuse to admit. As we have already seen, Kant is very much aware of our tendency to deceive ourselves in such matters. He even maintains, on these same grounds, that we can never be quite certain on what incentives we may be acting (G 4:407).

1.3. Volition and interest   Kant is sometimes misrepresented as holding that to act from duty is to act without (or even contrary to) *desire*,[6] for Kant denies that we could ever act without desire. We saw in Chapter 1, however, that sometimes desire is not a *cause* but is instead an *effect* of reason's determining the will (MS 6:211). This happens, for example, when we act from duty or respect for law. Here we do not do our duties because we have an independent desire to do them, which provides some indispensable conative augmentation to our recognition of them as duties. We desire to do our duties because we recognize them as duties and therefore choose to do them out of respect for a rational principle. The *feeling* of respect is not so much a cause of the will's determination as a necessary by-product of this determination in a being whose will is finite, natural, and thus susceptible to feeling (KpV 5:72, 76).

It follows that *willing* an end is not the same as desiring it. Desire is the passive experience of representing an object accompanied by a feeling of pleasure. Will is the activity of determining one's practical faculty to seek an end that has been set according to a maxim or practical principle.[7] The basic activity in willing is the adoption of normative principles for the regulation of our conduct. Desires involve the representation of objects (or states of affairs) whose existence we would experience as agreeable. But ends are possible states of affairs to whose actualization we are actively directing our powers. Willing an end is therefore quite different from merely *wishing* for something, since willing involves the subjection of one's actions to a norm and, to the extent that one acts on the norm, also the summoning of the agent's powers to produce it through actions chosen as appropriate means (G 4:394; VA 7:251).

When our understanding judges that a feeling of pleasure or displeasure is connected with a certain (kind of) object according to a rule, Kant says that we have an "interest" in the object (G 4:413, MS 6:212, cf. KU 5:204). Our awareness of inclinations (or habitual desires) creates interests because it enables us to anticipate the satisfaction of our desires and hence to adopt principles leading to their satisfaction. A brute power of choice, which acts from instinctive impulses rather than from principles or toward ends, thus involves no interest. When an interest arises from inclination, it is called "pathological interest." But interest is also present in actions done from duty or pure rational grounds (KU 5:207–209). For in setting an end from reason, we determine our faculty of desire by a rule in accord with which it will experience pleasure or displeasure in an object. Kant calls this "practical interest," and says that in such a case we "take an interest" in the object, even if we are not "acting from interest" (G 4:413).

A being with will, when it has a variety of desires to satisfy, has the capacity to adopt a set of principles that take account of the long-term or comprehensive satisfaction of its desires. This involves setting a comprehensive end, an idea of a "sum of satisfaction" or "happiness" (G 4:399). This idea, and the principles of action that correspond to it, are closely connected to "self-interest" because they involve an attempt to specify rules that connect actions to what we find comprehensively pleasant or satisfying. Since a brute has no conception of itself as an agent and does not act on norms, it has no conception of self-interest and no capacity to represent its own happiness. (Brutes can be pleased or contented but never consciously happy. Any conception we may form of what we could call the happiness or self-interest of a nonrational being is a regulative theoretical construct fashioned by a rational inquirer as a way of making the brute's life processes intelligible.)

1.4. The good   The only kind of being that is capable of understanding the concept 'good' is a practically reflective being, a being with will, a being that must choose what to aim at, what to do, how to employ its powers, and hence a being for which there are normative questions:[8]

"The will is a faculty of choosing only that which reason, independently of inclination, recognizes as practically necessary, i.e. as good" (G 4:412). We think of something as *good* whenever we regard ourselves as having a reason to constrain ourselves to pursue it even in the face of contrary inclinations that might tempt us not to pursue it.

Note that in this account of 'good' there is nothing specifically *moral*. Indeed, nothing we have been saying so far about the will or practical reason has brought in any specifically moral considerations at all. The point so far is merely that to set an end is to judge it as *good*, which means: as *worth* pursuing. To see an *action* as good is to see it as one that *should* be performed in consequence of a rational principle of some kind, irrespective of one's momentary impulses or inclinations (even if the adoption of the rational principle itself is based on inclination). We will get to moral considerations only later, when the rational principles are not *maxims*, but *laws* or *imperatives*, and indeed specifically *categorical* imperatives.[9]

Will involves the capacity to discriminate between actions one *should* perform (or should have performed) and acts one should not (or should not have). For this reason, will also presupposes and involves a conception of *oneself* as an agent, and the ability to be concerned about one's success or failure in pursuing the ends one has set, in following the principles one has chosen. This is why Kant identifies the dignity of our rational nature with the capacity to form the representation 'I' (VA 7:127). Raising normative questions about one's desires therefore leads to raising normative questions about one's actions, and therefore (even more fundamentally) to raising normative questions about *oneself.* A being with will therefore has a capacity to esteem or despise itself, which, as we shall see presently, lies at the ground of all its other volitional capacities.

2. *A priori* practical principles

Everything said about the will so far, in other words, applies to a rational being that acts solely on *empirical* practical principles adopted solely on the basis of inclinations. But Kant holds that for rational beings, who are capable of grasping the concept 'good', there must also be principles of reason, which are independent of inclination. Since "reason" is defined as the "faculty of principles" (KrV A299/B356), Kant also identifies will with "practical reason" (G 4:412). Reason is the highest of our faculties in the sense that it is the most independently active faculty because it is the one that unifies the exercise of all the others and in this sense "supplies [all] the principles of *a priori* cognition" (KrV A11/B24). Our theoretical knowledge of the world involves a combination of what is *a priori* (contributed by the exercise of our faculties) with what is given from outside (empirical data). Reason plays a similar role in the practical sphere when it responds to inclinations by generating principles of action or maxims, taking the objects of empirical desire into account in setting ends, selecting policies of action for their achievement, and forming an idea of our happiness in relation to which actions can be judged regarding the agent's self-interest.

2.1. The a priori   As we shall see in § 3, Kant thinks there is an indispensable place for *a priori* principles even in the pursuit of entirely empirical ends (whose pursuit is governed by hypothetical imperatives). But Kant holds that there are also practical *laws,* that is, "pure" or *a priori* practical principles that necessitate the will independently of all antecedent desires and all ends previously set. His most emphatic and controversial thesis on this score is that "pure reason can of itself be practical" (G 4:458, KpV 5:15).

This thesis may seem implausible or baffling for various reasons. Some of the obstacles to accepting it are simply empiricist prejudices about the whole notion of the *a priori*, whether used in a theoretical or a practical context. It may help to overcome them if we realize that in addition to practical *laws* (*a priori* moral principles that are categorically binding on the will), Kant holds that other *a priori* practical principles are necessarily and universally binding on the will even when it is acting on ends set in response to inclinations. Most of this chapter, in fact (through the end of § 4), will be devoted to the explication of these *nonmoral* (yet nonetheless *a priori*) practical principles.

Even the definition of *a priori* as "independent of experience" is opaque because it tends to suggest the quite absurd picture of your closing your eyes, stopping your ears, shutting yourself off from all external input – and *precisely thereby* acquiring some knowledge (which is all the purer for being untainted by sensory information). The picture may be suggested by the asceticism of Plato's *Phaedo* and by a certain Augustinian conception of spirituality (which was later put by Descartes to original epistemological uses on behalf of early modern natural science). But the Kantian *a priori* should not be associated with such images, and it is precisely to dispel them that Kant begins the *Critique of Pure Reason* by insisting that all cognition whatever (*a priori* as well as empirical) *begins* only with experience, hence even *a priori* cognition has experience as one of its necessary conditions (KrV A1, B1). The distinction is between cognition for which experience is merely an occasion and cognition that depends in a stronger way on the specific contents of experience as they are supplied by sensation.

Kant is convinced that some of our cognitions must be relatively independent of these contents because he thinks that some propositions needed in mathematics, natural science, and metaphysics have the form of strictly universal and necessary generalizations, while at the same time he is convinced by Humean skeptical arguments that no strictly universal or necessary propositions can be validly inferred from the particular contents of experience (KrV B3–6). Kant regards the idea of moral obligation as expressing universality and necessity, and hence as involving *a priori* principles, too (G 4:389, KpV 5:80). Since what is universal and necessary cannot be based on experience, it must have an *a priori* foundation.

2.2. *Practical universality and necessity* "Universality" and "necessity," however, don't appear to mean quite the same thing in practical contexts as in theoretical ones. Kant thinks rational principles (including but not limited to moral principles) are "universally valid" in the sense that they are normative for all beings capable of rational conduct (G 4: 389). This does not imply that all rational beings, irrespective of their nature or situation, must find exactly the same actions rational or irrational, or even that they must recognize the same rules about this. (Still less does it imply that any individual's or culture's view about the norms of rationality are ever infallible or incontrovertible.) It means only that insofar as what we take to be rational really is such (i.e., really is rationally binding); it must be understood in terms of the same *fundamental* principles (whatever the degree of understanding of those we may have acquired).[10]

What Kant means by "necessity" in moral contexts is that rational principles do not apply to us merely because we happen contingently to have some desire (G 4:389). Whether we are speaking of moral or nonmoral principles of reason, these principles "necessitate" in the sense that they *constrain* (or should constrain) me to do what they prescribe irrespective of what I may otherwise desire to do at the moment. In other words, the fact that I do not *want* to do something can never by itself defeat the claim that I am rationally required to do it. (This claim, once again, applies equally to moral and to nonmoral, i.e., instrumental and prudential, requirements of practical reason.)

Kant thinks universality implies apriority because if the practical principles were empirical, then we could know that they apply to all people only by induction from empirical features we happened to find common to all people. If there are genuine principles of reason, however (whether of instrumental rationality, prudence, or morality), then these principles must apply equally to all beings who have the faculty of will or practical reason, irrespective of any additional empirical features that these beings share or in which they may differ. Necessity implies apriority because an empirically grounded practical principle would be based on some empirical desire we contingently have. If a contingent empirical desire were the only reason we had for following the principle, then it could not claim universal validity.

But what if there are no practical principles at all that are "universal" and "necessary" in these senses? In that case, there would be no principles of reason at all. Throughout the first two sections of the *Groundwork*, Kant repeatedly reminds us that morality, as common rational cognition conceives of it, and as its philosophical concept is being developed, might be nothing but "high-flown fancy," a "chimerical idea," or "cobweb of the brain," and that the moral duties we take ourselves to have might be illusory (G 4:394, 423, 425, 429, 440, 445). If this were established, then we would not abandon all talk about reason and morality, but instead decide to mean something more modest by such talk, something that involves neither necessity nor universality nor (therefore) *a priori* principles of any kind. However, Kant has a strategy (sketched in Chapter 1, § 1) for showing that reason in general and morality in particular – in the undeflated sense of something based on principles whose claims are universal and necessary – is not an illusion.[11]

In the meantime, Kant's attempt to provide a philosophical account not only of morality but also of instrumental reason and prudence, has the aim of showing us that *a priori* principles play a vital role in what we actually recognize as the standards of practical reason (in both its moral and nonmoral uses). If there are no *a priori* normative principles, then not only morality but instrumental reason and prudence must be regarded as illusions. Thus moral reason cannot be rendered merely empirical by reducing it to prudential or instrumental reason, or deflated into a "system of hypothetical imperatives." If that is right, then the cost of adopting an empiricist deflationary account of moral reason is much higher than proponents of such accounts usually pretend.[12]

Kant argues that any cognitions that have the features of universality and necessity cannot be due to experience and must therefore be *a pri-*

ori. But this provides us with only a negative account of what we mean by '*a priori*'. In speaking of theoretical cognition, Kant holds (more positively) that all our cognition results from the operation of our faculties on sensible data given from outside us. Cognition is empirical, or *a posteriori*, if it is due to the external data, but it is *a priori* if it is due to our faculties. There is an obvious problem with drawing the distinction this way: If our cognition is always the result of our faculties operating on the data, then it looks as if all our cognition will be due to *both* factors. In that case it might seem as if every cognition is necessarily both empirical and *a priori*, so no cognition is simply empirical or wholly *a priori*, and hence perhaps there is no point in drawing the distinction at all.

Kant is aware of this problem and says that we may need practice before we can distinguish the *a priori* from the empirical (KrV B1-2, A23/B36). He thinks a detailed analysis of the way our faculties operate will reveal that some features of the objects of our cognition do not vary with varying empirical input and for this reason can be attributed wholly to our faculties. For example, Kant thinks that space and time, being mere forms of sensibility, are independent of the empirical sensations presented to us. Therefore, the spatio-temporal properties of things are knowable *a priori* in pure mathematics. The same is true of the features of the world that depend on the way in which our understanding must conceptualize it if we are to have a unified experience. For example, Kant thinks it can be known *a priori* that objects of experience are both intensively and extensively quantifiable and that changes are alterations of a mind-independent substance (an appearance) according to causal laws.

2.3. A priori *volition and enlightenment*   It is important that on Kant's theory, what is *a priori* is *produced by* our faculties, not *given to* them, whether through sensation or otherwise. This means that for Kant *a priori* cognition is utterly different from *innate* cognition, whose existence Kant emphatically denies (UE 8:221). What is innate is *implanted* in us at birth (by God, for example, or through our genetic constitution), independently of both sense experience and the exercise of our faculties. What is *a priori*, by contrast, we ourselves produce through the exercise of our faculties. This point is especially important in the case of practical principles. A moral law can be truly autonomous only if it is *a priori*; but an *innate* moral principle would be an instance of heteronomy. This is because an *a priori* principle is one we give ourselves, in contrast to one that we are given from outside (whether environmentally, by authority, custom, or tradition, or innately, by supernatural divine infusion or some nonrational genetic predisposition).[13]

Kant attaches *historical* significance to the philosophical enterprise of coming to be aware of our own faculties and what they contribute to cognition. This is the task of a *critical* (as opposed to a "dogmatic") philosophy. It characterizes an age of *enlightenment*, in which the human race collectively is entering into a condition of majority or adulthood (*Mündigkeit*). A critical or enlightenment moral philosophy is therefore one in which human beings achieve self-knowledge of their own cognitive capacities and justified confidence in them. This awareness is necessarily expressed in *a priori* principles, since to call a principle *a priori* is to say that it expresses a self-sufficient contribution of our faculties.

The Kantian *a priori* in practical philosophy is therefore *precisely the opposite* of what empiricist caricatures represent when they say that philosophers believe in the *a priori* only so as to hallow their received prejudices and immunize them against critical examination. For Kant, *a priori* principles are precisely those principles generated through *our own thinking*. They contrast to principles we owe to external sources, such as tradition, authority – or experience, which, apart from the use we make of it through our critical capacities of reason, would be equally a source of blind prejudice. That is why Kant associates *a priori* practical principles both with the idea of autonomy and with the maxim of enlightenment: always to think for oneself (O 8:146).

The idea of an *a priori* practical principle does involve a controversial thesis: that our practical faculties do not consist merely in the capacity to respond in various ways to desires that we find already there pressing in upon us, but rather that *we ourselves* (through the exercise of reason and independently of any empirical desire) can be the source of *principles* on which to act. In order for there to be *a priori* principles, there have to be some feelings and desires that do not arise in us merely passively, as a result of our undergoing certain experiences, but proceed from practical principles that are solely the products of our rational faculty. Kant usually emphasizes the importance of such principles for morality, but we shall now see that they are equally required for prudential, and even for merely instrumental, uses of practical reason.

3. Hypothetical imperatives

3.1. Kinds of imperatives   Kant conceives of two general kinds of will (or practical reason). A "holy will" necessarily follows rational principles, while a "finite" or "pathologically affected" will can fail to follow them and therefore must (at least sometimes) *constrain* itself to follow them (G 4:414). When addressed to a will of the latter kind, a rational practical principle is called an *imperative* (G 4:413). Kant also famously distinguishes between two kinds of imperatives. *Hypothetical* imperatives presuppose an end already set and command an action as a means to that end. Their constraint of the will is therefore conditional on the agent's having set the end in question. *Categorical* imperatives are not dependent in this way; they require the performance of actions (and the setting of ends) without being conditional on any prior setting of an end.

Kant's terminology here may mislead us in several ways. An "imperative" in his sense is not restricted to any grammatical form but is any principle that governs a will's rational self-constraint. Since (as we have seen) the term 'good' for Kant refers to that which reason recognizes as practically necessary, the statement 'That would be a good thing to do' is well-suited to function as an imperative (whether we mean 'good as a means' or 'good as an end,' and whether or not the good intended is moral in character). Nor are the terms 'hypothetical' and 'categorical' to be understood in a merely grammatical (or logical) signification. When it conveys the existence of a moral obligation, the statement 'If you make a promise, keep it' is a categorical imperative. The grammatically unconditional 'Look out!' functions as a hypothetical imperative if what it conveys is that I ought to turn my attention to the source of some imminent danger if I have the end of avoiding injury to my body.[14]

3.2. *Imperatives derived from ends*   To set an end is to undertake a self-given normative commitment to carry out some plan for achieving the end. Sometimes when I have set an end, I subsequently feel an impulse or desire either to perform some action that precludes achieving the end or else to refrain from an action that is necessary for achieving the end. In such cases, I must (on pain of a failure of rationality) make up my mind whether to abandon the end or to abstain from acting on the impulse. This is why any setting of an end also involves acting on *imperatives*. The general principle of these imperatives could be expressed as what I will call the 'imperative of ends' (EI):

EI: If you set an end Z (and as long as you retain Z as an end), then if possible perform some set of actions that will foreseeably result in the attainment of Z, and refrain from any action that would pre-clude the attainment of Z.

Kant never states any principle as encompassing as EI but confines him-self to a more limited principle, the principle of "hypothetical impera-tives" (HI), which may be regarded as one of the corollaries of EI:[15]

HI: If you set an end Z, perform whatever actions are indispen-sably necessary means to the attainment of Z that lie in your power (cf. G 4:414–417).

HI is more limited in scope than EI, since HI tells us only that we must perform those actions whose omission would preclude the achievement of our end Z, where EI tells us (more positively) to plan and carry out (if possible) some set of actions that may be reasonably foreseen to re-sult in Z. Kant maintains that HI is an imperative rationally valid for us because it is an *analytic* proposition:

> Whoever wills the end, so far as reason has decisive influence on his ac-tion, wills also the indispensably necessary means to it that lie in his power. For in willing an object as my effect, my causality as an acting cause, i.e. the use of means, is already thought, and the imperative de-rives the concept of actions necessary to this end from the concept of will-ing this end. (G 4:417)

Kant's claim that hypothetical imperatives are analytic is often puzzling to his readers, perhaps because it is easily misunderstood. Kant does not mean that the means-end connection represented in the imperative (which typically represents some sort of causal connection between the employment of the means and the coming about of the end) is analytic. That connection involves a purely theoretical proposition, which is typ-ically both synthetic and empirical. Nor does he mean that it is an ana-lytic proposition that everyone who sets an end will in fact perform the actions indispensably necessary to achieving it, for that, too, would be a theoretical proposition that is synthetic (and sometimes false). The proposition he is interested in is a *normative* one (HI). If I fail to per-form the actions indispensable to my end, then I am not acting ac-cording to a rational norm I have laid down for myself in setting the end, and hence reason does not have decisive influence on my actions. To violate HI thus involves a failure of instrumental rationality, a failure to comply with a normative principle that is contained in the very con-cept of the normative activity of adopting an end, and is in that sense analytic: The very concept of the normative act of willing an end Z contains within it the normative consequence: "You must will every indispensably necessary means to Z that is within your power." There would be a related failure of rationality in an agent that willed Z as an end, realized that M is indispensably necessary to achieve Z, but found in itself (when the time came) no desire to employ M. That this would involve a failure of rationality is analytic, even though it is a synthetic (and sometimes false) theoretical proposition that the desire in question is present in the agent.

A similar claim to analyticity could be made on behalf of the broader principle EI. If the concept of willing an end already contains the concept of willing a means, then a person who wills an end Z already wills to execute some rational plan through which Z is to come about. The plan may be as yet unspecified, but without the conception of such a plan or at least the intention to form one as well as a rational commitment to adhere to such a plan, we cannot regard the person as *willing an end* (as opposed to idly wishing for an object of desire). It is of course a synthetic (and sometimes false) proposition that an agent who sets Z as an end ever forms such a plan or has any desire whatever to carry one out. But the *normative* proposition (or imperative) that such agents *should* so act (and are otherwise guilty of a failure of rationality) is analytically true.

Every science that can be applied to practice provides us with information about how to achieve certain ends. Hence Kant says that every science contains hypothetical imperatives that he sometimes calls "problematic imperatives," sometimes "technical imperatives," and sometimes "imperatives of skill" (G 4:415; cf. Ak 20:200n). To illustrate such imperatives he offers examples from both geometry and medical science, which we could formulate thus: "If you want to bisect an angle, draw two arcs from each of its extremities" (G 4:417); "If you want to cure this disease K, then administer medication M to the patient in the prescribed dosage" (G 4:415). Following his principle HI, Kant apparently regards the actions commanded by these imperatives as indispensably necessary to achieving the ends in question.

"All imperatives are expressed by an 'ought' and thereby indicate the relation of an objective law of reason to a will" (G 4:413). This statement applies equally to hypothetical and categorical imperatives. An "objective principle" is distinguished from a mere maxim in that it is valid for or rationally binding on all rational beings. Therefore, Kant is claiming that hypothetical imperatives, no less than categorical ones, are universally binding on all rational beings and represent an action as objectively necessary. Of course a hypothetical imperative is not universally binding in the sense that all rational beings must *unconditionally* perform the actions it specifies. But it is universally binding in the sense that it tells *any* rational being that *if* it sets the end of bisecting an angle or curing disease *K*, then it ought to constrain itself to perform the prescribed actions.[16]

3.3. Instrumental rationality and desire   This is an important result for Kant's purposes, because it shows (what was hinted at toward the end of the previous section) that those who reject the idea of a categorical imperative because they think that all rationality is only instrumental are already committed to affirming certain things whose denial they are tempted to use in support of their rejection of categorical imperatives.

Some reject the idea of categorical imperatives, for example, because a categorical imperative is supposed to bind us irrespective of any desire for an end, and they think that actions are always produced by a desire for something plus a belief about how to get it. The desire supplies the motivation for the action, while the belief determines which actions are rational to perform once the end has been set. On this picture, "practical rationality" becomes nothing but the way new *theoretical* information may be thought of as altering the *content* of the desires we think of as causing behavior. I want *Z*, for instance; I then acquire the belief that if I do *M*, then this will result in *Z*. 'Practical rationality' consists only in the process by which my desire for *Z*, as a consequence of my acquisition of this belief, produces a new desire, the desire to do *M*.

In order to appreciate the inadequacy of this picture, we need only to emphasize that instrumental reason is *normative*. It is not merely the effect knowledge has on desire. The threat *to rationality* in pursuing an end is *not* that our desires will not be informed by the right beliefs about how to achieve the end, but rather that when the time comes to perform the necessary action, our desires may no longer conform to the norms of conduct we established in setting the end. The function of instrumental reason is not to inform desire regarding means but to constrain the will to hold to its rational plan to pursue an end, perhaps even in the face of distracting or contrary desires that tempt the will to abandon the plan.

Of course Kant does *not* deny that when you follow a hypothetical imperative there is also *desire* for the end, which moves you to act according to your plan. The only question is whether the desire is antecedent to or consequent upon determination of the will by an imperative. If it precedes determination of the will, then we are not dealing with a genuine case of practical reason at all, but only of action on a desire that coincides contingently with our rational pursuit of an end. The desire from which we act is a function of instrumental *reason* only if it is *produced by pure reason*, in accordance with an *a priori* principle such as EI or HI.

Those who reject the idea of a categorical imperative on the ground that it is an *a priori* principle must therefore be equally prepared to reject the idea of a hypothetical imperative and instrumental rationality, too. Or, contrapositively, those who find nothing problematic about instrumental rationality should recognize that they cannot consistently object to the idea of a categorical imperative on the ground that it is supposed to be universally valid, necessary, and *a priori* or that it is supposed to move the will independently of empirical desires, for those properties already belong to hypothetical imperatives.

4. Assertoric imperatives

4.1. Prudential reason Kant distinguishes two kinds of hypothetical imperatives. Some are grounded on a contingent end, which any rational being may either have or not have. These are "problematical imperatives," "imperatives of skill," or "technical imperatives" (G 4:414–416).[17] Other hypothetical imperatives are grounded on an end that may be attributed to all rational beings; these Kant calls "assertoric" or "pragmatic" imperatives (G 4:415–416). The sole end that may be attributed to every rational being is *happiness*. Therefore assertoric imperatives are also called "pragmatic imperatives" or "precepts of prudence" (G 4:415–416).[18]

Happiness, according to Kant, is "an idea in which all inclinations are summed up" (G 4:399), the idea of "an absolute whole, a maximum of well-being in my present and every future state" (G 4:418), or a "plan" for the greatest total satisfaction with our condition (G 4:395). An assertoric imperative would therefore be a precept that prescribes universally to all rational beings the actions that are required to achieve this greatest total satisfaction with life.

Kant holds that happiness is the sole end that can be presupposed for any rational being (G 4:415). This could be interpreted as a merely factual claim saying that no rational being ever fails to have its own happiness as an end. But this, too, could be understood as taking "happiness" either distributively (as each of the individual objects of desire that compose it) or collectively (as the idea of the sum of satisfaction combining these objects). Taken the first way, it would mean only that every rational being has some empirical desires, and therefore has as an end the satisfaction of some elements of its happiness. This would make the factual claim plausible, though uninteresting. Taken in the second way, however, it is not plausible, since Kant obviously realizes that imprudent people may place the satisfaction of a particular desire ahead of the pursuit of their happiness as a whole – as the incontinent gout sufferer does when he takes the drink that he knows will set off his ailment (G 4:399). On either interpretation, the claim is not plausible if it is interpreted to mean that we in fact make happiness an end by a kind of natural necessity (as Kant himself suggests at G 4:415). That would even contradict Kant's thesis that the setting of ends is always an act of freedom, never the result of natural necessity.

The claim that happiness is necessarily the end of a finite rational being is both more interesting and more plausible if it is taken *normatively*, as a distinctive *a priori* principle of prudential reason (with 'happiness' understood in the collective sense, as the idea of a sum of empirical satisfaction). What it says then is that it belongs to the essence of *rationality* that a rational being is bound to form the idea of its happiness and make that happiness an end. This is the most natural way to understand Kant's claim that happiness can be "presupposed surely and *a priori* in the case of every human being because it belongs to his essence" (G 4:415–416). In that case, the failure to make one's happiness an end or to give this end priority to the satisfaction of a momentary desire, would be the violation of a distinctive principle of reason.[19] A person might, for example, prefer the pleasure of the moment to his happiness on the whole (as Kant's incontinent podagrist appears to do). If he did, then it would constitute a distinctively *pragmatic* failure of practical rationality – that is, a failure to obey a distinctively pragmatic or assertoric imperative. The failure of rationality here would not be a failure of *instrumental* rationality,[20] for the imprudent person might unfailingly select the correct means to his momentary pleasure and could not be faulted from the standpoint of either EI or HI. The problem is not that he wills the end (happiness) yet fails to will a necessary means to it. The irrationality lies instead in the fact that he fails (at least on this occasion) to will the end of happiness, or at least prefers to it a momentary pleasure that (according to reason) he ought to will only on the condition that it is consistent with his overall happiness and constitutes a proper part of it.

4.2. *The pragmatic imperative* It is true in a sense that assertoric imperatives are only a species of hypothetical imperative because the rationality of the actions they command is contingent on our having an end, to which that action is a means. But assertoric imperatives also introduce a new species of rationality alongside the rationality of using means that are necessary for (or more generally, suitable to) a given end. For employing the idea of a total satisfaction with our state, we must judge not only the rationality of *actions*, relative to a given end, but also the rationality of *ends* relative to a whole of satisfaction, depending on whether they can be included within this whole. We could formulate this general principle as the "pragmatic (or prudential) imperative" (PI):

> **PI:** Form an idea for yourself of the greatest achievable sum of your empirical satisfaction (under the name 'happiness') and make happiness your end, always preferring it over any limited empirical satisfaction.[21]

According to PI, the pursuit of any end derived from empirical desire will be irrational if that pursuit is incompatible with the greatest overall satisfaction as represented in the agent's idea of happiness. Thus it will be irrational for a gout sufferer to prefer momentary pleasures of food or drink, which will exacerbate the illness and produce far greater pain than enjoyment in the long run, even if he rationally selects the right means to these short-term pleasures (G 4:399). The same may be said for the ends set by spendthrifts who ruin their lives through improvidence or people whose lack of social courtesy or self-restraint turns others against them to their overall disadvantage (G 4:418).

Kant never states PI explicitly. He isn't even entirely clear that there is such a principle distinct from the principles involved in hypothetical imperatives. So he doesn't ask how it (or how prudential rationality in general) is possible. It is not at all obvious that PI is an analytic normative judgment like EI and HI. Perhaps pragmatic reason has greater affinity with moral than with instrumental reason, and this fact (if Kant had acknowledged it) might require him to qualify his anti-eudaemonism – his view that the principle of morality and the principle of one's own happiness are direct opposites (KpV 5:25). Following up this last thought, some post-Kantians, such as T. H. Green, view the pursuit of happiness (or individual "self-realization") as occupying a middle position on a kind of continuum between mere desire-satisfaction and morality.[22]

4.3. There are no assertoric imperatives   Corresponding to EI, there are a large number of specific technical imperatives telling us how to bisect angles, cure diseases, and so forth. Useful assertoric imperatives would correspond to PI as technical imperatives do to EI. They would tell us what actions we must necessarily perform or omit in order to achieve happiness. Kant does not try to formulate the *specific* rational imperative violated by the imprudent gout sufferer or the spendthrift (except by representing them misleadingly as a violation of technical imperatives). It soon becomes clear why he omits to do so: Kant believes *there are no such imperatives*. An assertoric imperative would have to specify not merely which subordinate ends are to be pursued as parts of happiness, but also how far each should be pursued relative to all the others, and even which actions would achieve the correct balance between our ends. Perhaps this could be done if we had a sufficiently detailed conception of our happiness. But anyone's conception of happiness would clearly involve empirical details not only about the ends constituting it but about the means to those ends and the priorities to be given to the use of such means. For this reason, it is hard to see how an assertoric imperative could be *a priori* and valid for *all* rational beings (since the happiness of one person may differ greatly in content from the happiness of another).

Due to the variability of human nature, the complexity of life, and the impossibility of determining consistently what we really want out of life, it is impossible to provide a determinate concept of happiness relative to which the prudential rationality of ends and actions may be judged (G 4:417–418). Further, Kant thinks that human desires are so constituted that we are incapable of formulating any idea of a sum of satisfaction that is possible of achievement (KU 5:430). This is what Kant means when he says in the *Groundwork*, "It is impossible even for a most clearsighted and capable but finite being to form here a definite concept of that which he really wills" (G 4:418). In Part II we will look at Kant's reasons for holding that human beings are so made by nature that they can never be wholly satisfied with their lives.

What Kant calls "imperatives of prudence," therefore, are not really imperatives after all, for they cannot command us with the necessitating force of reason if obeying them may actually lead us to unhappiness rather than to happiness. Thus Kant explains why he modifies his account of them, saying that they are not "precepts" but only "counsels," "which are shown by experience best to promote welfare on the average" (G 4:418). For most people, most of the time, it is prudent to avoid overindulging in food or drink, to spend less than one makes, to behave politely toward others. But there are exceptional cases. Some people who follow these wise counsels end up unhappy anyway and are no happier for having followed them, while others become happier precisely through excess, improvidence, or arrogant rudeness.

4.4. Corollary: Morality cannot be based on prudence The thesis that there are no assertoric, pragmatic, or prudential imperatives can be seen to have an important implication that supports Kant's position in moral philosophy. It seems to be part of what we mean by a *moral* principle that the bindingness of such a principle on me should not be merely optional or dependent on what desires or ends I happen to have. It is never sufficient to defeat a claim that an action is *morally obligatory*, to show that the action fails to promote this or that end that I happen contingently to have.[23] Despite this, however, it would still be possible to represent moral obligations as founded on a hypothetical imperative if there were some end (i.e., my happiness) that I could not rationally disavow in this way, and rational precepts (assertorical or pragmatic imperatives) telling me what I must do to achieve this rationally necessary end. For then the necessity of moral obligation could be represented as the instrumental necessity of actions required by a pragmatically or prudentially necessary end. (This seems to be the way John Locke represents moral obligation – as depending on our inevitable desire for happiness, and our belief that we can achieve our greatest happiness in a future life only by obeying God's commands.[24])

Acting from duty, for example, could be represented as acting on the imperative to pursue one's good on the whole or one's happiness in the face of contingent desires that threaten to distract one from this end. In that case, moral imperatives could be represented as a species of hypothetical imperatives, namely, those that tell us what we must do in order to achieve happiness. A eudaemonistic ethical theory, such as Locke's, which regards moral imperatives as a species of assertoric imperative, could therefore do just as well as Kant's theory at meeting the condition that moral obligations must be independent of our desires or our (optional) ends.[25]

It is therefore important for Kant that relative to the end of happiness there are no universal precepts but only general counsels, all of which are only contingently valid and admit of exceptions. That means there is no way in which moral obligation can be presented under the guise of a hypothetical imperative telling us how to achieve the sole end that we as rational beings cannot disavow (namely, happiness). From these points and the thesis that moral obligations are universal prescriptions of reason that bind us independently of our contingent ends, it follows that if there is any such thing as moral obligation at all, then it cannot consist in rational imperatives that command only hypothetically (relative to an end, perhaps a necessary end), but rather it must consist in imperatives that command *categorically* (independently of any end, even a necessary one).

It is worth noticing that Kant's reason for rejecting the Lockean alternative depends in part on *empirical* theses about the conditions under which human beings pursue happiness. This means that Kant's *philosophical* argument for the conditional claim that if morality is real, then its principle must be a categorical imperative valid *a priori*, is not itself an entirely *a priori* argument. It is not based wholly on allegedly self-evident truths or the analysis of moral concepts, but is in part a consequence of Kant's empirical anthropology. Here again we see that the relation between the empirical and the *a priori* in Kant's philosophy is far more subtle and complex than is usually appreciated.

5. Categorical imperatives

The goal of Kant's discussion of imperatives is to introduce the conception of a *categorical imperative* (or "practical law"). A categorical imperative is a practical principle that constrains the will not relative to any end already given, but unconditionally and irrespective of any end. This does not mean that when a rational being follows such an imperative its actions lack an end (for Kant, no action can lack an end). It rather means that the law itself is capable of specifying what ends should be set (though as we shall see in Chapter 6, § 1, it is capable of this only by using empirical information about human beings).

5.1. The conceivability of a categorical imperative Kant realizes that the actuality of imperatives of this kind might be questioned (G 4:420). He asserts that no experience affords us any example of a categorical imperative, so any such principle must be *a priori*. But, in accord with the strategy of the *Groundwork* (discussed in Chapter 1, § 1), he postpones until the Third Section the question of whether there actually are categorical imperatives (G 4:431, 447). His aim in the Second Section is to investigate the *possibility* of a categorical imperative (G 4:419–420), determining what principles might be categorical imperatives if there are any.

Since a categorical imperative must constrain the will without reference to any object of desire, it must be *a priori*, since pleasure or displeasure associated with the representation of such objects provides only empirical grounds for volition. For a like reason, however, a categorical imperative must be *synthetic*, not analytic as EI and HI are. These principles begin with the concept of a will that has set an end, and draw from the very concept of that volition the constraint that the use of necessary means to the end must also be willed (G 4:417). But in the case of a categorical imperative, no prior volition of any kind can be presupposed. The connection of the will with any deed or end that ought to be willed must therefore be synthetic (G 4:420).

Behind many objections to the idea of a categorical imperative lie qualms about the entire idea that morality is grounded on *reason*. Kant belongs to a long tradition in Western philosophy that subscribes to this idea, and therefore holds that immorality involves a failure of reason (or that it is a species of irrationality). Obviously this is not the same as saying that wickedness is a form of insanity, and it does not deny that people may exhibit a high degree of rationality in pursuing evil ends. We have seen that Kant recognizes three kinds of reason – instrumental, prudential, and moral. It is an evident fact of life that people and their actions may exhibit a failure of rationality in any one of these ways while being perfectly rational in the others. Instances of this failure are sometimes comic, sometimes tragic; it is horrifying to behold the gruesomely rational manner in which highly intelligent people plan and carry out unspeakable (and morally irrational) acts of exploitation, war, or genocide.[26]

As we shall see in later chapters, Kant thinks that the human propensity to evil belongs to our rational capacity and develops along with it. Perhaps this is why it is easy for us to fall into "misology" (hatred of reason) (G 4:395). It is likewise why some find it hard to believe that reason (which is so conspicuously exhibited in so much evil) could also be the foundation of morality. But the view that morality is grounded on reason need not involve any illusions about the degree to which prudential rationality can motivate evil or instrumental rationality can be put in its service. On the contrary, the truly dangerous illusion is to think there could be some other (nonrational) compartment of human nature that somehow remains untouched by evil, and whose authority therefore deserves to override that of reason.

The most common objection to the possibility of a categorical imperative is based on the thesis that all practical reasoning must presuppose the desire for an end and consist in telling us how to achieve that end. In § 3, however, we saw that this thesis is false even in the case of hypothetical imperatives, which do rest on willing an end. When you act on a hypothetical imperative, you do not keep to your chosen end and your rational plan in pursuit of it only because there happens at the moment to be a resurgence of the original desire that occasioned your setting the end. Often you do it instead because you have acknowledged a universal practical *principle* that is binding universally on anyone who adopts the end you have set yourself.

A second objection to the possibility of a categorical imperative is that it is inconceivable that we could have a reason for following such a principle, since the unconditioned character of such an imperative – the fact that it rests on no prior end or volition – does away with even the very possibility of such a reason. To Schopenhauer, for example, the very notion of a categorical imperative seems self-contradictory. He can make sense of the notion at all only by supposing it to be a confused or disguised version of theological morality – for him, the categorical imperative must refer to the absolute command of God, though he thinks Kant falls into self-contradiction in trying to repudiate the ignoble motive of fear that must ground every such command.[27]

We can answer this sort of objection by pursuing a bit further the answer to the first one. For even in the case of hypothetical imperatives, the reason for following them does not consist in a desire for the presupposed end but rather in the ground we have as rational beings for taking the actions necessary to achieve an end that we have set (and continue to adopt, even if we feel no desire for it at the moment or find that other, stronger desires tempt us to omit the actions necessary to achieving it).

5.2. *Rational motivation and self-worth*   In this situation, what reason do you have for taking the necessary actions? Kant's method of exposition in the *Groundwork* requires him to postpone the answer to this question. It is only after he has formulated the principle of morality *formally*, based on the mere *concept* of a categorical imperative, that he turns to the will's ground or motive (*Bewegungsgrund*) in acting on such an imperative. This will lead to the Formula of Humanity as End in Itself (FH). His complete account, however, is given only with the thesis that categorical obligation must be grounded on autonomy of the will.

Because Kant discusses categorical imperatives for so long without explaining our rational ground for following them, some readers have the impression that it belongs to the very concept of such an imperative that there can be no such ground (other than the empty imperative form itself). This interpretation naturally leads them to reject the entire concept as nonsensical or self-contradictory (a "*sideroxylon*"), or at least as too metaphysical to play a meaningful role in any theory of rational action.[28] Another reason some philosophers may get the same impression is that they are wedded to the false dogma that all genuine reasons for action must consist in desires, and Kant is clear that a categorical imperative cannot be grounded on any desire.

Here it may help to recall that, as we saw in § 1.3, Kant thinks that desire *never* provides the fundamental reason for action. Even on the most subjective level, desires produce actions by being incorporated into maxims. Moreover, neither in instrumental nor prudential reason is action grounded *fundamentally* on desire. Rational principles such as EI, HI, and PI are needed, in fact, precisely in those cases where our *desire* for the end we have set or for our happiness has proven insufficient to get us to do what is needed to achieve the end or to choose the prudent course of action over a more immediately tempting course that will make us less happy in the long run. Not only in the moral case but even in the instrumental and prudential cases, rational principles operate on us by giving us a *reason* to act in a certain way, which *produces* in us a rational desire to act that way. And these reasons *never* consist in desires.

What, then, could such reasons be? Let me suggest the following answer on Kant's behalf, beginning with the case of instrumental reason. When you constrain yourself to take the necessary means to an end you have set, you follow the corresponding hypothetical imperative because you have a certain *conception* of yourself. You are someone who is *rational* in the pursuit of ends, and someone who has set a certain end. This conception not only describes you but makes demands on you. We say it is something you require yourself to *live up to*. You take the actions required by your purposive plan because otherwise you would not be living up to the conception of yourself as the person who set the end in question or as a person who pursues ends rationally. We could say something similar in the case of prudential reason. You have a reason to pursue your happiness because you conceive of yourself as one person, whose desires are not only individually worth satisfying but whose overall well-being or satisfaction is worth pursuing. You follow PI because you understand that to act imprudently would be to fail to live up to this self-conception.

It would be wrong to describe your reason for following the principles of instrumental and prudential reason as a *desire* to live up to
those self-conceptions. This is erroneous not because there is no such
desire (for there certainly is) but because the desire is only a *consequence*
of the reason you have, and cannot be the reason itself. For if it were,
then if I just happened to lack the desire to be a rational pursuer of
ends or a prudent person, then there would also be no reason for me
to follow principles such as EI or PI. But in fact I do have such reasons,
whatever my desires may be. For the absence of the desire to be a rational pursuer of the ends I set is all by itself a fundamental failure of
instrumental rationality. The absence of a desire to be prudent is already a failure of prudential rationality.[29] The desire to be rational
can arise only in consequence of the practically effective recognition of
reasons that are already there.

The ground of these reasons consists in a rational being's conception of its *self-worth*. It is not grounded on a *desire* to possess or live up to
such worth, but rather provides the necessary ground for all such desires. From this point of view, the difference between acting on technical imperatives and acting on prudential imperatives (or counsels of
prudence) may be seen as a difference in the *depth of the self-conception*
that gives these practical principles their authority. What binds me to
act on a technical imperative is the conception of myself as a rational
being who happens to have set a certain end. What binds me to act on
a counsel of prudence is something still deeper, the conception of myself as a single self with a conception of its own good. My commitment
to an end I have set can be abandoned at my discretion, but my rational
commitment to prudence cannot be abandoned as if it were an arbitrary end. It can only be overridden by ends or principles grounded on
a conception of myself that goes still deeper. Such a conception would
be independent even of the end that I as an individual self cannot renounce, the end of my own happiness. It would be the conception of
myself merely as a rational being, subject only to laws valid equally for
all rational beings. The imperative grounded on that self-conception
would not be technical or prudential, but categorical.[30]

Each of Kant's three formulations of the moral law in the *Groundwork*
may be seen as resting on a distinct way of approaching the value or self-
conception grounding a categorical imperative. The Formula of Universal Law (FUL) rests on the value of the good will, which is explicated
through the idea of "duty" as respect for universal law. This purely formal approach to the value is complemented by one that goes still

deeper: the Formula of Humanity as End in Itself (FH). It represents the substance of our absolute self-worth as the worth of our rational nature as such. These two values are then combined in the Formula of Autonomy (FA): Rational nature is seen as the source of universal legislation, which – in the Formula of the Realm of Ends (FRE) – is regarded as legislation for an ideal realm or commonwealth of rational beings, whose dignity is respected and whose ends are furthered through universal obedience to a system of legislation that systematizes their ends and brings them into necessary harmony. It will be the business of the next three chapters to explore these three formulas, their derivation, applicability, and their systematic interconnection.

THE FORMULA OF UNIVERSAL LAW

1. Objective practical principles

Kant's initial formulation of the principle of morality is "formal" because it is derived from the "mere concept of a categorical imperative" (G 4:420). A categorical imperative or "practical law," Kant says, must be "valid in the same form for all rational beings" (KpV 5:19, 21). Hence it must determine the will "on grounds which are valid for every rational being as such" (G 4:413). The reason for following it must be "the formal supreme determining ground of the will regardless of any subjective differences among human beings" (KpV 5:32). This must be a reason that is overriding for all rational beings, in the sense that it is the strongest reason they have (though not necessarily the reason that in fact motivates them the most strongly). It must also be *numerically the same* reason for all rational beings. A categorical imperative "must contain exactly the same determining ground for the will of all rational beings and in all cases" (KpV 5:25).

What sort of ground or reason might this be? Clearly, no empirical desire, not even the universal desire we all have for happiness, will meet the conditions required to ground a categorical imperative, for the desire for happiness is of merely empirical origin and not numerically the same reason for you as it is for me. Even if people found happiness in exactly the same states of affairs, there would be no numerical identity in their reasons, since my reason for seeking that universally felicific state would be that it is conducive to *my* happiness, while your reason would be that it is conducive to *your* happiness.

If we characterize the determining ground we are seeking merely formally, it would have to be something like *Because it is rational to do it.* But of course if an action is rational, then this has to be because there are *other* reasons for doing it. To some, this already provides a sufficient argument that no such reason could exist, and hence that the concept of a categorical imperative is unintelligible. As John Mackie puts it, the Kantian categorical imperative "demands obedience unmotivated by anything but respect for the categorically imperative form itself. No empirical self could be expected to comprehend or respond to such an 'ought'."[1] This objection is closely related to Hume's influential idea that "the first virtuous motive, which bestows a merit on any action, can never be regard to the virtue of that action, but must be some other natural motive or principle."[2] Hume thinks that because an action is called "virtuous" (or "dutiful") in part because of its motive, it would be viciously circular (and it would render "virtue" formal to the point of emptiness) if we characterize this motive as one of doing the virtuous (or dutiful) thing.

That thought is mistaken. That we can characterize the rational motive formally does not preclude its having some other characterization as well. The purely formal characterization, however, might be the most accurate way of specifying our reason to act. Nor would the moral motive, in order to move us, have to consist in a "natural" (i.e., empirical) motive such as self-love or sympathy. As we have just seen in Chapter 2, § 5.2, a rational being's conception of its own self-worth provides rational grounds independent of any desire, for following principles of instrumental and prudential as well as moral reason. We shall see in Chapter 4 that the worth of humanity provides us with an overriding reason grounding objective principles or categorical imperatives that is not dependent on our empirical desires but proceeds solely from our own rational faculties. In Chapter 5 we will look at Kant's definitive account of the reason grounding categorical imperatives, which is the autonomy of the will.

In the derivation of FUL, however, we are still considering the objective ground of action purely formally. This leads to a formula of the supreme principle of morality which abstracts from the objective value that grounds the imperative and considers only the categorical form of the obligation. No doubt Kant would have proceeded in a more reader-friendly manner (and provoked fewer charges of "empty formalism") if he had dealt from the start directly with the content of moral value, rather than proceeding (with proper scholastic pedantry) from form through matter to the moral principle in its systematic completeness (see Chapter 5, § 5). But it is important to him to present one and the same principle of morality first from a formal and only then from a material point of view, since otherwise it would be possible to think (as some of Kant's critics have actually thought) that no principle could simultaneously be a categorical imperative and be grounded on an objective value.[3]

2. The derivation of FUL and FLN

> If I think of a *hypothetical* imperative in general, I do not know in advance what it will contain until the condition is given to me. But if I think of a *categorical* imperative, then I know right away what it contains. For since the imperative contains besides the law only the necessity that the maxim should conform to the law, but the law contains no condition to which it is limited, then there is nothing remaining in it but the universality of a law, to which the maxim of the action is to conform, and which conformity alone the imperative really represents as necessary. (G 4:420–421; cf. 4:401–402)

2.1. Conformity to law   A "maxim" is a subjectively adopted normative rule or policy on which the person acts, a "subjective principle of volition," as distinct from an objectively valid principle or practical law (G 4: 400n, 420n). Kant supposes that every action, as an intentional deed of a rational agent, involves the adoption (whether conscious or tacit) of a maxim. Adopting a maxim means subjecting one's action to self-given norms. This includes such things as setting an end, choosing means to it, and selecting actions of a certain description to be performed under various circumstances. As Kant points out, the adoption of a maxim often involves the subject's specific inclinations, and it may also reflect the subject's ignorance (G 4:421n). A categorical imperative, however, tells us to act (to adopt maxims) in conformity with *objective* principles or "practical laws." Laws are based on *objective grounds* – reasons valid equally for every rational being as such. Hence they are universally and unconditionally valid rational constraints on action. The argument quoted above therefore infers that the conformity of maxims to universal laws as such follows from the mere concept of a categorical imperative. This first and most abstract version of the categorical imperative could be expressed as follows:

CI: Adopt only maxims that conform to universal law as such (cf. G 4:421).

The trouble with CI is that it gives us no idea at all what universal laws there are (assuming there are some, as Kant does, provisionally, in the

Second Section). This even seems to contradict Kant's claim that the content of a categorical imperative is immediately known. But what Kant means by the claim is that the content of a categorical imperative, unlike that of a hypothetical imperative, is not conditional on any independently given end. And this is obviously right, even if our only formulation of the categorical imperative is CI. However, CI does tell us nothing about the content of practical laws. The claim that our maxims should conform to universal law even seems to presuppose the existence of *another* universal law (or laws) whose content still remains unspecified.

Kant hastens to solve the problem by once more reformulating the principle he has just derived. Immediately following the passage quoted above he therefore says: "The categorical imperative is therefore only a single one, and specifically this":

FUL: *"Act only according to that maxim through which you can at the same time will that it should become a universal law."* (G 4:421; cf. 4:402)

Notice that FUL still does not directly specify the universal laws to which our maxims are supposed to conform. But it is not as formal as CI, because it proposes a *test* to use on any given maxim to determine whether that maxim conforms to these universal laws. The test is that a maxim is consistent with universal law only if a rational being can will that maxim itself to be a universal law. If this cannot be willed, then the maxim is contrary to universal law and hence impermissible.

This test is still very abstract, and Kant realizes that it may be hard to apply it. In order to make it easier, in the *Critique of practical reason* Kant provides a "typic of pure practical judgment" (KpV 5:67). This is supposed to be analogous to the "schemata" for the categories of pure understanding, only instead of relating a pure concept to intuition by way of imagination, it relates a law to concrete conditions of action in the natural world by representing the lawfulness of morality as the lawfulness belonging to *nature* (KpV 5:68–71). The resulting formula is the "Formula of the Law of Nature":

FLN: "Act as if the maxim of your action should through your will become a **universal law of nature**." (G 4:421)

The difference between FUL and FLN lies in the distinction between willing something to be a "law" (*simpliciter*) and willing it to be a "law *of nature*." Both sorts of laws consist in a general principle having *necessity*, but the necessity is not of the same kind. A "law" (*simpliciter*) is a principle that is necessary in the sense that, as rational *agents*, we *must* (i.e., we ought to) follow it. In other words, a law (*simpliciter*) is a *normative* principle. Hence to ask (using FUL), whether you could will your maxim to be a universal law, is to ask whether you could will that all others should be *permitted* to follow it.

Kant does this in his very first application of FUL to the example of the false promise, in the First Section of the *Groundwork*: "Could I indeed say to myself that everyone may make a false promise when he finds himself in difficulty and can get out of it in no other way?" (G 4:403). FUL thus provides a different test from FLN, and Kant's arguments about the false promise in the First Section are correspondingly different from those in the Second Section (where FLN is used). Supposing it were permissible to promise with no intention to do what is promised, then Kant argues first (and very plausibly) that "there would properly be no promises at all," and second, that "others would pay me back in my own coin" (i.e., make promises to me which my own will decrees that it is permissible for them to have no intention of keeping) (G 4:403). (Scholars sometimes notice that Kant's arguments about the false promise in the First Section are different from those in the Second, but they most often attribute this to confusion or indecision on his part rather than perceiving that different arguments are required by the different universalizability tests proposed in FUL and FLN.)

Yet it may not be entirely clear how these arguments show that I cannot will the maxim of the false promiser to be a universal (normative) law. Kant evidently thinks that it is easier to apply the test to a maxim if we think of it not as a normative law (a law *simpliciter*) but as a law *of nature*, that is, a law which is necessary in a different sense – a universal rule against which it is *causally impossible* for anyone to act. In other words, he thinks we will gain a more intuitive idea of which maxims we can will as universal laws (*simpliciter*) for all rational beings if we imagine a system of nature having our maxims as its causal laws, and then ask whether such a system of nature is something we can consistently will. It is in this form, as FLN (or the second Critique's "typic of pure practical judgment"), that Kant employs the first formulation of the law when he applies it to examples in the Second Section (G 4:421–423). It is not wholly clear what is supposed to be the force of natural necessity here, since maxims are themselves normative principles that can be acted on only by free beings, and Kant thinks that to view an act as free is necessarily different from viewing it as falling under natural necessity. In practice, to suppose that one's maxim is a universal law of nature is apparently to suppose that every rational being without exception adopts the maxim and acts on it unfailingly whenever it applies.

2.2. The fallacy in Kant's deduction   Before we try to understand the test (in either form), however, it is necessary to ask a prior question: Do either FUL or FLN follow merely from CI or from the idea of a categorical imperative or objectively grounded principle? The answer to this question unfortunately is, *No, they do not*.[4]

As in the derivation of FUL in the first section of the *Groundwork*, Kant introduces a criterion of lawfulness for which no reason has yet been given (see Chapter 1, § 5.5). Both FUL and FLN take what a rational being wills, or can consistently will, to be a valid criterion for what is consistent with a law objectively valid for rational beings in general. As in the First Section, Kant's only argument for this criterion is that when we have deprived the will of all material incentives, the only thing left to serve as a ground of the will is conformity to the universality of law in general (G 4:420–421; cf. G 4:401–402, KpV 5:29). Once again this tells us no more than that our maxims ought to conform to whatever universal laws there are. It does not tell us how to discover these laws, and it does not entail that maxims conform to the laws whenever they pass the tests provided for in FUL and FLN. More specifically, it does not follow from the mere concept of a categorical imperative that *the will of a rational being* – what a rational being wills or can consistently will – has any role at all to play in determining the content of universal laws.

We would have reason to accept the will of a rational being as such a criterion if we knew already that this will is the *author* of objective practical laws, hence that the moral law is a principle of *autonomy*. Kant does argue for this claim later (G 4:432), and his arguments do not depend in any way on the fallacious derivation of FUL and FLN. But they do depend on both the concept of rational nature as end in itself (FH) and the idea of the rational will as making universal law (FA). Thus since FUL and FLN already presuppose these later formulas, neither of them can be regarded as an adequate and self-sufficient formulation of the supreme principle of morality Kant is searching for in the *Groundwork*.

Though the universalizability test used in FUL and FLN involves the premature and surreptitious appeal to FA, these two formulas still fall significantly short of FA in that they provide no practical laws, but only a permissibility test for maxims. In §§ 7 and 8 we will see that Kant's invalid inference also infects the universalizability test itself, by mixing up what can be willed without contradiction to be a universal law (or law of nature) with what a rational will might itself give as universal law. This leads directly to some of the well-known counterexamples (of "false negatives") that plague FUL and FLN (see § 7.4).

The invalidity of Kant's derivation of FUL and FLN at G 4:420–421 is also evident if we consider the matter in another way. A practical law is a practical principle that is objectively grounded, that is, a principle such that there is a reason that every rational being as such has for following this principle. In other words, a practical law is a principle such that each rational being has an overriding and *a priori* reason (numerically the same reason) to follow it. But from the fact that a principle has this feature nothing may be validly inferred either way about whether you or I or anyone might will that *everyone* should follow the principle (that it should become a universal law or a universal law of nature).[5] Of course if we suppose (in the spirit of FRE) that it is up to rational beings to determine the content of such laws by framing them so as to unite the ends of all rational beings into a harmonious whole, then it is quite reasonable to regard it as a necessary feature of a putative practical law that it should be possible for each rational being to will that all rational beings follow it. But this once again presupposes a formula to be argued for later, which cannot be derived merely from the concept of a categorical imperative but depends on the crucial arguments for FH and FA.

From this standpoint one cannot blame Hegel and others for thinking that the Kantian moral principle is empty and that no practical conclusions can be derived from it unless some actual laws are introduced from outside to provide it with content.[6] Such critics can be faulted only for concluding prematurely that Kant's project in the *Groundwork* has failed before allowing the full argument of the Second Section to run its course. For once we see that FH, FA, and FRE are well-grounded, we can return to FUL and FLN, recognizing them as well-grounded, too, and we will also have a better appreciation of the limited role they have in Kantian ethics.

3. Applying FLN: suicide

Kant's procedure in the *Groundwork* is to illustrate FLN by applying it to four examples, each representing one of the basic categories of ethical duties according to a taxonomy that will be the organizing principle of Kant's presentation of ethical duties in the *Metaphysics of morals*. This taxonomy is in fact far more important for understanding Kant's ethical theory than is FLN and its universalizability tests. Moreover, the discussion of these four examples as illustrations of FLN is not Kant's final or definitive treatment of them. All four are dealt with again as illustrations of FH (G 4:429–430). In Chapter 4, § 7.4, we will see that the later discussion of them is not only a superior presentation of their relationship to Kant's ethical theory but also in each case sheds significant light on what is at stake morally in the arguments from FLN. All these points represent only so many ways in which Kant's theory is commonly misunderstood by exaggerating the role of FUL (or FLN).

In applying FLN to any example, the first question we must ask is: What makes it impossible to *will* that a given maxim could be a universal law? "Willing," as Kant uses the term, differs from merely wanting or wishing, in that to will x is to make x one's end, adopting a normative principle requiring us to apply means to achieve the end. (In the case of willing a maxim to be a universal law of nature, no such means are ever in our power; but the test involves a thought-experiment in which we must decide whether we can consistently commit ourselves to the volition whether or not we are ever in a position to act on it.) By contrast, one may *wish* for something without adopting any normative principle and which one would not be prepared to bring about through the use of means even if they were available (G 4:394).

Thus, first, it is impossible for me to *will* both of two contradictories, ——— since I cannot rationally subject my actions simultaneously to the norm that I will employ means to bring it about that Z and also the norm that I will employ means to bring it about that not-Z. I might *wish* for both Z and not-Z (for example, to have my cake and eat it, too), but I cannot *will* both. It is also impossible for me to *will* self-contradictory states of affairs, though we often wish for contradictions (e.g., we middle-aged people constantly wish to continue living but not to get any older).[7]

Second, there are certain things that I cannot in principle will that ◄——— another should do to me simply because they are by their very nature frustrations of my power to set and realize ends. People can sometimes want (i.e., wish) to be deceived or coerced, and even get pleasure from having their will thwarted. But one cannot self-consistently set as an end the thwarting and frustration of one's own power to set ends (as happens in coercion and deception).[8]

Finally, as we shall see in §§ 5 and 6, Kant also maintains that there ═══ are certain ends that a rational being *cannot fail to will*, either because it belongs to rationality itself to will them or because not willing them is rationally precluded by its other desires, needs, and circumstances. A rational being is therefore unable self-consistently to will something that is incompatible with these ends.

3.1. The two universalizability tests   These points provide Kant with criteria for determining whether one can will a maxim to be a universal law. Kant distinguishes two sorts of arguments here: The first claims that a maxim cannot even be thought of as a universal law of nature without self-contradiction; the second that it cannot be willed as a universal law of nature without falling into conflicting volitions. Using the terminology devised by Onora O'Neill, these two forms of the universalizability test are called, respectively, "contradiction in conception" (CC) and "contradiction in the will" or "contradiction in volition" (CW).[9] Kant claims that maxims that fail the CC test violate perfect duties (duties requiring specific actions or omissions), whereas those that fail the CW test violate imperfect duties (duties requiring only that we have certain ends but leave it up to us how far to pursue them and which actions to take in their pursuit). Later in this chapter we will return to this claim (which we will call "the Correspondence Thesis"; see § 7.1).

Kant's universalizability test has sometimes been reduced to CC alone and then further misunderstood as saying only that a maxim itself must not be self-contradictory or else that the proposition that everyone acts on the maxim must not be directly self-contradictory. Hegel, Mill, and others who have interpreted the test in this way have consequently concluded that it is a test even the most outrageously immoral maxims may pass.[10] Kant's own employment of the test in his four famous examples, however, *never* involves merely the claim that an impermissible maxim, when stated in the form of a universal law, involves a self-contradiction. As we shall see in this and the following three sections, although Kant's arguments are applications of an *a priori* law, they *always* rest mainly on claims about contingent, empirical matters of fact (as we would naturally expect in moral arguments of any kind about particular examples).

3.2. Testing a maxim   In the first example, concerning suicide, Kant argues that the following maxim fails the CC test:

M1:   "From self-love I make it my principle to shorten my life when by longer duration it threatens more ill than agreeableness." (G 4: 422)

In applying the CC test to M1, we must consider the universalized form of M1, namely:

U1: It is a universal law of nature that from self-love, all make it their principle to shorten life when by a longer duration it threatens more ill than agreeableness.

We must ask whether U1 can be conceived. Kant's argument that U1 cannot describe a law of nature is *not* based on the claim that U1 is directly self-contradictory (which it clearly is not). It is based instead on an alleged fact about the natural teleology of the feeling of self-love: that it is the natural function of this feeling to further life. Kant argues that there would be a contradiction in the conception of a teleological system of nature if this same feeling, under some circumstances, impelled human beings to end their lives according to a law of nature. Thus U1 is held to contradict an alleged (empirical) feature of the natural world as it actually exists, namely, the naturally purposive function of the feeling of self-love.

Kant's argument about suicide assumes a general *principle of natural teleology*:

NT1: If *F* is a feeling whose naturally purposive function is to bring about *P*, then it would be self-contradictory to suppose a system of nature one of whose laws is that under certain circumstances *F* systematically produces the contrary of *P*.

Note that Kant does *not* maintain that there could not be a system of nature in which self-love had a different function from its present one. In that sense, applying CC here depends on an (alleged) contingent, empirical fact about the world, namely that self-love has the function of furthering life. Kant is arguing from this alleged empirical fact that the feeling of self-love (in the *present* system of nature) has the function of promoting life, together with the regulative principle of teleological judgment NT1, to the conclusion that it would be self-contradictory for there to be a system of nature in which the feeling with this function should under certain circumstances bring about the end of life according to a law of nature. Since this is what would happen if U1 were a law of nature, Kant concludes that there is a contradiction in supposing that U1 is a law of nature, and hence that M1 violates FLN.

3.3. Assessing the argument Kant's argument about suicide is open to a number of formidable objections aimed not at FLN or the CC test but at the auxiliary premises required to show that M1 fails this test. Some, of course, may be suspicious of the whole idea of natural purposiveness, and others about NT1. Kant's views on these matters, which are crucial to understanding his ethical thought as a whole, will be discussed in Chapter 6, §5. Even waiving objections of that kind, however, Kant's specific claim about the natural purpose of self-love is unclear, perhaps doubtful even (or especially) to those who accept the idea of natural teleology. On some possible interpretations of that claim, his inferences from it are anything but self-evident.

The assertion that self-love naturally aims at the "furthering of life" could be interpreted, for instance, as saying that it aims at making life maximally enjoyable for living things. That might very well involve shortening life under many circumstances. Again, it could be read as saying that self-love aims at promoting the survival of biological *species*. This might best be done by ending the lives of some specimens under certain conditions, for example, to insure a more ample territory or food supply for the reduced number that remain. On these interpretations of "furthering of life," Kant's argument against M1 does not work.

If Kant's claim is to justify saying that it is impossible for U1 to describe a law of nature, then it has to mean something like that the natural purpose of self-love is to extend the life of the individual organism as far as possible under all circumstances. It is far from obvious, however, on empirical grounds, that *this* is the natural purpose of self-love. Given NT1, there may even be a problem reconciling that premise with the admitted fact that people are occasionally tempted to adopt M1 *from* self-love. (Also open to question is whether NT1 itself might need some qualification, since it is far from clear that there cannot be circumstances in which organs fail to achieve their natural purposes in accord with a law of nature. In Chapter 6, §§ 5.5 and 5.6, we will see both how Kant's commitment to NT1 is methodologically required by his theory of reflective teleological judgment and also why we post-Darwinians are apt to deny principles like NT1.)

Kant probably intended his four examples to illustrate duties that are both nontrivial and noncontroversial. The immorality of suicide was widely accepted in his time, though usually (as Kant himself elsewhere points out) on statutory religious grounds rather than rational ones (VE 27:370). But accepting FLN itself does not commit you to the immorality of suicide or even of suicide on M1. It may even indirectly tend to support Kant's principle that when we find his conclusions dubious, we also tend to doubt his derivation of them from his principle if our doubts are directed not to FLN but to some of the other premises he needs.

4. False promises and converted deposits

The suicide argument appeals to an alleged teleological fact about the system of nature in order to show that the maxim of suicide from self-love fails the CC test. The example of the lying promise seems to appeal to a different sort of empirical fact in order to derive a different sort of contradiction in conceiving a maxim to be a universal law of nature.[11] Here the maxim is:

M2: "When I believe myself to be in need of money, I will borrow money and promise to repay it, although I know I will never do so." (G 4:422)

The conception of this maxim as a universal law of nature is accordingly:

U2: It is a universal law of nature that when anyone believes they are in need of money, they will borrow it and promise to repay it without having any intention to do so.

To show that M2 violates FLN, Kant apparently must show that there is a contradiction in U2. His argument is this:

> The universality of a law that everyone who believed himself in need could promise whatever occurred to him with the intention of not holding to it would make the very promise and the end one had in making it impossible, since no one would believe what was promised him but rather would laugh at such an utterance as a vain pretense. (G 4:422)

4.1. The CC test: Two interpretations   Here it is unclear whether the contradiction is supposed to be (i) internal to U2 itself (or to the system of nature of which it would be a part) or (ii) between the end you would have in making the promise and the state of affairs you would have to will in willing M2 to be a universal law of nature. Christine Korsgaard has called (i) (which was once presented in an article of mine) the "logical" interpretation,[12] and (ii) (best known in Onora O'Neill's presentation of it) the "practical" interpretation.[13]

Let us look at the practical interpretation first. According to it, Kant's argument takes it to be a contingent empirical fact that if U2 described a law of nature, then it would be realized that promises made by people in need could not be trusted, and no one would ever lend money on the strength of such a promise, thus making it impossible to use a promise to achieve the end the agent has in acting on this very maxim. Since it is impossible to will to achieve an end by a certain means and simultaneously to will to act in such a way that one's end is rendered impossible of attainment through that means, it is impossible for the agent acting on M2 to will that U2 should describe a law of nature.

We might think there is no *contradiction* in the *conception* of either M2 or U2. The contradiction instead seems to be a contradiction in the agent's *will*, between what you will in following the maxim and what you would have to will, given certain empirical facts, in willing U2. M2 might seem, therefore, to run afoul of the CW test rather than the CC test. But there is another way of looking at the matter. Since the volition that conflicts with willing U2 is drawn from M2 itself (and doesn't appeal to anything else that rational beings will), it can be argued that the contradiction is still internal to the *conception of M2* as a universal law of nature. For, assuming certain contingent facts about human knowledge and motivation, it would then be self-contradictory to suppose that there is a system of nature of which U2 is a law and in which there are actual instances of acts (i.e., of people successfully acting on M2 to gain money) that fall under this law.

Even so, the logical interpretation would seem to provide a stricter conformity to the CC test. The starting point for such an interpretation is Kant's remark that if M2 were made a universal law "the promise itself" would be impossible. This suggests that U2 could not be even thought as describing a law of nature. For if U2 were the case then promises themselves would be impossible, but since U2 is a law involving the making of promises, it follows that the very conception of U2 as a law of nature is self-contradictory. Admittedly, it is not entirely clear what Kant means in saying that if U2, then "the promise itself" would be impossible. He might mean only that since no promises would be accepted, no one would in fact bother to make promises any more, and that would fall far short of making promises *impossible*. But Kant might also have meant to claim that a real or genuine promise, perhaps even the intention to promise, can occur only when it is possible for the promiser to have a reasonable ground to think that the promise will be believed. In that case, if U2 (even contingently) brought it about that no promises were ever believed and that all potential promisers knew this, then it would thereby bring it about that *promises* are impossible. Kant would not be claiming that the very *concept* of promising would then become self-contradictory – whatever that might mean – but only that such a natural law would render it impossible under the circumstances to engage in behavior that either the agent or others could regard as an act of promising. (Notice that even on the "logical" interpretation, the application of the CC test depends on contingent empirical facts.[14])

Obviously, Kant's argument about M2 is closer to his argument about M1 on the logical interpretation than on the practical interpretation. The argument itself, however, seems more convincing on the practical than on the logical interpretation. For it is far from self-evident that if M2 were a universal law of nature then there could be no promises at all. It is much easier to convince oneself that U2 as a universal law of nature would simply render it impossible to achieve one's ends by making false promises. As we have seen, even this would be enough to sustain Kant's position that the false promising maxim would fail the CC test on a slightly broader ("practical") interpretation of that test. (The practical and logical interpretations of the CC test may be viewed as yielding distinct interpretations of Kant's argument about M2, but they need not be seen as rivals, only as different versions, of the CC test.)

4.2. Universalizability and property   Kant twice puts forward an argument using the CC test in reference to another example quite similar to that of the false promise. He imagines a man with whom someone recently deceased has secretly left a sizable deposit and who now contemplates appropriating the money on the following maxim:

> **Md:**   "I will increase my property by every safe means." (KpV 5:27; cf. TP 8:286–287)

Kant argues that Md fails the CC test because "taking such a principle as a law would annihilate itself, because its result would be that no one would make a deposit" (KpV 5:27). This argument seems both to get and to require a "practical" interpretation, not a "logical" one. Kant never claims, namely, that the universalized form of Md,

> **Ud:**   It is a law of nature that everyone increases his property by every safe means

would make deposits *impossible.* Instead, the contention seems to be that if Md were made a universal law, then people would never trust others with deposits under circumstances where they might be converted without detection, and hence it would be impossible for me to achieve the end I set in Md in the manner proposed in the example, namely, safely increasing my property by converting a secret deposit.

To the argument about the deposit Hegel objects that since there is no contradiction in supposing that there would be no deposits, Md actually passes the CC test. Hegel further insists that Kant's argument presupposes the institution of property and the moral principles on which it is based.[15] These objections rest on misunderstandings we have already exposed. On the practical interpretation, the CC test does not require Kant to claim (what is obviously false) that the nonexistence of deposits would imply a self-contradiction; it requires only that if Md were a universal law of nature then the agent could not achieve the end he has set in Md itself through the means he now proposes (namely, appropriating the deposit).

As for Hegel's charge that the argument presupposes the existence of private property, in one way it is correct but not damaging to Kant, while in another way it is simply incorrect. It is correct insofar as the example focuses on deposits, appropriations, and such. Just as Md presumes the institution of property (and could be adopted only by someone living in a society that has such an institution), so the whole example presupposes empirical facts not only about the institution of ownership but also about human psychology (for instance, about what people would come to believe if Ud were a law of nature, and about what they would do if they believed it to be a law of nature that they could never trust others with deposits). But it is a misunderstanding of the CC test (on any interpretation) to think that Kant means his arguments to be independent of these sorts of empirical facts. Hegel's claim is incorrect, however, if it takes the sanctity of private property to be the central moral issue raised by the example. On the contrary, that issue is trust between people and its violation for selfish advantage. That issue does not depend on the existence of deposits or the institution of private property.

5. Rusting talents

Kant's third example is:

> **M3**: "I will neglect the development of my talents and instead devote my life entirely to idleness and pleasure." (cf. G 4:422–423)

The argument here is this:

> It is impossible to *will* that this maxim should become a universal law of nature or that it should be implanted in us by natural instinct. For as a rational being, he necessarily wills that all faculties should be developed in him, because they are serviceable and given to him for all sorts of possible aims. (G 4:423)

Here it is *not* a question of being able to will M3 in one case, but being unable to will it as a law of nature, that is, to will U3:

U3: Everyone will neglect the development of their talents and instead devote their lives entirely to idleness and pleasure.

What Kant asserts is rather that each of us as a rational being *must* will to develop our faculties (whatever the laws of nature are or might be).[16] In fact, the argument seems not merely to be that I can't will U3, but that I cannot rationally will even to adopt M3 for myself alone without contradicting something else that I must will simply as a rational being. For this reason, the argument about M3 might seem to contribute little or nothing to illustrating the universalizability tests.

In fact, however, it does contribute a very significant Kantian idea, which is easily lost sight of if we are too busy ratiocinating about universalizability. This is that there are some things that a rational being as such —— necessarily and unconditionally wills, such as that human talents should be developed so that they may be used to achieve the ends rational beings may set. Kant appears to treat this as an independent principle of reason. He might derive it from EI, since willing various sorts of ends includes willing the means to them, or from PI, since it might be deemed contrary to prudence not to provide oneself with the necessary means to achieve the components of happiness. Whatever its status, however, Kant's dependence on this principle suggests what will be discussed at greater length later: namely, that FUL and FLN are merely provisional and incomplete formulations of the principle of morality, which always depend for their application on other, independent rational principles.

6. Refusing to help

Kant's fourth example is that of a prosperous man who says, "May each one be as happy as heaven wills, or as he can make himself, I will take nothing from him or even envy him; but to his welfare or his assistance in need I have no desire to contribute" (G 4:423). This man recognizes moral constraints arising from the principle of not harming people and from the demand to respect what belongs to them (to respect their rights). He refuses only to make any voluntary contribution, by way of beneficence, to their happiness or to the pursuit of their ends. His maxim might be stated as follows:

M4: I will do nothing to harm others or deprive them of what is rightfully theirs, but I will refuse to help them or participate in their aims unless the assistance they need from me is one I owe them by strict right. (cf. G 4:423)

Corresponding to this would be the universalized form of M4:

> **U4:**   As a law of nature, no one will harm others or deprive them of
> what is rightfully theirs, but all will refuse to help others or to par-
> ticipate in their aims unless the assistance needed is owed by strict
> right.

6.1. The CW test   Kant begins his discussion of M4 by insisting that it
passes the CC test. Indeed, he goes further, claiming that a system of
nature that had U4 as one if its laws would in certain respects actually
be quite desirable, since it would mean that people never violate the rights
of others:

> Now to be sure if this way of thinking became a universal law, the human
> race could subsist and doubtless even better than when everyone prates
> about participation and benevolence, and also has the zeal to practice
> them on occasion, but, on the contrary, also deceives wherever he can,
> sells out human rights or otherwise violates them. (G 4:423)

Because Kant pretty clearly regards the latter state of human affairs as
the *actual* state, this remark is quite instructive regarding the CW test
for it shows that Kant regards U4 as incapable of being willed as a law
of nature even though he thinks that if it were one, then the human race
as a whole would get along better than it does now. That shows that John
Stuart Mill misinterprets the CW test when he provides the following
(charitably intended) gloss on it: "To give any meaning to Kant's principle, the sense put upon it must be that we ought to shape our conduct
by a rule which all rational beings might adopt *with benefit to their collective interest.*"[17] If he followed Mill's interpretation of the CW test, Kant
ought to hold that M4 is not only permissible but even a moral rule that
we ought to follow, since he thinks the human species would benefit (in
relation to its present condition) from M4's being universally followed.

What this shows is that the CW test is *not* based on the desirability,
in general, of the consequences of a maxim's being universally followed.[18] Both the CC and CW tests do rest in part on claims about
these (hypothetical) consequences, but their criterion is not the general desirability (either for the agent or for the world at large) of those
consequences. Instead, the CW test asks whether a rational being can
will without contradiction that the maxim should be universally followed.
Kant thinks that even if U4 as a law of nature would improve the human
condition, it still cannot pass the CW test:

Yet it is impossible to *will* that such a principle could everywhere hold as natural law. For a will which resolved on this would conflict with itself, since sometimes cases can occur in which he needs the love and partici-pation of others, but would rob himself, through such a natural law springing from his own will, of all hope of the aid he wishes. (G 4:423)

6.2. Misunderstandings   Even if we don't misunderstand the CW test in the way Mill has done, this argument is still easily misunderstood in other ways, perhaps because it involves premises about human life and psychology that may be controversial. But finding a cogent interpreta-tion of it will shed light both on the CW test and on Kant's theory of human nature.

i. Is the argument motivated by self-interest? One misunderstanding is displayed in Schopenhauer's criticism that the argument involves an ap-peal to self-interest and therefore reveals FLN to be surreptitiously based on eudaemonism or even egoism.[19] It is true that one of Kant's premises is an empirical claim about what a rational human agent must will on self-interested grounds: namely, that the agent may require the aid of others, and hence cannot rationally will a law that would deprive him of that aid. It is this volition, Kant contends, which will come into conflict with an agent's attempt to will U4. But obviously it is one thing — for the argument to *employ a premise about* what rational beings neces-sarily will from self-interest, and quite a different thing for the argu-ment to be *based on an appeal to* self-interest. If the argument is to do the latter, the reason given for excluding M4 would have to be that if I re-fuse voluntary help to others, then this will actually be detrimental to my self-interest (for instance, by making it more likely that others will refuse such help to me when I need it). But Kant's argument makes no such claim. It makes only hypothetical (or counterfactual) claims about how it *would* impact the agent's self-interest if U4 were a law of nature, and no claims at all about how agents can best promote their self-interest under the *actually existing* laws of nature.

ii. Does the argument commit a temporal fallacy? A subtler mistake is to think that Kant is arguing fallaciously from the fact that an agent may *someday* want aid from others to the conclusion that the agent *right now* does not will M4 to be a universal law.[20] The issue Kant means to pose, however, is not this, but whether it would be rational for me *at any time* to will to de-prive myself *for all times* (by a universal law of nature) of every possibility of voluntary help from others. Kant's contention is that, human beings and human life being what they are, this could not be rational.

iii. Can U4 be willed by some but not others? A third misunderstanding, to which we might be led by reflecting on this last point, is involved in the thought that the argument turns on whether it would be prudent for me to help others as an "insurance policy" against situations in which I might need the help of others. The question then would be whether the expenditure of my resources devoted to helping others when they need it would be a cost-effective way of insuring against the risk that I will someday be unfortunate enough to need someone else's voluntary help. On this interpretation, everything would depend on whether my welfare would be better promoted by allowing me, as well as others, to refuse voluntary help to others or whether I would be better off making some sacrifices if others were similarly willing to help me if the need arose. The problem then would be to weigh the likelihood of my needing the voluntary participation of others against the sacrifices it might impose on me to help them.

This way of looking at Kant's argument naturally leads to the thought that some (prosperous, ruggedly individualistic) agents could will M_4 as a universal law of nature, while others (who are needy or communistically disposed) could not. For the former, it seems, M_4 would be permissible, because they could will U_4 as long as they were willing, in circumstances of distress, to say consistently: "I didn't help others when they were in need, and now that I'm in need I don't want any help from them."[21] From this it might be concluded that the stingy man's maxim is impermissible for some people, but permissible for others.

Kantian principles do allow that different people may have different obligations, and also that obligations of beneficence allow for an area of latitude (*Spielraum*). But it does not follow that Kant's CW test is supposed to allow a maxim such as M_4 to be permissible for some and impermissible for others. It would be especially paradoxical (not to say offensive) if the CW test yielded the result that the refusal to help is impermissible for most people, but it is permissible for those who are exceptionally well off and by temperament stubbornly uncaring. The man in the example, after all, is explicitly described as one "for whom things are going well" (G 4:423), and we know from earlier in the *Groundwork* that Kant regards helping others as a duty even for the man "provided with special gifts of patience and fortitude, [who] expects or even requires that others should have the same" (G 4:398). Kant himself asserts that "many a man would gladly agree that others should not benefit him if only he might be excused from showing beneficence to them," using this as an objection to the Golden Rule as a moral prin-

ciple (G 4:430 note). If our interpretation of the CW test cannot show
why Kant thought M4 would be wrong even for a prosperous and independently disposed person, then either that interpretation is unac-
ceptable or else the CW test conspicuously fails to prove what Kant
thought it could.

6.3. Human interdependency   Kant's argument would be unproblematic
on this point if there were *no* human being who could rationally will M4
to be a universal law. It is easy enough to conceive of a natural species
of rational beings for whom this premise would not be true, even one
for which it would be true of no member of the species. All we need to
do is imagine a species of rational beings whose members are entirely
self-sufficient regarding their natural needs and can affect one another's
well being only by either respecting or violating one another's strict
rights. Any member of such a species certainly could will M4 to be a universal law of nature.

Kant's argument, on its most straightforward reading, is based on the
empirical claim that the human condition – the condition of any human
being whatever, however wealthy or individualistic – is not like that of a
member of this species. The premise needed is that we humans are
highly dependent and interdependent beings, whose ends, projects, and
general well-being are vulnerable not only to the violation of our rights
by others but to many other misfortunes, and they include many ends
that we can achieve only through a voluntary participation of others in
our ends that goes beyond what we can demand of them by right.

In fact Kant *does* take this view of the human condition. "Our self-
love," he says, "cannot be separated from our need to be loved (helped
in case of need) by others" and therefore "we make ourselves an end
for the others, and the only way this maxim can be binding is through
its qualification as a universal law" (MS 6:393). All human beings have
ends, projects, and needs that are sufficiently important to them and
sufficiently dependent upon the voluntary participation of others that
it would be irrational for any human being to resolve to abandon any
end or project, and to give up hope of satisfying any need, as soon as
it turned out to require the freely given aid of another. This need, Kant
thinks, is present even in the wealthiest and most powerful human beings, who can never lead satisfying lives without the friendship, love, and
affection of others (since these can never be demanded of anyone by
strict right). To be so ruggedly individualistic as to think you could leave
these needs unsatisfied would be to have an irrationally low estimate of

their importance to your personal good. To be so little risk-averse as to try to pursue your good while renouncing the hope of all voluntary participation of others in your ends would be to adopt an *irrational* plan for promoting your own welfare.[22]

If this interpretation of Kant's argument is correct, then the empirical premise to which it appeals is a *normative* premise in the sense that it declares a ruggedly individualistic or risk-loving policy for pursuing our own good to be an *irrational* policy for any human being. (Kant need not deny that such a policy might work if the person is lucky enough; betting your life savings on the Powerball Lottery is irrational, too, but it would certainly pay off if you happened to win.) Even so, there is still nothing question-begging about Kant's argument, because the normative premise is a *prudential* rather than a moral one. This empirical premise is controversial and would be impossible to test by any simple experiment. But that doesn't make it any less empirical or entail that it has no determinate truth value.

The worst problem for this straightforward interpretation of Kant's argument is not that rugged individualists might dispute Kant's premise. It is that the CW test, so interpreted, will obviously not disqualify many maxims besides M4, which obviously should be disqualified by the CW test on any reasonable interpretation of it as a moral standard. Consider, for instance, the maxim of refusing to provide *a particular sort* of voluntary help to others that many or even most people need but which I know for certain I shall never need from anyone. A law of nature according to which no one ever gave that specific kind of help might be disastrous for most people, but for me it would harmonize perfectly well with rational prudence.

What the CW test ought to tell us is which maxims, if universalized, would meet conditions of cooperation to which everyone would consent if they took a fair and impartial view of the matter. One way to think of the CW test, in the spirit of John Rawls's "veil of ignorance," would be to take it to be asking whether, given a complete knowledge of all the needs and resources of every human being but not knowing which human being you are, it would be rational for you to will U4 as a law of nature. In that case, if *any* human being is in such need that it would be contrary to reason to will this, then M4 fails the CW test. That would guarantee (what Kant obviously intended) that the results of the CW test are the same for everyone, regardless of their personal situations or tastes.[23]

The really big problem for Kant at this point is that, contrary to his allegations at G 4:421, neither FUL nor FLN (hence no form of the CC or CW tests) actually follows from the mere concept of a categorical imperative. Hence the argument of the Second Section of the *Groundwork* necessarily leaves it indeterminate how the CW test should be interpreted and whether its results should be allowed to depend on one's personal situation and tastes. Kant's sympathizers therefore try to reconstruct the most plausible version of the test while his critics, realizing that his arguments do not preclude versions of it having counterintuitive results, press objections that naturally flow from this point. I urge both sides to show greater appreciation for the overall argument of Section Two of the *Groundwork*. To do this is to consider FUL and FLN as expressions of the supreme principle of morality only from one limited point of view, as part of the entire system of formulas Kant works out between G4:421 and G4:437. (I try to identify their proper role in § 8 of this chapter and in Chapter 5, § 5.) For Kant's sympathizers, this means no longer trying to pretend that FUL and FLN are sufficient for moral deliberation. For the critics, it means appreciating that their objections to these formulas do not justify their closing the *Groundwork* at G4:424 in the self-satisfied conviction that they have just disposed of Kantian ethics once and for all.

7. The problems with FUL

In §§ 3–6 I have argued that given suitable empirical premises, Kant's arguments from the CC and CW tests do show that M1–M4 are ruled impermissible by FUL (or by its typic FLN). However, the most important claim I want to defend in this chapter is that FUL and FLN are themselves merely provisional formulations of the moral law. The universalizability tests represent a premature (and only partly successful) attempt to formulate and apply the principle for which Kant is searching. In the *Groundwork*, FUL (with its variant FLN) is not as well defended as are FH or FA (with its variant FRE). Nor are FUL and FLN as powerful or useful in moral deliberation as these other formulas. They have theoretical value —— at all only when they are considered as part of the systematic development that leads Kant to these other, more adequate and more practically useful formulations of the moral law. The remainder of the chapter will argue for these contentions by pressing a number of difficulties with FUL or FLN, and questioning some of the claims Kant makes on their behalf.

7.1. The Correspondence Thesis Kant regards the two universalizability tests as corresponding to a distinction between two different classes of duties. Let us call this the "Correspondence Thesis." Kant alleges that those maxims that fail the CC test violate duties that are "perfect," "narrow," "owed," or "imprescriptible," while those failing the CW test go against "imperfect," "wide," or "meritorious" duties (G 4:424).

Unlike the universalizability tests (whose importance in Kantian ethics has usually been greatly exaggerated by friends and foes alike), this classification of duties is absolutely vital to the structure of ethical theory as Kant conceives it. The taxonomy of duties is fundamental to the way Kant structures the system of ethical duties later in the *Metaphysics of morals* (MS 6:390–394, 421, 444; cf. the parallel distinction in the case of duties to others between duties of respect and duties of love, MS 6:448). If this distinction and classification is derivable from the distinction between the two FUL tests, then this helps to show that FUL is pivotal for Kant's theory as a whole. If, however, the Correspondence Thesis is false, then that undermines any claim for the privileged position of FUL, and lends further support to my contention that FUL and FLN are provisional and even defective formulations of the moral law.

A narrow or perfect duty is one requiring (or forbidding) a certain kind of action without exception, so that any violation of it constitutes an instance of moral wrongdoing and is blameworthy. An imperfect duty, by contrast, is one that requires only that we pursue a certain end but does not require us to do so to any determinate extent or through any determinate actions. An action fulfilling such a duty on a given occasion is meritorious, but the failure to perform such an action is not wrong or blameworthy; it merely lacks moral merit (cf. MS 6:390–394).

The Correspondence Thesis is not easy to disprove, since one cannot be sure in advance how Kantians would want to classify duties as perfect and imperfect, or how inventive they might be in constructing arguments to show that various maxims do fail the CC test. Of course, to the extent that these matters are obscure and difficult to determine, FUL and FLN also fail to provide any *perspicuous* route to Kant's taxonomy of duties. Naturally Kant chooses his examples of the CC test to be consistent with the Correspondence Thesis, since he holds that we have a perfect duty not to commit suicide or to make false promises (MS 6:422–423),[24] while developing talents and giving voluntary help to others are wide or imperfect duties (MS 6:444–445, 448). But there are nevertheless good reasons to doubt the Correspondence Thesis.

First, there seem to be some maxims that might lead one to violate duties of both sorts. For instance,

Mv: "I will not tolerate any unavenged insult." (KpV 5:19)

Acting on Mv, I might get even with someone who insulted me both by ——
refusing to help them when they are in need (thereby neglecting an
imperfect duty) and also by telling a malicious lie about them (thereby
violating a perfect duty). Whether Kant holds that Mv fails the CC test
or passes the CC test and fails the CW test, acting on it will involve the
violation of duties of a non-corresponding sort.

Next, there do appear to be some duties that appear *prima facie* to be
narrow or perfect duties if any are, and there are some maxims on
which one might violate these duties, which could nevertheless be conceived without contradiction as universal laws of nature. Consider duties of justice, those which violate the universal principle of right: "Any
action is *right* if it can coexist with everyone's freedom in accordance
with a universal law or if the maxim of choice of each can coexist with
everyone's freedom in accordance with a universal law" (MS 6:230).
This principle enjoins us not to do bodily violence to another, not to
violate another's freedom, and not to violate another's property. All
duties of justice are perfect or narrow duties (MS 6:240). But surely
there are some maxims involving the violation of such duties that could
be thought without contradiction to be universal laws of nature. Consider the maxim of "convenience killing":

Mk: I will kill other human beings whenever that is a safe and effective way of promoting my own self-interest.

It is easily conceivable that someone who followed this maxim would violate a strict or perfect duty to others, namely, the duty of justice, which
corresponds to their basic right not to be killed. But, as Barbara Herman
has cogently argued, Mk can be thought without contradiction to be a
universal law of nature.[25] Mk conceived as a law of nature would be

Uk: All human beings will kill other human beings whenever this
is a safe and effective way of promoting their own self-interest.

There is good reason to think that a rational being could not consis- ——
tently *will* to live in a world where Uk held as a universal law of nature.
But there seems no reason, either in general or contained in Mk itself,
why Uk could not be *thought* as a universal law of nature. Of course, in
a world where Uk held as a law of nature, human life might very well be
insecure (possibly also solitary, poor, nasty, brutish, and short). But such
a world would have even these noxious features only contingently, to

the extent that the ineffectiveness of rightful civil coercion makes convenience killing a safe and effective way of promoting one's interests.

Perhaps Herman's contention that Uk can subsist without contradiction as a law of nature is controversial. But it does not seem to be difficult to imagine maxims on which one might violate other strict or perfect duties (duties of others) – such as those forbidding bodily assault, or against defaming or ridiculing others (MS 6:466–467) – which could likewise subsist without contradiction as universal laws of nature. Surely it is *possible* that (i.e., there is no contradiction in the conception of a nature in which by natural law) people engage in such morally objectionable conduct whenever they have the opportunity. If this is possible, then there are evidently some duties that Kant categorizes as narrow or perfect, and a maxim on which they might be violated, such that the maxim passes the CC test and fails only the CW test.

7.2. *Only one positive duty from FUL*   Finally, the Correspondence Thesis is implausible in view of another serious shortcoming of both FUL and FLN. The capacity of the universalizability test, as illustrated in the *Groundwork*, to establish positive duties of any kind (perfect or imperfect) seems extremely limited. Hence it is implausible that one could use it to provide a taxonomical principle regarding such duties.

This is a direct consequence of the kinds of tests that the CC and CW tests are. These are tests of maxims, not of action-kinds, still less of omission-kinds. Their results can show only that it is permissible or impermissible to act on a certain maxim, never that we have a positive duty either to follow a maxim or to perform an action of a certain kind. For all Kant's arguments show, for example, there might be a maxim other than M1 enjoining suicide under certain circumstances or a maxim other than M2 enjoining the making of false promises, such that these other maxims can be rationally thought and willed as universal laws of nature.

Herman thinks that from the impermissibility of a maxim (e.g., M4), it follows that we are obligated to adopt its contradictory (which she formulates as: "To help some others sometimes").[26] But this certainly *does not* follow. Maxims, after all, are (subjectively) normative principles. From the mere fact that we may *not* adopt some specific principle as a norm (in this case, M4), it can never follow directly that we *must* adopt some other normative principle. For all the argument about M4 shows, it might be permissible to adopt no maxim whatever about helping others. The positive duty to help others (even where this duty is a wide one) is grounded on our duty to make their happiness our end. As we shall see in a moment, such a duty may be derivable from the same considerations that rule out M_4 according to FLN, but it does not follow merely from the fact that M_4 is an impermissible maxim.

It might also perhaps occur to someone to suggest that we could establish a positive duty (to do an action of kind K) by considering the maxim schema:

Mnk: I will never do actions of kind K.

Suppose Mnk is not universalizable. Then it seems to follow that one must sometimes do actions of kind K, and hence that there is a positive duty to do some such actions. But when we attempt to get a firmer grip on it, this suggestion dissolves like wet Kleenex between our fingers. The thought holds together quite well if all we want to establish is that it can be shown that there are kinds of actions such that we must not rule out on principle the performance of actions of that kind. (That is precisely the aim of Kant's discussions of M_3 and M_4.)[27] But as we have just seen, omitting to rule out a certain kind of action does not involve the adoption of any determinate maxim at all, and is compatible with omitting to regulate one's behavior by any maxims at all.[28]

There is in fact only one general duty for which Kant does argue using something like the CW test. In both the *Critique of practical reason* and the *Metaphysics of morals* he argues that we have a general (though wide and imperfect) duty to make the happiness of others our end (KpV 5:34–35, MS 6:393). Kant's argument rests on the same empirical premise as his argument regarding M_4: namely, that "our self-love cannot be separated from our need to be loved (helped in case of need) by others as well" (MS 6:393). Hence our naturally necessary maxim of self-love can be willed as a universal law only if mutual assistance is willed as part of the same law, and this gives rise to a law that every rational being should assist others and should include their happiness among its ends.[29]

It should be noted that this conclusion is distinct from (and stronger than) the conclusion of the fourth example in the *Groundwork*, which is only that M_4, a maxim of principled nonassistance to others, is impermissible. So it is once again quite consistent with the conclusion of the fourth example that there should be no general duty at all (even an imperfect duty) to assist others. That conclusion rules out only M_4's principled policy of not assisting them and does not show that we have a duty to adopt any contrary policy of making their happiness an end.

Even if we (somewhat generously) count this positive duty as derived from FUL (or FLN), its derivation remains entirely unique. We cannot expect any other duty to be derivable in a similar way. For the argument depends on the fact that one's own happiness is an end that can be attributed universally to all rational beings. But there are no other ends of this kind, so no analogous argument from FUL to any other positive duty is possible. This means that FUL (or FLN) should be considered an inadequate basis for the derivation of positive duties of any kind, and especially for the derivation of general categories of such duties, such as perfect or imperfect duties, duties to oneself and duties to others, and so forth. Since no positive duties of any kind can be derived from FUL or FLN, no perfect or imperfect duties can be derived from them on either the CC or the CW test. That by itself entails that the Correspondence Thesis is false.

7.3. *False positives*   The inadequacy of FUL and FLN regarding the derivation of positive duties is, however, only one respect in which it should be regarded as an incomplete or defective presentation of the fundamental principle of morality. Let us turn to some others.

A long line of distinguished critics, including Hegel, Mill, and Sidgwick, charge that FUL and FLN are incapable of disqualifying many obviously immoral maxims. This is the charge of "false positives" – that is, actions that FUL and FLN should rule out as impermissible but which (allegedly) pass their tests and therefore show up as permissible.[30]

These charges may not be sustainable regarding Kant's own four examples, but they are convincing in other cases.

Any maxim that tells us to make a false promise but sufficiently restricts the conditions under which we do so, would appear not to be excluded by the CC in the way that M2 is. Consider, for example, the maxim of making a false promise on Tuesday, August 21, to a person named Hildreth Milton Flitcraft. This maxim surely would not, if made a universal law of nature, make it impossible for me to gain money by making false promises. It is not even evident that such a qualified law would become well enough known to people named Hildreth Milton Flitcraft that one could not achieve one's purpose in following it.

The usual reply to this sort of objection is to insist that a "maxim" in Kant's sense is not just any principle that can be devised to fit a certain action; it must be a principle that accurately expresses the agent's actual intention. But actual people who want to gain money by making false promises would not desist on the basis of the day of the week or the name of the prospective creditor, so that is not the maxim adopted by any actual agent, and its permissibility is therefore not a real moral issue.

This reply is inadequate, for two reasons. First, if FUL is really supposed to supply us with a rigorous test of the morality of maxims, it ought to work not only for the maxims people commonly act on, but also, one would hope, even for strange maxims that would be adopted only under very unusual circumstances or by a very weird agent. If there is really something wrong with making false promises to repay money, then we should be able to show that the policy of doing this is wrong even if limited to false promises on Tuesdays in August and to people named Hildreth Milton Flitcraft.

Second, there is a deeper point the reply doesn't acknowledge. This is that the greater the specificity of an agent's intentions, as formulated in a maxim, the less sweeping will be the effect if the maxim becomes a universal law of nature, and hence the more likely it will be that even grossly immoral conduct will pass the CC and CW tests. Further, agents actually do form intentions at a wide variety of levels of generality and specificity. For example, I intend to get out of financial difficulty, to do this by borrowing money, by borrowing money without paying it back; I may also intend to borrow $500, to borrow it before lunchtime today, to borrow it from my gullible pal Hilly Flitcraft rather than my suspicious cousin Hester or my stingy colleague Hjalmar, to get Hilly to lend it to me by solemnly promising to pay him every cent by Friday, and so on, down to the last intentional feature of the particular action of which I may not be even subliminally aware. My intentions can be described – not artificially but quite accurately – in greater or lesser detail, at higher or lower levels of generality, by mentioning or omitting this or that feature of the situation. As we become more specific, all other things being equal, our maxim will have fewer consequences if made a universal law of nature, and therefore the less likely it is, all other things being equal, that a contradiction will arise in trying to conceive or will the maxim as a universal law of nature.

Thus it might be possible in some cases to describe my intention in borrowing the money in such detail (even without using indexicals or proper names) that its becoming a universal law of nature would foreseeably have *no* consequences beyond those of my acting on it on this particular occasion. In the case of such a maxim, the consequences of its being universally acted on could play no role in its disqualification under FUL or FLN. Unless the maxim is itself internally contradictory or aims at violating an existing law of nature it would necessarily pass the CC test. Unless, like M3, it directly opposes something that every rational being as such necessarily wills, it is bound to pass the CW test. In some cases, however, such as M2 and M4, the maxim is held to fail one of these tests precisely because of the hypothetical consequences of its being *universally* followed. Thus we could often (truly and accurately) formulate a maxim involving the same (morally objectionable) action with such specificity that its being universally followed would have no consequences except those of its being followed on the one intended occasion, and this more specific maxim would have to pass the corresponding universalizability test.

One might reply to this objection by claiming (following O'Neill) that in order for an action to be permissible under FLN, *every* applicable maxim must pass the universalizability test.[31] That means maxims involving the more general intentions would have to pass as well as those formulating highly specific intentions. But in the previous subsection we found it hard to make sense of applying the universalizability test to *all* the maxims on which a certain sort of action might be performed (e.g., all the actions falling under an instance of the schema Mnk). How could we hope to formulate a complete catalog of all the possible maxims for any action? In a similar way, we might also find it difficult to apply a procedure that would require one to canvass *all* the maxims (all the intentional descriptions) under which a given action might correctly be brought.[32] This may be the reason why O'Neill has more recently chosen to identify our "maxims," for the purpose of applying FUL or FLN, with "those underlying principles or intentions by which we guide and control our more specific intentions."[33] But this still doesn't tell us what is "underlying," that is, how deeply we should probe into an agent's intentions in order to find what is morally relevant.

In the false promising example "getting out of financial difficulty" or even "borrowing money from a friend when in financial distress" are, in an obvious sense, *more basic* intentions or principles than "borrowing money without intending to repay it." These more underlying maxims both pass the CC test and are morally permissible. What this shows is that it is crucial in giving the right assessment of the false promise that we include in our maxim the information that we intend to get out of financial distress by borrowing money *we don't intend to repay*, but not to include the information that we intend to borrow the money on Tuesday from good old Hilly Flitcraft, even though the latter might also be truly part of our intention. What we seem to need if the CC and CW tests are to be protected from this sort of objection is a way of describing our intention at *exactly the right* level(s) of generality. We want descriptions that are neither too superficial nor too basic and pick out the features of our intention that will be most relevant to the moral evaluation of our action in this case, the feature that I intend to borrow the money without paying it back.[34]

This is just another way of admitting something that is more damaging once it is made explicit: that in addition to FUL or FLN, we need a further specification of the moral laws themselves that FUL (in the empty form of CI, which does validly follow from the concept of a categorical imperative or objective principle) is commanding us not to violate. The CC and CW tests were ostensibly proposed as criteria for determining, in the absence of any such independent specification of the moral laws, which maxims violate those laws. The failure of these tests to operate reliably without a more precise specification of the morally relevant features of maxims to be tested is just a symptom of the fact that CI itself provides no clue for determining what the universal laws are. Even when, without argument, Kant introduces the criterion of what a rational agent can will to be a universal law of nature, this is still not enough.

7.4. False negatives The problems just mentioned have to do with "false positives" in regard to the CC and CW tests, that is, with maxims that might pass these tests even though they or actions performed on them seem intuitively to be contrary to duty. There are even clearer cases, however, of "false negatives," that is, of maxims that seem intuitively innocent but which the CC or CW tests appear to disqualify. Any number of such maxims can be found in the vast literature on this (much overworked) topic:

Ma: "I will buy a clockwork train, but never sell one."[35]

Mb: "In order to avoid crowded tennis courts, I will play on Sunday mornings (when my neighbors are in church and the courts are free)."[36]

Mc: "When the Dow-Jones average reaches the next thousand, I will sell all my stocks."[37]

All three maxims are intuitively quite innocent (unless you think there is immorality in skipping church or trading in stocks). Yet all three quite evidently fail the universalizability test. Ma fails the CC test on a logical interpretation, since if no one ever sold a clockwork train, then no one could ever buy one: There is a self-contradiction in the very conception of a system of nature one of whose laws is:

Ua: Everyone buys clockwork trains but no one ever sells them.[38]

Mb also fails the CC test, this time on a practical interpretation. For if, as a law of nature, everyone played tennis on Sunday mornings, the courts would be horribly crowded then, and the purpose contained in Mb itself would be frustrated. Finally, Mc fails at least the CW test, since if it were a universal law of nature, then as soon as the Dow reached the next thousand, the market would suddenly collapse in chaos and everyone's stock would be worthless – something no rational investor could will.

It might be suggested that we could avoid these counterexamples by reformulating the agent's maxims at a more general level – Mb, for example, as:

Mb':   I will make use of what others may be expected to do in order to secure advantages for myself.

But this suggestion is no good, because although Mb' may indeed pass the universalizability test and may be as true an expression of my intention as Mb, it is equally true that Mb' could perform exactly the same redeeming service in the case of the false promise, replacing M2 as a more general (and morally acceptable) expression of my intention. (In making the false promise, I am merely using to my advantage what my credulous chum Hilly Flitcraft may be expected to do if I ask to borrow money from him on trust.) In short, if we allow the suggested solution to the problem of false negatives, we only exacerbate the problems about false positives.[39]

There is actually a very simple point (and an utterly devastating one as far as Kant's universalizability tests are concerned) behind all false negatives such as Ma, Mb, and Mc (and such examples could of course be multiplied indefinitely). This point is that there are many maxims that could not themselves be (or be willed as) universal laws of nature but do not violate universally valid moral laws (on any plausible account of what these laws might be).

This merely reinforces the fundamental point made about FUL and FLN throughout this chapter. The principle CI that follows validly from the mere concept of a categorical imperative, practical law, or objective principle, says only that our maxim must not violate any universal laws (but tells us nothing about what these laws might be). To go beyond this, Kant (invalidly) infers FUL and then FLN, which commands us to act only on those maxims that can pass the universalizability tests (CC and CW). But this device fails because it is not true that we can equate "maxims which accord with universal laws" with "maxims which can themselves be willed as universal laws." Thus the problem of false negatives, like the problem of false positives, is merely another congenital defect the universalizability tests have inherited from their invalid derivation.[40]

In order to achieve systematicity in his presentation of the moral law, Kant began with FUL as a merely formal characterization of the law before introducing the substantive value that lies behind it (which appears only in FH). What Kant should have admitted is that a merely formal — characterization of the law, though necessary and entirely correct from a systematic standpoint, cannot provide us with a formulation well suited to be applied to particular cases. This is the full extent of the truth contained in criticisms of Kantian ethics as an "empty formalism." These criticisms completely ignore the fact that Kant does not provide merely a formal principle, but proceeds immediately to specify the substantive value on which the principle rests. Hence such critics behave as though they had suddenly stopped reading the *Groundwork* in the middle of the Second Section (at about G 4:425).

8. Exceptional behavior and self-preference

Through the CC and CW tests, FLN appears to provide something like an algorithm for testing the permissibility of maxims. This deceptive appearance, I think, is the main reason for philosophers' fascination with FUL and FLN, which appear to propose a universal moral decision procedure (the Kantian analogue of the act utilitarian's equally bogus ideal of precisely calculating the felicific tendencies of all practical alternatives now facing us). Unfortunately, however, human life and moral deliberation are too complex for any such procedure ever to exist. (Any moral theory that purports to offer one should *precisely thereby* have discredited itself in the eyes of any person of good judgment.) Instead of seeking for such an illusory procedure, what the philosophers should have sought is rather the *moral point* of FLN and its associated tests. *Why* should we act only on maxims that we can will to be universal laws?

One thought here starts from the fact that the CC and CW tests exclude maxims on the basis of *contradictions* in volition. We might then think: If the principle of morality is a principle of practical reason, then it should instruct us to avoid contradictions in willing, just as theoretical reason should avoid contradictions among our judgments. But maxims that fail the CC and CW tests do not necessarily involve conflicts or contradictions within our *actual* volitions. They involve contradictions between our actual volition in adopting a maxim and the (merely hypothetical) volition that this same maxim should be a universal law (or law of nature). In fact, Kant even maintains that when we will a forbidden maxim, we could never actually will its universalized form because we always already will precisely the opposite of that (G 4:424). The point that should interest us is why Kant thinks we do will that, and not why we should avoid volitional contradictions. We will return presently to this point.

A second account of the moral point of the universalizability test is given by Christine Korsgaard: "What the test shows to be forbidden are just those actions whose efficacy in achieving their purposes depends upon their being exceptional."[41] This is obviously mistaken because there are clearly any number of quite innocent actions that depend for their success on the fact that they will be exceptional, that others will choose not to do anything similar.[42] Herman's example of the Sunday morning tennis player (whose maxim is Mb) is one of these; so is her example of the person who saves money by buying next year's presents at "after Christmas" sales. Neither example involves any wrongdoing, yet both agents achieve their ends only by intentionally acting in ways they know will be exceptional. The principal kind of "exceptional" behavior which suits Korsgaard's remark is "free riding." But any plausible moral objection to free riding presupposes the existence of a determinate moral principle or duty with which everyone is supposed to comply. Morally objectionable free riding occurs only when you receive a benefit without assuming the associated burden that people eligible for the benefit are *obligated* to assume. [43] All moral objections to free riding thus presuppose determinate duties of the kind neither FUL nor FLN can by themselves establish.

Still less could the moral point of FUL and FLN be the *merely semantic* point that when I say that action A is right and action B is not right, I am committed to there being some *relevant difference* between A and B on which the moral difference supervenes. For that would be consistent with locating the relevant difference in the fact that it is Stan Spatz III who wants to make a promise without intending to keep it. From the purely formal semantic point of view, this difference would make as good a supervenience base as any other for the moral difference.[44]

The real moral point of FUL, however, is very simple: *It is wrong to make oneself (or one's inclinations) a privileged exception to universal moral laws that everyone else is rightly expected to follow.* Kant himself tells us this quite explicitly:

> If we attend to ourselves in the transgression of a duty, we find that we do not actually will that our maxim should become a universal law, for that is impossible for us, but rather that its opposite should universally remain a law; only we take the liberty of making an *exception* for ourselves or (also only for this time) for the advantage of our inclination. Consequently, if we weighed everything from the same standpoint, namely that of reason, we would encounter a contradiction in our own will, namely that a certain principle should be objectively necessary as universal law and yet subjectively it should not hold universally, but should permit exceptions. (G 4:424)

Note that Kant says *we do will* that the "opposite" of our immoral maxim should "universally remain a law," and find it *in our own will* "that a certain principle should be objectively necessary as universal law." This is as clear a confession as we could ask for that the application of FUL requires (besides FLN and the associated CC and CW tests) also *other* objectively valid laws or principles proceeding from our own will. "The opposite" of my maxim must refer to *some other specific principle*, which is *assumed* to be a *valid universal law.* Its validity, moreover, is asserted to derive from the fact that *we rationally will* it to be a universal law. Obviously neither FUL nor FLN (nor the CC and CW tests) contain by themselves anything capable of specifying or validating such universal laws, whose content and possibility are first given in the *Groundwork* only with the entire system of formulas leading from FUL and FLN through FH to FA and FRE. In other words, this is as clear an admission as we need that FUL and FLN are, by themselves, inadequate to test maxims or determine moral duties.

Kant makes another noteworthy observation in the passage just quoted, which is that FUL is addressed to a specific propensity of our *human* nature. The threat of conflicting volitions is a conflict between two points of view: the standpoint of reason, which puts us on an equal footing with all other rational beings, and the standpoint of self-preference, which wants to make exceptions to these same laws on behalf of ourselves or our inclinations. This shows that he considers the pertinence of FUL and FLN to moral choice to depend in part on a specific empirical propensity of the human will, namely, to give ourselves and our inclinations a rationally unjustifiable preference over other rational beings and their inclinations.

FUL does an incomplete job of calling attention to our propensity to self-preference, since this propensity does not show itself only when we make exceptions of ourselves when it comes to valid universal rules. As Nancy Sherman has pointed out, it can also show itself in our tendency to deceive ourselves about which maxims we are acting on – we may profess to be acting on a certain maxim, which is universalizable, and even believe we are acting on this maxim, while in fact our actions conform to quite a different maxim, which we know is not universalizable.[45] It would be entirely in the spirit of Kant's theory of human nature to acknowledge that point. Kantians may never claim, therefore, that FUL can provide any more than one out of many kinds of practical reflection to which we might submit a proposed course of action in deciding whether it is morally permissible.

Nor should they feel it necessary to claim more than this. For Kant, FUL is merely the first stage in a philosophical search for the supreme principle of morality, and we will not understand it until we see the role it plays in this systematic search. In Chapter 4, we shall see that Kant's formula of choice for applying the moral law is not FUL but FH. The formula that does the best job of displaying the ground of the principle is FA, and the formula that best conveys its spirit is FRE. Because FUL and FLN are the earliest and most abstract formulas Kant derives in the course of a progressive argument, they are also the least adequate expressions of the supreme principle of morality, and the poorest in practical consequences. The chief purpose of this chapter has been to discuss the standard disputes about them, which treat these formulas in abstraction from the system of which they are a part, in such a way as to show why we should leave those disputes behind.

THE FORMULA OF HUMANITY
AS END IN ITSELF

1. Ends and determining grounds of the will

1.1. Motives and incentives FUL does not take us beyond the mere concept of a categorical imperative. In order to derive a second formula of
the moral law, Kant turns to something more substantive. His aim is to
show how a categorical imperative or practical law could be "connected
(wholly *a priori*) with the concept of the will of a rational being as such"
(G 4:426). In other words, he turns our attention to what it would
require for a rational will to *obey* such an imperative or law. Kant distinguishes two kinds of grounds that can motivate a rational will: an objective ground, which is an end given by reason alone and valid for all
rational beings, and a subjective ground, which is an end based on
empirical desires. The former sort of ground he calls a "motive" (*Bewegungsgrund*), the latter an "incentive" (*Triebfeder*) (G 4:427–428).[1]

When Kant inquires into the nature of "motives," he is in effect trying to identify more precisely than he has already what it means to act
"from duty." Thus far it has been understood only as acting from respect
for law, but that account deals only with the "form" of the will, not with
its end or "matter." We could also put it by saying that the earlier account told us nothing about the substantive *value* that might be contained in the moral law and call forth our respect for it.

Earlier, Kant remarked that the determining ground of an imperative "connects it directly with the concept of the will of a rational being
as something that is not contained within it" (G 4:420n). This means
that he takes the claim he is making about the motivation of a rational
will to be *a priori* yet also synthetic. The second formula of the moral
law, therefore, is based on a synthetic *a priori* connection that holds between the concepts of a categorical imperative and a rational will. This

synthetic *a priori* proposition tells us what could motivate a rational will to obey a practical law, *if* there is such a law.

1.2. Ends and formal principles   The striking thing is Kant's insistence that the determining ground of a rational will must *always* be an end (*Zweck*), for this might be thought to contradict what he says elsewhere. Earlier in the *Groundwork* Kant stressed that the good will does not have its goodness in any end it might achieve (G 4:394) and that the moral worth of an act done from duty does not consist in its end but in its maxim (G 4:399). But on closer inspection there is no contradiction between saying that the good will is *motivated by an end* and saying that *its goodness does not consist in its usefulness in producing any end*. What Kant means to deny is that the goodness of a good will or the moral worth of an action is derivative from the desire for what it achieves or the end it aims to produce. We will see that the end that motivates the good will is neither an end to be produced nor an end whose worth is grounded in its being desired.

A more serious threat of inconsistency appears when we consider Kant's distinction in the *Critique of practical reason* between "formal principles" of the will, whose determining ground consists solely in the "legislative form" of the agent's maxim, and "material principles," whose determining ground is the end of the action. Formal principles alone, Kant says, can be practical laws; material principles are all empirical, fall under the principle of one's own happiness, and are opposed to the determination of the will by reason alone (KpV 5:21–22). Yet the distinction between "formal" and "material" principles is also drawn in the *Groundwork*, where material principles are said to be based on ends that rest on subjective grounds or "incentives," whereas formal principles disregard subjective ends and rest on "motives" (G 4:427). Moreover, for both the *Groundwork* and the second *Critique*, "material principles" are grounded on subjective ends or the *empirical* desire for an "object" (*Gegenstand, Objekt*). We will see presently that in the Second Section of the *Groundwork* "ends" are *not* restricted to "objects" (things or states of affairs) that are "effected" or brought about through actions. Kant also regards certain ends to be effected as necessary grounds of the will, when the desire for them is not an inclination but results from responding to a "formal principle" or categorical imperative. These are the "ends that are at the same time duties" that constitute the organizing principles of Kant's system of duties in the Doctrine of Virtue (MS 6:384–395; see Conclusion, § 4).

If there is a difference between the *Groundwork* and the second

Critique here, it consists only in the account of *formal* principles, whose determining ground the *Groundwork* identifies with a certain kind of end, an objective end or end in itself, which is valid for all rational beings, while the second Critique describes it as the "legislative form of the maxim," that is "the mere form of giving universal law" (KpV 5:27). The question, then, is what Kant means by 'legislative form' of a maxim and by an 'end in itself,' and whether these two phrases refer to a single determining ground of the will or to two different grounds.

That Kant intends these two descriptions to refer to the same ground (though perhaps regarded from two different points of view) is indicated a bit later in the *Groundwork*, where he describes the "ground of practical legislation" as lying "objectively [in] the form of universality," and "subjectively in the end" (i.e., the end in itself) (G 4:431). In order to see how these phrases might have the same referent, let us first try to be clearer about what Kant means by the 'legislative form of the maxim' or 'the mere form of giving universal law.' This last description seems to allude to the later formula FA and to the fact that the maxim with legislative form is regarded as conforming to a universal law *given* by the will. But the derivation of that formula depends on FH (G 4:431), so it would be premature to appeal to it here.

If we think of Kantian ethics primarily in terms of FUL, it is natural to take 'the legislative form of the maxim' to refer to some feature of the maxim already identified by that formula, in particular the maxim's passing of the CC and CW tests.[2] This would be a motive for action that is apparently distinct from any end. But the suggestion proves to be untenable as soon as we look more closely at what it would mean. For as we saw in Chapter 3, the CC and CW tests enable us only to distinguish permissible maxims from impermissible ones, and 'because it's permitted' is never a sufficient ground for doing anything. The very concept of obeying a categorical imperative thus requires that the legislative form of the maxim should be some positive value that goes beyond passing the universalizability tests. This entails that a new *formulation* of the moral law in terms of the motive for following a categorical imperative does not give us a *different principle* (which would be different from the categorical imperative conceived formally as FUL). On the contrary, the concept of a motive grounding obedience to a categorical imperative must be connected *a priori* (though synthetically) with the concept of such an imperative.

1.3. Ends and Kantian "formalism"   What we need to understand at this point is the relation between the "formal" principle FUL and the concept of an *end in itself* as its rational determining ground. Light is shed on these matters if we look at what Kant said about them more than twenty years earlier in his prize essay, *Inquiry concerning the distinctness of the principles of natural theology and morality* (1764). There Kant recognizes "formal grounds of obligation" to act and abstain, in the form of moral rules, but argues that: "No specifically determinate obligation flows from [them] unless they are combined with indemonstrable material principles of practical cognition . . . They cannot be called obligations as long as they are not subordinated to an end which is necessary in itself" (DG 2:298–299).

Kant's ethical theory has often been criticized as "formalistic" and "deontological" by those who insist that an obligation to follow a rule or principle makes sense only if there is some value or end that provides a reason for following the rule. To anyone tempted to think that Kant's theory is vulnerable to such criticisms, it should be of interest that Kant himself made exactly this point as early as 1764, and even made it the basis of the *Groundwork*'s argument that a categorical imperative can be binding on a rational will only if there is an objective end or end in itself. In fact, if a "deontological" ethical theory is one that *precludes* grounding a moral principle on substantive values or ends, then the aim of Kant's argument at G 4:427–432 is to show that no deontological theory is possible.

Kant's contention is that *humanity*, or "the human being and every rational being in general," is the end in itself that provides the categorical imperative with its objective ground (G 4:428). But the task of arguing for this contention must be approached cautiously, since it is a question of an ultimate end or value, which the prize essay described as an "indemonstrable principle of practical cognition."[3] In the *Groundwork*, Kant rejects the appeal to feeling as an alternative to demonstration, but he still has the same reasons as before for thinking that the goodness of the end he is seeking is *indemonstrable*. Hence the argument that humanity is such an end must proceed in a manner analogous to an appeal to feeling, such as by showing that humanity is something we already (perhaps tacitly or implicitly) acknowledge to be an objective end or end in itself.

2. Ends in themselves and existent ends

2.1. Value conceptions Kant begins with a bit fuller (though entirely hypothetical) account of the value he will ascribe to humanity or rational nature: "Supposing, however, that there were something *whose existence in itself* had an absolute worth, which, as *end in itself* could be the ground of determinate laws, then in it and it alone would lie the ground of a possible categorical imperative, that is, a practical law" (G 4:428). Here Kant supposes something to which he ascribes three distinct value conceptions:

1. *End in itself.* First, there is the conception of an *end in itself,* or *objective* end, whose worth, like the validity of the categorical imperative, is *unconditional* and independent of desire and valid for all rational beings. Because it is objective and independent of desire, it may constrain the rational will and thus "be the ground of determinate laws." The contrasting conception of an end would be that of a *relative* end, whose worth is relative to, conditioned by, and dependent on the subjective constitution of the faculty of desire of particular rational beings and varies from one such being to another. This sort of end could be the ground only of hypothetical imperatives (G 4:428).

2. *Existent end.* Second, there is the conception of an *existent* end, or, as Kant also calls it, a *self-sufficient end* (*selbständiger Zweck*) (G 4:437), that is, something that already exists and whose "existence is in itself an end," having worth as something to be esteemed, preserved, and furthered. Kant opposes this sort of end to an *end to be effected* (*zu bewirkender Zweck*), that is, some thing or state of affairs that does not yet exist but is to be brought about through an agent's causality (G 4:437).

3. *Absolute worth.* Third, Kant also speaks of something whose existence in itself has "absolute worth." He may mean by this only that it has *objective* worth as an end in itself, as distinct from a worth that is relative to inclination (in which case this would be an invocation only of conception (1) above). But Kant also ascribes to rational nature an "absolute worth" in the sense of a *dignity,* a value that cannot be compared to, traded off against, or compensated for or replaced by any other value (G 4:434). This is to be contrasted with an end with only relative worth, or *price,* whose value can be measured against the value of something else and may be rationally sacrificed to obtain something else of equivalent or greater worth. "Absolute worth" in this passage may be an allusion to the dignity of rational nature. Strictly speaking, as we shall —— see later, Kant ascribes dignity not to "humanity" but to "personality," that is, not to rational nature in general but to rational nature in its capacity to be morally self-legislative. Nevertheless, it will be useful at this point to distinguish "absolute worth" in the sense of "dignity" as a *third* crucial value conception both from the *first* conception, of the "objec-

tive worth" ascribed to an "end in itself," and the *second* conception of an existent or self-sufficient end.

2.2. *The concept of an existent end*   The second of these three value conceptions requires a bit more discussion. We are tempted to think that the concept of an end is *nothing but* the concept of a not yet existing object or state of affairs whose existence we desire and pursue. (Even Kant, as we have noted, often identifies the "end" of an action with the "object" to be produced by it.)[4] But we also include among our ends existing things or states of affairs that we merely preserve or do not act against, such as our own self-preservation and bodily well-being.[5] They are constantly ends for us, setting limits on what we are willing to do in pursuit of our other ends, even though our self-preservation in the future is something we present to ourselves as an end to be pursued only in rare and dire circumstances (such as those portrayed in Jack London's story "To Build a Fire").

In the broadest sense, however, an end is anything *for the sake of which* we act (or refrain from acting). Or, what I think amounts to the same thing, an end is that whose value provides an (at least relative) terminus in a chain of reasons for an action. This fits the usual case of an object or end to be effected, since when we build a house, our building activities are done for the sake of bringing the house into being, and the house's value to us is the reason why we build. It also fits an existent end such as self-preservation, because I cross the street at the crosswalk (rather than charging out into traffic) for the sake of preserving my life and also because the value I place on my life is my reason for what I do.

Other kinds of existent ends also play a role in our actions. When I build a house for myself, I not only build for the sake of bringing about the house but also for *my* sake; my reason for satisfying my needs is that I place value on myself. When I seek to relieve someone's suffering, my end to be effected is a certain state of affairs (the person's comfort); but I also act for the sake of a human being, whom I value in some way and is thus an existent end of my action. We are also familiar with existent ends in cases where there is no end to be effected, or at least none detachable from the existent end. When people kneel, bow their heads, or doff their hats to something (such as a flag or a religious object), they may have no end to be effected except the successful performance of the gesture of veneration itself. But they do act for an end, namely, for the sake of the revered object itself or the value it represents to them.[6]

Kant's theory maintains that to act morally is always to act for the sake of a person, or more precisely, <u>for the sake of humanity in someone's</u> <u>person</u>. In following a categorical imperative, the determining ground of the will is the objective worth of humanity or rational nature, as an object of respect. From this standpoint, all conduct is regarded fundamentally from the standpoint of what it *expresses* about the agent's attitude toward humanity. Morally good conduct expresses respect for humanity as an existent end, while bad conduct is bad because it expresses disrespect or contempt for humanity.[7]

We will be misled here, however, if we think of "valuing" or "respecting" humanity as some subjective state of mind, and interpret FH as commanding only that we put ourselves in such a state. If I make a promise to you I don't intend to keep, I am treating humanity in your person with disrespect, no matter what subjective thoughts or feelings I may have. On the other hand, in dealing honestly with you, I treat you with respect whatever my inner state may be. The actions commanded by FH (which conform to duty, whether or not they are done from duty) are those that express respect for humanity.[8]

2.3. Humanity as an existent end in itself   Now let us consider the three value conceptions we have distinguished in their relation to each other and to the value Kant intends to ascribe to humanity. Kant's position is that there is only one thing – namely, humanity, or rational nature – that satisfies the first conception, that of an end in itself. He further holds that it does so by instantiating the second conception, that of an existent or self-sufficient end. When considered as self-legislative, rational nature also satisfies the third conception: it has dignity or absolute worth. But as far as the three conceptions themselves are concerned, there is <u>no reason they would have to be found together</u>. It is perfectly possible to conceive of an end in itself that is an end to be effected. This would be some not yet existing thing or state of affairs that we have an objective reason to produce independently of any antecedent desire for it. An end in itself might also be an end with only relative worth or price, if rational deliberation might weigh objective ends against ends that depend on desires and find that a certain amount of what is objectively valuable might be rationally traded away to get a greater amount of what is merely desired. Conversely, there certainly seem to be existent ends, that is, existing beings for whose sake we act, which (at least in Kant's view) are not ends in themselves and do not have absolute worth or dignity. (<u>Nonhuman animals</u> are probably the most obvious examples of such beings.) Finally, an end having absolute worth or dignity might be both a relative end and an end to be effected. This would happen if there were an inclination to whose satisfaction it would be rational to give absolute priority over everything else in our scheme of values.

Therefore, Kant's attribution of all three value properties to humanity or rational nature is a claim not about any necessary relations between these properties, but rather about the kind of value belonging to that which in fact possesses the property in which he is primarily interested, namely, that of being an unconditioned or objective end, or end in itself. The contention, in other words, is that humanity is an end in itself by being an existent end having dignity or absolute worth.

3. Humanity and personality

3.1. Humanity as a predisposition   Before we look at the *Groundwork*'s defense of this contention, we need to understand what is meant by "humanity" (*Menschheit*) or "rational nature." In the *Religion*, Kant ascribes to human nature three fundamental global capacities or "original predispositions" (*ursprüngliche Anlagen*), to which he gives the names (1) "animality," (2) "humanity," and (3) "personality" (R 6:26).

Animality belongs to us merely as living beings, and it is the basis for our fundamental instinctual drives aiming at self-preservation (the drives for food, bodily well-being, and so on), the propagation of the species (the sexual instinct), and community with other members of our species (the social instinct). These drives provide for what Kant calls "mechanical self-love" (R 6:26–27). They give us (as they do nonrational animals) an instinctive urge to do what is necessary for our own survival and that of the species. But they operate at an entirely prerational level in that they involve no conscious representation of these natural ends and no deliberation as to how they are to be achieved.

The predisposition to personality is the rational capacity to respect the moral law and to act having duty or the moral law as a sole sufficient motive of the will. As we have already noted, Kant identifies personality with autonomy, in the sense of the ability to give oneself the moral law through reason, which is the ground of dignity (G 4:435, 439–440). As the basis of moral accountability (R 6:27–28), it is associated with the sensitive preconditions of morality in us: moral feeling, conscience, love of humanity, and self-respect (MS 6:399–403).

The predisposition to humanity lies in between the predispositions to animality and personality. It encompasses all our rational capacities having no specific reference to morality. Put most generally, humanity is the capacity to set ends through reason (G 4:437). In the *Anthropology*, Kant further subdivides the predisposition to humanity into the "technical predisposition" and the "pragmatic predisposition" (VA 7:322–324). The former includes our conscious, rational capacities to manipulate things as means to our arbitrary ends, including all learned skills, arts, and the deliberative abilities that fall under *technical* imperatives (see Chapter 2, § 3). Kant regards the pragmatic predisposition as the higher aspect of our humanity. It enables us not only to set ends but to compare the ends we set and organize them into a system (KU 5: 426–427). Hence humanity also involves the capacity to form the idea of our happiness or well-being as a whole. The pragmatic aspect of humanity is the basis of what Kant calls "prudence" (G 4:416) and is therefore the ground of the actual principles through which we seek happiness, which Kant calls "counsels of prudence" (G 4:418) (see Chapter 2, § 4).[9]

Humanity in this higher (pragmatic or prudential) aspect involves "rational" or "comparative" self-love, arising out of our social condition and the comparison of ourselves and our degree of well-being with that of others (R 6:28). For these reasons, Kant includes in the development of our predisposition to humanity everything belonging to culture and the cultivation of our social qualities (taste, manners, conformity to customs); for it is through these that we gain the esteem and approval of others and their willingness to contribute to our ends (VA 7:323–324).

The capacity to set ends through reason holds together the set of capacities constituting our humanity. It is this capacity alone that occasions the selection of means and hence the rational development of technical skills. It is also this capacity that makes possible the comparison and systematization of different ends into a whole. When it subjects my actions to rational guidance by an end, humanity in this sense also involves an active sense of my identity and an esteem for myself, which (as we saw in Chapter 2, § 5.2) is what holds me to my rational plan in the case of both the technical and the pragmatic use of reason. Humanity thus also presupposes a kind of freedom, namely the ability to resist the immediate coercion of desires and impulses. Kant calls this the "negative" concept of freedom (G 4:446, KpV 5:47–48).

"Humanity" clearly belongs to all mature members of our biological species who are not severely incapacitated. It is important to emphasize, however, it need not belong only to our species and therefore that the dignity of rational nature and the status of being an end in itself in no way privileges us over other possible rational beings. Kant is not a "humanist" (or a "speciesist") in the sense that he thinks we should place special value on our species or its members merely because it is —— ours. Likewise, because it is connected to the very concept of a rational being as such, Kant's contention that humanity (as rational nature) as an end in itself is the objective ground of the moral law in no way contradicts his frequent assertions that moral principles are not dependent on the constitution of human nature (in the ordinary sense) (G 4:388–390, 425–427).

3.2. *Why is* humanity *the end in itself?*   Once we see what Kant means by "humanity," it might surprise us that it is this, rather than *personality*, that he claims to be an end in itself. Personality seems "higher" than humanity in that it has essential reference to *moral* value, moral responsibility, and the "positive" concept of freedom, where humanity includes none of these. But Kant has at least two reasons for choosing humanity rather than personality as the end in itself.[10]

First, it is the whole of rational nature that constitutes such an end. Preserving and respecting rational nature means preserving and respecting it in all its functions, not merely in its moral function of giving and obeying moral laws. Furthering rational nature requires furthering all the (morally permissible) ends it sets, not merely the ends it sets in response to duty.

Second, it follows necessarily from the role played by the concept of an end in itself in grounding the categorical imperative that rational beings cannot be ends in themselves only insofar as they are virtuous or obedient to moral laws. For such an imperative is supposed to be *necessarily* binding on all rational beings. This could not be so if the sole ground that binds the will of a rational being to the law (namely, the worth of humanity as end in itself) were something whose existence were doubtful or even merely contingent. Yet it is contingent and even doubtful whether and to what extent the conduct of rational beings displays goodness of will by following the moral law and acting from duty (G 4:405–407).

Here we will be badly misled if we have been persuaded by the opening sentence of the First Section of *Groundwork* that everything in Kantian ethics turns solely on the value of the good will. If only the good will had the dignity of an end in itself, then the existence of such an end, and consequently the validity of categorical imperatives, would be doubtful. Kant, however, proposes to ground categorical imperatives on the worth of any being having humanity, that is, the capacity to set ends from reason, irrespective of whether its will is good or evil. That means that there is an objective ground of such imperatives as long as there are rational beings who can inquire after such a ground, even if they never act on it.

The same considerations tell us how Kant must deal with the fact that rational nature apparently comes in degrees. People have varying amounts of technical skill, pragmatic intelligence, or moral wisdom. Their actions exhibit various rational successes and failures. Even their rational capacities tend to develop as they mature and may be impaired in various ways by injury, disease, or old age. But being an end in itself cannot come in degrees, since a categorical imperative or practical law either has an objective ground or it does not. Kant's position therefore has to be that anything possessing the capacity to set ends and act according to reason is an end in itself, however well or badly it may exercise the capacity. It is a separate question (perhaps a much harder one to answer) how the requirement applies to beings in which humanity is found only partly or to an uncertain degree. The one option *not* open to Kant is to allow gradations of human dignity or differences in rank among members of the realm of ends.[11]

3.3. Rationality and value Perhaps the most fundamental proposition in Kant's entire ethical theory is that rational nature is the supreme value and the ground of whatever value anything else might possess. One natural reaction to this proposition is that even concerning human beings there are other things that we value besides rationality, such as capacities for feeling and emotion, such as sympathy, love, aesthetic sensitivity, or the *eros* and "divine madness" of which Plato speaks.[12] Such criticisms are due in part to false stereotypical conceptions of 'reason'. In Chapter 1, § 3.3, we saw that for Kant reason of itself is responsible for certain feelings: respect, moral feeling, conscience, and philanthropic love. He also regards the appreciation of natural beauty as closely allied to moral feeling (KU 5:298–303) and the capacity to be moved by the sublime as virtually identical with an awareness of the dignity of rational nature (KU 5:248–278). As for Platonic *eros*, reason is precisely the faculty that produces *ideas* – transcendent concepts whose objects can never be given in experience but which nevertheless represent our highest moral aspirations (KrV A312–333/B368–390). The term 'idea' is quite consciously an allusion to Plato (KrV A315–316/B372–373), and it is precisely the experience of the transcendence of the ideas over what is given as sensibly existing that Kant identifies with emotion (*Rührung*) of the sublime (KU 5:272–273). The primacy of reason is therefore anything but a denial of value to the emotional side of our nature, or to aspirations that transcend the real and ——the clearly conceptualizable. On the contrary, Kant holds that those capacities for feeling and emotion we have grounds to value belong to reason, and their worth is derivative from the dignity of rational nature.

It is quite true that Kant accords only limited value to certain feelings and emotions (such as love and sympathy). Nor would he use the term 'eros' (with its sexual connotations) to refer to reason's highest aspirations. Perhaps critics regard Kantian rationalism as hostile to "the emotions" because they think anyone who values human feelings and emotions at all must chiefly value *these* feelings and emotions, and a philosopher who is cool toward them can only be an enemy of *all* feelings. But Kant's views here are much more fine-grained and better worked out than the critics suspect. In Chapter 8 we will see why Kant withholds esteem from feelings like sympathy and love, and why his attitude toward sexual desire is largely negative. We may not end up agreeing with Kant on these topics, but we will see in due course how his account of human inclinations and affections follows from his general theory of human nature, and that if correct, it would fully support Kant's (no doubt controversial) evaluations. Once Kant's arguments are understood, they might even convince some of his sentimentalist critics to reassess the value of the specific emotions for which they feel such enthusiasm.

The unconditional value of rational nature thus includes the capacity for feelings and emotions. Only our rational capacities give human emotions the subtlety and complexity that make them as valuable as they are. Why, then, do so many people tend to think that a theory that grounds all value on reason needs to be supplemented in some way by objects of value lying outside reason (or even standing in opposition to it)? In Chapter 7, § 4.4, we will see that Kant has an interesting theory about human nature that can be used to provide a (rather unflattering) explanation for this common human tendency.

4. Things and persons

In the Second Section of the *Groundwork*, Kant is proceeding on the provisional assumption that there is a categorical imperative and tries to find out what it would have to be if we were able to act on it. One such condition, he has argued, is that there should be an objective end or

end in itself. He therefore provisionally assumes there is such an end
and asks, *If there is an end in itself, what could it be?* The first stage of the
search canvasses three kinds of things we consider valuable or sources of
value and argues that they cannot be considered ends in themselves:
(1) objects of inclination, (2) inclinations themselves, and (3) nonrational beings of nature whose existence doesn't depend on our will.

4.1. Objects of inclination   "All objects of inclinations have only a conditional worth; for if the inclinations and the needs founded on them
did not exist, their object would be without worth" (G 4:428). This first
exclusion is unproblematic. It is possible contingently to have an inclination for an object with objective or unconditional worth, but this
worth cannot rest on the inclination, since objective worth must ground
a categorical imperative. An imperative is categorical, however, precisely because it is rationally binding independently of any inclination.
An end in itself, by contrast, in order to ground a categorical imperative, must have a worth that is not conditional on inclination. Therefore,
no object of inclination as such can be an end in itself.

4.2. Inclinations themselves   "The inclinations themselves, however, as
sources of the need have so little of absolute worth that it must rather
be the universal wish of every rational being to be entirely free of them"
(G 4:428; cf. G 4:454). This remark has often appalled Kant's readers,
since it seems to suggest that he thinks it would be rational to mortify
all our empirical desires. In the *Religion*, however, Kant insists (against
the Stoics) that it would be not only futile and irrational but even morally
blamable to want to extirpate our natural inclinations (R 6:58). But for
Kant's purposes in the *Groundwork*, this whole issue is beside the point.
The only premises Kant needs for his present conclusion are first, that ——
inclinations themselves are not valued simply as such any more than
their objects are, and second, that even when we do value the object of
an inclination, it does not follow from this that we value the inclination
itself. Both premises are true, for it is surely true of *some* inclinations
(such as the smoker's craving for nicotine) that they are a nuisance, and
we would be better off if we had never had them. What Kant really
means to suggest here is that even when something is judged good
because it satisfies an inclination, it need not follow that the inclination,
as the *source* of this value, is something we judge to be good. This last
point is important to Kant because he will presently claim that, in contrast to inclination, the capacity to set ends according to reason is a

source of the value of those ends that *is* good – indeed, absolutely good, an existing end in itself.

Kant now infers: "Therefore, the worth of all objects *to be obtained* by our actions is always conditional" (G 4:428). In other words, whatever is an end in itself cannot have the character of an end to be effected, because such an end would have to be an object of inclination. So it must be an *existent* end. It is not clear, however, that this follows. For all that has been shown is that no object of inclination, *considered simply as such,* can be an end in itself. Some end to be effected (which is also an object of inclination) might still have the character of an end in itself in virtue of some characteristic other than simply being an object of inclination. Kant will actually give us a reason for thinking that the end in itself is an existing end only when he provides a positive argument for what the end in itself is.

4.3. *Nonrational beings*

> Those beings whose existence rests not on our will but on nature, if they are non-rational beings, have still only a relative worth, as means, and are therefore called *things,* while rational beings, on the contrary, are called *persons,* because their nature already distinguishes them as ends in themselves, i.e. as something that may not be used merely as a means, hence to this extent limits all arbitrariness (and is an object of respect). (G 4:428)

This is clearly the least well argued and (at least at this stage) the least plausible of Kant's three exclusionary claims. The commonly accepted distinction between "things" and "persons" may show that we tend to regard nonrational beings as of lesser value than rational beings. It does not show that everyone who accepts this distinction is committed to regarding nonrational beings as having value *only as means.* Clearly not everyone is prepared to accept the distinction if it has those implications. Once again, Kant's exclusionary claim can be made out only as a corollary of his positive argument that rational beings alone are to be regarded as ends in themselves.

5. The derivation of FH

Let us therefore turn to that argument. It has four steps, which will be numbered to facilitate discussion.

> The ground of [the moral principle] is: *Rational nature exists as end in itself.*

[1] This is how the human being necessarily represents his own existence; to this extent, therefore, it is a *subjective* principle of human actions.

[2] But every other rational being also represents its existence consequent to precisely the same rational ground which is valid for me;

[3] Therefore, it is at the same time the rational ground of an *objective* principle, from which, as a supreme practical ground, all laws of the will must be able to be derived.

[4] The practical imperative will therefore be the following: *Act so that you use humanity in your own person, as well as in the person of every other, always at the same time as end, never merely as a means.* (G 4:429)

(1) and (2) appear to be separate premises, though as we shall see, (2) is best understood as grounded on (1). In (3) Kant infers that rational nature as an end in itself is the ground of an objective principle, and (4) formulates the principle from the standpoint of the substantive value that grounds it.

5.1. Interpreting the crucial premise   The main difficulties with the argument concern the interpretation of (1). It may appear to be merely a universal empirical generalization about the worth people subjectively attribute to their existence. This reading only invites us to dismiss (1) as false, since people obviously sometimes do think of their existence as without value.[13] Kant presents it as he does, however, by way of acknowledging that as a claim about ultimate value, the proposition that humanity is an end in itself is indemonstrable. The only way to convince us that rational nature has such value, therefore, is to show that we already do (and that we must) value it in this way. Kant's procedure could therefore be aptly compared with Mill's idea that principles of ultimate value cannot be demonstrated but can be argued for rationally (and even "proven" in a looser sense of "proof"), by showing that what the principle takes to be valuable is already "in theory and in practice, acknowledged to be an end."[14] Any argument of this kind must begin with value judgments we already accept and then provide a convincing theoretical interpretation of these judgments that supports the pertinent philosophical claim about ultimate value.

Kant states (1) in the way he does because he wants to make the point that in humanity there is a close connection between three things: (a) having the *capacity rationally to judge* about what has ultimate value, (b) *thinking of oneself* as having value, and (c) being something that *actually has ultimate value*. Kant indicates this interconnection when he begins his lectures on anthropology with the arresting claim: "The fact that the human being can have the representation 'I' raises him infinitely above all the other beings on earth" (VA 7:127). Though Kant agrees with this judgment of self-worth, he does not necessarily accept or even condone all the forms it takes. For he soon follows this with the observation that "From the day a human being begins to speak in terms of 'I,' he brings forth his beloved self whenever he can and egoism progresses incessantly" (VA 7:128). The point is that Kant sees it as no accident that beings who are capable of judging what has value are beings who have a conception of themselves and also attach worth (even the highest worth) to themselves under that conception. This is why he takes the opinion of self-worth that human beings have – the fact that they already regard their own existence as an end in itself – as an appropriate starting point for deciding what really has ultimate value.[15]

With this in mind, let us return to (1). Even if it were a *true* empirical generalization, understanding it as no more than this would not go well with premise (2) in the context of this argument. For a merely subjective representation of my existence as an end in itself would have no connection with a *rational ground* having *objective validity* and making the existence of every other rational being also an end in itself. The interpretation of (1) as a contingent psychological generalization is also wrong because it fails to convey Kant's claim that every rational being *necessarily* represents its existence as an end in itself.

In order to fit both Kant's strategy and his explicit statements, (1) has to mean that rational beings necessarily represent their existence subjectively in some way that brings to light an objective ground for regarding them as ends in themselves. That Kant believes something like this is indicated by the account, in his essay *Conjectural beginning of human history,* of the first departure of human beings from the path of animal instinct through the use of reason to set ends and choose means to them. As a result of this first exercise of freedom, Kant says, the human being "came to understand, albeit only obscurely, that he is the true end of nature," and made "the claim to be an end in itself, estimated as such by every other, and to be used by none merely as a means to other ends" (MA 8:114).

—— Therefore, (1) means that when a rational being sets an end for itself, it thereby represents itself (if only obscurely or implicitly) as having some property that, as an objective ground of respect, makes it an end in itself. A bit later in the *Groundwork* Kant identifies one such feature simply as that of being able to set an end, since rational nature is the subject of all ends: "Rational nature is distinguished from others in that it sets an end for itself. . . . It is that which must never be acted against and which must never be valued merely as a means but in every volition also as an end. Now this end can never be other than the subject of all possible ends themselves" (G 4:437).[16]

I think Christine Korsgaard is on the right track in suggesting that Kant's reasoning here takes the form of a "regress on conditions."[17] It begins from the value we place on the ends we set, and infers that this value is grounded in the rational nature of the being who set the end, which (in Korsgaard's words) possesses a "value-conferring status" in relation to the end. Because humanity or rational nature is the source of all such value, it is regarded as absolutely and unconditionally valuable, and an end in itself.

5.2. The objective prescriptivity of the end in itself But it is far from clear from Korsgaard's account exactly how the argument is supposed to work or whether it really provides a convincing proof (even in a loose sense) of the value of rational nature as an end in itself. I hope the following reflections make some progress on that front.

Two points immediately seem crucial to Kant's argument: First, it requires us to concede that setting an end for ourselves involves ascribing *objective* goodness to it. Second, it involves an inference from the *objective* goodness of the end to the *unconditional* objective goodness of the capacity to set the end (which Kant calls 'humanity' or 'rational nature'). And it bases this inference on the fact that the capacity in question is supposed to be the *source* of the objective value of the end. On the first point, Kant maintains that goodness, whether moral or nonmoral, is that which reason represents as practically necessary, and hence as an object of volition for all rational beings (G 4:412–413). An action is *good as a means* if it is represented by reason (in a hypothetical imperative) as necessary for the attainment of an (actual or possible) end; it is *good in itself* if it is represented as required by reason irrespective of any end (in a categorical imperative) (G 4:414). In either case, what is good is represented as the object of a volition necessary to all rational beings (in the case of goodness as a means, only to those who set the end, but the volition is universally binding on all of them). On account of this universality, Kant thinks that when we set an end for ourselves, and consequently regard it as good, we thereby regard it as something of value universally for all rational beings. He thinks we are committed to this judgment of value simply in the act of setting something as an end.

Some may doubt that when I make my own happiness an end, for instance, I have to see it as "good for others," too, in the sense that others have a reason to make it their end as well. Those who doubt this may argue that when I make happiness my end I have only an "agent-relative" reason for pursuing my happiness, and not an "agent-neutral" reason (as Kant seems to suppose).[18] But Kant is at least consistent here, since he maintains that my desire for happiness involves *both* making a claim on others that they, too, should make my (permissible) happiness their end (G 4:423, 430; MS 6:393) *and also* ascribing to myself a worth in virtue of which my happiness has an objective value (KpV 5:74).

In response to the objection, Kant might say (using Francis Hutcheson's terminology) that the reasons in question have to be not merely *motivating* reasons but also *justifying* reasons, and that justifying reasons always require some universal grounding. This would not be an unreasonable interpretation of the thought behind (1) if we take Kant to be saying that people set ends to which they attribute genuine *value*, or take to be *good*. It would also go quite naturally with viewing human beings as rational agents, beings who are not merely shoved around by desires, but who act for *reasons*, with a view to achieving (what they take to be) *good* ends.

On this view of the matter, merely agent-relative reasons (simply as such) are never justifying reasons, hence not reasons at all in the sense that is relevant here. Agent-relative reasons might count as genuine justifying reasons, but only when they can be brought under a universal principle of value that gives them an interpretation in agent-neutral terms. Thus I have a (justifying) *reason* to seek my own happiness (as opposed to a mere *desire* for my happiness, providing me with a *motive* to pursue it) only if I bring my desire under a universal principle ascribing objective value to my happiness: for example, by seeing it as the desire of a being whose objective worth is such that the satisfaction of its desires is objectively good.

This is Kant's understanding of the scholastic formula: *Nihil appetimus, nisi sub ratione boni* ("We desire nothing except under the reason that it is good") (KpV 5:59). As we have seen, Kant rejects this saying if it is taken to mean that everything we *desire* (every object of inclination) is conceived by us as good, since rational beings are free to decide not to satisfy their inclinations and even to consider both an inclination and its objects as something worthless or bad. The object of inclination, considered merely as such, is not the good, but only "well-being" (*Wohl*) (KpV 5:59–60). To set an end, however, is an act of freedom (MS 6: 381), involving a judgment by reason that the end is good, at least relative to our desires and conditionally on the judgment that they should be satisfied (KpV 5:62, G 4:428).[19] Thus Kant's argument is based on the idea that to set an end is to attribute objective goodness to it and that we can regard this goodness as originating only in the fact that we have set those ends according to reason. The thought is *not* that all goodness is only subjective (because it depends on the choice of the being who sets the end and considers it good), but on the contrary, that rational choice of ends is the act through which *objective* goodness enters the world.

This last claim brings us to step (2) in the argument, which we may understand as the inference from the objective goodness of our ends to the unconditional goodness (as an end in itself) of the rational capacity to set ends, on the ground that it is the source of this goodness. In presenting Kant's reason for thinking this inference valid, it might prove illuminating to think of Kant's conception of objective value in relation to J. L. Mackie's contention that "objective goodness," if there were such a thing, would have to be a "queer" property because it would have to be "objectively prescriptive."[20] Mackie is operating within the options available within twentieth-century analytical metaethics, where it is usually held that either goodness exists only relative to our mind or will (in which case it is "subjective") or else it is something real out in the world (as something "objective"). In the latter case, goodness either itself necessarily provides reasons for action (if we hold what is called "internalism") or else such reasons must be added contingently to it (as "externalism" maintains). On the externalist view, however, the good gives me reasons to act only if along with it there is contingently present in me a desire or attitude disposing me toward the good (which once again reduces the authority of the good to something merely subjective). Hence the good has genuine practical authority only if we accept internalism. But then real goodness must be a property out there in the world that somehow of itself tells us what we must do – it must be Mackie's "queer" property of being "objectively prescriptive."

The options canvassed so far, however, do not include any Kant would find attractive. Kant holds that goodness is indeed objectively prescriptive, but not because external objects have some queer property that imposes itself prescriptively on the will (thus violating its autonomy). Instead, Kant locates objective prescriptivity in precisely the sort of thing that might naturally have been thought to prescribe objectively: namely, the rational will. He holds that the objectivity of the will's prescriptions comes from the rational capacity to set ends having objective value. The source of all such value is nothing but the value of rational willing itself, which can confer objective value on other things only if it is presupposed that it has objective value.

5.3. *The crucial inference*   Kant does infer from the premise that rational nature is the source or ground of the objective goodness of all ends to the conclusion that rational nature itself is the underivative objective good, an end in itself. The inference might be questioned on the ground that if y is something valuable and x is its source, it does not in general follow that x is something valuable, still less that it is objectively valuable or an end in itself. Sometimes in such cases we do not consider x good at all, but merely tolerate it as a necessary evil required to procure y. So even if we grant that the rational will is the source of all objective values, it does not seem to follow that it is valuable, still less that it is the basic value or an end in itself.

This objection misunderstands Kant's contention, however. For in Kant's argument rational nature is not being viewed as the source of *good things* (i.e., of their *existence*), but instead as the source of the fact of their *goodness* – indeed of the fact that anything at all is objectively good. If we are looking for a parallel, perhaps the best one is with our attitude toward an authority as a source of recommendations or commands. It makes sense for us to take someone's advice or prescription as authoritative only to the extent that we respect and esteem the authority itself as their ground. (If we have reason to think that what a person says can be relied upon as true, but do not esteem the source for its knowledge and judgment, then we do not regard it as an *authority* but only as a *reliable indicator* of the truth.)

Hence we have reason to regard as good the ends we ourselves set only to the extent that we (at least implicitly) respect and esteem our own rational nature as that which sets them. More generally, if something is good only through being made the object of rational choice, then the capacity to make such choices is thereby taken as the sole authority over goodness, or as Kant puts it, "the subject of all possible ends" (G 4:437). If rational nature is in this way the prescriptive source of all objective goodness, then it must be the most fundamental object of respect or esteem, since if it is not respected as objectively good, then nothing else can be treated as objectively good.

In representing its rational nature as the ground of the goodness of its ends, however, every rational being implicitly also acknowledges that it is *its rational nature* that makes it such an end. Hence, as (2) tells us, every rational being also represents its existence as an end in itself from "the very same rational ground" that holds for every other (namely, the rational nature that they all have in common). This means that it understands its status as an end in itself in such a way that this status is an objective one, valid *of* all rational beings, just as it is valid *for* all rational beings. That is, (3) all beings possessed of rational nature are to be regarded as ends in themselves, and this status must be viewed as making an objective claim on all rational beings to recognize both themselves and others as ends in themselves. This leads to (4): the formulation of the categorical imperative, as the requirement to use humanity in every rational being always as an end and never only as a means.

By Kant's argument, rational nature is presented as the only thing that could answer to the concept of an objective end or end in itself. In the Second Section of the *Groundwork*, Kant has provisionally assumed that there is a categorical imperative. He has argued that if there is such an imperative, then the possibility of its determining the will depends on their being an objective end or end in itself. He has now tried to argue that implicit in our activity of setting ends according to reason is the acknowledgment that rational nature is the only thing that could answer to the conception of an end in itself. Therefore, he is entitled to conclude that if there is a categorical imperative capable of determining the will of rational beings, it must be grounded on the worth of rational nature as an end in itself.

This conditional character of the argument is indicated by Kant, when he attaches a qualification to premise (2), which says that every rational being represents its existence by the same rational ground that holds for me. To this he adds: "Here I put forward this proposition as a postulate. The grounds for it will be found in the last section" (G 4:429). It is not surprising that Kant regards some element in the derivation of FH as provisional, since the *Groundwork*'s strategy, described in Chapter 1, § 1, takes all formulations of the moral law in the Second Section to be derived merely provisionally. But it requires explanation that Kant attaches the qualification specifically to (2), at just the point where the argument extends self-esteem to a like valuation to others by means of an identical "rational ground" applying equally to all.

I suggest that it be understood as follows: (1) cites an attitude that every rational agent (whether explicitly or implicitly) necessarily takes toward its own existence. This attitude rests on a rational ground that is presupposed by that self-esteem, but Kant thinks the attitude of self esteem is sufficiently natural that it will not be removed merely by casting metaphysical doubt on the rational ground it presupposes. This rational ground, however, lies in our capacity to set ends, which will later be seen to imply autonomy of the will and hence to presuppose transcendental freedom. That presupposition will be vindicated (from a practical standpoint) only in the Third Section of the *Groundwork*. Until then, the genuine existence of the rational ground suggested in (1) and made explicit in (2) is subject to a metaphysical doubt based on the theoretical indemonstrability of transcendental freedom. That is why at G 4:429 Kant regards (2) as (for the time being) only a "postulate."[21]

It is by no means universally granted that all human beings are ends in themselves – especially since, as we will see momentarily, this entails that the comparative self-worth of all rational beings be *equal*. It is also not universally granted that human beings (as rational beings) enjoy *any* distinctive moral status, or that rationality (as distinct, for example, from sensibility to pleasure and pain) is what is crucial to determining moral status. Finally, these fundamentally important claims of Kant's moral theory are defended only in this brief argument in the Second Section of the *Groundwork*. For all these reasons, it is important that Kant should at this point present a good *argument* that rational nature is an end in itself. Whether we decide he does have such an argument depends on whether we think he provides a convincing interpretation of what we presuppose and commit ourselves to when we exercise our rational capacities in setting ends. No doubt a wide array of alternative metaethical theories could be offered as alternative interpretations. But few of them, I submit, are very compelling when considered in precisely that light, and none is as compelling as Kant's. If we accept the view, shared by Kant and Mill, that all propositions of ultimate value are "indemonstrable," then we ought also to agree that this is the proper light in which all such theories are to be considered.

6. The equal worth of all rational beings

6.1. Absolute worth is noncomparative   The thesis that every rational being is an end in itself with absolute worth has an immediate but radical corollary: The worth of all rational beings is *equal*. In other words, the worst rational being (in any respect you can possibly name) has the same dignity or absolute worth as the best rational being in that respect (or in any other). As the *Conjectural beginning of human history* puts it, as soon as our first parents began using their reason to direct their lives, they stepped into "a position of *equality with all rational beings*, whatever their rank" (MA 8:115).[22] Thus the serpent was not lying when it told Eve that the faculty of practical reason (which Kant equates with the "knowledge of good and evil") would make her the full equal even of God. Kant takes the serpent's statement to be confirmed by the *Genesis* story through the admission that "Behold, man has become like one of us, to know good and evil" (*Genesis* 3:22; cf. MA 8:115).[23] FH implies that all the normal (comparative and competitive) measures of people's self-worth – wealth, power, honor, prestige, charm, charisma, even happy relationships with others – are expressions of an utterly false sense of values.

6.2. Inner worth and humility   We might wonder, however, whether human self-worth might vary at least on *moral* grounds. If the good will is the only unqualified good, it might be wondered, how can Kant regard a person with a bad will as the equal of a person with a good will? Earlier in this chapter, however, we saw that Kant cannot consistently hold that the status of end in itself belongs only to the good will, since this would render the existence of a motive for obedience to that law only contingent and hence undermine the categorical status of the moral imperative. It is quite consistent, moreover, for Kant to consider all rational beings equal to one another based on their common possession of the *capacities* to set ends and give themselves laws, even though each such being might regard its will as better, measured by those laws, insofar as it lives up to them, than it is if it fails to do so. It is not self-evident that judgments of the latter sort entail any judgments about the different worth of rational beings as compared with each other. The logic of Kant's position, therefore, requires him to maintain his strict egalitarianism even in moral contexts, even if he were reluctant to maintain it.

But in fact he shows no such reluctance. Kant does say that "a thing has no other worth than that determined for it by the law" (G 4:436). The law, however, as formulated in FH, tells us that the worth of rational nature is absolute, an end in itself. Hence "a human being must be judged only by what constitutes his absolute worth" (G 4:439), that is, by the dignity of humanity. And Kant often insists that even the worst human beings have dignity. Although he identifies dignity with the *capacity* for morality or for having a good will, he never makes it contingent on *acting* morally or on actual goodness of will (G 4:428, 435; MS 6:329–330, 402–403, 462–463).

Kant also says that people may give themselves, their actions, and their characters moral worth through goodness of will, and that this is what makes them and their actions objects of esteem (G 4:397–399). In this connection, though, what he stresses is that the morally good person has greater "inner" worth. By "inner" worth he means worth as measured solely by comparison to the person's own self-given moral law or idea of virtue. When I am conscious of doing my duty, I feel an "inner self-contentment" (KpV 5:88, MS 6:387, 391); transgressions of duty occasion "self-contempt and inner abhorrence" (G 4:426).

The *merit* attaching to the fulfillment of imperfect duties must also be understood as wholly *inner* – a relation to the moral law or idea of virtue but not legitimating moral comparisons *between people*. "Moral self-esteem, which is grounded in the worth of humanity, should not be derived from comparison with others, but from comparison with the moral law. . . . Moral humility, regarded as the curbing of our self-conceit in the face of the moral law, can thus never rest on a comparison of ourselves with others, but with the moral law" (VE 27:349). Differences in *inner* worth do not in the least disturb the absolute equality of self-worth between human beings, which is entailed by FH: "All human beings are equal to one another, and only he who is morally good has a superior inner worth" (VE 27:462).

Sometimes Kant speaks of those who transgress a duty (especially a duty to oneself) as "surrendering" their personality (MS 6:425), "degrading" or "violating" humanity in their own person (MS 6:423, 429) or even "annihilating their dignity as a human being" (MS 6:429), and "taking away their entire worth" (VE 27:341). Yet he does not mean that the transgression of duty actually deprives them of the status of being ends in themselves, but only that their conduct (when compared with the moral law) appears *unworthy* of the humanity, personality, or dignity that they possess as rational beings. "I cannot deny respect even to a vicious man; I cannot withdraw the respect that belongs to him in his quality as a human being, even though by his deeds he makes himself unworthy of it" (MS 6:463).

Of course Kant regards externally wrongful (illegal) *conduct* as deserving of punishment, and the state not only may but must use such coercion to protect people's rightful freedom (MS 6:231–233, 331–332). But deserving punishment is not the same as being worth less than others. Perhaps a criminal forfeits his right to external freedom or even to life, but criminal acts involve no forfeiture of the dignity of humanity. In punishing a criminal, we must always respect humanity in the criminal's person, and this makes it wrong to inflict forms of punishment that humiliate or degrade (MS 6:333). What is more to the point, it is *contrary to ethical duty* for anyone "inwardly to look down on some in comparison with others" (MS 6:463).

> Humility *in comparing oneself with other human beings* . . . is no duty; rather, trying to equal or surpass others in this respect, believing that in this way one will acquire an even greater inner worth, is *ambition (ambitio)*, which is directly contrary to one's duty to others, while belittling one's own moral worth merely as a means to acquiring the favor of another, whoever it may be (hypocrisy and flattery) is false (lying) humility, which is contrary to one's duty to oneself since it degrades one's personality. (MS 6:435–436)

Kant's consistent position, then, is that the *inner* worth of a person, measured solely by comparison to the moral law, may be greater or less according to one's virtue in fulfilling the law one gives oneself; but the worth of a person never varies in comparison to others, since the good and the bad alike possess the dignity of humanity. Or as we might also put it, following Thomas Hill, Jr., the respect we owe others simply as rational beings is not a respect they have to *earn*.[24]

Saying only this much, however, does not convey the full, radical import of FH. For it is sometimes represented as the view of moral common sense that every person is owed a certain minimal respect (simply as a person), which they do not have to earn (though sometimes it is held that they can forfeit it through bad conduct), and beyond that, respect must be earned (whether through good conduct or by displaying nonmoral excellences of various kinds). But if this is the view of common sense, then FH contradicts common sense in important ways, for FH claims that the worth of rational nature in the person of every rational being is *absolute*. It can be neither forfeited nor augmented, whether by having a good or bad will or in any other way.

Because respect for the dignity of humanity is identical with the respect for law grounding morality in general, to demand that others earn it (or any part of it) is in effect to hold that our obligations to others rest (at least in part) on their distinctive excellences rather than fully and unconditionally on their humanity. To require that respect be earned is to hold that people are to be respected in part for what *distinguishes* them from others; it thereby places respect squarely within the comparative-competitive conception of self-worth. Kant not only regards all such conceptions of self-worth as distinct from a moral conception of it, but, as we will see in Part II, it is no exaggeration to say that Kant even regards them as the sole and exclusive ground of all moral evil.

6.3. Moral comparisons   Kant's reference to "false (lying) humility" might seem to imply that there could be *true* (moral) humility in comparing one's moral worth unfavorably to that another, as long as the comparison is sincere and not made with a sycophantic (self-serving) intent. This implication is correct only in a trivial sense, though, because it is Kant's position that people's self-worth cannot be measured comparatively, even on moral grounds. Kant also urges against comparing oneself morally with others because he thinks this has a bad effect on one's character, leading to self-deception, envy, and malice. "When a human being measures his worth by comparison to others, he seeks either to raise himself above the other or to diminish the worth of the other. The latter is envy" (VP 9:491).

Paradoxically, Kant's opposition to any form of moral comparison between people is confirmed most decisively by just those passages in which Kant discusses the humility induced by respect for the moral merits of others:

> Fontenelle says: "I bow to a great man, but my mind does not bow." I can add: before a humble plain man, in which I perceive an uprightness of character in greater measure than I am conscious of in myself, *my mind bows* whether I choose or not, however high I may carry my head in order that he may not forget my superiority. Why? His example holds a law before me which strikes down my self-conceit when I compare my own conduct with it. (KpV 5:76–77 cf. G 4:401 note)

Here Kant is in effect proposing that we reinterpret the moral judgments we make comparing ourselves with others. Such judgments really involve a comparison of ourselves only with the moral law, *not with others at all.* When I consider the moral merits of the humble plain man, what really happens is first, that I become aware of the hollowness of my own pretensions to greater self-worth based on social superiority, and second, that I experience humility when I compare my conduct with the *moral law.* Later in the same passage, Kant gives precisely the same account of respect for the *nonmoral* merits of another:

> The respect we have for a person (really for the law, which his example holds before us) is, therefore, not mere admiration. This is also confirmed by the way the common herd of amateurs gives up their respect for a man when they think they have found out the badness of his character (as in the case of Voltaire); but the true scholar still feels respect at least for his talents, since he is himself involved in a business and vocation which makes the imitation of him to some extent a law. (KpV 5:78)

The judgment of the true scholar is a genuine case of respect for Voltaire's talents but that of the herd of amateurs is not. This is because it is only for the scholar that the comparison provides an occasion for reflecting on one's own duty, whereas the amateurs are caught up in false, competitive standards of self-worth, where even moral judgments serve merely as an excuse for the envious to flatter themselves that they are superior to a man of great intellect.

It still might be thought that there has to be an inconsistency in Kant's position. For if a virtuous person is entitled to inner self-contentment and a vicious person must feel inner self-abhorrence, how could it be consistently maintained that the moral worth of the former does not exceed that of the latter? This could be done, however, as long as there is no common measure in terms of which your virtuous character could be compared with my vicious one. This would be the case if the moral task of each person is utterly unique and incomparable to that of any other, so that each of us can be measured morally by our own "inner" standard, but there exists no common or comparative standard. Kant urges just such a noncomparative view of people's moral tasks when he insists that people's characters are ultimately unknowable to us and their unique situations, temperaments, and temptations make the moral challenges they face utterly incommensurable: "For if even [a human being] is a scoundrel, I can still think: 'Who knows what drove him to it? Perhaps with his temperament what he did was no worse than a trifling misdeed would be for a person with mine?'" (VE 27:418). "How many people who have lived long and guiltless lives may not be merely *fortunate* in having escaped many temptations?" (MS 6:392–393).

It also follows from this, of course, that I cannot really know whether the "humble plain man" really has an "uprightness of character superior to my own." But when we see the point of Kant's reinterpretation of our moral respect for others, we also see why *that doesn't matter.* For the whole point of Kant's interpretation of respect for another's merit is that every comparison between people drops out, and the only real comparison is between my own conduct and the moral law. The merits I *suppose* to be present in the humble man would be enough to occasion the comparison Kant intends, even if the humble man were (unbeknownst to me) actually a scoundrel as measured by his inner standards.

There are two claims, however, that would be equally consistent with the above remarks about people's differing circumstances, temperaments, and temptations. On the first, which I have been urging, no comparison can be made between the moral worth of different people; on the second, people's moral worth can be compared, but we are (epistemically) in no position to make the comparison. What has been argued above is that given Kant's conception of the dignity of rational nature, the second (purely epistemic) claim (whether or not it might be defensible on its own) is too weak to be the entirety of his position; if he is to be consistent, we must understand him to be making the first claim as well (or instead).

Kant's remarks about the uniqueness and unknowability of each person's moral predicament are often read as if they were motivated by a (perhaps exaggerated) sense of moral "fair play": A person's moral worth must depend solely on that person and on nothing else because the competition for self-worth must take place on a "level playing field," and nothing like "luck" must be permitted to enter into the contest. On the reading I am proposing, however, this interpretation of Kant is subtly but profoundly mistaken. For the point is *not* that the competition for self-worth must be *fair,* or that people should be compared with one another solely on their *intrinsic merits* and not on externalities subject to luck. The point is instead that human dignity, properly understood, rules out the very idea of any *comparison* or *competition* regarding self-worth (whether fair or unfair). We could put Kant's position by saying that the only way to measure the worth of rational beings "fairly" is not to compare them at all but simply to attribute absolute worth to every rational being, looking away from every feature other than their common rational nature.

The equality of all rational beings does not entail that they must be treated exactly alike in any particular respect. It does not preclude valuing the abilities and accomplishments of other people, both as means to various ends and as ends in their own right. (Regarded as part of their happiness, these abilities and accomplishments are even ends that morality *requires* us to have.) Even so, Kant's moral principle does (and is intended to) have some radical implications for our everyday attitudes toward ourselves and others. In the Introduction, we saw that some of Kant's early ethical reflections expressed outrage at the "general injustice" prevailing in society, and insisted that people should demand what is theirs by right. Kant's mature ethical thought is grounded on a conception of the human condition which sees human nature as locked in a struggle between two incompatible conceptions of human self-worth: one arising out of our nature as social beings, founded on comparison, competition, rivalry, and jealousy; the other arising from the cultivation of moral reason, enjoining equal respect for the dignity of humanity of every rational being and constraining us to act on principles which would unite all human ends into a harmonious system. It is to our progress on the path from the first conception of self-worth to the second that Kant is referring when he remarks that "culture, considered as the genuine education of the human being as human being and citizen, has perhaps not even properly begun, much less been completed" (MA 8:116–117). The discomfort with ourselves that critics notice in Kant – his distrust of our feelings and inclinations, his intolerance of our tendencies toward moral complacency and laxity – all these are chiefly expressions of how far he thinks we still have to go on that historical path of progress toward the proper recognition of our equal human dignity.

7. Applying FH

"Always use humanity at the same time as an end, never only as a means." The commandment has often struck readers of the *Groundwork* as high-sounding but too abstract to yield determinate moral principles or duties. Kant clearly does not see things that way, however, since he regards FH, along with FLN and FRE, as "bringing the idea of reason closer to intuition" (G 4:436–437).[25] Our impression that FH is too abstract to be easily applicable might best be understood by seeing that FH is rather like the Sermon on the Mount, the principles of communism, or other admirable utopian visions of human society, whose demands require such a radical departure from our customary practices and accepted attitudes toward ourselves and others that we are at first perplexed when we try to apply them. Kant views our ordinary moral duties as the first small steps we must take in the direction the moral law directs, hoping that in human history our species may eventually transform itself so that eventually "art will be strong enough to become a second nature" (MA 8:117).

7.1. FH as the preferred formula of application   In the *Metaphysics of morals*, where Kant systematically derives ethical duties, we find very little about formulating maxims and testing them for universalizability. Instead we find that FH is by a wide margin the formula of choice in justifying the system of duties (see the table in Conclusion, § 3). So dominant is FH in the role of justifying particular duties that it is worth pausing a moment to document this fact.

It is from FH that Kant derives our innate right to freedom in the Doctrine of Right. He glosses Ulpian's principle of natural right, *honeste vive*, as "asserting one's worth as a human being in relation to others, a duty expressed by the saying: 'Do not make yourself a mere means for others but be at the same time an end for them'" (MS 6:237). The innate right to freedom is said to "belong to every human being in virtue of his humanity" (MS 6:237). There are fourteen ethical duties explicitly enumerated by Kant in the Doctrine of Virtue. Of these, only (1), beneficence to others, is grounded on FUL (MS 6:389, 451, 453). (As we noted in Chapter 3, § 7.2, this is the only positive duty that *could* be grounded on anything like FUL, since the derivation depends on the fact that happiness is an end necessary to all rational beings, and happiness is unique in this regard.) Eleven of the remaining fifteen ethical duties are explicitly based on FH, and the other four are based on it by implication.

The emphasis on FH is most explicit in the case of duties to oneself. (2), The duty against suicide, is based on the fact that "disposing of oneself as a mere means to some discretionary end is debasing humanity in one's person" (MS 6:423); (3), the duty against lust or carnal self-degradation, on the fact that it "violates humanity in one's own person" (MS 6:425); (4), that against drunkenness, on the fact that the drunkard is "like a mere animal," and cannot be "treated as a human being" (MS 6:427). (5), Lying, "violates the dignity of humanity in one's own person" (MS 6:429) and (6), the self-respect opposed to servility, is a duty "with reference to the dignity of humanity within us" (MS 6:436). (7), The human being's duty to develop our natural perfection, is one "he owes himself (as a rational being)" because it is "bound up with the end of humanity in our own person" (MS 6:444, 392). (8), Violation of the duty of gratitude, is "a rejection of one's own humanity" (MS 6:454) based on "pride in the dignity of humanity in one's own person" (MS 6:459), while (9), the duty to sympathize with others, holds insofar as "the human being is regarded not merely as a rational being but as an animal endowed with reason" (MS 6:456). (10–12), All three duties of respect to others (those against self-love, contempt, and giving scandal), are grounded on "the dignity in other human beings" (MS 6:462).

There is no explicit appeal to any formula in the case of four duties: (13) our duty to ourselves not to be avaricious (MS 6:432), (14) our duty as self-judge (MS 6:437–440), (15) our duty to increase our moral perfection (MS 6:446–447), or (16) our duty to ourselves regarding nonrational beings (MS 6:442–443). But (14)–(16) are all duties that

Kant derives from the duty to promote our own moral perfection by acting from the motive of duty. That duty (as we have just seen) is explicitly grounded on our dignity as rational beings. (13), our duty to avoid avarice, is defended on the ground that it impairs our rational nature in respect of the use of money (self-impairment is also used as the basis for (4)). Reference to FH also grounds Kant's discussion of five of the six enumerated vices that are opposed to duties to others: envy, ingratitude, arrogance, defamation, and ridicule (MS 6:458–461, 465–467). (No explicit appeal to any formula occurs regarding the vice of gloating (MS 6:460).)

7.2. *Expressive reasons for action*   As this catalog indicates, it would be impossible to overestimate the importance of FH for applying the principle of morality. Hence FH is much more important to Kant's theory ——— than FUL or FLN, and it is crucial to any understanding of Kant's ethical thought to understand *how* FH is to be applied.

One reason FH may strike us as too abstract, vague, and high-sounding to yield specific moral requirements is that it involves a *kind* of moral appeal that is largely unfamiliar in philosophical theories of morality.[26] Consequentialist theories represent the fulfillment of our duties as bringing about desirable *states of affairs*. Deontological theories (including Kant's own theory, insofar as it is interpreted exclusively through FUL) represent them as obedience to an obligatory *rule* or *commandment*. FH, however, bases duties instead on the *absolute worth* of rational nature ——— as an end in itself. Though FH takes the form of a rule or commandment, what it basically asserts is the existence of a *substantive value* to be respected. This value does not take the form of a desired object to be brought about, but rather the value of something existing, which is to be respected, esteemed, or honored in our actions. As Korsgaard has emphasized, Kantian ethics breaks with the utilitarian tradition most fundamentally by denying that the most basic objects of value are states of affairs, and that "the business of morality is to *bring something about*."[27]

What FH fundamentally demands of our actions is instead that they *express* proper respect or reverence for the worth of humanity. *Expressive* reasons for doing things may have been largely overlooked in moral theory, but they are not unfamiliar in everyday life. People shake hands, congratulate or condole with others, and say "Please," "Thank you," and "You're welcome," in order to manifest respect, gratitude, benevolence, or esteem for them. As we noted earlier, this is also the sort of reason why people salute the flag or bow their heads in the presence of religious objects. Yet if we think only of examples in which expressive reasons are seen in abstraction from more familiar kinds of reasons, expressive reasons may seem suited only to matters of etiquette or ritual, and they may therefore appear an unlikely ground for a comprehensive rational morality. But that impression is misleading, since every action that is done for a reason (as distinct from being merely a response to an impulse) is based on regarding something as objectively *valuable*. When it is done for that kind of reason, the performance of the action is most fundamentally an expression of esteem for that value, and this expressive reason for performing the action is therefore the ground of any other reason we may have for performing it (such as a reason framed in deontological or consequentialist terms).

From the standpoint of reasons for action, even our furtherance of an end to be effected is fundamentally a piece of expressive behavior, since it expresses how we value the end. When we desire an end for a reason, this desire itself is grounded on our valuing the end, and is thus also basically an expression of valuation. This is why we praise people for caring about the things they should and blame them if they don't desire good ends strongly enough. A desire for an end to be effected, when it is grounded on reasons, is always grounded on the esteem or respect for an existent end. We care about someone's good (as an end to be effected) only to the extent that we think of the *person* as worth caring about. This is true even about our concern for our own good, and even about our satisfaction of our own desires, insofar as the latter can be regarded as guided by reasons. When I choose to satisfy a desire (as distinct from responding automatically to an instinctive impulse), I do so because I judge the desire to be worth satisfying. This, in turn, expresses a judgment about my own worth.[28] This is how we should understand the worth of the ends Kantian ethics holds to be obligatory: our own perfection and the happiness of others. These ends have worth based on the dignity of the rational beings whose perfection and happiness they are. The same is true of acting on a principle, since such action makes no sense unless the principle is seen as expressive of a value. This is why FUL requires FH to complement it.

7.3. Respecting humanity   FH says "Act so that you use humanity, whether in your own person or in the person of any other, always at the same time as an end and never merely as a means" (G 4:429). As H. J. Paton long ago pointed out, this does not forbid us to use a person (whether ourselves or another) as a means to our ends. It forbids only *omitting* to treat a person "*at the same time* as an end."[29] In fact, according to Kant's conception of an ideal "realm of ends" (which we will be examining in § 4 of Chapter 5), moral laws "have as their purpose just the relation of [rational] beings to one another as ends and means" (G 4:433). Thus — to be a member of a realm of ends you *must* be a means to the ends of other rational beings (just as they have to be means to your ends).

No misinterpretation of FH is more elementary than that which starts from the fact that certain conduct treats a person as a means and then (invalidly) infers the conclusion that this conduct fails to treat the person as an end in itself. From this point, however, it follows directly that the phrase "never merely as a means" actually *plays no role whatever in the actual content of FH*. For if we are permitted to use a person as a means whenever we *also* use the person as an end, then the *entire* force of the injunction lies in telling us to treat persons as ends. If we do that, then we have thereby avoided treating them *merely* as means no matter what use we may (also) make of them as means.[30]

What, then, could be Kant's purpose in including "never merely as a means" so ostentatiously in the verbal statement of FH and of his equally conspicuous use of like phrases in many of his arguments from FH? One answer is that the phrase calls special attention to what Kant takes to be a fundamental pattern in human wrongdoing. He thinks it is a propensity of human nature to show disrespect for the dignity of humanity not because we altogether fail to value it, but because we tend to place things of lesser value ahead of it, treating rational nature (which is an end in itself) as a mere means to these merely conditioned goods. As he puts it in the *Religion*, both morality and self-love are always incentives for us, but we have a propensity to invert the proper order of incentives (R 6:36–37). Despite the dignity we share with other rational beings, we tend to place our value ahead of theirs, and we do this because we value ourselves in the wrong way, for the wrong reasons. When we fail to treat humanity as an end in itself, this is always because we have decided to use its dignity as a means to something that has mere price. This point *about human nature* gives Kant reason enough to emphasize that FH forbids us to treat humanity "merely as a means."

Kant probably also uses that phrase in stating FH in order to state a characteristic doctrine of his, namely, that whatever lacks humanity and personality (which would make it an end in itself with dignity), is a mere thing, and a thing has value only as a means (G 4:428; cf. VA 7:127). His view seems to be that to respect humanity is always to respect it *in the person* of some being who has it. We may call this the "personification principle." This principle seems to underlie Kant's most fundamental division of ethical duties in the *Metaphysics of morals*, that between duties to oneself and duties to others.

The personification principle gets Kant into trouble in several ways. It forces him to analyze our duties regarding nonrational nature (e.g., regarding animals and the natural environment) as duties *to* a person – he argues that they are really duties to oneself (MS 6:442–443). It even entails that all nonrational beings must be regarded *only as means* (to some person as an end in itself or to the ends of a person). It even creates problems about the treatment of some human beings. For recall that in FH, "humanity" is a technical term, referring to the rational capacity to set ends. This means that very small children do not have it, nor do people whose rational capacities have been lost (e.g., through Alzheimer's disease) or are temporarily absent or impaired through illness (or even just because they are now asleep). This means that small children and the severely mentally impaired are not literally "persons" at all in the sense meant in FH. Of course it would be absurd to suggest that FH has nothing to say about how we should treat such people. For we surely would dishonor rational nature if we did not cherish its development in children or failed to strive for its recovery in men and women who have temporarily lost it.[31] What this shows, I think, is that the basic idea behind FH does not include the personification principle and is even inconsistent with it. To treat humanity (or rational nature) as an end in itself requires more than treating humanity *in persons* as an end in itself. Elsewhere I have argued that Kantian ethics both is more self-consistent and does a better job of handling duties regarding nonrational nature if it abandons the personification principle.[32]

Sometimes Kant's readers have exactly the opposite worry about the injunction to respect *humanity* (or *rational nature*) in someone's person. They fear that it means respecting only an abstraction and not the persons themselves. Kant's answer to these worries, of course, is that rational nature is precisely what makes you a person, so that respecting it *in* you is precisely what it means to respect *you*. Or, if you prefer, it is only because we are instantiations of this abstraction "rational nature" that we deserve any respect at all. Once again, to say this is not to disvalue human feelings or emotions, or to treat even the animal side of our nature as valueless. For as we have seen, our capacities for feeling and emotion and even our animality are parts of our rational nature.

There certainly are people who value themselves chiefly for attributes other than the rational nature they share with other human beings: Some value themselves as wealthy, powerful, handsome, intelligent, talented, or educated, or for being of a certain social class or race, gender, religion, or ethnic affiliation. Kantian ethics must reject all such modes of self-valuation except insofar as they are derivative from valuing *humanity* and are grounded on the acknowledgment that every person's humanity is deserving of equal respect. It is not inconsistent with FH (on the contrary, it is required by it) that we should honor the different ways of life people choose and the different ways they unfold the common capacities that make them human. Participating in a certain culture, for example, or cultivating a certain religious disposition, are certainly ways of developing our common humanity and exercising our rational nature. It is only to the extent that people value themselves for such things *instead of* for their humanity that FH charges them with valuing themselves wrongly.

Respect is not only a subjective feeling. It is also a relationship between people, which can exist only if the person respected as well as the person respecting fulfills certain requirements. It is not possible for you to respect me except for qualities for which I also respect myself. Thus homophobic Christians cannot genuinely respect gay people who affirm their identity as gay as long as the Christians regard homosexual feelings and behavior as something unnatural, degrading, and hateful to God. Likewise, it would seem that Kantians cannot respect people who do not respect humanity in themselves. For example, they apparently cannot respect Aryan-supremacists who refuse to respect themselves for being rational persons or who even despise humanity in themselves simply because it is found equally in people they regard as inferior to themselves.

Kant's answer to this problem lies in his insistence that whether they realize it or not, all responsible moral agents do in fact respect themselves as rational beings. For that is simply what it means for morality to be an incentive for them. And morality must be an incentive for any being that is held morally responsible for what it wills (R 6:35). No one who truly is a person and a moral agent can entirely refuse to respect their own rational nature, just as no being with moral personality can entirely lack conscience or moral feeling (MS 6:399–403). The Aryan racist, if he has humanity and personality at all, also has respect for these qualities in himself, even if he disavows it in his words and acts directly contrary to it in his deeds. Kant's contention, in other words, is that to regard him as a moral agent at all is to attribute certain feelings and attitudes to him as preconditions of moral personality, and among these is respect for rational nature.

This will not solve the whole problem, though, because even people who respect rational nature in themselves may prefer to be respected more for other qualities and achievements, and may not feel they are being duly respected by Kantians unless they are respected more than other people (who, they might say, have not *earned* as much respect as they have). Here Kantians cannot, consistent with their principles, respect these people in the way they want to be respected. But this is a kind of problem that any radical ethical principle is bound to encounter when we try to apply it to a social world whose lived practices, feelings, and perceptions are deeply at odds with it. The only real solution to that kind of problem is to change the world so that people's expectations and motivations (starting with those of Kantians themselves) are brought closer to the demands of FH. In the meantime, the fact that all moral agents as such must have some respect for their own rational nature at least guarantees that the Kantian will respect *something* in others that they also respect in themselves. It may help some that many people already at least pay lip service to the principle that all human beings have equal dignity, even if their lives, social practices, and natural feelings are still deeply at odds with that professed conviction.

A more radical problem is raised by those who insist that it is simply an *empirical fact* that there are moral agents (extremely evil ones) who have no conscience or moral feeling or respect for humanity (they might be said to deserve blame *most of all* precisely because they have none of these). To this the first Kantian response is to point out that no judgment could be grounded on experience if it is not even conceptually coherent. And it is indeed incoherent to claim that someone is evil while denying that morality is an incentive for them, since this is a necessary condition of any moral responsibility at all. To regard someone as simultaneously incapable of good and blamable for evil seems rather to be a projection of irrational resentment, hatred, and moral despair, which are characteristic on the one hand of those who have been wronged, and on the other, of those whose moral sense has been distorted by bigoted hatred of people who have been socially marginalized, stigmatized, or scapegoated.

The reply must be similar to those who assert first that people subjected to extremely degrading conditions (such as the people reduced to being so-called *Musulmänner* in Nazi death camps) are literally deprived of their human dignity – or even, second, that such people constitute empirical counterexamples to the Kantian assertion of the dignity of humanity itself. Regarding this last contention, as far as the *philosophical* issue is concerned, if Kant's arguments are convincing, then humanity does have absolute worth as an end in itself and the <u>objectivity</u> of value is not dependent on its being acknowledged (that is the whole point of the *objectivity* of value). Admittedly, settling the issue glibly on an intellectual level can do little to alter the aftereffects of the unimaginable experiences that might lead someone to make such terrible assertions.

As to the first claim: People may of course lose their rational capacities, temporarily or permanently, through injury, disease, or the deliberate evil deeds of others (I make no judgment about whether this is what happened to the *Musulmänner*). Strictly speaking, it is true that human beings deprived of their rational capacities are no longer "persons" (since they lack "humanity" in the technical Kantian sense). But if we respect the dignity of rational nature, we cannot regard these people as mere things. We have a duty to attempt to restore the rational capacities if they have been lost, and if the loss is due to the deliberate act of others, we must continue to treat the people as persons (in every way possible) if only to express our implacable opposition to what has been done to them.[33]

7.4. The four examples again How do we decide when conduct treats, or fails to treat, humanity according to its worth as an end in itself? Kant uses the same four examples to illustrate both FLN and FH. FH commands conduct that expresses respect for the worth of humanity as an end in itself, and FH forbids conduct that fails to treat humanity with due respect or esteem. His arguments clearly indicate that the value appealed to in FH is expressive in character. The arguments also show that positive duties can be derived from FH, as they could not be from FLN. Further, in each case the arguments from FH are distinctly superior to the arguments from FLN in another respect: They help us to understand better the moral substance of the arguments from FLN at points where those arguments remain opaque.[34] Finally, from a brief discussion of these examples we may also learn a little more about the general way in which Kant thinks we may argue from FH to specific practical conclusions. The latter topic, however, will be thematized mainly in the following section.

1. *Suicide.* Kant alleges that killing oneself is always wrong because it involves disposing of a person (a being with absolute worth), merely as a means to some discretionary end, such as maintaining a tolerable condition up to the end of life (G 4:429). The general duty not to commit

suicide is therefore derived from the expressive meaning of the act itself, which Kant holds to be "degrading to the humanity in one's own person" (MS 6:422–423).

Interpreting Kant's argument against suicide from FLN in light of FH helps us to understand that argument better. For that argument depended on the claim that suicide uses the impulse of self-love contrary to its natural purposiveness. In the *Metaphysics of morals,* Kant argues that we should respect the natural purposiveness involved in our instinctive impulses (such as those for food, drink, and sex), since they belong to the predisposition to animality which is the underpinning of our rational nature. Hence to use natural impulses contrary to their natural ends is to show disrespect for humanity in one's own person, and not to treat oneself as a human being (MS 6:424–427). We may therefore see the argument against suicide based on FLN not so much as an argument about whether M1 passes the CC test as an appeal to treat our instinct of self-love with a proper respect for its natural purposiveness. The basis of this appeal, in turn, is the worth of humanity to which this purposiveness belongs.

2. *False promising.* We have a duty not to make promises we don't intend to keep because the making of such a promise treats those we deceive merely as means, "without considering that, as rational beings, they must always at the same time be esteemed as ends" (G 4:430). The explicit ground of this duty is the failure of our act to express proper esteem for rational nature; moreover, the duty applies to false promises generally, not merely to those made on M2 (or on any other particular maxim). Also highlighted in the argument is the *disrespect* shown to humanity in the person of the one to whom the false promise is made. Kant points out that the false promiser "wants to make use of another human being *merely as a means,* without the other at the same time containing in himself the end. For he whom I want to use for my purposes by such a promise cannot possibly agree to my way of behaving toward him, and so cannot himself contain the end of this action" (G 4:429–430).

Again this helps us to understand the argument from FLN. For in that argument it was never entirely clear why action on M2, if it became the universal law U2, would render the promise itself and its end impossible. If, however, the giving and accepting of a promise requires the promiser and the promisee to *share* their ends, then it is clear why the promises falling under U2 would be impossible, since they preclude such sharing. It is also clear why the promise made on M2 could not achieve its end if made a universal law, since the promisee, who (according to Kant's argument for FH) necessarily regards his own existence as an end in itself, cannot consent to be treated in a way that disrespects that existence and reduces it to a mere means.

3. _Rusting talents._ I have a positive duty to develop my capacities in order that my actions should "harmonize" with the (existent) end of humanity in my person (G 4:430). Kant emphasizes that this duty is not grounded on the advantages we may acquire by cultivating our talents but instead on the requirement to be "in a pragmatic respect a human being equal to the end of his existence" (MS 6:445). In other words, we ——— show respect or honor to our rational nature by putting at its disposal the capacity to achieve all sorts of ends, and it is this, rather than any interest in the ends themselves, which is the basis of our duty to perfect ourselves. This line of reasoning is made more explicit in the _Metaphysics of morals_:

> The capacity to set oneself an end – any end – whatsoever is what characterizes humanity (as distinguished from animality). Hence there is also bound up with the end of humanity in our own person the rational will, and so the duty, to make ourselves worthy of humanity by culture in general, by procuring or promoting the _capacity_ to realize all sorts of possible ends. (MS 6:392)

Once again, the argument from FH illuminates the corresponding argument from FLN: For the argument from FLN appealed to the fact that "as a rational being he necessarily wills that all the capacities in him be developed, since they serve him and are given to him for all sorts of possible purposes" (G 4:423). We noted in the last chapter that FLN does nothing to show why a rational being would necessarily will such a thing. But FH does show this.

4. _Refusing to help._ My positive duty to further the ends of others is also based on the requirement to bring my actions into "harmony with humanity as an end in itself." "For the ends of any person, who is an end in himself, must as far as possible also be _my_ end, if that representation of an end in itself is to have its _full_ effect on me" (G 4:430). The representation of an end in itself is the representation of human beings as objectively valuable, existent ends, or beings having dignity. To let this conception have its full effect on me is to allow my valuation of rational beings according to their dignity to be exhibited in my actions toward them. Thus the reason that we should help others in need is that we thereby exhibit proper esteem for their worth as rational beings. Kant

therefore maintains that it is no true benefit to help others in such a way that they are humbled by it in their own eyes; instead, a true bene-factor "must show that he is himself put under obligation by the other's acceptance [of the benefit], or honored by it" (MS 6:453). And he al-ways is honored because the beneficiary of his charity is a being with absolute worth.

One puzzle about Kant's argument from FLN against M4 was why it would be impossible for a prosperous rugged individualist to will that others should not help him on the condition that he should be exempt from helping them. It was argued in Chapter 3, § 6.3 that Kant's argu-ment requires some possibly controversial empirical assumptions about what is rational given the facts of human vulnerability and interdepend-ence. But FH enables us to provide a less questionable argument.[35] The reason it would be impossible to will that others not help me is that their refusal would show contempt for my humanity, which I must regard as an end in itself. Insofar as their existence contains the same rational ground for respect, it is equally impossible for me rationally to will that I should not extend the same help to them.

Most readers of the *Groundwork* think of Kant's four examples mainly in terms of his arguments from FLN. When they have found these de-fective (for reasons such as those presented in Chapter 3, § 8) they dis-miss Kant's entire moral theory simply on that basis. They do not even consider the possibility that the parallel arguments from FH might make good the defects in the arguments from FLN. I hope the preceding dis-cussion has shown why all such readers are deeply mistaken.

8. The structure of arguments from FH

8.1. FH and "particularism"   It is traditional to treat the application of any moral principle as a piece of deductive reasoning from that prin-ciple, together with some further propositions about the circumstances, to a conclusion that we should or should not do something. In the *Cri-tique of practical reason*, Kant uses terminology implying that he views the application of moral principles as proceeding according to practical syl-logisms (KpV 5:18–19). But FH tells us only to act in such a way as to express proper respect for the worth of humanity. Proper expression of respect, however, surely is a contextual matter; it is not evident that it could be reduced to any set of rules or generalizations that could serve as premises in a deductive argument. It might instead be something that has to be apprehended in each set of particular circumstances, perhaps by a sort of educated moral perception. Allan Gibbard is doubtless correct that it is impossible to codify "respect for persons" into any determinate set of unexceptionable rules (a project Kant wisely never undertakes). If that is right, then Kantian ethics, on the basis of FH, might have quite a bit in common with some current views in moral theory (or antitheory) that sail under the banner of "moral particularism," remind people more often of Aristotle than of Kant, and are associated with names such as John McDowell, Martha Nussbaum, and Jonathan Dancy.[36]

Kant holds that every application of a general rule or concept to a particular case involves an act of judgment that eludes formulation in generalizations (KrV A134/B173; R 5234–5243, Ak 18:127–129). On this basis, he would clearly insist that there is an irreducible particularity to the application of any rule of duty and of concepts of virtues and vices, such as beneficence and malice, gratitude and ingratitude, or self-respect and servility. Though some of the moral rules for which Kant argues strike many of us as harsh and uncompromising, he quite explicitly allows that it requires careful consideration of particular circumstances to determine precisely what falls under these rules (regarding the conspicuous cases of suicide and lying, see G 4:429, MS 6:423, 431). The "casuistical questions" that Kant appends to the discussion of many ethical duties are mainly intended to raise issues that have no clear or general resolution but are left to individual judgment depending on the particular circumstances. They are "not so much a doctrine about how to *find* something as rather a practice in how to *seek* truth" (MS 6:411).

Kant's theory nevertheless applies FH by deriving determinate categories of duty, formulated in general terms. He differs from "particularists" chiefly by *mistrusting* our particular moral perceptions. Perhaps he mistrusts even more the training these receive on the basis of customary approval and the examples commonly set before us for our admiration and imitation (G 4:408–409; KpV 5:153–154; MS 6:479–480). In teaching ethics, he opposes the "catechistic" method, which tests only the pupil's memory, and favors the "erotetic" (Socratic) method, which develops the pupil's own reason (MS 6:411–412, cf. 6:480–482, KpV 5:151–161). Kant's Enlightenment view is that the principle of morality is an idea each of us possesses in our reason. This idea starkly opposes much of the human conduct around us, including the customs and traditions of our societies, and therefore the habits, feelings, and perceptions that have been trained into us. Abstract reasoning has the advantage over particular perceptions and feelings that the self-alienation involved in it serves to protect us against the prejudices and self-deceptions that present themselves to us as self-evident moral truths when they take the form of immediate feelings and perceptions. If people were by nature good and generous and if their social relationships and institutions tended to make them more so, then particularism would provide us with a sound moral epistemology. As long as the truth remains closer to the opposite of this, particularism will yield unreliable results and can easily serve to underwrite complacent moral corruption.

It seems more faithful to Kant's best insights, therefore, to portray the application of FH in terms of a process of deductive reasoning from that principle and intermediate premises to a set of general conclusions, requiring clear argument from such a fundamental principle, about what we have a duty to do and not do. Only subsequently, on the basis of further critical reasoning and a faculty of judgment irreducible to general rules, can we draw conclusions about what these duties require of us under particular circumstances.

8.3. Intermediate premises   We may regard every argument from FH to a general duty as resting on an intermediate premise, logically independent of FH itself, which tells us what a kind of action (or its maxim) expresses or fails to express concerning the worth of humanity. Viewed in this light, Kant's argument against suicide, for instance, might look something like this:

1. FH: Always respect humanity, in one's own person as well as that of another, as an end in itself.
2. Ps: The act of suicide always fails to respect humanity in one's own person as an end in itself.
3. Cs: Therefore, do not commit suicide.

One cannot reach the conclusion Cs from FH without Ps or some other intermediate premise connecting FH with the act of suicide by means of some claim about what the act of suicide expresses concerning the worth of humanity. But Ps is logically independent of FH, as we can see easily from the fact that it is possible to deny Cs by accepting FH and denying Ps. For example, some people think that it is degrading to humanity for a person afflicted with a horrid and debilitating terminal disease to live on in a virtually subhuman condition. They might argue that for a person faced with this prospect, the act of suicide expresses respect for the worth of humanity and protects the dignity of rational nature in the face of the degrading condition with which the person is threatened.[37] Two people who equally accept FH can therefore disagree about a conclusion such as Cs because they disagree about Ps.

Probably fewer of us will quarrel with Kant's conclusion in the case of the argument about false promising, for coercion and deception obviously violate FH because they achieve their end precisely by frustrating or circumventing another person's rational agency and thereby treat the rational nature of the person with obvious disrespect. Kant's argument for this conclusion might be stated as follows:

1. FH: Always respect humanity, in one's own person as well as that of another, as an end in itself.
2. Pf: A false promise, because its end cannot be shared by the person to whom the promise is made, frustrates or circumvents that person's rational agency, and thereby shows disrespect for it.
3. Cf: Therefore, do not make false promises.

We may be tempted in the case of Pf, as we were not in the case of Ps, to think that it follows immediately from FH itself, as part of its very meaning. This temptation should be resisted. For although Pf may be less controversial than Ps, it is still possible without contradiction to affirm FH while denying Pf. There certainly are actions that frustrate or restrict someone's agency through deception or coercion, whose end therefore cannot be shared by the patient, but which nevertheless do not fail to respect the patient's humanity. Kant himself would cite an act of just punishment as an example of this, since he maintains that it is impossible to will one's own punishment, yet clearly regards just punishment as respecting the dignity of the criminal (KpV 5:37–38; MS 6: 331–337).

There are in any case significant questions about the circumstances under which paternalistic interference might be permissible in the name of the worth of humanity, in order to prevent people from harming their rational capacities or behaving in ways that they will later regard as dishonoring their humanity. It is implausible to suppose that the right answer to such questions can always be found right in FH itself through an analysis of what is meant by "using humanity as an end in itself." If we suppose Kant is committed to this, then we are bound to conclude that FH is so empty and vague, and that its meaning is so flexible and disputable, that no determinate conclusions can be drawn from it. And we will naturally charge that FH is useless because it provides no "substantive criterion" for moral rightness and wrongness.[38]

A better way to look at the matter, however, is this: The meaning of FH is clear and determinate because the concepts of humanity (or rational nature) and existent end in itself are both reasonably clear and determinate. But the use of FH in moral deliberation always requires an intermediate premise, logically independent of FH, which does the work of Ps or Pf in the above arguments; and such premises are often doubtful or controversial. We badly misunderstand Kant's theory if we suppose he thought the *a priori* principle of morality (in any formulation) could determine what to do apart from such empirical principles of application.[39]

The intermediate premises are disputable because rational nature reveals itself only under particular cultural and historical circumstances and our views on it are corrigible (as we learn more about ourselves). We do have quite a bit of knowledge about rational nature, however – not only from science (including philosophy), but perhaps even more stored up in folklore, literature, and religion. This knowledge is what we must use to guide our judgments about how the dignity of humanity should be respected in action. Admittedly, it sometimes does so in frustratingly unsystematic, ambiguous, and even conflicting ways, and (as some of Kant's own moral conclusions conspicuously illustrate) part of what passes for such knowledge at any given time is really pernicious prejudice, which it is the task of enlightenment to remove.

A premise such as Pf is easier to accept than a premise such as Ps because the direct frustration of a rational being's agency through deception is by virtually all accounts a more direct affront to the worth of humanity than a rational being's termination of its own life-processes. Ps, in turn, is easier for us to accept than some of Kant's other premises, such as that we always dishonor our humanity when we lie or enjoy sexual pleasure (Ak 8:427–430, MS 6:424–425, 429–431). Kant also regards the absolute equality of all rational beings as compatible with social inequalities that nearly everyone today would regard as intolerable, such as the subordination of wives, children, and servants to the male heads of households and the exclusion of most people from all political participation (MS 6:282–284, 313–315, 329–330). We disagree here because we justifiably believe we know more about what respect for humanity requires in these matters.

The intermediate premises connecting FH with conduct are *hermeneutical* in nature: They involve interpreting the *meaning* of actions regarding their respect or disrespect of the dignity of rational nature. There can be no neat algorithms or decision procedures for the interpretation of human actions. But such intermediate premises may be accepted or rejected on the basis of reasons; they do not depend merely on blind intuitions or irrational prejudices. If the dignity of humanity provides the *correct* basis for deciding moral questions (and even gives the correct explanation of why we ought to care about people's welfare at all), then Kantians need not apologize for the fact that their principle does not lead to tidy utilitarian calculations (whose pretense to precision turns out in practice to be illusory anyway). No fundamental moral principle should be seen as directly solving all moral problems (especially controversial ones). Its task is rather to provide a correct framework within which problems can be raised and discussed.[40]

THE FORMULA OF AUTONOMY
AND THE REALM OF ENDS

1. The ground of obligation

Autonomy of the will as the ground of moral obligation is arguably Kant's most original ethical discovery (or invention). But it is also easy to regard Kant's conception of autonomy as either incoherent or fraudulent.[1] To make my own will the author of my obligations seems to leave both their content and their bindingness at my discretion, which contradicts the idea that I am *obligated* by them. If we reply to this objection by emphasizing the *rationality* of these laws as what binds me, then we seem to be transferring the source of obligation from my will to the canons of rationality. The notion of *self*-legislation becomes a deception or at best a euphemism.

One way of responding to this dilemma would be to trace the prehistory of autonomy in early modern ethical thinking, as has been done in two excellent recent studies by Stephen Darwall and Jerome B. Schneewind.[2] They describe the process involved in the transformation of "self-government" from a political metaphor applied to individual conduct into a fundamental conception relating to individual persons, which is then capable of making revolutionary demands on political institutions themselves. Once we understand this movement of thought in historical context, we see that the paradoxes about obligation based on self-legislation arise only insofar as we fail to recognize (or try to resist) the change in moral conceptions underlying the best thinking modern moral philosophy has to offer us.

Perhaps the best way to convince those who are deeply skeptical of the idea of moral autonomy is to pursue this historical path. But that would lead me away from my topic and has already been done better by others. So I will remain within Kant's own arguments, which go on the offensive against the above objections by arguing that moral obligation in general can be made intelligible _only_ by grounding it on autonomy of the will. If these arguments are successful, they show that we resist the idea of autonomy only on pain of having no satisfactory account of moral obligation.

Kant's search for the principle of morality began with the concept of a categorical imperative, resulting in FUL (and its more intuitive variant FLN). The search then led to a consideration of the motive determining a rational will to follow a categorical imperative, resulting in the concept of an end in itself and FH. From these two formulas, Kant says, "there follows now the third practical principle of the will, as supreme condition of its harmony with universal practical reason, the idea _of the will of every rational being as a will giving universal laws_" (G 4:431). This third formula is the formula of autonomy (FA).

1.1. The idea of autonomy It is significant that Kant formulates FA using the word 'idea' (_Idee_). An idea is a concept of reason to which no object in the world of appearance can be adequate (KrV A310–320/B366–377). Thus to ground morality on the _idea_ of the will of every rational being as legislative is _not_ to ground it on what particular rational beings arbitrarily decree. On the contrary, we regard ourselves as _categorically bound_ by norms only to the extent that we see them as proceeding from reason, which has the _critical_ capacity to recognize its errors and correct them. The volition that is author of categorical obligations is thus the will toward that (unattainable) _idea,_ which is the same for every rational being.[3]

Regarding the author of the moral law as an idea is really only a corollary of Kant's statement in the _Critique of pure reason_ that "Nothing is more reprehensible than to derive the laws about what I ought to do from what is done, or to limit it to that" (KrV A318–319/B375). It is a special case of this reprehensible procedure to identify the moral law with what any (or every) rational being might in fact think about it. To ground the moral law on the _idea_ of the will is therefore to distinguish moral _truth_ from what any finite rational being (or all such beings) might believe. Since Kant holds that moral truth is irreducible either to what people think or to the results of any verification procedures, he is a moral _realist_ in the most agreed-upon sense that term has in contemporary metaphysics and metaethics.[4] Kant is a moral realist because realism is the only way of preserving the _critical_ stance necessary to all moral thinking, the openendedness of moral inquiry. To say that the moral law rests on an *idea* is to say that it is always in principle possible for us to be mistaken about what we think is right, no matter who we are, how many of us there are, or what decision procedures we may have applied in arriving at our moral beliefs.[5]

1.2. The derivation of FA   In what sense does FA "follow" from FUL and FH? We get nowhere trying to deduce any verbal statement of FA from the verbal statements of FUL and FH. We do better if instead we attend to the basic thoughts behind these two formulas and then try extending both thoughts by combining them. FUL is based on the mere concept of a categorical imperative, and that thought naturally leads us to inquire after the authority that could ground such a principle. FH identifies rational nature as the fundamental value behind all moral principles, which prompts us to investigate what principle might rest on this fundamental value. Putting these two thoughts together and addressing the two questions they provoke, we come to a third thought, namely, that the value of rational will might serve as the authority for an objective universal law commanding categorically. That also extends the conception of *humanity*, the capacity for *setting ends* having objective value, to that of *personality*, the capacity for *giving laws* which determine all objective value. It gets us to FA, "the idea *of the will of every rational being as a will giving universal laws*" (G 4:431).

No law whose bindingness rests on an external interest can be truly universal, that is, valid categorically for every rational will simply as such. For the interest that grounds it applies to the will only through a contingent inclination grounding the interest. Hence such a law "would itself need yet another law that would limit the interest of its self-love to the condition of a validity for universal law" (G 4:432). But a law so limited could not command unconditionally or categorically. The only way to conceive of a law that does command in that way is to suppose that its ground is the supreme worth of the rational will itself which obeys the law. This worth is present as much in others as in myself and requires respect for them as much as for myself.[6] It is objectively valid, moreover, only if it accords with the idea of the will, and not merely with the *fiat* of some fallible being such as myself. To the extent that I esteem myself as a rational being, a law conceived in this way is given by my will, too, the very will that is to obey it. Thus it is possible to regard this same law as categorically obligatory by viewing it as proceeding from my own will.

A law proceeding from a self-legislating rational will obligates us only through *respect*. To use the terms we borrowed earlier from Korsgaard

(Chapter 4, § 5.1), we can now say that the rational will not merely *confers value* on *ends* but also *confers validity* on the normative *laws* that establish the fundamental standards for the dutifulness of actions. We can therefore argue that rational nature has an even higher value than we ascribed to it before, because we now see it as grounding not merely the objective value of ends but also the obligatoriness of laws. Rational nature, that is, can be seen not only to be an end in itself (with fundamental objective worth), but to have dignity (absolute or incomparable worth).

> Nothing can have a worth other than that which the law determines for it. But the lawgiving itself, which determines all worth, must for that reason have a dignity, that is, an unconditional, incomparable worth; and the word *respect* alone provides a becoming expression for the estimate of it that a rational being must give. *Autonomy* is therefore the ground of the dignity of human nature and of every rational nature. (G 4:436)

Every other source of the law would have to bind the rational will to it by some *other* volition grounded contingently on a value different from that of the law. A law grounded on happiness would have to appeal to our will to be happy. A law grounded on the will of God would have to appeal either to our love of God's perfections or our fear of his power. These further volitions would turn the categorical demand of the law into a merely hypothetical demand, by referring it to some other volition as its ground. This line of thinking convinces Kant that the principle of autonomy is the only possible solution to the riddle of obligation, and that all other principles of obligation must fail to solve it because they must be grounded on heteronomy of the will (G 4:441–445; KpV 5:34–41).

1.3. Principles of heteronomy   There are two natural rejoinders to Kant at this point. The first is to deny that there really is such a thing as categorical obligation and insist that volition can be grounded only on something contingent and subjective, such as a moral feeling or a desire for happiness. This says in effect that moral obligation, as Kant has been depicting it, is (in his words) nothing but a "high flown fantasy," "chimerical idea," or "cobweb of the brain" (G 4:394, 407, 445). The favored deflationary alternative is then dressed up in its Sunday best, and through the pressure of skeptical arguments against the real thing, we are blackmailed into accepting the sad imitation.

In the Second Section of the *Groundwork* Kant mentions several views of this kind: the moral sense theory of Hutcheson (which, as we have seen, once tempted Kant himself), the hedonistic eudaemonism of Epicurus, which bases morality on the desire for pleasure (G 4:442, cf. KpV 5:40), and conventionalist theories that ground morality solely on the force of social custom, either that of education (Montaigne) or of civil constitution (Mandeville) (KpV 5:40). There are still plenty of such views around today.

Kant seems to dismiss such views peremptorily, but his real strategy is to postpone his response to them. For in the First and Second Sections, he is *provisionally assuming* that morality (as he conceives it) is not an illusion. After inquiring into the conditions of its possibility, he will present a positive argument for his account only in the Third Section (see § 4). In the First and Second Sections, however, he has already been arguing subtly in this direction. For if he can persuade us that morality, as we already understand it and are committed to it, requires respect for law, categorical obligation, and treating persons as ends in themselves, then he will have given us strong reasons to resist any deflationary account of it.

Obj. # 2   *1.4. Theological morality*   The second line of objection concedes that moral obligation as Kant presents it is real but tries to account for it in some way other than autonomy of the rational will. These include divine command theory (familiar to Kant from the writings of Christian August Crusius) and the theory of perfection (which Kant found in Christian Wolff and the Stoics) (G 4:443, KpV 5:40–41). Although Kant's official objection is that these positions involve principles of heteronomy, a closer look shows that his real argument takes the form of a dilemma: Either these principles are principles of heteronomy, and unsatisfactory because they cannot account for the categorical character of moral obligation, or else their account is opaque and requires the dignity of self-legislating reason to explain or complete it.

Kant has no objection to our thinking of ourselves as obeying God when we do what morality requires. His own (favorable) account of "religion" is "the recognition of all duties as divine commands" (R 6:153–154; see Chapter 9, § 4.4). But he denies that the appeal to God's commands can provide a satisfactory account of moral obligation. Kant distinguishes the *legislator* of a law, the one who issues a command and may attach positive or negative sanctions to it, from the law's *author*, the one whose will imposes the obligation to obey it. In these terms, Kant has no objection to regarding God's will as the legislator of the moral law but thinks only the rational will of the person obligated can be its author (MS 6:227, R 6:99, G 4:448). If I regard a will other than my own as author of the law, then the law obligates me only through some interest (such as love or fear) that I have in obeying that other will. This interest would undermine the categorical nature of obligation.

If my motive for obeying God's will is fear, then I seem to be representing God as a cosmic despot, motivated by a desire for glory. The authority of his commands to us – his groveling minions – rests on our dread of divine vengefulness or our hope of gaining divine favor for our own aims (G 4:443). Such a picture demeans both the Deity and ourselves, and degrades virtue into mere hired service (ED 8:339; VpR 28:1115, 1118). We don't do much better by representing our obedience to God as grounded on love if our love is merely another volition on which our reason for obedience depends, since that equally destroys categorical obligation. We truly preserve the character of moral obligation only if we hold that God's will itself is inherently worthy of obedience because what God commands is in itself right (i.e., categorically obligatory). But this means we are still faced with our original problem of determining what makes something categorically obligatory, toward the solution of which we now see that appeals to the divine will can contribute nothing.

Theological morality also fails as an account of how we know what is obligatory, because its account is either circular or presupposes theoretical knowledge we cannot have. Kant maintains that we have no concept of God and no cognition of his will through experience. Our only conception of this will must be based on the pure rational concept of God as a supremely perfect will. Our concept of such a will can come only from our own rational idea of goodness or perfection.[7]

1.5. Perfectionism Kant regards the principle of perfection the alternative to autonomy that comes closest to a correct account of obligation (G 4:443). The problem is what you mean by 'perfection'. You get a thoroughly unsatisfactory theory of obligation if 'perfection' is understood as the fitness of an object to some (arbitrarily chosen) end, since that directly undermines the categorical character of duty. You do no better by understanding 'perfection' as relative to a concept of the general kind of thing (e.g., a perfect fruit knife as one that is sharp, safe, easy to use, and so on), since that makes the value of perfection conditional on our interest in that kind of thing (G 4:441–442; cf. KpV 5:22–26).

'Perfection' might also refer to the goodness of the will itself. One version of such a view, found in Aristotle and the Stoics, would be a form of eudaemonism that identifies happiness not with subjective satisfaction but with a person's objective good, and equates this good (or its dominant component) with moral virtue or the exercise of practical reason. Kant's objection here is not that perfection is a principle of heteronomy but that this concept of perfection is too indeterminate and empty to provide a determinate account of moral obligation. Just as even the most satisfactory form of theological morality still leaves in the dark our categorical *reason* for obeying God's will, so this form of perfectionism leaves it still to be determined why we are rationally bound to seek perfection (G 4:443).

Perfectionists might say at this point that they do exactly what Kant does – they rest obligation on our rational esteem for the worth of something. For Kant this is rational nature; for the perfectionist it is perfection or the objective good. Why does Kant think there is greater clarity in conceiving the ground of obligation as the dignity of rational will than as objective perfection or goodness? (Theological moralists might make an analogous objection, saying that they stop with the transcendent goodness of the Deity.) Kant's reply is that the recognition of a law as categorically binding presupposes the unconditional and incomparable worth of the source of the legislation, which in relation to practical reason is adequately conceived not as perfection or divinity but only as rational self-legislation. For only this has such a worth to the rational will originally rather than derivatively, making its commands truly categorical.

Let us try to state the argument in a slightly different way. When I judge an action to be good or obligatory or rationally binding on me, I thereby exhibit respect *at least* for my own rational capacity to make this judgment. In this way, we might well say, along with Andrews Reath, that I regarded myself as the *author* of the moral law only because I am *subject* to the law.[8] For it is from my recognition of myself as *subject* to the law that Kant proposes to derive the proposition that its obligatoriness is grounded on my rational self-legislation. Just as Nietzsche says that "He who despises himself at least esteems the despiser within himself,"[9] so we must also say that she who subjects herself to an obligation presupposes the authority of the rational nature in herself that recognizes her subjection to it.

If my recognition of an obligation is supposed to be based on something over and above the dignity of my legislating reason (such as the value of objective perfection or divine goodness), then a further ground would be needed to explain why my will values that object. If that ground is distinct from my respect for rational nature as self-determining, it thereby renders my acceptance of the obligation conditional on some other volition of mine, and the categorical nature of the obligation has been forfeited. If it turns out to be the same ground as respect for my rational nature, then perfectionism or divine command morality becomes acceptable, but only because its account of obligation turns out to be parasitic on an appeal to the autonomy of reason. It follows that no property of any object could provide me with a reason for regarding any act as categorically obligatory except insofar as that property plays a reason-giving role in following some principle legislated by the idea of my rational will.[10]

2. FA as a moral principle

2.1. Formulating FA   The idea of every rational will as universally legislative is not directly a formula of any moral principle but only a way of representing the ground or authority of other moral principles (such as FUL or FH). Kant does, however, present FA through various other verbal formulas, indeed, through more (and more diverse) verbal articulations than any of the other formulas. There are at least fifteen distinct statements of it in the Second and Third Sections of the *Groundwork*, of which the following seem to me the most fundamental and prominent. (In § 3 we will discuss the Formula of the Realm of Ends (FRE), which Kant presents as a more intuitive version of FA.)

1. "The idea of the will of every rational being as a will giving universal law" (G 4:431, 432).
2. "The *principle* of every human will as *a will giving universal law through all its maxims*" (G 4:432). Or, from Kant's late lectures: "So act that by the maxim of your action you may present yourself as a universal legislator" (VE 27:518).
3. "To choose only in such a way that the maxims of your choice are also included as universal law in the same volition" (G 4:440). Or: "Act on no other maxim than that which can also have as object itself as a universal law" (G 4:447).
4. "Act on a maxim that at the same time contains in itself its own universal validity for every rational being" (G 4:437–438).
5. "*Act in accordance with maxims that can at the same time have as their object themselves as universal laws of nature*" (G 4:437).

(1) expresses FA explicitly in terms of the idea of the rational will as moral legislator. (4) makes the point that some maxims are universally valid (or obligatory) for all rational beings and commands us to act on them. (3) and (5), by referring to our *maxims* as *universal laws*, make FA sound very similar to FUL. (5) sounds like FUL's variant, FLN. It is the only formulation of FA to employ the conception of a law of *nature* (as a "typic of pure practical judgment" (KpV 5:67–71)). (4) seems also to inherit at least one problem we noted with FUL and FLN: That is, it gives rise to the problem of "false negatives" discussed in Chapter 3, § 7.4. By commanding us to act *only* on maxims that could themselves be universal laws, it apparently forbids us to act on maxims that merely conform to universal laws without qualifying to serve as universal laws.

2.2. *Distinguishing FA from FUL*   In every one of its formulations, however, FA is quite distinct from FUL. It is crucial for our understanding of the *Groundwork*'s account of the fundamental principle of morality not to confuse the two formulas. By passing off elements of FA as contained already in FUL, such confusions play a significant part in reinforcing the false and mischievous notion that FUL is Kant's definitive statement of the moral law.

FUL and FLN provide only tests for the *permissibility* of any given maxim, but do not tell us positively what kind of maxim we must act on. By contrast, FA, especially in formulations (3)–(5), positively commands us to act on certain maxims: either those that contain the volition that they themselves should be universal laws or those that are "universally valid" for the rational will. The positive command corresponds to a very different test from those involved in FUL and FLN. The latter test maxims by what a rational being might *possibly* will (without contradiction in conception or conflicting volitions) as universal law. FA tests them by whether they *actually* belong to the universal legislation of an ideal rational will or *actually* contain in themselves the volition that they should belong to such a legislation.

Closely related to this is the fact that several formulations – (2), (3), and (5) – significantly speak of "maxims" in the plural. FA says not that we should act on *a* maxim having a certain property (universalizability), but that we should act on a *set of* maxims that *collectively* qualify as a *system* of rational legislation. It is only this idea that makes the connection essential to FA, namely, that maxims as universally valid laws proceed from the rational will as their author. The term "universal law" in all these formulations is most naturally treated as a collective noun (as in a phrase like "the law of the land"). This is not a natural way to read the corresponding phrase in FUL or FLN.

Thus the crucial difference between FA and the FUL test, which is ——
the criterion of being a *possible* universal law, is that FA demands of the
maxim that it be an *actual* law belonging to an entire *body* of laws. If FA
is regarded as a test on maxims, then it is both a different and a more
stringent one than the tests involved in FUL and FLN. For it is not evident that every maxim that can be willed without contradiction as a
universal law can qualify as an *actual* universal law, because in order
to do this, it would not only have to pass the CC and CW tests, but it
would also have to harmonize with all the other universal laws given by
the idea of a rational will into a single harmonious system of rational
legislation.[11]

In Chapter 3, § 2, I argued that the principle that actually follows
from the concept of a categorical imperative is not FUL, but rather:

CI: Adopt only maxims that conform to universal law as such.

The above formulas of FA are all very close to CI, adding to it only the ——
decisive new thought that universal law is to be given through the idea
of the will of every rational being (or through the maxims of this will).
In Chapter 3, § 8, we saw that Kant's own comment immediately following his examples of FLN presupposes that there are determinate
universal laws, proceeding somehow from the rational will of the deliberating subject. FUL and FLN are formulations of this idea that are
premature in that they were introduced at a point when Kant was not
yet in a position to justify all that they contain.

3. The realm of ends

Along with FH, the most striking formulation of Kant's moral principle
is the formula of the realm of ends:

FRE: *The Formula of the Realm of Ends:* "Act in accordance with the
maxims of a universally legislative member of a merely possible
realm of ends" (G 4:439; cf. 4:432, 437, 438).

FRE is introduced in conjunction with FA, and in some passages,
Kant even seems to be intending FRE to be an expression of FA itself
(G 4:436). He thereby equates the laws corresponding to the idea of
the will of every rational being as universally legislative with the laws of
a merely possible realm of ends. But what is a "realm of ends"?

FRE

Kant defines a "realm" (*Reich*) as "a systematic union of different rational beings through common laws" (G 4:433). He distinguishes a "realm of ends" as a union under moral laws from a "realm of nature" as a system under mechanical laws – noting, however, that the latter realm may also be considered by natural teleology as involving ends which explain what *exists*. (We will look at Kant's theory of natural teleology in Chapter 6, § 5.) The realm of ends, by contrast, is a *moral* realm, the idea of which determines what *ought* to exist (G 4:436, 438). Kant says that nature is considered a "realm" only because it contains rational beings as ends (G 4:438).[12]

Rational beings constitute a *realm* to the extent that their ends form a *system*. This happens when these ends are not only mutually consistent, but also harmonious and reciprocally supportive. Thus regarded as laws of a realm of ends, moral laws "have as their end the relation of [rational] beings to one another as ends and means" (G 4:433). The laws of a realm of ends are such that universally following them would result in the agreement and mutual furthering of the ends of all rational beings in a single unified teleological system. The idea of a "realm" of ends is thus far more than "the liberal's ideal" of "a good society" as "one in which the ideals and interests of all are given equal consideration" (as R. M. Hare interprets the Kantian realm of ends).[13] A "realm" requires a harmony or even an organic unification of ends so that the ends of all can be pursued in common. Even the most liberal society would still be far from achieving the total unity and unanimity required for a realm of ends.

FRE makes it explicit that moral laws are "universal" in a new sense – not one contained in the mere concept of a categorical imperative but one required by esteem for rational nature as an end in itself. The first sort of universality is a categorical imperative's bindingness on all rational beings, which provides each one the same *a priori* rational ground for following it. But it is not contained in the mere concept of a categorical imperative that the *result* of *everyone's* following it is something any (still less, every) rational being must will.[14]

3.1. The derivation of FRE   FRE is derived by combining ideas drawn from all the previous formulations of the moral law. This makes FRE the formula most adequate for expressing the spirit of the supreme principle of morality.

> For rational beings all stand under the *law* that each of them shall treat himself and all others *never merely as means* but always *at the same time as*

ends in themselves. But from this there arises a systematic combination of rational beings through communal objective laws, that is, a realm, which, because what these laws have as their end is just the relation of these beings to one another as ends and means can be called a realm of ends (admittedly only an ideal). (G 4:433)

FRE first combines the form of law (from FUL) with the substantive value of rational beings as ends in themselves (FH). Kant then draws on something else that was justified only when these two formulas were combined to arrive at FA, namely, that all rational beings stand under the same common or *communal* (*gemeinschaftlichen*) objective laws. Kant later alludes to FLN by comparing the moral realm of ends with nature regarded as such a realm (G 4:436 note). Kant takes for granted that since all rational action involves the setting of ends, these communal laws must also have an end. Since the content of the laws is that all rational beings shall be treated as ends in themselves, and this involves bringing our ends into agreement with those of a being that is so treated (G 4:430), it follows that an end for the communal objective laws is thinkable only through the concept of a single end in which the ends of all rational beings are combined or brought into agreement. That is just the concept of a "realm" in which the ends of all rational beings are systematically united as a single shared end. "When the will is subordinated to the dictate of ends universally valid, it will be in harmony with all human ends" (VE 27:257). "Morality is an absolutely necessary system of *all ends*, and it is just this agreement with the idea of a system that is *the ground of the morality of an action*" (VpR 28:1075). To put it another way, if all rational beings truly honored the rational nature in themselves and one another, the result would necessarily be utter unanimity among all their ends, and ultimately no antagonism or competition of any kind between them.

3.2. Applying FRE   In the *Groundwork*, second Critique, and *Metaphysics of morals*, Kant never attempts to use FA as a formula determining specific duties through FRE.[15] But he does suggest how to do this in some of his lectures, though attempts along these lines are not many and not well worked out. One of the few explicit attempts at an *argument* from FRE is this: "For example, if all human beings speak the truth, then among them a system of ends is possible; but if only one should lie, then his end is no longer in connection with the others. Hence the universal rule for judging the morality of an action is always this: If all human beings did this, could there still be a connection of all ends?" (VpR

28:1100). Being able to will a maxim as a universal law (or law of nature) is therefore seen as equivalent to the maxim's being such that if all followed it, then this would be compatible with a systematic unity (reciprocal community, collective agreement) of all the ends of all rational beings.

We can also easily see how FRE might apply to Kant's fourth example. Everyone necessarily has their own happiness as their end. Thus if I make another's happiness my end, I thereby bring about a harmony or coincidence of ends, and to this extent contribute to a realm of ends, whereas to the extent that I refuse to make the happiness of others my end I prevent a realm of ends. FRE seems to have less obvious application to duties to oneself, but it might be so applied by enjoining a harmony between the ends I actually set and either ends of nature (such as my self-preservation) or ends I cannot rationally act against (such as the development of my capacities to further all sorts of ends). Although Kant never derived his four duties from FRE (the more intuitive and applicable version of FA) as he did FLN (the applicable version of FUL), I think the above considerations show that he obviously could have done so.

But it is not as clear how FRE could be used to derive an entire system of duties. In the real world we often cannot act without thwarting someone's end. If, for example, *A* and *B* have conflicting ends, then I cannot harmonize with the ends of either *A* or *B* without thwarting the ends of the other. In order to apply FRE we seem to need some way of deciding how to resolve or prevent such conflicts. This means knowing how to determine which ends belong to the universal system and which stand outside it or in opposition to it. The little that Kant says here is confusing, possibly even inconsistent:

> Now since laws determine ends in terms of their universal validity, if we abstract from the personal differences of rational beings as well as from all the content of their private ends, we shall be able to think of a whole of all ends in systematic connection (a whole both of rational beings as ends in themselves and of the ends of his own that each may set himself).
> (G 4:433)

First we are told that the laws of a realm of ends must "abstract" both from the "personal differences" among rational beings and from "all the content of their private ends." Yet the result of following these laws is supposed to be "a whole of all ends," including "the ends of his own that each may set himself." It is hard to see how the agreement of *all* ends, including the ends of his own that each may set himself, can be achieved by *abstracting* from the content of a great many of these same ends, especially *all* the private ends of individuals. If 'private ends' here just *means* those ends that cannot agree with the harmonious system, then Kant can be saved from inconsistency, but his statement then becomes trivial and uninformative.[16]

What FRE seems to require is the *exclusion* of ends that *in principle* cannot be shared between rational beings (such as those requiring deception or coercion) and the *furthering* of ends that unite people (such as those involving mutual respect and mutual aid). Sometimes when a person thwarts my ends, I have to admit that I regard it as reasonable for them to do so, because if the situation were reversed I would consider myself entirely justified in thwarting their ends. FRE rules out ends that cannot be shared because they *essentially* involve thwarting the ends of other rational beings in situations where it is not the case that those whose ends are thwarted cannot withhold approval from the attempt to thwart them. Conversely, ends are "good ends," or belong necessarily to the realm of ends, when they can be everyone's ends and their pursuit is necessarily approved by everyone.

Kant himself states this conception of a "good end" quite elegantly in his lectures on pedagogy: "Good ends are those which are necessarily — approved by everyone and which can be the simultaneous ends of everyone" (VP 9:450).[17] This still requires a criterion for determining which ends everyone must approve. But since we already have FH at our disposal, we may leave this to be determined according to the criterion that rational nature must always be treated as an end in itself. Ends are *possible* candidates for universal approval if they do not involve disrespect for rational nature, and they are necessary objects of rational approval if their pursuit shows respect for rational nature.[18]

3.3. Conflict and competition FRE forbids only those conflicts among ends that would make a system of ends impossible. It permits any conflict that involves no disrespect for rational nature because it rests on a more basic convergence of the ends of rational beings. Two people playing a game of cards, for example, have conflicting ends insofar as they both seek to win, and each one's winning means that the other must lose. But card-playing need not violate FRE, if we regard this competitive behavior as the manifestation of a more fundamental agreement. Both players have the end of getting enjoyment out of the game, and by playing they will both achieve this more fundamental end whoever wins. The concept of a "good end" also fits here, since I could not reasonably disapprove of your trying to win a game we have both chosen to play. Political or economic competition might accordingly be squared with FRE by seeing them as resting on mutual respect and hence on a more basic convergence of ends. This is how political and economic conflicts are represented by those who see the political process and the market as grounded in a fundamental community between people, who all rationally and voluntarily accept these systems as the right way of adjudicating political differences and distributing wealth and power.

Yet it remains doubtful whether people really do (or rationally can) regard political processes and the market mechanism in such a way. For to meet the demands of FRE, the competitive system would also have to be accepted *for the specific reason that it harmonizes everyone's ends*. It would not be enough to accept the economic system, for example, because it maximizes aggregate or average welfare. It is not plausible that the political or market systems harmonize everyone's ends, because they systematically result in some acquiring political power that they use to rule others, and in some becoming fabulously wealthy while even more remain destitute, hungry, and homeless. It seems utterly impossible to reconcile war with FRE by appealing to any deeper harmony of ends underlying the conflicting ends of mortal antagonists. We can reconcile warlike behavior with FRE only if we regard our ends as belonging to the realm of ends and the ends of our enemies as opposing that realm, by being necessary objects of rational disapproval. The plausibility of such representation will vary greatly from case to case. In actual wars, the ends of all sides usually fall outside any conceivable realm of ends. Nearly always they are necessary objects of the rational disapproval of some (e.g., of the innocent civilians inevitably killed even by the "good" side).[19]

People sometimes also regard the ends of their political foes as lying outside and opposed to the realm of ends. But it would threaten the civility of political and economic life to regard all one's competitors as objects of necessary rational disapproval. Surely if economic competition cannot be based on an end shared by all, then it violates FRE. Kant appears to accept this consequence to the extent that he holds the maxim of trying to become wealthier than others to be in violation of the moral law.[20] I tentatively conclude that FRE is violated by the kinds of competitive behavior to which most wealthy, honored, and successful people devote most of their lives.[21]

4. Freedom and the moral law

Throughout the First and Second Sections of the *Groundwork*, Kant repeatedly indicates that his search for the moral law is conditional or hypothetical. He is *provisionally assuming* that there are a good will, action from duty, and categorical imperatives binding on the finite rational will. He is seeking the principle of morality that follows from these assumptions. He promises to discharge the assumptions in the Third Section by arguing that morality is not an illusion and there is indeed a categorical imperative binding on rational beings.

Kant's argument for the moral law is complex and difficult to interpret. The argument he presents in the *Groundwork* was obviously unsatisfying to him by the time he wrote the *Critique of practical reason* three years later. Insofar as it involves speculative issues about transcendental freedom, this argument also lies outside the intended scope of this book. My discussion here is therefore an unashamed reconstruction and a deliberate simplification. It makes no pretense of being a close reading of any single text but tries instead to call attention to the elements of Kant's argument in the *Groundwork* that seem most characteristic of his thinking throughout the critical period and also have the greatest lasting interest for moral philosophy. I will focus attention chiefly on what Henry Allison has called the "preparatory argument" of Section Three of *Groundwork*.[22]

The basis of Kant's deduction of the moral law is what Allison calls the "Reciprocity Thesis."[23] The reciprocity is a mutual entailment between the following two propositions:

F: The rational will is free.
M: The moral law is unconditionally valid for the rational will.

For short, we will refer to the reciprocity thesis as 'F↔M'. The reciprocity between F and M is especially emphasized in the *Critique of practical reason* (KpV 5:28–29), where Kant seems to have abandoned the hope of deriving the moral law from the practical postulate of freedom. In the *Groundwork*, on the other hand, the emphasis is on the inference from freedom of will as a presupposition of the practical standpoint to the validity of the moral law (G 4:446–447). Thus in the second Critique, Kant appears to hold that the moral law needs no "deduction" of any kind, but must be accepted as a self-evident "fact of reason" (KpV 5:31–32).[24] In this respect, the argument as I present it will be closer to the procedure of the *Groundwork*, since it will attempt to ground the moral law on F→M and on F as an indispensable presupposition of all rational judgment.

4.1. Freedom as causality through norms   Kant distinguishes several senses of 'freedom'. *Transcendental* freedom is the capacity of a cause to produce a state spontaneously or "from itself" (*von selbst*) (KrV A533/B561). A transcendentally free cause, in other words, is a "first cause," one that can be effective independently of any prior cause. This is distinguished from *practical* freedom, which we attribute to ourselves as agents. Kant's metaphysical contention is that the will can be practically free only if it is transcendentally free, and transcendental freedom could exist only in a noumenal world, not in the empirical world. Here, however, we will be mainly concerned with practical freedom – which even Kant himself sometimes thinks can be treated independently of speculative issues about transcendental freedom (KrV A800–802/B829–831). Practical freedom is in turn taken in two distinct senses: In the "negative" sense, a will is practically free if it acts independently of external causes determining how it acts; in the "positive" sense, it is practically free if it has the power to determine itself in accordance with its own law (KrV A534/B562, G 4:446, KpV 5:33).

The key to understanding the Reciprocity Thesis is Kant's conception of freedom as a special kind of causality. From this he infers that it must operate according to a *law*. In the case of a free cause, the law must be "of a special kind" (G 4:446). A *natural* cause is a state of a substance upon which another state of some substance follows in accordance with a necessary rule; this rule is the pertinent causal law (KrV A189/B232, A534/B562). Since a will acts not only according to laws but according to their *representation* (G 4:412), the "law" of a *free* cause must be one it *represents* to itself. But this does not mean merely that a free will is aware of the law it follows. The law is one under which it considers its actions from a practical standpoint. In the case of an imperfectly rational will, which does not always act as reason directs, the law is represented as a principle according to which it *ought* to act. We could describe such a law, in contrast to a natural law, as an imperative, or a *normative* law.[25]

The notion of a cause acting according to normative laws may strike us as odd, but it is not. We often explain human actions by reference to norms the agent recognizes. A chess player moves the bishop only diagonally because that is the rule in chess. In constructing the sentences they speak or write, people choose words that accord with the rules of grammar, and we use these rules to explain why the sentences are formed as they are. Norms also explain why a composer avoids parallel fifths, and why a batter keeps his weight on his back foot as long as possible.

Explanations of actions according to the agent's *intentions* are normative law explanations. Intentions are constituted by the normative principles the agent adopts in forming the intention. It is only because intentions are norms that people can bungle intended actions or fail to carry through their intentions. Despite such cases, we do not regard explanations by reference to intentions as defective, pointless, or merely bad substitutes for natural law explanations. We even use normative laws as part of explanations of actions that *contravene* them, by describing the actions as *failed attempts* to comply with the norm. (The utterance of an unparsable string of words can be explained by informing us what the speaker was trying – unsuccessfully – to say.) We might think that normative law explanations could make no sense because, depending on what 'ought' to happen rather than what does happen, they would be divorced entirely from the actual occurrences we are trying to explain. But this thought is mistaken as applied to explanations that refer to intentions. In the interpretation of people's behavior, we also tend to attribute to them the intentions that make best overall sense of what they actually do, and there is a conceptual limit on our ability to make sense of what agents do while ascribing to them intentions they do not fulfill. (This is one way of looking at Donald Davidson's famous "principle of charity.")

Normative law explanations are highly appropriate to voluntary, rational actions because rational actions are by their very concept freely chosen and norm-guided. All our purposive actions fall under normative explanations insofar as every intention to pursue an end requires subscribing to certain norms, such as the principles EI and HI (discussed in Chapter 2, § 3.2) or various technical imperatives of which the agent is aware.[26]

Kant is convinced that natural cause explanations require the natural necessitation of an event by preexisting states of the world independently of the adoption of any intention or normative principle by the agent (KpV 5:94–96). If this (incompatibilist) view is correct, then normative law explanations of human actions cannot be reconciled with natural law explanations at all except through a desperate expedient such as Kant's infamous distinction between phenomenal and noumenal causality. We should be careful here to distinguish between Kant's incompatibilist views (and the metaphysical theory of freedom he needs in order to accommodate them) and the theory of agency we are now examining as part of his conception of practical freedom (which is *not* committed to incompatibilism). Above all, we should avoid thinking that Kant means to say the moral law stands in the same relation to actions as a natural causal law to its effects. For then we will also think (along with Henry Sidgwick and countless other critics since) that Kant is committed to say that the will acts freely only if it actually follows the moral law. And that commits him to say that if the will transgresses this law, then it is not acting freely (and so the agent cannot be held responsible).[27] But it should be clear from the above why he neither holds nor is committed to any such view.

4.2. Freedom as a presupposition of reason   The first step in Kant's deduction of the moral law in the *Groundwork* is an argument for a conditional proposition that is half the Reciprocity Thesis:

F→M: If the rational will is free, then the moral law is unconditionally valid for it.

Kant argues for F→M on the ground that freedom is a kind of causality and of an analysis of what 'causality' must mean in the case of freedom. It must mean being subject to an unconditional and self-given normative law. (If the will is perfect or holy, the normative law tells us what its self-determined volitions necessarily *are*; if it is finite and imperfect rather than holy, then this law is a categorical *imperative*, determining what its volitions *ought* to be.) The argument of the Second Section of the *Groundwork* has shown that the moral law, in its fully developed formulation as FA, is exactly such a law for any rational will. Therefore, if there is a free will, then the moral law is valid for it (i.e., F→M).

To complete the argument, Kant now needs only to discharge the antecedent of the conditional by showing that we have reason to assert F. Kant does not think that the freedom of the will can be theoretically demonstrated (or theoretically cognized in any way at all). In the *Critique of pure reason*, Kant argues that the idea of a free will is a transcendent idea to which no experience can ever be adequate. From this he draws two conclusions: (1) that freedom cannot be attributed to the will as an object of experience, and (2) that it can never be shown that the will is not free, if it is considered as a noumenon or thing in itself (KrV A532–558/B560–586). He reiterates these arguments in both the

Groundwork and the *Critique of practical reason* (G 4:451–463; KpV 5: 41–57, 94–106). But the transcendental idealist metaphysics involved tends to distract us from what is relevant to Kant's deduction of the moral law. We will understand that deduction better if we focus solely on the (quite unmetaphysical) way in which Kant considers freedom in the deduction itself.

In the *Groundwork* Kant claims that "freedom must be presupposed as a property of the will of all rational beings" (G 4:447). Freedom is not being proved theoretically, but it is claimed to be a *presupposition* of taking the practical standpoint at all – which we unavoidably do, even when we are engaged in theoretical inquiry:

> Now, one cannot possibly think of a reason that would consciously receive direction from another quarter with respect to its judgments, since the subject would then attribute the determination of his judgment not to reason but to an impulse. Reason must regard itself as the author of its principles independently of alien influences; consequently, as practical reason or as the will of a rational being it must be regarded of itself as free. (G 4:448)

Notice that these remarks, focusing not on actions but only on *judgments*, concern the way in which we must regard ourselves in making judgments of any sort, even wholly theoretical ones. If even there we must regard ourselves as free, then there is no room in any sort of understanding of ourselves for a conception of ourselves as other than free.

Kant holds that we must think of ourselves as free in all our rational judgments in the sense that we must regard our judgments as acts we perform under norms. Because it is conceived as action under a norm, 'freedom' as meant in F is not at all the same as *arbitrariness*, and is even close to its opposite. If I judge that q based on the evidence that p *or* q and *not-p*, then I can regard this as a *rational judgment* on my part only if I am prepared to give it a normative explanation, by viewing it as proceeding from my correct application of the logical rule *modus tollens*, regarded as a *normative* principle which I, simply as a rational being, recognize as valid and therefore impose on my own judgments. Thus to say that judgment is an exercise of free agency in this sense is precisely *not* to say that I may judge any way I please. On the contrary, my judgment can go contrary to the norm only if it involves a failure or mistake.[28] If I think of my judgment as prompted by some conscious *cause* external to my free and rational norm-guided activity (e.g., if I see it as prompted by fear of what my logic teacher will do to me if I don't give the answer of which I know she approves), then to that extent I cease to regard it as a judgment which is *rational* by the standard of the relevant norms (logical rules of inference). If my fear of my logic teacher leads to my giving the right answers, that will be because those happen to be the ones the teacher wants; but the rightness of my judgments would be only contingently the result of anyone's applying rational norms (and the rationality of my judgments would have to be ascribed to my logic teacher, not to me). The verdict would be the same if I came to regard my judgment as the result of some unconscious process (of neurotic compulsion or posthypnotic suggestion) whose results accord only contingently with the rules of logical inference. Not all my reasoning processes need be entirely conscious and explicit, but to regard them as successful processes of reasoning, they must be regarded as the result of my freely (though perhaps habitually and unreflectively) following rational norms. Even mistakes in reasoning are regarded as rational processes only to the extent that I see them as falling under such norms and as trying to comply with them.

For this argument to be relevant to moral freedom, Kant must maintain that the norms of theoretical reasoning, like those of morality, are both self-given and unconditional. But Kant's argument is *not* that logical rules are a species of moral rule or that moral rules are merely rules of logic. What he needs to claim is that the capacity we ascribe to ourselves in regarding ourselves as subject to moral obligations is of exactly the same *kind* as that we ascribe to ourselves in thinking of ourselves as judging according to rational norms, so that if we cannot intelligibly doubt that we have such a capacity in one case, we have no good ground for doubting that we have it in the other. And this he *can* claim. We do not accept logical rules only conditionally – because, for example, we think that reasoning according to *modus tollens* will be advantageous to us. On the contrary, following *modus tollens* is unconditionally necessary in order to preserve the truth of our judgments. From the standpoint of one who judges, seeing myself as following the norms required to judge truly is no different from merely seeing myself as judging.

Therefore, to understand myself as capable of judging is to assume that I am free in precisely the sense meant in F→M, and to understand myself as judging rationally is therefore to presuppose that F. Since we have already established that F→M, all those who think of themselves as making rational judgments already presuppose something that commits them to M.

4.3. The practical incoherence of fatalism   Let a *fatalist* be someone who denies practical freedom (where this freedom is understood in the Kantian way, as causality according to norms). The fatalist, therefore, holds that ~F. She must regard her own acts of judgment *solely* as the necessary effects of natural laws, denying that they can be correctly explained by reference to reasons or normative rules of inference (such as *modus tollens*).

If fatalism is to be an interesting position, then the fatalist must be prepared to give *arguments* for ~F, assert ~F on the basis of those arguments, and expect those to whom she gives the arguments to be convinced that ~F on the basis of them. Yet fatalism itself says that all judgments (including the fatalist's judgment that ~F) are to be explained solely by reference to natural laws and can never be correctly explained by reference to norms of reasoning. Fatalism itself, therefore, undermines the fatalist's claim that she, and those she tries to persuade of fatalism, can hold fatalism on rational grounds.

In 1783, Kant reviewed a book on moral philosophy by Johann Henrich Schulz, whose position he described as a "universal fatalism, which ... turns all human conduct into a mere puppet show and thereby does away altogether with the concept of obligation" (Ak 8:13). In the review, Kant stated his argument against fatalism quite explicitly:

> Although he would not himself admit it, [Schulz] has assumed in the depths of his soul that understanding is able to determine his judgment in accordance with objective grounds that are always valid and he is not subject to the mechanism of merely subjective determining causes, which could subsequently change; hence he always admits freedom to think, without which there is no reason. (Ak 8:14)

This argument makes the point that we can doubt the reality of freedom only if we also doubt our capacity to judge rationally, including even our capacity to judge whether to entertain those very doubts. A fatalist might still assert fatalism and even present arguments for it. But she would be unable to represent herself or those to whom she offers the arguments as holding fatalism rationally on the basis of those arguments.

Classical compatibilist (or "soft determinist") approaches to the free will problem would accept the fatalist's idea that rational judgment is a natural causal process but would try to show that it could *at the same time* be a case of free action or conformity to rational norms. Here Kant sides with the fatalist, holding the compatibilist project to be impossible. Note, however, that the argument for freedom we have just seen is even more basic than Kant's arguments for incompatibilism. For they say that whatever we may or may not hold about the compatibility of freedom and natural causality, we must presuppose our own freedom, as the capacity to act under norms of reason, in order even to represent ourselves as competent to decide on rational grounds whether fatalism or compatibilism is true.[29] Our agreement or disagreement with Kant's incompatibilism therefore should make no difference to our acceptance of his argument that F is a necessary presupposition of all rational judgment.

It bears repeating that to represent freedom as a presupposition of rational judgment is by no means to provide a *theoretical proof* that we are free. Still less is it to cite an *experience* of our freedom, or a piece of *empirical evidence* that shows we are free. For all such an argument shows, there might even be strong evidence or arguments that we are *not* free and that freedom is an illusion. What Kant shows is that we would face an insuperable difficulty if we were confronted with such proofs or evidence. For even to represent ourselves as considering such proofs on their merits is to presuppose that we have the capacity to judge according to norms of reasoning, hence to presuppose that what such proofs are trying to show is false.

This way of vindicating the principle of morality is thoroughly consistent with the transcendental strategy Kant employs throughout the critical philosophy. Kant's argument attacks skepticism about morality by showing that the skeptical doubts undermine the very conditions of their own intelligibility. It is grounded on the typically Enlightenment appeal to that critical self-confidence in reason without which it would be impossible even to acknowledge on good grounds the limits and fallibility of reason.[30]

4.4. Freedom and nature   One of the greatest stumbling blocks to the acceptance of Kantian ethics has always been its association with his view that we belong simultaneously to two different worlds, the natural or sensible world of phenomena (the realm of appearance), in which everything is causally determined and causal spontaneity is unthinkable, and the noumenal world of things in themselves outside nature, outside space, and even outside time. I have elsewhere argued that Kant's attempt to solve the metaphysical problem of free will is both coherent and well-motivated (even if we do not find it convincing).[31] It lies beyond the scope of this book to discuss those issues further here, but I do not want to ignore or underestimate the costs incurred by Kant's approach. Since the noumenal world for Kant is a timeless realm, his solution requires us to regard even such basic features of the moral life as moral striving and moral progress as having only figurative or allegorical and not literal truth. Another problem is that because Kant's approach is committed to regard free will as something falling entirely outside the realm of nature or experience, it necessarily precludes the possibility of any empirical investigation of the natural conditions of moral responsibility, and hence any empirical theory concerning when we should and should not hold people responsible for their actions.

To many, these features of Kant's metaphysical theory of freedom have seemed sufficient reasons to reject his entire ethical system. Before drawing such drastic conclusions, we ought to ask how far Kant's ethical theory proper, including his deduction of the moral law from the presupposition of freedom, really depends on the controversial metaphysics of transcendental idealism. Kant's deduction of FA depends on regarding ourselves as free in the sense of being capable of guiding our thoughts and actions by self-given rational norms. The substantive values that ground Kant's ethical theory are respect for the worth of rational nature and the dignity of personality as rationally self-legislative. It may be controversial whether personality and humanity have the objective worth Kant's theory attributes to them, but it does not go beyond ordinary common sense to ascribe to ourselves the rational capacities to set ends and guide both our reasoning and our conduct by the rational norms we recognize.

It contradicts Kant's incompatibilist intuitions but not informed common sense in the late twentieth century to suppose that those rational capacities might be part of our natural equipment – a result of wholly natural processes of biological evolution and historical development. Nothing in Kant's argument for his three formulas or in his deduction of the FA from the presupposition of freedom provides those persuaded by a naturalistic view of human reason with any reason for suddenly thinking that our abilities to recognize values and govern ourselves by rational norms requires a supernatural or idealist metaphysics.[32]

This of course does not mean that Kant's theory of noumenal freedom is necessarily mistaken. Those persuaded by a naturalistic view of reason might be wrong.[33] If Kant's incompatibilist views are correct, then despite the counterintuitive features of his theory of noumenal freedom, it might be the best we can do to resolve the problem of freedom and natural determinism. The point I mean to emphasize is only that we badly err if we suppose our disagreements with Kant on incompatibilism and the metaphysics of freedom give us any good reason for rejecting his moral philosophy (unless of course we are fatalists and think we have some way around his argument that fatalism cannot coherently represent itself as being held on rational grounds).

4.5. Kant's naturalistic understanding of freedom   There are good reasons, moreover, for exploring the possibility of combining Kant's ethical theory (including its presupposition of freedom) with a naturalistic picture of human beings. For it is a remarkable fact that what we find in Kant's historical and anthropological writings is precisely an attempt to integrate human freedom into a naturalistic understanding of human beings as a biological species.

Especially for those unfamiliar with the writings just referred to, this may be hard to accept, for at first glance it seems completely to contradict Kant's most conspicuous statements about freedom and nature in his metaphysical works, which have determined the image most readers have formed of his views about freedom, agency, and our empirical knowledge of human actions. Consider, for instance, the following:

> All actions of human beings in the domain of appearance are determined in conformity with the order of nature, . . . and if we could exhaustively investigate all the appearances of the wills of human beings, there would not be found a single human action we could not predict with certainty and recognize as proceeding necessarily from antecedent conditions. So far, then . . . there is no freedom. (KrV A550/B578)

> Since the past is no longer in my power, every action I perform is necessary from determining grounds which are not in my power; that means that at the time I act I am never free. (KpV 5:94) If it were possible for us to have so deep an insight into a human being's character . . . that every, even the least incentive . . . were known to us, then his future conduct would be predicted with as great a certainty as the occurrence of a solar or lunar eclipse. (KpV 5:99)

From a few such eye-catching statements, it is easy to form vivid expectations about Kant's conception of the natural or empirical study of human nature and conduct (the study he calls 'anthropology'). We think he must project a mechanistic natural science that excludes freedom altogether and treats human behavior as merely part of the mechanism of nature. We do not expect to find any empirical investigation of human beings as free agents, much less a naturalistic investigation of the development of the rational capacities which presuppose freedom. Kant's talk of two "standpoints" and of considering ourselves in "speculative" and "practical respects" (G 4:455) are easily interpreted as a theory positing two radically different and wholly incommensurable conceptions on ourselves: that of the "spectator," from which I must view all human beings (including myself) as causally determined natural automata, and that of the "agent," from which I view myself as a free but wholly uncognizable member of a supernatural noumenal realm.[34]

The truth about Kantian anthropology, however, is very different from this picture. Although Kant never pretends to seek or find empirical *proofs* of human freedom, his empirical anthropology always proceeds (as the argument discussed in § 4.3 should lead us to expect) on the fundamental presupposition that human beings are free. Kantian anthropology even emphasizes those very features of human life which he takes to be empirical manifestations of freedom – the development of new capacities, the variability of ways of life, the progress of human culture, the development of reason and the historical phenomenon of enlightenment. Though he approaches anthropology from what he calls a "pragmatic viewpoint" (the standpoint of human action), he never suggests that this viewpoint is radically incommensurable with the viewpoint of an empirical observer of human affairs. Kant places anthropology right alongside physical geography, seeing these two studies as the two main divisions of our empirical acquaintance with the natural world in which we live (VPG 9:157; cf. KrV A849/B877).

Surprising or not, this is actually just what we should have expected. For statements like the ones quoted above from the first two Critiques must always be read in light of the fact that *Kant denies that we can ever be in a position to have anything approaching an exhaustive knowledge of the appearances of the human will.* We must read Kant's statements as expressing only metaphysical propositions; the "if" clauses in them about our knowledge of the causes of human actions are never true and can never be true. Thus in speaking of the unpredictability of human history Kant says explicitly that the future "is not discoverable from known laws of nature (as with eclipses of the sun and moon, which can be foretold with natural means)" (SF 7:79). There is no prospect that we will ever be in a position to have detailed knowledge of the psychological causes of individual human actions or to predict human actions as we predict astronomical events. In Kant's view, any study of human nature or behavior that followed such a model would be doomed before it starts.

Metaphysically we know that as natural beings we fall under the universal causal mechanism, but our capacity to investigate this causality empirically is virtually nonexistent. Commonsense guesswork may enable us to foretell what people will do some of the time, but there can never be anything approaching a *predictive science* of human behavior.

One factor here is Kant's denial that there is any solution to the mind-body problem (KrV A381–404). We can never know whether the empirical self is a material or an immaterial thing, and any noumenal self wholly transcends our powers of empirical cognition. No causal connections between the corporeal and the mental can even be made intelligible to us, much less empirically investigated. Hence any mechanistic laws governing acts of the mind would have to involve a psychological determinism cut off from the causality of objects of outer sense that is investigated by physics. A second crucial factor is that, as we shall see in Chapter 6, § 2, Kant thinks our awareness of the appearances of inner sense is characterized by uncertainty and deceptiveness, and no study of them can ever achieve the precision of a genuine natural science (Ak 4:471, cf. VA 7:121). Anthropology can never attain to a precise knowledge of causal laws or causal connections. Insofar as Kant has a conception of its methods at all, he thinks of anthropology as following the looser method of biology, based on regulative principles of teleological judgment.

5. Formulating the moral law

The aim of the *Groundwork* is to discover and establish the supreme principle of morality (G 4:392). Many readers of the *Groundwork* identify this formula with FUL. There are a number of passages, both here and in other works, where Kant identifies a "universal formula of the moral law" (G 4:436–437, KpV 5:30; MS 6:225); most readers have taken the formulas so designated to be expressions of FUL. Throughout Part I of this book, however, we have been looking at some strong reasons to doubt that FUL deserves this privileged position. In § 5.5 we will show that the textual evidence itself, if read correctly, indicates that it is FA rather than FUL which should be considered the "universal formula."

We have seen that the derivation of FUL both from the concept of duty (in the First Section of the *Groundwork*) and from the concept of a categorical imperative (in the Second Section) is invalid. FUL uses what

a rational being can will as a criterion of universal law, even though this
anticipates FA, which is not justified until much later. It still does not import enough, however, to turn FUL into a principle from which positive
duties can be derived or even to afford satisfactory tests for the conformity of individual maxims to universal law. It is FH that provides both
the objective value on which the moral law is based (namely, that of rational nature as an end in itself) and the explicit basis on which Kant
derives nearly all the duties of right and ethics enumerated in the *Metaphysics of morals*. FA, derived from FH in combination with FUL, then
supplies Kant with the formulation of the moral principle that serves in
its deduction from the necessary rational presupposition of freedom.

5.1. *A system of formulas*   Kant views all three formulas as constituting
a *system*, presenting a single moral principle to us from three different
sides. In that sense, there is no reason to accord any of the three formulas an absolutely privileged place. But from a systematic standpoint
the formulas developed later in the exposition are less inadequate than
the earlier ones (hence FA is in this sense superior to FH, which is in
turn superior to FUL). The *Groundwork*'s search for the supreme principle of morality should thus be seen as ending only when we grasp *the
moral law as a system of formulas*. Kant presents the system as follows:

> All maxims have, namely,
> (1) a *form*, which consists in universality; and in this respect the formula
> of the moral imperative is expressed thus: that maxims must be chosen as
> if they were to hold as universal laws of nature;
> (2) a *matter*, namely an end, and in this respect the formula says that a ra-
> tional being, as an end by its nature and hence as an end in itself, must
> in every maxim serve as the limiting condition of all merely relative and
> arbitrary ends;
> (3) a *complete determination* of all maxims by means of that formula, namely,
> that all maxims from one's own legislation are to harmonize with a pos-
> sible realm of ends as with a realm of nature. (G 4:436)

Kant formulates the moral law as a *system* of formulas in order to insure
the *unity* of the principle he is seeking. There is nothing inconsistent
about formulating the moral law *first* in terms of a certain kind of *principle* (a categorical imperative or universal law), *then* in terms of a *value*
to be esteemed, respected, and furthered (humanity as an end in itself)
and *finally* in terms of its *ground* in the rational will which legislates universally, recognizing no authority except its own autonomy. These three
standpoints do not constitute three different moral principles, but only

three different ways of regarding one and the same principle. This is shown by the ways the different formulas arise from considering the categorical imperative from different sides: FUL in terms of its form alone, FH in terms of the motive for following it, FA in terms of the ground of its authority. It is also shown by the way the various formulas themselves constitute a whole and complete one another.

In constructing the system of formulas, Kant alludes to analogies with several other parts of his own philosophical system. There is always only a limited amount to be learned from such architectonic considerations, but here they do help us.

5.2. *Complete individual concepts*   In the context of Kant's ontology, the triad *form, matter, complete determination* refers to the conditions for the possibility of the concept of an individual thing. The formal condition of a concept is its logical possibility or noncontradictoriness; the material condition is the givenness of some reality as the matter of thought; and "thoroughgoing determination" refers to the Leibnizian idea that the concept of an individual, in contrast to that of a universal, is determined with regard to every possible pair of contradictory predicates (KrV A166/B207–208, A218–224/B265–272, A266–268/B322–324, A571–573/B599–601).[35]

Form, matter, and complete determination together constitute the necessary and sufficient conditions for the complete concept of a possible individual. We may take this allusion as an indication that the three formulas together are supposed to complement one another, and that only together do they specify the moral principle completely.

The first formulation of the principle corresponds to the form of generality in every maxim, the fact that it is a general principle or policy of action. FUL (presented here in its more intuitive form, FLN), which is supposed to express the universal concept of a categorical imperative, specifies the *formal* condition that a maxim must satisfy if it is not to contradict the moral principle.

Every maxim, however, equally has a matter, that is, an end for the sake of which the action is performed (G 4:400, 427; KpV 5:21–23). FH specifies the moral principle in terms of the objective end that serves as the motive of the will that follows a categorical imperative: This is the existent end of humanity as end in itself.

"Complete determination" is not a component of any individual maxim, but it is a necessary requirement of an entire system of moral legislation governing the conduct of a rational agent. As we noted earlier in § 2.3, FA differs from FUL chiefly in the fact that it formulates the moral law in terms of such a system, and this is most explicit when FA is formulated as FRE, since this spells it out that the laws must unite all rational beings as ends in themselves, together with all their particular ends, into a harmonious organic system.[36]

5.3. The categories of quantity If Kant's primary allusion emphasizes the interdependence and collective completeness of the system of formulas, a second allusion indicates both the progression of Kant's argument through the formulas and the way in which they complement one another in their practical application: "A progression takes place here, as through the categories of the *unity* of the form of the will (its universality), the *plurality* of the matter (of objects, i.e., of ends), and the *allness* or totality of the system of these" (G 4:436). Kant refers this time to his three categories of quantity in the *Critique of pure reason*: unity, plurality, and totality (KrV A80/B106).

Let us first consider the point about complementarity. The three formulas correspond to the categories of quantity in that they refer to complementary ways in which the moral principle is applied to maxims. FUL corresponds to the category of unity in that it refers to the universal validity of each single maxim; FH, to plurality through directing us to the many rational beings who must be treated as ends; and FA (once again as FRE), to totality in presenting these ends as an organic system.

The most intriguing claim, however, is that there is a "progression" within the three categories that corresponds to the progression from FUL through FH to FA. There is a progression through these categories in the sense that the unit provides the standard for constructing plurality and because (as in the other triads in the table of categories), the third category of the triad can be viewed as a synthesis of the first two (as a totality is a unity made up out of a plurality of items) (KrV B110–111).

FUL corresponds to unity in that it refers to the "legislative form of the maxim" as the *single* pure determining ground of the good will, "which must be exactly the same determining ground for the will of all rational beings and in all cases" (KpV 5:25). FH represents plurality because there are *many* rational beings, each containing humanity as an end in itself. FA (as FRE) corresponds to totality, since it represents these beings as ends in an *organized whole* or "realm" under a *system* of laws. Just as the unit provides the basis for plurality, so the concept of the legislative form of a maxim leads in Kant's argument to the search for the objective end or motive which could serve, subjectively, to represent this legislative form, and this end is located in the plurality of rational beings as ends in themselves. Likewise, just as unity and plurality combine to form totality, so FUL and FH are put together to yield FA, in which the worth of rational nature (which grounds FH), conceived as the idea of rational will, is represented as the author of the universal laws (which are presupposed in FUL).

5.4. *The "very same law"*   This puts us in a position to understand better Kant's most striking claim about the three formulas: "The above three ways of representing the principle of morality are only so many formulas of the very same law, and any one of them of itself unites the other two in it" (G 4:436). This need not be taken to mean that the three formulas are intended to be logically equivalent, so that given a verbal statement of any one of them, verbal statements of the other two could simply be deduced from it. That sort of equivalence is even *precluded* by the claim that there is a "progression" between the formulas from FUL, through FH, to FA (which follows from the first two). For it means that FH is richer in content than FUL, and FA (as FRE) is still richer than FH.

Nor does it make sense to attempt to demonstrate that the three formulas are "equivalent" in the sense that their practical consequences must be identical (that they will necessarily require and forbid exactly the same things under all conceivable circumstances). This is not because their consequences could be *different,* but rather because none of the formulas, considered alone, has consequences that are determinate enough for such an *a priori* "equivalency proof" to make sense.

We have seen that FUL is best interpreted as presupposing determinate moral laws (distinct from it) with which the maxim is to be tested by its agreement or disagreement (G 4:424). It is therefore misunderstood when interpreted as a universal and self-sufficient criterion of moral rightness. FH tells us to treat rational nature in every person as an end in itself. This injunction is by no means empty of consequences, but to arrive at them we require premises telling us what is the expressive meaning of various courses of action regarding the dignity of rational nature. FA and FRE are merely general characterizations of the entire system of moral laws, which resist direct application to individual cases. Any formulation of the law yields practical consequences only when combined with intermediate premises through which it is applied. (Kant articulates the need for such intermediate principles when he distinguishes between the purer and the more intuitive forms of his formulations and also when he distinguishes the moral law itself from the "typic of pure practical judgment" in the *Critique of practical reason* (KpV 5:67–71).) But the intermediate premises are not of the same kind. For FUL and FLN, they are premises about what a rational being can will as a universal law (of nature); for FH they are premises about which acts do and do not treat rational nature as an end in itself; for FA and FRE, they would be claims about which maxims could constitute themselves a rational system of legislation that would unite the ends of all rational beings into a realm. Kant has no reason to deny that different moral issues might be seen more clearly by looking at them in the light of different formulas. Kant's remark that the three formulas express "the very same law" might best be read as an invitation to understand each formula, and even its application to empirical circumstances, only in light of the others. Instead of making us look for an *a priori* equivalency proof, it should place a constraint on the way we interpret all three formulas. This is just another way of stating Kant's main point about the three formulas, namely, that the supreme principle of morality is *adequately* expressed only in the *system* of all three (which Kant is about to present when he makes this remark). Each formula "unites the other two in itself" in the sense that none of them is adequately understood except in its systematic connection with the other two, which includes its distinctive role relative to the formulas that complement it.

5.5. The "universal formula" Kant's chief task in the *Groundwork* is not to construct an ethical theory to be applied to our actions, but only to lay the ground for such a theory by discovering and establishing its fundamental principle. But he is also trying to make the principle easier to apply by giving it intuitive appeal for us as moral agents. In the system of formulas, Kant chooses the variant of each formula which he regards as "closer to intuition": FUL is presented there in the form of FLN and FA in the form of FRE. Kant makes this intent explicit when he concludes his systematic presentation with the following remark:

> But one does better always to proceed in moral *appraisal* by the strict method and ground it on the universal formula of the categorical imperative: *Act in accordance with a maxim that can at the same time make itself a universal law.* If, however, one wants also to provide access for the moral law, it is very useful to bring one and the same action under the three concepts mentioned above, and thereby, as far as possible, bring it closer to intuition. (G 4:436–437)

Kant wants to make the law applicable and to draw on moral feeling in order to do this. At the same time, he wants to warn us about the human tendency to take any opportunity to pervert the law in its application to particular cases and to cater to the "dear self" by indulging our inclinations and relaxing the strict demands of duty (G 4:405–408). So even as he employs the more intuitive formulas, he warns us against them and urges us to appraise our actions by as austere a standard as we can manage: "the universal formula of the categorical imperative":

> **FG:**   "Act in accordance with a maxim that can at the same time make itself a universal law." (G 4:436)

Which of his three formulas is Kant invoking here? Most readers conclude without a second thought that FG is identical with FUL.[37] Perhaps they do so because Kant calls the quoted formulation the "universal formula" immediately after identifying FUL (or its more intuitive representative FLN) with the "form" of maxim "which consists in universality." But FG is presented in the same paragraph (3) devoted to FRE, the intuitive variant of FA. From that one might conclude instead that Kant intends FG to be simply a more abstract and austere version of FRE – in other words, FA. Further arguments for identifying FG with FA can be drawn simply from *what FG says*. Like the formulations of FA considered in § 2.2, FG specifies no universalizability test for individual maxims in terms of what can be willed as a universal law, but instead commands us positively to act on certain maxims. It identifies them as maxims that can *make themselves* universal laws. I take this to be equivalent to "include within themselves the volition that they should be universal laws," an idea found in formulation (3) of FA (G 4:440, 4:447; cf. G 4:432) but never in any formulation of FUL. The injunction to present oneself in all one's maxims as a universal legislator (which is clearly a statement of FA, not of FUL) is explicitly presented in Kant's lectures as a universal formulation of the categorical imperative, "conveying the essential character of the moral principle" (VE 27:518).

FG also closely resembles the wording of the formulations used in the *Critique of practical reason* and the *Metaphysics of morals* as the most general formula of the categorical imperative:

> **FK:**   "So act that the maxim of your action could always at the same time hold (*gelten*) as a principle of universal legislation." (KpV 5:30)
>
> **FM:** "Act upon a maxim that can also hold as a universal law." (MS 6:225)

The difference between FG and these other two formulas is that FG commands us to act on a maxim that *can make itself* a universal law, whereas FK and FM command us to act on a maxim that *can* (or *could*) *hold* (or be valid, *gelten*) as a universal law. In § 2.2 we saw that Kant sometimes expresses the idea that a maxim *holds* as a universal law by saying that it *makes itself* such a law or has itself as universal law for its object. On closer examination, then, FK and FM, as well as FG, are better seen as statements of FA than of FUL. They do not refer to testing maxims for their permissibility by the criterion of what *can be consistently willed* as universal law, but instead command us positively to act on maxims that *can hold or be valid* as universal laws, which means, as we saw above, that they can belong to a total *system* of universal legislation.

FG, FK, and FM swerve in the direction of FUL only insofar as they include the modal "can" (or "could") whereas other formulations of FA speak (simply in the indicative) of what *is valid* as a universal law or *makes itself* one. But FG, FK, and FM can be read as equivalent to FUL only if the phrase 'can (could) hold as universal law' or 'can make itself universal law' is taken to mean the same as 'can be willed to be a universal law' (and assuming the CC and CW tests for that). But as we saw in § 2.2, no such equation is tenable. The possibility of being willed as universal law refers only to the fact that the maxim, considered in isolation, might (without contradiction or volitional conflict) be willed as such a law. But for a maxim to (be able to) *hold* or *be valid* as a universal law, it would have to (be able to) belong to a system legislated by the idea of a rational will. That is the criterion for maxims proposed in FA (but absent from FUL). Note also that FK is presented in close conjunction with the Reciprocity Thesis (KpV 5:28–30). In the *Groundwork* it is clear that the only formulation of the law in terms of which this claim can be made is FA, since it alone represents the law as proceeding from the will of a rational being (G 4:446–447). Therefore, it is reasonable to suppose that FK is also FA, not FUL. And since the wording of FM is very close to that of FK, it seems reasonable to think that FA (rather than FUL) is intended by it, too. (That the "universal formula" FK is meant to be FA rather than FUL was already recognized by both Paton and Beck.[38])

In that case, when Kant says that we should use the "universal formula of the categorical imperative" as our standard for "moral *appraisal*," he cannot mean that we should judge actions or maxims, or derive more specific principles of duty from it. What he means, I suggest, is rather that unless we use the most austere moral standards in appraising our conduct, our moral reasoning is likely to degenerate into comfortable and corrupt rationalizations. He is warning us that although from the standpoint of applicability there may be advantages in formulations of the law (such as FLN, FH, and FRE) that bring it "nearer to intuition," such formulas may also (and for the very same reason) make it easier for us to perpetrate convenient self-deceptions on ourselves about what duty demands. The "purer" formulas FUL and FA are more difficult to apply but also less susceptible to abuse. Kant's point, in other words, is not one about the *a priori* law, but about human psychology. It refers us to a complex empirical theory of human nature and history, which has been sadly neglected by students of Kant's ethical thought. To remedy that neglect is the next item on our agenda as we begin Part II.

II

ANTHROPOLOGICAL APPLICATIONS

THE STUDY OF HUMAN NATURE

1. Practical anthropology

1.1. Metaphysics of morals and anthropology The *Groundwork* divides moral philosophy into two distinct parts: the metaphysics of morals and practical anthropology (G 4:388). The first of these alone is said to be "morals proper," and it is supposed to provide us with the "laws according to which everything ought to happen." These laws are to be entirely unmixed with any information about what *does* happen. Hence it is to be completely separate from everything we know about human nature through experience. In the *Groundwork* Kant regards the two departments of moral philosophy as so separate that he even wonders whether they shouldn't be pursued by different researchers in order to take advantage of the benefits of an intellectual division of labor (G 4:388–389).

In the *Groundwork* it remains extremely unclear what either a "metaphysics of morals" or a "practical anthropology" would look like. The *Groundwork* is not a metaphysics of morals but only lays the ground for one by formulating and establishing its first principle. It is unclear what it would be to go beyond the fundamental principle of morality and develop a system of practical laws and duties, while still making no use whatever of empirical information about human beings.

Kant seems to want to have even less to do in the *Groundwork* with practical anthropology, since he appears to cast himself for the purposes of that work as someone better suited to the metaphysical side of moral philosophy than the empirical or anthropological side. Yet even in the *Groundwork* he cannot abstract entirely from empirical anthropology. His illustrations of the moral principle depend on substantive assumptions about human nature – about the natural purposiveness of self-love and of natural talents, about our dependency on the charitable aid of other human beings, and about the likely consequences for the practice of promising if it became a law of nature that those in need of money would borrow with no intention to keep their promises to repay. But there is no attempt to show how any of this knowledge is related to a systematic study of human nature. Perhaps that is why many readers, despite Kant's explicit statements to the contrary, think that for him moral philosophy as a whole contains no such study and has no need of one.

It was not until a dozen years later that Kant actually wrote a work entitled *Metaphysics of morals*. In the introduction to that work he once again contrasts "metaphysics of morals" with "practical anthropology." But the sameness of the terminology may cause us to overlook the major change that has occurred in the way the two parts of moral philosophy are conceived. In the Preface to the *Groundwork*, a 'metaphysics of morals' contains *only a priori* principles; *everything* empirical is consigned to 'practical anthropology'. In the Mrongovius transcription of his lectures on moral philosophy, which is probably contemporaneous with the *Groundwork*, Kant remarks that the second part of moral philosophy may be called

> *Philosophia moralis applicata*, moral anthropology. . . . Moral anthropology is morals that are applied to human beings. *Moralia pura* is built on necessary laws, and hence it cannot base itself on the particular constitution of a rational being, of the human being. The particular constitution of the human being, as well as the laws which are based on it, appear in moral anthropology under the name of 'ethics'. (VE 29:599)

A metaphysics of morals is, namely, a "pure moral philosophy, completely cleansed of everything that might be only empirical and that belongs to anthropology" (G 4:389). The duties of *human* beings can be discussed only by 'ethics' or 'practical anthropology', which must be kept entirely distinct from a pure or metaphysical treatment of moral principles.

One striking feature of Kant's conception of practical anthropology is that it is taken to be a part of *morals* or *practical* philosophy, not of theoretical philosophy (G 4:388–389). The consistency of this classification has been called into question by H. J. Paton and Mary Gregor, on the ground that factual information about human nature forms no part of the principles determining what we ought to do. "There is no reason," Paton says, "why we should regard such a psychology as practical; it is a theoretical examination of the causes of certain morally desirable effects."[1] He supports this charge by citing the (unpublished) first introduction to the *Critique of the power of judgment*, where Kant criticizes those who treat information that tells us how to produce an object under the heading of "practical philosophy" (Ak 20:197–201).

Kant's inclusion of practical anthropology as part of moral or practical philosophy seems to me, however, both consistent with Kantian principles and quite illuminating as to the way Kant conceives of the system of moral philosophy. Paton and Gregor see an inconsistency between the *Groundwork* and the first introduction only because they suppose that practical anthropology must be restricted to giving information about *means* to the fulfillment of moral duties or the achievement of moral ends. But in fact Kant regards empirical information about human nature as well as *a priori* or metaphysical principles as determining the *content* of moral ends and thereby of ethical duties. Such information is to be used not merely in choosing *means* to moral ends but in determining which *ends* we ought to set as moral beings (the "ends which are also duties," which the *Metaphysics of morals* calls "duties of virtue") (MS 6:382–395). (This makes it implausible to say, as Thomas Hill once did, that "in his formulation of the Categorical Imperative, Kant suggests that one can decide what is morally right in isolation from facts about the frailty and corruption of other human beings."[2])

Nor is it difficult to see how on Kantian principles empirical anthropology might play this indispensable role in practical philosophy. In Chapter 4, §§ 7–8, we saw that FH determines duties through the judgment that certain actions express the respect and esteem for humanity required by the moral law. It will obviously require empirical knowledge of human nature to determine which ends will suitably honor the rational nature of human beings and which ends are contrary to the respect we owe to human dignity. Further, no attempt to determine the laws that will unite the ends of rational beings into a realm can afford to ignore what ends such beings are empirically disposed to adopt.

1.2. The new conception of a "metaphysics of morals"   In fact, it is only such a conception of practical anthropology that makes possible a significant shift in meaning which the term "metaphysics of morals" undergoes in the work with that title. There Kant concedes that the system of duties falling under the title of "metaphysics" consists of pure moral principles insofar as they are applied to human nature. A metaphysics of morals itself, he says, "cannot dispense with principles of application, and we shall often have to take as our object the particular *nature* of human beings, which is known only by experience" (MS 6:217).[3] Accordingly, a metaphysics of morals *itself* now includes some empirical anthropology because it must contain "principles of application." A metaphysics of morals is now bounded on the empirical side only by the fact that it limits itself to those duties that can be derived from the pure principle as applied to *human nature in general.* The only duties that fall outside of a "metaphysics of morals" are those involving reference to particular conditions of people or to special relationships between them (MS 6:468–469).[4]

In shifting the content of a "metaphysics of morals" toward the empirical, Kant is in no way abandoning or modifying his fundamental thesis that the *supreme principle of morality* is wholly *a priori* and borrows nothing from the empirical nature of human beings. He is withdrawing only his earlier claim that a "metaphysics of morals" can concern only "the idea and the principles of a possible *pure* will and not the actions and conditions of human volition generally" (MS 4:391; cf. G 4:388–389). In other words, Kant now no longer regards a metaphysics of morals as constituted solely by a set of pure moral principles (with the pure moral law as its only foundation). It is instead the system of duties that results when the pure moral principle is applied to the empirical nature of human beings in general.

2. The difficulty of self-knowledge

Neither in the *Groundwork* nor the *Metaphysics of morals* does Kant ever give any systematic account of the methods of the specifically empirical part of moral philosophy, 'practical anthropology'. Accounts given elsewhere are also both hazy and tentative. There is good reason to believe that this omission reflects serious methodological worries Kant had about anthropology as a discipline and some longstanding doubts about the very possibility of human self-knowledge in general. We find these worries expressed as early as *Universal natural history and theory of the heavens* (1755):

> It is not even known at all to us what the human being now is, although consciousness and the senses ought to instruct us in this; how much less will we be able to guess what one day he ought to become. Nevertheless, the human soul's desire for knowledge snaps very desirously at this object, which lies so far from it, and strives, in such obscure knowledge, to shed some light. (AN 1:366)

Some of Kant's worries are due to his view that the study of human nature is still in a relatively early and unsatisfactory state in comparison to

what it might someday become. Kant's desire to lecture on anthropology and even to reconceptualize the study of human nature was apparently stimulated in 1772 by his dissatisfaction with the 'physiological'
approach to the subject taken by Ernst Platner. According to a 1773
letter to Marcus Herz, Platner's popular treatise on anthropology provoked Kant to institute an empirical study of human nature aimed at
avoiding Platner's "futile inquiries as to the manner in which bodily organs are connected with thought" (Ak 10:146).[5]

Yet Kant is also doubtful about our capacity to study human nature
even when we do it as well as we can. Some of his doubts are due to general epistemological considerations, such as the standards for scientific
knowledge and the fact that the subject matter of anthropology cannot
meet them. Still other doubts could be described as due to the findings
of anthropology itself. Kant thinks that what we do know about human
nature gives us reason for distrusting our abilities to know ourselves.

2.1. Empirical psychology   In Kant's time the study of human nature was
generally treated under the heading of "empirical psychology" (it was
Baumgarten's treatment of this science that Kant used over many years
as the text for his lectures on anthropology).[6] Though his earliest lectures on anthropology (1772–1773) appear to equate anthropology
with empirical psychology (VA 25:8), he later refers to 'empirical psychology' as the part of anthropology that deals only with appearances
of inner sense (VA 25:243, KrV A347/B405). Kant was always dissatis-
fied with the way his predecessors dealt with both subjects. Both in his
earliest lectures and in the *Critique of pure reason*, he criticizes the practice of confusing the questions of empirical psychology with those of
metaphysics or transcendental philosophy, which must claim *a priori*
status (VA 25:8, 243, KrV A848–849/B876–877). Yet in the *Critique* he
also makes the following strange concession:

> Nevertheless, in accord with the customary scholastic usage one must
> still concede [empirical psychology] a little place (although only as an
> episode) in metaphysics, and indeed from economic motives, since it is
> not yet rich enough to comprise a subject on its own and yet it is too im-
> portant for one to expel it entirely or attach it somewhere else where it
> may well have even less affinity than in metaphysics. It is thus merely
> a long-accepted foreigner, to whom one grants refuge for a while until
> it can establish its own domicile in a complete anthropology (the pen-
> dant to the empirical doctrine of nature). (KrV A848–849/B876–
> 877)

From this remark it is evident that Kant regards neither empirical psy-chology nor anthropology as currently in a satisfactory state. It is equally evident that he regards empirical psychology as only one part of an-thropology, which in turn is a subfield of the empirical doctrine of na-ture, and hence a branch of "applied' rather than "pure" philosophy (KrV A848/B876). But he regards such a subject as incapable of math-ematical treatment, hence incapable of becoming a natural science in the proper sense (Ak 4:471).

> We must concede [he says] that psychological explanations are in very sad shape compared to physical ones, that they are forever hypothetical, and that for any three different grounds of explanation, we can easily think up a fourth that is equally plausible. . . . Empirical psychology will hardly ever be able to claim the rank of a philosophical science, and prob-ably its only true obligation is to make psychological observations (as Burke does in his work on the beautiful and sublime) and hence to gather ma-terial for future empirical rules that are to be connected systematically, yet to do so without trying to grasp these rules. (Ak 20:238)

Here again Kant's skepticism about empirical psychology contains two elements: first, doubts in principle about its prospects as a natural sci-ence, and second, doubts arising from the fact that the study of empir-ical psychology is presently still in a highly unsatisfactory state even rel-ative to its limited possibilities. Kant seems to be recommending that anthropology content itself for the moment with making unsystematic observations, which are only later (as the science matures) to be taken up into empirical rules. But even when empirical psychology reaches a more satisfactory state, Kant seems to think that psychological expla-nations will never be more than hypothetical or conjectural. For this reason he has little to say about the scientific structure of empirical psy-chology. The same seems to be true of empirical anthropology (the larger study of which empirical psychology is a part). This dissatisfaction pre-sumably applies also to practical anthropology, that study which is supposed to form the empirical part of moral philosophy.

2.2. The indefinability of human nature   Kant sometimes places the question *What is the human being?* at the very center of philosophy (VL 9:25). But he never attempts to provide a systematic answer to it.[7] Kant even thinks it is *impossible* to define what is peculiar to the human species. For this species is only one possible variant of rational nature, yet we are acquainted with no other variants with which to compare it and arrive at specific differentia (VA 7:322). Whatever we say about human nature, its predispositions and its propensities can have only a provisional character.

Kant rejects the traditional definition of the human being as *animal rationale*, allowing only that the human being is an *animal rationabilis* – that is, a being *capable* of acting rationally but not a being that necessarily or even typically exercises this capacity successfully (VA 7:321). Further, rational capacities themselves open our nature to modification by being the source of perfectibility. For reason is precisely our capacity for an *indeterminate* mode of life, one that is open-ended and self-devised, in contrast with the life of other animals, which is fixed for them by instinct (MA 8:111–115). So understood, the traditional definition itself is only a confession that human nature is in principle indefinable.

Since Kant's time "anthropology" has come to refer primarily to the study of the customs and folkways of different peoples. Kant's sense of the term includes this meaning since he thinks the empirical observation of human behavior can be extended through travel or through reading the accounts of travelers (something Kant did avidly) (VA 7:120).[8] Histories, plays, and novels – Kant specifically mentions Shakespeare's tragedies, Molière's comedies, Fielding's novels, and Hume's history of England – are also "auxiliary" sources for the anthropologist, even though fictional works often represent human nature in an exaggerated fashion (VA 7:121, 25:7, 472, 734, 858, 1212–1214).

"Anthropology," however, "is not a description of human beings but of human nature" (VA 25:471). Kant thinks that a "local knowledge of the world" must rest on a "general knowledge of the world" (a knowledge of human nature as such) if it is to be useful to us, since what it represents is valid only for a limited time and place unless it contributes to a knowledge having cosmopolitan validity (VA 25: 734). We may also see Kant's rejection of a "merely local" anthropology as grounded on moral considerations. FRE tells us that we must seek to realize a realm of ends with all rational beings, which must include at least all human beings. In order to do this, anthropology cannot content itself with the study of what makes each people different but must be oriented from the start to what they have in common.

The real difficulty of anthropology lies in discerning regularities in human behavior that might be indicative of human nature as such. Most regularities in people's behavior, Kant observes, are due to *habit*. But habits provide reliable information only about how they act in familiar situations. We could tell which regularity a habit really displays only if we could see how it might make the person behave in unusual circumstances. Yet if we look at human beings in varying situations, we see that different circumstances merely produce *different habits*. What habits tell us about a person's underlying principles of action is always ambiguous, for any habit is consistent with a variety of traits or dispositions. Further, habits *must* be ambiguous in this way if they are to perform one of their essential psychic functions, which is to conceal and disguise people's real motives and principles (from others and from themselves). This makes it difficult in principle to formulate any reliable generalizations at all about human dispositions. Kant concludes that it is "very difficult for anthropology to raise itself to the rank of a formal science" (VA 7:121).

2.3. Self-deception and self-opacity   Kant's anthropology involves a complex individual psychology, but it is one arrived at only through a teleological theory about the collective tendencies of the human species in history. And the positive theory itself helps to underwrite some of his doubts about the possibility of human self-knowledge. Not only are laws governing human behavior extremely variable, but their discovery is also blocked by obstacles thrown up by human nature itself. Kant denies that we can know even in our own case the principles on which we act. Kantian anthropology says that human beings have a strong tendency to conceal and disguise the truth about themselves: "The human being has from nature a propensity to dissemble" (VA 25:1197). If someone notices we are observing him, then he will either become embarrassed, and hence unable to show himself as he really is, or else he will deliberately dissemble, and refuse to show himself as he is (VA 7:121, 25:857–859).

In order to see human nature as it truly is, we would have to observe behavior that is unselfconscious. But human nature in its full development occurs only in civilization, and it is one of the effects of civilization to make people more vulnerable to the opinions of others, hence more sensitive to the way others perceive them. "In crude people their entire humanity is not yet developed," but if we observe more cultivated people, "then [we] run into the difficulty that the more educated (*gebildet*) the human being is, the more he dissembles and the less he wants to be found out (*erforscht*) by others" (VA 25:857).

If we try to avoid this difficulty by engaging in self-observation, then we must either do this when we are in a purely contemplative mood, when the true nature of our desires is not displaying itself, or we must attempt it when we are agitated, when our own motives are bound to distort both the data and our observations. "When our incentives are active, we are not observing ourselves; and when we are observing ourselves, our incentives are at rest" (VA 7:121).

Kant distinguishes between merely "noticing" oneself (which we do haphazardly all the time) and "observing" oneself (in a methodical way). The latter (he claims) would be necessary for a scientific anthropology, but it is inherently untrustworthy. When a person is being observed by others, "he wants to *represent* himself and makes his own person into an artificial illusion" (VA 7:132). It is just the same when we study ourselves: "Without noticing what we are doing, we suppose we are discovering within us what we ourselves have put there" (VA 7:133). Kant is thus very much in agreement with Nietzsche's critique of "naive empiricism": the "inner" world of our sensations and feelings is even less trustworthy and more "phenomenal" than the world of external objects.[9]

Hence those who have sought to make a meticulous record of their inner lives usually record only lies and self-deceptions; zeal in self-honesty leads sooner to enthusiasm and madness than to truth. For those who undertake "this hard descent into the Hell of self-knowledge" (VA 25:7),[10] coming to know the deeper truth about oneself usually produces only anguish and despair, which unfits them equally for knowledge and for action (VA 7:132–133). "Nothing is more harmful to a human being than being a precise observer of himself" (VA 25:252); "All self-scrutinizers fall into the gloomiest hypochondria" (VA 25:863, cf. 25:477–478, 865).

Kant's principal targets here are religious self-observers, such as Pascal, Haller, Gellert, and Lavater (VA 7:132–133, 25: 863). He speaks approvingly of Montaigne's cooler and more skeptical style of self-examination because he sees it not as a morbid exercise in introversion but as an invitation to put oneself in the author's place, and hence to make observations of universal validity (VA 25:472, 735). Knowledge of oneself as an individual is for Kant a moral duty, always burdensome and always to be undertaken soberly, with a view to moral improvement (MS 6:441–442). Those to whom self-examination is an occasion either for pleasure or for the moral paralysis of religious enthusiasm are not discharging that duty properly, and are substituting lies and deceptions for the sober self-knowledge they should be getting.

When Kant's readers come across statements of his view that individual human motivation is self-opaque (e.g., at G 4:407), they tend to associate it with his metaphysical theory of freedom, which locates our free agency in the intelligible world. But it would make little sense to draw empirical conclusions about how far we can understand human behavior from a metaphysical theory whose truth, in any case, Kant insists we can never know. In fact, matters make sense only if viewed just the other way round. Kant's conjectures about noumenal freedom are possible only because we can never have satisfactory empirical knowledge of the mind. If we had reliable access to the natural causes of our behavior, then it would be quite untenable to claim that the real causes are different from these and transcend all experience.[11]

Kant's view that we are psychologically opaque has less to do with his transcendental idealism than with a set of ideas more often associated with later thinkers, such as Nietzsche and Freud. Kant holds that most of our mental life consists of "obscure representations," that is, representations that are unaccompanied by consciousness; if we ever learn about them at all, we must do so through inference (VA 7:135–137). This is partly because many representations are purely physiological in origin and never *need* to reach consciousness. But in some cases, Kant thinks, we have a tendency to *make* our representations obscure by pushing them into unconsciousness. "We play with obscure representations and have an interest, when loved or unloved objects are before our imagination, in putting them into the shadows" (VA 7:136). The paradigm example of this, he thinks, is the way people deal with their *sexual* thoughts and desires.

3. Pragmatic anthropology

3.1. Kant's interest in anthropology   Kant's reservations about the study of human nature might lead us to think that this is an area of study about which he did not trust himself to say very much. But in fact the very reverse turns out to be the truth. In his teaching duties at the University of Königsberg, Kant lectured on the topic of anthropology as often as he lectured on any subject, and those lectures were the most popular he gave. The most recent addition to the Academy Edition of Kant's writings is the critical edition of eight manuscript versions of Kant's lectures on anthropology, dating from 1772–1773 to 1788–1789 (VA 25). Kant's own notes on these lectures, *Anthropology from a pragmatic standpoint* (1798), was one of the very last works he published. It is the only set of lecture notes on any subject that Kant allowed to be published under his own name without someone else as editor. Its contents largely reflect Kant's view that for now anthropology must content itself

with empirical observations, which can yield important theoretical results only on the basis of a scientific revolution still to come. In the *Anthropology* there is very little discussion of the aims, methods or structure
of anthropology as a branch of human knowledge. What information
we do get about this is either contained briefly in the Preface, Prolegomena, or Proemium to his lectures, or must be inferred from clues
Kant provides by the way he structures the material he presents.

3.2. Four senses of 'pragmatic'   Kant employs the term 'pragmatic' in his
title in four distinct senses.

1. *Pragmatic vs. physiological.* Kant distinguishes the *pragmatic* approach to the study of human nature from the *physiological.* The latter,
he says, studies only what nature makes of the human being, whereas
pragmatic anthropology considers "what the *human being* as a free agent
makes, or can and ought to make, of himself" (VA 7:119). Pragmatic
anthropology deals with human actions, and with human nature as
something that is in part self-produced by free action.

From this description, it looks as though pragmatic anthropology is
intended to include 'practical anthropology', since that study is also
supposed to deal with human nature in light of human freedom and
what human beings *ought* to do. This impression is confirmed by some
of the manuscript versions, especially by the Mrongovius version (1784–
1785), which is most contemporaneous with the *Groundwork.* There the
part of pragmatic anthropology entitled "Characteristic," which deals
with human character and action, is called the "practical part of anthropology" (VA 25:1367).[12] The scope of pragmatic anthropology is
broader than that of practical anthropology, since it seeks knowledge
of human nature in light of *all* the uses we may choose to make of this
knowledge, and not only for its moral use.

The "self-making" of the human being denoted by "pragmatic anthropology" includes the way each of us is (and ought to be) made through
the actions of others and the influence of society. In Kant's view, human
beings are human at all only through the actions of others who educate
them: "A human being can become human only through education.
He is nothing but what education makes of him" (VP 9:443). Kant also
holds that the development of our human predispositions is a social
process, a result of the collective actions of society (most of which are
unknown to and unintended by individual agents) (I 8:17–18). Moreover, as we shall see in Chapter 9, in Kant's view the evil in human nature is a social product, and our fulfillment of our moral vocation must

equally be social in nature: Our only hope for human moral improvement lies in our being members of an ethical community with shared or collective moral ends. (On all these points, the common characterization of Kant as a moral "individualist" could not be more mistaken.)

2. *Pragmatic vs. scholastic.* Kant intends pragmatic anthropology to be a 'knowledge of the world' (*Weltkenntnis*) as distinct from a *scholastic* knowledge (VA 7:120). The latter involves knowing or being acquainted with the world (*die Welt kennen*), but a truly pragmatic knowledge of human nature involves 'having a world' (*Welt haben*): "The one only *understands* the play (*Spiel*), of which it has been a spectator, but the other has *participated* (*mitgespielt*) in it" (VA 7:120, cf. 25:9, 854–855, 1209–1210). In other words, pragmatic anthropology is supposed to involve the oriented sort of knowledge of human nature that people gain through acting and interacting with others, rather than the theoretical knowledge of a mere observer. At the same time, however, Kant emphasizes (as we saw earlier) that anthropology must be *Weltkenntnis*[13] also in the sense that it is *cosmopolitan* in its scope. It must be a universal knowledge involving acquaintance with and reflection on the entire species (VA 7:120).[14] (It is the worldly contrast between the scholastic and pragmatic attitudes toward the study of human life, not the metaphysical contrast between the allegedly incommensurable standpoints of "agent" and "spectator," that plays a decisive role in Kant's thinking about anthropology.)

3. *Pragmatic as useful.* The term 'pragmatic anthropology' refers not only to our knowledge of human nature insofar as it is a *result* of human actions, but also to knowledge acquired with the aim of *using* it in action. When we study memory, for example, as pragmatic anthropologists, we are not mere "spectators of our play of ideas" but we "use our observations about what has been found to hinder or stimulate memory in order to increase its scope and efficiency" (VA 7:119). (This use of 'pragmatic' is explicitly derived from the idea of "pragmatic history," or the study of history undertaken for the purpose of utility in action (VA 25:1212). In Germany the term was particularly applied to Hume's historical writings.)[15] 'Utility' here is meant to encompass technical knowledge, prudential knowledge, and moral knowledge. Kant's emphasis on the *pragmatic* character of his anthropology is partly to be explained by the popular intent of the lectures, which leads him to advertise the utility as well as the worldly character of the information he is providing.[16]

4. *Pragmatic as prudential.* Yet in naming his lectures 'pragmatic' Kant is also sometimes thinking of his theory of the three kinds of rational-

ity, contrasting the *pragmatic* with both the *technical* and the *moral* (see Chapter 2, §§ 3–5). That aligns the pragmatic with prudence – with a knowledge that furthers our happiness, especially through the use we make of other people (VA 25:469, 1210). In the lectures Kant's audience is often being told what will help them to use their own capacities to advance their ends, especially their well-being, and also what will help them make use of the characteristics of others for their own advantage (VA 7:312).

3.3. The structure of pragmatic anthropology Kant organizes the *Anthropology* into two main divisions: "Anthropological didactics" and "Anthropological characteristics." The first division is subdivided according to the three principal human faculties of mind: the cognitive faculty, the feeling of pleasure and displeasure, and the faculty of desire (VA 7:127, 230, 251; cf. KU 5:198). It is subtitled: "On the way of recognizing the inner as well as the outer of the human being" (VA 7:125). Since this division deals with human faculties, the title apparently regards capacities for cognition, feeling, and volition as the inner, contrasting this with their external effects or operations.

The second division deals with human *character* – that is, what human beings make of themselves through their own free volition. This is divided into four main sections, dealing respectively with the character of individuals, sexes, nations (*Völker*), and of the human species as a whole (VA 7:285). (The character of races is apparently an appendix to the discussion of nations (VA 7:320–321).)

The discussion begins with two features of the human being, which are to be distinguished from character. Temperament *(Temperament)* concerns the basis of an individual's *inclinations* insofar as it is related to bodily constitution (VA 7:285–291, 25:218, 426, 1156, 1370); the "individual nature" (*Naturell*) of human beings is constituted by their *mental powers* (*Gemüthskräfte*), which are the basis of their natural abilities or *talents* (VA 25:226, 436, 1156, 1368–1369).[17]

Kant contrasts both 'individual nature' and 'temperament' with the "way of thinking" (*Denkungsart*), which takes over this natural basis and transforms it through freedom into *character* (VA 7:29–295, 25:1156, 1384, 1530). Under this heading Kant considers first the expression of character through the immediate features of the face (VA 7:295–301). Then he goes on to treat the special propensities of the two sexes, of various (European) peoples, of the (four) races, and finally of the entire human species (VA 7:321–333). It is noteworthy that he

regards gender, national, and racial differences as matters of *character* —
that is, as the results of free agency when it takes over differences in physiological endowment or a geographically conditioned mode of life.
Such differences are never seen as mere consequences of a biological
determinism (which Kant apparently meant to be rejecting along with
Platner's "physiological" approach to anthropology). This also indicates
that Kant regards under the heading "effects of freedom" a good deal
that would not be considered "voluntary" in the legal or moral sense.

Kant is concerned instead with the *expression* of character (freedom)
in aspects of ourselves that are distinct from freedom. Anthropological
didactics is accordingly subtitled: "On the way of recognizing the inner
of the human being from the outer" (VA 7:283). Here the "inner"
might be taken as the appearances of inner sense, while the "outer"
would be its corporeal or physiological basis. The contents of Kant's discussion might give some credence to this interpretation, but Kant's more
frequent emphasis on capacities and the activities through which they
are developed compels us to understand the "inner" as an operation of
human freedom and the "outer" as its expression mediated by what is
empirically given in our bodies, psyches, and environment. The aim of
anthropological characteristics would then be to understand how freedom expresses itself through the medium of nature.

The pragmatic approach to anthropology serves to indicate the great
distance separating Kantian anthropology from traditional empirical
psychology and also from what Kant's metaphysical theory of freedom
and nature might lead us to expect. Kantian anthropology is anything
but a deterministic natural science of human behavior conceived exclusively from the standpoint of a detached observer. As the arguments
we examined in Chapter 5, § 4 should lead us to expect, Kantian anthropology *assumes* from the start that human beings are free (since even
as theoreticians we cannot avoid making this assumption about ourselves and about those with whom we propose to communicate). Kant's
anthropology also has little to do with an introspective science of inner
sense, since it concerns itself primarily with people's active use of their
faculties, and especially with their characters and tendencies in their in-
teractive relationships with one another. It recognizes no discontinuity
between the perspective of the observer and that of the agent. The pragmatic anthropologist is conceived not as a detached inquirer but as an
agent who must be capable of participating in the standpoint of other
agents and their freely chosen practical projects.

3.4. Natural teleology in pragmatic anthropology Another noteworthy feature of Kant's anthropology is its continual appeal to natural teleology in the understanding of human capacities and characteristics. Kant attempts teleological explanations, for example, of sleep and dreaming (VA 7:166, 175, 190), anger and weeping (VA 7:262–263), and even of the coquetry of married women (VA 7:305–306, 310). Such explanations, however quaint or whimsical they may seem to us, are fundamental to a *naturalistic* study of human nature as Kant conceives of it. "Naturalism" in the study of human beings is sometimes only an empty slogan, expressing the vague (though not entirely uncontroversial) idea that we are no more than natural creatures, or else the pious wish for an entirely satisfactory theory of ourselves from a natural scientific standpoint. Or it may be a form of "scientism" – an attempt to understand distinctively human capacities or activities through the methods and theories of some specific natural science (as Julien La Mettrie tried to do in the eighteenth century through mechanistic physics or as some have tried to do more recently through evolutionary biology or neuroscience).

For reasons discussed in Chapter 5, § 4, Kant is not usually considered a naturalist in good standing in the first sense of the term. But this common opinion may be too hasty. Kant, after all, was (in our sense of the terms) a natural scientist even before he was a philosopher. His first important intellectual contribution was a wholly naturalistic account of the origin of the solar system, and his theory of human history was cast from the same mold. It is "naturalistic" also in the second (or "scientistic") sense, in that it does attempt to understand humanity as a biological species in the same way other animals are to be understood. For historical reasons, however (chiefly consequent on the Darwinian revolution), it is all too easy for us to misunderstand Kantian biology and even easier for us to mislead ourselves about the extent to which Kant's approach to anthropology and history might still be available to us and how we ought to view it in order to appropriate it. The remainder of this chapter will attempt to shed light on these matters.

4. Human history as a natural phenomenon

The aspect of Kant's anthropology that is best worked out methodologically is his philosophy of history.[18] Those who do not think of Kant as a significant philosopher of history, or even think of his philosophy as "ahistorical," have a profoundly false image of the critical philosophy. (The historical self-consciousness of Kant's project in the *Critique of pure reason* is evident in both Prefaces, where Kant locates what he is doing in the history of metaphysics (A vii–xiv, B vii–xxxvii).) Kant's historical self-consciousness belongs to him as a philosopher of the Enlightenment, the first historically self-conscious age, and the age whose (rationalistic, cosmopolitan, progressive) historical consciousness is still the definitive model for all sound historical self-consciousness.

Kant's philosophy of history is "naturalistic" in that he treats history as a branch of *biology*. For Kant, however, biology can never be a strict science, because it deals with a realm of objects whose comprehensibility comes not from their conformity to mechanistic laws but to the applicability to them of principles of reflective judgment which are only regulative in character. Kant's philosophy of history is guided by a philosophical idea that understands the historical change as the development of the natural predispositions of the human race as a living species. To say that the study of history is to be guided by an 'idea' is to say that we approach history using an *a priori* concept of what would make the course of human events maximally intelligible to us and look for ways in which history corresponds to this idea. We cannot count on finding such a correspondence in any specific instance, but because in general Kant thinks reason can understand objects only by approaching them with a self-devised plan (KrV Bxiii–xiv), the idea that guides our inquiry into history will be the measure of the degree to which it will ever be intelligible to us at all.

4.1. The idea toward a universal history Although I will argue that Kant's philosophy of history is indispensable for an understanding of his ethical thought, his principal writings on the subject are all brief essays, apparently the products of contingent literary occasion. On February 1, 1784 the *Gotha Learned Papers* printed a short article by Kant's colleague and follower Johann Schultz,[19] containing this intriguing remark:

> A favorite idea of Professor Kant is that the final end of the human race is the attainment of the most perfect political constitution, and he wishes that a philosophical historiographer would undertake to provide us in this respect with a history of humanity, and to show how far humanity has approached this final end in different ages, or how far removed it has been from it, and what is still to be done for its attainment. (Ak 8:468)[20]

In November of the same year, Kant made good on Schultz's hint by publishing in the *Berlin Monthly* a short essay, *Idea toward a universal his-*

tory with a cosmopolitan aim in which he explained more fully the sort of history he had in mind.

The *idea* on which Kant proposes to base the study of history is constructed on the basis of the regulative maxims of reason, which Kant thinks should be followed in the theoretical investigation of living organisms. Yet in the course of such an investigation, as applied to the human species, Kant argues for the importance of another idea, that of a perfectly just political constitution, which (he argues) will turn out to play a vital role in giving direction to the historical progress of the human race as a living species (I 8:23).

Kant thinks it is very difficult to discern a rational meaning in human actions, not only our individual actions but even more human actions considered collectively and on a large scale. He takes the causes of our acts often to be hidden from us. Even when we think we understand what individuals do, the collective result of their actions appears to have no regularity or meaning. People seldom project any collective aim over time, and still less often do they attain any such aim. Kant despairs of ever understanding the broad panorama of human history in terms of the conscious aims of individuals. The only hope is that when considered *on a large scale* (i.e., collectively) history may be able to understand them as exhibiting the development of the natural predispositions of the species as a whole.

Marriages, births, and deaths result from the free actions of individuals and appear to occur entirely fortuitously. "And yet the annual statistics for them in large countries prove that they are just as subject to constant natural laws as are changes in the weather" (I 8:17). Weather is also beyond our power to predict on the basis of mechanistic physical laws applied to the molecules of atmospheric or terrestrial matter, yet it follows general regularities when considered on a large scale, which can be perceived in the way that the weather sustains geographical and biological features of the earth (such as rivers and vegetation). Kant thinks our only hope for understanding human history is to discern similar macro-level regularities in the behavior of human beings considered as a biological species. In effect, he holds that the repudiation of what has come to be known as 'methodological individualism' is a necessary prerequisite for any rational understanding of history (see Chapter 7, § 1).

Kant thinks the only way to conceive of the relevant natural regularities in history is *teleologically*. We must form the concept of an *end* served by the events of history and unify our cognition of these events by understanding the way that they contribute to it. As we have already seen, no such end is consciously pursued by human individuals. On the contrary, the reason we need to form the concept of such an end is precisely that individuals, and even entire nations, consciously set themselves vastly different – often mutually opposed – ends. The problem is that just as human beings do not follow instinct, so they also do not act according to a common plan, "like rational citizens of the world" (or members of a realm of ends). We therefore must try to understand them as guided by an "aim of nature" (*Naturabsicht*) on behalf of which they are working collectively even though individually "they would scarcely care about it if it were made known to them" (I 8:17).

As we might expect from Schultz's report, in the *Idea toward a universal history* this aim turns out to be a perfect political constitution administering legal justice. Yet we totally misunderstand Kant's methodology if we think he means that philosophical historians should simply postulate some aim of history that appeals to them (perhaps on moral grounds) and then try to understand history as working toward it. To the extent that Kant's idea plays a role in his practical anthropology, it would involve a vicious circularity to base a conception of human history on the ends of morality. For as we saw above, the ends of morality are first to be determined by applying the principle of morality to practical anthropology. So at this stage of inquiry they are not yet available to anthropological research.

This need not prevent Kant from appealing, as he does at several points, to our practical strivings toward these ends to justify the *hope* that we will make progress toward them in history (TP 8:307–313, EF 8:365, SF 7:83–84). Even in the *Idea toward a universal history* itself, it does not prevent Kant from observing that there is a *convergence* between the theoretical idea of history and a "*justification* of nature – or better of *providence*" which is bound up with our morally inspired hopes (I 8:30).[21] These hopes, however, can receive their content only from an understanding of human nature which depends on empirical investigations guided by a *theoretical* idea.

4.2. Predispositions and their development Kant starts by considering human beings simply as a species of natural creatures. He applies to the human species a general principle that has both wide-ranging empirical confirmation and a fundamental place in teleological sciences of nature:

All the natural predispositions of a creature are someday determined to
be developed completely and suitably to their end. In all animals this is
confirmed by external as well as internal or anatomical examination. An
organ which is not to be used, or an arrangement which does not attain
its end, is a contradiction in the teleological theory of nature. (I 8:18)

A "predisposition" (*Anlage*) is a "ground for a determinate development" – that is, a feature of a living thing's nature that accounts for its
developing in a certain way. Kant calls such a basic teleological feature
of an organism a "germ" (*Kern*) when it determines the development
only of a particular part or organ; but a "predisposition" when it is a
global feature of the organism, determining the relationships between
its parts, hence its organic form as a whole (RM 2:434). The principle
from which Kant begins therefore says that in studying any organism we
should suppose that all such predispositions will sooner or later reach
their full development and that nature has suited the organism to its
environment so that this will be the case. (His methodological reasons
for accepting this principle will be discussed below in § 5.)

Rational creatures, however, are different from other living things,
whose predispositions determine them through instinct to a single determinate mode of life. Reason is the capacity to set one's own ends and
to choose or even invent means to them, making possible a self-devised
mode of life, which can be taken over and further modified by other
beings of the same species. The natural predispositions of other animals – to find food, escape predators, construct dwellings, and so forth –
are fully exhibited within the lifetime of a single normal specimen (or, if
reproduction and the rearing of young is included, a pair of specimens). In the case of human predispositions, however, no single human
being, not even any group of people, nor even all human beings living
at any given time or up to any given time, will ever fully exhibit all the
rational capacities of the human species. This is the feature of human
beings Rousseau calls 'perfectibility'. As Kant does after him, Rousseau
holds it responsible for what raises the human species above the rest of
nature, as well as for all the moral evils, and the greater part of the miseries, which afflict human beings (MA 8:116–118; Rousseau, *Discourse
on the origin of inequality*, 3:142–144).

Thus the predispositions of a rational species must take a distinctive
form: "Those natural predispositions which aim at the use of reason are
fully developed in the species only, and not in the individual" (I 8:18).
Rational capacities for Kant are *learned* capacities, acquired through

interaction (and especially communication) with other human beings, and subject to historical development by later generations. Hence rational capacities are historical in their mode of acquisition and also essentially open-ended in their content. "Reason knows no bounds to its projects"; by means of "experiments, practice, and instruction, it progresses from one stage of insight to the next" (I 8:18–19). Perfectibility is also the trait which makes the human species essentially *historical.* As Kant asserts in his review of Herder, "No single member of all the generations of the human race, but only the species, attains its destiny completely" (RH 8:65).[22]

When we seek for natural purposiveness in the human species, we must look not only at the structure and development of individual specimens but at the development and perpetuation of human capacities through reason and historical tradition. We must try to understand how nature has provided for people to develop capacities that are mainly of use to *other* (later) members of the species; and we should consider the effect of social arrangements on people's ability to transmit and further develop their learned capacities over long periods of time.

4.3. Human discontent   Kant notes two remarkable facts about human life that may look counter-purposive at first, but can be explained teleologically when considered from a social and historical standpoint: first, the role of individual *discontent* in fulfilling nature's purposes, and second, the pervasive fact of *social antagonism.*

> Nature has willed that the human being should produce entirely out of himself everything that goes beyond the mechanical arrangement of his animal existence, and should participate in no other happiness or perfection but what he has created for himself without instinct and through his own reason. (I 8:19)

Human beings do not have the bull's horns, the lion's claws, the dog's teeth. But they do have a remarkable ability to adapt themselves to different environments and to live under a variety of conditions. They must themselves make the choice of how they want to live and then develop for themselves the skills required to implement this choice. And they find the means to do this chiefly by cooperating and communicating with one another.

The natural conditions of this sociability, however, are also conditions of discontent and conflict. "It is as if [nature] had cared more about [the human being's] rational *self-esteem* than his being well off" (I 8:20).

Nature has not arranged human life so that people will be happy; on the contrary, "nature does not seem to have been concerned with seeing to it that the human being should live agreeably" (I 8:20). In fact, nature has arranged that we should forever be discontented and uses our discontent to spur us on to the development of new capacities.

4.4. Unsociable sociability The connection of this discontent with the human concern about self-esteem is apparent in human social relations. In society, people show a strong sense of comparative self-worth. Each individual wants to have his own way and to achieve a position of superiority over all others. This makes human social life fundamentally a struggle, each individual tending to resist the efforts and frustrate the ends of every other. "Yet it is this resistance which awakens all the powers of the human being, making him overcome his propensity to laziness; and it drives him, by means of the mania for honor, domination, or property, to seek status among his fellows, whom he cannot *stand*, but also cannot stand to *leave alone*" (I 8:21). It is above all this *social* discontent, arising from self-esteem and mutual hostility, which nature has apparently used to develop the natural capacities of human beings. People are thus placed in a condition simultaneously of mutual interdependence and mutual hostility.

The argument of *Idea toward a universal history* is based on the ambivalence of social conflict as a device for developing the predispositions of the species. Discontent and competitiveness provoke us to develop our capacities but only as long as there is sufficient order and peace in society. As human culture grows, the degree of peace and order required for further progress also tends to increase, for these capacities themselves involve increasing interdependence and cooperation, and they are increasingly vulnerable to destruction by violent human conflict. This means that as culture progresses, human reason is challenged to devise ways of creating a well-ordered society in which people's antagonistic tendencies can be kept in check. "The means nature employs to bring about the development of all [human] predispositions is the *antagonism* [of human beings] in society, insofar as this antagonism is in the end the cause of a lawful order in it" (I 8:20).

Nature's devices for developing our rational predispositions thus set us a problem, which nature leaves to human reason to solve: "The greatest problem for the human species, the solution of which nature compels him to seek, is that of attaining a *civil society* which can administer justice universally" (I 8:22). The same antagonism that spurs human beings to develop their natural predispositions also makes it necessary for them to create a legal order among themselves, not only to make life tolerable but even, after a certain point, to make it possible for their rational capacities to develop further. Nature's purposive arrangements for the development of our predispositions will therefore reach an impasse unless human beings themselves find a way of controlling their mutual antagonism. This makes the problem of finding a just civil constitution the "last and most difficult problem to be solved by the human race" (I 8:23).

Solving this problem turns out to involve the further difficulty of attaining stable and lawful relations between states. For no state can achieve internal justice as long as it is oriented toward constant preparation for war, owing to "the taxing and neverending accumulation of armaments, and the want which any state even in peacetime must suffer internally" (I 8:24). War is thus the means through which nature forces the human species "to make the first inadequate and tentative attempts; and finally, after devastations, revolutions, and even complete exhaustion, she brings them to that which reason could have told them at the beginning, . . . to advance from the lawless condition of savages into a federation of nations" (I 8:24). This is the route by which Kant finally reaches his "favorite idea": "One can regard the history of the human race as a whole as the completion of a hidden plan of nature, in order to bring about an internally perfect state constitution – and to this end also an externally perfect one – as the sole condition in which it can develop all the predispositions of humanity" (I 8:27).

The attempt to work out a philosophical history of humanity on the basis of that goal, he concludes, may even be seen as furthering nature's purpose itself (I 8:29). Notice that Kant does *not* argue on moral (or other) grounds that we should set a perfect civil constitution as our goal, and then infer that we should ascribe the goal to nature, viewing human history as the process of its realization. (As we mentioned earlier, this would render his procedure viciously circular.) The starting point of his inquiry is a purely *theoretical* proposition used in judging natural teleology: that nature arranges for the predispositions of every species to be fully developed. In light of this principle, Kant uses general facts about what our predispositions are and how they develop in order to reach conclusions about nature's means for developing them, and what would have to be done by human beings in order to fulfill nature's purposes. The teleology in Kant's philosophy of history is not a *moral* teleology, supporting a belief in nature's purposes from a practical standpoint. On the contrary, the only connection he draws between our goals and nature's operates in exactly the *opposite* direction: The problem of a civil constitution is one set for us *by nature*. The ends of morality are to be devised subsequently, with this natural end as something given.

Nor is this derivation based on the general thesis (articulated in various forms in the ancient world by the Stoics, Cynics, Skeptics, and Epicureans and analogously in Kant's own century by Rousseau, Swift, Hume, and Helvetius) that we should arrange our lives "according to nature" by adopting nature's ends as our own. Thus Kant holds *neither* that morality should ascribe its purposes to nature *nor* that nature's purposes are always ends of morality. He does believe that the attainment of a just civil constitution harmonizes with moral ends. But this harmony plays a role *neither* in his argument for a just civil condition as a natural purpose *nor* in his reasoning that such a constitution is an end of human reason. In Kant's philosophy of history, some arrangements of natural teleology (such as the ends of internal justice in states and external peace between states) are also ends of morality, while other forms of natural purposiveness (such as human discontent and social antagonism) work directly contrary to the ends of morality. The theoretical argument that something is an end of nature is always distinct from the practical argument that it is an end of reason or morality (though the latter argument *sometimes* makes use of the former).

5. Natural teleology

Kant's frequent references, in both his anthropological writings and *Idea toward a universal history*, to nature's purposes, aims, plans, and intentions are bound to arouse our curiosity, even our suspicion. Kant was interested in natural teleology at least since his essay *The only possible ground of proof for a demonstration of God's existence* (1763). But he was not to give it definitive treatment until the *Critique of the power of judgment* (1790). He firmly believes in the modern scientific conception of nature as matter governed by mechanistic causal laws and from very early on was deeply skeptical of any attempt to employ conceptions of divine design or providential purpose in the theoretical cognition of nature.

This poses a serious theoretical problem because Kant does not think that biological phenomena can be understood entirely in mechanistic terms. He holds that a theoretical approach to nature employing final causation must supplement a causal-mechanistic account if we are to provide a theoretical account of nature that approaches the ideas of coherence and systematicity, which ought to guide reason's inquiry. In a book on Kant's ethical thought we cannot give this topic a thorough treatment. But we cannot ignore it either, if, as I am arguing here, Kantian ethics cannot be understood without Kantian anthropology, and Kantian anthropology makes essential use of a teleological conception of nature.

5.1. Teleology as a regulative principle   In the first Critique, natural purposiveness is treated as part of reason's "regulative" use of ideas (specifically, the idea of God). If we view nature as having been produced by a supreme intelligence ordering things in accordance with wise intentions, then we will look for the kinds of unity in experience that reason demands. The worst that can happen is that we fail to find what we are looking for in particular cases, but even this does not discredit the search, which is prescribed to us by the nature of our reason itself (KrV A685–688/B712–716). In the *Critique of the power of judgment*, Kant redescribes the role of teleology in the investigation of nature, but it is still crucial to natural science, perhaps even more so than before. The search for purposes is now assigned not to the faculty of reason but to judgment, the faculty that relates universal concepts to their particular instances. More specifically, it is assigned to *reflective* judgment, the capacity to find an appropriate universal concept to fit a given particular (as distinguished from *determining* judgment, which applies already given concepts to particulars) (KU 5:179).

For example, as Kant had already pointed out in the first Critique, we can discover universal generalizations in experience (such as causal laws) only if our judgment can search for suitable universals in terms of which to frame empirical hypotheses; in this search, it must be guided by a "problematic concept" of the universal it is looking for, as "a mere idea" (KrV A646–647/B674–675). More generally, he thinks that reason supplies some determinate general principles we use in classifying objects: these are the "law of homogeneity" (different natural kinds may always be brought under higher kinds or genera, in virtue of some common feature), the "law of specification" (every natural kind may be further specified in terms of differences, which create subclasses), and the "law of affinity" or "continuity" (the transition between different kinds is always gradual, with no "gaps" or "leaps") (KrV A651–662/B679–690; cf. KU 5:182).

5.2. *Teleology and reflective judgment*   In the *Critique of the power of judgment*, however, Kant insists that our faculty of judgment can neither prescribe to nature the concepts we need in order to frame systematic theories about it nor take these concepts from somewhere else. The former alternative is ruled out because the concepts are empirical; the latter is ruled out because it would presuppose that we already have an adequate theory that judgment needs only to apply; but then we would be dealing with a problem for determining rather than reflective judgment. From this Kant infers that reflective judgment itself must contain an *a priori* principle guiding its search for the right sort of *empirical* concepts (KU 5:180). The third Critique is chiefly interested in those concepts which provide a unity to experience going beyond that supplied by the causal laws required (as Kant argued in the Second Analogy) for events in experience to have an objective temporal order (KrV A189–211/B232–256). However, because our understanding is discursive, combining sensible data given independently of it, causal laws leave much of the content of experience contingent, confronting us with an indeterminate variety of "empirical laws" (KU 5:405–410). Thus in reason's striving for systematic unity in experience, it needs a way of conceptualizing the causally contingent elements of experience.

"The power of judgment must assume as an *a priori* principle for its own use that what to human insight is contingent in the particular (empirical) laws of nature does nevertheless contain a law-governed unity, unfathomable but still conceivable by us" (KU 5:183). Because this unity is to be conceivable by us, the particular empirical laws, "must, as regards what the universal laws have left undetermined in them, be viewed in terms of such a unity as would have been given by an understanding (even though not ours) so as to assist our cognitive powers by making possible a system of experience" (KU 5:180). The idea of a unity given by an understanding, however, is that of an *end* or purpose (*Zweck*). Or again, an end is the representation of an object which is the ground of the object's actuality (KU 5:180). Kant thus infers that "the principle of the formal purposiveness of nature must be assumed by us as a transcendental principle of judgment" (KU 5:181).

5.3. *Natural and intentional teleology*   In the case of the *intentional* purposiveness involved in the faculty of desire of a rational being, this representation is the thought in the mind of that being, determining the being's powers to produce the object. In the case of natural purposiveness, however, the representation of the object is a concept in the under-standing of the rational *inquirer,* such that it increases the intelligibility of nature to regard the object as if this concept were the ground of its actuality. Kant is emphatic that we are not entitled to ascribe the pur-posiveness we find in nature to any *intention,* for example God's, which is supposed to produce the objects according to his representations of them. Kant favors the expression *Naturzweck* (end or purpose of *nature*) precisely because "no one would attribute an intention to lifeless mat-ter" (KU 5:383). When he considers the hypotheses that might be ad-vanced with the further aim of explaining natural purposiveness, Kant regards the theistic hypothesis as the closest to being satisfactory (KU 5:394–395). But he insists that no such explanation can ever re-ally be satisfactory. This is first because we cannot exclude the possibil-ity that natural purposiveness is merely a result of the mechanism of na-ture (KU 5:395), and second, more fundamentally, because the entire idea of natural purposiveness always has only regulative use in organiz-ing our cognitions; it is misunderstood if viewed as an explanatory hypothesis of any kind, or even as an object inviting such hypotheses (KU 5:395–397).

5.4. The idea of an organized being There are at least two types of pur-posiveness in nature, or two ways in which the concept of a natural end can be employed in our attempts to comprehend order in nature. The first could be called *general* or *taxonomic* purposiveness. It involves the heuristic assumption that beings in nature can be classified according to a system of concepts that satisfy the ideas of parsimony and continuity which reason brings to nature (KU 5:182–186; cf. Ak 20:211–216). The second concept of purposiveness could be called *special* or *organic.* It is involved in the structure and functioning of certain beings we find in nature, those that correspond to the idea of an *organized being.* The ra-tional principle for judging the purposiveness of such beings, accord-ing to Kant, "which is also the definition of organized beings," is the fol-lowing *principle of natural teleology*:

    NT: *An organized product of nature is one in which everything is an end and reciprocally also a means*" (KU 5:376). This involves the assump-tion: "Nothing in such a being is in vain (*umsonst*)" (KU 5:376, 379, 437). "Regarding [living beings], reason must assume as a neces-sary principle that no organ, no faculty, nothing superfluous, or disproportionate to its use, hence nothing purposeless is to be encountered, but rather that everything is to be judged as precisely suitable to its function." (KrV B425)

The idea of an organized being is thus a theoretical idea, a concept that *maximizes* intelligibility. To judge *teleologically* concerning the life processes of a plant or animal is to investigate it on the heuristic hypothesis that it is an organized being in this sense. This tells us what to *look for* in experience but does not guarantee that we will find it, since the form of a natural purpose "is, as far as reason is concerned, *contingent* as regards empirical laws" (KU 5:370). Kant does not think that we will ever *find* the maximal reciprocal relations of means and end between the parts of any living thing. But he holds that the *assumption* of NT is *always beneficial* to inquiry (because it tells us how to maximize the sort of intelligibility in the object that our discursive understanding is capable of comprehending) and *never harmful* to it (because the worst that can happen is that we merely fail to find the maximal intelligibility we are looking for).

Hence even when NT leads us to find something that makes a living thing more intelligible to us, Kant thinks we cannot assert definitively that we have found an "organized being" or "natural end"; in fact, he denies that we can ever establish even the *real possibility* of a natural being that is grounded on its concept (KU 5:395–396). There are at least three reasons for this. First, we cannot show about the organism in question that it corresponds to the definition of an organized being, because we can never hope to show it actually to be true of it that in its life processes nothing is in vain. The maxim NT (or: "Nothing in vain") holds only regulatively (or for heuristic purposes) in our reflective judging; it never attains the status of a constitutive principle telling us how the organism is constituted. Hence "even experience cannot prove that there actually are [natural] ends" (KU 5:359). Second, we can never hope to show, even of those arrangements in the organism that we comprehend under the principle of purposiveness, that they could not be explained entirely as a result of mechanical causality (KU 5:395). The most we can say here is that our understanding is such that judging the thing as a natural end is the best way for us to maximize its comprehensibility (KU 5:405–410). Finally, in consequence of this second point, we can never establish that the object really is (causally) grounded on a representation of it – such as an idea of it in the mind of a divine artificer. All we can say, once again, is that the intelligibility of the thing *to us* is maximized if we regard it as if its actuality were somehow grounded on the concept *we* form of it when we *judge* its processes as falling under the idea of an organized being.

5.5. Maxims of teleological judgment   Because the concept of a natural end is one of whose very possibility we can never have determinate cognition, natural teleology can never belong to a *science* of nature (*Naturwissenschaft*). It belongs to no *doctrine of nature* (*Naturlehre*). It forms an indispensable part of our *investigation* of nature, yet only as it pertains to the *critique* of our cognitive power of judgment (KU 5:417). Teleological judgment investigates nature, and especially living organisms, in light of a set of heuristic maxims, which in the first Critique are called "maxims of reason" (KrV A666/B694). These maxims will hold of the objects under investigation to the extent that these objects instantiate the concept of a natural end or organized being. We can never know the precise extent to which living things actually do instantiate this concept, but it is in the interest of our reason as theoretical inquirers to *assume* at every point that they do. The heuristic maxims in question are all corollaries of NT or versions of the principle "nothing in vain" which governs teleological judgment.

One such maxim of teleological judgment is the principle NT1, employed in Kant's argument about suicide in the Second Section of the *Groundwork* (see Chapter 3, § 3.2):

> **NT1**:   If *F* is a feeling whose naturally purposive function is to bring about *P*, then it would be self-contradictory to suppose a system of nature one of whose laws is that under certain circumstances *F* systematically produces the contrary of *P*.

One reason why readers of the *Groundwork* question Kant's argument about suicide is that they find NT1 dubious. But if we understand it in the context of Kant's theory of reflective teleological judgment, we can see why he found such a principle compelling. He thinks that for heuristic reasons we would not count anything as the natural function of a feeling if under any circumstances it tended to bring about the contrary of its natural end according to a law of nature. To do so, in fact, would be to misapply the concept of a natural function, since the point of that concept is to maximize the intelligibility of what happens regularly or systematically by understanding it as the result of natural purposiveness.

A second teleological maxim, found also in the *Groundwork,* is:

NT2: "In the natural constitution of an organized being, . . . we assume as a principle that there will be found in it no instrument for some end other than what is also most appropriate to that end and best adapted to it." (G 4:395, cf. 4:398)

Once again, readers of the *Groundwork* often take this heuristic maxim for a dogmatic empirical claim, and therefore often question or deny its truth on empirical grounds.[23] However, once we understand the point of such a maxim in Kant's theory of teleological judgment, we see that in his view it would be counterproductive to rational inquiry to look for empirical counterexamples to it and methodologically wrongheaded to rest content with them even if we think we have found them. For under the principle of teleological judgment, it belongs to the concept of something as an organ O with natural function F that it fulfills F to the maximal degree. If we were to find that O does not do so under our present concept of F, then what we ought to do is modify our concept of F, framing a new concept F' such that O *is* best adapted to fulfilling F'.

This discussion should put in perspective a third heuristic maxim, the one through which we apply the principle of purposiveness to the predispositions of organisms. This is, of course, the fundamental one appealed to in Kant's *Idea toward a universal history*:

NT3: "Nature arranges things so that eventually all the natural predispositions of an organism are fully developed." (I 8:18)

Here, too, we would misunderstand the status of the maxim if we set about looking for empirical counterexamples to it. For the point is that we should look at the growth process of every organism as consisting in the development of predispositions, which thus constitute part of the concept of the organism which teleological judgment regards as the ground of its actuality. We should not count anything as a predisposition in a given species unless it is something that normally gets fully developed in the life of that species.

Kant's philosophy of history clearly involves an *extension* of the concept of a predisposition, since it applies this concept to capacities that are not given in the species through instinct but are devised by reason and then transmitted from one generation of human beings to the next. But to extend it in this way is inseparable from Kant's attempt to understand *naturalistically* the history of free and rational beings.

5.6. Teleological judgment and the theory of natural selection   The biological method Kant employs in theorizing about history was rendered obsolete sixty years later by the Darwinian theory of evolution by natural selection. But it is not at all clear how this fact should bear on our assessment of Kant's philosophy of history. For although Kant's theory of teleological judgment was evidently devised to deal with the study of living organisms and then extended to human history, its fundamental epistemic motivation was not based on anything peculiar to problems of biology, and this motivation in relation to the philosophy of history survives the theoretical revolution through which the theory has ceased to be either necessary or useful in the general study of living things. Or so I will contend.

It now always raises eyebrows when people read in the *Critique of the power of judgment*:

> We may boldly assert that it is absurd for human beings ever to attempt [an explanation of organic nature in terms of mechanical principles], or to hope that perhaps someday another Newton might arise who would explain to us in terms of natural laws unordered by any intention, how even a mere blade of grass is produced. (KU 5:400; cf. 5:378, 409, 415)

No one writing after Darwin would ever make such a statement. If we look closely, however, we must acknowledge that Kant's main contention here is still literally correct: No one *has* produced a causal explanation of the production of any individual blade of grass (or any other such specific biological phenomenon) purely in terms of the laws of mechanistic physics as it existed in the seventeenth and eighteenth centuries; nor is it likely that they ever will. Evolutionary biology, along with modern genetics and biophysics, certainly makes intelligible how animals and plants have arisen purely through the operations of matter as we understand it in accordance with physical laws (as we now understand them), apart from any order imposed on them by any intention. But they do not do so by directly producing a mechanistic explanation of the origin of a blade of grass, still less by relying solely on the physics of Kant's age.

Nor does modern evolutionary theory directly call into question the theoretical rationale for the kind of teleological investigation of organisms Kant proposes. Kant was *not* claiming that we ought to explain biological phenomena through divine intentions (or any others). He thought the existence of natural ends will always be *inexplicable* by us (whether naturally or supernaturally) and that our inquiry into them must accept this fundamental limitation as a starting point. Since Kant's methodology of teleological judgment assumes the inexplicability of natural ends, it is also entitled to suppose that the maxims of teleological judgment will always be valid, since they are dictated solely by general heuristic considerations. Their use therefore cannot be constrained by detailed knowledge of the nature of the processes whose investigation they are supposed to guide. It is on precisely this point that evolutionary theory proves Kant wrong.

The theory of evolution by natural selection proposes a general type of naturalistic explanation for the existence of living organisms. It thereby calls into question the kind of considerations that lead Kant to recommend the teleological investigation of nature, and thereby enables us to find empirical reasons for questioning maxims of judgment that cannot be empirically questioned as long as the ground for them is not empirical. In short, it gives us empirical grounds for holding that the living organisms around us *do not* instantiate the regulative idea of an organized being, and that they sometimes deviate from this idea in determinate ways that are both empirically identifiable and empirically explicable.

Stephen Jay Gould has argued at length, citing phenomena as varied as the nectar cups of orchids and the thumb of the panda, that it is one of the strengths of evolutionary theory that some of these arrangements are precisely *not* as we would expect them to be if they had been designed from scratch by a first-rate engineer. They seem instead to be jerry-built constructions contrived by an opportunistic tinkerer using a limited set of tools and sometimes cleverly making something perform a function for which it looks as if it had not originally been intended.[24] To understand the evolution of an organ, therefore, is sometimes to see precisely why it is *not* perfectly adapted to its function.

This is why we are so quick to look for exceptions to NT3 when Kant uses it in the First Section of the *Groundwork* (thereby misunderstanding the status it had for him). The same might be true of NT1: Understanding how a feeling developed through natural selection might make it quite intelligible that under changed circumstances it systematically produces a contrary result from the one it was originally its function to produce. Likewise, evolutionary theory might lead us to expect that organisms that evolve in one environment, with a corresponding survival strategy, might have to find new ways of surviving under quite different circumstances. In such cases, the "predispositions" adapted to the earlier environment might tend to atrophy, while those needed for the new survival strategy might look like they are just barely up to the task and not fully developed. That would call NT3 into question, and with it the biological ground of Kant's philosophy of history.

Yet to criticize Kant's general theory of teleological judgment in this way is still to misunderstand it in at least two important ways. First, it treats this theory as if it were an empirical theory, like the theory of evolution. Second, it views it exclusively as a theory about biological organisms. In fact, however, Kant holds that the need to employ teleological concepts in the study of nature arises *a priori* from our need to employ our own concepts regulatively in the enterprise of finding maximal systematicity in nature (KU §§ 75–78, 5:397–415). This enterprise is necessitated by the fact that our understanding does not produce the data of cognition, but instead unifies data given independently in intuition, and so in addition to inquiring after the lawfulness constituting the conditions of any possible experience, we must attempt to discover a lawfulness that is contingent in respect of those conditions. The latter lawfulness corresponds to the general conception of an 'end' (*Zweck*), as a "representation which makes its own object possible": hence "the lawfulness of the contingent is called purposiveness" (KU 5:404). But here the representation is present solely in the mind of the investigator, who uses it regulatively to conceptualize (though *never to explain*) an order found in nature that exceeds the order grasped through the concept of a mechanistic cause.

This means that while living organisms may *suggest* to us the rational project of judging nature purposively, that theoretical project does not depend on the empircal fact that large numbers of something like organized beings are found in our experience in the form of living things. On the contrary, Kant's general *a priori* argument is that we should expect to deal purposively with any domain of nature that is characterized by contingency and incapable of integration into explanations on the basis of the mechanism of nature. The use of the concept of a natural end is simply the way our cognitive faculties must proceed in seeking the "lawfulness of the contingent." Kant thought biology was such a domain, and in his time that thought was completely justified. But the theory of evolution has since shown us that it is wrong.

Human history is above all a domain characterized by contingency, in which, however, our reason requires that we seek for some lawful order. Thus Kantian natural purposiveness is still well suited to the study of history, even if not to biology. Kant's philosophy of history is based on NT3, treating as "predispositions" all the capacities human beings invent in the course of adapting to different natural environments, and even of devising new forms of social cooperation and cultural expression. Further, Kant takes these predispositions to be indefinitely perfectible, so that human beings have an open-ended capacity to acquire new skills and devise new and different modes of life.

It is not clear that evolutionary biology can explain this feature of human capacities, nor is it even evident that evolutionary considerations by themselves would lead us to expect human beings to be endlessly inventive in the way we find them to be. Indeed, much of the (pseudo-)science that has been undertaken under the names of "social Darwinism" and "sociobiology" has even drawn *pessimistic* (and socially conservative) conclusions about the capacity of human beings to alter their modes of life, especially their social relationships. Hence those sympathetic to NT3, in the anthropological form of humanity's indefinite perfectibility, have more often than not taken the position that, contrary to the speculations of sociobiologists, biological evolution cannot be responsibly used either to explain the course human history has taken or to set limits to what the human species might accomplish in history.[25] Philosophers and evolutionary biologists still attempt to speculate about the biological function of complex systems of rational thought, feeling, and social interaction, and to draw philosophical conclusions about the nature of ethical norms and concepts on the basis of such speculations. Their oversimplified and dismissive reductions of subtle ethical concepts to crude biological constructs are the obvious symptoms of a misguided and excessive scientistic zeal that should expect to encounter deep skepticism from reasonable people.[26]

Perhaps someday there will be a credible theory of human psychology, sociology, and even history based on human evolution by natural selection. But since any such theory will have to be empirical, we have no *a priori* reason for thinking that such a project will ever succeed. Until it does, Kant's reasons for applying a theory of teleological judgment to this domain of inquiry remain entirely reasonable. This is why the Kantian philosophical approach to history – including the more famous versions it later assumed in his direct followers, namely Hegel and Marx – still remains viable even after the Kantian approach to biology has long since been discredited by the theory of evolution.[27]

THE HISTORY OF HUMAN NATURE

1. Herder vs. Kant

Kant became interested in the philosophy of history at about the time he first articulated his mature moral philosophy in the *Groundwork*. It is reasonable to conjecture that this is no mere coincidence. As we have already seen, some of the arguments of the *Groundwork*, especially toward the beginning of both the First and Second Sections, depend significantly on Kant's theory of human nature and history. More generally, the *Groundwork* articulates a moral philosophy suited to Kant's philosophy of history and to the time in history in which he saw himself as living.

The rise in Kant's interests in both history and moral philosophy also occurred at the same time he was becoming critically engaged with the highly original historical reflections of his former student Johann Gottfried Herder (1744–1803). Herder had studied with Kant between 1762 and 1765, but while in Königsberg he had also come under the influence of Kant's eccentric friend Johann Georg Hamann (1730–1788). Hamann's views on reason, religion, science, and society were very much at odds with those of the Enlightenment. Herder subsequently rose to prominence as a writer on a wide variety of topics and as a critic of Enlightenment thought, especially its views of society and history. His greatest work, *Ideas for the philosophy of history of humanity*, was published in several volumes beginning in 1784.[1]

Kant reviewed the first two volumes of the *Ideas* for the *Allgemeine Literaturzeitung* (RH 8:45–46) between January and November of 1785, but then declined to review further volumes on the ground that he was too busy working on the *Critique of the power of judgment* (Ak 10:490). The third Critique itself, however, with its attempt to distinguish critical uses of teleological judgment in nature from illegitimately metaphysical ones, can profitably be read as a systematic reply to Herder.[2] Kant also continued his critical discussion of Herder's thoughts early in 1786 with a satirical essay *Conjectural beginning of human history*. Though it never mentions Herder by name, the *Conjectural beginning* obviously refers to Book 10, Chapters 5–7 of Herder's *Ideas*.

1.1. Herder on the beginnings of human history   In Book 4 of the *Ideas*, Herder ascribes all of humanity's characteristic powers and dispositions to the erect posture of human beings (Herder, *Ideas* 13:129–150). At the same time, Herder treats all the physical powers of human beings as expressions of *spiritual* forces – divine living powers continuously at work in the natural world, displaying diverse development under different environmental conditions (Herder, *Ideas* 13:170–175). In Book 10, Herder applies this view to human origins through an imaginative interpretation of the Mosaic history in the book of *Genesis*. Kant's satire involves using the same sacred texts, but in wry and sometimes irreverent ways, to tell an alternative story about the early history of our species.

Both Kant and Herder conceive human nature fundamentally in terms of the historical process through which the capacities of the human species are developed. Their opposing ways of employing this idea are derived from different strands in the complex social thought of Rousseau. The controversy between Kant and Herder represents one of the earliest discussions of a set of fundamental issues about humanity and society first raised in the Enlightenment that have been central to thinking about modernity during the last two centuries.

History for Herder is the process through which the nature of reason itself is developed and modified into a wide variety of cultural forms through poetic inspiration and folk tradition, both of which he sees as the immanent workings of divine revelation. Herder sees human nature as grounded on a continuity between the natural and supernatural, and reason as an animal capacity that is nevertheless grounded in a spirituality greater than reason and transcending nature. Every cultural tradition was brought to life by a divine spark and should be cherished for the unique way it reveals an aspect of spirituality. The danger, he thinks, is that reason will cut people off from their own spirituality, as has happened in modern societies. They then perversely regard their self-inflicted spiritual impoverishment as a mark of superiority. Other cultures and their own past seem worthless to them or are valued only as so many stepping stones on the way to their own "enlightened" condition.

Herder depicts the first humans as "soft, defenseless creatures" who lived in harmony with nature, with each other, and with the spiritual powers to which they stood in a much easier relationship than we do (Herder, *Ideas* 13:431). Their ability to reason and speak is due to their instruction by "the Elohim" (*Genesis* 2:16–17).[3] People are naturally sociable, and peace is the natural relation between them as long as their societies remain small and their reason remains rooted in the divine spirituality from which it originally arose. All wildness and strife in human nature are a result of subsequent "degeneration." "The oldest tradition of the world's earliest peoples knows nothing of those jungle monsters who, as naturally inhuman beings, prowl around murdering, and thus fulfill their original vocation in this way" (Herder, *Ideas* 13: 430–431).

Human beings for Herder were destined by God for a life of harmony and innocent contentment. They enjoyed such a life as long as they remained under the benevolent tutelage of divine traditions. But "when the human being illicitly aspired to become like the Elohim in the knowledge of evil, he attained this knowledge to his own detriment and henceforth occupied a new status, adopting a new and more artificial way of life" (Herder, *Ideas* 13:435). God's aim in history is the happiness of human individuals. People introduce evil into the world when they detach their reason from these roots and, arrogantly aspiring to the independent status of gods (cf. *Genesis* 3:5), create for themselves an artificial way of life (the modern or "civilized" political state that can be held together only by war and coercion).

Thus in the same book of the *Ideas*, Herder attacks as "an evil proposition" Kant's claim, in the *Idea toward a universal history*, that "the human being is an animal who needs a master" and therefore requires the coercion of a political state in order to fulfill the destiny of the species (I 8:23; Herder, *Ideas* 13:435). Herder maintains that "each human individual has the measure of his happiness within him," and "it was a benevolent thought of providence to give the more easily attained happiness of individual human beings priority over the artificial ends of large societies, and to save those expensive machines of state as far as possible for a later age" (Herder, *Ideas* 13:342).

For Kant, by contrast, the individual's desire for happiness is merely nature's means of stimulating the development of the powers of the species. Thus Kant views natural purposiveness *holistically* in two senses.

First, he sees the skills developed by individuals not in terms of their usefulness for the individuals as such, but in terms of the contribution they make to the cumulative powers of the species over time. Second, Kant is especially interested in the devices nature uses to develop *cooperative* capacities, such as those needed to establish a law-governed civil order.

Herder fears that if we view history in this way, we will turn mere abstractions into final ends and treat the unhappiness of human individuals as a mere means, which could not be reconciled with the aims of a wise and benevolent providence (Herder, *Ideas* 13:341–342).[4] Herder is especially disturbed by the fact that Kant's conception of historical progress places such stress on the modern state, founded on coercion and on complex social institutions devised by unaided human reason, which seem to do so poorly at achieving human happiness. Herder considers it pernicious to represent state coercion as the necessary foundation of human society. For the same reason, he thinks it outrageous to represent the miserable and wicked social conditions found in modern states as a "higher end" not only in relation to the unhappiness of individuals but even in relation to the existence of all earlier periods of human history.

Each individual, culture, and age, Herder thinks, has its own conception of happiness, which serves as its proper end. Herder views reason itself, insofar as it is a real and valuable human capacity, as identifiable with what is agreed upon by consensus within specific social traditions. Reason and truth are therefore always bound down to a traditional consensus. The Enlightenment attempt to posit a universal human reason independent of social consensus is never anything but an expression of individual prejudices and fancies.[5] Thus Herder thinks the philosophy of history should value each part of the whole for its own sake. It should not turn earlier ages (which were actually more peaceful, contented, and more in accordance with the aims of providence than modern states are) into mere stages on the way to a self-styled age of 'enlightenment'. His own age, as Herder sees it, has purchased its overdeveloped capacity for ratiocination at the cost of its capacities for poetry and religion. Its states have grown large and powerful mainly through war and corruption.[6] It is probably unnecessary to point out that Herder's reaction to modernity and the Enlightenment is by no means a historical curiosity. Herder's name is not as famous today as Kant's, but his view of modernity has long been fashionable and is in that sense at least as characteristically modern. (It is especially fashionable just now among those most deluded of all moderns who flatter themselves that they have transcended modernity.)

1.2. The historical defense of reason   Kant's view of human nature is bleaker, yet its promethean outlook on the forces of modern society is ultimately more hopeful. Kant's critique of Herder starts with his critical strictures against speculative knowledge of the supernatural. Kant holds that even if there were empirical revelations of God, we could not recognize them as such (SF 7:63). Consequently, our reason cannot be grounded on supernatural gifts or hyperrational inspirations but only on its own capacity for self-criticism and self-correction. Kant holds that our *use* of reason develops through history but that reason itself is a single faculty with unchanging principles. History is not the emergence *of reason* out of tradition or revelation but the development *through reason* of the entire range of human capacities and dispositions.

The issue between Kant and Herder at this point is not whether reason develops historically or is always historically situated (both affirm that it is). The question is whether reason also has the capacity to transcend its situation, to generate higher universal standards (which Kant calls 'ideas') through which social traditions may be criticized and changed. Or the issue might be put more sharply if stated this way: Is the ultimate aim of reason merely to make us *happy* by bringing us into harmony with what history and tradition have made us, or is it instead precisely reason's function to make us *discontented* with all this, driving human culture to perfect itself further? Herder's position is the former one; Kant's is the latter.

Kant grants no historical reality to the thought of a peaceable kingdom in which "soft and defenseless" human beings lived in natural harmony with the supernatural. For him, the only reason we have is a reason whose essential use is to devise "artificial" modes of life, which have thus far always led people mainly into strife, suffering, and evil. The puzzle he tries to solve is why the very capacities whose development is to blame for our wickedness and unhappiness are also the ground of our self-esteem, setting us incomparably above the rest of nature.

The solution lies in rejecting Herder's principle that the natural (or providential) end of the human species must be found in people's happiness. It would contradict a regulative principle of natural teleology (NT2) to take as the natural end of a developmental process something that that process tends only to frustrate and make more difficult. The natural human desire for happiness must itself be regarded only as nature's means to another end, which is the development of those very faculties which make happiness impossible. The true ends of human life, however, are not posited for us by nature or providence, but by human reason once nature has brought it to historical maturity.

Herder insists that each individual, each culture, and each age contains its own measure of happiness, which is incommensurable with that of other cultures and ages. From this he infers that each individual, culture, and age must be regarded as constituting a unique end in itself. Kant accepts the incommensurability of different people's standards of happiness, but for him it implies something quite different. If the happinesses of different people, ages, and cultures are so relative and indeterminate that they cannot even be compared according to a common measure, then happiness could not be the objective end of human history.

> But what if the true end of providence were not this shadowy image of happiness which each individual creates for himself, but the ever continuing and growing activity and culture which are thereby set in motion, and whose highest possible expression can only be the product of a political constitution based on concepts of human right, and consequently an achievement of human beings themselves? (RH 8:64)

Nature's purpose in history must therefore be located precisely in the autonomous use of reason. The task of history is not to make people happy but to produce a political constitution in which the culture of reason can develop to the full. Finally, the value of human life is to be measured not by *happiness* but by *self-worth*. Our vocation cannot be to make ourselves content – irrational animals do that better than we ever can – but to give our lives meaning and value by perfecting and exercising the capacities that no other animal has, which are worthier than anything any other animal can even dream of.

> Does our author really mean that if the happy inhabitants of Tahiti, never visited by more civilized nations, were destined to live in peaceful indolence for thousands of centuries, it would be possible to give a satisfactory answer to the question why they should exist at all, and of whether it would not have been just as good if this island had been occupied by happy sheep and cattle as by happy human beings who merely enjoy themselves? (RH 8:65; cf. I 8:21, G 4:423)

Kant does not count human happiness among the ends of nature, but it is among the ends of morality and hence of providence. For him human happiness exists only as an idea self-devised by human beings, whose content is multifarious due not to nature's bounty but to the

endless creativity of human choices. As an end of morality and providence, the happiness of rational beings is to be achieved only through
their own rational efforts, and as something for which they have made
themselves worthy by struggling to develop and exercise their rational
nature. It is not a gift to be bestowed on us as soft, defenseless innocents
by a maternally affectionate nature or a paternally indulgent Deity.

1.3. Social "Averroism" Kant not only denies that individual happiness
is nature's end in human history, but he even denies that nature's end
concerns individuals as such. As we have seen, in *Idea toward a universal
history* Kant maintains that nature's end is the development of human
capacities – and not individual capacities but the *collective* capacities of
the human species. Herder rejects as "Averroistic" the thesis that "it is
not the individual human being but the human race which receives an
education." "Race and species," he says, "are only general concepts except insofar as they exist in individual beings" (Herder, *Ideas* 13:345–
346; cf. RH 8:65).[7]

Kant replies that locating the human end in the species rather than
the individual is *not* like saying that no individual horse has horns but
the species of horses is horned. For the human species is not being considered as a universal, in contrast with individual human beings as its
instances, but as itself a unique individual – "the totality of a series of
generations which goes to infinity (i.e., indefinitely)" (RH 8:65). Individual human beings contribute to the progress of the species insofar
as they leave the human world better than they found it. We relate consciously to the species insofar as we reflect – as Kant does in his historical writings – on the nature and extent of human progress. Because
human history has no final endpoint, its purposiveness must be thought
of as an endless progress, which reaches fulfillment at no definite time
and in no human individual. "In other words, no single member of all
the generations of the human race, but only the species, attains its destiny completely" (RH 8:65).

This exchange between Kant and Herder affords us a new perspective on some twentieth-century ideas because it is perhaps the earliest
modern prefiguration of the debate between "social holism" and the
"methodological individualism" that is now familiar from liberal individualist critiques of Hegel and Marx.[8] Herder is not interested in finding "microfoundations" for social theories. Still less is he worried about
the metaphysical wooliness of the notion of a collective spirit animating
a group, culture, or nation. (It was Herder rather than Kant who was,

in fact, one of the chief modern originators and proponents of such notions.) Herder's real motivations (like those of many methodological individualists) are moral rather than theoretical. Their target is Kant's Enlightenment universalism.

The issue is really about whether we can understand history in terms of an end seen first as implicitly and unconsciously animating the progressive efforts of the entire human species and later as something grasped by reason and pursued consciously and collectively as a common purpose. Herder looks upon such an idea with fear and repugnance because he thinks it threatens to destroy our humanity through sterile homogenization and the privileging of cultural forms in which reason has become overdeveloped and the complementary sides of our humanity have been left to wither. Like some recent critics of Enlightenment universalism, Herder views it as a dangerous pretext for all kinds of tyrannical abuse: "The universal dress of philosophy and philanthropy can conceal repression, violations of the true personal, human, local, civil, and national freedom, much as Cesare Borgia would have liked it" (Herder 5:578). Also like these critics, Herder frequently finds it necessary to appeal to universal values to support both his philosophy of history and his political convictions (thus raising serious doubts about the internal consistency of his views). Chief among these values, perhaps, is his ideal of *Humanität,* which is intended to "comprehend everything I have said hitherto about humanity's formative education (*Bildung*) toward reason and freedom, toward finer senses and desires, toward the most delicate and robust health, toward occupation and domination of the earth" (Herder, *Ideas,* 13:154).

Kant views the ideal of a universal humanity created through history with equal favor, but more consistently and hopefully, as the ideal of a realm of ends, and the collective task of bringing rational concord and unity to a species that, if left to nature and particular traditions, will never achieve the dignity of self-government but will forever be sunk in internal discord and antagonism. The modern contest between these two views of history is still far from being decided.

2. Historical conjectures

Kant's *Conjectural beginning of human history* is an attempt to argue for his alternative while satirizing the vehicle Herder used to present his views in Book 10 of the *Ideas.* Kant also makes use of the biblical history, "sketching a different route" through the same "trackless desert" – that is, the unrecorded history of humanity's origins (RH 8:64). He begins with the insistence that historical conjectures based on sacred documents can never attain the status of a narrative based on genuine records. It can be only a "pleasure trip" of the mind, not a serious scientific account. On the other hand, he says that a "history of the first development of freedom from its origins in a disposition in human nature" is necessarily different from any history in the ordinary sense. It can only be "derived from the philosophy of nature" – that is, "deduced from experience, assuming that what was experienced at the beginning of history was no better or worse than what is experienced now" (MA 8:109).

Kant's conjectural history is a kind of thought experiment. It starts with the faculty of reason as we find it operative in human beings now and attempts to abstract from the rational capacities we have acquired as a result of *using* reason. Kant imagines the first employment of reason by beings like ourselves, assuming that up until that point their behavior resulted solely from faculties like those found in nonrational (nonhuman) animals. This conforms to the aims of Kant's *Idea toward a universal history*, since that essay directs us to see history in terms of the natural purpose of developing the capacities of the human species on the basis of human predispositions.

Unlike Herder, Kant begins with a being who can stand and walk, speak and think. He emphasizes that even these skills would have to be acquired by human beings for themselves, rather than being innate, since otherwise they would even now be inherited rather than learned (MA 8:110). His aim is obviously to suggest that human powers of reasoning could have been exercised and developed entirely by human beings themselves, without any need for instruction by "the Elohim." On the contrary, Kant thinks they could count as *rational* powers only to the extent that they developed through being exercised autonomously by human beings. Accordingly, he interprets "the voice of God" in the biblical story as the guidance of natural instinct, which all nonhuman animals obey (MA 8:111). This divine voice is benevolent, but its commands are without moral content, for they are merely the leading strings that guide human beings as long as they exist in a pre-moral condition of tutelage to nature. Disobedience to them will therefore be not a sin but an act of self-emancipation.

As we saw in Chapter 2, Kant holds that brutes as well as human beings possess a faculty of desire, a capacity to actualize objects of representation by means of those representations (KpV 5:9; MS 6:211). A brute faculty of desire merely responds to impulses that trigger behavior predetermined by instinct (KrV A534/B562, G 4:448). Rational beings can deliberate about their actions, choosing which ends to set and which means to take to them. This requires a disengagement from the process by which representations in brutes give rise to impulses and thereby to instinctive actions. Where reason sets an end independently of preexisting desires, the end-setting act produces the feeling of pleasure accompanying the representation of the object, thus *causing* a desire for it (KpV 5:9; MS 6:211–212). This means that the first use of reason must involve the creation of a *new desire*, which is a product of reason, independent of and even opposed to instinct.

3. The first free choice

3.1. First step: the creation of new desires When we find Kant praising reason for setting ends opposed to natural instinct, we are apt to suppose he is thinking about moral laws and the imposition of duties. In the *Conjectural beginning*, however, the first use of reason to produce desires involves nothing of the kind. In a playful allusion to the biblical history, Kant suggests that the first human beings might have begun by using the sense of sight rather than taste to compare their usual diet (a fruit) with something else that had a similar visual appearance (cf. *Genesis* 3:6). This act of comparing – one not involved at all in the exercise of a brute faculty of desire – then gave rise to a desire to eat this new fruit. This was the first exercise of "the peculiar capacity of reason," which, "with the help of imagination," is able to "invent desires which not only *lack* any corresponding natural impulse, but which are even *opposed* to the latter." In their original form, these rational desires have nothing to do with morality – on the contrary, "such desires in the beginning get the name of *lasciviousness* (*Lusternheit*), and through them flourish a whole swarm of superfluous or even unnatural inclinations, under the name of *luxury*" (MA 8:111).[9] Moral principles descend from such unnatural desires.

3.2. Second step: "anxiety and fright" The creation of artificial desires by reason is the *first* of the four steps through which the first people began to assume their humanity. Confronted for the first time with conflicting wants, people now take a *second* step: They become aware of what it means to *choose* (MA 8:112). They become conscious of what Kant elsewhere calls "negative freedom," the absence of the "pathological necessitation" or mechanical coercion of their will by instinctive impulses (KrV A564/B562, G 4:445, KpV 5:29). Through the first experiment in free choice, Kant says, the human being "discovered the faculty for choosing a way of life for himself, and not being bound to a single one like other animals" (MA 8:112).

The awareness of this ability, he conjectures, must at first have been a source of pleasure, because through it people became aware of their superiority over the brutes. Like Herder, Kant sees reason as making possible an "artificial" way of life, devised by human beings themselves, and representing an aspiration to superiority over the rest of creation. But whereas Herder contrasts this with an earlier benign use of reason under the guidance of the Elohim, Kant sees the alienation from instinct and the institution of a self-devised mode of life as the original and basic function of reason. For Kant it was the use of reason itself that made it impossible for our first parents to live any longer in paradise.

The pleasure they took in the ability to choose could therefore be only short-lived. It soon gave way to "anxiety and fright" when people began to realize how ill-equipped they were to create satisfactory alternatives to the life of instinct they had now left behind. Freed from the coercion of impulses, faced suddenly with self-generated desires, yet no longer having any way of identifying their true needs and still ignorant of the properties of things that would be capable of satisfying their new wants, human beings "stood on the brink of an abyss" (MA 8:112).

3.3. Third step: awareness of the future   Forced to plan for the satisfaction of their wants, people now had to take a third crucial step. As long as their present needs are satisfied, brutes are content. They are wholly absorbed in the present and led from it to the future only by instincts telling them at every moment what to do. By contrast, human beings must depend on themselves to chart the perilous temporal course that leads from their setting of an end to the relatively distant time when it can be achieved. Thus their attention is increasingly drawn to the future. Following the biblical story, Kant describes this as the source of new and terrible miseries of which no other creature can even form a conception: Human beings are subject to *labor* (present toil for the sake of future satisfaction) (*Genesis* 3:17) and the *fear of death* (*Genesis* 3:19). Realizing how unhappy it had made them, Kant says, people came to "decry as a crime the use of reason which had been the cause of all these ills" (MA 8:113).

Herder gives a relatively orthodox account of Adam's fall as an act of wickedness, motivated by pride, in which people misuse their reason, disobeying the benevolent commands of the Elohim and establishing an artificial mode of life, which expels them from the original paradise. Kant interprets the myth less traditionally, as the origin not of sin but of "misology" (the hatred of reason).[10] Eating the new fruit was not a crime, but an act of liberation. It was "decried" as a crime because people held it responsible for the new sufferings it brought on them. Kant's ironical exegesis thus attributes to early humans (or perhaps rather to the priestly narrators of the biblical story) a pattern of thought he regards as typical of religious superstition. Religious people feel guilty not because they have done something *wrong* but because they have become *unhappy* through imprudent behavior. Deceptively concocted guilt feelings lend some measure of dignity to the humiliation of having only their own foolishness to blame for their misery (R 6:24).[11]

Human beings are subject to misology as soon as they begin to realize two important truths. First, reason turns out not to be a good instrument for making rational beings happy or contented (G 4:395–396). It complicates their lives, generating new desires and creating new and more complicated circumstances in which people must devise ways of satisfying them. And by depriving people of comfortable illusions and superstitions, reason also alienates them from nature, their social traditions, and their natural feelings. Second, the development of reason also arouses a profoundly vicious side of human nature – self-conceited, self-centered, insatiably greedy, and prone to all kinds of pernicious errors and delusions. The two truths even reinforce one another, for we naturally take refuge from our discontent both in our natural feelings and in our cultural, social, and religious traditions (as Herder recommends). But one of the enlightened person's chief sources of discontent is the rational perception that our natural affections are full of deception and resistant to moral goodness, while it is social tradition and custom that we have chiefly to blame for inequality, injustice, tyranny, and superstition. We therefore find it hard to forgive reason for depriving us of our illusions of innocence (Herder and his followers merely exemplify this human foible).

Kant thinks that misology, like discontent and vice, is a by-product precisely of the development of reason. In fact, it is merely another aspect of the discontent with themselves which Kant takes to be the peculiar fate of finite rational beings. He views this discontent as itself part of the system of natural teleology, since it serves the function of inciting rational creatures to employ their reason in the further development of their capacities. For reason is first and foremost the capacity to which Rousseau gave the name 'perfectibility' – the capacity to adopt

new and varied ways of life and to develop varied abilities and modes of
behavior in response to new situations and new needs.

4. The origin of morality

4.1. The sovereignty over desire   In his Note to this account, however, Kant
says that from a moral point of view the first use of reason represented
a fall because before there were commands, there could be no violations and because the cultivation of reason itself occasioned the growth
of moral vices (MA 8:115). His point is once again to answer Herder's
criticisms. Kant holds that nature's purpose in history is progress for the
species at the expense of the individual but that this gives us no cause
to accuse providence, since all the losses we sustain as individuals are
our own fault, due to our own exercise of freedom.

> For the individual, who looks only to himself in the exercise of freedom
> [the development of reason] represented a loss; for nature, whose end
> in relation to humanity concerns the species, it represented a gain. The
> individual therefore has cause to blame himself for all the ills which he
> endures and for the all the evil he perpetuates; but at the same time, as
> a member of the whole (of a species) he has cause to admire and praise
> the wisdom and purposiveness of the overall arrangement. (MA 8:115–
> 116)

Kant does not see the myth of the fall as directly involving moral evil because he holds that the development of people into moral beings involves a long process, whose overall shape is barely discernible at the
beginning. It starts with the capacity of reason, aided by imagination,
to produce new and artificial desires. Morality arises in consequence of
a new employment of this same capacity, which applies it not to the
desire for food, but to the *sexual* instinct. This time the desires it creates
are not in oneself but in another.

   Kant points out that in contrast to the sexual impulses of the brutes,
which are transient and periodic, human sexual desire is much more
constant and plays a far more powerful role in the life of the species.[12]
Kant ascribes this difference to the rational ability to exercise control
over impulses through the deliberate withdrawal of their object. Human sexuality involves a desire for another whose satisfaction involves
overcoming the other's resistance. He interprets the biblical fig leaf
(*Genesis* 3:7) as a device for *stimulating* sexual desire through concealment. "*Refusal* was the device which invested purely sensuous stimuli

with an ideal quality" (MA 8:112), thereby prolonging and intensifying sexual desire.

4.2. Sittlichkeit *and* Moralität   This alteration of the sexual impulse through reason may not seem to have any direct connection with morality at all. But, Kant insists cryptically, "it is a small beginning which is nevertheless epoch-making because it imparts a whole new direction to thought that is more important than the whole endless series of cultural developments based upon it" (MA 8:113).

We are told right away, however, how the development of human sexuality through reason is related to morality. The use of clothing (as a symbolic refusal and incitement to the imagination) to manipulate the sexual desire of others has such significance because it marks "the proper foundation of true sociability" among people. Human sociability, that is to say, is grounded on the intention to influence others by behaving toward them in such a way as to affect their attitude toward oneself. This means that human moral sense arose in close connection with the attempt to gain control over others through their sexual appetites while at the same time retaining their *respect.* The sense of morality (*Sittlichkeit*) thus arises historically from "the sense of *propriety* (*Sittsamkeit*), the inclination to infuse in others a respect for ourselves through good behavior (*guten Anstand*) (the concealment of whatever might excite low esteem)" (MA 8:113).

Our first parents felt superior to all creation when they became aware of their ability to choose. With the developments just described, this sense of superiority has now taken on a social dimension. Each person wants to maintain self-esteem by seeing it reflected in attitudes of respect and approval others take toward them. This leads directly to a need to subject one's behavior to those customs (*Sitten*) through which people gain one another's approval, which is closely joined to a need to conceal from others the less estimable side of oneself. For Kant as for Nietzsche, the social origin of morality is closely related to lying, deception, and pretense.[13]

On Kant's account, then, morality emerges out of custom in the form of the social control over natural impulses, achieved through the desire of individuals to have their self-esteem confirmed by the good opinion of others. But this is only the starting point of morality. Obviously there is a wide gap between *Sittsamkeit* and *Moralität*, or between *Sittlichkeit* (in the sense of customary mores) and genuine morality as Kant understands it. True morality is conformity to a rational principle of autonomy or self-rule based on respect for one's own reason; this is entirely different from conforming to received customs with a view to gaining the approval of others. Anticipating Hegel, Kant himself makes this point explicitly in his lectures. "The word *Sittlichkeit* has been taken to express morality (*Moralität*); but (*Sitte*) expresses only the concept of decorum (*Anständigkeit*). Some peoples can have *Sitten* but no virtue, while others can have virtue but no *Sitten*" (VE 27:300).

Kant helps us to bridge the gap between custom and genuine morality by pointing to yet another significance we may attribute to the modification of the sexual impulse by reason. Concealment of the sexual organs involves not merely the creation by reason of a new desire out of an old (instinctual) one, but also an attempt to control desire through reason: "For to render an inclination more intense and lasting by withdrawing its object already displays a consciousness of some rational control over the impulses, and not just an ability, as in the first stage of rationality, to obey the impulses to a greater or lesser extent" (MA 8:112–113). It is noteworthy that in this first attempt, the aim is to control the *other's* desire through *my* reason. I want the other's desire to be more predictable, and hence a more useful tool for manipulating the other's conduct to serve my ends.

This shows that we are still not dealing with genuine morality in the Kantian sense. For in order to be truly moral, the rational control of desire must be the regulation of a subject's own desires by the subject's reason, just as the rule of custom will become true morality only when our attempt to confirm our self-esteem takes the form of acting according to a law our reason gives itself. But this brings out yet another respect in which Kant is not an "individualist" about morality. Historically regarded, moral reason is from the start a *social* capacity. At every stage in the rational control of desire, what must be overcome is a dependence on the *natural* conditions of human *society*, which enslave rather than liberate the rational subject. Before there can be a morality of autonomy, the subject must learn to act toward other subjects according to objective rules given through its own faculty of reason, or in other words, according to *a priori* laws.

4.3. Fourth step: human dignity and self-conceit   Kant concludes with a *fourth* step through which people took possession of their humanity. This step, however, involves only a sharper focusing of the self-esteem they gained in the course of their first experience of freedom: Through the use of reason, Kant says, the human being "becomes aware, although only obscurely, that he is the true end of nature" (MA 8:114). Kant finds the idea that the human being is the end of nature expressed in the biblical story when it is said that after expelling them from the garden God took the pelts of animals to make clothing for the man and woman (*Genesis* 3:21).

> When the human being said to the sheep: "The fleece you wear was given you by nature not for your own use but for mine," he became aware of the prerogative which, by nature, he enjoyed over all the animals; from now on, the human being views non-human things no longer as fellow creatures but as mere means to ends at his discretion. (MA 8:114)

As presented here, there is a fundamental ambivalence in human self-esteem. The dignity of the human being consists in an absolute worth as the end of nature. The source of this superiority is the freedom to choose, the human being's capacity to set ends through reason. "This, rather than reason considered merely as an instrument for the satisfaction of various inclinations, is the basis of the human being's equality with higher beings" (MA 8:114). The Bible says the serpent promised the woman that through eating the fruit from the tree of the knowledge of good and evil, she and the man would become equal to gods (*Genesis* 3:5). On Kant's reading of this story, the serpent did not lie but spoke the literal truth:

> [Through the use of reason] the human being attained a position of equality with all rational beings, whatever their rank, because he could claim to be an end in itself, to be accepted as such by all others, and not to be used by anyone else simply as a means to other ends. Even if they are incomparably superior to him in natural gifts, they do not have the right to use him as they please. (MA 8:114)

When the human being thinks of his dignity or absolute worth by contrasting himself with the other animals, he expresses it in a *comparative* judgment, asserting the superiority of his natural being over that of brutes and other nonhuman natural things. This prepares the way for the self-conceited assertion of his natural superiority over other *rational* beings or (what is equivalent to this) of the priority of his natural desires over the universal laws of reason. For Kant the human condition is fundamentally to be caught in the struggle between these two interpretations of self-worth. The rational idea of humanity's historical development is to be the story of the victory of the rational–moral conception over the natural-social conception. The natural-social interpretation of self-worth is based on my existence as a natural being and on contingent features of myself in terms of which I can compare myself with others and claim superiority over them. The rational–moral interpretation grounds my worth solely on my freedom as a rational being.

For Kant it is the natural–social (or comparative) interpretation that has played the major role in human history up to now, since it leads to competition and the natural development of human capacities through social antagonism. It is also the root in human nature of all evil. The rational–moral (or absolute) interpretation of self-worth is something of which people are at first aware only obscurely. They become clear about it only insofar as they achieve enlightenment, and actualize their rational nature only by governing their lives according to this standard of self-worth.

4.4. The expulsion from paradise   As Kant presents it, the disobedience of God's command in the Garden is the human being's "release from the womb of nature" – from the merely animal condition of pre-rational guidance by instinct. This first use of reason leaves human beings restless, frightened, discontented, and careworn, but also with an awareness of self and a powerful self-esteem. This transformation of animality into rationality "does honor" to human beings, providing a ground for their self-esteem, but also delivers them over to danger, suffering, and moral corruption.

The difference between the merely animal condition and the human one is so fundamental and the transition from one condition to the other involves such a profound mixture of good and evil that Kant sympathizes with the deep ambivalence people are bound to feel whenever they bring themselves to contemplate it clearsightedly. The archetypal expression of this ambivalence for Kant is the notion of a perfect mode of life, one that would combine their humanity as rational creatures with the animal contentment that always remains beyond their reach: "In the future, the hardships of life would often arouse in him the wish for a paradise created in his imagination, a paradise where he could dream or idle away his existence in quiet inactivity and everlasting peace" (MA 8:114).

Paradise (the Golden Age or Garden of Eden) is perhaps the most characteristic delusion of misology. We find it in the fantasies that more developed cultures project on earlier stages of their own history or else on foreign peoples, which (in their imperfect comprehension of other ways of life) they often fancy correspond to a happier and less corrupted version of themselves (MA 8:122–123).

We should recognize it also in the human tendency (noted earlier in Chapter 4, § 3.3) to separate off feeling and emotion, *eros* and inspiration, from human reason, treating them as valuable apart from it (even as "correctives" in opposition to it). For in ourselves we desperately want to see something innocent and unspoiled by reason, so that through it we may recapture some part of that elusive original happiness of which we think reason has deprived us. The sentimentalism that wishes to "correct" reason through feeling belongs to this species of self-deception. Its actual role in our moral economy, however, is most often to provide a pretext under which we may exempt our (often corrupt) feelings and emotions from rational criticism. The pretense of innocence is therefore both hollow and treacherous.

The wish to return to paradise, whatever the form it may assume, is always deeply deluded. Paradise never did (and never could) exist in the form we imagine it. The innocence and self-wholeness we seek in natural feelings were never there to be had (at least, not for rational beings, who are the only ones capable of understanding or appreciating them as something valuable). The wish is also a delusion because the natural purpose of these longings is precisely the opposite of the one projected in the wish, namely, to make us discontented with our condition so that we will develop our rational capacities further, taking us ever farther from the original paradise we wish for.

Paradise is never a historical possibility, neither in the past nor in the future. It is certainly not (as Herder thought) the condition in which all peoples naturally find themselves before aspiring reason arrogantly separates them from the spiritual wisdom revealed by the poets and prophets of folk culture. On the contrary, to be contented under such tutelage would be to leave reason dormant, a condition that would only degrade those who occupied it.

"Restless reason impels [the human being] to develop his innate capacities, [yet] stands between him and that imagined seat of bliss, not allowing him to return to the condition of crude simplicity from which it originally extracted him" (MA 8:115). Every step forward is a step toward paradise in the sense that it takes us toward a fuller development of our reason. It is equally a step away from paradise in the sense that it separates us even further from animal contentment. What cuts us off from the paradise behind us is that we have a rational nature enabling us to conceive of paradise. What separates us from the paradise before us is the endless, unhappy struggle to perfect our rational nature. In both directions, what separates us from blessedness is nothing other than our human dignity, which is worth incomparably more than our happiness, and is even the ground of whatever value our happiness may possess.

5. Kant's historical materialism

5.1. Antagonism as the engine of history   Kant thus agrees with Herder that in the course of history, the development of our faculties has made human life harder, more miserable, more corrupt. In the period following the development of reason, "humanity went from the period of leisure and peace to that of *labor and discord,* as the prelude to uniting in society" (MA 8:118). Though he still makes a point of alluding to the Mosaic legends, the final main section of *Conjectural beginning,* headed "Close of the story" (MA 8:119–120),[14] ceases to be a mere thought experiment and seeks to construct a program for understanding the actual historical development of the human species. Kant's program was doubtless inspired by Rousseau's *Discourse on the origin of inequality,* but it goes beyond Rousseau in a number of ways and bears a noteworthy resemblance to Marx's materialist conception of history.

Kant's *Idea toward a universal history* proposes that we view history as the process through which human beings develop their rational capacities. Along with Marx, Kant understands the basis of history as the development of people's *socially productive powers,* their collective capacities to produce their means of subsistence in distinctive ways that vary with historical conditions. Through history these capacities change and grow, and human history therefore passes through different stages, which correspond to the dominant mode of productive activity. Along with Marx, Kant also views history as a scene not only of conflict and strife but of deepening inequality and oppression. And as in Marx's theory of history, the root of this conflict is a struggle between groups of people with antagonistic economic interests, where the different groups represent different stages in humanity's economic development.

5.2. The economic stages of history   Kant divides the early history of the human race into stages distinguished by the modes of economic or productive activity predominant in them: the age of hunting, the pastoral age, and the age of agriculture. The first two stages comprise the first main epoch of human history, which was marked by primitive simplicity and comparative tranquillity. A second epoch, marked by strife, arose when people began to cultivate and harvest crops. At the basis of this strife was a conflict over property relations. Agriculture requires the introduction of property in land, which did not exist in hunting or herding societies and is inimical to them (EF 8:363–364). A pastoral society will tend to own land in common (MS 6:265), and will resist the introduction of property in land (MA 8:118). In order to establish land ownership, farmers had to drive herdsmen off their fields by force. There began a state of war between the two economic modes, resulting in a victory for the higher mode of production.

This is how Kant interprets the biblical story of the murder of the shepherd (Abel) by the farmer (Cain) (*Genesis* 4:2).

> The farmer may have seemed to envy the herdsman as someone more favored by heaven (*Genesis* 4:4), but in fact the herdsman was a great inconvenience to him as long as he remained in his neighborhood, for grazing animals did not spare his crops. . . . Thus the farmer had to use force against such incursions, which the other could not regard as impermissible. (MA 8:118–119)

The story of Cain and Abel thus depicts not the origin of fratricide or blood guilt but the first violent social revolution necessitated by economic progress. In this light, Kant regards Cain's act of homicide as *justified,* since in a condition of society prior to the founding of a civil state (which itself rests on an agricultural mode of production) farmers and herders have an equal right to resist each other by force (MS 6:266). The result of the strife in this second epoch was the "distancing" of the farmers from the herdsmen (cf. *Genesis* 4:16), in other words, the establishment of an agricultural economy over against the pastoral economy (MA 8:119).

5.3. Private property and the origin of the state   Kant's theory of history is *proto*-Marxist. Both regard the growth of the social powers of production as the fundamental natural tendency in human history.[15] Both view this tendency as working itself out through a dynamic of social struggles, with economic and political forms changing in response to the need for further development in the collective capacities of the species. From Kant's account of the struggle between the pastoral and agricultural modes of production, however, we can already see three important ways in which it differs from Marxian historical materialism.

First, Kant views the conflict between modes of production as a simple conflict between those who carry on different forms of productive activity; he does not view it as a struggle between classes internal to a single economic structure. In this respect, Kant goes beyond Rousseau, seeing historical epochs as representing distinct stages of economic organization and the dynamic of history as a conflict between the representatives of different stages. But in another way he ignores a prominent Rousseauian theme that was to be developed by Marx: namely, the social dynamic generated by internal social inequalities (compare Rousseau, *Discourse on the origin of inequality*, 3:179–182).

Second, Kant regards the institution of private property established by the agricultural mode of production as the basis of all civil society based on right, and thus for all subsequent developments of civilization. There is no suggestion that any of the social struggles subsequent to the agricultural revolution will ever call the principle of private property itself into question.

A third major difference between Kant and Marx is already hinted at in Kant's description of the epoch of "labor and discord" as a "prelude to uniting in society." It will become even more apparent in Kant's account of human history subsequent to the establishment of an agricultural mode of production. Kant views the early development of civilization as a prelude to "civil society" (a social union under coercive laws or a political state). Kant lacks the *Hegelian* concept of civil society as a social system of economic activity distinct from the state. Still less does he anticipate the Marxian position that civil society in this sense is the "real foundation" of the political state, a mode of collective human activity that might someday evolve in such a way as to render the political state superfluous. For this reason, there is also no room in Kant's theory of history for the prospect of abolishing the state at any point in the historical future.[16]

Like Engels, however, Kant sees the founding of political states as *the* pivotal event in human history.[17] Thus the third major epoch of history begins after the agricultural mode of production has established itself over against the pastoral. Farming requires permanent settlements and the protection of harvests from hostile incursions. Kant therefore sees an agricultural mode of life as requiring greater cooperation between people than was found in earlier economies. In order to defend their property against hordes of nomadic herders, farmers had to band together. They could no longer live in family units – as people had in hunting and herding societies – but began to settle together in villages (MA 8:119).

Only with the formation of towns do people enter into a *civilized* condition. Urban life meant the beginnings of a division of labor within society and an economy based on exchange. This gave a new impetus to the development not only of practical crafts but to art and culture. (This is Kant's interpretation of the biblical account of the varied trades practiced by Cain's children; *Genesis* 4:17–23.) The most beneficial fruits of civilized life were "sociability and civil security"; they enabled agricultural societies with urban centers to colonize new territories, increasing the geographical area dominated by the new and more civilized way of life (MA 8:119).

A plurality of different ways of life existing in close proximity also enabled the seeds of human conflict to germinate. Civilization gave rise to new and subtler forms of competition, rivalry, and domination, involving vanity, envy, malice, and deceit (R 6:27, 33). It is in the civilized condition that we really begin to see the close connection between the development of reason, including the beginnings of morality, and the increase of human vice and unhappiness (compare Rousseau, *Discourse on the origin of inequality*, 3:175–180). "With this epoch there also began the *inequality* among human beings, that rich source of so much evil, but also of all good; and henceforth this inequality was only to increase" (MA 8:119).[18]

Civilized life thus provides the proper medium for developing the fundamental human trait of "unsociable sociability" – the simultaneous interdependence between people and their mutual antagonism and hostility. Kant explains the creation of political states through increasing conflicts between people when they enter into civilized life. In the earliest stages, these conflicts took two main forms: private violence and revenge, requiring a system of public justice, and war, at first chiefly a perpetuation of the conflict with pastoral peoples (MA 8:119–120). At a later stage, he thinks, civilization tends eventually to be victorious over pre-agricultural peoples, who are "drawn into the glittering misery of the towns" (MA 8:120). He understands the "sons of God" in *Genesis* 6 as a reference to these nomads, and their marriage with "the daughters of men" as their absorption into civil life.

Kant portrays a cyclical dynamic in early civil society: The threat of external conflict requires preparation for war, and hence a strong economic base, which can be maintained only if the ruler allows a measure of civil freedom. The absorption of civil society's enemies makes for a time of peace and luxury, but this permits civil rulers to become tyrants and destroys the freedom of citizens. The resulting corruption of civil society, which thus "becomes unworthy of its very existence" (MA 8:120), is Kant's way of interpreting the biblical story of the flood (*Genesis* 6:5–7).

Elsewhere he indicates that this state of corruption is usually prevented by the ever-present threat of war between states, and that the hostility between states itself serves the end of progress toward rightful political constitutions (EF 8:367; TP 8:310–311; I 8:26).[19]

5.4. The historical presuppositions of right   The first part of the *Metaphysics of morals* presents a theory of right (*Recht*), that is, of legal justice within a political state (see Conclusion, § 2 and Note 3). There Kant asserts that right is grounded on "immutable principles" deriving *a priori* from pure reason alone (MS 6:229–230). In his view, however, right is nevertheless historically conditioned. The *principles* of right, like those of morality, derive solely from the exercise of our rational faculties, but the exercise of these faculties is historically conditioned. It is only after people achieve the social forms of civil society and landed property that they actually become aware of pure principles of right and begin to apply these principles to their social relationships. Kant thinks private property in land began because it was necessary for agriculture, but was established conclusively only after the increased productivity of farming facilitated the growth of towns, practical arts, and the concentration of military power to enforce property in land by holding at bay the hordes of pastoral nomads and submitting private quarrels between landholders to a system of legal justice (MS 6:267).[20]

In Kant's theory of the state, as in the theories of Locke and Rousseau, private property in land plays the decisive role. For Kant, property in land is the foundation of all forms of acquisition (MS 6:261–262). The state is necessary because it is the condition for enforceable property rights (MS 6:264–267). Prior to entry into a state, the right to property can be only "provisional." "Peremptory" acquisition is possible only when people leave the state of nature and enter into the civil condition (MS 6:257). "Therefore something external can be *originally* acquired only in conformity with the idea of a civil condition, that is, with a view to it and to its being brought about, but prior to its realization" (MS 6:264).

This theory is, of course, intended to apply directly to the present. To say that property is only provisional prior to the civil condition is to hold that we acquire genuine property rights only under the conditions specified by public laws given through a general will (MS 6:256). Kant rejects the Lockean idea that in a state of nature we may have full-fledged property rights (acquired by means of our labor) that may be rightfully enforced against others. It is rather the function of public law to determine the conditions under which people may acquire a genuine and enforceable right of ownership over things. This means that in Kant's theory the state has broad redistributive powers. If it so chooses, the general will may rectify natural and social inequalities. If the wealthy complain that they are being taxed for the benefit of the poor, then it must be pointed out to them that they hold their property by right only insofar as they submit to the state whose general will has determined that they be taxed for these purposes (MS 6:325–326).

At the same time, however, Kant's theory of acquisition, and of property as the basis of the state, refers literally to the historical origins of landed property and the civil condition. Kant opposes the state of nature not to a social condition but to a *civil* condition (MS 6:242). A society in the state of nature is a literal historical reality at many times and places. In the earliest stages of the agricultural mode of production, farmers began to lay claim to private property in land, but there was as yet no organized civil society in terms of which their property rights could be adjudicated and publicly enforced. It is this historical period Kant means by "the state of nature" when he contrasts this with the "civil condition" (MS 6:242). When Kant speaks of leaving the state of nature and entering into a civil condition, he is referring quite literally to a kind of historical event. Kant's entire theory of right thus presupposes a post-agricultural form of society and takes for granted the social relations appropriate to a mode of human life centered on an urban civilization.[21]

HUMAN INCLINATIONS
AND AFFECTIONS

1. Natural desire

1.1. Reason and inclination   There is a long tradition in Western ethical thought, going back at least as far as Socrates, that says the right sort of life is one guided by reason rather than by emotions, passions, or natural appetites. There are harsher and milder versions of this view, and it has also been controverted both by hard-headed empiricists and by tender-minded enthusiasts. Kant's version of the rationalist view is both milder and subtler than its common reputation, but it is still relatively harsh. This chapter explores Kant's reasons for thinking that reason must oppose and regulate the satisfaction of natural appetite and the prompting of natural feeling. These reasons are not derived *a priori* from Kant's conceptions of metaphysics or morality but are empirical and anthropological in character.

In the *Groundwork* Kant says prominently: "The human being feels within himself a powerful counterweight to all the commands of duty, . . . the counterweight of his needs and inclinations" (G 4:405). Such remarks have been a rallying point for attacks on Kant's position, beginning with those on Kant's "rigorism" and "formalism" by milder rationalists (such as Schiller and Hegel). Kant's moral psychology presents a relatively easy target in the abstract form it assumes in his foundational ethical works, where it can be associated with his "two worlds" metaphysics of the self, and blamed either on his pietist background or the Stoic ethical tradition Kant seems to represent. The criticisms are harder to make out if Kant's suspicion of natural desire is seen in light of the empirical theory of human nature developed in his writings on anthropology and history. Even then, Kant's views will still no doubt strike many as extreme (or just plain nasty). But they can no longer be dismissed in the same condescending way they were before. For the mistrust of inclination (or natural desire) in Kant's rationalism is not about hostility to anything so innocent as "finitude" or "the senses" or "the emotions" or "the body." The focus instead is on the (far from innocent) *social* character natural desires must assume in the natural process through which our rational faculties develop in history.

What do we mean here by "natural" desire when inclinations (empirical desires) are said to be *natural?* For Kant *all* human desires are "natural" in the sense that they result from the operation of faculties developed by a natural process. This is especially true of the rational or moral desires that arise from pure reason. However, *all* action, even on the most basic instinctive inclinations, is "nonnatural" (or even "supernatural") insofar as Kant holds that it must be an effect of freedom and cannot be merely an effect of natural mechanism. Thus neither of these routes yields a useful distinction between "natural" and "rational" desire in the context of Kant's philosophy. We do get one, however, if we understand "natural" desires and feelings as those that serve *natural* ends, especially nature's most fundamental end in human history, that of developing human species capacities through our discontent and unsociable sociability. For empirical desires serve nature's ends through these human propensities in a way that purely rational desires do not.

Kant holds that even natural desires in this sense are by nature good. That is, they are placed in us *for* good, and it would be not only futile but even contrary to duty to attempt to extirpate or rid ourselves of them (R 6:26, 57–58). But natural desires in this sense lie outside of and opposed to the moral principles of reason. They do so because the fundamental maxim on which we act in following them represents a fundamentally opposed standard of value, especially of self-worth. Our fate is therefore to struggle discontentedly between *two* opposed principles: one self-legislated by our reason, the other an evil principle belonging to our misuse of our rational freedoms and hiding within our natural desires. Wantonly yielding to inclinations and ascetically seeking to mortify them would be merely two ways of trying to overcome the inevitable self-alienation of our finite rational condition – that is, to evade our discontent, to flee from ourselves, to renounce our duty.

1.2. Affects and passions   Desire in general is the self-determination of a subject's capacity to determine itself through the representation of something future as an effect of this capacity (cf. KpV 5:9, MS 6:211, VA 7:251). When the source of desire is the senses (the feeling of pleasure or displeasure accompanying the representation of a future object) and the desire is a habitual one, it is called *inclination* (*Neigung*) (MS 6:212, VA 7:251). In his pragmatic discussion of the faculty of desire, Kant's chief aim is to identify the natural desires that resist the self-government of reason, since they threaten both prudence and morality. Kant identifies two such phenomena of our faculty of desire that deserve special attention.

The first are "affects" (*Affekte*), powerful and sudden feelings of pleasure or displeasure that take away our capacity for reflection on whether we should give ourselves over to them (MS 6:408, VA 7:251). Among the affects Kant counts anger, fright, grief, shame and exuberant joy (VA 7:254–256). Patience and courage, he says, are qualities whose chief moral function is to make us less susceptible to harmful affects (VA 7:256–257). Some affects promote bodily health through their operations on the body (e.g., he thinks weeping has a soothing effect; VA 7:262–263). But many are directly responsible for failures of rationality, threats to morality, counterproductive to our well-being, and sometimes they even diminish our capacity to achieve the very ends they themselves presuppose. A fit of anger makes us more vulnerable to our enemies. Being overcome by shame takes away the self-assurance we need in order to act in a way we can be proud of (VA 7:260–261).

The "apathy" Kant praises as a presupposition of moral virtue consists in an *absence of affects*. Kant emphasizes, however, that there is nothing conducive to virtue in a general absence of feelings or a general indifference to things (MS 6:408–409). So he is not praising "apathy" in either of those senses. Like most Enlightenment thinkers, Kant distrusts feeling as a guide to action when it is unregulated by rational reflection, but he also rejects the Stoic view that action from reason excludes action from feeling or emotion.[1] As we saw in Chapter 1, §3.3 (as regards respect, moral feeling, conscience, and love for human beings), Kant holds that some feelings are essential expressions of reason, so that a human being without the capacity for them would be incapable of acting rationally on moral principles.[2]

A deeper threat to reason's control over desire are certain inclinations that reason is capable of subduing only with difficulty or not at all. To such inclinations Kant gives the traditional name "passion" (*Leidenschaft*) (VA 7:251, MS 6:408). Not only are passions contrary to morality, but they are also opposed to prudence since a passion is "an inclination for something which prevents reason from comparing it with the totality of all our inclinations when making a choice" (VA 7:265).

Not all human inclinations for Kant are passions. Only some inclinations – those involving other people – are even capable of becoming passions. But it is in the form of passions that inclinations most dramatically display their tendency to become a counterweight to rational principles. In his anthropology lectures, Kant most often organizes his discussion of the passions (or even just the "inclinations") around the objects for two "formal inclinations": those for *freedom* and for *resources* (*Vermögen*), which are "the means of satisfying his inclinations" (VA 25:1141, cf. VA 25:214, 417–418, 1354). "Resources" are then subdivided into talent, power (*Gewalt*), and money, each of which is the object of a possible passion, characterized by "addiction" or "mania" (*Sucht*). The inclination for resources gives rise to the three passions of ambition (*Ehrsucht*, the addiction to honor), tyranny (*Herrschsucht*, the addiction to domination), and greed (*Habsucht*, the addiction to possession) (VA 25:1141–1142).

In his published lectures of 1798, however, Kant distinguishes passions arising from *nature* from those produced by *culture* (VA 7:267). Throughout all his lectures he regards *all* passions (even the natural ones) as *social* in the sense that they have other human beings as their objects (VA 7:268–270, 25:733, 1141, 1359).

According to the 1798 version, we have two *natural* passions: for *freedom* and for *sex* (VA 7:268; for an earlier anticipation of this division, see VA 25:1359). As we shall see in §§ 2 and 3, the passion for freedom is a desire to be rid of the limitations imposed on us by the existence of others (by their power over us or by our obligations to them); this easily passes over into a desire to deprive them of freedom. Sexual passion is understood as an inclination to use the body of another for our pleasure. The social passions, on the other hand, aim at obtaining the resources needed to satisfy our inclinations. In the social condition, these resources consist mainly in our ability to use other people as means to our ends. There are three ways in which Kant thinks we exercise power over others: through their *fear*, their *interest*, or their *opinion*. Consequently, the desire to use others for our ends takes three basic forms: tyranny, greed, and ambition (VA 7:272).

2. Natural passions

2.1. The passion for freedom Kant regards the passion for freedom as the strongest of all human inclinations. He interprets the cry of the newborn infant as a wail of rage occasioned by the child's incapacity to make use of its limbs, which it experiences as external constraint (VA 7:268). We have such a powerful need to be free of all the restraints imposed on us by the existence of others that, however fortunate we may be in other respects, being subject to the will of another is usually sufficient by itself to deprive us of happiness: "A human being whose happiness depends on another human being's choice (no matter how benevolent the other may be) rightly considers himself unhappy" (VA 7:268).

In society, however, people are always dependent on one another's existence and activities for the satisfaction of their needs. Hence the conclusion Kant draws from this is *not* the Stoical one that we should seek happiness in objects that are wholly independent of the choice of others. It is rather that our condition is such that in certain respects we are necessarily unhappy. As we have seen, happiness is not an end of nature. Our desire for happiness even adds to our needs as we sum up our inclinations into a lasting whole and make this whole into an object of desire that may rob us of contentment even when our present needs are satisfied. This discontent serves nature's purpose by stimulating us to employ our reason and develop the predispositions of the species. In other words, our desire for happiness serves its natural purpose precisely by making us *unhappy*. This is why Kant says in the *Groundwork* that promoting our happiness cannot have been nature's purpose in giving us reason (G 4:395–396), and why he says in the third Critique that even if a human being were omnipotent, complete happiness would still be impossible (KU 5:430–431).[3]

We can achieve freedom not by separating ourselves from others but only by standing in some relationship to them in which their will offers no resistance. Yet we live *naturally* in an antagonism with our fellow human beings and can anticipate at every point that they will resist our desires. Hence our natural desire for freedom necessarily becomes a desire to deprive others of their freedom. "The human being's self-will is always ready to break forth into hostility toward his neighbors, and always presses him to claim unconditional freedom, not merely independence of others but even mastery over other beings that are his equals by nature" (VA 7:327).

It is his emphasis on the passion for freedom that leads Kant to the assertion that "if he lives among others of his own species, the human being is an animal who needs a master." To this, Herder took the strongest exception: "It would be an *easy* principle [he said], but an *evil* one, to maintain in the philosophy of human history that the human being is an animal who needs a master, and who expects from this master, or from his association with him, the happiness of his ultimate destiny" (*Ideas* 13:383). But Kant approves of paternalistic government no more than Herder does, calling it "the greatest despotism thinkable" (TP 8:291). His point is not that the human being needs a master in order to be *happy*, but that he naturally abuses his freedom to such an extent that unless there is external constraint on his unjust actions, even external freedom itself will not be possible for him: "For he certainly misuses his freedom in relation to others who are like him; and although as a rational creature he wishes a law to impose limits on the freedom of all, his selfish animal inclinations mislead him to except himself from it wherever he is able to" (I 8:23). (Kant's view at this point may remind us of Hobbes. But if we look deeper, we will see that the differences between the two philosophers are much greater than the similarities.[4])

Until people have become accustomed to the yoke of coercive laws in civil society, their desire for freedom keeps them in a state of constant conflict. "The savage (who is not yet habituated to submission) knows no greater misfortune than falling into [the power of another]; and he is right, as long as there is no public law to protect him. . . . This accounts for his state of constant warfare, by which he intends to keep others as far away from him as possible" (VA 7:268). Kant relates the passion for freedom to the conflict between the different forms of economy prior to the founding of civil society. Once people have adopted a certain way of life, they identify themselves so firmly with it that any challenge to it is experienced as a restraint on their freedom. Thus Kant says of nomadic pastoral peoples that it is this attachment to their way of life, springing from the passion for freedom, that makes them "look down with contempt on settled peoples" and often causes them to cling to their way of life even despite the hardships involved in it. "Peoples who are purely hunters (like the Olenni-Tungusi) have really ennobled themselves by this feeling for freedom (which has separated them from other tribes related to them)" (VA 7:269).[5]

But Kant does not really regard the passion for freedom as "ennobling" those who have not had it subdued by the discipline of state coercion. For since even in preagricultural and prepolitical societies people understand their self-worth only competitively, they seek to assert it not only negatively by separating themselves from others, but also more positively by subduing or killing other people. Kant sees this as the source of the cruelty of "savage" peoples and of the primitive attraction of war (which he thinks has survived down to the present day) as something worth carrying on for its own sake because it provides an opportunity for warriors to show their courage (EF 8:364–365). We might be tempted to admire this, he says, were it not for the fact that "we see in the complacency with which the victors praise their great deeds (massacring whole peoples, swooping down on them without sparing any, and the like) that what they really value in these deeds is only their own superiority and the destruction they are able to wreak" (R 6:33).

When people follow reason's laws of freedom, uniting them in a realm of ends, the freedom of one cannot conflict with that of another, because all their ends form a single harmonious system. But this *rational* freedom, grounded on human dignity, is the direct contrary of what we seek under the influence of the *natural* passion for freedom, grounded on competitive self-conceit.

2.2. Sexual passion   Kant understands sexual desire as the desire to use another person's body for the gratification of merely animal impulses (VA 7:136). Sexual inclination is not directed at the whole person, but only at the pleasure the person's sexual organs afford. However, the parts of a person's body constitute a single whole, in which the integrity of a person consists, so that to use a part is to use the whole. This entails that an essential result of sexual pleasure is to degrade a person, to use a person as a mere means (MS 6:278).

Kant allows, however, that sex may be combined with genuine love for the person, and treats this combination – along with the acquisition of aesthetic taste and a moral sense – as one of the morally beneficial effects of civilization (MA 8:113). But he does not think that love changes the essential character of sexual desire or the degrading effect of the sex act itself (VE 27:384):

> Because sexuality is not an inclination which one human being has for another as such but is an inclination for the sex of another, it is a principle of the degradation of humanity, a source of the preference of one sex to the other and of dishonoring it so as to satisfy an inclination. The inclination a man has for a female is not directed to her as to a human being; rather, for the man the humanity of the female is indifferent and only her sex is the object of his inclination. (VE 27:385)

Kant holds that the sex act reduces both man and woman to the status of things. Hence the pursuit of sexual pleasure for its own sake also displays contempt for oneself as a person (MS 6:424–425). Nevertheless, as the above quotation suggests, Kant treats sex chiefly in terms of a man's desire for (and degradation of) a woman. This is not because he denies that women experience sexual desire or sexual pleasure (indeed, he asserts the direct contrary of such a denial; R 6:80–81). It is rather because he recognizes that the social power relations between the sexes has always made the man's satisfaction or frustration, not the woman's, the main issue.

Since men are physically stronger, sexual passion originally involves the total and forcible subjection of women to men (VA 7:309, MA 8:113). "In the crude state of nature, . . . the woman is a domestic animal" (VA 7:304). With increasing culture, Kant thinks, women begin to acquire compensating capacities. Women, in Kant's view, have less intellect than men, but they are more sensitive to social propriety and decorum, and they are shrewder and more self-controlled in personal interactions (VA 7:306–307). Thus women are better capable of emotional independence and the manipulation of desire through allurement.[6] A woman's acknowledgment of sexual desire is therefore more shameful than a man's because to be too open about her desire for the man would deprive her of the principal weapon she needs in the struggle to resist his domination (VA 7:307).[7]

MARRIAGE. Even at its best, the marital relationship as Kant portrays it is fundamentally a system of mutual exploitation: Each partner uses the other by taking advantage of the other's vulnerabilities.[8] The man victimizes the woman's physical and intellectual weakness, which is ramified in her position of social and economic dependence. The woman uses her allurement, emotional sensitivity, and self-control to play on the man's passions and affections. As we shall see in § 5.2, love as a natural inclination depends on the superiority of the lover over the beloved; reciprocal love therefore always depends on a kind of mutual superiority, in which each partner has some decisive advantage over the other. Sexual love is the most extreme instance of this: It is a struggle of wills in which each employs weapons against which the other is defenseless.

This makes it easier to understand Kant's infamous theory that marriage is a contract between two people for the mutual use of their sexual capacities (MS 6:277). Kant breaks with tradition when he refuses to regard procreation as the end of marriage (MS 6:277). Its function is rather to enable people to engage in sex without violating their right of personality.

The woman's humanity is especially vulnerable because her position

is weaker both naturally and socially. Kant considers this natural inequality as unalterable; for that very reason, he thinks that any additional inequality favoring the man – as occurs in prostitution, concubi-
nage, or morganatic marriage – turns the relationship into one of
wrongful domination (MS 6:279). In sex outside marriage "woman would
be degraded to a mere means for satisfying man's desires" (VA 7:309).
The violation of a person's body, which is inherent in the sex act itself,
can be made consistent with the fundamental rights of humanity only
by imposing on it a legally enforceable mutual limitation to a single
partner.[9]

For Kant the aim of marriage is to guarantee, by means of a contractual relationship, that the degradation of humanity involved in being used by another sexually is at least mutual and formally voluntary.
Precisely because Kant regards women as naturally inferior to men, he
thinks of marriage as more protective of their dignity. In marriage the
loss of one's personality in the sex act is compensated for by the fact
that one acquires the other's personality in turn.

> In [the sex act] a human being makes himself into a thing, which con-
> flicts with the right of humanity in his own person. There is only one con-
> dition under which this is possible: that while one person is acquired by
> the other *as if she were a thing*, the one who is acquired acquires the other
> in turn; for in this way each reclaims herself and restores her personality.
> (MS 6:278)

This may seem nonsensical – as if Kant thinks two wrongs make a right
or as if sex is improved by making it part of a contractual agreement,
like prostitution. We probably see things this way because we expect his
theory to show how marriage legitimates the sexual enjoyment of another in itself. For Kant, however, that would be to ask the impossible.
In marriage, prostitution, and in every other form, sexual pleasure is
derived from a use of another's person that inevitably threatens to degrade the other. Marriage preserves the right of humanity only by
adding *another* feature to the relationship (the cold contractual one),
that gives the person used a compensating right that counteracts the
threat and insures that the person is not *merely* a thing to be used. In
marriage, the other has the right to use your sexual organs, but you
have the right to use theirs, and moreover you have the *exclusive* possession of that use (a right never enjoyed by either prostitutes or their
customers).

Kant's view of sex as inherently degrading is repugnant to most of us.

But we should not dismiss it too quickly or attribute it condescendingly to the quirks of his personality or lifestyle. Kant's view of marriage as a sexual contract was just as offensive to many of his contemporaries as it is to us and for similar reasons.[10] Moreover, some of our contemporaries hold very similar views of sex, which cannot be accounted for by the condescending explanations just mentioned. According to Andrea Dworkin, the essential function of sexual intercourse is to violate the woman's bodily integrity, to reduce her from the status of a person to that of an object.[11] Even if we reject this picture as portraying sex only in a morbid and degenerate form, we still must admit that there is a dark side of sexual desire, that sexual relations inherently involve power and the threat of domination. The social regulation of *this* side of sexuality may be required to protect the rights of human beings, especially of women. Kant's theory of marriage may be repugnant and no longer tenable, but it addresses problems that cannot be so quickly dismissed.

Seen in that light, perhaps the most dubious feature of the theory turns out to be Kant's respectable bourgeois opinion that traditional legal monogamy is a satisfactory way to secure the rights of humanity in the sexual sphere. Taking marriage as Kant knew it, we cannot help asking how far exclusive possession of her husband's sexual capacities could really go toward protecting a woman's personality as long as she remained economically dependent on him and her life-activities were confined by both law and custom to the domestic sphere. What social changes would still be necessary even today for women to be treated as free persons in the context of sexual relationships? Here the prejudices of Kant's time and his own personal insensitivity to the problems of women may indeed explain why he failed to ask the right questions.[12]

3. Social passions

The passions of culture arise from inequality, which emerges along with an urban culture and the many-sided development of human faculties. Differences between people, combined with our basic natural-social propensity to self-conceit, produce a propensity to think that our will deserves to prevail over the wills of others. This leads us to seek superior status among our fellow human beings and hence a position of dominion over them.

Kant even says that the foundation of all the passions of culture is the inclination to gain *power* over others (VA 7:271). This inclination to rule is closely connected to *prudence*. In one sense, "prudence" refers merely to the capacity to choose the correct means to our happiness, but in a narrower sense it refers to the capacity to exercise control over other people through using their own passions and inclinations against them (G 4:416; KU 20:200n). The relation between the two senses is clear. We are social beings whose chief means to happiness lies in controlling and manipulating other people. Gaining that power, through fear, interest, or opinion, is the aim of the social passions.

> This inclination [to power over others] comes closest to technically-practical reason, that is, to the maxim of prudence. For getting other human beings' inclinations into our power, so that we can direct and determine them according to our own purposes, is almost the same as *possessing* other human beings as mere tools of our will. (VA 7:271)

3.1. Tyranny (Herrschsucht) Tyranny is the least subtle of the social passions. It seeks, through use of the other's fear of what one may do to them, to turn one's own selfish will as such into a coercive law over them. This directly violates the fundamental principle of justice, that all rational beings should enjoy external freedom under universal laws (VA 7:273; cf. MS 6:230).[13] Curbing this passion by force is the most basic function of an organized civil society.

> [Human beings] feel ever more keenly the ills they do to one another through selfishness as culture increases, and since they see no other means against them, they submit, though reluctantly, to a discipline (of civil coercion), subjecting the private mind (of the individual) to the common mind (of all united). (VA 7:329)

At the same time, tyranny is also the most direct *cause* of civil order, since states are founded through the might of self-willed rulers who find they can maintain their dominion over others only by defending the rights of their subjects under a system of legal justice (EF 8:365–366). Tyranny tends to be self-undermining in the long run because it seeks omnipotence, which is beyond anyone's reach. Those who inspire fear in others thereby acquire grounds to fear for themselves, which can be removed in the long run only by setting limits to everyone's possible dominion over others, including their own. For Kant the basic problem of designing a political constitution is that legal justice comes about because "the human being is an animal who needs a master," but at the same time "this master will also be an animal who needs a master" (I 8:23). Although this problem is virtually insoluble in principle, it can be addressed in Kant's view through a republican constitution with divided governmental powers and constitutional provisions for protecting the rights of individuals to freedom, equality, and independence (I 8:23; EF 8:351–353, MS 6:313–318).

3.2. Greed (Habsucht) Greed is the desire to possess things not as useful objects but as objects of exchange. Hence it is above all the desire to possess *money* – which (relying explicitly on Adam Smith) Kant defines as "the universal means by which human beings exchange their industriousness with one another," or "that material thing the alienation of which is the means and at the same time the measure of the industry by which human beings and nations carry on trade with one another" (MS 6:287–289).

We are greedy because exchangeable commodities, especially money, give us power over others by means of their interests (VA 7:274). "Wealth is power: purchasing power. . . . Money gives me the power to put the powers of others at my service" (VE 27:398). Kant emphasizes that wealth excites the respect and esteem of others because it makes the wealthy person appear independent of others (VE 27:398). The rich seem to rely only on the justice of others, requiring no one's beneficence, and hence never have to appear in the inferior relation to others of needing to be grateful (MS 6:455, VE 27:341–342, 439–440).

Kant is especially interested in the psychology through which greed can turn into miserliness or *avarice* (Geiz). Avarice is the passionate disposition to hoard money even to the point of depriving oneself of the useful goods money represents. Kant's explanation of avarice is that the representative capacity of money makes us prey to the illusion that we already possess whatever our money can buy. We have the illusion that we simultaneously possess all the mutually exclusive objects we might purchase with it.

> Here an illusion arises in us, that as long as we still possess our money, we can pay for things disjunctively, by using it either for this or for that. But we consider it collectively, and believe we have everything we can get for it. [Thus money becomes] the repository of all pleasures I can enjoy, if I will, in their totality. (VE 27:403)

In reality, however, avarice accustoms us to do without pleasures and thus actually deprives us of the useful things our money might obtain for us. The motive of avarice is really "fear of want," or else "a yearning for power and authority, and money is the best way to get them"

(VE 27:405). In short, avarice is a victory of social illusion over rational truth.

According to Kant, misers tend to be very devout people. They are also prey to superstition, which is the propensity to see nature as governed by causes arising from our subjective wishes rather than from the objective laws of the understanding (VA 7:275; KU 5:294). Misers are used to substituting imaginary powers for real objects of desire: money in place of goods we will never enjoy, divine favor or good luck in place of well-being in the here and now, which we forgo to no real purpose (VE 27:401–402). Because misers benefit neither others nor themselves, they are despised by everyone, but they cannot understand why because they feel they possess great power, hence are deserving of great respect (VE 27:400–401). But the miser's illusion has a powerful hold because it is based on the twisted version of a profound truth about civilized life: "Money brings power, it is the universal means to all ends" (VE 27:403). Hence the illusion "can never be corrected by reason, just as it would itself be irrational to offer advice to a man suffering from a hallucination" (VE 27:402). This makes avarice a nearly incurable vice. (There is obviously much in Kant's discussion of greed and avarice that anticipates Marx's later theories of alienated labor, the objective social illusions of the market, and the fetishism of commodities.)

3.3. Ambition (Ehrsucht)   Ambition is the addiction to *honor* (the good opinion of others). Ambition, Kant says, is the passionate desire that others should despise themselves when they compare themselves with us (MS 6:465, cf. VA 7:273). We have an instrumental interest in being well thought of because people who admire us will want to benefit us. To be admired by others, and especially to have them think of us as superior to themselves, is already a kind of power over them (VE 27:409). But we also want the good opinion of others for its own sake.

Kant distinguishes the desire to be *loved* by others from the desire to be *respected* or *esteemed* by them. The former corresponds to "self-love" (*philautia*), the latter to "self-conceit" (*arrogantia*) (MS 6:462). People love what benefits them, and this love depends on their inclinations; but esteem or respect involves power over them, and it is taken to depend more on the qualities of its object than on the likings of the esteemer. Consequently, ambition is not a desire to be loved but a desire to be esteemed by others (VE 27:406–407). A petty form of ambition is vanity, the desire to be admired for dress or other things incidental to our person; ambition proper focuses on self-worth (VE 27:409).

Ambition involves three distinct but closely related things: (1) a tendency to *think yourself better than others*, (2) a *desire* that *others* think of you as better than they are, and (3) a desire to *be* better than they are. Kant sees these three desires as closely linked in the psychology of comparative self-worth that is built into all our natural inclinations in virtue of our social condition. People are capable of ascribing to themselves a superiority in relation to others only to the extent that they think of their superiority as confirmed by the opinion of others. That is because comparative superiority among people is entirely a function of their ambition – their desire to be esteemed in the opinion of others. This in turn is because people are in fact all of equal worth, hence there is nothing for the (illusory) superiority of one individual over another to consist in except the fact that people hold false opinions.

Tyranny and greed, in their insatiability, make us prey to delusions. Ambition, however, insofar as honor is desired for its own sake and not merely as a means to other benefits, rests *entirely* on a delusion. The closest I can come to achieving true superiority over others is that they should come to share my own self-deception that I am superior to them. "Honor is a delusion; the ambitious person seeks only the praise of another and their submission, according to which they assign themselves to being less than he is" (VA 25:1147).

Kant maintains that "ambition," "desire for honor" (*Ehrbegierde, ambitio*) or "haughtiness" (*Hochmut, superbia*), is different from "pride" (*Stolz, animus elatus*) or the "love of honor" (*Ehrliebe*), which are equivalent to "proper self-respect" (MS 6:465–466; VE 27:408–409, VA 25:1522). Ambition may look similar to self-respect, but Kant argues that they are in fact exact contraries of one another. "The haughty person expects of others that they should *despise* themselves in comparison with him; such a thought could occur only to someone who feels ready to abase himself; so haughtiness already provides an unmistakable sign of such a person's abject mentality" (VA 7:273).

The basic difference is that ambition rests on judgments about the *comparative* worth of human beings, while self-respect rests on a self-esteem that is not conditional on one's superiority to others. Self-respect ascribes no greater worth to oneself than to anyone else and involves no partiality toward oneself. It rests solely on the "dignity" of humanity, the absolute worth belonging to rational nature as such. To respect oneself is therefore to repudiate the entire enterprise of comparing people's personal worth (MS 6:434–436; G 4:434–435; VE 27:348–350).

VICES OF FAILED AMBITION. Ambition inevitably fails in reality, since it aims at the impossible (having a worth superior to that of another). Usually it fails to reach even the attainable goal of winning over the opinion of others to that necessary falsehood. The most extreme form of ambition Kant calls "haughtiness" (*Hochmuth, superbia*) (VE 27:457–458). When we try too hard to force others to accept our self-serving delusion, we easily make ourselves the object of derision and contempt (VE 27:408).

Failed ambition leads to two contrasting things (which, however, are not mutually exclusive, but rather tend to form a sort of homeostatic pair, reinforcing one another). The *first* is self-degradation before one's successful competitors in the struggle for honor and resentment against them. When we measure our self-worth competitively and feel ourselves to have lost the competition, then we lose self-respect and seek to do the best we can for ourselves by "waiving our claim to moral worth" and adopting the servile position of a flatterer or lackey (MS 6:435). Servility is often associated with hypocrisy because our self-conceit (if not our obscure awareness of our absolute worth as persons) seldom allows us to believe wholeheartedly in the superiority of others (MS 6:436). Thus Kant associates servility with lying. Both are vices displaying cowardice and lack of self-respect (MS 6:429–430, VE 27:449).

The *second* product of failed ambition is antagonism toward one's successful competitors in the struggle for illusory superiority. There are a rich variety of such antagonisms. They constitute the greater part of the natural-social life of human beings. Kant distinguishes the following ones: jealousy, grudgingness, spite, envy, ingratitude, gloating, malice, hatred, and cruelty. "Jealousy" (*Eifersucht*) is the painful awareness of the respects in which another is seen to be superior to us; it leads us to deprecate the other's qualities, an attitude Kant calls "grudgingness" (*Mißgunst*) (VE 27:437). We naturally begrudge others any happiness we do not enjoy because we interpret it as a sign of their superiority. This tendency sometimes leads us to begrudge someone even a happiness that poses no such threat to us; this nasty trait is "spite" (*Abgunst*) (VE 27:438). When grudgingness takes a more principled form and expresses itself in actions that try to rob others of happiness, Kant calls it "envy" (*Neid*) (MS 6:458–459; VE 27:439).

Envy follows from our basic tendency to consider ourselves happy only when we think ourselves better off than others (R 6:27). When we receive some favor from another, we naturally resent the position of dependence in which this places us and the superiority of the other involved in their capacity to help us. This is the source of "ingratitude" (*Undankbarkeit*) (MS 6:459).

Our general sense of our rivalry with others gives rise to the direct delight we take in another's misfortune, called "gloating" (*Schadenfreude*) (MS 5:460). The natural rivalry between people leads them to hate each other, and just as knowing you are loved tends to produce love in return, so when I know that you hate me, my frustrated desire for your approval, arising out of my ambition, leads me to hate you in return. This phenomenon of reciprocal or reactive hatred (*Gegenhaß*) is Kant's explanation for the strong human tendency toward cruelty (*Grausamkeit*). "Thus when kings know that their subjects hate them, this makes them all the more cruel" (VE 27:444).

Servility and the antagonistic vices of failed ambition are in a sense opposites, since servility seems to be an acceptance of defeat in the struggle for self-worth, while the various antagonisms are attempts to avenge that defeat. But just as haughtiness already displays a kind of self-abasement, so servility and the antagonistic vices of failed ambition also express fundamentally the same attitude of mind. In Kant's view, servility is not really a renunciation of one's claim to self-worth but rather an attempt to substitute a false self-worth for one's true dignity. The social sycophant hopes to better his position through flattering his patron; the religious hypocrite denies any worth to himself in order to be compensated by the borrowed worth he imagines divine beings will bestow on him in return for his act of self-contempt: "Waiving any claim to moral worth in oneself, the belief that one will thereby acquire a borrowed worth is morally false servility (*humilitas spuria*)" (MS 6:435). The rancor contained in vices such as envy, ingratitude, and malice also expresses the same inner contempt for oneself displayed in servility, for the envious, ungrateful, malicious, or cruel person does not inflict pain on another in order to vindicate his self-worth but rather to avenge himself against the other for failing to achieve the superiority he sought. Hence such vices not only violate one's duty of love to others but "add meanness (*Niederträchtigkeit*) to one's neglect of duty to one's neighbor, so that one also violates a duty to oneself" (MS 6:458).

4. Desire and deception

4.1. Moral ambiguity   Kant is usually thought of as asserting the rigorous separation of right from wrong, good from evil. Yet the reason he thinks we must struggle so hard to keep good distinct from evil is that they are so inextricably intertwined in the human heart. There is nothing in human nature that evil does not corrupt, and nothing so evil that it cannot also be made to serve the good.

The foundation of all goodness is the esteem rational beings have for themselves, yet this is also the source of their self-conceit and the vices that spring from ambition. On the other side, ambition is fundamentally evil, but the desire for honor from which it springs is placed in us for good and serves nature's purposes. By exciting competitiveness, it serves to develop human faculties. Our concern about the opinion of others can even promote the moral end of rational harmony between people. Since what gains the approval of others sometimes approximates to the common good, ambitious behavior sometimes has a tendency to mimic moral virtue. Our ambitious desire for the good opinion of others serves to open our minds (VE 27:410). By making us attend to the opinions of others, ambition therefore also directly serves the development of critical reason, since the only effective way we have of correcting our erroneous opinions is to try to bring them into agreement with the opinions of others through expression and communication (KrV A743–751/B771–779, KU 5:293, O 8:144, VA 7:219).[14]

4.2. Delusion (Wahn)   Kant describes inclination as the "deceiver within ourselves" (VA 7:151). Passions subject us to "delusion," which Kant defines as "the internal practical deception of taking what is subjective in a motive for something objective" (VA 7:274; cf. R 6:168). This definition is intended to fit the delusions of insanity or dementia (in which people take figments of their imagination to be real things) (VA 7:215). But it also encompasses human tendencies that are more common and less extreme, as when we enjoy playing imaginatively with objects of fantasy, pine for imagined goods we hope for but can never enjoy, or ascribe to real things imaginary properties corresponding to our wishes (as in superstition) (VA 7:275).

Kant thinks delusion itself is a human passion (an inclination that reason controls only with difficulty). Human nature is especially prone to "present objects of imagination as real ends (ways of acquiring honor, dominion, and money)"; inclinations focusing on such delusions "are apt to become passionate in the highest degree, especially when they are applied to *competition* among human beings" (VA 7:275). Avaricious people represent something subjective as objective when they enjoy their money because in their imagination it represents all possible forms of power and happiness. We bend the requirements of morality so that our conduct can more easily conform to them. Our aim is self-conceitedly to picture ourselves as morally better than we are. We jealously project bad qualities on others whom we see as rivals for moral excellence so as to make ourselves look better by comparison in our own eyes.

Each of the passions of culture appears to its subject as a desire for freedom from the constraint of another's will. This is what tantalizes us about the prospect of gaining tyrannical power, acquiring the wealth needed to place others in a position of dependence, or being honored by them so that they regard us as their superior. It is the delusory character of these prospects that makes our desires insatiable and turns them into passions. But the freedom at which passions aim is also delusory in another way since every passion is actually "a slavish disposition, through which another, having gained power over it, acquires the capacity to use one's own inclinations to serve his aims" (VA 7:272).

The social life that results when people follow their natural inclinations is always grounded on domination and subjection. The domination is grounded partly on the fear, interest, or opinion of the dominated, but also on their delusory hopes, when they fancy themselves on the way to achieving a dominant position in relation to someone else. This makes social relationships based on natural desire not only relations of *domination* but also of *deceit*. People are dominated in part precisely through their acceptance of the delusory hope that they may become dominant themselves. (How many poor people, who envy and hate the rich, nevertheless tolerate monstrous inequalities of wealth merely because they hope eventually to be among the few who rise to the top? Some even consider this vicious delusion admirable: "the American Dream.")

Insofar as we are social beings, all our inclinations take on a deceptive quality, not only for others, but even for ourselves. This is one reason for Kant's cautious attitude toward the study of anthropology itself, noted earlier: "To obscure something is the art of clever brains" (VA 25: 737). "Human beings are one and all actors – the more so the more civilized they are" (VA 7:151). "It belongs to the basic constitution of the human creature and to the concept of his species to explore the thoughts of others, but to withhold one's own – a nice quality that does not fail to progress gradually from *dissimulation* to *deception* and finally to *lying*" (VA 7:332). When Kant wants to display the radical evil in human nature as it shows itself in the civilized condition, the *first* evils he fastens on are those involving deception: "the secret falsity in even the closest friendship," the universal distrust of all our fellow humans which prudence demands, the propensity to hate those who have benefited us, the malicious joy in the misfortunes of even our best friends, and the "many vices concealing themselves under the appearance of virtue" (R 6:33–34).

In the civilized condition, people advance their interests mainly by hiding their faults and pretending to merits they do not have. Those who care about the truth rather than the opinion of others are therefore imperfectly socialized, and we condescendingly call them "naïve":

> Naïveté is conduct where one does not pay attention to whether one is being judged by others. Whoever has not yet become shy before others, e.g. a young innocent girl, says something entirely correct, but one notes right away that she does not fear being judged by others, and then it comes across as naïve . . . Such naïve remarks arouse laughter, which, however, is to the advantage of those who say them. (VA 25:866–867)

For Kant, our social relationships involve not only conscious deception but also an even more insidious falsehood woven into the fabric of the natural feelings through which people relate to each other. Obsequious behavior conceals the self-interest of the hypocritical flatterer. Sincere esteem leads to jealousy and envy. Gratitude easily gives rise to the resentment of being put by one's benefactor in a position of dependence. My passions make me a victim of delusions that deliver me into the hands of those prudent enough to exploit them.

In the social (and especially in the civilized) condition, elementary prudence dictates that we never entirely trust others and that we behave in ways that will probably inspire their distrust. This is such common knowledge that everyone takes it for granted that no one is what they seem and no one means what they say: "[People] put on a show of affection, respect for one another, modesty and impartiality, but without deceiving anyone, since it is generally understood that they are not sincere" (VA 7:151).

4.3. Permissible deceptions Surprisingly, Kant does not entirely disapprove of this. He thinks we are so entangled in deceptions that we have no choice but to "deceive the deceiver within ourselves " by using some of the deceptions of civilized life in such a way as to improve ourselves. In particular, he thinks that pretending to virtues we lack can sometimes lead, through a beneficial self-deception, to the acquisition of the virtue itself.

Kant agrees with the advice Hamlet gave his mother: "Assume a virtue if you have it not."[15] "If human beings keep on playing these roles, then the real virtues whose semblance they have merely been affecting for a long time are gradually aroused and pass into their attitude of will" (VA 7:151). "A *dignified bearing* is an outward show that instills *respect* in others. . . . *Modesty*, a self-restraint that conceals passion, is a salutary illusion that keeps the sexes sufficiently far apart that one is not degraded into a mere tool for the other's enjoyment" (VA 7:152). "We must value even the semblance of good in others," since we thereby become more benevolent to them and by trying to live up to our opinion they may develop the virtues they pretend to have.

The matter is quite otherwise regarding ourselves. "It is only the semblance of good *in ourselves* that we must wipe away; we must tear off the veil with which self-love covers our moral defects" (VA 7:153). This is not easy to do because the basic motive for self-concealment and dissimulation is simple self-protection.

> The human being is inclined to be reserved and to dissimulate. . . , being reserved about his weaknesses and misdeeds, and also dissimulating and creating semblances. The inclination to reserve and concealment rests on caution; the human being must not be completely open because he is full of faults, . . . which are objectionable to others, and we don't want to show ourselves to others as foolish and hateful. (VE 27:444)

If we let others know too much about us, they will not only come to despise us, but they will also use this knowledge to their advantage and our discredit. "Therefore no human being in his right mind is candid" (VE 27:445). Kant applies this point even, or rather *especially*, to close friendships:

> We must conduct ourselves toward a friend in such a way that it would do us no harm if he became our enemy, we must not put anything in his hands. . . . If I rely completely on my friend, and confide to him all the secrets that could threaten my happiness if he became my enemy and blabbed them around, then that would be extremely careless of me. (VE 27:429–430)

5. Sympathy, Love, and Charity

In surveying Kant's conception of human nature we have thus far emphasized the sinister passions. We must take care not to ignore Kant's treatment of the more likable inclinations: sympathy, love, charity, and friendship. We do this not to provide a "balanced" account but only so as not to underestimate Kant's shrewdly bleak vision of all interpersonal relationships based on natural feelings. For Kant's view of sociable inclinations will in the end do very little to cheer us.

Kant distinguishes several meanings of "love." "Practical love" or "love of good will" is the policy of benefiting others on moral principle from the motive of duty. Only this kind of love can be a direct duty (KpV 5:82–84, MS 6:449–453). We also have philanthropy or love of human beings as part of our moral predisposition (MS 6:401–402). Like the feeling of respect, moral feeling, and conscience, philanthropy is not a natural inclination but an immediate effect of reason on sensibility (MS 6:401–402). Philanthropy is impartial love, and acting from it is acting from duty rather than inclination. In this section, however, our topic is love as an inclination, arising out of our natural sociability.

Sociable inclinations are part of our predisposition to animality. They are naturally purposive for the life of both the individual and the species. They are also purposive for morality because they usually manifest a good will and help it to achieve its ends. Since we have a duty to make the happiness of others our end, we have moral reasons to value these inclinations and even a *duty* to cultivate them (MS 6:456–457; VA 7:253; VE 27:417–420, 459–460). At times Kant goes so far as to suggest that our imperfect wills may not succeed in doing duty consistently without the presence of love to assist the incentives of reason (ED 8:337–338). Despite their usefulness to morality, however, the amiable inclinations still stand entirely outside it and are not to be trusted.

5.1. Sympathy   Kant holds that nature has put sympathetic feelings (*Mitfreude, Mitleid*) in us in order to bring us closer to one another through sharing one another's joys and sorrows (KU 5:208). They can serve as a substitute for morality "*provisionally,* until reason has achieved the necessary strength" (VA 7:253). We tend to feel compassion for those we take to be weaker than ourselves, and this often coincides with our duty to protect them (VA 7:263). Yet compassion is unreliable because, like all inclinations, it goes its own way and follows no rule (VE 27:419). Compassion is also a poor basis for action because it can become an affect, hindering our ability to pursue ends chosen rationally (VA 7:252–253; cf. KU 5:272). Such an affect might paralyze a villain, preventing an act of cruelty, but this is only good luck, not good will. Compassion makes us *sentimental,* we dwell self-indulgently on our own feelings rather than acting effectively toward good ends (KU 5:273; VE 27:420–421). There can be no duty to cultivate feelings of that kind (MS 6:457).[16]

5.2. *Love* We are more likely to see something moral in sociable feelings if we think not of momentary rushes of emotion but of *love*, as an abiding inclination to promote someone else's welfare. Kantian ethics, however, is not an ethics of love in this sense. We will see why when we understand the role love plays, according to Kant's theory, in the economy of our unsociable sociability.

Love as *feeling* must also be distinguished from love as *desire*. "Aesthetic love" or the "love of well-pleasedness" (*Wohlgefallens*) is a feeling of pleasure (whether intellectual or sensual) taken in the perfections of another. "Pathological love" or the "love of benevolence" (*Wohlwollens*) is a desire to benefit another (VE 27:416; KU 5:276; cf. MS 6:449). The two are connected because taking pleasure in another (or in another's perfections) is closely associated with taking pleasure in the representation of the other's happiness, which is the same as having a desire for it. But this should not be understood in the sense that I love the other only as a means to feeling the pleasure I take in her perfections. To represent the other's perfections with a feeling of pleasure should rather be seen as triggering a representation of the other's happiness also with a feeling of pleasure, and that means desiring the beloved's happiness for its own sake, not as a means to my pleasure or happiness.[17]

Kant thinks there is a basic tension in human nature between *loving* people and *respecting* them (VE 27:406–407, MS 6:449).[18] Respect and love are not mutually exclusive: In rational philanthropy they even go necessarily together. But in our natural inclinations they make for an unstable combination. Love as inclination is based on the pleasure we take in another (or her perfections), but respect for others pains us by striking down our self-conceit. Love as an empirical inclination, however, is not opposed to self-conceit and indirectly it is even an expression of it.

Kant brings love, along with all other inclinations, under the egoistic principle of self-love or one's own happiness (KpV 5:22). This does not mean that love seeks the other's happiness only as a means to my happiness. Kant's point is rather that empirical love falls under the principle of self-love by selecting its objects partly on the grounds of self-love. Love exhibits a kind of second-order self-partiality; its objects are subject to limits set by "the dear self."

Because we tend to take pleasure in what is advantageous to us, we also tend to feel aesthetic love, and hence pathological love, for those whose qualities or actions please or benefit us (VE 27: 407). But this is

in tension with our disposition to hate benefactors when the benefit obligates us or makes us dependent and puts the benefactor in a position
of superiority. Since our first need is to be honored rather than benefited, we fear rivals for this honor but love those over whom we can exercise superiority.

Consequently, love more often selects as its objects those who please
us without threatening our self-esteem. We tend to love those to whom
we can feel superior, those we can trust, and those we have in our power.
Kant tries out different theories on this point, some making only the
point that an absence of rivalry is required for love, others insisting that
love requires a decisive superiority over the beloved. The common theme
is that where love as a natural inclination is concerned, we tend to love
only those whom we feel we do not need to respect.

> We need more to be honored than to be loved, but we also need some-
> thing to love with which we don't stand in rivalry. So we love birds, dogs,
> or a young, fickle and cheerful person. Even love between men and
> women is partly grounded on this, since no struggle for superiority oc-
> curs between people of different kinds. (R 1471, 15:649)
>
> We love everything over which we have a decisive superiority, so that
> we can toy with it, while it has a pleasant cheerfulness about it: little dogs,
> birds, grandchildren. Men and women have a reciprocal superiority over
> one another. (R 1100, 15:490)
>
> Love, like water, always flows downward more easily than upward.
> (VE 27:670)

From these remarks it is easy enough to see why Kant thinks *sexual* desire
is easily combined with love. The object of our desire gives us pleasure,
and over it we feel a decisive *superiority* (for the man this superiority is
physical and social, taking the form of power and dominion; for the
woman it is emotional and erotic, taking the form of manipulation).
Since in such a relationship one is always at the same time (and in another respect) *inferior* to the object of one's desire, sexual love is simultaneously a condition of superiority and vulnerability. Each is subject to
manipulation and control by the other.

If Kant's theory of love as inclination is correct, then he is quite right
in regarding it as he does in the *Groundwork*: as an amiable feeling, but
one whose production of morally good actions is only "contingent and
spurious" (G 4:390) and from which we are correct in withholding esteem (G 4:398). Because the selection of its objects is an indirect expression of self-conceit, empirical love is not motivated by the dignity

of rational nature and cannot be counted on to combat the competitive conception of self-worth which is the ground of moral evil.

5.3. *Charity* (Gütigkeit)   Defenders of an ethics of love might concede that Kant is right about love as just described, but assert that the love they mean to defend is a natural inclination to kindness or generosity toward others that is not partial in this way. Kant accepts the existence of such an inclination, which he calls *Gütigkeit* ("charity" or "kindness"). He regards charity, like love, as both likable and worthy of encouragement, but it too is unreliable in producing dutiful actions and has no claim on our rational esteem.

If charity were the only motive behind human actions, Kant says, then no one would ever have to put forth special effort for their own good, but everyone's needs would be met spontaneously by the inclinations of others. Charity could be the sole motive only in a world of abundance, in which there is no need to distinguish what is mine from what is yours or to worry about the competing desires of others. Plainly, we do not live in such a world. Kant does not even think it would be good if we did, since then we would have had no incentive to develop our faculties through struggling to meet our own needs (VE 27:416–417).

Like love, but in a different way, charity is circumscribed by the more fundamental inclinations of our unsociable sociability. People do not usually feel benevolent unless they think highly of themselves and regard their own circumstances as comparatively enviable. "One wishes others well only when one feels oneself to be well off" (R 6600, 19:104). What makes us charitable is still that the act of benefiting another establishes the benefactor's superiority. Charity is very often merely the smiling mask worn by oppression and injustice ("capitalism with a human face"). "Kindnesses (*Gütigkeiten*) occur only through inequalities" (Ak 20:36).[19]

> The greatest and most common miseries of humanity rest more on the injustice of human beings than on misfortune. Since respect for rights is a consequence of principles, but since human beings are lacking in principle, providence has implanted in us another source, namely the instinct of charity, through which we replace what we have previously gotten in an unjust manner. . . . We participate in the general injustice even if we do no injustice according to civil laws and institutions. When we show beneficence to a needy person, we do not give him anything gratuitously, but only give him some of what we have previously helped to take from him through the general injustice. . . . Thus even actions from charity are

acts of duty and obligation, based on the rights of others. (VE 27:415–416, cf. 27:455–456)

This is both what makes people charitable and also why people receive charity only reluctantly. "Good deeds make us ungrateful because we fear being despised" (R 1471, 15:649).

Not far beneath the surface of charity Kant always sees the self-conceited delusion of moral sentimentalists, who want to pretend they need no constraint in order to do good deeds (VE 27:455–456). "It is the mark of actions done from charity that the ground of obligation is turned into another ground" (R 6585, 19:96). This explains why a person overflowing with the milk of human kindness is likely to feel insulted by Kant's sour-faced assertion that actions have moral worth only when done from duty. "Such a person will do a great deal out of charity, but if someone came to him in great need to demand something as owed, speaking in the ordinary language of indebtedness, then he would call this vulgar, and say the other wants everything by compulsion" (VE 27:416; cf. R 6736, 19:145).

It is significant that Kant points up the flaw in charity by imagining a *counterfactual* situation in which the charitable person *ceases* to feel and act charitably. Kant is *not* claiming (as simple-minded psychological egoists often do) that charitable actions are merely a surreptitious means to assert one's superiority or feed one's self-conceit. But he sees nothing at all in charity to combat the firmly rooted human tendency to self-conceit, and thus refuses to see it as worthy of esteem (G 4:398, KpV 5:82).

Of course if I do not measure self-worth in the competitive way characteristic of natural–social inclinations, then my sympathy, love, and charity need not be selective in this self-serving manner. If I respect the dignity of rational nature and accept my equality with all others, these feelings only make it easier to fulfill my duties to others. What that shows, however, is that our sociable feelings, like all other gifts of nature and fortune, are good only on the condition that they follow the guidance of reason so that their evil tendencies can be corrected through the influence of a good will (G 4:392–393).

5.4. Sociability and misanthropy   Why do we have inclinations toward the good of others? In order to understand Kant's answer to this question, we need to keep in mind that the basic principle of our empirical desires is unsociable *sociability* – social antagonism within the context of mutual need and interdependence. Our antagonistic impulses tend to break society up, so by themselves, they would lead people to live separately. Without sociable inclinations, we would reason that since we cannot stand others, we should simply avoid them. In that case we might succeed in avoiding the social antagonism that makes us unhappy but is nature's device for unfolding our predispositions. This is what the cynical hermit tries to do when he dispenses with civilization and avoids contact with other people. Kant calls this attitude of "negative misanthropy" a "flight from humanity." It is a form of "timidity" or "anthropophobia" (*Leutescheuen*), "which cuts itself off from all human beings because it regards them as enemies and fears harm from them" (VE 27:672).

Nature foils that option, however, by implanting sociable inclinations in us that make such a life a basic denial of our humanity. By means of our sociable inclinations, nature insures that we are "unable to *do without* living peacefully side by side but also unable to avoid constantly offending one another" (VA 7:331; cf. I 8:21, KU 5:276). Negative misanthropy is a vice akin to positive hatred of humanity. Cynical withdrawal from society is not a way of avoiding social antagonism but only a cowardly form of that antagonism. It is related to the other misanthropic vices of failed ambition: jealousy, envy, spite, and gloating. These characteristics coincide in suppressing sympathy, love, generosity, friendship, and the other sociable feelings that, though untrustworthy and devoid of moral worth, are still the most likable inclinations nature has given us.

6. Friendship

Friendship is an important theme both in Kantian ethics and Kantian anthropology. One would have to go back as far as Aristotle to find a major philosopher for whom friendship is as important to ethics as it is for Kant.[20] Since Kant's theory of friendship has some fundamental points in common with Aristotle's, but also some deep points of contrast, it will be useful to compare them.

Like Aristotle, Kant distinguishes three kinds of friendship, regarding only one of them as true or complete friendship and the other two as imperfect likenesses or incomplete forms of friendship. Aristotle distinguishes the friendship of advantage, the friendship of pleasure, and the friendship based on moral character.[21] Analogously, Kant distinguishes between the friendship of need, the friendship of taste, and the friendship of disposition (*Gesinnung*) or sentiment (*Sentiment*) (VE 27: 424–426). Kant regards friendship of need (or mutual advantage) as the original foundation of all friendship, but the friendship of taste (pleasure in the company of the other) as only an analogue of friendship (VE 27:425).

6.1. The true form of friendship   Since Kant regards the friendship of disposition or sentiment as the true or complete form of friendship, unless otherwise indicated we will refer to it henceforth simply as "friendship." This form of friendship bears a complex relation to morality. Its *natural* end (the need it serves in relation to human nature) is not a moral end. But both moral virtue and action on moral principles turn out to be required for friendship to reach its natural end. Further, though the natural end of friendship is not moral, it nevertheless stands in close relation to the ends of morality. Finally, because friendship turns out to involve a disposition that makes us worthy of happiness, Kant also argues that friendship is an ethical duty for human beings.

In describing the highest kind of friendship, Aristotle emphasizes the mutual esteem and admiration friends have for one another's characters. According to his account, virtuous friends wish good to one another because they perceive one another to be good, and to be similar in goodness.[22] For Kant, however, the basic thing in all forms of friendship is not mutual admiration but mutual benevolence. In the friendship of disposition or sentiment, it is even more fundamentally mutual revelation and understanding: "Each participating and sharing sympathetically in the other's well-being through the morally good will that unites them" (MS 6:469).

Friendship for Kant is furthered by a morally good will, and it cultivates a good will. But the source of benevolence to one's friend is *not* esteem for the morally good will one might find in one's friend. For Kant, to put friendship on that basis would only invite the deceit and enmity that would come inevitably from a competitive struggle for honor in which flawed beings attempt to persuade one another that they are better than they really are. Instead, friendship evolves originally from the "general love of humanity" (or rational philanthropy) that arises from appreciating the absolute worth of the other's person, irrespective of the goodness of the other's will (VE 27:422).

This general basis of friendship, therefore, cannot explain why I am friends with one individual rather than another. On Kant's view, the explanation is rather this: If I am Paul's friend rather than Peter's, that is not because Paul seems more virtuous to me than Peter, nor is it because Paul and I are more alike in virtue. It is rather because I have somehow succeeded in developing a special relation of intimacy and mutual trust with Paul and not with Peter (MS 6:471–472, VE 27:428, 430, 677–678).[23] It is this relation of intimacy that provides friendship with its natural end in relation to our human needs, since our sociability involves a fundamental need to reveal ourselves to others, despite the dangers this always involves for social creatures like ourselves.

Moral virtue first enters into Kant's account of friendship *not* (as with Aristotle) through the fact that *you must be virtuous* for me to have a reason to wish you well.[24] It enters instead through the perception that *I must seek to be virtuous and to act virtuously in relation to you* in order to be *worthy* of the trust and benevolence I hope you will show me as a friend (VE 27:429). Kant agrees with Aristotle that virtuous people will be better friends than vicious people, but he does not think that we do (or should) select as friends those who are especially virtuous (or those with virtues like our own). Rather, virtuous people make better friends because they are more likely to follow the principles that preserve the intimacy and mutual trust we need in friendship (VE 27:429).

Aristotle appears to hold that only good people can share in the best kind of friendship because bad people are unworthy of it. For Kant, that would annihilate all friendship among human beings, since by that standard no one would qualify for friendship. If my friend's bad conduct threatens our friendship, this is not because it gives me reason to think (self-conceitedly) that she is no longer worthy of my friendship but rather because it threatens the mutual trust between us that is required to sustain our intimate self-revelation to one another.

Kant and Aristotle agree that friends must tend to agree in their moral principles. But for Kant this is *not* because friends must be *alike* in virtue. Instead it is only because some fundamental agreement of this kind is needed for trusting communication between friends. In fact, Kant positively denies that friends must in general be alike or think alike. He even argues, on the contrary, that friendship thrives on differences in cases where "each supplies what the other lacks" (VE 27:428–429).[25]

For Kant the mutual benevolence involved in friendship rests fundamentally on the rational philanthropy we feel toward others.[26] Nevertheless, the benevolence involved in friendship is not typically grounded on the thought of duty. Kant explains that by describing it as the friendship of "disposition" or "sentiment" he means "dispositions of sensation and not dispositions of performance" (VE 27:426–427). For Kant what matters most in friendship is the mutual communication of thoughts and feelings. Our natural need for friendship is the need to share our condition with others unreservedly, to be "wholly in society" (*gänzlich in Gesellschaft*) with our friend (VE 27:427). It is this need, not the thought of duty, that leads friends to behave benevolently toward each other. The same need to share their inner lives leads friends also to unite their ends into a common end, encompassing their separate ends which they then consciously pursue in common.

Our need for friendship arises from a powerful "need to reveal [ourselves] to others (even with no ulterior end)" (MS 6:471). As we saw earlier, in social intercourse people must be cautious and defensive about revealing themselves; elementary prudence dictates that they not be wholly honest with one another. But as sociable beings, we nevertheless have a profound need for it to be otherwise, to be fully with and open to, or "wholly in society" with, one another.

> Even if we are among our acquaintances and in society we are still not wholly in society. In every society one holds back most of one's sentiments, dispositions and judgments. Everyone expresses the judgments that seem advisable under the circumstances: everyone is under constraint, everyone mistrusts everyone else. . . But if we can release ourselves from this constraint and give the other what we really feel, then we are wholly in society. (VE 27:427; cf. MS 6:470–471)

This need can be satisfied only through friendship, which is "the human being's refuge in this world from the distrust of his fellows, in which one can reveal his disposition to another and enter into community with him; this is the whole human end, through which he can enjoy his existence." (VE 27:428)

6.2. The elements of friendship   Kant formulates the nature of true friendship in the following way: "A complete love of benevolence (*Wohlwollens*) and also of well-pleasedness (*Wohlgefallens*) among equals in regard to their moral disposition and inclinations" (VE 27:680). This formula summarizes a detailed analysis of friendship he has just provided, involving five distinct elements. Let us briefly consider each in turn:

1. *Reciprocal benevolence.* The ground of friendship is always the general or philanthropic love that we rationally feel for every human being as a rational nature. This is a benevolence (*Wohlwollen*) grounded on the well-pleasedness (*Wohgefallen*) we experience in the dignity of the

other's rational nature as an end in itself. "Benevolence changes into friendship (*amicitia*) through being a reciprocal love or *amor bilateralis*" (VE 27: 675–676).

2. *Equality.* Kant denies that there can be any true friendship at all between unequals (VE 27:676).[27] Any inequality between friends, anything that puts one of them in a position of superiority over the other, undermines the fragile trust required by the intimacy that makes it possible for friends to "possess one another" and share their thoughts, feelings, and lives with one another (VE 27:683). Friendship requires equal love but more importantly equal respect (MS 6:469). In civilized life this is always a fragile balance, and it is threatened when one friend becomes too dependent on the other or owes the other too heavy a debt of gratitude for favors received (MS 6:471). Kant thinks this also entails that marriage can never involve true friendship, since the wife is economically dependent on the husband and her respect for him must therefore be greater than his respect for her (VE 27:683).[28]

Although love, in the sense of the disposition to benefit the other for her own sake, is an element of friendship, there is also a sense in which loving someone, in the sense discussed in § 5.2 above, constitutes an obstacle to being her friend. For friendship requires mutual equality, while as we saw there, love requires superiority over what is loved, and mutual love requires mutual superiority (such as obtains necessarily, in Kant's opinion, between men and women). The fact that a husband and wife have this kind of love for each other would therefore seem to be another obstacle to their being friends.

3. *Reciprocal possession.* Kant thinks that friendship *is* like marriage in one way. Regarding human ends and sentiments, friendship is what marriage is regarding coercive right – namely, something like a mutual surrender or alienation of two persons to each other. Kant resists the Platonic inference that the common possession of one another requires the pooling of resources, but even so, he holds that each friend "belongs to the other": "Each mutually shares in every situation of the other as if it were encountered by himself" (VE 27:677).[29] This is what Kant means by the formula "each participating and sharing sympathetically in the other's well-being" (MS 6:469). In this way, friendship is also the clearest real model in human life for the ideal realm of ends, in which the ends of all rational beings are united into a single system. Kant indicates this when he regards friendship as a relation in which one's happiness is effectively promoted not through one's own striving but through a common striving toward an end in which both happinesses

have been included: "This is the idea of friendship, where self-love is swallowed up in the idea of a generous mutual love" (VE 27:423).

4. *Intimate communication.* This for Kant is the final end of all friendship. He describes this element of friendship simply as "the [friends'] reciprocal enjoyment of their humanity." "This mutual enjoyment, which arises in that one shares his thoughts with the other, and the other conversely with him, is the foundation of openheartedness, *animus apertus sinceritas aperta*" (VE 27:677). "Moral friendship" is therefore described as "the complete confidence of two persons in revealing their secret judgments and feelings to each other, as far as such disclosures are consistent with mutual respect" (MS 6:471).

5. *Love toward reciprocal well-pleasedness* (*die Liebe zu dem wechselseitigen Wohlgefallen*) (VE 27:680). What Kant means by this phrase is that people are truly friends only if in addition to loving one another, they also cherish (or love) something of great moral value that friendship instantiates, namely, the fact that two human beings really do reciprocally esteem one another, show benevolence toward one another, communicate intimately, and unite their ends, swallowing up the happiness of each into a shared end. It is only this fifth feature of friendship, in fact, that makes friendship an ethical duty: "Even though it does not produce complete happiness of life, the [friends'] adoption of this ideal [of friendship] in their disposition toward one another makes them deserving of happiness; hence human beings have a duty of friendship" (MS 6:469).

These five elements of friendship constitute necessary conditions for it, but in different ways. (1) identifies the ultimate foundation of friendship in the objective value of the persons who enter into it, without which nothing like friendship would be possible. (2) is the necessary condition of its possibility in the relationship of the two who are friends. (3) is the unique effect friendship has on the rational volition of the individuals, which accounts for its moral value and importance. (4) is the final end of friendship from the standpoint of our natural needs, and (5) is the final end of friendship from the standpoint of morality.

Kant emphasizes that no stable friendship can be based on natural feelings and desires alone, because a relationship based on feelings can never sustain the trust required either for intimate communication or for the persisting commitment to a shared end required for mutual possession. "Friendship is something so delicate (*teneritas amicitiae*) that it is never for a moment safe from interruptions if it is allowed to rest on feelings." This is not because feelings are sensuous or empirical but because even such feelings as sympathy, love, and charity rest on the natural-social propensity to self-conceit, which can only threaten the equality and mutual possession required for friendship. This is why true friendship can exist only as "moral friendship," based on a common commitment to ends and principles (MS 6:471).

Friendship is the only relationship between people that is based on natural needs and natural desires that also requires morality. This is how it leads us in the direction of a common life (the realm of ends) based on shared ends adopted through rational principles.

Kant's theory of friendship is indispensable for understanding his ethical thought. This is not only because friendship is the most concrete example of pursuing the moral realm of ends, but also – as we shall see in Chapter 9 – because it is the best way of understanding his conception of the religious community, which is the social formation in which Kant invests most of his historical hopes for the moral progress of humanity.

Any appreciation of Kant's theory of friendship must immediately give the lie to the false image of Kant's ethical thought as "individualistic." For although Kant is an uncompromising defender of the dignity of human individuals and the rights grounded on it, we can hardly regard "individualist" as an accurate classification of any moral philosopher who thinks we have an ethical duty to enter into personal relationships involving us in the mutual surrender of ourselves, the common possession of each other, and the swallowing up of our happiness in commitment to collective ends.

6.3. The limits of friendship   Kant insists that friendship is always an *idea* to which actual friendships can never perfectly correspond (MS 6:469; VE 27:423–424). In that respect friendship is like our virtues and our moral principles, which always exist in an imperfect form, forever standing in need of correction and striving endlessly toward perfection. As part of the condition of finite rational beings, it shares in the insuperable self-alienation of that condition.

One obvious way in which Kant thinks even the best friendships are inevitably imperfect is in regard to the complete equality required for friendship. For the social condition is essentially a condition of inequality, and (at least up to the present stage of history) it becomes more so the more culture and civilization progress. Moreover, the self-conceit built into all human feelings and inclinations constantly tends to upset the equality between any two individuals. This limitation of friendship is inseparable, of course, from the unsociable sociability on which it is grounded. For from the standpoint of natural teleology, we need friendship in order to prevent us from being misanthropic and hence anthropophobic, separating ourselves from society. But nature's purpose in bringing us into society is to make us compete with and seek superiority over one another so as to develop our species capacities.

A second crucial limitation on friendship has to do with what Kant takes to be its most fundamental end as regards our natural feelings and desires, namely, intimacy of communication. We saw earlier that Kant advises us on grounds of prudence never to open ourselves fully to our friend but always to conduct ourselves to our friend as one who might later be our enemy and use our revelations against us (VE 27:429). Friends must also be cautious in the giving and receiving of favors, in view of the tension within friendship between love and respect. Perfect friendship requires mutual respect, which will be threatened by too much love, too much familiarity, too much openness (MS 6:261). Further, friends must be careful not to go too far in their generosity to one another, since friendship requires perfect equality, and if the benefits conferred are too one sided, then the debt of gratitude incurred by one friend may undermine the respect of the other (VE 27:425). Finally, because – as we shall see at the beginning of Chapter 9 – the deepest truth about human beings in the social condition is always morally abominable, the desire of friends to open their hearts to one another always remains under constraint even on grounds of love:

> The trust and confidence goes as far as disposition and sentiment, but decency must still be observed; for we all have certain natural frailties and must be reserved regarding them lest humanity be outraged. Even to one's best friend one must not reveal oneself as one naturally is and knows oneself, for that would be loathsome. (VE 27:427–428)

Our sociability gives us a desperate need to be "wholly in society"; yet our unsociable nature frustrates this need in manifold ways. So in relation to others we must forever pretend to be the friend that both we and our friend know we can never be. Kant therefore finds the deepest truth about friendship in a saying sometimes attributed to Aristotle: "My dear friends, there are no friends" (MS 6:470; VA 7:152; VE 27:424; cf. G 4:408).[30]

THE HISTORICAL VOCATION
OF MORALITY

Kant's ethical thought is self-consciously addressed to the historical needs of an age of enlightenment. Kant views the human race – even (or especially) its most cultivated part – as confronted by crucial questions imposed on it by the natural teleology of human history and the stage in that history which it has reached.

The human species, beset collectively by an innate propensity to evil, finds itself still in the historical epoch of nature. It has long since become "civilized" and therefore finds itself sunk in a condition of social antagonism, misery, inequality, war, and injustice. Yet it also finds itself at the beginning of a new epoch of freedom, struggling to "moralize" itself by combating its evil propensity and discipline the wills of individuals to follow the rational law of autonomy. In individuals, the enemies of morality are passion and self-conceit, the obstacles to moralization are fear, intellectual indolence, and the deadly comfort of deference to authority. In societies, the obstacles to progress are inequality and injustice, the external unfreedom of political tyranny, and the inner unfreedom of traditional superstitions. In Kant's view, the indispensable condition for the historical struggle for good is freedom of thought and communication. But the most powerful historical force for good is an enlightened religious community. Our task in this chapter will be to look at Kant's ethical thought from the perspective of its historical self-conception.

1. The radical evil in human nature

1.1. The propensity to evil   Kant's most striking anthropological doctrine is that human nature contains a radical propensity to evil. The doctrine scandalized some of Kant's contemporary admirers because it seemed to them a deplorable concession to the unenlightened misanthropic Christian doctrine of original sin. Recent scholars have more often puzzled over its meaning and the kind of proof Kant intends to give for it.

'Radical evil' does not refer to a special kind of evil that is especially "radical." Kant's doctrine is that all the evil we commit has a common *root* in human nature, that the human will has an innate *propensity* (*Hang*) to make choices against the moral law. A "propensity" (*Hang*) is a dispositional property of the free will. Kant characterizes it as "the predisposition to desire an enjoyment which, when the subject once has experience of it, produces an *inclination* for it" (R 6:28). I have an innate propensity toward alcohol addiction, for example, if drinking alcohol gives me a compulsive desire to drink more (R 6:29 note). Kant thinks of the propensity to evil as a predisposition to have inclinations of a certain pattern, namely, those that prefer nonmoral incentives to the incentive of the moral law, even though reason commands us to prefer the moral incentive to all nonmoral ones.

Because this propensity belongs to our nature only insofar as we are rational beings with free choice, it is something for which we are responsible. Since all good or evil must lie in a maxim or rule made by the will (R 6:21), the radical evil in human nature thus consists in a "fundamental maxim," adopted by free choice, which underlies all the evil actions we perform (R 6:25). In his writings before the *Religion*, Kant sometimes says or implies that the moral law is an imperative for us merely because we have, besides reason, natural needs or desires that can come into conflict with its laws (G 4:405, 454; KpV 5:25). But whether there is any conflict between reason and our other desires obviously depends on the *content* of those desires, not on their mere existence. And even if inclinations differ from duty in what they bid us do, it cannot be part of their nature as empirical desires that *our will* (or our "power of choice," *Willkür*) has a propensity to act as they bid in the face of the rationally stronger incentives of morality. Kant already realized this when he said that the law becomes an imperative for us "only if the will is not *in itself* completely in conformity with reason (as is actually the case with human beings)" (G 4:413).

In the *Religion*, Kant finally makes it explicit that we can regard the human will as necessarily under constraint in following rational laws only by locating in our power of choice itself a propensity to resist reason. The enemy of the moral law is not "the natural inclinations that merely lack discipline and openly display themselves unconcealed to everyone's consciousness, but is rather as it were a secret enemy, one who hides behind reason and is hence all the more dangerous" (R 6:57). We might understand this in either of two ways (or both at once). Our power of choice, through its maxim, determines either the *content* of our natural desires (as opposing the demands of reason) or their *motivational strength* as incentives (when we give them subjective priority over the rationally stronger incentives of morality).[1]

The doctrine of radical evil does not hold that people do evil for evil's sake, at least if this means that to them the morality of an action is a positive *disincentive* to doing it. Kant holds that if the moral goodness of an action did not present itself to us as a positive incentive for doing it, then we would not be moral agents at all and could not be held accountable for our transgression of the moral law. If the morality of an action presented itself to us simultaneously as both an incentive for doing it and an incentive for not doing it, then our moral condition would be incoherent, and once again we could not be considered responsible agents. We can be held responsible for following the law only if our reason always regards the morality of an action as a positive incentive for doing it, even when our will, acting to this extent contrary to reason, prefers other incentives, and disobeys the law on account of them. Kant's doctrine is therefore that duty always constitutes a positive incentive, but we have a motivational propensity to prefer the rationally weaker incentives of inclination to those of duty (R 6:36).[2]

1.2. Three degrees of evil   The propensity to evil shows itself not only in the highest degree – depravity, the "corrupt," "vicious," or "perverse" tendency to neglect moral incentives in favor of nonmoral ones – but also in two lower degrees. The lowest (or least corrupt) of these is the will's "frailty" – the tendency, even where the right choices have been made, not to carry them through consistently (R 6:29–30). A second degree is "impurity" – where in order to do the right thing, the will requires incentives of inclination in addition to those of duty (and would act contrary to duty if these nonmoral incentives were not present).

The highest degree of evil exhibits evil openly and directly. The two lower degrees are cases of evil lurking even in conduct that is good on the surface. Frailty consists in the fact that even when we have apparently done well by adopting a good maxim, our occasional failure to live up to this maxim is not merely a random deviation from it but in fact exhibits a different (contrary and hence evil) *maxim* – namely, that of preferring nonmoral incentives to moral ones. Impurity consists in a disposition to do evil that may be built into the motivational structure of actions that accord with duty. Even when I do the right thing, it may be true of me that I would not have done it unless nonmoral incentives had been present. In that case, of course, the dutiful act itself is not blameworthy, but it does not exhibit as much virtue – that is, strength in fulfilling the law (MS 6:405–406) – as it seems to; and though the action is not blameworthy itself, behind it is a volitional act that is evil and blameworthy, namely, that of having adopted the *maxim* that I will do my duty *only* when I have sufficient nonmoral incentives to do it.[3]

Kant describes the propensity to evil as "innate" in the sense that "it must be posited as a ground prior to every use of freedom in experience," but human beings themselves are to be regarded as the cause of it. We are to think of it as present in us at birth, though being born is not its cause (R 6:22). The claim that there is radical evil in *human nature* means that this propensity is part of the "character of the species." Though it is not biologically inherited, it is present in all human beings without exception (R 6:20–22, 25–26).[4]

1.3. Evil as a product of society   The doctrine of radical evil is an ambitious thesis, and it would be quite astonishing if proving it turned out to be a simple matter. But the *Religion* is surprisingly unclear about how it is to be established. Since it purports to be a thesis about human nature, it makes most sense to look for its foundation in Kantian anthropology (and I will presently conclude that this is where its foundation really is). But some of Kant's most prominent and explicit remarks appear to suggest either a quite different argumentative procedure or even that he regards no proof of the doctrine as necessary at all.

Near the beginning of his discussion, Kant says "in order, then, to call a human being evil, it must be possible to infer *a priori* from a number of consciously evil actions, or even from a single one, an underlying evil maxim, and from this, the presence in the subject of a common ground, itself a maxim, of all particular morally evil maxims" (R 6:20). This remark seems to propose a highly demanding – not to say wildly implausible – standard of proof for the doctrine. How could it be possible to infer *a priori* from a *single* action an underlying ground of all morally evil maxims (not only for the agent but for the entire human species)?[5]

On the other hand, when Kant comes to the point of concluding that human nature is radically evil, he is disarmingly direct and even seems to spurn rigorous argument altogether: "We can spare ourselves the formal proof that there must be such a corrupt propensity rooted in the human being, in view of the multitude of woeful examples that the experience of human *deeds* parades before us" (R 6:32–33).

Perhaps the confusion engendered by these remarks explains the wide disagreement among commentators, whose opinions run all the way from my own naïve conjecture long ago that the doctrine of radical evil is intended simply as an empirical generalization[6] to Henry Allison's equally implausible proposal that it is not a far-reaching indictment of the human will but only a trivial practical corollary of our finitude. He reasons that if the human will is finite and therefore not holy, then there must be in it some propensity not to obey the moral law.[7]

Kant helps us to resolve the confusion when he says that no *a priori* arguments based on a single act can "demonstrate the existence of this propensity to evil in human nature," which comes instead from "experiential proofs"; such arguments rather only "teach us the essential character of the propensity" (R 6:35). In other words, the point of considering a *single evil act* is only to specify the precise character of the fundamental maxim to which we must ascribe it in considering it as an instance of a propensity to evil. Whether or not we decide human beings have such a propensity depends not on *a priori* inferences from a single evil act but on "experiential proofs." These proofs, however, do not consist in induction from isolated instances of evil acts; instead, the doctrine of radical evil "can only be demonstrated if it transpires from anthropological research that the grounds that justify us in attributing [an evil propensity] to a human being as innate are of such a nature that there is no cause for excepting anyone from it, and that the character therefore applies to the species" (R 6:25). Apparently in the *Religion* itself Kant chose not to follow up this hint by providing the relevant piece of anthropology. He relied instead on the "multitude of woeful examples" to convince us of the doctrine of radical evil.

An approach to Kant's doctrine of radical evil that does follow up the hint has been suggested by Sharon Anderson-Gold.[8] On her view, the doctrine of radical evil is based on Kantian anthropology, that is, on his theory of the purposive development of the human race's collective predispositions, which nature has brought about through the human trait of unsociable sociability. This makes radical evil an empirical thesis without reducing it to a mere inductive generalization. On this interpretation, radical evil would pertain to us insofar as we are social beings; the evil in our nature is closely bound up with our tendencies to compare ourselves with others and compete with them for self-worth.

On first reading Kant appears to locate radical evil not in our social nature but in each person's fundamental maxim (perhaps present only in a worldless, timeless noumenal self). Radical evil is said to consist in a propensity to prefer the incentives of inclination to those of the moral law. Yet this is not after all so far from our unsociable sociability once we realize that what the law commands most fundamentally is that we treat ourselves and others according to our absolute worth as rational beings. Our natural inclinations resist reason because they manifest our self-conceit. This is why we want to make exceptions of ourselves to rules we will others should follow (violating FUL), use others as mere means without treating them as ends (violating FH), and set ends that cannot be united with theirs (violating FRE). From that point of view, the propensity to prefer incentives of inclination to those of the law would be precisely the same as the propensity to self-conceit.

Kant's discussion of evil in the *Religion* confirms that relationship. The vices grafted on to our predisposition to humanity[9] arise out of our "inclination to create a worth for oneself in the opinion of others, [occasioned] by the concernful attempts of others to gain a hated superiority over us." This is really an inclination to "create for ourselves for the sake of our safety some superiority over others as a precaution, yet this leads inevitably to "the unjust desire to gain [superiority] over others" (R 6: 27). Out of it arise the "vices of culture," including envy, ingratitude, and gloating – "the greatest vices of secret or open hostility against all whom we regard as alien to us" (R 6:27). In the Vigilantius lectures on ethics (contemporaneous with the *Religion*) Kant indicates the social content of evil when he describes depravity of heart as "a wickedness in the way of thinking *about others*" (VE 27:691, emphasis added).

So, first, the *Religion* confirms the anthropological *content* of evil, which focuses on vices of human competitiveness. But second, the anthropological reading of the doctrine of radical evil also implies that evil has its *source* in social comparisons and antagonisms. Does the text of the *Religion* confirm the anthropological reading on this second point, too? Yes, it does. Kant explicitly attributes the corruption of human nature to the *social* condition of human beings, and more specifically to the concern over comparative self-worth that characterizes people whenever they live in proximity to one another. Considered in abstraction from the effects of society, the natural desires of human beings are moderate, and they are disposed to contentment. What disturbs this contentment is the human being's fear of his own worthlessness in the sight of others:

It is not the instigation of nature that arouses what should properly be called the *passions*, which wreak such great devastation in his originally good predisposition. His needs are but limited, and his state of mind in providing for them is moderate and tranquil. He is poor (or considers himself so) only to the extent that he is anxious that other human beings will consider him poor and despise him for it. Envy, tyranny, greed, and the malignant inclinations associated with these, assail his nature, which on its own is undemanding, *as soon as he is among human beings*; nor is it even necessary to presuppose that these are sunk into evil and are examples to lead him astray; it suffices that they are there, that they surround him, and that they are human beings, and they will mutually corrupt one another's moral predispositions and make one another evil. (R 6:93–94)

Finally, the anthropological reading of the doctrine of radical evil can be confirmed as regards its *natural purposiveness* in human history. The relation of evil, as unsociable sociability, to the teleology of history is also explicit in the *Religion*, where Kant defends the natural goodness of this antagonistic arrangement in the same terms he used in the *Idea toward a universal history*: "For nature willed the idea of such a competition (which in itself does not exclude mutual love) only as an incentive to culture" (R 6:27).

Kant is no "individualist" about the *nature* and *source* of moral evil. He holds that our propensity to evil belongs to us only as social and historical beings. It attaches to us insofar as we enter into social relationships, and even plays a role in the historical plan of providence for the culture of the whole species. But Kant can be called an "individualist" about *moral responsibility* for evil. Though Kant holds that history is to be understood in terms of collective actions and his ethics requires us to adopt shared ends, he recognizes no category of "group responsibility" or "collective guilt." Evil is always the deed of an individual's free power of choice, which therefore bears the entire moral responsibility for it. The social character and source of evil, and its role in the teleology of history, do not give us any excuse to transfer to nature, providence, or other people the blame for what we do. We would entirely misunderstand the regulative role of natural teleology in guiding our reflective judgment if we were to think of natural ends as *intended effects* of *voluntary efficient causes* (such as God or nature). To blame nature or divine providence for evil on the grounds of its natural purposiveness would be a particularly flagrant instance of that misunderstanding.

1.4. Ambition as the root of all evil   We saw a bit ago that in speaking of the social nature of the propensity to evil, Kant mentions two of the three passions of culture: tyranny and greed. The third (ambition) is replaced by envy (a representative vice of failed ambition). But Kant may omit explicit mention of ambition also because it is not so much an expression of radical evil as the root of evil itself. Kant regards ambition as the *first* social passion, hence the earliest of the three social passions to develop in most people; the other two tend to follow (VA 25:1356): "The three [passions] follow one another according to difference in age. In the beginning is ambition, soon after tyranny, and at last greed" (VA 25:1148).

In the same passage from the *Religion*, Kant also claims that all three passions seek to obtain means to satisfying our inclinations, but illustrates this only with respect to greed and tyranny. I want wealth in order to rule others by means of their self-interest, and power in order to rule them by means of their fear. I might also want to be honored because people will serve those they honor. But honor is also sought for its own sake, and both power and wealth are often sought because people are honored for having them.

We have already seen that honor is sought fundamentally for the sake of achieving a real superiority of one's self-worth over that of others. Hence the passion for it is grounded essentially on delusion, since the closest thing to this that I can have is the (necessarily false) opinion of others that I am worth more than they are. Insofar as power and wealth are sought in order to achieve superiority over others, this opinion is even the final end of all the social passions. Thus they are grounded collectively on a single fundamental delusion, which is the root of all evil.

We can see that ambition is the root of all evil by considering what Kant says about radical evil and the human propensities it involves. Radical evil consists in the maxim of subordinating the laws of reason to my inclinations (R 6:36). This maxim is equivalent to self-conceit, the propensity to make my inclinations legislative for all willing in general (KpV 5:74). But that would be the same as the propensity to ascribe greater self-worth to oneself than to others, preferring one's own interest to theirs through the delusion that one is better than they are. From this standpoint, the radical propensity to evil is a predisposition to form inclinations that involve delusions of self-conceit. The systematic satisfaction of these inclinations would amount to my "always being on top" (*immer oben zu schwimmen*), that is, my being regarded by others as having greater worth than they do – which is simply Kant's definition of *ambition* (MS 6:435, 465).

2. Nature and culture

We have already mentioned that the doctrine of radical evil scandalized some of Kant's Enlightenment contemporaries because they saw it as a reversion to the Christian doctrine of original sin.[10] It would be pointless to deny that it represents an interpretation of that doctrine, since Kant himself presents the doctrine of radical evil as an interpretation of Christianity from "within the boundaries of mere reason."[11] We will understand the doctrine better, however, if we also see how it *differs* from Christian orthodoxy. The doctrine of radical evil is anthropological, not theological, in both its ground and its content. Its basis is not religious authority but naturalistic anthropology. If radical evil is rebellion, it is chiefly rebellion against the legislation of our own reason. If it is prideful self-assertion, then this self-will is directed not against God's majesty but against the dignity of rational nature in the person of other human beings. We deceive ourselves if we dismiss the thesis of radical evil as some sort of superstitious or premodern misanthropy. It is based on a shrewd perception of how people have made themselves in society – especially in modern bourgeois society.

2.1. Rousseau and Kant   Perhaps Kant's doctrine that human nature has an inborn propensity to evil also shocked his contemporaries because it seemed diametrically opposed to Rousseau's (modern, enlightened, philanthropic) doctrine that human beings are by nature good. In that case, Kant's critics were taken in by appearances. For if we look closely, we can see that these two doctrines are not only compatible, but they are actually *one and the same doctrine.*

Rousseau considers humanity to be good in the "natural" (i.e., presocial) state, because he considers all human wickedness and misery to be the consequence of the social condition, and the trait of *amour-propre*, which human beings begin to display as soon as they enter it. This is, of course, the same trait as "self-conceit," or "ambition" – the sense of comparative self-worth and the desire to achieve superior worth in the eyes of others – which constitutes, in Kant's view, the radical propensity to evil in human nature.

Rousseau opens *Emile* with the declaration that "Everything comes good from the hand of the author of things; everything degenerates between the hands of men" (Rousseau, *Emile* 4:35). Kant echoes these words in the *Conjectural beginning*: "The history of *nature* begins with goodness, for it is the *work of God*; but the history of *freedom* begins with evil, for it is the work of *the human being*" (MA 8:115). For both philosophers this applies chiefly to human nature itself, since it is fundamentally our nature which comes good from God but degenerates into evil when social human beings get their hands on it. For both philosophers, it is only in *society* that human beings come to be their own work, because it is only with others that people perfect themselves and devise their own modes of life. Human beings therefore become responsible for themselves only through their social relations (this is the fundamental antiindividualism in both Rousseau's and Kant's theories of evil).

There are good reasons, however, why Kant and Rousseau express one and the same doctrine in diametrically opposed words. Kant insists on the natural goodness of the human "predispositions" (to animality, humanity, and personality), but he does not speak of the "original goodness of human nature." For that would imply that there once was (or at least there might have been) a presocial condition in which the propensity to evil had yet to develop. Rousseau entertains the idea of such a condition, but Kant does not.

This issue about the far distant past (or even the merely hypothetical past) may look like only a point of metaphysical (or even mythical) speculation. We begin to see what is at stake when we recognize that Rousseau also thinks he can discern a "path of nature" in relation to the education and conduct of *present* human beings. By following this path, he thinks we can in some fashion recapture the original self-contentment and harmony with the natural world that has been disrupted by the development of our faculties and the disordered social relations that this development has produced.[12] Like Herder after him, Rousseau holds that nature aims at the contentment of human beings. Therefore it originally proportioned the individual's capacities exactly to the individual's needs, which is the condition of greatest happiness for any being. We are still happiest, Rousseau thinks, when the two are in balance. Trying to perfect ourselves by acquiring powers in excess of what we need leads to capricious desires and, consequently, to vice and unhappiness.[13]

By contrast, Kant views nature's end as the development of the species capacities of humanity; he sees in human discontent not merely something bad but also something purposive. The hope of "returning to nature" is akin to the historical idea of a "natural paradise." Both are delusions, symptoms of the condition of fundamental dissatisfaction in which nature has placed us for the purpose of developing our species capacities. "Nature" (in any sense that could be contrasted with reason) can *never* serve as the guide for *human* beings, for to be fully human is to have attained the condition of maturity or enlightenment, where we have nothing but reason to guide our struggle against the terrible evils our corrupt use of reason has brought upon us in the course of reaching maturity.

In Rousseau's writings Kant sees two tendencies that seem to go in opposite directions. In his two *Discourses*, Rousseau argues that there is an inevitable conflict between the natural ends of the human species and the effects of culture. Rousseau condemns culture for having deprived us of both goodness and contentment. In *Emile* and the *Social contract*, however, Rousseau surprisingly makes progressive recommendations about education, politics, and other aspects of culture. Kant proposes to bring Rousseau's ideas into agreement "both with reason and with each other" by arguing that Rousseau never meant us to *go* back to the state of nature but only to *look* back at it from the perspective of the condition in which we now find ourselves (MA 8:116, VA 7:326–327). The lesson we should draw from "looking back" is *not* that civilization is a bad thing, which we should flee, nor even an ambivalent one, from which we must try to detach a part of ourselves. What Rousseau shows us is instead that "culture, considered as the genuine education of the human being as human and as citizen has perhaps not even been properly begun, much less completed" (MA 8:117). The antagonism and inequality of the social condition, we should recall, are the source not only of *many* evils, but also of *everything* good (MA 8:119). Kant resolves the tension in Rousseau's attitude toward civilization by deciding that what we need is not less civilization or correctives to civilization but only a fuller development of the capacities civilization has begun to provide us.

2.2. *The irony of history*   Unsociable sociability develops the capacities of the human species but at the cost of individual human beings. Nature has been frugal with means to meet our self-expanding needs, but liberal in providing us with incentives to expand our own powers to meet them (that is, generous in doling out misery and discontent): "The human being's own absurd *natural predispositions* land him in troubles that he thinks up for himself, and make him put others of his own species in great misery through oppressive domination, barbaric wars, etc." (KU 5:430).

The consequence of nature's plan for us as *moral* beings is even worse. Nature has given us the rational capacity to be conscious of ourselves and recognize our self-worth, but while our reason is still unripe this takes the form of the ambitious desire to achieve superiority over others. This desire deludes us regarding the real source of our self-worth and causes us consistently to fall short of our rational vocation. Consequently, our history gives us no ground for complaint against the nature (or providence) that arranged things this way. The misery we must endure through our own discontented nature, as well as the misery we inflict on our fellows, is in general no more than we deserve.

"In human affairs," Kant says, "nearly everything is paradoxical" (WA 8:41). The natural purpose of our unsociable sociability is to develop human reason, the faculty enabling us both to comprehend purposes and to set them; yet the purposes reason sets are fundamentally at odds with the human nature that made reason possible for us.

Kant describes this as a systematic conflict between the *natural* and *cultural* predispositions of our species. What is naturally purposive for the development of our faculties at one stage in their development turns out to be counter-purposive at a later stage, after it has served its purpose and brought those faculties to maturity. He cites three examples. First, the early onset of reproductive urges is better suited to a less civilized animal than we have become. Second, the capacity of talented individuals to contribute to the faculties of the species is severely limited by the brief span of life and activity nature has imposed upon them. Finally, the freedom and reason of human beings, which decree human equality by right, are contravened by the inequalities that culture establishes, and which it is bound to establish, Kant says, "as long as [the development of culture] proceeds, as it were, without a plan" (MA 8:117; VA 7:325–326).

A more general instance of this same conflict would be the general principle behind Kant's historical materialism. The conflicts between historical stages of human culture, e.g., between a nomadic pastoral society and a property-owning agricultural society, are really conflicts between the more *natural* (i.e., undeveloped) mode of life of the former and the more *cultivated* mode of life of the latter. This is Kant's anticipation of the Marxian idea that human history develops through the conflict between social relations of production suited to one stage of humanity's economic development and the growth of new productive forces which press the human species on toward a higher stage. In Kant's theory, the more precise character of this conflict is that it pits *reason* against the *natural* conditions under which reason has developed. On one level, this is a conflict between the moral law and natural inclinations. But that conflict should always be seen in Kant's philosophy as a *historical* conflict between nature and culture, or between earlier and later stages of social life. Kant gives Rousseau the chief credit for this insight:

"In his writings *on the influence of the sciences* and *on the inequality of human beings*, he shows quite correctly that there is an inevitable conflict between culture and the nature of the human race as a *physical* species in which every individual is entirely to reach his determination; but in his *Emile, Social Contract,* and other writings he seeks once more to solve the harder problem of showing how culture must progress in order to suitably develop the predisposition of humanity as a *moral* species to its determination, so that this determination no longer conflicts with humanity as a natural species. From this conflict (since culture as in accordance with true principles has still perhaps not even properly begun his education as human being and citizen, still less completed it) arises all the true ills which oppress human life and all the vices that dishonor it, while the stimulus to the latter, which one holds responsible for them, are in themselves good and purposive as natural predispositions, but since they were adapted to the state of nature, they suffer interference from the progressive culture and in turn interfere with it, until perfected art again becomes nature, which is the moral determination of the human species considered as an ultimate goal. (MA 8:116–118)

The same conflict, as we have seen, can also be represented as a struggle within each of us between the natural–social and the rational–moral conceptions of self-worth. From this point of view, the demand of reason is not merely to subordinate our inclinations to reason's principles but also to reconstitute our disordered social relationships on the basis of rational principles. In this sense, human history works backwards: It makes us rational through an irrational society, leaving us the task of remaking society through reason: "Nature within the human being tries to lead him from culture to morality and not (as reason prescribes) from morality and its law, as the starting point, to a culture designed to conform with morality; which inevitably gives [to human history] a *perverse* and *counter-purposive* tendency" (VA 7:328).

It is only through culture that the human race can move toward a condition respecting the dignity of rational nature. Under its influence, "merely animal desire gradually becomes love, the feeling of the merely agreeable becomes taste," and the sense of propriety (attaching to social custom, especially as regards sexual modesty) eventually develops into a genuine sense of morality (MA 8:113). Though culture by itself cannot produce goodness of will (which is a work of freedom), our idea of morality, and in that sense our awareness of freedom itself, is a product of history, a work of civilization (I 8:26). Through the "cultivation of social qualities [the human being] may become a well-bred (if not yet moral) being, destined for concord" (VA 7:323–324).

The moral vocation of the human species in Kant must therefore always be seen as a contribution to this *social* revolution. That is why, as we shall see in the remainder of this chapter, Kant sees *social and political changes* (the perfection of a civil constitution, the creation of a rightful condition of peace between states, the enlightenment of a communicating public, the reform and propagation of an ethical community or rational religion) as the vehicles of human progress.

2.3. The epoch of nature and the epoch of freedom   Kant's ethical thought is fundamentally about the human race's collective, historical struggle to develop its rational faculties and then through them to combat the radical propensity to evil that alone made their development possible.[14] It is precisely because human beings must in this way turn against their own nature that their history is one of self-conflict, self-alienation, and consequently self-liberation. Human history is "nothing other than [the human being's] transition from a rude and purely animal existence to a condition of humanity, from the leading strings of nature to the guidance of reason – in a word, from the guardianship of nature to the condition of freedom" (MA 8:115).

Kant's philosophy of history represents it as having two overlapping phases, to which (following the above quotation) we we may give the names: the "epoch of nature" and the "epoch of freedom."

During the *epoch of nature*, unsociable sociability serves to develop the capacities of the species. The epoch of nature began with the struggle of an agricultural economy against the hunting and pastoral ways of life, which led to urban civilization and the founding of civil societies which give coercive protection to property and a condition of right (Kant's account of this process was discussed in Chapter 7, § 5). It continues today with the struggle in political states toward a just constitution.

Kant thinks that the chief problem in the present phase of the epoch of nature is that state coercion checks social antagonism only on a local level. The conflict between states endangers the natural development of human predispositions. On the most obvious level, this is because the constant threat of the destruction of civilization by war removes the incentive for people to exercise their faculties in a productive way. But a deeper problem is that the despotic injustice characterizing states whose economies are oriented toward military power tends to suppress, either openly and forcibly or else more subtly, the civilized and civilizing activities of their citizens. As long as different nations remain in this lawless and mutually hostile condition, there can also be no civilizing influence of one people on another. (As we shall see in the next subsection, this is why Kant thinks we should not expect European conquest and colonization to spread civilization to other parts of the world.) In the long run, there can be no justice in the relations between individuals, and so no natural development of human capacities, without peace between states (I 8:24–27).

But here, too, nature comes to the rescue. For it turns out that the strongest states militarily tend to be those that are the strongest economically, and the economic strength of a state rests on the "commercial spirit" of its citizens, which cannot develop unless they are given a measure of freedom by their rulers (EF 8:368). This provides states with an impetus to develop constitutions that protect the rights of citizens, pushing them, in fact, in the direction of a *republican* constitution, which checks despotism through the rule of law and the separation of state powers.

Thus even the separation of people into mutually hostile states is a device of nature. Without it, a single despot might achieve domination over the whole of humanity, blocking forever the progress of the human race. The constant threat of war between states gives each one an incentive to develop itself economically and hence in the long run to become more just, more republican (EF 8:367). This, in turn, leads through nature's purposiveness toward a lessening of the threat of war itself. For in republican states, decisions about war and peace will be increasingly referred to the citizens themselves, who must fight the wars and pay for them (EF 8:350). Kant looks forward to a time when all political constitutions will be of this form. That will make possible a federation of states introducing a right of nations into their mutual relations (EF 8:354–357; TP 8:310–311; MS 6:350–353). The *federation of states* will lead to a *state of nations*, a political union of free republics governing international relations through a system of law (TP 8:312, EF 8:354). This will introduce what we could call the *period of perpetual peace*, the final period in the epoch of nature. It will make possible an endless progress in political constitutions toward justice (I 8:27–28). *Peace with justice* thus constitutes a rational end for the human species, which fulfills nature's purpose by counteracting the effects of unsociable sociability so that it is not counterproductive to nature's purpose of fully developing human faculties.

In a sense we could also consider the period of perpetual peace the *end* of the epoch of nature as a whole. For in Kant's view the unconscious natural teleology that leads first to a cosmopolitan federation of states and then to a state of nations seems to be the end of *nature's* devices for developing the capacities of the human species during its period of natural tutelage. Once the human race reaches perpetual peace, its further progress (political, cultural, moral) will be due not to nature's unintended work but solely to conscious human intentions.

In this respect Kant's view of history is like Marx's. Both see past human history (and future history, too, as long as the epoch of nature lasts) as "naturally evolved" (*naturwüchsig*), but look forward to the future as something to be posited *through freedom*.[15] Kant says that inequality between people is the basis of history as long as it "proceeds, as it were, without a plan" (MA 8:113). What brings the epoch of nature to a close is people's achievement of their collective ability to develop the faculties of human species according to a common rational plan. In that sense the achievement of perpetual peace for Kant could be described (as Marx describes the end of class society) as the close of "the prehistory of human society."[16] Only what comes after this will be truly *human* history, that is, a history made consciously and collectively by human beings.

Nature's own purposes require that human beings should emerge at a certain point from the tutelage of nature and begin to set rational collective ends. This emergence from tutelage is *enlightenment*. Individuals become enlightened as they begin to think for themselves, but Kant argues that since they can do this only through free communication with one another, the precondition for individual enlightenment on a significant scale is the existence of *an enlightened public*. Enlightenment of the human species will eventually turn it into a cosmopolitan community of world-citizens. Kant thinks he is living at a time when this process of enlightenment is going on.

The collective enlightenment of a communicating public is the beginning of the *epoch of freedom*. Long before the end of the epoch of nature – while that epoch is still in the period of war and injustice – the epoch of freedom is beginning to get underway; and this is even necessary for the achievement of nature's purposes within the epoch of nature itself.

2.4. European civilization and colonialism   Prominent among Herder's reservations about Kant's philosophy of history – and about the Enlightenment generally – is the fear that privileging the "rational" ways of modern European culture will sanction the arrogant destruction of the riches of folk cultures that are regarded as "backward" by comparison. (In this Herder has many followers today.) Kant's view on these points was mentioned briefly in the Introduction, but it is worth pausing now to look at it more closely.

> If we compare [our idea of a cosmopolitan constitution] with the *inhos-pitable* conduct of the morally civilized (*gesitteten*), especially the commercial states of our part of the world, then the injustice they practice in *visiting* foreign lands and peoples (which to these states seems to mean the same as *conquering* them) goes to terrible proportions. America, the Negro lands, the Spice Islands, the Cape, etc. were looked upon at the time of their discovery as belonging to nobody; for they counted the inhabitants as nothing. In East India (Hindustan) foreign troops were brought in on the pretext of intending to set up trading posts, but this led to the oppression of the natives, the incitement of different Indian states to extensive wars, famine, insurrection, treachery, and the whole litany of evils affecting the human race. (EF 8:358–359)

Like Herder, Kant accepts the imperialist's premise that the Europeans have a more advanced culture than the people they have conquered. Unlike Herder, he sees nothing of irreplaceable value in the conquered cultures themselves that should make us regret the advance of greater civilization among them. To wish that they remain in an uncultivated state would even be to demean their humanity. We have already seen, in fact, that in response to Herder, Kant credits "visitation" by "more civilized nations" with lifting "the happy inhabitants of Tahiti" out of the "thousands of centuries of quiet indolence," which have given their lives no more worth than those of "happy sheep and cattle" (RH 8:65). It is significant that Kant regards contact with civilized peoples as having a civilizing *effect* on the Tahitians, yet without ascribing this effect to the visitors' *intentions*. For, as he makes quite clear elsewhere, he does not approve of the conduct of those who have acted with such intentions, nor does he think that such "visitations" have in general had a civilizing influence on either the visitors or the visited.

Kant does not deny (as Herder sometimes does) that making backward peoples more civilized would be a good end (MS 6:266). For we should regard this as a good end among ourselves, and not to applaud and support it for others is only to suggest that we think less of them.

(Herder might not have to accept this argument since he has mixed feelings about the development of culture even for us.) But Kant insists that even the best end may not be pursued through means that violate people's rights. "It is easy to see through this veil of injustice," he says, through which colonizers pretend to bring native Americans, Africans, and others "into a condition of right" (MS 6:266). In Kant's view, civilization does not equip a nation to treat others justly (R 1445 15:631). "We are *cultivated* to a great extent through art and science, *civilized* to excess by all sorts of social artifices and proprieties. But a lot is lacking before we can consider ourselves *moralized*" (I 8:26). In fact, the respects in which Europeans are more civilized directly *unfit* them for civilizing other peoples, since *thus far* civilization has made them no more just, only more competitive, exploitative, violent, and deceitful.

The Kantian view of the matter is this: The task of people everywhere is to cultivate and perfect *themselves*. They should encourage self-perfection in others, but only in ways that respect their rightful freedom to perfect themselves by setting their own ends, following their own concepts of self-perfection. This follows from Kant's doctrine that the ends of morality (duties of virtue, ends that are at the same time duties) include the happiness of others, but not the perfection of others (MS 6:386, 393–394). Hence we may pursue the self-perfection of others only insofar as it is included in the ends they adopt for themselves, whose totality is their happiness.

3. Reason, communication, and enlightenment

Radical evil is a propensity of human reason as it develops under social conditions. The propensity to self-conceit corrupts all human inclinations and affections, making them expressions of unsociable sociability. But self-conceit is evil only because it is opposed to the moral law of reason, which is the only power in human life capable of radically combating radical evil.

Reason is the highest of our mental powers, and it sets rational beings the most ambitious set of tasks it is possible to conceive. In its theoretical use, reason provides principles for thinking in general. In this sense, it encompasses all cognitive faculties, of sense, understanding, and judgment (KpV A298/B355, KU 20:195). As we saw in Chapter 5, § 4, reason's capacity to give unconditioned principles is identical with the capacity to act freely (KU 5:172, VA 7:199). This freedom governs theoretical inquiry by seeking the unconditioned, which means bringing all cognitions, concepts, and principles into systematic unity (KrV A300–302/B356–359, KU 5:195–198, Ak 20:195–211).

In the practical sphere, to act freely is chiefly to choose the end of actions, so reason is the capacity to set ends (G 4:427, MS 6:395; cf. KpV 5:57). But since the power to set ends is the power to direct one's life independently of instinct, reason is also the ground of perfectibility, the power to develop all human predispositions (VA 7:321). As the unconditioned capacity to make choices, reason is also the faculty through which we become aware of all values, and (as we saw in Chapter 4, §§ 3–5), this makes rational beings aware of the dignity of rational nature as an end in itself. In relation to all ends, reason also imposes the architectonic task of bringing them into systematic harmony (G 4:436). To this task Kant gives the name "philosophy" regarded as a "doctrine of wisdom" (KpV 5:108).[17]

3.1. The pluralism of reason   Like the propensity to evil, reason is a product of society. Kant holds that human beings can accomplish the tasks set by reason only through interacting with one another. We can develop our reason only by communicating with others (VA 7:227–228; VE 27:411). Our capacity to think at all, and especially to think accurately, depends on our thinking "in community with others to whom we *communicate* our thoughts, and who communicate their thoughts to us" (O 8:144). Kant therefore concludes that "reason depends for its very existence on the freedom to communicate" (KrV A738/B766). Since reason is our only hope for achieving peace with justice during the epoch of nature or cultivating reason and moral virtue in the epoch of freedom, free communication is the most indispensable condition for all human progress. The freedom to communicate is "the one treasure which remains to us amidst all the burdens of civil life, which alone offers us a means of overcoming all the evils of this condition" (O 8:144).

The standpoint of self-conceit, not only in relation to will, but even in relation to thoughts and feelings, is "egoistic." This egoism involves a threefold "presumption" (*Anmaßung*): of understanding, taste and interest (VA 7:128). "Logical egoism considers it unnecessary to test one's judgment by the understanding of others, as if one had no need at all for this criterion (*criterium veritatis externum*). But we cannot dispense with this means of assuring the truth of our judgments" (VA 7:128). The "aesthetic egoist" seeks the criterion of beauty only in his own feelings, and this prevents him from progressing to better standards of judgment (VA 7:129–130). Worst of all is the "moral egoist," who "locates the supreme determining ground of his will merely in his own happiness and what is useful to him, not in the thought of duty" (VA 7:130).

The opposite of egoism is "pluralism," which is "the disposition of not being occupied with oneself as the entire world, but regarding and conducting oneself as a cosmopolitan [or citizen of the world]" (VA 7:130). The standpoint of reason is *pluralistic* because it takes account of the thoughts, feelings, and volitions of others. To consider Kant's philosophy as "monological" or "solipsistic" (as Habermas and his followers do) is *fundamentally* to misunderstand the Kantian conception of reason.[18] Or to use a term coined by Adrian Piper, rationality is *xenophilia*: It values and seeks out what is other or different, because without this it would be impossible to find anything having universal validity.[19]

3.2. Three maxims of thought   Several places in his works, Kant proposes three principles to guide human thought and communication:

1. Think for yourself.
2. Think from the standpoint of everyone else.
3. Think consistently. (KU 5:294–295; cf. VA 7:200, 228–229, VL 9:57)

The first he calls the maxim of *unprejudiced* thought, which opposes *superstition*; the second is the maxim of *broadminded* thought, which strives for *universality*; and the third is the maxim of *consistent* thought, which Kant regards as the most difficult of the three maxims to apply successfully (KU 5:295).

The first maxim is necessary because no real communication can take place between parties unless they are independent participants in the process, who can provide a genuine critical check on one another's thinking. The second is necessary if there is to be any *communication* at all, as opposed to a mutual venting of private feelings or thoughts in which there is no critical interaction between them. The third is required if thinking is to count as the exercise of a *skill* and to achieve reason's end, which is unity under principles (KU 5:294–295; VA 7:227).

Thinking itself is a *social* activity because it must be critical, testing what is thought from a plurality of standpoints in order to achieve unity. This is possible through imagination, but only partially, and imagination must in any case be regularly stimulated through actual communication with those in whose standpoint one is trying to place oneself. This is why Kant says that reason depends on freedom of communication for its very existence.

We can understand why Kant regards the third maxim as the most difficult if we realize that it is associated with reason's search for principles. "Consistent" thought requires not merely avoiding contradictions (which, however, may be hard enough to do), but also the successful unification of thoughts under principles. In the context of communication, the third maxim requires us not only to seek to reach agreement with others (so that my thoughts do not contradict yours) but also to give systematic unity to our thoughts under common principles.

3.3. Culture and taste Culture prepares the way for reason chiefly by increasing our capacity for communication. This begins with a desire to make our representations and feelings communicable. That is why it constitutes cultural progress when animal desire becomes love and the feeling of the agreeable becomes taste, for love involves the extension of animal desire to include the thoughts and feelings of the other and taste involves an interest in pleasures which can be shared with others and brought under standards of taste that claim universal validity.

Kant defines a judgment of taste as one involving a "disinterested liking," that is, a pleasure that is not connected with any desire (whether sensuous or moral) for an object (KU 5:204–205). This is the pleasure we take in *beauty* (KU 5:211). Judgments of taste depend on the possession by human beings of a "common sense," or a faculty of feeling, which is the same *a priori* for all human beings (KU 5:237–238). The fact that judgments of taste are disinterested does not mean that we cannot *take an interest* in the beautiful by regarding its universal communicability itself as an object of rational desire (KU 5:296). In fact, culture involves an increasing interest in beauty. This is both an empirical interest and an intellectual interest.

The empirical interest in the beautiful is our interest in pleasures that can be shared with others and about which we can communicate according to standards claiming universal validity. This interest plays a role in preparing human beings for rational concord.

> A concern for universal communication is something that everyone expects and demands of everyone else, on the basis, as it were, of an original contract dictated by our very humanity. Initially, it is true, only charms are important in society and become connected with great interest, e.g. the dyes people use to paint themselves. . . , or flowers, sea-shells or beautifully colored feathers; but eventually also beautiful forms (as in canoes, clothes, etc.) that involve no gratification whatever, i.e. no liking or enjoyment. In the end, when civilization has reached its peak, it makes this

communication almost the principal activity of refined inclination, and sensations are valued only to the extent that they are universally communicable. (KU 5:297)

The empirical interest in artistic (or artificial) beauty, Kant thinks, involves no direct advantage to reason or morality, because it constitutes a merely "social joy" often only feeding the "obstinate vanity" and "ruinous passions" of civilized people (KU 5:298–299). In the form of fashion, it exhibits merely "the natural human tendency to compare oneself, in one's behavior, with others more important than oneself" (VA 7:245). Through the empirical interest in it, taste tends to degenerate into mere fashion, which consists in giving oneself airs, pretending to participate in genuine communication with others as an independent voice, but in fact merely bowing to custom or novelty for their own sakes (VA 7:245).

Kant thinks it is otherwise with the beauties of nature. For their enjoyment is not based on an interest (e.g., the interest in creating or owning beautiful objects or in displaying to others one's superior taste in the appreciation of them). Natural beauty instead gives rise to an immediate *intellectual* interest in universally communicable harmony for its own sake. That interest is closely related to moral feeling, even a stage in its development (KU 5:300). Moral feeling, that which disinterestedly approves or disapproves actions, involves an immediate relation of reason to sense, and claims objective validity (universal validity for everyone) (MS 6:400). Pleasure in the beauty of nature also involves a harmony among our active and passive faculties (understanding and imagination), a claim to universal validity, and a pleasure in something that is free from interest. The appreciation of natural beauty therefore prepares the way for a moral disposition and prepares us for moral autonomy.[20]

Judgments of taste accustom us simultaneously to exercise our own capacities to judge and to compare our judgment with that of others. In this process, which Kant calls "reflection," we learn to "abstract from the limitations that may attach to our own judging" (KU 5:294). Reflection is the essential prerequisite for all communication based on claims to universal validity. It involves the transition from *sapor* (savor, taste) to *sapientia* (wisdom): "This is how the organic feeling that comes through a particular sense could give its name to an ideal feeling: namely, the feeling of a sensuous choice that is universally valid" (VA 7:242). Judgments of taste provide a transition from feeling to understanding

(VA 7:241), which is a prerequisite for rational communication in general. Taste therefore matures into reason: "Beauty is the blossom, while science is the fruit" (VA 7:249).[21]

3.4. *Thinking for oneself* Kant defines "enlightenment" as "the human being's emergence from his self-incurred condition of minority or tutelage (*Unmündigkeit*)" (WA 8:35). Kant defines *Unmündigkeit* as "being incapable of using one's understanding without the direction of another"; *Unmündigkeit* (a "condition of tutelage") is opposed to *Mündigkeit*, "adulthood," "majority," or "maturity" – the condition in which one is empowered to speak (hence to think) for oneself. Any person in such a condition is an intellectual and moral dependent, not an autonomous personality.

The condition of tutelage is "self-incurred" (*selbstverschuldet*, i.e., something for which those in this dependent condition are themselves responsible) whenever it is due not to a lack of understanding but to a lack of "resolution and courage." A child's tutelage to its parents is not self-incurred because its powers are still immature and incapable of fully functioning without parental guidance.[22] But people who do not need to submit to tutelage often do so because they find it convenient to have others guide them. Being unaccustomed to think for themselves, they are often frightened by the prospect of having to do so.

For most of human history the vast majority of the human race has remained in minority or tutelage. In all traditional religions (or "ecclesiastical faiths"), a priesthood usurps the role of individual conscience and revealed statutes take the place of self-legislated moral principles (R 6:175–180). In his essay *What is enlightenment?* Kant concentrates on religious enlightenment because he regards spiritual tutelage as "the most harmful and also the most degrading of all" (WA 8:41). But there are other forms of intellectual tutelage that are almost as bad. Paternalistic governments are less interested in protecting the rights of their subjects than in deciding for them what their happiness should consist in (TP 8:290–291). People also remain in self-incurred tutelage when they subscribe to dogmas and formulas or rely uncritically and unthinkingly on medical advice and on the printed word (WA 8:35–36).

People with an interest in directing the lives of others (such as tyrants, priests, and authorities of all kinds) keep them in this degraded condition by playing on their fears. Having "carefully prevented the docile creatures from daring to take a single step without the leading-strings to which they are tied, they next show them the danger which threatens them if they try to walk unaided" (WA 8:35). Kant does not deny that the masters' arguments have merit, but the dangers they cite are only examples of the moral evil and discontent inseparable from the human condition. Enlightenment is a duty, but fear of the dangers that come with the emancipation of reason is often sufficient to keep the pupil subordinated to the master indefinitely.

Thinking for oneself is a duty because to remain in a condition of self-incurred tutelage is degrading to our humanity (WA 8:41). It is also a duty to the human race generally, because reason can exist and fulfill its vocation in human history only through free rational communication between independent thinkers (O 8:146–147).

3.5. *The public use of reason*   Kant is an impassioned defender of freedom of communication. For this reason he is rightly regarded as a representative of *enlightenment liberalism*. But Kant's views on this topic are surprisingly at odds with some attitudes and assumptions we usually think of as liberal, or even as "Kantian."

First, Kant's defense of freedom of public communication is strikingly *consequentialist*. It is not based on any presumed *right* of people to "have their say" (whether or not what they say is ever heard, or worth hearing). Kant defends freedom of communication as the indispensable means for promoting the collective development of people's rational powers and their effective use to discover and agree on what is true. Kant is therefore entirely at one with John Stuart Mill in thinking that freedom of expression must be defended entirely on the basis of the way it promotes the "permanent interests of man as a progressive being."[23]

Second, because he thinks the primary concern should be with the conditions for freeing the human race *collectively* from self-incurred minority, Kant's 1784 essay *What is enlightenment?* defends freedom of communication as a means to this end. Kant asserts no individual right of free speech or expression. He even argues that narrow constraints on civil freedom are often advantageous to promoting people's intellectual freedom during the period when people are becoming enlightened (WA 8:41).

Finally, Kant also regards the ends of free communication, important as they are, as having to be weighed carefully against other vital human ends, such as the maintenance of public order (without which there would be no hope for the progress of reason anyway). Kant therefore accepts that state policies regarding free communication must insure that free thought and speech do not undermine the civil authority and right. Free communication, both in the printed word and in universities, must therefore occur within a special context that has been carefully devised for it (WA 8:36–42, SF 7:21–36), and those who value this freedom must use it responsibly, under the discipline of reason, if they do not want to lose it (O 8:144–147).[24]

Kant recommends that freedom of communication must be confined to a special sphere, where it cannot threaten right or civil order. Within this sphere freedom should be absolute because making it so is the only way to promote public enlightenment and intellectual progress. Outside it, however, freedom of expression may be regulated as much as may be necessary for the promotion of other ends, especially the maintenance of public order.[25]

People should be completely free in the *public* use of their reason, though the *private* use of their reason may be restricted (WA 8:36–38). By the "public use of reason" Kant means its use "as a *scholar or man of learning* (*Gelehrte*) addressing the entire *reading public*"; by "private use," Kant means what a person may think or say "in a particular civil office with which he is entrusted." Thus a soldier may not quarrel with the orders given by his superiors, and a clergyman may not question the doctrines of his church in the course of performing his official duties. But both may argue against these same things (or say anything they like about the army or the church) in a published article or treatise addressed universally to the learned public.

Kant's proposals are unclear in certain respects, and they are open to some obvious objections in light of our experience of the process of public enlightenment in the past two centuries. It is not clear how far the policies Kant advocates would involve the protection of people's freedom to express themselves on political or religious questions in private conversations with their friends. No doubt it could be argued that freedom of public communication would be seriously compromised if people's personal conversations were spied on and regulated by the state or by their employers. But if the powers that be regard the restriction of speech as promoting their legitimate ends – maintaining political stability or the discipline of the workplace – then Kant's proposal would seem to give them wide discretion to restrict free communication. Although Kant favors a republican form of government with representative institutions, his proposals regarding freedom of communication recognize no right to use free speech deliberately as a way of effecting political change (by stirring up resistance to government policies) or reforming the practices of social institutions (by criticizing from within the policies of the church or the army or by inciting employees to organize against the wishes of their employers).

Kant intends that the public sphere, in which freedom of expression is to be unbounded, should be one in which people address themselves solely to one another's intellects and consciences. Communication is to effect social and political change only by employing reason to convince those in power how to use their legally unfettered discretion. When addressed to the unjustly powerful, it can only attempt to persuade them to relinquish their power voluntarily. It is easy enough to agree with Hamann when he satirized Kant's proposal, characterizing the "public use of reason" as merely a "sumptuous dessert" to be enjoyed only after the private use of reason supplies one's "daily bread."[26]

Of course even that freedom was much more than could be taken for granted in eighteenth-century Prussia (or indeed, in most other European states at the end of the eighteenth century). As proposals motivated by consequentialist considerations, they were adapted to the situation they addressed. The Prussia of Frederick the Great was an absolute monarchy, where much of what we think of as potent political expression (e.g., that designed to elect public officials or influence elected representatives) could have no application. Viewed in its context, therefore, Kant's limited defense of freedom of communication must be seen as both progressive and liberal. Kant understands the fundamental importance of freedom and defends it with vigor; but even allowing for the circumstances of his time, his defense makes too many concessions to the fear of disorder, and his "public" sphere provides reason with far too little social or political power to combat injustice or achieve progressive social change.

Kant expects a great deal from rational communication. He does so not because he thinks it has a proven record of accomplishment but because he regards it as our only hope. Kant does not dispute Herder's charge that the only reason we have is limited and corrupt and that when it has gone off on its own it has made us evil and unhappy. But he nevertheless insists that reason alone claims sovereignty over our lives because it is the only power capable of combating evil and improving our lot. Natural feelings, as expressions of our unsociable sociability, must always be disciplined if they are not to lead us into disaster. The culture and social institutions handed down to us are a dangerous mixture of good and evil, and can serve human interests only if they are subjected to constant rational criticism leading to relentless progressive reform (KrV A xi note). Nothing that reason *necessarily* destroys could be worth preserving, and following reason gives us our only real chance of protecting what is valuable even against the destructiveness of reason.

4. The ethical community

Free communication and enlightenment are necessary conditions for the historical progress of the human species. But if enlightened human beings are to be truly agents of this progress, they must direct themselves consciously toward rational collective ends. It is the task of philosophy in an age of enlightenment to make these ends explicit and then to look for social institutions and historical tendencies that promote them. This is how Kant understood the historical vocation of his ethical thought.

4.1. Moral teleology Rational nature is an end in itself but not an end to be produced. All action, however, requires also an end to be produced by action, and reason has the task of setting ends and then, in its systematic function, of unifying them. In the third Critique's "Methodology of teleological judgment," Kant attempts to harmonize the natural ends used as regulative principles of reflective judgment in the *theoretical* cognition of nature (and thereby also of human history) with the ends of freedom set by *practical* reason.[27]

In the *Critique of the power of judgment*, Kant distinguishes between the "ultimate end" (*letzter Zweck*) of nature and the "final end" (*Endzweck*) of creation as a whole.[28] An *ultimate end* is a single end with reference to which it is possible to think of a teleological system as a unified whole; we are entitled to employ the idea of such an end regulatively as a principle of reflective judgment in giving systematic unity to the teleology we find in nature (KU 5:429). Kant claims that because rational nature alone is capable of setting ends and organizing them into a system and human beings are the sole examples of rational nature with which we are acquainted in the natural world, the human being is the only being that could answer to the concept of an ultimate end of nature (KU 5: 427; cf. R 6:6–7n).[29]

What is it *about* human beings that could be the ultimate end of nature? Kant denies, first of all, that this could be human happiness. For that is not observed to be an end of nature at all, much less the ultimate end (KU 5:430–431). In nature's teleology, our desire for happiness serves only as a means to "culture" (*Kultur*), the development of our species capacities. Could that culture, then, be the ultimate end? Kant distinguishes two kinds of "culture": the "culture of skill" and the "culture of discipline." The former is the development of capacities to achieve various other ends set by rational choice; the latter, the capacity of the human will to "liberate itself from the despotism of desire." The culture of skill cannot be the ultimate end of nature. Skills themselves are only means to other ends, and nature's purposive mechanisms for developing the culture of skill contain much that is at the same time counterpurposive, such as social inequality and war. Even such pursuits of culture as art and science often merely feed our vanity, tending to frustrate the ends of reason, so they seem ill-suited to the idea of an ultimate end of nature (KU 5:432–433).

The culture of discipline looks like a better candidate for the ultimate end, since it prepares the human being to prevail over the counterpurposive tendencies in his inclinations "which interfere very much with the development of our humanity" (KU 5:433). But it, too, merely enables human beings to actualize some of the *other* rational ends they set. Kant's conclusion appears to be that human beings are the ultimate end of nature only insofar as they are capable of *setting* a *final end*: "It is the human being's vocation (*Bestimmung*) to be the ultimate end of nature, but always subject to one condition: he must have the understanding and the will to give both nature and himself reference to an end that can be independent of nature, self-sufficient and a final end" (KU 5:431).

What is a "final end"? It is "an end that requires no other end as a condition of its possibility." In other words, it is an end (like the one Aristotle is seeking at the beginning of the *Nicomachean ethics*), which must be thought of as pursued *only* for its own sake, and *cannot* be thought of as a means to any other end.[30]

An ultimate end is *ultimate* through its relation to *other* ends (since it is what unifies a plurality of ends into a system or "realm"). Without an ultimate end, every aggregate of ends is incomplete. Without an ultimate end, there would have to be either a plurality of ends in which the teleology terminates, or else every member of the aggregate had a further end somewhere else within the aggregate. In the former case, the aggregate would lack unity and not constitute a true system (or realm) of ends. In the latter case, the resulting chain of ends would run on endlessly and the whole would be without an end. If either nature or morality (or both) is to constitute a system of ends, it must have an ultimate end.

A final end, on the other hand, is in its concept related to other ends only negatively, as presupposing no end beyond itself to which it might serve as a means. A final end could be the ultimate end in relation to an aggregate, but that is not what would make it a *final* end. (There could also be more than one final end, if there were more than one end that is sought solely for its own sake.)

We might think that every rational being is a final end, because humanity in every rational being is an end in itself. But we are speaking now of ends to be effected by action, and although the dignity of rational nature may be the foundation of the principle grounding all ends to be effected, it is not itself one of them. Further, no human being can be a final end because every person, though an end in itself, may also be a means to other ends, and thus cannot be a final end. Hence no human being (nor all human beings taken together) can be a final end. Their rational capacity, however, is distinguished from everything else in nature in that it alone can not only set ends and systematize them but also set a final end.

The connection between nature's ultimate end and the final end is this: Because human beings are the only beings in nature that can set a final end, they may be considered as the ultimate end of nature insofar as they do set a final end. Nature has no ultimate end except *through* human beings; or, what comes to the same thing, it has no ultimate end at all *until human beings give it one* by setting a final end. That is what it means to say the human being's *vocation* (*Bestimmung*) is to be the ultimate end of nature (KU 5:431). Kant's philosophy of history can be regarded as a theodicy or theory of divine providence, as he himself also regularly regards it (I 8:30, MA 8:120–123, TP 8:312, EF 8:362, SF 7:93). But if so, it is a highly novel and perhaps an unorthodox one. For in Kant's view, the plan of providence remains incomplete until *we human beings* complete it.

4.2. The highest good Kant's name for the final end, through which we complete the system of moral ends and simultaneously the system of natural ends, is the "highest good" (*summum bonum*) (KU 5:451). A final end must be by its concept something good for its own sake. Human beings can set two general kinds of ends that fit this description: (1) *morality* (goodness of will) and (2) *happiness*. In the *Critique of practical reason*, Kant names these two goods (respectively) the "good" (*Gut*) and "well-being" (*Wohl*) (KpV 5:59–60). He also calls them the "moral" good and the "physical" (or "natural") good (VA 7:276–277). Kant regards the two goods as *heterogeneous*. They must not be confused with each other, and the lack of one cannot be compensated for by more of the other (VA 7:277).

This might make it seem as though there were two heterogeneous final ends and no single final end. But Kant thinks it is possible to unite the ends of morality and happiness in a systematic way. What makes this possible is that there is a difference between them as ends. Though each is an end valued solely for its own sake, the moral good is good unconditionally, while the natural good (happiness or well-being) is good only conditionally. It is crucial to Kant's moral teleology that an end can be good *conditionally* without being good only *instrumentally*. Every bit as much as morality, happiness (when we are worthy of it) is good for its own sake or (to use Christine Korsgaard's terminology) a "final good." Neither is good as a means, but both, when they are good, are good entirely for their own sake. This is required of anything that is to form even a conditioned part of a *final end*. But morality is an "intrinsic" good, having its goodness entirely in itself, while happiness is an "extrinsic" good, because its goodness is dependent (or conditional) on the goodness of morality.[31]

Kant puts this by saying that the moral good is the "supreme good" (*das oberste Gut, bonum supremum*) (KpV 5:110). As the supreme good, it is also the condition of the goodness of the natural good. There is no circumstance in which a good will would not be good, but happiness is good only if the person who enjoys it is worthy of it through goodness of will (G 4:393). When the *bonum supremum* of morality is accompanied by the extrinsic or conditioned good of happiness, then it includes *everything* that belongs to the concept of a final end, and is therefore the "highest good" in the strictest sense, called the "completed good" (*vollendete Gut, bonum consummatum*) (KpV 5:110).

We can think of the highest good either as having two components related lexically or conditionally (the moral good/the natural good). Or we can think of it as having two distinct components, each of them good in itself and entirely for its own sake:

1. Morality or goodness of will
2. Happiness proportional to worthiness[32]

The latter way of representing the highest good will be misleading, however, unless we keep in mind that (1) is precisely the condition specified under (2), so that the two components of the highest good do not constitute merely an aggregate, but are a systematic whole bound together by the conditional relation between them.

The highest good is "the goodness of a possible world" or "the final end for creation" (KpV 5:110, R 6:6). Or it is "the sort of a world [a morally disposed human being] would create, under the guidance of practical reason – the world within which, moreover, he would place himself as a member" (R 6:5).[33]

The practical import of the highest good in Kant's writings is misunderstood if it is associated with the "immanent" teleology of our duties of virtue (particular ends, falling under the headings of our own virtue and the happiness of others, which it is our duty to have). If we understand it this way, then it will be hard to see why we should be concerned about it at all, since everything included in it would be conceived in more practical terms as a particular perfection or happiness of some rational being.[34]

Kant's most prominent use of the concept is as part of his argument for the practical rationality of moral faith in God, as the sole agency through which we can conceive the possibility of the highest good.[35] But this does not mean that the highest good is not also seen by Kant as an object of *human* striving. As the sole conceivable *final* end, it is the sole end in which we can see the strivings of all well-disposed rational beings as united, and therefore it is the only conceivable end that can be universally shared by all human beings and regarded by them as a *common end* of all their strivings (insofar as these strivings accord with morality). "Harmonizing with this end does not increase the number of morality's duties but rather provides these with a special point of reference for the unification of all ends" (R 6:5).

But why is it important for us to form a unified conception of our final end? Is this merely a (characteristically Kantian) metaphysical demand for architectonic unity in the abstract? Perhaps it is this, but it is unquestionably more besides. For Kant it is crucial that human beings think of themselves as belonging to a moral community, of which all rational beings could regard themselves as members. This community is to be united through the concept of a single final end that its members consciously pursue *in common* as a *shared* end. Such a community could be called the "realm of ends" if it is represented as "only an ideal" (G 4: 433). However, it is vital to Kant's ethical thought that such a community should not remain that but should also acquire actual earthly reality in human history.

4.3. The common pursuit of virtue   "It is our universal duty to elevate ourselves to the ideal of moral perfection" (R 6:61). Owing to the radical evil in human nature, we always begin this striving with an exactly contrary propensity. Moral goodness is therefore not a gradual change in "mores" (*Sitten*) but instead a radical "change of heart" or "conversion": if there is to be a "gradual reformation in our mode of sense" then "a revolution is necessary in our mode of thought" (R 6:47). We must adopt a moral "disposition" or "attitude" (*Gesinnung*) that opposes the propensity to evil innate in us:

> So long as the foundation of the maxims of the human being remains impure, [virtue] cannot be effected through gradual *reform* but must rather be effected through a *revolution* in the disposition of the human being (a transition to the maxim of holiness of disposition). And so a 'new man' can come about only through a kind of rebirth, as it were a new creation and a change of heart . . . From this it follows that a human being's moral education must begin not with an improvement of mores, but with the transformation of his attitude of mind and the establishment of a character. (R 6:47–48)

Kant does not think I can ever achieve this inner revolution toward goodness entirely on my own. The origin of evil is social, and so must be the struggle against it.

> Human beings (as we have remarked above) mutually corrupt one another's moral predisposition, and even with the good will of each individual, because of the lack of a principle which unites them, they deviate through their dissensions from the common goal of goodness, as if they were *instruments of evil*, and expose one another to the danger of falling once again under its dominion. (R 6:97)

Hence the struggle against evil can be effective only if it assumes a social form. "The highest moral good will not be brought about solely through the striving of one individual person for his own moral perfection but requires rather a union of such persons into a whole toward that end" (R 6:97–98).

The pursuit of my own morality can be distinguished from the moral progress of the human race, but the above argument shows that the two ends are necessarily linked in their pursuit.[36] Because it can be effectively pursued only in concert with others, the duty to promote one's own morality leads inevitably to a "duty *sui generis*, not of human beings toward human beings but of the human race toward itself. For every species of rational beings is objectively – in the idea of reason – destined to a common end, namely the promotion of the highest good as a good common to all" (R 6:97). Because this end must be universal, so that no rational being can be excluded from the common striving, it must be conceived only as the final end, the highest good. At this point, the highest good ceases to be merely a requirement of Kant's rational architectonic and becomes, through its shared pursuit by an ethical community, "a duty which differs from all others in kind and in principle" (R 6:98). The moral progress of the human race, in Kant's view, is possible only through the progressive extension of such a free moral community to more and more people, until it eventually encompasses the entire human race (R 6:94).

Such an "ethical community" can be regarded as under *only ethical* legislation, *never* under laws of right that may be coercively enforced (R 6: 98). "It would be a contradiction for a political community to compel its citizens to enter into an ethical community" (R 6:95). Nevertheless, the moral legislation for this community is to be considered "public legislation, regarded as the commands of a common legislator" (R 6: 98). The laws of the community are purely ethical, *universal* in scope, comprehending all humanity, and *purified* of everything alien to rational morality (R 6:96). As principles of reason, its laws are in principle *unchangeable*, but membership in the community must be entirely *free*, so it may have nothing resembling a *political constitution*. There can be no hierarchy of authorities, no binding creeds, no statutory observances (R 6:101–102):

> It could best of all be likened to the constitution of a household (a family) under a common though invisible moral father, whose holy son, knowing the father's will and yet standing in blood relation with all other members of the family, takes his father's place by making the other members better acquainted with his will; these therefore honor the father in him and thus enter into a free, universal and enduring union of hearts. (R 6:102)

For Kant, true community involves the collective pursuit of ends set in common with others. It follows that community and external coercion are mutually exclusive. Setting ends is an act of freedom. It would be impossible to compel people to adopt a shared end; it would be a violation of their right as human beings to compel them to serve ends set by others on the pretense that they shared those ends. In the political state, people are subject to common coercive laws regulating their external conduct. For that reason, the state cannot be an institution in which people share ends or live a common life. Its function is only to protect the external freedom of individuals and maintain the general conditions of public order that make that protection possible.

From the fact that Kant denies that the state (or any other coercive institution) can unite people in a common life, it does *not* follow that he fits the familiar communitarian caricature of a "liberal individualist" – someone who values only the external freedom of individuals and places no value on community, a shared life or the pursuit of collective ends. On the contrary, Kant thinks our nature as sociable beings gives us a profound need for this kind of community, and our vocation as moral beings cannot be fulfilled without it. The natural need for a common life with others makes friendship indispensable to us; our moral vocation makes it an ethical (hence noncoercible) duty to belong to a free ethical community, to join a *church,* and to practice *religion.*

Kant claims that due to a weakness of human nature, no ethical community can be founded on pure reason alone. Such a community can arise only through a claim to particular divine revelation, as embodied in a holy book or scripture (R 6:103). We should view this as Kant's acknowledgment that historical progress can be expected only when rational principles are embodied in empirical social institutions. We witnessed a similar pattern of thinking on Kant's part regarding the way a morality of autonomy grows out of an "ethical life" of custom (Chapter 7, § 4), and the way a rightful state grows out of despotism (Chapter 7, § 5).[37]

Kant speaks of the ethical community metaphorically as a (specifically patriarchal) "family." But the best Kantian model for the ethical community, based on his own theory of social relations is not domestic (filial or fraternal) – at least not as Kant conceives of domestic society.[38] It is instead the relation of *friendship,* though extended beyond the confines of two individuals to a community that is ultimately to encompass the entire human race.

Like friendship, the ethical community involves a common or shared end. Its "free union of hearts" strongly resembles the voluntary self-surrender and mutual possession of friends by one another, which grounds the shared end of friendship. Further, if the religious community is to effect a fundamental change of heart or revolution in the moral disposition of its members through their wholly voluntary cooperation, they would have to relate to one another on terms of extraordinary intimacy, self-revelation, mutual influence, and mutual trust. Finally, the ethical community shares with friendship the very special property (which Kant attributes to no other sort of social institution) that individuals have a purely ethical duty to enter into it.[39]

Kant's model for the ethical community is obviously an idealized Enlightenment version of the Christian church, with its evangelical mission one day to unite the whole human race into a single "Kingdom of God."[40] Kant's historical hope is obviously that existing religious communities throughout the world, both Christian and non-Christian, will gradually purify their doctrines and practices through the progress of culture and the influence of enlightened reason. As they do so, they will loosen their attachment to practices, beliefs, doctrines, and authorities whose foundation is parochial and exclusive. They will become less sectarian, more ecumenical, more cosmopolitan. Kant expects them to preserve their traditional cultural identities, but reason will require them to distinguish between the "historical shell" of each limited ecclesiastical faith and the "rational kernel" of pure moral religion – which alone can be the basis for a universal moral community. Each ecclesiastical faith will come to regard itself not as the one true path to salvation, but as one possible historical vehicle (along with others) of the pure rational religion by which humanity will be united in the collective fulfillment of its moral vocation.

4.4. Religion Kant defines "religion" as "the recognition (*Erkenntnis*) of all duties as divine commands" (R 6:153). This definition is in need of explication in at least three respects.

1. Why should we think of our duties as divine commands? Though moral laws are thought of as *public*, they nevertheless do not proceed, like juridical laws, from the united or general will of the individual members of the moral community. Human beings know only one another's external actions, which may suffice for laws involving external coercion, but the laws for a moral community must be wholly ethical. The moral community at any given time is always limited in extent, and the wills of its members are fallible, but the ideal moral community must be thought of as entirely universal and its laws holy. Therefore, only God is a suitable legislator for the moral community (R 6:98–99).

2. Kant denies that any theoretical cognition of God is required for religion.[41] This is natural enough, since he denies that any such cognition is available to us (R 6:153–154). He infers from this that there need not be any special duties *to* God in order for there to be religion. In fact, because God is not a possible object of experience, the class of such duties must be empty (MS 6:241). The duties we regard as divine commands are simply the duties we have as human beings to human beings.[42]

3. The formula "the recognition of duties as divine commands" must be understood as meaning that religion is "the moral disposition to observe all duties as [God's] commands" (R 6:105). The point of religion is that we may think of the human species as a single community united by a common set of principles and ends, even though their content may remain somewhat indeterminate, open to controversy and correction, and thus a matter of each individual's conscience.

Kant was an opponent of Protestant orthodoxy in his own day. He protested the rule of religious ideas over the human mind in the form of creeds and catechisms, and he refused on principle to participate in religious services, which he regarded as superstitious counterfeit service of the Deity. He was strongly anticlerical, and – man of science that he always was – he had no patience at all for the mystical or the miraculous. Nevertheless, we must say that Kant is fundamentally a *religious* thinker. For his highest hopes for human history are pinned on religious values and religious institutions.

It may be easier to comprehend the absolutely central role of religion in Kant's ethical thought if we remind ourselves that the Enlightenment was a time of revolution even more in religious than in political thinking. Though he lived in an absolute monarchy, Kant hoped someday that the representative republic would be widely accepted as the only political constitution compatible with the idea of right. On this point, his hopes have not been disappointed. Kant clearly entertained parallel hopes for religious institutions, and even more was riding on these hopes because they concern the ultimate ends and common vocation of humanity. What the state is to the epoch of nature, the church is to the epoch of freedom.

Kant was looking forward to the day when membership in churches would be entirely voluntary, their members no longer subjected to the humiliating tutelage of a priestly hierarchy. In such a church, true divine service would be recognized as coinciding entirely with rational morality, and religion would be gradually purged of superstition and slavish attitudes of mind, just as political progress toward a rightful constitution will gradually purge the state of despotism and injustice.

In Kant's time, these hopes were not as unreasonable as they must now seem to us. In his experience raised as a pietist, religion represented the interests of our deepest spirituality. Its aim was to transform human life from within. Its final aim was to actualize the realm of ends (the "realm of grace" or "Kingdom of God") on earth. In this context, as in American abolitionist movements of the nineteenth century and in the African-American church during the twentieth, it was quite natural to think of religion as the principal historical agent representing the cause of humanity, the natural vehicle for progressive social change. In eighteenth-century Germany, moreover, there flourished a remarkable variety of rationalistic, deistic, and liberal theological views. They exercised strong influence on institutionalized religion and they resisted, with considerable success, the efforts of religious conservatives to enforce unenlightened orthodox opinions.[43]

Since the Enlightenment, religion has come to constitute itself far more often as a center of resistance to Enlightenment ideals and values. Much of popular religion now sees itself as "correcting" the "one-sidedness" of modern Enlightenment culture by privileging what is irrational and parochial, defending tradition, authority, and superstition. It would reject such descriptions, of course, for it pays fervent lip service to spiritual freedom, even to the point of treating rational doubt and secular culture as sinister forces attempting to encroach on that freedom. But the " religious freedom" it seeks to protect has little in common with the Enlightenment spirit of thinking (rationally, universally) for oneself – a spirit that courageously accepts the anxiety, instability, discontent, and self-alienation that rational thinking inevitably brings with it. Instead, religion "corrects" this "bad side" of the Enlightenment by offering people a way of fleeing back into the security of self-incurred tutelage. This tutelage is less often now to priests and inquisitors, but more often to ossified dogmatic interpretations of old holy books, to timeworn, unenlightened moral ideas, to familiar, comforting delusions about human life and in short to old, narrow, bigoted, complacent ways of thinking.

Perhaps Kant's undeserved reputation as an "individualist" is due in part to the fact that the community in which he placed his strongest hopes is of a kind to which we now find it impossible to relate. A philosopher who views the coercive powers of the state with suspicion, and advocates a religion of reason as the only true human community is easily perceived as condemning individuals to loneliness and advocating social atomism.[44] From a Kantian standpoint, however, the right conclusion to draw is that the state was always the wrong institution in which to place one's hopes and that religion has thus far failed humanity.

Looking back to the century that preceded it, Kant's view of history looks like a rationalistic version of the apocalypse expected by egalitarian German Pietism. Looking ahead to the next two centuries, it might just as easily be interpreted in terms of Marxian communism or, as some neo-Kantians did in the late nineteenth and early twentieth centuries, as a radical *socialist* vision lying at the heart of Kantian ethics and showing itself most explicitly in Kant's religious thought.[45] No such view would agree with Kant if it expected a sudden, transfiguring apocalypse in human affairs. The only hope Kant thinks we may justifiably entertain is for an endless, uncertain, painful (and occasionally interrupted) progress from bad toward better. But such a view would be Kantian in holding that if we are to fulfill our collective historical vocation, we will need to find (or invent) a form of ethical community that is capable of gradually reshaping our deeply corrupt social life by revolutionizing and uniting the hearts of individuals through the free power of reason. For Kant himself, however, the human race can no more expect to fulfill this moral vocation apart from organized religion than it can expect to achieve justice through anarchy.

CONCLUSION

1. The final form of Kant's ethical theory

More than thirty years elapsed between Kant's first announcement that he was producing a "metaphysics of morals" and the publication of his work with that title.[1] Kant's final system of ethics is even now not studied by philosophers with the same care as the *Groundwork* and *Critique of practical reason*.[2] Consequently, the projections they make on the basis of these more abstract, foundational works often do not fit what Kant says about the moral life in the book that was most explicitly devoted to it. Although a systematic exposition of the *Metaphysics of morals* lies beyond the scope of this book, in the preceding chapters I have tried to interpret Kant's ethical thought, and especially the *Groundwork*, in light of the ethical system it was supposed to ground. In these concluding remarks it will be appropriate to devote some space to showing how Kant's final system of practical philosophy reflects the spirit of Kant's ethical thought as I have presented it.

The *Metaphysics of morals* (*Sitten*) is divided into two main parts. The first is a Doctrine of Right (*Rechtslehre*). The second deals with "ethics" (*Ethik*), which is a Doctrine of Virtue (*Tugendlehre*). The doctrine of right is independent of the doctrine of virtue because right is the task of the epoch of nature, while virtue is the task of the epoch of freedom. Right protects the external freedom of individuals, which is a condition for the development of the predispositions of the human species, including both the culture of skill and the culture of discipline. The ends of morality, specified in a system of ethical duties and summed up in the idea of the highest good, are the concern of ethics.

Because right promotes an end of nature but that end also requires practical reason for its complete achievement, the relationship between

321

right and ethics is complex. Right and ethics are two distinct spheres of practical philosophy, or "morals" (*Sitten*), but the values grounding ethics also show themselves in the system of right.

2. The sphere of right

Right deals with the permissible use of external coercion, or the limits of external freedom. Its principle is:

> **R:**   "Any action is right if it can coexist with everyone's freedom according to a universal law, or if on its maxim the freedom of choice of each can coexist with everyone's freedom in accordance with a universal law." (MS 6:230; cf. TP 8:289–290)

R bears a superficial verbal similarity to FUL, but the differences between it and all forms of the principle of morality are far more significant than the similarities. R does not directly command us what to do (or not to do). It tells us only what is *right* (*recht*), that is, what is externally just.[3] This is because commands of right are to be issued not by moral reason but by an authority with the coercive power to guarantee that people will comply with them. Kant holds that we have a *moral* obligation to limit ourselves to actions that are right, but that duty is no part of R itself. R grounds only *juridical* duties, which are distinguished from ethical duties by the fact that their concept contains no determinate incentive for complying with them. Yet it is contained in the concept of ethical duties that duty itself is the primary incentive for fulfilling them (MS 6:218). For juridical duties the incentive may be moral but it may equally be prudential or (more often) something even more direct and empirical than abstract prudence – namely, immediate fear of what a legal authority will do to us if we violate the obligation. An action fulfilling an ethical duty has greater *moral* merit if it is performed from duty, but the incentive from which we perform a right action makes no difference to its juridical rightness.

To say that an act is "right" (i.e., externally just) is only to say that, by juridical standards, it may not be coercively prevented. These juridical standards of permissibility are not moral standards but are determined entirely by what a system of right (of external justice) demands in the name of protecting external freedom according to universal law.[4] The sphere of right does not exist to promote morality but only to guarantee external freedom (or civil peace with justice).[5]

R no doubt *suggests* to us (by something like conversational implicature) that right, or external freedom according to universal law, is something valuable. This implied value is also obviously an expression of the principle of morality. This is easiest to see if we consider FH, since respect for humanity requires granting people the external freedom needed for a meaningful use of their capacity to set ends according to reason. That is why Kant says that the "innate right to freedom," which is the sole ground of all our rights, "belongs to every human being by virtue of his humanity" (MS 6:237). The value we accord to external freedom, based on the dignity of rational nature as an end in itself, is the rational foundation for systems of right and for the standard of *natural* right by which systems of positive law are to be judged and corrected.[6]

R and the juridical duties that fall under it are nevertheless a distinct sphere of duties. They are not to be derived from the principle of morality.[7] One point of keeping the sphere of right independent of morality in this way is that our external freedom would be inadequately protected if we had to rely on people's moral virtue in order to get what is ours by right. A system of right cannot presume any virtue or good will even on the part of those who legislate and administer right (even the master, as Kant says, will always be an animal who needs a master). Kant earnestly argues and remonstrates with political authorities, urging them to subject their official conduct to moral principles (EF 8:370–386). But he would deny that their compliance with moral principles is a qualification for holding external authority. He is resigned to the fact that rulers will be morally imperfect, even morally corrupt. Kant thinks a representative republic with divided power is the only satisfactory way to address this problem, though he doubts that any solution will ever be perfect. Reason requires that there be a just civil society in which external coercion would be sufficient to protect the rights even of rational beings who are entirely lacking in moral virtue. The problem of establishing such a civil order, says Kant (in one of his most famous formulations) "must be soluble even for a nation of devils (if only they have understanding)" (EF 8:366).[8]

3. Ethics as a system of duties

As presented in the *Metaphysics of morals*, ordinary moral reasoning consists in deliberating about the bearing on one's action of one's ethical duties. The material of one's ethical duty is constituted by "duties of virtue" or "ends that are at the same time duties" (MS 6:382–391). Formulating maxims and deciding whether they are universalizable is sel-

dom mentioned in the Doctrine of Virtue (as we saw in Chapter 3, §
7.2, only a single duty of virtue is justified by appeal to anything like it).
Central to Kant's ethical system is instead a *taxonomy* of ethical duties.
The basic division is between duties toward oneself and duties toward
others. Within duties toward oneself, Kant distinguishes perfect duties
(those requiring specific actions or omissions, allowing for no latitude
in the interests of inclination so that failure to perform them is blameworthy) from imperfect duties (where one is required to set an end, but
there is latitude regarding which actions one takes toward the end, and
such actions are meritorious). Perfect duties to oneself are further divided into duties toward oneself as an animal being and as a moral being (MS 6:421–442). Imperfect duties toward oneself are divided into
duties to seek natural perfection (to cultivate one's powers) and duties to seek moral perfection (purity of motivation and virtue)
(MS 6:444–447). Duties toward others are subdivided into duties of love
(which correspond to imperfect duties) and duties of respect (which
correspond to perfect duties) (MS 6:448). Duties of love are further
subdivided (MS 6:452), as are the vices of hatred opposing these duties
(MS 6:458–461). Regarding duties of respect, there is a subdivision
only of the vices that oppose them (MS 6:465).

Metaphysical duties of virtue are those pertaining to human nature
in general, not arising out of particular conditions of people or our relations to them (MS 6:468–474). A complete taxonomy of metaphysical duties of virtue may be represented in the following table (cf. MS 6:
417–468):

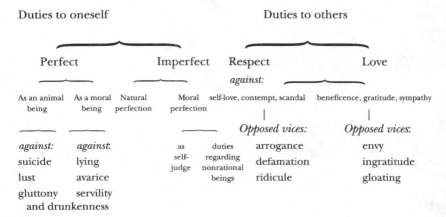

DUTIES OF VIRTUE

Duties to oneself   Duties to others

Perfect   Imperfect   Respect   Love
                                       against:

As an animal As a moral Natural   Moral   self-love, contempt, scandal   beneficence, gratitude, sympathy
   being   being   perfection perfection

                                              Opposed vices: *Opposed vices:*

against: *against:*   as   duties   arrogance   envy
suicide   lying   self- regarding defamation   ingratitude
lust   avarice   judge nonrational ridicule   gloating
gluttony   servility   beings
  and drunkenness

Kant makes an attempt (which we saw in Chapter 3, § 7.1 to be unsuccessful) to ground the distinction between perfect and imperfect duties on FLN. He never even tries to use FUL or FLN to draw the more basic distinction between duties to oneself and duties to others. Both distinctions, however, are quite easily explicated in terms of FH. A duty *d* is a duty toward (*gegen*) *S* if and only if *S* is a rational being and the requirement to comply with *d* is grounded on the requirement to respect humanity in the person of *S*.[9] A duty is wide or imperfect (or, if toward others, a duty of love) if the action promotes a duty of virtue (an end it is a duty to set); an act is required by a strict or perfect duty (or a duty of respect to others) if the failure to perform it would amount to a failure to set this obligatory end at all, or a failure to respect humanity as an end in someone's person. An act violates a perfect duty (or duty of respect) if it sets an end contrary to one of the ends it is our duty to set, or if it shows disrespect toward humanity in someone's person (as by using the person as a mere means).

Moral reasoning for Kant consists mainly in seeing how one's duties bear on one's actions. Imperfect or wide duties should guide us in setting the ends of our life. Not all ends need be duties or contrary to duty (some ends are merely permissible), but morally good people will include duties of virtue among the central ends that give their lives meaning. Kantian morality thus leaves a great deal of latitude in determining which ends to set and how much to do toward each end. The pursuit of our ends, once they have been decided upon, is constrained only by juridical duties, perfect duties to ourselves, and duties of respect to others. No doubt both our ends and our actions toward them will be further constrained by duties we have to others on account of their circumstances or our relationships to them, which Kant makes no attempt to discuss in a *metaphysical* system of ethical duties (MS 6:468–469; see Chapter 6, § 1.2).

4. Ethics as a system of ends

Viewed historically, all ethical duties belong to the epoch of freedom. Ethics is concerned with the free self-government of rational beings (as FA expresses it) and the pursuit of a community of ends universally shared among them (according to FRE). The foundation of ethics is the incentive of duty (self-constraint by pure reason). Hence the first (though merely formal) ethical duty is to do all duties from the motive of duty (MS 6:219, 383). All other ethical duties are what Kant calls "duties of

virtue," namely, duties to set and pursue certain ends (MS 6:379–384).
"For this reason ethics can also be defined as the system of *ends* of pure
practical reason" (MS 6:381). Kant argues that there must be ends of
pure practical reason:

> For since there are free actions there must also be ends to which, as their
> objects, these actions are directed. But among these ends there must be
> some that are also (i.e., by their concept) duties. For were there no such
> ends, then all ends would hold for practical reason only as means to other
> ends; and since there can be no action without an end, a categorical im-
> perative would be impossible. (MS 6:385)

This argument is based on Kant's thesis that every action must have an
end to be effected (G 4:427, KpV 5:58, KU 5:196–197). Some of these
ends are valued for their own sake, some only as means to other ends.
Kant argues that actions commanded by the categorical imperative
must, in their concept, have some ends of the former kind. That is, a
categorical imperative must command us to set certain ends that we are
to pursue for their own sake. Otherwise, all the ends of dutiful actions
would be valued merely as means to other ends (not required by morality). That would make the commands of morality conditional upon our
contingent choice to set these further ends and thereby contradict the
concept of a categorical imperative. Therefore there must be some ends
which are "by their concept duties."[10] These ends are all grounded on
the dignity of rational nature as an existent end in itself, but they are
ends to be effected.

Kant identifies two ends of practical reason, which it is our duty to
set: our own perfection and the happiness of others (MS 6:385). 'Perfection' includes both our natural perfection (the development of our
talents, skills, and capacities of understanding) and moral perfection
(our virtuous disposition) (MS 6:387). A person's 'happiness' is the
greatest rational whole of the ends the person set for the sake of her
own satisfaction (MS 6:387–388). Even Sidgwick agreed that because
we naturally have our own happiness as an end, it cannot be a duty except insofar as we need to be constrained to pursue it from grounds of
reason (e.g., in order to promote one's own perfection).[11] Because we
must respect the autonomy of others their perfection is a duty only insofar as it belongs to their ends (hence their happiness) (MS 6:386,
388).[12] Sidgwick also argues that Kant's concept of 'perfection' has implicit reference to some end beyond itself to which the perfection is to
serve as a means, and since the sum of all such ends is the happiness of

rational beings, it follows that for Kant all the ends which are at the same time duties have at least implicit reference to happiness.[13] Sidgwick would be correct if 'perfection' referred only to technical perfection (the suitableness to a given end); however, since 'perfection' also includes moral perfection, which is something good for its own sake (and even unconditionally so), Kant's theory of duties does not collapse into a system of eudaemonistic consequentialism.

The Doctrine of Virtue is, however, overwhelmingly *teleological*. In fact, *within* the *system of ethical duties* (this is a crucial qualification[14]), Kant is not (in the now commonly accepted sense of these terms) a 'deontologist' but a 'consequentialist'. For he asserts the priority of the 'good' (of the end to be effected) over the 'right' (taking this term not in Kant's sense but only in the Anglophone philosopher's sense, meaning an action that conforms with our *ethical* duty). Further, he accepts no properly *ethical* constraints on our actions except what are required by the setting of obligatory ends.[15] In the system of duties of virtue, even perfect ethical duties, those absolutely requiring certain actions or omissions, have to be grounded on *teleological* considerations. Only *juridical* duties, grounded from outside the system of ethical duties, can command us how to act irrespective of ends (MS 6:219, 388–389).

The general formula is that an action is a perfect ethical duty if omitting it means refusing to set a morally required end, or means setting an end contrary to a morally required one; an action violates a perfect duty if it involves setting an end contrary to one that is morally required. The duty not to lie, for example, regarded as a perfect ethical duty toward oneself, must be grounded on the fact that all lying involves an end that is contrary to the end of one's own perfection (MS 6:429–431). The analogous perfect ethical duties not to behave with contempt toward others, to defame, mock, or ridicule them, would be based on the claim that such behavior involves an end contrary to morally required ends (MS 6:463–468).[16]

Kant's ethical theory of ends, however, does not conceive of our pursuit of obligatory ends in the way most consequentialist theories do. Standard devices of prudential rationality, such as summing and averaging, maximizing, and satisficing, do not necessarily apply to our moral reasoning about these ends. My duty to promote the happiness of others is *not* a duty to maximize the collective happiness of others. My duty to promote my own perfection is not a duty to achieve any specific level of overall perfection, still less a duty to make myself as perfect as I can possibly be.

This is because duties of virtue are in their concept wide, imperfect, and meritorious duties (MS 6:390–391). I behave meritoriously insofar as I act to promote an end falling under the concept of the required ends. But I deserve no blame for failing to promote the end on any given occasion, and *a fortiori* no blame for not promoting it maximally. In general, it is up to me to decide whose happiness to promote and by what means and to what degree. Ethics allows me latitude or "playroom" (*Spielraum*) in deciding such matters (MS 6:390).

For Kant there is more virtue and more merit in working harder and sacrificing more for moral ends. But there is not more merit *per se* in making two people happy rather than one, or in making one person twice as pleased as you might have, or in developing two talents rather than one.[17] The obligatory ends may be ends of pure reason insofar as they fall under the headings "my perfection" and "others' happiness," but it is always the particular instances as such that are the ends of reason. Kant's view is *not* that the real ends of reason are only the larger categories and promoting the particular instances is meritorious only insofar as it contributes to the maximum achievement of the good represented by the larger category.

The latitude of ethical duties will be bounded mainly by the duties I have to specific individuals on account of their particular circumstances or their special relationships to me. My duty to promote my family's welfare is considerably stricter than my duty to promote the welfare of strangers. In general it is meritorious for me to help strangers who need it, but not blameworthy if I do not help them. Yet it would sometimes be blameworthy to refuse aid to someone who might die without my assistance. Kant asserts the existence, and does not deny the importance, of these special duties; but spelling them out would require more empirical detail than pertains to a "metaphysics of morals" (MS 6:468–469).

The fact that duties of virtue constitute an indeterminate plurality governed by no aggregative or maximizing principles entails that moral agents themselves, as free agents and not the theory or moral principles or duties, are responsible for the design of their individual life plans. People are responsible for dedicating their lives to *some* ends that are at the same time duties. For example, I fulfill my duty to make my own perfection an end if I take up weight-lifting, learn to play the violin, study quantum physics, or learn how to interpret the poetry of Wallace Stevens. To make the happiness of others my obligatory end is to work to relieve hunger in distant lands, devote myself to cheering up a lonely friend, to make a profession of healing or teaching. I may act more meritoriously by *devoting myself more* to these good ends. But there is nothing aggregative in the quantity of my perfection or others' happiness that necessarily enters into the measure of my devotion. (I do not necessarily devote myself more to the ends of morality merely by devoting myself to more such ends or by taking a greater quantity of good as my end.) Finally, since the duties in question are wide or meritorious, I never deserve *blame* for aiming at less good rather than more or even for being less devoted to good ends than I might have been.

This picture makes it highly unlikely that what Bernard Williams calls my "ground project" could fall outside the scope of my ethical duties.[18] Duties of virtue for Kant are not mere "side constraints" on the pursuit of the ends that give meaning to our lives. On the contrary, if I am a decent person, I will choose to give my life meaning by pursuing some set of ends that fall under the general descriptions "my own perfection" and "the happiness of others." Where that is so, morality *underwrites* our ground projects, regarding them as morally meritorious.[19] Of course, it is quite possible to give one's life meaning by pursuing ends contrary to morality, such as wealth, power, or other forms of superiority over others. Kantian ethics does condemn that sort of life (along with the meaning chosen for it) as contrary to morality. This also entails that the ground projects of such a life are ultimately contrary to reason (even if their goals are pursued in accordance with technical or prudential rationality). Hence for one's life as a rational being to have meaning, its ground projects must be among those falling under the (relatively loose) confines of those ends that are at the same time duties.

5. Ethics as virtue

The title of Kant's system of ethical duties is the "Doctrine of virtue." His name for the obligatory ends of pure practical reason is "duties of virtue." This should be enough to make us think twice before accepting the common allegation that Kant's ethical theory is concerned only with willing and acting, with moral doing rather than ethical being, that it neglects the importance of virtue.[20]

In the *Critique of practical reason*, Kant describes "virtue" as "a naturally acquired faculty of a non-holy will" (KpV 5:33) or, more specifically, as "the moral disposition in the struggle" (*im Kampfe*) (KpV 5:84). Virtue, then, presupposes a moral disposition but is the acquired ability of a non-holy will to struggle successfully against inclinations to achieve the performance of duty.[21] In the *Metaphysics of morals*, virtue is characterized as "the moral strength of a human being's will in fulfilling his duty" (MS 6:405; cf. 6:394). "Moral strength" is an "aptitude (*Fertigkeit, habitus*) in acting and a subjective perfection of the power of choice" (MS 6: 407). Because we are finite and flawed beings whose conformity to reason must take the form of self-constraint, virtue is required if we are to follow rational principles, which may command unconditionally but become subjectively "irresistible" only through virtue (MS 6:405). Since freedom is the capacity to follow self-given rational laws, virtue is therefore equivalent to "inner freedom," "being one's own master," and "ruling oneself" (MS 6:407).

Our inclinations are a counterweight to the moral law, which requires strength to overcome it. Therefore, there can be no reliable fulfillment of duty without (some degree of) virtue. Because virtue is the fundamental presupposition of ethical conduct, the theory of ethical duties is called a Doctrine of Virtue. Obligatory ends are called "duties of virtue" because virtue is required to adopt and pursue them.[22] Virtue may also be characterized as the strength of our commitment to these ends.[23] There is only a single fundamental *disposition* of virtue, which is required for all conformity to duty. But because the ends which it is our duty to have are many, there are many different virtues (MS 6:383, 410).[24] I can have one virtue and lack another if my commitment to one end (e.g., respecting the rights of others) is strong (I will promote this end even in the face of contrary temptations), but to another end (e.g., the happiness of others) it is weak (e.g., I seldom have enough moral strength to overcome selfish impulses and perform acts of generosity).

Alasdair MacIntyre writes: "To act virtuously is not, as Kant [held], to act against inclination; it is to act from inclination formed by cultivation of the virtues."[25] This both misdescribes virtue and caricatures Kant's conception of it. Virtue for Kant is the strength of our commitment to a rational end. To act virtuously is to act from a (rational) desire for those ends. To act virtuously is to act against inclinations only to the extent that virtue is measured by its power to resist those specific inclinations (*empirical* desires) that tempt us not to pursue the rational end. Insofar as Aristotle holds that virtues are dispositions to rational choice, it is not clear that he would agree with MacIntyre that virtuous action is action from inclination (i.e., from empirical rather than rational desire).[26] A person whose inclinations spontaneously harmonize with the demands of morality is not *per se* more virtuous than one whose inclinations are less favorable to morality. It's rather that the former person will find it easier to comply with those demands, and therefore will have less *need* of virtue in order to comply with them.

Kant agrees with Aristotle that a virtue is a habit (*habitus*), but he insists that virtue must be a "free habit" (*habitus libertatis*), *not* merely an *assuetudo* – "a uniformity in action that has become a *necessity* through frequent repetition" (MS 6:407).[27] Kant also agrees with Aristotle that virtue involves desire, pleasure, and pain.[28] Because virtues involve the setting of ends according to reason, and setting an end produces a rational desire for the end, virtues involve desires; because desire is a representation accompanied by a feeling of pleasure or displeasure, virtues also involve such feelings. But being virtuous does not consist in having *inclinations* (empirical desires) that happen to be conducive to morality, or in an *empirical* propensity to be pleased or pained in ways that make dutiful conduct easier, or in a *temperament* that makes good conduct easier.[29] Kant holds that we have duties to cultivate such feelings and inclinations and also to acquire a temperament suitable to morality (MS 6:457). But he does not equate *virtue* with success in fulfilling that duty (MS 6:409). Virtue is needed, in fact, precisely to the extent that good conduct is hard for us, since it consists in the strength we need to perform a difficult task. A person whose temperament is happily constituted so that virtue is less often necessary, may still be virtuous, but virtue is a quality of *character*, not of temperament.

It should be clear by now that virtue is at least as important to Kant's ethical theory as it is to any "virtue ethics." Owing to Kant's moral psychology, however, his conception of virtue differs significantly from those involved in the views that usually go by that name. Advocates of these views often charge Kant with seeing only the standpoint of the individual agent, ignoring the individual's social surroundings, and also with grasping this standpoint in an objectionably abstract and intellectual way and alienating agents from their feelings, desires, perceptions, and contextual judgments. I think we are now in a good position not only to see the element of truth in such charges but also to understand the ways in which they both misunderstand Kant's view and fail to appreciate the strength of his reasons for rejecting their so-called virtue ethics.[30]

Kant emphasizes the moral predicament of individual rational agents because the human species, at the present epoch in its history, can make moral progress only through *enlightenment*: self-thinking or the pure self-legislation of human beings as autonomous rational agents. He insists that only action from pure reason and the motive of duty can be relied upon to produce dutiful action because he thinks that our empirical desires, as expressions of our unsociable sociability, are thereby in general also expressions of the radical evil in human nature. They sometimes contingently coincide with what is good but cannot be trusted to produce good actions.

Thus it is utterly false to claim that Kant views the moral life "individualistically" in the sense that it abstracts from social and historical realities. On the contrary, Kant thinks enlightenment will be possible for individuals only through the free give and take of ideas of an enlightened *public* and that the struggle against evil can be effective only if it is carried out through an *ethical community*, in which the virtuous disposition of individuals to pursue moral ends grasps these explicitly as common ends and objects of collective striving.

We saw in Chapter 4, § 8.1, that Kant thinks there is an irreducible role for judgment about particular cases in the application of any rule, theoretical or practical. He acknowledges the flexibility of many moral rules in the "Casuistical Questions" appended to the discussion of duties in the Doctrine of Virtue. Any virtue, as the practical commitment to an end which is a duty, will at the same time involve a commitment to search for means to achieve the end. That should result in a heightened awareness of opportunities to promote it and sensitivity to dangers which threaten its achievement.[31]

Nevertheless, Kant does not regard skill in practical judgment as part of virtue; nor would he endorse any view that identifies virtue with a disposition to make morally sensitive judgments about particular cases without reference to universal principles. His theory of human nature even shows why people's moral perceptions are untrustworthy to the extent that they have been acquired from socialization in traditional institutions, which reflect our unsociable sociability. For Kant, the most important part of moral education must be to teach people to employ rational principles so as to criticize their perceptions and intuitive judgments about particular cases. To a certain extent, Kant agrees with those who would prepare a child to follow moral principles by training it to be pleased and pained by the right things, so that rational morality will be experienced as continuous with attitudes they have already developed. Like Rousseau, however, he thinks this should take the form not of rewarding and punishing, but of showing the child the natural advantages of good conduct and the disadvantages of bad conduct (Rousseau, *Émile* 4:317–321). For example, a child who tells a lie should be made to see that people will not believe him in the future (VP 9:480). But Kant thinks there is also a real danger in producing too comfortable a fit between a person's affective dispositions and the moral principles they are taught. This danger is that the unreflective harmony between principles and perceptions will make it harder for people to stand back from those feelings and rationally criticize them. It is already difficult to do this if, as Kant holds, our natural inclinations and affections are inherently untrustworthy, forever in need of correction by rational thought and moral motivation.

The advantages of Kant's position are particularly obvious in times of moral change and moral progress. For example, a man who was brought up in middle-class America in the mid-twentieth century typically has habits, feelings, perceptions, and judgments that ill equip him to deal with women in the workplace in the 1990s. Such a man is likely to resist many changes in attitude that are rightly expected of him.[32] If he relies on the feelings and perceptions consequent on the character he has been educated to have, then he will experience these expectations as the tyrannical imposition of "political correctness" on "natural" and "normal" human feelings and relationships. He will vote Republican and may join an organization like the Promise Keepers. He would do better to ignore the recommendations of virtue ethics and become more Kantian, alienating himself from the gentlemanly "virtues" he has been taught, and struggling to reform his habits and feelings by following the abstract principle of equal respect for all rational beings.

Kant's historical theory of moral progress in effect places us in an uncomfortable condition of "permanent revolution." Rational principles, constantly subjected to reflection and criticism, are our only reliable guide. Good people are always alienated to some degree from their habitual perceptions and natural feelings. This, at any rate, is what Kantian anthropology tells us. Virtue ethics no doubt presupposes a contrasting empirical–historical vision of human nature, which is more trusting of our empirical feelings and perceptions. This means it cannot help being more complacent regarding the traditional social practices in which they are rooted. Kant rejects that vision not because he denies or ignores the fact that ethics has social and historical foundations, but because he has carefully argued for an alternative (critical enlightenment) conception of them.

6. What is Kantian ethics about?

My aim has been to present Kant's ethical thought in a new light, in order that it might be easier to understand and more relevant to ethical questions of today. By attacking the view that Kant's moral principle can be identified with FUL and the universalizability tests and by stressing the importance of Kant's theory of human nature and philosophy of history for his ethical thought, I have been trying to change the common image of Kantian ethics to show that Kant's ethical thought is not only different from what it is usually taken to be but also subtler and more complex. But in this way I have also been trying to make it *harder* for anyone to make any final assessment of Kant's ethical thought as a whole. My attempt to change the image of Kant's ethical thought will have been successful if the readers of this book find that the issues they are thinking about when they consider the cogency of Kantian ethics are different from the ones that have usually been associated with controversies about it.

Despite the care and insightful detail (too seldom appreciated by his readers) with which Kant works out this troubling vision of human society, some may dismiss it as one-sided and excessively cynical. Kant understands virtually everything in human life as an expression of unsociable sociability, self-conceit, or the radical propensity to evil in human nature (three different names for the same reality). The result is an unpleasant (some might say a truly poisonous) slant on a broad range of human desires, feelings, and relationships, one that finds deceit, competitiveness, and the "dear self" everywhere, even in our most benevolent feelings of sympathy, love, and charity. Some will find Kant's view of human nature no more than a caricature.

Clearly, both Kant's moral principles and his theory of human nature are designed only to add to our discontent with ourselves. For Kant the task of philosophy is not (as it is for Hegel), to *reconcile* us to the human condition.[33] Kant thinks that as rational creatures our condition must be one of dissatisfaction, self-alienation, and endless striving. Philosophy should not try to transcend that condition but only to help us live with its inevitability, and more important, to make progress in the painful tasks it sets us. To some this aim may seem unhealthy, perhaps even dangerous. From a Kantian standpoint, however, any other way of representing our condition appears complacent, cowardly, and dishonest.

A moralist can be expected to make enemies if his message is that there is something radically unsatisfactory about most of the ways we usually act, think, and feel. But Kant's picture of human beings as arrogant, antagonistic, deluded, and unhappy may merely be the way the facts of human life *must* appear to someone who takes seriously the moral demand that people should act in accord with the laws of a community of ends in which all human beings are treated with equal dignity. In Kant's unflattering portrait of human nature, it is easy enough to recognize ourselves as modern capitalism has made us. If our dismissal of his unflattering portrait is functioning as an apology for that system, then we should at least not conceal from ourselves that that is what is going on. Something like this is doubtless an important part of the appeal of the invidious images of Kantian ethics that focus on his extreme views about lying or sex or his unenlightened opinions about race or about women. It is easier to fend off ideas that make you uncomfortable if you can see them as expressions of attitudes you know you can rightly reject than if their source appears to be a radical principle with which you cannot help agreeing.

The demands of Kantian morality *are* radical. They ground morality solely on the idea of one's own rational will. Kantian principles require treating all human beings as ends in themselves with absolute, hence equal worth. They demand that human beings unite their ends into a single, reciprocally supporting teleological system, or "realm." The ideals of Kantian ethics are *autonomy, equality,* and *community.* Or, to put these ideals in the political language of his own time: *Liberté, égalité, fraternité!*

Kantian ethics is about the opposition between the social conflict natural to human beings and their rational striving toward concord and community. It is about the process of enlightenment enabling us to form the idea of the laws and principles of such a community, and about the hope that gradually, through the historical progress of reason, we may overcome the conflict that is natural to us and make progress toward an ideal realm of ends on earth.

Kant maintains that social antagonism and inequality belong to human culture as long as it develops "without a plan" (MA 8:118). In an age of enlightenment, the historical vocation of moral philosophy is to work toward an explicit formulation of the conscious, collective plan through which human beings are eventually to overcome the natural discord between them.

The Kantian ideals of *autonomy, equality,* and *community* can be grasped and pursued only as a unity. If we find a tension between them, if we think that we have to sacrifice one of them in order to realize another, then that shows only that we are still so far from realizing any of them that even our conceptions of them are still defective. For example, to think that greater equality can be had only at a proportional cost in human freedom is to confuse the liberties necessary for human dignity with the license to dominate and exploit others, which is inimical to it.[34]

Above all, the three ideals can be pursued effectively only in common with others, on terms of reciprocal respect and rational agreement. For Kant, they are to be pursued in a cosmopolitan spirit by the entire human race. The proper model for that collective pursuit is neither a closed society based on pious adherence to tradition nor an ever-shifting nexus linking people solely through self-interest, strategic bargaining, and exploitation. Real solidarity between mature human beings can grow only from their shared commitment to universal principles that are given content and universal validity by an ongoing process of free, enlightened communication. At present, we see only fragments of such a community, which we must nurture like seedlings, hoping that they will someday grow into a single social whole uniting all people, whose actions accord with a shared, rational plan for our common human destiny (I 8:29–31, MA 8:117–118). Precisely that hope was literally Kant's own last word on the human condition. For it concludes the handbook for his lectures on anthropology, which he published at the end of his teaching career:

> In working against the [evil] propensity [in human nature] . . . our will is in general good, but the accomplishment of what we will is made more difficult by the fact that the attainment of the end can be expected not through the free agreement of *individuals*, but only through the progressive organization of citizens of the earth into and toward the species as a system that is cosmopolitically combined. (VA 7:333)

NOTES

PREFACE

1. *Hegel's Ethical Thought* (New York: Cambridge University Press, 1990). The discussion of Hegel's critique of Kant is mainly in Chapters 8 and 9, especially pp. 144–174.
2. See *Hegel's Ethical Thought*, p. 156.
3. One clear symptom of the overemphasis on the Formula of Universal Law is the notion that the central idea behind Kantian ethics can be formulated as a "procedure" for testing maxims. Perhaps the most influential recent version of this idea is the "CI-Procedure" devised by John Rawls, "Themes in Kant's Moral Philosophy," in R. Beiner and J. Booth (eds.), *Kant and Political Philosophy: The Contemporary Legacy* (New Haven: Yale, 1993), pp. 292–293. Compare Rawls, "Kantian Constructivism in Moral Theory," *Journal of Philosophy* 77 (1980), pp. 515–572. Much impetus was given to this reading of Kant by an earlier book that also did much to make Kantian ethics respectable in Anglophone philosophy: I mean, Onora Nell (O'Neill), *Acting on Principle* (New York: Columbia, 1975).
4. This paper was subsequently published in English and in German, in two slightly different versions: "Unsociable Sociability: The Anthropological Basis of Kantian Ethics," *Philosophical Topics* 19, No. 1 (1991), "Ungesellige Geselligkeit: die anthropologischen Grundlagen der Kantischen Ethik," B. Tuschling (ed.), *Kants Metaphysik des Rechts und Geschichtsphilosophie*. Berlin: Duncker & Humblot, 1997. Much of it was also incorporated into my lectures on "Idealism and Revolution: Human Nature and the Free Society in Kant, Fichte and Hegel," which were published in *Philosophy and the History of Science* 4 (1995).
5. Chapter 4 is an expansion of "Humanity as End in Itself," in H. Robinson (ed.), *Proceedings of the Eighth International Kant Congress*, Volume I.1 (Milwaukee: Marquette University Press, 1996), reprinted as "Humanity as End in Itself," in P. Guyer (ed.), *Critical Essays on Kant's Groundwork of the Metaphysics of Morals*. Totowa, NJ: Rowman and Littlefield, 1998. Chapter 7, § 5 incorporates part of "Kant's Historical Materialism," in Jane Kneller and Sidney Axinn (eds.), *Autonomy and Community: Readings in Contemporary Kantian*

Social Philosophy. Albany: SUNY Press, 1998. Chapter 5, § 5 is an abbreviation of "The Moral Law as a System of Formulas," in H. F. Fulda and H. D. Klein (eds.) *Architektur und System in der Philosophie Kants* (Hamburg: Meiner, 2000). Individual passages in the book may often overlap with the papers listed in the next note.

6. (1) "Rol religii v Kantovoi filosofskii istorii" (Russian tr. by L. Kalinnikov), *Kantovskyi Sbornik* 18 (1994) (no English version of this paper exists). (2) "Kant's Project for Perpetual Peace" (Opening Plenary Address), in H. Robinson (ed.), *Proceedings of the Eighth International Kant Congress*, Volume I.1 (Milwaukee: Marquette University Press, 1996), reprinted as "Kant's Project for Perpetual Peace," P. Cheah and B. Robbins (eds.), *Cosmopolitics: Thinking and Feeling Beyond the Nation.* Minneapolis: University of Minnesota Press, 1998, and translated as "Kants Entwurf zum ewigen Frieden," R. Wittmann and R. Merkel (eds.), *Zum ewigen Frieden nach 200 Jahren.* Frankfurt: Suhrkamp, 1996, and "'Vyechnyi mir' spustia dva vyeka" (Russian tr. by B. Glazov), *Kantovskyi Sbornik* 20 (1996). (3) "Self-Love, Self-Benefit and Self-Conceit," in J. Whiting and S. Engstrom (eds.), *Aristotle, Kant and the Stoics: Rethinking Happiness and Duty.* New York: Cambridge University Press, 1996. (4) "The Final Form of Kant's Practical Philosophy," *The Southern Journal of Philosophy* 36 Supplement (1997). (5) "Kant on Duties to Nonrational Nature," *Proceedings of the Aristotelian Society* Supplement, Volume LXXII (1998). (6) "Kant's Doctrine of Right: Introduction," in O. Höffe (ed.), *Immanuel Kant: Metaphysische Anfangsgründe der Rechtslehre* (Klassiker Auslegen) (Berlin: Akademie Verlag, 1998). (7) "Kant vs. Eudaemonism," in Predrag Cicovacki (ed.), *Kant's Legacy: Essays in Memory of Lewis White Beck.* Rochester: University of Rochester Press, 2000.

INTRODUCTION

1. John Rawls, *A Theory of Justice* (Cambridge, MA: Harvard University Press, 1971), p. 256.

2. When he speaks of 'paederasty' it is unclear whether Kant means homosexuality in general or more specifically the sexual abuse of children. His association of paederasty with rape might suggest the latter. (Lara Denis suggested this reading of the passage to me.) But it has been quite common (and still is today) for homophobes (such as Kant obviously was) to imagine there is some association between consensual relations between adults of the same sex and the sexual abuse of boys by older men. So the two readings are not mutually exclusive.

3. Kant holds that all human races share a common biological origin, rejecting Georg Forster's theory that their origins were separate (Ak 8:157–184). Kant's theory is that in human nature there were originally four different "germs" (*Keime*) associated with four sets of racial characteristics. Which germ develops in a given individual or genetic line depends on geographical conditions (Ak 8:167). Thus Kant regards the physical characteristics of race as hereditary. But he holds that the determining factor developing these characteristics is the geographical situation and the consequent adaptation to a

distinctive mode of life (BM 8:94ff, EF 8:364–365). Like Herder, Kant appears to regard different races and nations as playing complementary (though not equal) roles in the complete development of the human species. Kant does not give the white race sole credit for *past* progress of the human species, but he does appear to think that *future* progress is to be expected chiefly from Europeans. The following passages are representative:

> [Native Americans] are deficient in feeling (affects and passions), and resist civilization. [Africans, by contrast] are excessive in feelings; they have a strong sense of honor, and can be educated, but chiefly for servitude. [Asians ("Hindus" or "Yellow Indians")] are educable in the highest degree, but only for arts and not for sciences; they do not advance culture, and have a strong degree of composure (*Gelassenheit*): They all look like philosophers. (VA 25:1187)

> We find some peoples who seem not to progress in the perfection of human nature, but have come to a standstill, while others, as in Europe, are always making progress. If the Europeans had not discovered America, then the Americans would have remained in their condition. And we believe that even now they will not attain to any perfection, for it seems that they will all be eradicated – not through murder, that would be gruesome! but rather they will die out. For we calculate that only a twentieth part of all the previous Americans are still there. Since they only retain a small part, since the Europeans take so much away from them, there will arise internal struggles between them, and they will be in friction with one another. China and Hindustan is a land in which there is much art and also an analogue to science; indeed, we are much indebted to this land. If we consider this people, then we ask: has it come to the bounds of its destiny? We have conjectured that it will not proceed further, since it lacks spirit." (VA 25:840)

> The Americans have such relations in their nature that they will not become more perfect. The Negroes are also not susceptible of further civilization, but they have instinct and discipline, which the Americans lack. The Indians and Chinese appear to be at a standstill in their perfection; for their history books show that they now know no more than they have for a long time. (VA 25:843)

Some have concluded that Kant's principled moral universalism is implicitly qualified by a white racism, in effect restricting moral status to white males. See Reinhard Brandt, *D'Artagnan und die Urteilstafel: Über die Ordnungsprinzip der europäischen Kulturgeschichte* (Stuttgart: Franz Steiner, 1991), pp. 135–136 and Emmanuel Chukwudi Eze, "The Color of Reason: The idea of 'Race' in Kant's Anthropology," in E. Eze (ed.), *Race and the Enlightenment* (Oxford: Blackwell, 1997), pp. 103–140. But Kant never explicitly draws such a conclusion or denies moral status to any human being on the basis of race. For a more balanced account of Kant's racism and its ethical implications, see Robert Louden, *Kant's Impure Ethics*, Chapter 3, final section, "The Whole Human Race" (Oxford: Oxford University Press, 2000).

4. Kant regards the ethical disposition of women as more a hindrance than a

help in achieving public enlightenment, since he thinks women fear more than men the dangers of thinking for oneself (VA 7:303–311, MS 6:279, WA 8:35). Regarding Kant's views on women, see Susan Mendus, "Kant: An Honest But Narrow-Minded Bourgeois?" in Howard Williams (ed.), *Essays on Kant's Political Philosophy* (Chicago: University of Chicago Press, 1992), pp. 166–190. Far more progressive views were expressed by Kant's close friend Theodor Gottlieb von Hippel in *Über die bürgerliche Verbesserung der Weiber* (1792). For a good brief summary of Hippel's views, see Hannelore Schröder, "Kant's Patriarchal Order" in Robin May Schott (ed.), *Feminist Interpretations of Immanuel Kant* (University Park: Pennsylvania State Press, 1997), pp. 275–282. Hippel's book was published anonymously, and when it came to light that Hippel was the author, there was public conjecture that it must really have been authored (or coauthored) by Kant. Even though Kant himself later explicitly denied any association with the book (Ak 12:386), some still think he made a contribution to it (see Ursula Pia Jauch, *Immanuel Kant zur Geschlechterdifferenz: Aufklärische Vorurteilskritik und bürgerliche Geschlechtsvormundschaft* (Vienna: Passagen, 1989), pp. 203–236).

5. See Howard Williams, *Kant's Political Philosophy* (New York: St. Martin's, 1983), pp. 178–182. Kant's reason for such exclusion is that he regards it as pointless to include as active participants in the state those who are economically dependent on others, since they will be coerced by their patrons to vote as the patrons will and cannot therefore enter actively into civil society as free individuals. There is an important point here that we should not overlook, since even in our societies (which recognize the principle of universal adult suffrage) the political choices of many are constrained by the electorate's knowledge of what the propertied may do to those who are economically dependent on them. Taxation of the wealthy or too much public assistance for the poor will result in increased unemployment or other evil consequences inflicted on the working class by those who own a disproportionate share of society's financial resources. Today we are not much closer than Kant was to drawing the right conclusion from this, which is that no society can be considered politically free as long as it tolerates large disparities of wealth between its members.

6. John Dewey once wrote about Kantian ethics:

> Idealism and personality separated from empirical analysis and experimental utilization of concrete social situations are worse than vague mouthings. They stand for realities, but these realities are the plans and projects of those who wish to gain control, under the alleged cloak of high ends, of the activities of other human beings. (John Dewey, *German Philosophy and Politics* (1915) (2nd edition, New York: Putnam, 1944), pp. 29–30.)

Insofar as Dewey's remarks reflect the common image of Kantian ethics as "formalistic" and unconcerned with empirical psychological and social reality, we will see that they are just false. Regarding the political effects of Kant's ethical doctrines, if Dewey's claim is that the principles Kant articulated have always (or even most often) been used to defend the plans and projects of tyrants and dictators, then it too is obviously false. If the claim is that Kantian principles *can* be (and sometimes have been) so used then it is true, but it does not distinguish Kantian principles from any other influential moral or political doctrine, since anything many people believe can be (and probably has been) used as that sort of pretext. (So has "empirical analysis and experimental utilization of concrete social situations"; twentieth-century social science has lent itself far more easily and more often to the justification of oppression than have Kantian moral principles.) See Julius Ebbinghaus's reply to Dewey in "Interpretation and Misinterpretation of the Categorical Imperative," *Philosophical Quarterly* 4 (1954), reprinted in Robert Paul Wolff (ed.), *Kant's Foundations of the Metaphysics of Morals: Text and Commentary* (Indianapolis, IN: Bobbs-Merrill, 1969), pp. 105–107.

7. Annette Baier is one of the most forceful in criticizing Kant for "individualism." Annette C. Baier, *Moral Prejudices* (Cambridge, MA: Harvard University Press, 1994), Chapters 12 and 13. There are many different propositions that might be asserted by saying that Kant is an 'individualist'. In the course of this book, however, we will see that most of the interesting ones are false. Two true ones are (1) that a strong component of Kant's ethical thought is its defense of the rights and dignity of individual human beings, and (2) that Kant acknowledges no such thing as collective responsibility or guilt (though he does think that both moral good and evil are fundamentally social products, and hence is an antiindividualist in that important respect). Baier's own charge rests heavily on Kant's remark that one should prefer to shun all society than to wrong anyone (MS 6:236). But to see this echo of Rousseau (cf. *Émile*, 4: 340–341) as an expression of individualism is clearly to misinterpret it. Even more than Rousseau, Kant regards it as neither possible nor morally permissible for a rational human being to shun all human society. Surely the obvious point of the remark is not that one can evade the claims the rights of others make on us by shunning human society, but rather that these claims are impossible for human beings to evade. Baier is fair and perceptive enough, however, to make the following observation: "['Individualism'] is only one strain in Kant's thought, and it is in some tension with the version of the Categorical Imperative that tells us to act as members of a realm of ends" (*Moral Prejudices*, p. 249).

8. Typical is Fritz Medicus, who charges Kant with failing to appreciate that "human beings are not equal in their ethical education. . . . With primitive peoples, who lack concepts of right, treaties cannot be made, as Kant demands." Medicus cites Kant's demand that European peoples respect the rights of non-Europeans as a "proof of Kant's incapacity to judge of cultural-historical things" (F. Medicus, "Kant's Philosophy of History," *Kant-Studien* 54 (1900), pp. 61–67). See Georg Cavallar, *Pax Kantiana* (Vienna: Böhlau, 1992) pp. 235–241.

9. The real modern originator of this idea is Bernard Mandeville (1670–1733), in his poem *Fable of the Bees* (1705):

> Much of Rousseau comes almost word for word from the writings of Bernard Mandeville, a Dutchman living in England, whose famous *Fable of the Bees* appeared early in the eighteenth century. Mandeville's thesis was

that one could not raise a people into a populous and flourishing nation without the assistance of evil, both natural and moral. The advancement of knowledge on which material progress depends must enlarge men's desires, refine their appetites, and increase their vices . . . A choice has to be made between accepting the consequences of scientific progress and a consistent and total rejection of the desire for its benefits. (W. D. Falk, *Ought, Reasons and Morality* (Ithaca, NY: Cornell Press, 1986), p. 266.)

We find Mandeville's problem posed strikingly, and in varying forms, by many thinkers in the Enlightenment tradition, including Rousseau, Smith, Swift, Turgot, Kant, Hegel, and Marx. Kant's solution is to accept Mandeville's claim that evil necessarily accompanies the development of reason for the historical past but not necessarily for the future. As rational beings we must work for a historical future in which the benefits of developed reason can be freed of the moral evil necessary for reason's development, and it is rational to hope that such a future may be possible.

10. Bernard Williams, "Evolution, ethics and the representation problem," in *Making Sense of Humanity* (Cambridge, UK: Cambridge University Press, 1995), p. 104.
11. Alasdair MacIntyre, *After Virtue* (Notre Dame, IN: Notre Dame Press, 1984), p. 52. In Chapter 6, § 2, we will see that the conception of anthropology that MacIntyre ascribes to Kant is precisely the approach whose *rejection* (in Platner's version of it) motivated Kant's attempt in the 1770s to refound the study of human nature on an entirely different ("pragmatic") basis.
12. Richard Rorty, "Justice as a Larger Loyalty," in P. Cheah and Bruce Robbins (eds.) *Cosmopolitics* (Minneapolis: University of Minnesota Press, 1998), p. 49.
13. Philippa Foot, "Does Moral Subjectivism Rest on a Mistake?" *Oxford Journal of Legal Studies* 15 (1995), p. 7.
14. To rid ourselves of false images we need at the same time to free ourselves from longstanding prejudices about the Enlightenment itself. Enlightenment thought was by no means ahistorical. It was in fact with this movement that modern historical self-consciousness first arose; it is with the Enlightenment that European culture first became clearly aware of its historical specificity. This point was established long ago by Ernst Cassirer, *The Philosophy of Enlightenment* (1932) (Boston: Beacon Press, 1955), Chapter I. As Michel Foucault has observed, this is evident from the very fact that this is the first age such that our name for it coincides with the name it gave itself (Foucault, 'Un cours inédit,' *Magazine litteraire* (Paris: May, 1984), p. 36).
15. "In fact Kant is far from insisting, as he has often been charged with insisting, that there is a natural opposition between sense of duty and inclination; what he does insist on is that there is complete indifference between the two" (Sir David Ross, *Kant's Ethical Theory: A Commentary on the Grundlegung zur Metaphysik der Sitten* (Oxford: Clarendon, 1954), p. 17). Here Ross is trying to be charitable to Kant, but in fact he could hardly be more mistaken.
16. August Wilhelm Rehberg, "Recension von *Kritik der praktischen Vernunft*, von Immanuel Kant," *Allgemeine Literaturzeitung*, August, 1788. Christian Garve, *Versuch über verschiedene Gegenstände aus der Moral und Literatur* (Bres-

lau, 1792) I, pp. 111–116. Friedrich Schiller, *Über Anmut und Würde in der Moral* (1792).

17. This book (especially Part Two of it) can claim kinship with other recent studies of Kantian ethics that also stress the anthropological side of Kant's ethical thought. See especially: G. Felicitas Munzel, *Kant's Conception of Moral Character: The 'Critical' Link of Morality, Anthropology and Reflective Judgment* (Chicago: University of Chicago Press, 1999) and Robert B. Louden, *Kant's Impure Ethics* (see Note 2). Another expositor of Kant's moral theory who does not neglect the role of anthropology and history is Roger J. Sullivan, *Immanuel Kant's Moral Theory* (New York: Cambridge University Press, 1989), pp. 235–239. But following Kant's *Idea toward a universal history*, Sullivan considers Kant's philosophy of history chiefly in relation to political philosophy. Louden, Munzel, and I think its significance must be appreciated for Kant's entire practical philosophy.

PART ONE: METAPHYSICAL FOUNDATIONS

CHAPTER 1: COMMON RATIONAL MORAL COGNITION

1. On the number and relation of these formulas, see H. J. Paton, *The Categorical Imperative* (New York: Harper, 1965), Ch. XIII; A. R. C. Duncan, *Practical Reason and Morality* (Edinburgh: Nelson, 1957), pp. 165–185; T. C. Williams, *The Concept of a Categorical Imperative* (London: Oxford University Press, 1968), pp. 20–36; and this book, Chapter 5, § 5.

2. Stephen Engstrom, "Kant's Conception of Practical Wisdom," *Kant-Studien* 88 (1997), pp. 24–25.

3. Kantian ethics cannot regard wisdom and virtue as special cognitive abilities that only some moral agents possess. The capacity for them comes with the rational capacities required for moral agency in general. But Kant need not (and should not) deny that we sometimes correctly regard *good judgment* as part of what constitutes a person's moral worth, and *bad judgment* as something for which we are to blame. Where this is so, however, good judgment must be viewed as excellence in the exercise of moral capacities (and bad judgment as deficiencies in their exercise). Moral ends may sometimes be better furthered by those who have special technical knowledge of how to achieve them, but that knowledge itself is not part of a person's moral worth, nor is the lack of it something for which we can be blamed (except insofar as the agent had a specific duty to acquire it). For a contrasting account, compare Alasdair MacIntyre, *After Virtue*, pp. 154–155.

4. David Ross is in error when he attributes to Kant the views that (1) "that which is good without qualification must never unite with anything else to produce bad results" and (2) "it must never unite with anything else to produce a bad whole" (Sir David Ross, *Kant's Ethical Theory: A Commentary on the Grundlegung zur Metaphysik der Sitten* (Oxford: Clarendon, 1954), p. 10. About the cases Ross mentions, Kant's only claim is that the worth of *the good will itself* is never diminished by its results or by being combined with bad things. On (2) Kant takes no clear position at all as far as I can see. He does think that talents,

capacities, and other goods are themselves good and contribute to the goodness of any whole of which they are parts, only insofar as the will that uses them is good. On (1) it is clear that the good will, when encumbered with misfortune or "the niggardly provision of a stepmotherly nature," *can* produce results that are bad (i.e., results directly contrary to what the good will wills them to be). It is easy to imagine the good will producing bad results because it is combined with the contraries of the conditioned goods Kant lists (understanding, wit, judgment, resoluteness, etc.). If a person lacks the strength of will to overcome these defects of temperament, Kant considers this a lack of *virtue*, but not a lack of *good will* (MS 6:407). Surely we could also imagine cases where, due to the unpredictable ironies of fortune, the good ends intended by a good will are not reached by the good will, but they would have been attained by a person in the same situation acting with a bad will.

5. Alasdair MacIntyre, *A Short History of Ethics* (Notre Dame, IN: Notre Dame Press, 1997), p. 192. Contrast the more accurate remark of Paton: "It must not be thought that a will is good only because it overcomes obstacles. On the contrary, if we could attain to the ideal of complete goodness, we should have so disciplined our desires that there would be no further obstacles to overcome. Obstacles may serve to make the goodness of a good will more conspicuous, and we may be unable to measure goodness except by reference to such obstacles; but a good will must be good in itself apart from the obstacles it overcomes" (Paton, *The Categorical Imperative*, p. 46). However, in speaking of measuring the good will by obstacles overcome, Paton may be confusing the good will with virtue, which is distinct from the good will in Kant's theory. See Note 7 .

6. Kant roundly rejects as "fantastical moralism" any view of morality that would have a person "strew all his steps with duties as with man-traps," so that duty would have to be at stake in every choice (MS 6:409).

7. It is not clear whether this hypothesis would be correct, however, or even that it is intelligible. A good will is that which strives for good ends, but it is not obvious that having a good will is among the ends of a good will. If I *have* a good will, it makes no sense for me to *strive* to have one. But it also makes no sense to suppose that a will that is not good might strive to have a good will. Here it is again important to recognize that for Kant good will is not the same as virtue (MS 6:408), since virtue (as moral perfection of the will) is an *end* of morality (MS 6: 386–387, 391–393). See also, Conclusion, Note 17.

8. Schiller, *Xenien,* "The Philosophers"; see Goethe, *Werke* 1, ed. Erich Trunz (Munich: Beck, 1982). (The *Xenien* were published jointly by Goethe and Schiller.)

9. See Marcia Baron, *Kantian Ethics (Almost) Without Apology* (Ithaca, NY: Cornell Press, 1995), pp. 188–193. See also Henry Allison, *Kant's Theory of Freedom* (New York: Cambridge University Press, 1990).

10. See Paul Dietrichson, "What Does Kant Mean By 'Acting From Duty'?" in R. P. Wolff (ed.), *Kant: A Collection of Critical Essays* (Garden City, NY: Doubleday, 1967).

11. Notice, however, that no example of this is ever discussed in the First Section of the *Groundwork*. That suggests that we have probably misunderstood the

point of his discussion if we think it turns on his view of such examples. I am grateful to Marcia Baron for pressing me to clarify the point discussed in this paragraph.

12. Probably the best of the many discussions of these topics is by Barbara Herman, *The Practice of Moral Judgment* (Cambridge, MA: Harvard University Press, 1993), Chapter 1 (first published in the *Philosophical Review* 90 (1981)). One discussion that avoids raising these irrelevant questions (though more because of its philosophical approach than its reading of Kant's ethics or his aims in the *Groundwork*) is Richard Henson, "What Kant Might Have Said: Moral Worth and the Overdetermination of Dutiful Action," *Philosophical Review* 88 (1979). Conspicuous (to me at least) among the discussions that do raise questions Kant was not answering are those found in *Kant's Moral Religion* (Ithaca, NY: Cornell Press, 1970), pp. 40–68, and *Hegel's Ethical Thought* (New York: Cambridge University Press, 1990), pp. 146–153.

13. For good discussions of what Kant does and does not claim here, see Thomas Hill, Jr., "Is A Good Will Over-rated?" *Midwest Studies in Philosophy* Vol. 20: *Moral Concepts* (1996), pp. 299–317, Marcia Baron, *Kantian Ethics (Almost) Without Apology*, Ch. 4, Tom Sorell, "Kant's Good Will and Our Good Nature," in Paul Guyer (ed.), *Kant's Groundwork of the Metaphysics of Morals: Critical Essays* (Lanham: Rowman and Littlefield, 1998), pp. 81–100, and the exchange between Julia Annas, "Personal Love and Kantian Ethics in *Effi Briest*," and Marcia Baron, "Was Effi Briest a Victim of Kantian Morality?" in Neera Kapur Badhwar, *Friendship: A Philosophical Reader* (Ithaca, NY: Cornell Press, 1993), pp. 155–191. My thinking about Kant on the motive of duty received much stimulus from discussions with Sigurdur Kristinsson.

14. Henry Sidgwick, *The Methods of Ethics* (1874) (Indianapolis, IN: Hackett, 1981), p. 223.

15. On this point see Christine Korsgaard, "The Argument of *Foundations* I", *Monist* 72 (1989), pp. 324–327, reprinted in *Creating the Kingdom of Ends* (New York: Cambridge University Press, 1996), Chapter 2.

16. Whether philanthropic love is *pathological* love is harder to say. It is if any love as feeling (*pathos*) counts as pathological love. But sometimes Kant equates what is 'pathological' with what has empirical origins and therefore precludes motivation by pure reason (KrV A802/B830). But if philanthropic love is not pathological, then the distinction between pathological and practical love is not exhaustive, since philanthropic love belongs to neither category. I am grateful to Daniel Guevara for pressing me to clarify this point.

17. From this Kant wants to infer also that the worth of an action done from duty is not to be located in the end or object, that is, the thing or state of affairs the action intends to bring about. (Kant does not deny, but affirms, that the action must always have such an end, MS 6:385). Strictly speaking, however, this does not follow. We could value an action not for its results but for itself, and yet what we value about it might be the fact that it *intends* a certain result. But it would be difficult to imagine why we would value an action fundamentally for the end it seeks to produce if we did not value it for the sake of that end. There is a similar problem for certain rule utilitarians, who think we value actions for their own sake insofar as they follow certain rules, namely

those rules whose acceptance, observance, or intended observance promotes the general happiness. But why should we accord special value to the actions simply because they follow moral rules rather than valuing the actions for the sake of the happiness they promote (via following the rules)?

18. John Stuart Mill, *Utilitarianism*, ed. George Sher (Indianapolis, IN: Hackett, 1979), pp. 35–37.

19. I owe this formulation of the relationship between the three propositions to remarks made in discussion by Dieter Schönecker.

20. On this distinction see Mary J. Gregor, *Laws of Freedom* (Oxford: Blackwell, 1963), Chapter VII.

21. There is a very good discussion of this famous example in Christine Korsgaard, "From Duty and for the Sake of the Noble: Kant and Aristotle on Morally Good Action," in S. Engstrom and J. Whiting (eds.), *Aristotle, Kant and the Stoics: Rethinking Happiness and Duty* (New York: Cambridge University Press, 1996), pp. 203–236.

22. "Respect is a feeling . . . whose biological function is to stabilize the results of bargaining – bargaining understood broadly" (Allan Gibbard, *Wise Choices, Apt Feelings: A Theory of Normative Judgment* (Cambridge, MA: Harvard University Press, 1990), p. 269. This analysis would appear to make the respect owed to people proportional to the bargaining chips they hold (of course, understanding these "broadly"). A Kantian, however, will regard the respect for human dignity as having greatest importance of all when the demand for respect is unsupported by the results of bargaining. Perhaps Gibbard would understand "bargaining" so broadly as to include all moral reasoning, even reasoning that dictates going directly against the results of "bargaining" in the usual sense, because it requires respect for those who lack the bargaining power to get it by negotiation. In that case, though, the term "bargaining" would seem to be highly (or even objectionably) misleading.

23. Nelson Potter accurately describes the situation by saying that either FUL does not follow from the propositions on the basis of which Kant infers it or else "it does not express all that Kant thought it did" ("The Argument of Kant's *Groundwork* 1," Guyer (ed.), *Kant's Groundwork of the Metaphysics of Morals: Critical Essays*, p. 35).

CHAPTER 2: RATIONAL WILL AND IMPERATIVES

1. "The end justifies the means" is a slogan passed freely in moral or political argument like a currency of dubious value. Taken literally, the slogan is a virtual tautology and hence necessarily true. The end always justifies the means because once something is described as a 'means', it follows that the pertinent end is the only thing that could possibly justify it. It should be annoying to philosophers, therefore (since we are a stubbornly literal-minded lot) that the slogan's normal use is in despite rather than because of its self-evident truth. Sometimes people seek an end in circumstances where the best (or the only) means to it are morally impermissible. The slogan is commonly used by their critics to state the (morally corrupt) principle on which they are supposed to be acting. However, the *real* moral principle the agent is usually violating is

one Judith Jarvis Thomson calls a "second cousin" of Kant's claim that whoever wills the end wills the means, namely, "one may will the end if and only
if one may will the means" (*The Realm of Rights* (Cambridge, MA: Harvard University Press, 1990), p. 108). What such agents ought to accept is that they
must either *give up their end* (at least temporarily), or else limit their pursuit
of it to means that are morally permissible (even though they are less justifi-
able in relation to that end). Perhaps the rhetorical function of taunting
them with the slogan "The end justifies the means" (suggesting that to think
this way is corrupt, perhaps even implying that the slogan itself is false) is to
persuade them that they must renounce the most rational means to their end
without in the least renouncing their end itself (which agents in such situations usually persuade themselves is so noble that it must be achieved at any
cost). If we care more about literal truth than rhetoric, what we should tell
them is that their end, however noble in itself, is worth less than they think,
and that under the circumstances other ends or moral principles should take
precedence over it. The fact remains that once we have decided, all things
considered, what ends we should be pursuing, they will always justify the
means to them.

2. Like many early modern philosophers, Kant seems to have underestimated
the mental (including volitional) capacities of nonhuman animals. It would
often seem as though higher mammals do not always respond immediately
to impulses but sometimes deliberate, set ends, select means to them, even
hesitate whether to pursue an end. But part of the problem is that it is inherently problematic to apply to nonhuman creatures any of the terms we
have devised to designate the set of mental capacities we attribute to ourselves. Since our rational capacities are conceptualized both holistically and
in relation to the entire normal range of human behavior, we will be faced
with impossible choices if we are forced to describe the behavior of animals
by unequivocally applying some of these terms to them and denying that others should be applied. What is really needed is a separate set of conceptions
to describe the distinctive capacities of different animals. Kant's conception
of the "brute power of choice" is therefore probably useless to describe any
existing creature, but it may be useful in bringing out by contrast something
distinctive about ourselves as volitional agents.

3. On the *Wille/Willkür* distinction, see Lewis White Beck, *A Commentary on Kant's
Critique of Practical Reason* (Chicago: University of Chicago Press, 1960),
pp. 176–181, and Henry Allison, *Kant's Theory of Freedom*, pp. 129–136.

4. Henry Allison, *Kant's Theory of Freedom*, pp. 40–41 and passim.

5. Kant's view, as is clear in the Paralogisms of Pure Reason (KrV A338–405, especially A361–366, cf. B406–432, especially B409), does not involve any
commitment to the idea, challenged by Derek Parfit, that being a person
involves being a "Cartesian ego," or the presence of a "deep further fact"
beyond my mental states (Parfit, *Reasons and Persons* (Oxford: Clarendon,
1984), pp. 205–211). It does require that we think of ourselves as agents, and
our identities as held together by the practical requirements of agency and
the commitments we undertake as agents. See Christine Korsgaard, "Personal
Identity and the Unity of Agency: A Kantian Response to Parfit," *Philosophy*

and Public Affairs 18 (1989), pp. 101–132, reprinted in *Creating the Kingdom of Ends*, Chapter 13.

6. Robert Paul Wolff also realizes that Kant wants to reject the Humean view that "desire sets the ends of action and reason chooses the means" (Wolff, *The Autonomy of Reason* (New York: Harper, 1973), p. 120). But in his account of the Kantian doctrine that "pure reason can determine the will" Wolff, like Hume, treats "reason" as functioning solely in the production of *beliefs*. Hence he opposes the "desire" to do something to the "belief" that it is morally wrong and supposes that reason can determine the will only if this *belief* can somehow overcome desire – not this or that desire, but desire in general, making us act in precisely the way we *don't want to*. Kant's view, however, is that pure reason can determine the will because it is also *a source of desire*. The big mistake is to think that Kant regards moral *truths* (or our beliefs about them) as bringing about action in a way that is entirely distinct from (and even precludes) desire. For example:

> A distinction between "having a motive" and "desiring" was introduced by Kant. For, according to Kant, we have in the thought that we ought to do some act a motive for doing it: but "having a motive" does not here entail "having a desire." (W. D. Falk, *Ought, Reasons and Morality*, p. 24)

In Kant's view, however, to be aware of a moral incentive to do *A* (or to bring about *E*, which is the end of *A*) is to be aware of a feeling of pleasure accompanying the representing of *E* (and thus of the doing of *A*). That combination of representation and feeling, however, is precisely what it is to have a desire. See following note.

7. Even as confirmed an empiricist as John Stuart Mill is not unaware of this point. Mill recognizes that people who *desire* an end through a passively experienced impulse can come to will the end actively, and then they may subsequently desire the end only because they have come to will it (Mill, *Utilitarianism*, ed. G. Sher (Indianapolis, IN: Hackett, 1979), pp. 38–39). Empiricist absurdities remain in Mill's account, however. Mill thinks that active will arises only out of passive desire, through a mechanical process of habituation. In other words, the empiricist theory is that activity consists in a passivity repeated so often that it begins mechanically to repeat itself.

8. This point is developed by Christine Korsgaard in Onora O'Neill (ed.), *The Sources of Normativity* (Cambridge, UK: Cambridge University Press, 1996), Lecture 3.

9. A *maxim* is a "subjective principle of action," that is, a principle the subject makes for itself to govern its action. The principle is "subjective," however, in that it is "valid only for the subject" – binding on or normative for only the individual who actually adopts it, and it is valid for this subject only for as long as the subject chooses to accept it as a rule of action. In these respects a "maxim" contrasts with a "law," a principle on which the subject *should* act (whether it does or not). A law is binding on the subject through its rational faculty but independently of the subject's arbitrary adoption of the rule (G 4:400, KpV 5:18–19). Laws take the form of *imperatives* when they apply to a

will that is not perfectly rational or "holy," that is, a will that can fail to follow them, and hence must *constrain itself* to follow them (G 4:413–414).

10. In Kant's view, the very concept of morality (i.e., of principles unconditionally binding on us simply as rational beings) rules out the possibility of "different moralities" (i.e., disjoint or conflicting *fundamental principles* of morality) (EF 8:367). Different cultures do recognize very different moral obligations, and even have very different conceptions corresponding more or less closely to "moral obligation." But different obligations, or even different conceptions of what is to be done and not done, might be expressions of the same fundamental principle under widely differing circumstances or widely differing interpretations of the world. There are also, no doubt, errors in the beliefs of many (most likely, of all) cultures, both about what morality fundamentally demands and about the world to which these demands are applied; if all err in varying ways, then of course they may disagree. To infer moral relativism directly from moral disagreement shows no awareness of the important distinction between everyday moral beliefs (and prejudices) and fundamental principles. It also fails to appreciate the absolutely compelling reasons we have as moral agents, both in making our own decisions and in dealing with others on terms of mutual understanding and respect, for proceeding on the presumption that there is a single fundamental moral principle that is valid for all rational beings. See Chapter 9, § 3.2.

11. There is a more general strategy in Kant for vindicating reason as a guide to both belief and practice. It has been recently expounded and defended by Onora O'Neill in *Constructions of Reason: Explorations of Kant's Practical Philosophy* (Cambridge, UK: Cambridge University Press, 1989), Chapters 1 and 2 and "Vindicating Reason," in Paul Guyer (ed.), *The Cambridge Companion to Kant* (New York: University Press, 1992), pp. 280–308.

12. The continuing challenge Kant poses to some popular varieties of empiricist deflationary naturalism about moral motivation is well presented by Samuel Scheffler, *Human Morality* (New York: Oxford, 1992), pp. 61–72.

13. See Lorne Falkenstein, "Was Kant a Nativist?" *Journal of the History of Ideas* (1990), pp. 573–597, reprinted in Patricia Kitcher (ed.), *Kant's Critque of Pure Reason: Critical Essays* (Lanham, MD: Rowman and Littlefield, 1998). Kant has no doubt that something natural (and innate) is a factor in generating both *a priori* and empirical knowledge. In the practical sphere, our innate predispositions (especially what Kant calls our rational predisposition to "personality") provide us with the *capacity* to give ourselves moral principles. But *a priori* principles themselves arise only as a result of our *exercise* of those innate capacities. Rational capacities, as Kant understands them, are distinguished from others in that they make it possible for the beings that have them to devise and select their own way of life. Moral principles arise in us, in Kant's view, only when these capacities are exercised under certain historical and social conditions, which is *not* the same as saying that they owe their *content* to empirical factors. This makes *us* their author as rational agents, not our genes or our empirical conditioning.

14. Kant has sometimes been accused of confusing an imperative which is

categorical because (1) it is not contingent on the setting of an end, with an imperative that is categorical because (2) it is not contingent on anything at all. He is supposed to have missed the point that there could be imperatives that are categorically binding but admit of exceptions. See A. N. Prior, *Logic and the Basis of Ethics* (Oxford: Clarendon, 1949), pp. 40–41; Marcus Singer, "The Categorical Imperative," *Philosophical Review* 63 (1954), p. 581. Kant may be less willing than we would like to make exceptions to some moral rules (such as those forbidding lying). But it is a crude misunderstanding to attribute this disposition to the fact that he grounds his theory on a categorical imperative. (On this, see Singer, *Generalization in Ethics*, p. 225, and Thomas Auxter, *Kant's Moral Teleology* (Macon, GA: Mercer University Press, 1982), pp. 143–144 and Lewis White Beck, "Apodictic Imperatives" in R. P. Wolff, *Kant's Foundations of the Metaphysics of Morals: Text and Commentary*, pp. 155ff.) Kant holds that the supreme principle of morality is categorical in sense (2) as well as (1), simply because it is the *supreme* principle, so that there could be nothing outside it grounding any exceptions to it. But he certainly allows that the various moral rules derived from this principle admit of exceptions, since rules of exceptions (*exceptivae*) are one of his categories of pure practical reason (see KpV 5:66), and the main point of the many "casuistical questions" discussed in the *Doctrine of Virtue* is to explore possible exceptions to standard moral rules.

15. HI, as a general principle, is close to the principle Thomas Hill, Jr. has called "The Hypothetical Imperative," *Dignity and Practical Reason* (Ithaca, NY: Cornell Press, 1992), pp. 17–37.

16. Sidgwick does not get this point quite right when he says that if I do not happen to have the end presupposed by a hypothetical imperative, then the imperative is "not addressed to me" (*Methods of Ethics*, pp. 6–7). For the imperative is already universally binding on all, hence *already* binding on me. In that sense, it is already *addressed* to me as a rational agent. It is only that if I do not now have the relevant end, then the imperative does not at present rationally require any specific action of me. The case is quite analogous to that of the moral rule "Keep your promises" (assuming it to be a categorical imperative). This moral rule is binding on me already even if I have made no promises, and as a moral rule we would normally think of it as addressed to all moral agents without exception, even though it requires specific actions only of agents who have made promises. John Mackie displays a similar misunderstanding of hypothetical imperatives when he writes:

> "If you want *X*, do *Y*" (or, "You ought to do *Y*") will be a hypothetical imperative if it is based on the supposed fact that *Y* is, in the circumstances, the only (or the best) available means to *X*. The reason for doing *Y* lies in its causal connection with the desired end, *X*; the oughtness is contingent upon the desire. (J. L. Mackie, *Ethics: Inventing Right and Wrong* (New York: Penguin, 1977), pp. 27–28)

That you ought to do *Y* is conditional on your having set *X* as your end (this is true whether or not your present *desire* for *X* is enough by itself to get you to do *Y*). The *"oughtness" of the imperative*, however, is not conditional upon your desiring *X*, or having *X* as an end. It rests only on the causal fact that *Y* is an indispensable means to *X* and on the analytical connection between willing an end and being rationally required to will the indispensable means.

17. In the *Groundwork*, Kant uses the term "problematical" imperatives, but later he rejected this in favor of the term "technical" imperatives (Ak 20:200n). His reason was doubtless that the former term seemed misleading or even oxymoronic, since it might suggest that even in the presence of a valid imperative commanding an action it might still be problematic whether the action ought to be performed. The term "problematic," however, was probably chosen because in the case of technical imperatives, it is possible to refrain from the commanded action while still conforming to reason, if one abandons the contingent end. This is not an option in the case of assertoric imperatives, because the end is not a contingent one, and it is not possible in the case of categorical imperatives because their validity does not depend on the prior adoption of any end (but instead provides the ground for setting rationally necessary ends).

18. See Norbert Hinske, "Die Ratschläge der Klugheit im Ganzen der *Grundlegung*," in O. Höffe (ed.), *Grundlegung zur Metaphysik der Sitten: Ein kooperativer Kommentar*, pp. 131–147.

19. W. D. Falk writes:

> One says sometimes "I ought to save because I *want* to be prudent," but sometimes "because I *ought* to be prudent." One may also decide that in one's own best interest one ought to be prudent rather than daring or daring rather than prudent, as the case may be. Now, that one ought to do something because it would be prudent is a dictate of prudence. But that one really ought to be prudent, in one's own best interests, would not be a dictate of prudence again." (Falk, *Ought, Reasons and Morality*, p. 205)

The first thing Falk reports one as saying here is an example not of prudential but of instrumental reason. For it tells me only that I ought to do what will get me what I want (what I have made my end, which in this case just happens to be prudence). Only the second thing is an example of properly prudential reasoning, since it gives as the ground for acting that the action will conduce to prudence (to happiness). What Falk goes on to say involves a confusion between two senses of 'prudence'. In the sense Kant means, 'prudence' is doing what is conducive to your own greatest happiness. But in another familiar sense it refers to a policy of caution as opposed to daring or risk-taking. A person whose desires and tastes are such that they can be happy only by taking risks would behave imprudently in the first sense if they adopted too strict a policy of prudence in the second sense. Once this ambiguity is sorted out, it is easy to see that (using the term 'prudence' in Kant's sense) Falk is wrong to deny that one ought to follow dictates of prudence in the interests of prudence.

20. Sullivan writes: "All particular prudential maxims presuppose and instantiate the same ultimate, formal prudential principle: Insofar as any agent acts rationally, willing an end also means willing whatever means are within that agent's power and (which the agent knows) are necessary to get it."

(*Immanuel Kant's Theory of Morality*, p. 33). The quoted principle, however, is a principle of instrumental, not of prudential rationality. Perhaps particular cases of prudential reasoning presuppose instrumental rationality, insofar as they dictate the right means to happiness. But the essence of prudential reason is that happiness has a rational claim on us distinct from and superior to that of any arbitrarily chosen end. Sullivan does realize the two are distinct when he distinguishes technical from prudential imperatives (pp. 34–36), but (like Kant himself) he seems confused at times about what the difference consists in.

21. There is a familiar problem about PI: It is often self-defeating to pursue your own happiness in a focused and single-minded fashion (i.e., people who do this tend to make themselves *unhappy* as a result). (As we shall see later, Kant agrees with this commonplace; it is part of his reason for holding that human happiness would have been better provided for by nature through instinct than it is by our having reason, G 4:395.) This does not show that PI is not a rational principle or that we should not follow it. Instead, it bears only on the strategy we should use in following PI. Some ends can be better pursued by not focusing attention on them but letting them influence the choice of other things to pursue and avoid. I will not achieve the end of not thinking about purple cows by focusing my attention on the thought of that end. But I can easily achieve it by concentrating on some of the many other things I have more reason to think about. Our happiness is often best sought by pursuing other ends (including the happiness of others and the means to or various proper parts of our own happiness) or else by avoiding doing things we might be tempted to do that will make us unhappy. That's precisely the sort of conduct that falls under PI.

22. See Thomas Hill Green, *Collected Works,* ed. Nettleship (London: Longman Green, 1885–1888), Volume 2: Lectures on Kant §§ 105–122; *Prolegomena to Ethics* (Oxford: Clarendon, 1883) §§ 173–202. See also T. H. Irwin, "Morality and Personality: Kant and Green," in A. Wood (ed.), *Self and Nature in Kant's Philosophy* (Ithaca: Cornell, 1984), pp. 31–56.

23. Philippa Foot maintains that moral imperatives must be considered hypothetical because imperatives are supposed to represent requirements of practical rationality and (so she alleges) it is a conceptual truth that "irrational actions are those in which a man in some way defeats his own purposes, doing what is calculated to be disadvantageous or to frustrate his ends" ("Morality as a System of Hypothetical Imperatives," in Foot, *Virtues and Vices* (Berkeley: University of California Press, 1972), p. 162). But she gives no argument that this is a conceptual truth, and it seems to be a falsehood not only regarding moral rationality but even regarding prudential rationality. For it would not defeat either PI or a counsel of prudence falling under it that the agent has not made happiness one of his ends, and hence that his imprudent behavior does not frustrate his ends or defeat his purposes. On the contrary, that would show only that the agent's deficiency in prudential rationality is quite profound. See also Michael Smith, *The Moral Problem* (Oxford: Blackwell, 1994), pp. 77–84.

24. This idea also seems to play a role in Kant's argument that we can have no di-

rect ethical duty to make our own happiness an end, since we do this inevitably by natural necessity and therefore cannot be constrained to do it (MS 6:387–388). That we have a natural and inevitable desire for our own happiness was a commonly held view among Kant's predecessors, notably Locke; see *An Essay Concerning Human Understanding*, ed. P. Nidditch (Oxford: Clarendon Press, 1975), Book II, Ch. XXI, §§ 42–43. See also Stephen Darwall, *The British Moralists and the Internal 'Ought'* (New York: Cambridge University Press, 1995), pp. 43–50, 170. Darwall also mentions such a view in others, such as Cudworth (p. 145) and Shaftesbury (p. 184) – though, like Kant, they do not think that our natural desire for happiness is rationally irresistible and do not consider it the ground of all practical reason, as Locke does.

25. Locke, *Essay*, Book II, Ch. XX, § 2, Ch. XXVIII, §§ 5–11. See Darwall, *The British Moralists and the Internal 'Ought'*, pp. 36–50.

26. In the course of an earnest article attacking Kant's argument for FH, Pepita Haezrahi writes:

> It never occurred to Kant that men could, on rational grounds, refuse to treat other men as ends. To our generation, however, this possibility has occurred, indeed the question has been brought home to us with great emphasis. ("Man as End-in-himself," in R. P. Wolff (ed.), *Kant's Foundation of the Metaphysics of Morals: Text and Critical Essays* (Indianapolis, IN: Bobbs-Merrill, 1969), p. 296)

This possibility obviously did occur to Kant, since otherwise the entire strategy of the *Groundwork* would not have been devised to help clarify in what sense it is possible rationally to refuse to treat people as ends, and to show in what sense it is not. Haezrahi is correct (and agrees with Kant) when he says:

> As a matter of fact, very few people actually feel that all people are endowed with dignity. Mostly the innate emotional regard for other people's persons embraces a restricted and definite group (who are thought of as endowed with dignity in virtue of their class, profession, nationality, etc.). Almost always the purely emotional respect for other people's persons excludes certain groups on more or less defensible rational reasons, or on irrational, sometimes even unconscious grounds. (pp. 315–316)

Kant does think that all people are *susceptible* to the feeling that all rational beings are endowed with dignity, insofar as their reason recognizes this and has an impact on feeling (producing respect, love of human beings, and other such feelings). But the fact that people seldom have these feelings "innately" is precisely why a principle like FH requires a *rational defense*. For it is the function of reason to produce these feelings in people not born with them. See also Chapter 4, Note 14.

27. As we shall see later, Kant's ethical theory holds that there are two other ends that every rational being is *required* to set in obedience to the moral law: namely, my own perfection and the happiness of others (MS 6:385–388, 391–394). But these are ends represented as necessary *consequent on* the moral law; they are not ends that might be appealed to in grounding it. What would be required for an end of that sort is that it should be rationally necessary inde-

pendently of the moral law. My own happiness, for Kant, is the sole end that might meet that condition.

28. Schopenhauer, *On the Basis of Morality*, tr. E. J. F. Payne (Indianapolis, IN: Bobbs-Merrill, 1965), pp. 52–58.

29. Christine Korsgaard (*Creating the Kingdom of Ends*, p. 50) correctly distinguishes Kant's theory from any that would "reduce the motive of obligation to a desire for self-approval." The desire to approve of oneself, insofar as it reflects a genuine moral disposition, is rather grounded on the principle that one should live up to certain objective standards and also try to know that one has lived up to them. This conformity and knowledge will therefore result in self-approval, which one should desire only under these conditions. A mere desire for self-approval could often be more easily satisfied by not living up to the standards but deceiving yourself into thinking you have. To think of *that* desire as the basis of moral motivation is to adopt a position that is conspicuous for its moral bankruptcy. Thus Bernard Williams gets off on the wrong foot right away when he attempts to reconstruct Kant's argument for the rationality of moral conduct by taking as the fundamental question: "Is there anything that rational beings necessarily want?" (Williams, *Ethics and the Limits of Philosophy* (Cambridge, MA: Harvard, 1985), p. 55). Kant does think that there are things rational beings necessarily want (insofar as reason determines their wants), but these wants are not what is fundamental to his ethical theory. What is fundamental are the (*a priori*) *reasons* we have for wanting those things, and those reasons are not wants.

30. In citing a person's self-conception as the source of our reason to follow a hypothetical imperative, I am once again agreeing with Korsgaard (*The Sources of Normativity*, Lecture 3, especially § 3.3.1–4). See also Harald Köhl, *Kants Gesinnungsethik*, pp. 147–155. A historically rich version of the idea of the self as source of normative force is worked out by Charles Taylor in *Sources of the Self* (Cambridge, MA: Harvard, 1989). I do not follow Korsgaard, however, in holding that being motivated by a normative self-conception is a *sufficient* condition for acting from a genuine reason. I would not agree, namely, with her reaction to G. A. Cohen's example of the (idealized) Mafioso who lives up to a self-conception of strength and honor, when she declares there is a sense in which the obligations arising from this self-conception are real "not just psychologically but normatively" (*The Sources of Normativity*, p. 257). Korsgaard admits that the example causes her discomfort, but she is willing to endure it. I think she is too willing because she is too eager to embrace a position too close to Taylor's. She wants, namely, to reconcile her version of Kantianism with communitarian views that regard "thick" self-conceptions deriving from personal commitments and ethnic, national, or religious sources as providing the only "real" reasons people have for living up to norms (and consequently balk at what seems to them the abstract and impoverished self of the Kantian agent). In the real world, the "thicker" conceptions celebrated in the theories of communitarians are not only great sources of spiritual comfort (and moral complacency) but are often closely allied with ethnic or religious bigotry and are responsible for some of the most terrible evils human beings ever commit against one another. What gen-

uine normative force they have should be regarded as borrowed from the fact that rational beings ("thinly" conceived) have chosen them. A conversation with Bill FitzPatrick helped me to clarify this point.

CHAPTER 3: THE FORMULA OF UNIVERSAL LAW

1. J. L. Mackie, *Ethics: Inventing Right and Wrong*, p. 224.
2. David Hume, *A Treatise on Human Nature*, ed. L. A. Selby-Bigge and P. H. Nidditch (Oxford: Clarendon, 1978), p. 478. Cf. also Hume's discussion of the motive of just acts, pp. 492–501, the parallel discussion in Hume, *Enquiry Concerning the Principles of Morals*, ed. L. A. Selby-Bigge and P. H. Nidditch (Oxford: Clarendon, 1975), pp. 282–283, and Christine Korsgaard's perceptive discussion of "Hume's Dilemma" in *Creating the Kingdom of Ends*, pp. 47–67.
3. This doubt was raised in conversation by Robert Pippin. For a well-known reply to it, see Barbara Herman, *The Practice of Moral Judgment* (Cambridge, MA: Harvard University Press, 1993), Chapter 10.
4. This point has been noted by Bruce Aune, *Kant's Theory of Morals* (Princeton: Princeton Press, 1979), pp. 29–30, and conceded by Henry Allison, *Kant's Theory of Freedom*, p. 210. Cf. Allison, *Idealism and Freedom: Essays on Kant's Theoretical and Practical Philosophy* (New York: Cambridge University Press, 1996), pp. 143–144.
5. This seems to be the point of Gilbert Harman's objection to Kant in *The Nature of Morality: An Introduction to Ethics* (New York: Oxford, 1977), pp. 76–77. But Harman's argument tacitly depends on supposing that what is "rational" has reference solely to what are sometimes called "agent-relative" reasons. We will see Kant's reasons for rejecting this supposition in Chapter 4, § 5.2 (and Chapter 4, Note 17).
6. See § 8.1.

7.   I often do things in spite of motives impelling me not to do those things. From the fact that my will would be at variance with itself if it willed the universal adoption of my maxim it does not follow that I cannot will the universal adoption of my maxim. All that follows is that I cannot will it wholeheartedly. (Jonathan Harrison, "Kant's Examples of the First Formulation of the Categorical Imperative," in R. P. Wolff (ed.), *Kant's Foundations of the Metaphysics of Morals: Text and Commentary*, pp. 219–220)

This remark displays a fatal confusion between "willing" and "wishing" or between 'willing' in Kant's sense and 'willing' in some looser sense in which it means something like "wanting" or "having motives to want."
8. It does seem possible to will (and even take steps to bring it about) that one's power to set and realize certain ends should be frustrated in certain ways. But one cannot will that *this very act of willing* itself should be frustrated through coercion or deception. Thus a masochist might will to put himself under the power of a sadist but cannot will that he be deceived or coerced into the very act of submission which he is supposed to be willing (though a masochist, in his delusive attempt to flee from his own freedom, might *wish* for this impossible situation). The same sort of impossibility of volition arises in

common and egregious violations of a person's will, such as deceit, oppression, and rape. See Onora O'Neill, *Constructions of Reason*, pp. 133–138.

9. Onora Nell (O'Neill), *Acting on Principle*, Ch. 1. One common mistake is to think that Kant regards a maxim as immoral because *it* (or action on it) is alleged to involve a contradiction (see Wolff, *The Autonomy of Reason*, p. 172).

10. See Hegel, *Phenomenology of Spirit*, tr. A.V. Miller (Oxford: Oxford University Press, 1977), §§ 429–431; cf. Mill, *Utilitarianism*, ed. G. Sher (Indianapolis, IN: Hackett, 1979), p. 4.

11. In his famous discussion of FLN and the universalizability test, H.J. Paton argues that the laws of nature Kant appeals to throughout the test are teleological rather than causal (Paton, *The Categorical Imperative* (New York: Harper, 1967), Ch. XV, § 6, pp. 150–152). Such an appeal is explicit only in the suicide argument, where the content of the teleological law remains conspicuously obscure and the argument itself far from convincing. There is no good reason to interpret any of the other three arguments as appealing to natural teleology, and Paton only distorts them when he so interprets them. See Note 16.

Compare the caricature of Kant's argument presented by Alasdair MacIntyre: "This is as if someone were to assert that any man who wills the maxim 'Always to keep my hair cut short' is inconsistent because such willing 'contradicts' an impulse to the growth of hair implanted in us all" (MacIntyre, *After Virtue*, p. 45). It might be pedantic to reply to a criticism that seems to be offered in bad faith, except that MacIntyre seems really to believe that Kant's argument about suicide is no better than this, and he is apparently not alone. Even those (such as myself) who reject both Kant's argument and its conclusion can easily see why it should be taken seriously, while MacIntyre's parallel argument about hair-cutting should not be. Kant thinks that committing suicide merely to avoid pain is wrong because it shows disrespect for the natural purposiveness involved in our self-love. One can see the point of that argument even if one does not agree with it. In the parallel case, it would be immoral to cut our hair short only if the growth of our hair involved an organic purposiveness in our constitution that is treated with contempt when we cut our hair. No one thinks this is true in general about cutting their hair, since hair is naturally useful for certain purposes but is sometimes more useful kept short and sometimes it only gets in the way and should be shaved off. Kant does apparently think that when a woman cuts off her hair in order to sell it, it is a violation of a duty to herself (though not a very serious one) (MS 6:423). Here the point seems to be that the beauty of her hair is something about *herself* that she should value and therefore should not sell as a commodity. MacIntyre may object that in my defense of Kant's argument from FLN, I am bringing in considerations based on FH. I accept that point, but would defend my procedure by generalizing it. As we shall see in Chapter 4, § 7.4, it is in general true that the point of Kant's arguments from FLN is elucidated by looking at the parallel arguments from FH, and more generally, FLN must never be seen as more than a provisional statement of the moral principle more adequately expressed in FH.

12. Allen Wood, "Kant on False Promises," in L. W. Beck (ed.), *Proceedings of the Third International Kant Congress* (Dordrecht: Reidel, 1972), pp. 614–619.

13. Nell (O'Neill), *Acting on Principle*, pp. 63–82. Christine Korsgaard, *Creating the Kingdom of Ends*, p. 78. Korsgaard also distinguishes the "Teleological contradiction interpretation," in order to capture the view of Kant's arguments put forward by Paton, *The Categorical Imperative*, pp. 149–164 (see Note 11 and Note 16).

14. This was the way I understood Kant's claim in "Kant on False Promises," loc. cit. pp. 616–619. Compare a similar reading by Robert Paul Wolff, *The Autonomy of Reason*, pp. 166–167.

15. Hegel, *On the Ways of Treating Natural Right Scientifically*, *Werke* (Frankfurt: Suhrkamp, 1970), 2:462; *Natural Law*, tr. T. M. Knox (Philadelphia: University of Pennsylvania Press, 1975), p. 77.

16. I owe my interpretation of the rusting talents example to remarks by Nicholas Sturgeon. This is a good place to challenge H. J. Paton's interpretation of the rusting talents example in terms of an alleged natural teleology (H. J. Paton, *The Categorical Imperative* Ch. XV, § 10, p. 155). Contrary to Paton's account, Kant's contention is clearly *not* that laziness is contrary to our natural instincts or their purposiveness. He often asserts, in fact, that human beings are naturally indolent and that nature has had to institute special (to us very painful) arrangements in order to overcome their inborn inertia and propensity to animal contentment (I 8:21, RH 8:65, MA 8:114–115, VA 7:276). Kant's argument is rather that *reason* (even in defiance of our natural laziness) unconditionally requires us to develop our faculties, because it is incompatible with reason's laws to adopt the principle of not acquiring means to (at least some of the) possible ends *we* (and not nature) may set.

17. Mill, *Utilitarianism*, p. 51. Ross is guilty of a similar misinterpretation when he says (apparently of the CW test) that it involves asking "whether we could wish our maxim to be universalized" (Ross, *Kant's Ethical Theory*, p. 30). The CW test asks not what our *wishes* are, but only whether there would be conflicting *volitions* if we tried to will our maxim to be a universal law of nature. Consider the maxim: "For identification, I will write my name in the flyleaf of every book I buy" (cf. Lewis White Beck, Introduction to *Kant: Foundations of the Metaphysics of Morals*, tr. L. W. Beck (New York: Macmillan, 1990), p. xix). This maxim is permissible, but it is also permissible to adopt the contrary maxim of never writing my name in my books for identification. In neither case do many of us have the *wish* that either maxim be a universal law of nature, nor does the permissibility of either maxim hinge on having such wishes. Regarding M4, I can imagine someone's wishing that all people should be so independent that they never need help from others. My own wish, by contrast, is that all people should sometimes need the help of others and always find someone willing and able to help. Neither of these wishes, however, has the least bearing on the permissibility of M4. It is equally impermissible for me and for the person with the wish contrary to mine.

18. This point might also have been made with respect to the maxim of the converted deposit. Assume *arguendo* that leaving deposits in trust is a bad

practice and that the human race would be better off without it. This would not show that appropriating deposits is universalizable, even assuming as an empirical fact (as Kant's argument does) that if the maxim were a universal law, the practice of making deposits would cease to exist. On the contrary, the argument is supposed to show that even those who want to abolish this practice may not convert the deposits left in their care, at least if this is an instance of following Md.

19. Arthur Schopenhauer, *The World as Will and Representation*, trans. E.F.J. Payne (New York: Dover, 1969) 1:525–526.

20. Fred Feldman, *Introductory Ethics* (Englewood Cliffs, NJ: Prentice Hall, 1978), p. 114.

21. This formulation is quoted from Feldman, *ibid.* p. 114.

22. This is not to deny that you might successfully promote your own happiness by having the self-deceptive thought that it would be rational to do without the voluntary help of others and thereby persuading yourself that it is permissible for you not to help them. That is a quite common rationalization people use for selfish conduct. Applied at the social level, this deception is even a successful political program for advancing the interests of the wealthy.

23. This suggestion is very much in the spirit of the ideal contract theory of morality worked out by Thomas M. Scanlon (see also Chapter 5, § 3.2 and Note 15). For thoughtful discussions of what would be involved, see Barbara Herman, *The Practice of Moral Judgment*, Ch. 3; and Thomas Nagel, *Equality and Partiality* (New York: Oxford, 1991), pp. 47–52.

24. It is not clear, however, that everything Kant says about the examples is easy to reconcile with the Correspondence Thesis. In the First Section's discussion of the false promising example, Kant argues that M2 cannot be willed as a universal law in part because, even if others "rashly" did believe my promises, they would "pay me back in like coin" (G 4:403). Here Kant seems to be envisioning the possibility that U2 might be a law of nature without either making promises impossible or making it impossible to obtain money in time of need by means of one. He seems to be supposing, however, that one could not *will* U2 of a law of nature because one necessarily wills not to be deceived by false promises oneself. This volition, however, is clearly not internal to M2, and it is therefore an argument that M2 fails not the CC test but the CW test.

25. Herman, *The Practice of Moral Judgment*, pp. 116–119. Herman's argument was anticipated by Paul Dietrichson, "Kant's Criteria of Universalizability," in R. P. Wolff (ed.), *Kant: Foundations of the Metaphysics of Morals: Text and Critical Essays* (Indianapolis, IN: Bobbs-Merrill, 1969). This version of the argument is discussed by Korsgaard, *Creating the Kingdom of Ends*, pp. 82–84. Her conclusion is that "the perfect duties of virtue require a more complex derivation than Kant gives them in the *Groundwork*" (p. 83). I take this to be a kinder, gentler way of agreeing with my more blunt contention that such duties show the Correspondence Thesis to be false.

26. Herman, *The Practice of Moral Judgment*, p. 63. It is quite easy to see that Herman's inference here is invalid if we think of some of Kant's other examples. From the fact that we cannot will M2 or Md to be a universal law of nature, it obviously *does not follow* that we are obligated to *make* promises we intend to

keep or *accept* deposits we don't intend to convert. It *certainly* does not follow from the disqualification of M2 that we must keep whatever promises we do make, because for all the argument about M2 shows, there could be some other maxim that is universalizable on which one might make a promise one does not intend to keep. Herman's inference is probably easier to draw in the case of M4 because Kant thinks that our happiness is an end we necessarily have, whose pursuit cannot be separated from the need of help from others. This justifies positing a positive duty to aid others based on FLN (the only such positive duty derivable from it). We might also be thinking of Kant's remark, which we will discuss in §8.1, that when we fail to will a maxim to be a universal law of nature this is because we do will "its opposite" as such a law (G 4:424). But as we will see there, this shows only that FLN *presupposes* a set of moral laws, which by itself it cannot derive or justify.

27. In the case of rusting talents, as we have seen in § 5, the argument actually makes no appeal whatever to the universalizability tests, but instead rests on the claim that every rational being necessarily wills to develop its talents. M3 runs afoul of the CW test only because if I can't rationally will that I neglect to develop my talents, then *a fortiori* I cannot will that all should neglect them according to a universal law of nature.

28. If all we are given to test is, "Under circumstances *XYZ*, I will omit action *A*," then we do not as yet have any *maxim* at all to test, since the mere conditional omission of an action is too indeterminate to constitute an intelligible norm of action. In order to have something to test, we would at least need to be told something about our ends in omitting *A* under these circumstances, and why omitting *A* promotes them. But any further information of this kind will leave us with a maxim far too specific for it to be the case that the positive duty to do *A* (or to do it under these circumstances) will follow merely from the fact that this maxim cannot be, or be willed to be, a universal law or a law of nature. We could of course include such information under the heading of "circumstances *XYZ*." But that would once again show only that we must *not* follow *some* particular maxim, not that, in those circumstances but independently of that maxim, we must do *A* (e.g., keep our promises or even omit to make promises we don't intend to keep). (My thinking about such cases was helped along by objections from Ralph Wedgwood and Desmond Hogan.)

29. Notice that it does not imply what order of priority it must have among these ends. That this should remain flexible is part of the meaning of the claim that the duty to aid others is wide or imperfect. Kant even argues for the *impermissibility* of the maxim of sacrificing our happiness, or the satisfaction of our own true needs, in order to assist others, since, if universalized, that maxim would destroy itself by frustrating the happiness of all (MS 6:393).

30. Hegel, *Elements of the Philosophy of Right*, § 135; R. A. Mill, *Utilitarianism*, p. 4; Sidgwick, *Methods of Ethics*, pp. 209–210.

31. Nell (O'Neill), *Acting on Principle*, pp. 40–41, 79–80. But her real reply is that FUL supports positive duties because some ends can be shown to be obligatory because no rational being could be without them (*Acting on Principle*, pp. 47, 82). This is a more successful reply, and it is correct that in his argument M4,

Kant appeals to the claim that happiness is such an end, just as in M3 he appeals to the claim that every rational being must will to have capacities to realize its ends. But it should be observed that while Kant may make use of such claims in applying FUL, FUL has no role to play in arguing for these claims.

32. Compare the criticism of O'Neill's earlier approach by Herman, *The Practice of Moral Judgment*, p. 142.

33. O'Neill, *Constructions of Reason*, p. 84.

34. Here Ross seems to me to get it right (*Kant's Ethical Theory*, p. 33). See Herman, *The Practice of Moral Judgment*, pp. 141–143.

35. Nell (O'Neill), *Acting on Principle*, p. 76; Bruce Aune, *Kant's Theory of Morals* (Princeton: Princeton Press, 1979), p. 122.

36. Herman, *The Practice of Moral Judgment*, p. 138.

37. This example is adapted (to booming stock market conditions) from Fred Feldman, *Introductory Ethics*, p. 116.

38. Herman claims (*The Practice of Moral Judgment*, pp. 138–139) that counterexamples involving maxims like M2 do not arise if we use the logical interpretation of the CC test. But I take examples such as Ma to show that she is wrong about this.

39. Here I again agree with Herman, *The Practice of Moral Judgment*, pp. 139–140.

40. "[FUL] would be all very well if we already had determinate principles concerning how to act . . . But in this case, the principle itself is not yet available, and [Kant's criterion] is non-productive [of it]" (Hegel, *Elements of the Philosophy of Right*, ed. Wood, tr. Nisbet (Cambridge, UK: Cambridge University Press, 1991), § 135A, p. 163). Whatever other mistakes Hegel may have made about FUL, that statement is exactly right, as Kant himself even admits at G 4:424.

41. Korsgaard, "Kant's Formula of Universal Law," in *Creating the Kingdom of Ends*, p. 92.

42. See Herman, *The Practice of Moral Judgment*, p. 138.

43. There wouldn't even be anything wrong with *literal* free riding if a mass transit system were publicly subsidized by taxing automobiles and riders weren't expected to pay. (Actually, this ought to happen, since mass transit systems are clearly both more egalitarian and more environmentally sensible than the use of private vehicles, and public subsidies of mass transit derived from heavy taxation on private vehicles would be not only good environmental policy but would also be socially progressive.) In other words, if literal free riding isn't all right, then it ought to be.

44. See Marcus Singer, *Generalization in Ethics* (New York: Knopf, 1961), pp. 22–25.

45. Nancy Sherman, *The Fabric of Character: Aristotle's Theory of Virtue* (Oxford: Clarendon, 1989), pp. 23–26.

CHAPTER 4: THE FORMULA
OF HUMANITY AS END IN ITSELF

1. In later works, *Triebfeder* is used more broadly, so that there are incentives of pure reason as well as empirical incentives (KpV 5:71–72; R 6:23–27; MS 6:218). "Incentives," in the narrower sense of the *Groundwork*, are all empir-

ical and contingent, so it is only through "motives" that a categorical imperative can be connected *a priori* with the will of a rational being. Throughout Kant's writings, *Triebfeder* means "*subjective* ground of determination of the will," but this formula is not always understood in the same way. In writings after the *Groundwork*, it is taken to mean any determining ground (roughly, motive or reason) that determines the will, including grounds that have objective validity, when these are considered as possibly determining the will. Thus a chapter of the *Critique of practical reason* is entitled "the *Triebfedern* of pure practical reason" (KpV 5:71). The term "incentive" is a good translation of this use of *Triebfedern*, since it refers to anything that is present to the will as a possible ground on which it might choose to act. (We may speak, in this sense, of competing incentives, moral vs. nonmoral, and incentives having objective validity vs. those not having it.) In the *Groundwork*, however, the meaning of the formula appears to be restricted to merely subjective determining grounds and applies to them whether or not they actually (subjectively) determine the will. Thus a ground having objective validity (valid *a priori* for all rational beings) cannot count as *Triebfedern* in this sense, even if the will is in fact determined by it (i.e., even if an agent chooses to act on it), and the term "*Triebfedern* of pure practical reason," with *Triebfedern* taken in this sense, would be a *contradictio in adjecto*. Hence there is a need in the *Groundwork* for a contrasting term (*Bewegungsgrund*), referring to grounds of the will's possible determination which *do* have this objective validity.

2. This is what Korsgaard does; but then a bit later she says: "So a maxim of duty is not merely one that you can will as a universal law, but one that you must will as a universal law" (*Creating the Kingdom of Ends*, p. 63). In other words, she shifts from FUL and its tests of permissibility to FA and the very different idea that what makes a principle valid as a universal law is that it necessarily is willed as such by a rational being. The latter idea is not part of FUL and it does not follow from the mere concept of a categorical imperative. Kant reaches it only through combining that concept with the dignity of the rational will as end in itself, which is the basis of FH. So this provides us no route to a "formal principle" independent of FH.

This may also be Lewis White Beck's understanding of "legislative form" when he writes that the legislative form of a maxim is the "skeletal 'ought'," and that "what is derivable from this, unlike what is derivable from any specific content, is addressed to all rational beings who act, and the rules derived from it are fitted to be universal in application" (Beck, *Commentary on Kant's Critique of Practical Reason*, p. 72). Beck may mean only that the legislative form of a maxim is *whatever* makes it the case that we unconditionally ought to follow it, and makes it the case that it obeys rules which ought to be universally obeyed. Passing the CC and CW tests, however, makes a rule only permissible, not universally binding. And what makes a rule universally binding may consist in its being a necessary condition of treating humanity as an end in itself. If Beck and the second *Critique* are read in this way, however, then there is no longer even any appearance of contradiction between what they say and what Kant says in the *Groundwork*.

3. Kant regarded it as indemonstrable because he held that the only way of

demonstrating a principle of practical cognition would be to show that it can be represented as a necessary means to something already taken as an end (or, in his later terminology, that it is something required by a hypothetical imperative) (DG 2:298). Kant therefore argued that the ultimate good is known not by demonstration but by a feeling of pleasure combined with the representation of the object. At this point he alluded approvingly to Hutcheson's conception of moral feeling as the starting point for knowledge of the good (DG 2: 299–300).

4. The charge is common that Kant is not using the term 'end' in its normal sense here. "[Kant] describes man, i.e. all men, as ends. This, in the ordinary sense of the word, men are not. For an end is an object of desire, and an object of desire is something that does not yet exist" (Sir David Ross, *Kant's Ethical Theory: A Commentary on the Groundwork of the Metaphysics of Morals* (Oxford: Clarendon, 1954), p. 51). Even some who rightly wish to place emphasis on FH in Kant's theory accept the charge:

> As Ross and others have pointed out (and this view can be substantiated by the Oxford English Dictionary and the standard German dictionaries), in our ordinary language the word 'end', when it refers to an object of an action, always designates something or some state of affairs not yet existing, which is to be brought into existence . . . . [Thus] I am ready to concede that in the standard and ordinary sense of the word 'end' (in the context of discussing human actions) existent things or states of affairs are not really ends. (P. C. Lo, *Treating Persons as Ends* (Lanham, NJ: University Press of America, 1987), p. 90)

As for dictionaries, they are usually written by people who aren't concerned with the philosophical issues involved in the meaning of words. Where these issues are at stake, dictionaries often merely record common philosophical confusions and unthinking prejudices. Note that Lo feels he must add the qualification "when it refers to an object of an action" – since an existent end is precisely an end that does *not* refer to "an *object* of an action"! Existent ends are ends in the perfectly ordinary sense of the terms 'end', 'purpose', and *Zweck*. They are *that for the sake of which* an action is done.

Compare the remark by Robert Paul Wolff: "Can a person *be* my purpose? No. The question makes no grammatical sense . . . When I say, for example, that I took my son to the dentist for his sake, I mean that I did it in order to further his well-being . . . It was *his end* that I took as my end, not *him*" (*The Autonomy of Reason*, p. 175). Often we promote people's well-being or their ends for their sake, but we can also do this not for their sake but for our own sake or for some third person's sake, which shows that the "for his sake" is not eliminable or reducible to the ends effected in the way Wolff proposes.

Existent ends are indeed counterexamples to common philosophical prejudices (unthinkingly repeated by philosophers and dictionaries alike) about the range of things to which the term 'end' (in this ordinary sense) applies. Korsgaard correctly diagnoses the prejudice as the false view "that the business of morality is to bring something about" (*Creating the Kingdom of Ends*, p. 275). The alternative she would put in its place is that the business of morality is "how we should relate to one another." This is closer, but still not quite right. The authentically Kantian view (which in this case is also the correct view) is that the business of human action is to act according to principles of reason; the specific business of morality is to act according to the rational grounds consisting in the objective worth that rational beings have as ends in themselves (this includes my own worth as well as that of others to whom I may relate). It is this worth that gives us objective reason to seek the objects rational beings (including ourselves) desire or set as their ends to be effected. Thus existent ends are not only ends in good standing, but they are presupposed by all other ends, including all ends to be effected. According to Alan Donagan, the foundation for a rational being's presumption that his own desires should be satisfied is the "judgment that a being such as himself is one whose natural inclinations are worth satisfying . . . Human beings think of their actions as done for the sake of beings – themselves or others – who are ends in themselves, and who are therefore considered to be beings for whose sake . . . purposive actions [are] rationally performed" (*The Theory of Morality* (Chicago: University of Chicago Press, 1977), pp. 228–229).

5. Korsgaard, "Kant's Formula of Humanity," *Kant-Studien* 77 (1986), p. 185; reprinted in *Creating the Kingdom of Ends*, p. 108.

6. This is only an example of how people might *treat something* as an existent end. Perhaps I should hasten to add that it is *not* an example Kant would endorse: "Kneeling down or prostrating oneself on the ground, even to show your veneration for heavenly objects, is contrary to the dignity of humanity, as is invoking them in actual images; for you then humble yourself, not before an *ideal* represented to you by your own reason, but before an *idol* of your own making" (MS 6:436–437).

7. It is illuminating to view Kant's conception of "acting from duty" from this new perspective. For once we realize that the worth of humanity in someone's person is the sole *Bewegungsgrund* of moral action, we are in a position to see that to act "from duty" (in the sense described in the First Section of the *Groundwork*) can consist only in acting from this motive. We will then recognize that when Kant regards the cold-hearted man who helps others from duty as more deserving of esteem than the sympathetic man who helps them because he enjoys spreading joy around, he is not saying that it is bad to care about people and good only to follow abstract moral rules. Instead, he is saying that it is better to care about people because we value and respect them as beings with worth and dignity, who have an objective claim on our concern, than because we just happen to like them or because in our present mood helping them makes us feel good.

8. Of course, Kantian ethics is concerned also with the motive behind such actions. An action that expresses respect for humanity but is not done from respect for humanity has no moral worth, but it is still an action that accords with duty and should be praised and encouraged. As I noted in Chapter 1, § 3.2, an action that conforms to duty but involves an *end* contrary to morality can be blamed, not for its motive but for the vice of character it displays in pursuing a bad *end*. A discussion with Carol Rovane helped me to clarify this point.

9. The same term, however, is applied more narrowly to a special ability he regards as particularly crucial to this end, namely skill in manipulating other people's wills to serve our purposes (G 4:416, VA 7:324; cf. KU 5:172, Ak 20:209).

10. Bruce Aune, (*Kant's Theory of Morals*, pp. 112–113), distinguishes the principle that we should respect *rational nature* from the principle that we should respect *humanity*, taking the former to be the "purer" variant of FH and the latter the more empirical or applicable variant (analogous to Kant's distinctions between FUL and FLN and between FA and FRE). There is certainly room in Kant's system for drawing such a distinction. Nearly all the intermediate premises I will argue that we need in order to apply FH (see § 8.2) are premises not about rational nature in general but about human beings (many of them may even be premises about human beings under quite determinate social and historical conditions). As an account of *Kant's* formulation of FH, however, Aune's distinction is without foundation. "Humanity" (as the set of capacities involved in setting ends according to reason) would apparently belong to any rational being whatever, and has no special reference to our biological species.

11. Are humanity and personality necessarily coextensive? When discussing FH, Kant speaks of "humanity" and "personality" as though the terms were interchangeable. He says that rational beings as ends in themselves are called "persons" ". . . because their nature already marks them out as an end in itself" (G 4:428). Though the two concepts are distinct, it would seem that personality is always found where humanity is found, because the rational capacity to set ends involves the capacity to recognize humanity as an end, and hence both the capacity to give oneself the moral law and to obey that law out of the motive of respect for the worth of humanity. There is no indication anywhere in Kant's writings that there might be a class of beings which have humanity (and are thus ends in themselves) but lack personality (and therefore lack the capacities required for moral agency, and the dignity that follows upon these capacities). Yet the one passage in Kant's writings that explicitly addresses the issue seems to return just the opposite answer:

> We cannot consider [personality] as already included in the concept of [humanity], but must necessarily treat it as a special predisposition. For from the fact that a being has reason it does not at all follow that, simply by virtue of representing its maxims as suited to universal legislation, this reason contains a faculty of determining the power of choice unconditionally, and hence to be 'practical' on its own; at least, not as far as we can see. The most rational being in the world might still need certain incentives, coming to it from the objects of inclination, to determine its power of choice. It might apply the most rational reflection to these objects – about what concerns their greatest sum as well as the means for attaining the goal determined through them – without thereby even suspecting the possibility of such a thing as the absolutely imperative moral law which announces itself to be an incentive, and indeed, the highest incentive. Were this law not given us from within, no amount of subtle reasoning on our

part would produce it or win our power of choice over to it. Yet this law is the only law that makes us conscious of the independence of our power of choice from determination by all other incentives (of our freedom) and thereby also of the accountability of all our actions. (R 6:26)

Kant is correct that the *concepts* of humanity and personality are distinct and that it is therefore correct to present them as different predispositions of our nature. It is far less clear, however, that there could be a reason that reflects on objects of desire and combines them into a sum of satisfaction but fails to recognize morality as an incentive. For if humanity involves the rational capacity not only to set ends but also to compare their objects and fashion a whole based on priorities among these values, then reason would seem to include the capacity to make comparative judgments of value, hence an (at least implicit) awareness of the rational standards of value – whose ultimate foundation, Kant claims, is the dignity of humanity or rational nature as an end in itself. It is unclear whether it would be coherent to describe a being as having a *rational* capacity to deliberate and make choices if it were entirely lacking in any appreciation at all for the most fundamental standard of value.

Perhaps Kant's thought is that a being might be instrumentally or prudentially rational without being transcendentally free. But a being capable of either instrumental or prudential rationality must already be practically free in the negative sense, since it is capable of resisting sensuous impulses to act on ends it has set or for the end of its own greatest well-being. If transcendental freedom is necessary for practical freedom, then such a being must already be transcendentally free.

Kant's lack of clarity on this issue is closely related to two other points on which he is also unclear. First, as we saw in Chapter 2, Kant never unambiguously acknowledges that prudential or pragmatic reason is a species of reason distinct from technical reason, and he is therefore unclear as to the grounds on which a rational being should form the idea of an overall sum of satisfaction and subordinate its particular desires to this idea. The possibility of a being having humanity but lacking personality depends on there being a ground of this sort, which is distinct from the worth of humanity (or personality), that is, distinct from grounds which are specifically moral. It is unclear, however, whether there could be such a ground. Second, at the end of the passage just quoted, Kant is quite evidently equating the possibility of a being having humanity but lacking personality with that of a being having the *empirical* features of a free will but lacking the *transcendental* features Kant thinks are required for freedom. But Kant never tells us what it would be like to understand people's actions empirically without regarding them as the effects of a power of choice that recognizes the incentives of morality. It would even create a serious problem if he did so: for if he were to admit the possibility of creatures having humanity but lacking in personality, his own doctrine of the theoretical unprovability of transcendental freedom would also commit him to the admission that we have no way of empirically distinguishing human beings from such creatures. That would entail that there could be no way in principle of answering a moral skeptic who argues that people are prudentially rational but not morally accountable. For practical purposes, then, Kant must assume that personality is found wherever humanity is found.

12. Plato, *Symposium*, 203b–212c; *Phaedrus*, 265e–266b. The criticism that Kantian rationalism is hostile to *eros* in all its forms is the fundamental idea behind Robin May Schott, *Cognition and Eros: Critique of the Kantian Paradigm* (Boston: Beacon, 1988; reprinted University Park, PA: Penn State Press, 1993).

13. For such a denial, see Alan Donagan, *The Theory of Morality*, pp. 229–230.

14. Mill, *Utilitarianism*, pp. 4, 34, 37–38. Near the end of his article, Haezrahi exclaims: "The synthetic proposition 'All men-qua-men are possessed of dignity' is therefore incapable of any proof whatsoever" (Pepita Haezrahi, "Man as end-in-himself," in Wolff (ed.), *Kant's Foundations of the Metaphysics of Morals: Text and Commentary*, p. 316.) He concludes that human dignity "can only be classified as a postulate" (like freedom and the existence of God) or "a necessary hypothesis without which moral experience would neither be possible nor explicable" (p. 317). Haezrahi here offers us two alternatives. The first is exceedingly unpromising. Perhaps Haezrahi thinks that to call FH a "practical postulate" is to lower our standard of proof and thereby to make FH easier to justify. If he thinks that, then he is mistaken. For the only effect of his proposal would be to make FH entirely unjustifiable. Since the practical postulates presuppose a rational moral principle, and FH is indispensable to formulating that principle, no practical postulates at all could be justified if FH is demoted to that status. The second alternative, treating FH as a "necessary hypothesis of moral experience" is actually quite close to the strategy I am attributing to Kant in justifying FH. The main difference is that the strategy as I interpret it does not depend on (question-beggingly) assuming the validity of so-called "moral experience," but instead argues that we best make sense of our conduct in setting ends we regard as valuable if we regard our own rational nature as the absolute ground of that value.

15. Kant is *not* supposing that in attaching ultimate value to themselves, human beings always value themselves in the right way (or according to the kind of objective worth they really have). On the contrary, as we will see, Kant thinks that human beings have an innate propensity to value themselves *excessively* (in comparison with others), since both they and others are beings whose worth is absolute and hence beyond comparison. The egoistic self-regard through which people think of their own existence as an end in itself must be the starting point for our consideration of what is ultimately valuable. But it cannot be taken at face value. There is nothing illegitimate in such a pattern of argument, for it merely illustrates the general pattern of rational criticism used in philosophy at least since Plato and Aristotle. It begins with ordinary opinion, not resting content with it but reaching truth through its interpretation, critical examination, and correction.

16. A similar thought is expressed in the *Critique of the power of judgment* where the status of rational beings as the ultimate end of nature is inferred from their capacity to conceive of ends and organize them into a system: "The human being is the ultimate end of creation here on earth because he is the only being on earth who can form a concept of ends and use reason to turn

an aggregate of purposively structured things into a system of ends" (KU 5:427).

17. Korsgaard, "Kant's Formula of Humanity," pp. 194–197, *Creating the Kingdom of Ends*, pp. 122–125.

18. "There is no reason on earth why something should not be good for me or why I should forgo something that seems good to me simply because it may not be good for everybody" (Pepita Haezrahi, "Man as end-in-himself," in R. P. Wolff (ed.), *Kant's Foundations of the Metaphysics of Morals: Text and Commentary*, p. 310). This is true only if prudential reasons alone count as reasons. (Even then what he says would be false if what "*seems* good to me" is not actually good for me, for then prudential reason would require me to forgo it.) If, however, there exist moral reasons as well as prudential ones, then I may very well have a *moral* reason to forgo something that is good for me simply because it is not morally good for me to have it. And if prudence in general is based on the judgment that my happiness is something *good*, then I have reason to pursue my own happiness only insofar as I regard it as worthy of pursuit on the basis of agent-neutral reasons (in that sense "good for everybody").

For one influential account of the distinction between agent-neutral and agent-relative reasons, see Thomas Nagel, *The View from Nowhere* (New York: Oxford University Press, 1986). The distinction was introduced earlier by Nagel (using the terms "subjective" and "objective") in *The Possibility of Altruism* (Oxford: Clarendon, 1978). The terms "agent-neutral" and "agent-relative" were introduced by Derek Parfit, *Reasons and Persons* (Oxford: Clarendon, 1984). A critical discussion of the distinction and Nagel's use of it is presented by Korsgaard, *Creating the Kingdom of Ends*, Chapter 10. I do not agree with Korsgaard that the distinction is indefensible but do think that "agent-relative" reasons apply only where the reasons under consideration are merely instrumental or prudential reasons, since that makes them relative either (in the case of instrumental reason) to the setting of an arbitrary end or (in the case of prudential reason) to the self-interest or happiness of a single person. But if the goodness of these ends also requires a grounding in reasons that are universally valid, then ultimately there are no merely "agent-relative" reasons. For that means that an end (or a happiness) whose goodness cannot be based on (agent-neutral) reasons is not something we have any genuine reason to pursue. On the other hand, it is easy enough to understand why agent-relative reasons matter a great deal to those who believe that instrumental or prudential reasons are all the reasons there are. Such views even make it difficult to see how there could be any reasons that aren't agent-relative, which is probably the most serious objection that could be raised against them since intersubjective argument can be only about agent-neutral reasons.

19. Korsgaard, "Kant's Formula of Humanity," pp. 190–192; *Creating the Kingdom of Ends*, pp. 118–121.

20. John L. Mackie, *Ethics: Inventing Right and Wrong*, pp. 15–45.

21. The need for this postulate shows that Kant does not regard the extension to others of the status one naturally claims for oneself as self-evident or merely a requirement of logical consistency. In this respect he differs from Alan

Gewirth, *Reason and Morality* (Chicago: University of Chicago Press, 1978), pp. 135–161.

22. See Jerome B. Schneewind, *The Invention of Autonomy* (New York: Cambridge University Press, 1998), pp. 509–513. Schneewind emphasizes Kant's commitment to the proposition that all rational beings are equal in their capacity to know and comply with the demands of morality more than in holding that rational beings have equal dignity – though for Kant the former equality entails the latter. Schneewind acknowledges Kant's originality in holding both positions, though he also provides an informative account of the views which prepared for and anticipated Kant on these matters.

23. Not surprisingly, Kant elsewhere seeks to qualify this conclusion (which might have been regarded as blasphemous). In the *Metaphysics of morals* he remarks that "humility in comparing oneself with other human beings (and indeed with any finite being, even a seraph) is no duty" (MS 6:435), conceding that it might be a duty to be humble in comparing oneself with an infinite rational being. There is a similar qualification when he says that any human being "possesses a *dignity* (an absolute inner worth) by which he exacts *respect* for himself from all other rational beings in the world, can measure himself with every other of this kind and value himself on a footing of equality" (MS 6: 435). Here the phrase "in the world" once again exempts the (extramundane) Deity. Setting aside fears about being charged with blasphemy, though, it is not clear that Kant has any reasons for these qualifications. And whatever Kant may think or say about comparisons with deities or seraphim, it is clear that he intends his position to imply that all human beings, as ends in themselves, are of equal worth. But in this passage there is every reason to believe that the Deity is explicitly to be included in the referent of the phrase "whoever it may be." One of Kant's most persistent criticisms of traditional religious services and petitionary prayer is the way extravagant praise of God and self-belittlement are combined with wheedling solicitations of (self-confessedly undeserved) divine aid (R 6:51, 185n, 194–196, VpR 28:1102, 1112, 1118).

24. Bernard Williams gets Kant right on this point: "The ground of the respect owed to each man thus emerges in the Kantian theory as a kind of secular analogue of the Christian conception of the respect owed to all men equally as equally children of God. Though secular, it is equally metaphysical: in neither case is it anything empirical about men that constitutes this ground of equal respect" (Williams, "The Idea of Equality," in Joel Feinberg (ed.), *Moral Concepts* (Oxford: Oxford University Press, 1969), p. 158). Of course, it can be known only empirically that a given entity has rational nature. But Kant would agree that rational nature is a metaphysical feature of a person in the sense that it presupposes freedom, which is a metaphysical attribute he thinks is not knowable empirically. Thus Alan Donagan also takes the authentically Kantian position when he criticizes Rawls for including the self-esteem that is proportional to success in achieving one's aims as among the conditions for self-respect (John Rawls, *A Theory of Justice*, p. 440). Donagan explains:

> Respect, in this sense, has no degrees: you either respect somebody or you do not; and you respect him for what he is, not for what he does. The dis-

tinction here implied between respect and esteem shows itself in syntax. It makes sense to say of somebody what Falstaff constantly implies about Prince Hal: that he esteems himself too much. But it makes no sense to say of anybody that he respects himself too much." (Donagan, *The Theory of Morality*, p. 240)

See also Thomas Hill, Jr., "Must Respect Be Earned?" Grethe B. Peterson (ed.), *Tanner Lectures on Human Values* 18 (Salt Lake City: University of Utah Press, 1997).

25. This has been seen clearly by Thomas Auxter, *Kant's Moral Teleology,* p. 134.

26. The role of expressive reasons for acting in moral value has, however, recently been explored by Elizabeth Anderson, *Value in Ethics and Economics* (Cambridge, MA: Harvard Press, 1993).

27. Korsgaard, *Creating the Kingdom of Ends*, p. 275.

28. When people consider themselves worthless, they tend to care less about their own ends, and even their own happiness may cease to matter very much to them. (Their self-interested and self-protective conduct then often ceases to take the form of rational concern for their long-term good and regresses to the level of a blind, habitual pursuit of short-term ends or even an instinctual response to immediate impulses.) This pathology expresses a piece of consequent reasoning, though if Kant is right, its premise is necessarily false, since their humanity always has absolute worth.

29. "Every time we post a letter, we use post-office officials as means, but we do not use them simply as a means. What we expect of them we believe to be in accordance with their own will and indeed to be in accordance with their duty" (H. J. Paton, *The Categorical Imperative*, p. 165).

30. This point was first called to my attention by Shelly Kagan. Thomas Hill suggests that the point of the phrase "never only as a means" is to insure that we do not reverse the priority of dignity to price, placing something with only relative and exchangeable worth ahead of something with absolute or incomparable worth. In his argument against suicide, Kant claims that the act of suicide "makes use of a person *merely as a means* to maintain a tolerable condition up to the end of life" (G 4:429). "To take the life of someone with humanity for the sake of something of mere price is always wrong, an undervaluation of humanity. Pleasure and pain, and the particular goals one has because of what one desires to achieve, are thought to have only conditioned value or price, and so suicide . . . for the sake of increasing pleasure, diminishing pain, or achieving any contingently desired goal is wrong" (Thomas Hill, Jr., *Dignity and Practical Reason*, (Ithaca, NY: Cornell Press, 1992), p. 52). Hill sees suicide as exchanging something with dignity (humanity) for something with mere price (pleasure or the absence of pain). Our previous reflection about the redundancy of "never only as a means," however, applies equally well to Hill's reformulation of the same idea. In order to claim that in suicide something with dignity is *exchanged* or *sacrificed* for the sake of something with mere price, it must already be conceded that the taking of my life fails to treat my humanity as an end and dishonors the dignity of humanity. If this is granted, then it has already been admitted that I have violated FH

whether or not I do it for the sake of something with mere price. If it is not conceded, however, then the fact that in taking my life I thereby gain something with mere price does not show that I have behaved disrespectfully toward the dignity of humanity. In either case, my acquisition of something with mere price is irrelevant to whether my act is a violation of FH.

31. Kant does not directly address the moral issue of abortion. About infanticide, when performed by the mother in order to escape the dishonor of unmarried motherhood, he regards it as a crime of murder which, however, is not properly punishable by death and perhaps is not properly punishable at all. (In the same passage, Kant takes a similar line about dueling among military officers.) At first he suggests that the killing of an illegitimate child might be ignored by the state because the child has come into existence in a way which the state is not required to recognize (MS 6:336). This argument has horrified more than one reader, because they take it to mean something Kant never affirms and obviously does not intend: namely, that the fact of illegitimate birth might deprive a person (perhaps even in adulthood) of the right not to be killed. Kant's concern here, however, is manifestly restricted to the killing of illegitimate infants by their unmarried mothers and has to do not with the child's juridical status but with the way the mother's act of homicide is to be viewed. Thus his final pronouncement on the issue leaves the horrifying thought entirely behind and takes quite a different tack:

> Here penal justice finds itself very much in a quandary . . . But the knot can be undone in the following way: The categorical imperative of penal justice remains (unlawful killing of another must be punished by death); but the legislation itself (and consequently also the civil constitution) as long as it remains barbarous and undeveloped, is responsible for the discrepancy between the incentives of honor in the people (subjectively) and the measures that are (objectively) suitable for its purpose. So the public justice arising from the state becomes an *injustice* from the perspective of the justice arising from the people. (MS 6:336–337)

In a less barbarous society than the present one, people would set less store by the present ("subjective") criteria of honor, and the bearing of an illegitimate child would not be such a disgrace that the mother would be impelled to end its life. In such a world, infanticide by the mother would be a crime punishable by death. But as long as current attitudes prevail, such cases of infanticide must be treated with leniency, because the blame for the crime rests more with social attitudes than with the woman who kills her child. Analogously, in a more rational society, the honor of a military officer would not depend on his fighting in a duel when challenged. But in our society, his honor is perceived to be at stake and hence we must regard killing under such circumstances as different from a case of murder. Although no reasonable person could simply equate abortion with infanticide, Kant's verdict on the latter issue in his own day may still be able to teach us something about the issue of abortion as we presently face it, namely this: If society took greater responsibility for the living conditions of illegitimate children and their parents, abortion would cease to be the only acceptable choice many women have.

32. The claims discussed in this last paragraph are made by Emil Fackenheim in "Kant and Radical Evil," *University of Toronto Quarterly* 23 (1954) and *To Mend the World* (New York: Shocken, 1982). The same ideas are certainly being hinted at by Haezrahi, "Man as end-in-himself" (see Note 14). I am grateful to Seth Limmer for thoughtful discussions of this issue. A less despairing alternative view of the experience of those who survived the death-camps is offered in Viktor Emil Frankl, *Man's Search for Ultimate Meaning* (New York: Insight, 1997) and Frankl, *From Death-Camp to Existentialism: A Psychiatrist's Path to a New Therapy* (tr. by Ilse Lasch of *Psycholog erlebt das Konzentrationslager*) (Boston: Beacon, 1959). For further discussion of the personification principle, and how to deal with cases of actual or potential human beings who lack 'humanity' in Kant's technical sense, see my article "Kant on Duties Regarding Nonrational Nature," *Proceedings of the Aristotelian Society* Supplementary Volume LXXII (1998), especially pp. 196–200. By denying the personification principle and emphasizing the respect required for rational nature when it exists merely potentially, Kantian ethics might similarly defend a moral claim on behalf of the life of fetuses. At the same time, however, it is not easy to see how this claim could prevail over the right of a fully autonomous human being to control the life-processes going on in her own body. Nor is it easy to see how a fetus could have a *coercive right* to life (or any *coercive* rights at all) on Kantian grounds (MS 6:230, 237). For an alternative way of dealing with the moral status of actual or potential members of the human species who are only potentially or virtually rational beings, see Ludger Honnefelder, "The Concept of a Person in Moral Philosophy," in K. Bayertz (ed.), *Sanctity of Life and Human Dignity* (Dordrecht: Kluwer, 1996), pp. 139–160. We should not expect FH all by itself to decide questions like the morality or external rightfulness of abortion. On the contrary, it is an advantage of FH as a moral principle that both sides in profound moral disputes can use it to articulate what they regard as their strongest arguments.

33. To the extent that we entertain the Kantian-Nietzschean suspicion that people consumed by *ressentiment* are susceptible to such irrational deceptions, we also have reason to eschew the Humean-Strawsonian strategy of constructing our philosophical conception of moral responsibility using our feelings of resentment as its natural basis. An insightful, clearheaded, and highly sympathetic examination of this highly questionable strategy is to be found in Paul Russell, *Freedom and Moral Sentiment: Hume's Way of Naturalizing Responsibility* (New York: Oxford University Press, 1995). A good critique of it along the same lines I am suggesting here can be found in Samuel Scheffler, *Human Morality*, pp. 66–72.

34. By this of course I do *not* mean to claim that further illumination necessarily reveals that the arguments are convincing or that their conclusions are correct.

35. Alan Donagan argues that M4 cannot be excluded by FUL, though it can be by FH, in "The Moral Theory Almost Nobody Knows: Kant's," in J.E. Malpas (ed.), *The Philosophical Papers of Alan Donagan* (Chicago: University of Chicago Press, 1994), 2:144–152.

36. The most detailed (and extreme) defense of "particularism" is Jonathan

Dancy, *Moral Reasons* (Oxford: Blackwell, 1993). See also John McDowell, "Virtue and Reason," *Monist* 62 (1979), pp. 331–350, and Martha Craven Nussbaum, *The Fragility of Goodness: Luck and Ethics in Greek Tragedy and Philosophy* (New York: Cambridge University Press, 1986). My understanding of particularism has been helped by discussions with Jennifer Whiting, Karen Jones, and Lisa Rivera. My thoughts on arguments from FH were stimulated by a discussion with Shelly Kagan.

37. Perhaps surprisingly, Kant shows some sympathy with this line of thinking, though his examples are not medical. He wonders about Curtius and Seneca, and about Frederick the Great's policy of keeping poison with him while leading his troops, so that if captured he might, by suicide, avoid being held for ransom by an enemy, to the detriment of his country (MS 6:423). Perhaps the closest parallel to the argument we are presently considering is one present in his lectures:

> Cato killed himself when he saw that it was not possible to evade the hands of Caesar, though the whole people still depended on him; as soon as he had subdued him, as the defender of freedom, the others would have thought: if Cato submits, what shall we do? But if he killed himself, then the Romans could devote their last ounce of strength to defending their freedom; so what should he do? It appears, then, that he saw his death as necessary; he thought: since you can no longer live as Cato, you cannot go on living at all. In this example, one must freely concede that in such a case, where suicide is a virtue, it has a great appearance of plausibility in its favor. But this is also the sole example that the world furnishes us in which suicide can be defended. (VE 27:370–371)

Those who accept FH but reject Ps might accept every word of this, with the sole exception of the final (extremely implausible) sentence. In place of it, they might claim that anyone faced with a dehumanizing terminal illness is in a position to say something of the form: "Since you can no longer live as Cato, you cannot go on living at all."

38. This complaint is made by Wolff, *The Autonomy of Reason*, p. 176.

39. It is not entirely clear why Jürgen Habermas says that Kant "neglects" the problem of applying practical rules (Habermas, *Justification and Application: Remarks on Discourse Ethics*, tr. C. Cronin (Cambridge, MA: MIT Press, 1994), pp. 13–14, 35). No doubt part of the explanation is that Habermas makes the common (but deplorable) assumption that the "Kantian" approach to any ethical question consists in formulating maxims and applying an abstract universalizability procedure to them. He could not have said what he does if he had been thinking about Kant's use of FH in the *Metaphysics of morals*. However, Habermas has some pertinent remarks to make especially about the epistemic conditions and limitations of applying moral principles which a Kantian should take seriously (*Justification and Application*, pp. 13–14, 37–38, 128–130, 152–160).

40. We also need some principle like FH (in its purest, most abstract, most universal form) as an incentive to sharpen our moral perceptions and even to reform them. If the meaning of FH is to be properly understood, the dis-

covery of what it demands can only be regarded as a never-ending critical process. An excellent recent contribution to these reflections is to be found in Thomas E. Hill, Jr., "Respect for Humanity," *The Tanner Lectures on Human Values* 18, pp. 1–76.

CHAPTER 5: THE FORMULA OF AUTONOMY AND THE REALM OF ENDS

1. For one influential version of such an attack, see G. E. M. Anscombe, "Modern Moral Philosophy," *Philosophical Review* 33 (1958), reprinted in Anscombe, *Ethics, Religion and Politics* (Minneapolis: University of Minnesota Press, 1981).

2. Stephen Darwall, *The British Moralists and the Internal 'Ought'*, New York: Cambridge University Press, 1995; Jerome B. Schneewind, *The Invention of Autonomy*, New York: Cambridge University Press, 1998. There is a more philosophically oriented attempt to discuss some of the same Kantian pre-history in Christine Korsgaard, *The Sources of Normativity*, Lectures 1–2.

3. Iris Murdoch dramatically declares that

> It is not such a very long step from Kant to Nietzsche, and from Nietzsche to existentialism and the Anglo–Saxon ethical doctrines which in some ways closely resemble it. In fact Kant's man had already received a glorious incarnation a century earlier in the work of Milton: His proper name is Lucifer. (*The Sovereignty of Good* (London: Routledge, 1970), p. 80)

Compare Onora O'Neill's forceful comment on this passage:

> This is a grand accusation, and misplaced. Autonomy is not the special achievement of the most independent but a property of any reasoning being . . . On Kant's understanding [existentialist] freedom, if found, would be a 'lawless', merely 'negative' freedom and the antithesis of autonomy. (O'Neill, *Constructions of Reason*, p. 76)

O'Neill is right in rejecting Murdoch's remark as a misunderstanding of Kant, but she identifies only one way in which Kantian autonomy differs from satanic self–assertion, and not even the most essential way at that. For it is arguable that when Lucifer declares "Evil, be thou my Good!" (Milton, *Paradise Lost*, IV.108) he *is* laying down a law of sorts for his new Kingdom and for himself, so that his freedom need not be seen as merely negative. The more important point is that Lucifer's *fiat lex* is self-enclosed, he is open to nothing but his own arrogant, resentful arbitrariness in determining its content. Lucifer might represent what Robert Adams calls "autonomy in the extreme sense":

> A person who is autonomous in this extreme sense will rely exclusively on her own reasoning and/or feelings in adopting moral principles, values and priorities. Her moral judgments will not be totally insulated from what is going on outside her, for she will have to learn the facts of her situation in order to apply her moral principles to them. But what the rest of the world is to contribute to her moral thinking is just the nonmoral material

for it. (Robert Adams, *Finite and Infinite Goods* (New York: Oxford, 1999), Chapter 11, Section 5)

As we shall see in Chapter 9, § 3, Kant holds that just because "thinking for oneself" claims universal rational validity, this thinking must also strive to "think from the standpoint of everyone else," which is possible for beings like ourselves only through free communication between people, and also to "think consistently" so that the thinking from different standpoints can achieve a unity with universal validity for all thinkers (KU 5:294–295, VA 7:200). The autonomous will is this threefold striving, which aims at the idea of every rational will as universally self-legislative. Kant's name for "autonomy in the extreme sense" is "theoretical solipsism," which he regards as the exact opposite of rational autonomy (VA 7:128–130). Jürgen Habermas writes: "In Kant, autonomy was conceived as freedom under self-given laws . . . . In discourse ethics, the idea of autonomy is intersubjective" (Habermas, "Morality and Ethical Life: Does Hegel's Critique of Kant Apply to Discourse Ethics?" in R. Beiner and J. Booth, *Kant and Political Philosophy*, p. 329). I submit that any interpretation of Kant that takes account of his conception of reason as grounded on public communication must display Kantian autonomy as intersubjective already. Only when we appreciate how important this theme is to the Kantian idea of autonomy can we also appreciate how *utterly wrongheaded* are the following remarks by Bernard Williams (which are explicitly intended to apply to *Kantian* morality):

> [When] ethical considerations are in question, the agent's conclusions will not usually be solitary or unsupported, because they are part of an ethical life that is to an important degree shared with others. In this respect, the morality system itself, with its emphasis on the 'purely moral' and personal sentiments of guilt and self-reproach, actually conceals the dimension in which ethical life lies outside the individual. (Williams, *Ethics and the Limits of Philosophy*, p. 191)

4. See Richard N. Boyd, "How to Be a Moral Realist," in G. Sayre-McCord, *Essays on Moral Realism* (Ithaca, NY: Cornell Press, 1988), pp. 181–228; Boyd, "Scientific Realism and Naturalistic Epistemology," in P. D. Asquith and R. N. Giere (eds.), *Philosophy of Science Association*, Volume 2 (East Lansing: Philosophy of Science Assocation, 1982); and Adams, *Finite and Infinite Goods*, Chapter 2, § 4. Kant's realism precludes identifying moral truth with what is "constructed" through any (Rawlsian) "CI-procedure." It is precisely the adherence of some contemporary Kantians to a Rawlsian "constructivism" or "proceduralism" that leads them to deny that Kantianism is metaethically realistic. See John Rawls, "Kantian Constructivism in Moral Theory," The Dewey Lectures 1980, *Journal of Philosophy* 77 (1980), pp. 515–572; Rawls, "Themes in Kantian Moral Philosophy," in R. Beiner and J. Booth (eds.), *Kant and Political Philosophy*, pp. 302–308. Rawls insists that only a theory is "constructed," repudiating the locution that "moral facts" are constructed by the procedure. The latter way of talking, he says, is "at odds with our ordinary idea of truth and matters of fact" (p. 308). But it is hard to see any but a ver-

bal difference between this and the position he and his followers take. See also Christine Korsgaard, "Reasons We Can Share," in *Creating the Kingdom of Ends*, p. 278; Korsgaard, *The Sources of Normativity*, pp. 19, 246–247; Onora O'Neill, "Constructivisms in Ethics," *Constructions of Reason*, pp. 206–218; Jürgen Habermas, *Justification and Application*, pp. 25–26; Habermas, *Moral Consciousness and Communicative Action*, tr. Christian Lenhardt and Shierry Weber Nicholsen (Cambridge, MA; MIT Press, 1990), pp. 102–109.

5. This makes it especially wrongheaded for R. M. Hare to associate Kantian autonomy with moral antirealism and the "is-ought gap":

> The reason why heteronomous principles of morality are spurious is that from a series of indicative sentences about 'the character of its objects' no imperative sentences about what is to be done can be derived, and therefore no moral judgment can be derived from it either. (Hare, *The Language of Morals* (Oxford: Clarendon, 1952), p. 20)

6. George Schrader thinks there is a dilemma facing Kant in his attempt to maintain both FH and FA as formulations of the same moral principle: To treat the other as an end in itself is to acknowledge the other's existence as a ground of obligation, but to regard the moral law as a principle of autonomy seems to be to treat all obligations as established solely through our own will:

> If [Kant] acknowledges that our action is in any way instrumental in establishing the reality of the other as an end-in-himself, he attributes to moral action an influence upon the subjectivity of others which he characteristically denies. But if he fails to acknowledge it, it remains unexplained just how we can treat others as ends rather than means merely. This is no minor dilemma! (George A. Schrader, "Autonomy, Heteronomy and Moral Imperatives," in Wolff (ed.), *Kant's Foundations of the Metaphysics of Morals: Text and Commentary*, pp. 130–131)

There is such a dilemma, however, only if we misinterpret both FH (as mere deference to the will of the other in its contingency) and FA (as the arbitrary laying down of moral laws by my contingent will). Both sides then become something quite different from what Kant intends. (FH would then be reduced to a mystical worship of "The Other" – the sort of thing that attracts giddy minds to the philosophy of Emanuel Levinas; as for what FA would become, see Iris Murdoch's misunderstanding quoted in Note 2.) Schrader's solution to the dilemma, which he says he is sure Kant accepted "in fact if not in explicit theory" is "to affirm the twofold status of the other as a person both in actual capacity and in ideal possibility" (p. 131). If I understand this correctly, then it seems to me half right. Kant does recognize the "twofold status" of the other when he says that what we respect in the other is always *humanity* (Schrader's "ideal possibility") in her *person* (Schrader's "actual capacity"). But Schrader completely ignores the other half – the crucial "twofold status" of one's own legislative will both as an *idea* and as the actual perpetual striving to approximate it in one's moral judgments.

7. Robert Adams advocates a form of divine command theory that seems to go at least as far in this direction as Kant would:

God is distinct from any ideas we may have about God, and more perfect than they can be. One's loyalty toward God may therefore be manifested in one's critical examination of all claims and beliefs about what God has commanded, and hence about what is right and wrong. Indeed, it may be manifested in critical scrutiny of the claim that God issues commands at all . . . There certainly are forms of religious belief and life that have not encouraged such a critical stance, but I see no reason why a divine command morality should not encourage it. (Adams, *Finite and Infinite Goods*, Chapter 11, Section 5)

However, it is hard to see how the ideas of devotion or obedience to God play any positive role in Adams' account of our critical moral practice. *Any* form of moral realism distinguishes what is good from our (always provisional) opinions about it. This is the role played in Kant's theory by the claim that the author of the law is the *idea* of every rational will as universally legislative. The most natural way to express the critical stance is to regard one's own best actual thinking (including one's respect for the best critical thinking of others) as the closest available approximation to such an idea, to which one is endlessly aspiring without ever reaching it. It only tends to falsify the picture to regard this striving as one's deference and self-subjection to an alien (divine) will.

8. Andrews Reath, "Legislating the Moral Law," *Nous* 28, No. 3, December 1994.
9. Nietzsche, *Beyond Good and Evil*, Fourth Article, § 78.
10. If I suppose that even my acceptance of the obligation is due to some alien power (as some Christians teach that divine grace, *coming from outside our reason and even in opposition to it*, is the ground of saving faith) then I thereby confess that my judgment is ungrounded and even ungroundable (at least internally, for me – which is what ought to matter to me in making it). From the standpoint of someone else, who rationally knows the goodness of the power which induces my belief, my faith may be seen as a benevolent miracle. From my standpoint it can be only a piece of irresponsible conduct; any judgment *of mine* that its origin is miraculous or good must be regarded by me as equally irresponsible, for precisely the same reason. To that extent, my acknowledgment of the worth of my reason's self-legislation seems to be the ground of every acceptance of an obligation as well-grounded, or even groundable at all, from my own point of view.
11. This point is emphasized by Thomas Pogge, "The Categorical Imperative," in O. Höffe (ed.), *Grundlegung zur Metaphysik der Sitten: ein kooperativer Kommentar* (Frankfurt: Klostermann, 1989), reprinted in Guyer (ed.), *Kant's Groundwork of the Metaphysics of Morals: Critical Essays*, pp. 189–214.
12. The notion of a "realm" was probably consciously derived from Leibniz, who referred to the Kingdom of God as a "realm of grace." See *Discourse on Metaphysics*, §36, Gerhardt (ed.), *Philosophische Schriften* 4:461–462; *Monadology* §§ 84–90, *Philosophische Schriften* 6:622–623. FRE is actually Kant's first published formulation of the moral law, insofar as it may be identified with the *Critique of pure reason*'s formula: "The idea of a moral world [conceived as] a *corpus mysticum* of the rational beings in it, insofar as the free will of each, under

moral laws, is in complete systematic unity with itself and with the freedom of every other" (KrV A808/B836). The system is teleological, or composed of ends, because it resembles an "organized being," a plant or animal organism, whose parts or organs combine into a whole. The parts or organs of a living thing, Kant says, are mutually cause and effect of one another, and in which the parts and the whole stand in the same reciprocal relation (KU 5: 369–376). Thus in FRE, Kant is in effect employing the concept of a living organism as the metaphor for an ideal human society, as did Plato before him and Hegel after him. But he has in mind not a political state, nor any actually existing society, but rather a purely ideal republic of rational beings governing their behavior by moral laws, whose validity depends not on external coercion of any kind but solely on the objective internal motive (*Bewegungsgrund*) of each rational will.

13. See Hare, *Freedom and Reason* (Oxford: Clarendon, 1963), p. 179.

14. On this point, see *Hegel's Ethical Thought*, pp. 161–167.

15. This claim is true taken literally, but needs to be qualified if (3) is, as I have argued, a formulation of FA. For (3) is analogous to FLN, which is taken to be the more easily applicable form of FUL; thus it also seems analogous to the "typic of pure practical judgment" (KpV 5:67–71), which Kant regards as the form through which the moral law in general is to be applied. But Kant's actual application of the law in the Doctrine of Virtue never explicitly appeals to (3), or indeed to any other statement of FA or FRE.

16. There seems to be a resemblance – and perhaps more than that – between Kant's unclarity here and some of the unclarities found in Rousseau's famous distinction between the "general will" (*volonté générale*) and the "will of all" (*volonté de tous*):

> There is often a lot of difference between the will of all and the general will; the latter regards only the common interest, the former regards private interest, and is nothing but the sum of particular wills: but remove from those same wills the pluses and minuses that cancel each other and the general will remains as the sum of the differences. (Rousseau, *Social Contract* 3:371)

Here the "common interest" corresponds to the rationally harmonious *system* of ends, while "private interest" corresponds to the ends that are outside the system. Rousseau's arithmetical metaphors don't provide much help in determining how the general will might result from combining private wills.

17. This Kantian formulation is suggestive of the ideal contractarian moral theory developed by Thomas M. Scanlon: "An act is wrong if its performance under the circumstances would be disallowed by any system of rules for the regulation of behavior which no one could reasonably reject as a basis for informed, unforced general agreement" (Scanlon, "Contractualism and Utilitarianism," in A. Sen and B. Williams (eds.), *Utilitarianism and Beyond* (New York: Cambridge, 1982), p. 110).

18. According to Kant, a person's happiness is an idea of imagination representing a maximum of total satisfaction of their inclinations with the prospect of an indefinite continuation of contentment (G 4:393, KpV 5:25, MS 6:387,

cf. KpV 5:124). But happiness is also an *end* determinative for rational principles (or at least counsels) of prudence (see Chapter 2, § 4). Thus if an agent limits her ends to *good* ends by the criterion of FRE, then this should shape her idea of happiness, bringing it into closer conformity with the ends of morality. In a world where everyone followed FRE, the ends determinative of their ideas of happiness could be expected to harmonize with one another, and in this way everyone's happiness would come to coincide with the ends of morality. In such a world there might still be a struggle between inclination and duty, but it would coincide with the struggle between immediate inclination and rational prudence. Kant's assertion would no longer be true that the principle of morality is opposed to the principle of one's own happiness (KpV 5:21–27). I think this line of thinking lies behind Fichte's endorsement of the apparently anti-Kantian proposition that "*only what is* [morally] *good makes us happy*. No happiness is possible apart from morality" (Fichte, *Lectures concerning the scholar's vocation*, in D. Breazeale (ed.), *Fichte: Early Philosophical Writings* (Ithaca, NY: Cornell Press, 1988) p. 151). But it may also be what Kant has in mind when he says that the conflict between nature and culture in human life (which in his view grounds the conflict between moral reason and inclination) will continue "until perfected art again becomes nature, which is the moral determination of the human species considered as an ultimate goal" (MA 8:117–118). See Chapter 9, § 2. The thesis that our conception of "personal good" (happiness or welfare) is dependent in this way on our (moral) ideal of what a person should be is convincingly argued by Connie S. Rosati, "Persons, Perspectives, and Full Information Accounts of the Good," *Ethics* 105 (January, 1995).

19. For a Kantian discussion of the morality of war, and specifically of the use of nuclear weapons at Hiroshima and Nagasaki, see Alan Donagan, "The Relation of Moral Theory to Moral Judgments: A Kantian Review," in J. E. Malpas (ed.), *The Philosophical Papers of Alan Donagan*, pp. 194–216.

20. Paul Menzer (ed.), *Eine Vorlesung Kants über Ethik* (Berlin: Heise, 1924), p. 52; cf. VE 27:399.

21. Of course it is a separate question how far economic behavior is contrary to *right* and therefore subject to coercive regulation by the state. Here the proper criterion is not merely FRE, but it must rest on the claim that the competitive behavior infringes the external freedom of others according to universal law (MS 6: 230–231). Kantian theory is nevertheless in a strong position to argue for some economic regulation on these grounds. The point is well stated by Wolfgang Kersting:

> When one considers the dangers that threaten right, freedom and the dignity of humans from a marketplace unsupervised by a social state and from radical libertarianism's politics of minimal state restriction, then one sees that the philosophy of right must require a compensatory extension of the principle of the state of right through measures toward a social and welfare state in the interest of the human right to freedom itself. (Wolfgang Kersting, "Politics, freedom and order," in P. Guyer (ed.), *The Cambridge Companion to Kant* (New York: Cambridge University Press, 1992), p. 357)

Compare Allen D. Rosen, *Kant's Theory of Justice* (Ithaca: Cornell, 1993), Chapter 5; and Leslie A. Mulholland, *Kant's System of Rights* (New York: Columbia, 1990), pp. 293–298, 388–396.

22. Henry Allison, *Kant's Theory of Freedom* (New York: Cambridge Press, 1990), pp. 214–218. A good discussion of the difficulties in the Third Section of the *Groundwork* are Dieter Henrich, "Kant's Deduction of the Moral Law: The Reasons for the Obscurity of the Final Section of Kant's *Groundwork of the Metaphysics of Morals*" in Guyer (ed.), *Kant's Groundwork of the Metaphysics of Morals: Critical Essays*, pp. 303–341. See also Dieter Schönecker, "Die 'Art von Zirkel' im dritten Abschnitt von Kants *Grundlegung zur Metaphysik der Sitten*," *Allgemeine Zeitschrift für Philosophie* 22.2 (1997), pp. 189–202.

23. Allison, *Kant's Theory of Freedom*, pp. 7, 201–222.

24. See the discussion of Kant's argument in Beck, *A Commentary on Kant's Critique of Practical Reason*, pp. 164–175. Beck concludes that in the second Critique, Kant's position is that "The moral principle neither has nor needs a deduction" (p. 172; cf. KpV 5:42–50).

25. As I understand Kant, he does not want to presuppose that every will is free. (He does not want to agree with Hegel that freedom is the essence of will as gravity is the essence of matter (Hegel, *Elements of the Philosophy of Right*, tr. Nisbet (Cambridge, UK: Cambridge University Press, 1991), § 4,A, p. 35.) An unfree will would be one that acts according to a normative law which it represents to itself, but one which is not given by this will itself. An unfree will would be a heteronomous will, which is therefore incapable of acting on categorical imperatives or, therefore, of moral personality.

Yet the laws of *every* will must be *normative*. I therefore disagree with Dieter Schönecker who (in some comments he made on a draft of this chapter) argued that describing the laws of the free will as 'normative' precludes discussing the pure or holy will (as Schönecker thinks Kant is doing throughout the Third Section until he introduces the idea that we are subject to imperatives because we belong to two worlds at G 4:453). I see no reason why saying that laws of freedom are normative is inconsistent with this. The divine will, as Kant conceives it, is a cause, and acts according to laws. What kind of laws? Not *natural* laws, surely. Nor could they be laws that in any other way necessitate (constrain or coerce) divine volitions or actions. The laws of a holy will, just because it is a *will*, have to be normative, but they are not *obligating*, since obligation implies the need for *self-constraint* in following normative laws, and in the case of the holy will, there is no room for any sort of constraint. The holy will follows normative laws freely and infallibly, with no possibility that it may fail to follow them, and therefore it is not subject to them as imperatives or obligated by them as our finite and fallible free wills are. On the other hand, it is a nice question whether an unfree will would be capable of adopting a practical standpoint on its own actions. Apparently not, since it is this standpoint, according to Kant's argument, that requires us to presuppose that we are free. But what would it be like to represent something as a *normative law* to oneself without taking a practical standpoint regarding it?

An unfree will, since it is a will, would have to be capable of action on norms, but since it acts on no unconditionally self-given norms, it is incapable of action on categorical imperatives. Perhaps we might try to think of it as capable of instrumental or even prudential rationality, but not capable of morality. In Chapter 4, Note 11, however, we have already seen that the concept of such a being is of doubtful coherence. There we noted that for practical purposes, Kant must regard the predispositions of humanity and personality as coextensive, yet he is committed at the same time to denying that we can ever infer from the fact that a being has humanity that it has personality. On Kant's account, moreover, no empirical information about the being could ever be relevant to this inference. So it is not clear that an unfree will, any more than a free will, is a concept for which conditions of its empirical application can be satisfied. It could be that it is not merely the concept of *freedom* that must be regarded as an idea of reason, but even the concept of *will*. Or maybe Hegel is right after all, and the concept of an unfree will is simply incoherent. (That is my tentative conclusion.)

26. Perhaps there are always natural law explanations of such failures (and likewise of normative successes). If so, however, such explanations do not compete with normative law explanations as long as their function is either to *supplement* the normative explanations (by telling us why the person bungled or succeeded on this occasion). Nor do they compete if they take on the more ambitious task of providing the natural "underpinnings" of normative explanations according to intentions.

Freud's explanations of slips of the tongue are not causal explanations, but could better be understood as an alternative (or supplementary) kind of normative explanation. When someone misspeaks, the garbled utterance can be explained as a failure to follow norms the speaker intended to follow, but Freud also tries to explain it as a case of *successfully* following norms governing an intention of which the speaker is not conscious. See Note 28.

27. Sidgwick, *Methods of Ethics*, pp. 511–516. This view of Kant's theory of freedom seems to lie behind Robert Paul Wolff's highly critical discussion of it in *The Autonomy of Reason*, Chapter 3. The results of the discussion are summarized on pp. 210–212.

28. To the extent that such mistakes are regarded as the result of something other than action under rational norms, they are no longer seen as cases of rational judgment – even of failed or mistaken rational judgment. We could say in such a case that we made the mistake because the judgment was only apparently a rational judgment, but really an instance of some other mechanism. Note, however, that *Freudian* explanations of such slips typically represent them as unconsciously *motivated*, for example, by strategies for reducing psychic tension or giving expression to repressed wishes. Such explanations actually attribute a certain kind of *rationality* to unconscious mechanisms, that is, see them as guided by rational norms about how tension is best to be reduced or the wishes most painlessly and effectively expressed. To that extent, Freudian unconscious processes, too, would have to be seen as functions of *freedom*, though only of a free agency in the service of certain desires and one that is defective in that it has been separated from the principal (and conscious) free agency defining the ego. Kant, incidentally, recognizes the existence of unconscious mental states and mechanisms of repression,

though of course he does not call them by the Freudian names and does not explain their relation to conscious free agency (VA 7:135–137).

29. It is essential to locate this presupposition precisely, however. For it is not necessary to *assert* that we are free (or to take any position at all on this issue) merely in order to consider theoretical questions or to make judgments according to normative laws of thinking and judging. Nothing in the process of raising the question of freedom and coming to a fatalist conclusion about it would necessarily require us to assert the contradictory of fatalism. We do, however, have to make such an assertion as soon as we try to give any reflective account of our coming to draw the conclusion through conforming to normative laws. Fatalists could elude Kant's argument, therefore, if they were able to give some reason why we cannot or should not reflect on our thought processes or why we should not be able to give an account of them as conforming to norms. They could also elude the argument if they could satisfactorily explain why we should not expect the answers to such reflective questions to cohere with the first order conclusions we draw on the basis of rational arguments. Admittedly, the prospects for *plausibly* eluding the argument in either of these ways look pretty desperate, but then fatalism itself, once its implications are understood, won't appeal to anyone who is fainthearted about adopting desperate measures. The Kantian defense of freedom I am defending here has much in common with the conceptions of "pragmatic justification" and "ultimate grounding" (*Letztbegründung*) advocated by Karl-Otto Apel and his followers. See K.-O. Apel, 'The *a priori* of the Communication Community and the Foundations of Ethics: The Problem of a Rational Foundation of Ethics in the Scientific Age," in Apel, *Selected Essays*, Volume 2 (Totowa, NJ: Humanities Press, 1996), Volume 2, pp. 1–67; and Apel, *Towards a Transformation of Philosophy*, tr. G. Adey and D. Frisby, 2 vols. (London: Routledge, 1980). Compare Jürgen Habermas, *Justification and Application*, pp. 79–88.

30. Kant's deduction of the supreme principle of morality admittedly does not address (or even appear to take seriously) some of the more extreme forms of skepticism about value which have dominated twentieth-century metaethics. To these skeptics, the Kantian argument I have been reconstructing may be a big letdown. The argument draws no distinction between our *having* to take ourselves, from a practical standpoint, to be capable of judging according to objective reasons, and there *actually being* such reasons for us to judge according to. Analogously, and perhaps more controversially, it draws no distinction between our taking ourselves (from a practical standpoint) to be capable of setting ends with objective worth and there really being objective worth for those ends to have. Still more controversially, it draws no distinction between our taking ourselves (from a practical standpoint) to be responding to moral requirements that are unconditionally obligatory and the actual existence of such categorical requirements. To some twentieth-century metaethical skeptics, that may seem extravagant. But then to someone trying seriously to decide on the basis of the best reasons she can find what she absolutely ought to do, a lot of twentieth-century metaethical skepticism will seem extravagant.

31. Allen Wood, "Kant's Compatibilism," in A. Wood (ed.), *Self and Nature in Kant's Philosophy* (Ithaca: Cornell Press, 1984), pp. 73–101. Reprinted in Patricia Kitcher (ed.), *Kant's Critique of Pure Reason: Critical Essays.*

32. If our natural sciences cannot at present explain how we have these abilities, then that looks like unfinished business for those sciences. If our conceptions of causality and natural law seem to preclude our having these capacities, then that looks like a glaring defect in those conceptions and a good reason to abandon them in favor of more empirically adequate ones.

33. The free will problem is an old and intractable one. The unreflective common-sense view of the free will problem – that we are free, that our actions are causally determined, and that freedom and determinism are incompatible – remains commonsensical only because common sense never brings its parts together. As soon as philosophical reflection takes a step beyond this, something dear to common sense has to be abandoned. Although we may take ourselves to be natural beings, and suppose that our experience, mentality, and agency can all be comprehended by our natural sciences, we still are far from achieving such comprehension, and it even remains highly controversial – not only regarding our free agency, but also regarding the fact of consciousness and the qualitative character of experience – which phenomena generate only philosophical pseudo-problems and which are to be regarded as real objects of scientific explanation. (The best recent study of this problem with regard to consciousness and qualia is David Chalmers, *The Conscious Mind: In Search of a Theory of Conscious Experience* (Oxford: Oxford Press, 1996).)

34. "Kant does not and cannot offer a single model of human action that can both serve for empirical explanation and guide choice" (Onora O'Neill, *Constructions of Reason*, p. 70). This way of reading Kant's doctrine of the "two standpoints" is extremely common, even among those who are uncomfortable with his theory of noumenal freedom. Cf. Paton, *The Categorical Imperative*, p. 267; Lewis White Beck, *Commentary on Kant's Critique of Practical Reason*, pp. 194–196; Beck, *The Actor and the Spectator* (New Haven, CT: Yale, 1975); Wolff, *The Autonomy of Reason*, p. 222; Wood, "Kant's Compatibilism," in Wood (ed.), *Self and Nature in Kant's Philosophy*, pp. 57–72; Korsgaard, *Creating the Kingdom of Ends*, pp. x–xii. And Kant is often appealed to by those who think that there is a radical difference between the standpoint of an agent and that of an observer, so that the former view of ourselves is radically opposed to any scientific or naturalistic picture of ourselves. (For instance, see Georg Henrik von Wright, *Explanation and Understanding* (Ithaca, NY: Cornell Press, 1971), pp. 198–199.) The interpretation may even be largely correct as an account of Kant's solution to the metaphysical problem of free will, and is well supported by those foundational texts (such as the Third Antinomy in the *Critique of Pure Reason*, the Third Section of the *Groundwork*, and the Analytic of the *Critique of Practical Reason*, which focus on the metaphysical issue). But this view goes wrong whenever it projects metaphysical hypotheses used only problematically in this highly abstruse part of Kantian doctrine onto Kant's theory of our empirical knowledge of human nature. In the event, this theory (as presented in Kant's writings on anthropology and

history) turns out to be much more interesting and plausible than the false projection. One recent attempt at a different view is Allison, *Kant's Theory of Freedom* and *Idealism and Freedom*, Chapter 8. But Allison seems to me to go wrong in the opposite direction by trying to integrate too much of Kant's practical theory of action into his metaphysics of freedom.

35. See Béatrice Longuenesse, *Kant et le pouvoir de juger* (Paris: Presses Universitaires de France, 1993), pp. 185–196; English version: *Kant and the Capacity to Judge* (Princeton, NJ: Princeton University Press, 1998), pp. 292–310. Cf. Allen W. Wood, *Kant's Rational Theology* (Ithaca, NY: Cornell Press, 1978), pp. 28–34, 37–55.

36. For a fuller presentation of the analogies between the three formulas in the *Groundwork* and other themes in Kant's theoretical philosophy, see my article "The Moral Law as a System of Formulas," in H. F. Fulda and H. D. Klein (eds.), *Architektur und System in der Philosophie Kants* (Hamburg: Meiner, 2000). For another account of the relation between the three formulas and the argument of the *Groundwork*, see Paul Guyer, "The Possibility of a Categorical Imperative," *Philosophical Review* 104 (1995), reprinted in Guyer (ed.), *Kant's Groundwork of the Metaphysics of Morals: Critical Essays*, pp. 215–246.

37. For example, H. J. Paton, *The Categorical Imperative*, p. 130; Onora O'Neill, *Constructions of Reason*, p. 127; Paul Guyer, "The Possibility of a Categorical Imperative," in Guyer (ed.), *Groundwork of the Metaphysics of Morals: Critical Essays*, p. 216; Brendan E. A. Liddell, *Kant on the Foundation of Morality: A Modern Version of the Grundlegung, Translated with Commentary* (Bloomington, IN: Indiana University Press, 1970), p. 177. In a conversation with me, Jerome B. Schneewind also took it to be obvious that by FG, Kant meant FUL.

38. H. J. Paton, *The Categorical Imperative*, p. 130, and Lewis White Beck, *Commentary on Kant's Critique of Practical Reason* (Chicago: University of Chicago Press, 1960), p. 122 and Note 22. Paton even notes the incongruity of identifying FG with FUL and FK with FA, remarking that it is a curious difference between the *Groundwork* and the second Critique (p. 130). Kant certainly has employed FUL earlier in the second Critique in discussing the example of the deposit (KpV 5:27–28) and he appears to introduce FLN later on as the "typic of pure practical judgment" (KpV 5:67–70). My claim, however, is not that he ever *abandons* FUL or FLN (or any other formula), but only that when he wants to refer to the purest and most universal formula of the moral law, it is FA rather than FUL that he must have in mind.

CHAPTER 6: THE STUDY OF HUMAN NATURE

1. H. J. Paton, *The Categorical Imperative*, p. 32; Or as Mary Gregor puts it "the precepts derived from practical anthropology . . . do not prescribe duties," Mary J. Gregor, *Laws of Freedom* (Oxford: Blackwell, 1963), p. 8. It is significant, however, that Paton distinguishes between two senses of 'applied ethics': In the first sense "we apply the supreme moral principles to the special conditions of human nature"; in the second applied ethics concerns "the conditions which favour or hinder the moral life" (p. 32). He claims (probably based on MS 6:217) that Kant means only the latter sense, which he inter-

prets as being concerned only about the means of making ourselves better or worse. If in the *Groundwork*, Kant is using the term in the first sense, in which practical anthropology is used along with the *a priori* principle to "prescribe duties," then Paton's charge would be mistaken, though Paton (via his first sense of 'applied ethics') could be credited with recognizing the most important point, namely, that Kant thinks empirical information about human nature must be used in setting moral ends. (Paton also remarks that "Kant may have thought more of his *Metaphysics of morals* was pure ethics than is in fact the case" (p. 32).) It is only in the *Groundwork* that Kant does think a 'metaphysics of morals' is entirely pure ethics; hence 'applied ethics' in Paton's first sense belongs to 'practical anthropology'. In the *Metaphysics of morals*, however, as we shall see directly, the meaning of the term has shifted so that it includes some empirical anthropology, combined with pure ethical principles. Now the referent of 'practical anthropology' is restricted to 'applied ethics' in Paton's second sense (see Note 3), and this is arguably (as Paton says) not a part of practical philosophy.

2. Thomas Hill, Jr., "Kant's Utopianism" (1974), Ch. 4 of *Dignity and Practical Reason*, p. 72. There is no doubt that Kant's stance on various moral issues strikes many as "utopian" in its highminded adherence to moral principle in contempt of practical consequences; this is especially true of his views about the role morality should play in politics (TP 8:275–278, 287–289, EF 8:370–380; see Christine Korsgaard, *Creating the Kingdom of Ends*, Chapter 5). It is a mistake, however, to attribute this feature of Kant's ethical thought to his reliance on *a priori* principles, or to the (utterly false) notion that Kant thought moral principles can be directly applied to practice without taking empirical facts into account (including facts about human frailty and corruption). Some of Kant's recommendations do explicitly take into account the fact that common moral opinions and practices are deeply flawed (see Chapter 4, Note 31, and Chapter 8, § 4.2). Kant's insistence on following principles is better understood as the assertion of a certain *way of dealing* with human imperfection, frailty, corruption, and the general absurdity of the world in which we have to act. This is an attitude that insists above all on the integrity of the agent as a rational being and accepts that maintaining this integrity will sometimes be costly in terms of the immediate goals and consequences of action. It is an attitude that comports well with Kant's rational faith that the world is ultimately governed by reason, and that the human species will in the long run sustain its progress in history as long as human beings remain true to rational principles. Thus Kant's "utopianism" is sooner to be explained by his philosophy of history than by his belief that moral principles are categorical or *a priori*. The converse attitude might be called a "pragmatic" one (though not in Kant's sense of the term). It is concerned with relatively short-term consequences of our actions (the outcome for the individuals immediately affected or at most the fate of a given political movement or cause or generation). Perhaps this attitude recognizes no reality to be taken account of beyond that, because it thinks of history as nothing but the chance combinations and successions of the contingent fates of individuals, movements, or nations. Alternatively, this "pragmatic" attitude might be

the "Cold War" thinking (common to both sides) that casts aside all principles because it thinks we must effect (or prevent) some urgent (or disastrous) change on which all subsequent history is alleged to depend (for better or worse).

An articulate defense of the Kantian position on issues involving a conflict between principle and pragmatism is to be found in Alan Donagan, *The Theory of Morality* (Chicago: University of Chicago Press, 1977), pp. 143–200. In times when human affairs are extremely disordered, a principled stance such as Kant's can look not merely "unpragmatic" but downright heartless or even insane. This is the way Kant's principled objections to lying looked to Benjamin Constant when he considered them in relation to the situation he and others had to face in France during the worst times of the Revolution. (For an excellent brief discussion of this issue, see Stephen Holmes, *Benjamin Constant and the Making of Modern Liberalism* (New Haven, CT: Yale, 1984), pp. 107–109.)

The whole truth cannot lie with either the "principled" or the "pragmatic" attitude. Sophocles' *Antigone* is about the conflict between two people who suffer shipwreck by taking the principled (or "Kantian") course in such a situation. The dangers of the "pragmatic" course are even more familiar to us, since they are exhibited in the conduct of those who remain "constructively engaged" with evil, benefiting from their collaboration while resolving to "do what they can" to alleviate the evils in which they are complicit. Max Weber is right that "one cannot prescribe to anyone whether he should follow a [principled, Kantian] ethics of disposition or a [pragmatic] ethics of responsibility, or when one and when the other" ("Politics as a Vocation," Gerth and Mills (eds.), *From Max Weber* (Oxford: Oxford University Press, 1958), p. 127. In this book, *Gesinnungsethik* is (mis)-translated as "ethic of ultimate ends" or "ethic of absolute ends." Cf. Harald Köhl, *Kants Gesinnungsethik* (Berlin: deGruyter, 1990).) When we are confronted with dilemmas that force us to choose between principle and pragmatism, the only satisfactory solution consists in finding a way of *reconciling* adherence to principles with meeting the practical demands of the situation (as Thomas Hill argues in a later article, "Making Exceptions without Abandoning the Principle: or How a Kantian Might Think about Terrorism," *Dignity and Practical Reason*, Chapter 10 (1991)). Contingent circumstances sometimes make this reconciliation impossible. In that case, the situation is tragic. Both extremes in the dispute are right, and the only utterly untenable position is the "moderate" one that tries to sell us some "compromise" as a satisfactory outcome.

3. See Ludwig Siep, "Wozu Metaphysik der Sitten?" in O. Höffe (ed.), *Grundlegung zur Metaphysik der Sitten: ein kooperativer Kommentar* (Frankfurt: Klostermann, 1989), pp. 31–44, and Mary J. Gregor, *Laws of Freedom*, p. 11.

4. It is doubtful that Kant holds consistently even to this restriction, since in the *Metaphysics of Morals* he deals with juridical duties arising out of family relationships, and ethical duties pertaining to friendship, as well as the relationship between benefactors and beneficiaries. As the scope of a metaphysics of morals expands in the direction of the empirical, that of practical anthropology is correspondingly constricted to concern with "the subjective

conditions in human nature that hinder human beings or help them in *ful-filling* the metaphysics of morals" (MS 6:217). "Practical anthropology" in this new and more restricted sense will not even qualify as a part of "practical philosophy" in the sense described by Kant at Ak 20: 195–201. This change in the scope of a "metaphysics of morals" brings "anthropology" into "metaphysics" itself, in a way analogous to (but different from) the way Kant thinks the empirical concept of matter needs to be brought into the metaphysics of nature. The metaphysics of matter, namely, begins with its empirical concept, of which it provides a mathematical construction (Ak 4:472–479). The metaphysics of morals begins with an *a priori* practical principle and applies it to empirical human nature to derive a set of duties for human beings. But Kant does pursue the parallel at one point in the Doctrine of Right (MS 6: 232–234).

5. Ernst Platner, *Anthropologie für Ärtzte und Weltweisen* (Leipzig: Dukische Buchhandlung, 1772). The book was reviewed by Kant's friend Marcus Herz in the *Allgemeine deutsche Bibliothek* 20 (1773); Kant's comments about his own lectures on anthropology are in reference to this review.

6. The first discussion of Kant's source for these lectures in Baumgarten is: Benno Erdmann, *Reflexionen Kants zur kritischen Philosophie* (Leipzig: Fues, 1882). The more recent, definitive treatment of Kant's relation to Baumgarten's empirical psychology is found in: Norbert Hinske, "Kants Idee der Anthropologie," in Heinrich Rombach (ed.), *Die Frage nach dem Menschen* (Munich: Alber, 1966).

7. To be sure, Kant's requirements for a "definition" (in the strict sense) are very demanding, and he even holds that "definitions," properly speaking, are possible only in mathematics (KrV A727–732/B755–760). But his worries about characterizing the human species go far beyond these general considerations. "[This question] is encountered neither in the lecture notes nor in Kant's notes for the lectures. It appears in the field of anthropology only in a Kantian manuscript (still kept today in Rostock) in which Kant set down the text for the [*Anthropology from a Pragmatic Standpoint*], but was not transferred into the book. It contradicts the sober inventory of experiences with which Kant wanted to introduce students to ways of dealing both with themselves and with other human beings" (Reinhard Brandt, "Kants pragmatische Anthropologie: Die Vorlesung," *Allgemeine Zeitschrift für Philosophie* 19 (1994), p. 43) (cf. VA 25:859).

8. It is well known that Kant never traveled outside the boundaries of East Prussia. As if to anticipate the obvious criticism of his own qualifications to lecture on such a subject, he notes that the study of literature and reading about the travels of others can provide the acquaintance with humanity needed for pragmatic anthropology. He even argues in a footnote that the city of Königsberg, because it is a large city, a university city, a seat of government, a commercial center, and a seaport with worldwide connections, which is also connected by a river to the interior of the country, is a suitable location from which to undertake a pragmatic study of human nature even without traveling (VA 7:120–121 and note). It is more to the point merely to ponder the remarkable fact that just as it was possible for Beethoven to write some of the

most original music the world has ever known after he was completely deaf, so it was possible for Kant to be the most cosmopolitan of philosophers while never traveling forty miles from his birthplace.

9. Nietzsche, *The Will to Power*, tr. W. Kaufmann and R. J. Hollingdale (New York: Vintage, 1968), §§ 476–480.

10. Kant is borrowing this phrase from J. G. Hamann, *Abälardi virbii Chimärische Einfälle über den Briefe die neueste Literatur betreffend*, J. Nadler (ed.), *Sämmtliche Werke* (Vienna: Herder, 1949–1957), 10:164: "This descent into the Hell of self-knowledge paves the way for deification" (cf. SF 7:55).

11. One suspects that this, even more than metaphysical extravagance, is probably why Kant's theory of freedom has seemed hopelessly artificial and implausible to traditional empiricists, who often naively take it for granted that we can know the mental causes of our own behavior by introspection.

12. Kant's terminology on this point in the lectures is somewhat fluid, however. Sometimes the pragmatic is identified with the moral (VA 25:1211), other times it is distinguished from it (VA 25:1436). Sometimes the anthropology that encompasses both prudence and morality is described as "practical" (VA 25: 1208, 1436).

13. As already mentioned, Kant distinguishes two parts of *Weltkenntnis*: pragmatic anthropology and physical geography (VA 25:733).

14. The explicit division into "didactics" and "characteristics" is found only in Kant's published version (VA 7:123, 284). But 'characteristic' is distinguished by a new heading in Collins (1772–1773) (VA 25:218), Parow (1772–1773) (VA 25:426), Friedländer (1775–1776) (VA 25:624), Pillau (1778–1779) (VA 25:814), *Menschenkunde* (1781) (VA 25:1156), Mrongovius (1784–1785) (VA 25:1367); in Busolt (1788–1789), character is discussed under the heading "Doctrine of Method" (VA 25:1530).

15. For example, by Herder. See also Reinhard Brandt and Werner Stark, Einleitung, VA 25:xv, and Reinhard Brandt and Heiner Klemme, *Hume in Deutschland* (Marburg: Schriften der Universitätsbibliothek, 1989), pp. 53–55.

16. Kant contrasts his "pragmatic" approach to anthropology with the "pedantic" approach of Platner, and in this connection even makes a virtue of the popularity of his approach, which he thinks is necessitated by the inherent limits and the unsatisfactory state of our present knowledge of human nature: "Our anthropology can be read by everyone, even by ladies while getting dressed (*bei der Toilette*)" (VA 25:856–857).

17. Sometimes Kant distinguishes *Talent* from *Naturell* (VA 25:626), but more often he identifies the two or discusses talent in place of individual nature (VA 25:1156–1157).

18. The most influential recent exposition of Kant's philosophy of history, which argues persuasively for its importance in understanding Kant's philosophy as a whole, is Yirmiyahu Yovel, *Kant and the Philosophy of History* (Princeton, NJ: Princeton University Press, 1980). A good discussion of the theme of history throughout the works in which Kant discusses it is to be found in Pauline Kleingeld, *Fortschritt und Vernunft: Zur Geschichtsphilosophie Kants* (Würzburg: Königshausen und Neumann, 1995).

19. Johann Schultz (or Schulze) (1739–1805), referred to in this issue of the

Gotha Learned Papers as "Chief Court Chaplain Schulze," was a Professor of Mathematics at the University of Königsberg, to whom Kant is said to have referred in the 1790s as "the most faithful of my followers." In 1784 Schultz also published *Elucidations on the Critique of Pure Reason,* a compendium Kant occasionally used in his lectures; the purpose of Schultz's article in the *Gotha Learned Papers* was actually to announce this publication. See Karl Vorländer, *Kants Leben* (1911) (Hamburg: Meiner, 1986), pp. 121–122, 136.

20. J. Schulze, "Kurze Nachrichten," *Gothaischen Gelehrten Zeitungen* 12 (11.2.1784), p. 95.

21. "Teleological convergence" is a happy phrase for this, coined by Thomas Auxter, *Kant's Moral Teleology,* Chapter 9.

22. Like Herder, Kant finds it troubling that earlier generations should appear to labor and suffer for what only the later generations will possess. Unlike Herder, he does not shrink back from this view of human history on that ground. On the contrary, Kant insists that this is necessary if there is to be a "class of rational beings, who all die, but whose species is immortal, attaining to a complete development of its predispositions" (I 8:20). See Chapter, 7, § 1.2.

23. For example, Harald Köhl, *Kants Gesinnungsethik,* p. 31.

24. Stephen Jay Gould, *The Panda's Thumb: More Reflections on Natural History* (Boston: Norton, 1980).

25. For a critique of such theories, see Philip Kitcher, *Vaulting Ambition: Sociobiology and the Quest for Human Nature* (Cambridge, MA: MIT Press, 1985).

26. The *best* example of this sort of project (the one with the greatest philosophical subtlety and sophistication) as applied to ethical topics is probably found in Allan Gibbard, *Wise Choices, Apt Feelings.* It is admirably candid in its dismissal of the possibility that ethics is based on reason (a dismissal far more aprioristic than the *a priori* theories it is dismissing):

> No one has been able to show how the foundations of ethics can be laid *a priori.* This claim is controversial, since some think they have done so [here Gibbard lists: Kant, Sidgwick, Moore, Ross, Gewirth, Donagan and Gauthier]; but it is widely shared and widely argued [Gibbard here cites Brandt and Williams]. Indeed it would make no sense for a reader to proceed with me if he thought any such *a priori* foundation to be firm. (*Wise Choices, Apt Feelings,* p. 25)

27. On the affinities and differences of Kant's philosophy of history and Hegel's, see Yovel, *Kant and the Philosophy of History,* pp. 9–25.

CHAPTER 7: THE HISTORY OF HUMAN NATURE

1. For a sympathetic and perceptive exposition of Herder's views, see Frederick C. Beiser, *The Fate of Reason* (Cambridge, MA: Harvard, 1987), Chapter 5; and Beiser, *Enlightenment, Revolution, Romanticism: the genesis of modern German political thought, 1790–1800* (Cambridge, MA: Harvard, 1992), Chapter 8. There are also good discussions of Herder in Charles Taylor, *Hegel* (Cambridge: Cambridge University Press, 1975), Chapter I, especially pp. 11–27 and Taylor, *Sources of the Self* (Cambridge, MA: Harvard, 1989), Chapter 21.

See also H. B. Nisbet, *Herder and the Philosophy and History of Science* (Cambridge: Modern Humanities Research Association, 1970).

2. This is argued with great erudition by John Zammito, *The Genesis of Kant's Critique of Judgment* (Chicago: University of Chicago Press, 1992).

3. The Hebrew noun for the Deity is in the grammatical plural. Herder's studied use of the plural probably reflects his intention *not* to restrict the guidance of early peoples to the monotheistic God of the Judaeo-Christian tradition but also to embrace pagan polytheism as well as the variety of different gods worshipped by different peoples.

4. Herder was the first to articulate a moral objection to Kant's philosophy of history, which is repeated in a lot of recent literature. Usually this objection is presented as an internal inconsistency in Kant's philosophy, as it is by Hannah Arendt:

> In Kant himself there is this contradiction: Infinite progress is the law of the human species; at the same time, man's dignity demands that he be seen (every single one of us) in his particularity, and, as such, be seen – but without any comparison and independent of time – as reflecting mankind in general. In other words, the very idea of progress – if it is more than a change in circumstances and an improvement of the world – contradicts Kant's notion of man's dignity. It is against human dignity to believe in progress. (Hannah Arendt, *Lectures on Kant's Political Philosophy*, edited by Ronald Beiner (Chicago: University of Chicago Press, 1982), p. 77)

Similar charges are found in William Galston, *Kant and the Problem of History* (Chicago: University of Chicago Press, 1975), pp. 231–235, Paul Stern, "The Problem of History and the Temporality of Kant's Ethics," *Review of Metaphysics* 39 (1986), pp. 535–539, and Louis Dupré, "Kant's Theory of History and Progress," *Review of Metaphysics* 52 (1998). A common version of the objection is that Kant's philosophy of history somehow itself involves a violation of FH because it treats the efforts and sufferings of earlier generations as *means* to the development of the faculties of later generations. See Emil Fackenheim, "Kant on History," *Kant-Studien* 48 (1957), pp. 396–397 and Susan Meld Shell, *The Embodiment of Reason: Kant on Spirit, Generation and Community* (Chicago: University of Chicago Press, 1996), p. 161. Those who charge that Kant's philosophy of history violates FH do not trouble to reply to the obvious objection that it involves an elementary fallacy of the form: "*x* is being treated as a means, therefore *x* is being treated *merely* as a means." It also remains unclear why *Kant* (or his philosophy of history) would be guilty of violating FH. For what it claims is only that according to Kant, *nature* treats human individuals in ways that would (allegedly) violate FH (if nature were a human moral agent – which, of course, it is not).

On both these points, Herder's argument is conspicuously more lucid and cogent, making it easier to see what is at stake. Herder presents the objection explicitly as an objection to the implications *for theodicy* of Kant's philosophy of history. Kant's philosophy of history is alleged to represent *God* as violating FH by using the unhappiness of earlier generations as a means to the happiness of later ones. As Kant sees quite clearly, this charge depends on presupposing that *human happiness* must be God's final end in history; hence God would violate the dignity of the earlier age if its unhappiness is used as a means to the happiness of a later one. Kant's response to the objection is that because happiness is not an unconditioned good, it is entirely consistent with God's benevolence and wisdom that nature should use the unhappiness that morally imperfect human beings bring on themselves as a means to the end of developing the predispositions of the human species. This is an end that (in Kant's view) honors the dignity both of those in whom the capacities are developed and those whose efforts and sufferings serve as means to develop them.

5. For an exposition of this aspect of Herder's views and their later influence on Hegel (especially in his Jena period), see Michael Forster, *Hegel's Idea of a Phenomenology of Spirit* (Chicago: University of Chicago Press, 1998), pp. 222–244.

6. Cf. Herder, *Auch eine Philosophie der Geschichte zur Bildung der Menschheit*, *Sämmtliche Werke* 5:547–554.

7. Herder does not explain what makes Kant's view "Averroistic." Ibn Rushd (Latin transliteration: "Averroes") (1126–1198) was an influential Islamic philosopher and commentator on Aristotle active in Moorish Spain. His Aristotle commentaries arrived in Western Europe in the early thirteenth century, about the same time as the *libri naturales* of Aristotle (the *Metaphysics*, *Physics*, and other works on natural science). Herder may have had in mind Averroes' interpretation of the "passive intellect" in Aristotle, which involved a religiously heterodox belief in collective (but not individual) immortality. This view made Averroes an object of persecution by his fellow Muslims, closing their minds to free philosophical thinking for centuries afterward – in some places down to the present day. It was also a source of resistance in Christian Europe to Averroes' version of Aristotelianism. But the sudden, creative thirteenth century reception of Aristotle in the West, fateful to all philosophy and science since then, would have been unthinkable without Averroes' brilliant commentaries on the *libri naturales*. Averroes is therefore one of the greatest enlighteners in the history of philosophy. Kant's view that there are collective natural ends in history that are not the ends of individuals may have seemed to Herder a denial of the dignity of individuals which is comparable to that involved in Averroes' denial of individual immortality.

8. This is only one of many respects in which Hegel's philosophy of history is anticipated by Kant. Once again, see Yovel, *Kant and the Philosophy of History*. The similarity of Kant's philosophy of history to Marx's historical materialism will be explored in § 5 of the present chapter.

9. An interesting discussion of the theme of reason's creation of new desires in Rousseau and Kant is presented by Richard L. Velkley, "The Crisis of the End of Reason in Kant's Philosophy," R. Beiner and J. Booth (eds.), *Kant and Political Philosophy: The Contemporary Legacy*, pp. 76–94.

10. For the likely historical origin of the term "misology," see Plato, *Phaedo* 89d–91b.

11. We see more everyday secular examples of the same pattern of self-deception when people "feel guilty" about smoking or overeating. Kant thinks this is the

psychology of the "self-torment of the repentant sinner" who, instead of reforming his conduct, imposes punishments on himself for his sins (real or
imagined – imagined ones are better, both because they allow us to dignify
our imprudence and because they distract us from moral demands to change
our actual conduct) (R 6:24).

12. By understanding our sexuality as foundational to the moral disposition, he
is explicitly acknowledging human sexual desire is as much a function of reason and human society as of our biological nature. Unfortunately, Kant does
not employ this insight to confront his more commonly expressed (and more
traditional) belief that our sexuality embarrasses us because it reminds us of
our similarity to irrational animals (R 6:80n, MS 6:425).

13. Nietzsche, *Twilight of the Idols*: The "Improvers" of Mankind, § 5.

14. I see no ground at all for Fackenheim's and Nisbet's translation of *Beschluß
der Geschichte* as "The End of History" (Beck (ed.), *Kant on History* (Indianapolis, IN: Bobbs-Merrill, 1963), p. 63; Reiss (ed.), *Kant: Political Writings*
(2nd edition, Cambridge: Cambridge University Press, 1991), p. 229). There
is nothing Fukuyamaesque about this section. It concludes with the human
species "turning away from the task assigned it by nature, the progressive cultivation of its disposition to goodness," which has made it "unworthy of its
destiny" (MA 8:120). What the heading means is simply that Kant is now
going to describe the "close" or concluding portion (*Beschluß*) of the "story"
(*Geschichte*) (i.e., the biblical narrative from *Genesis* 2 to *Genesis* 6) that he and
Herder have selected to guide their conjectures about the *beginnings* of human history. There is an awful lot of the biblical history still to come at that
point (starting with the Flood, to which the quoted phrases are an allusion) – not to mention all the secular events that have happened since things
dried out again.

15. For expositions of Marx's historical materialism, see G. A. Cohen, *Karl Marx's
Theory of History: A Defense* (Princeton, NJ: Princeton University Press, 1978)
and Allen Wood, *Karl Marx* (London: Routledge, 1981), Part Two (pp. 61–
121).

16. We will see later, however, that even without access to the Hegelian notion of
civil society, Kant does regard the political state as something less than the
true social life of humanity, and he does look forward to a social form which
will go beyond the state by being a non-coercive social unity posited freely by
the united power of rational human individuals.

17. Friedrich Engels, *The Origin of the Family, Private Property and the State*
(1884), Marx-Engels *Selected Works* (New York: International Publishers,
1968), pp. 455–593.

18. Here again we are dealing with what I earlier called "Mandeville's dilemma"
(see Introduction, Note 9).

19. Kant's apologists are in the habit of praising his noble insistence on the evils
of war and the need to overcome hostility between nations through a federation of states; they are also in the habit of contrasting Kant's views on war
favorably with Hegel's nasty idea that occasional wars are necessary to preserve the ethical health of peoples. But this is misleading, since Kant too
maintains that until civil society has been firmly established on the basis of

republican principles of right, the threat of war serves as nature's principal means for protecting individual liberty and keeping social progress alive within the state (MA 8:119–120). Of course for Kant war serves its historical purpose chiefly by making it increasingly *intolerable* for states to retain pre-republican constitutions and to exist outside a universal federation which will maintain perpetual peace between them (I 8:24–25). The form of the paradox Kant thereby embraces – that war is historically necessary as a means to peace – is characteristic of his philosophy of history, which in general treats the evils of human life purposively as means to the goods opposed to them. The paradox can be dissipated if we realize that the end in question is not a good provided to the human race through nature's bounty, but rather an achievement of human beings themselves: It is as if nature "had willed that the human being, having finally worked his way up from the greatest barbarism to the greatest skill, the greatest perfection in his way of thinking and thus to happiness (as far as it is possible on earth), should take sole credit for this and have only himself to thank for it" (I 8:20).

20. Kant does not accept Hegel's inference from the fact that right is based on historical-economic conditions to the conclusion that people in pre-agricultural societies have no rights against developed states and only "formal" independence, which these states need not respect (Hegel, *Elements of the Philosophy of Right*, § 351). His view seems rather to be that once a society acquires the conception of right, it must constrain its behavior accordingly, understanding the customs and institutions of pre-agricultural peoples in such a way as to grant them the rights belonging universally to all rational beings. Kant holds, for example, that the nomadic peoples of Mongolia should be regarded as owning in common the lands across which they travel: "since all the land belongs to the people, the use of it belongs to each individual" (MS 6:265). He also asks whether a hunting people can resist a herding or a farming people who wish to make a different use of the land, and answers: "Certainly, since as long as they keep within their boundaries the way they want to *live* on their land is up to their own discretion (*res merae facultatis*)" (MS 6:266). See the following note.

21. Common ownership of land was characteristic of pre-agricultural societies, but such societies also lie outside a condition of right, since they were prior to the founding of states. Kant does recognize the existence of present-day non-agricultural societies where land is owned in common by the whole people; but in order to regard this as rightful he thinks we need to interpret it as the result of an agreement between the citizens to alienate their private holdings (MS 6:251; cf. 6:265–266). Kant does hold that some features of his theory of right – such as the original common ownership of the earth and the social contract – are misunderstood if they are taken as historical facts. Both, he says, are instead "ideas" (or even "fictions") in terms of which we should conceive presently existing institutions (MS 6:251–252, TP 8:297; cf. MS 6:315, EF 8:349–351). It would be mistaken, however, to infer that he means the same to apply to the transition from provisional to peremptory acquisition or between the state of nature and the civil condition (which are never described as mere ideas or denied historical reference). Kant's theory of history

has no place for events and conditions such as the social contract and original common ownership of land. For according to it states were first founded only through the violence that turned provisional property rights into peremptory ones.

CHAPTER 8: HUMAN INCLINATIONS AND AFFECTIONS

1. Compare, for example, the following from the *Encyclopedia* article "philosopher" (*philosophe*), which has often been attributed to the grammarian César Chesnau Dumarsais (1676–1756):

> Other men are carried away by their passions; their actions are not preceded by reflection: they are men who walk in darkness. A philosopher, on the other hand, even in moments of passion, acts only according to reflection: he walks through the night, but he is preceded by a torch . . . [The philosopher] is far removed from the impassive sage of the Stoics. The philosopher is a man, while their sage was only a phantom. They were ashamed of their humanity, he takes pride in his. (*Encyclopédie, ou Dictionnaire raisonné des sciences, des arts et des métiers, par une société des gens des lettres. Mis en ordre à publié par M. Diderot* (Paris: Briasson, 1751–1765) XII: 509–510. (English translation from *Encyclopedia (Selections)*, tr. N. Hoyt and T. Cassirer (Indianapolis: Bobbs-Merrill, 1965), pp. 285, 288–289.)

Of course, Dumarsais does not mean by "passion" the same thing Kant does, since for Kant a passion is an inclination that resists rational reflection, whereas Dumarsais regards the true philosopher as acting by such reflection "even in moments of passion."

2. An important theme in the *Critique of the power of judgment* is the positive contribution aesthetic feeling makes to morality, both in the form of feelings of pleasure in the beautiful (KU §§ 42, 59) and the emotion (*Rührung*) we experience through the sublime (KU §§ 27–29). Kant regards such emotion as an expression of moral feeling, hence inseparable from our susceptibility to morality (KU 5:256–266). Thus Paul Guyer quite accurately describes Kant's view of what such feelings mean to us in the title of his book: *Kant and the Experience of Freedom* (New York: Cambridge, 1993). For treatments of the role of aesthetic feeling in morality, see Chapters 1, 6, 9, and 10.

3. For more on this point, and its role in Kant's view that the principle of happiness cannot be the supreme principle of reason, see Allen W. Wood, "Kant vs. Eudaemonism" in Predrag Cicovacki (ed.), *Kant's Legacy: Essays in Honor of Lewis White Beck* (Rochester, NY: University of Rochester Press, 2000).

4. "[The human being] thus needs a *master* to break his self-will and force him to obey a universally valid will under which everyone can be free" (I 8:23). This may remind us of Hobbes's idea that the state of nature is a war of all against all which can only be ended through the establishment of a sovereign authority with the power to coerce. Kant confirms the comparison himself:

> As Hobbes maintains, the state of nature is a state of injustice and violence, and we have no option save to abandon it and submit ourselves to the

constraint of law, which limits our freedom solely in order that it may be
consistent with the freedom of others and with the common good of all.
(KrV A752/B780; cf. R 6:97)

But apparently similar conclusions should not lead us to ignore the fundamentally different starting points of the two philosophers. As Kant makes explicit in his essay on theory and practice, the most basic difference is that
Hobbes proceeds from the will to live, but Kant proceeds from the idea of
freedom (TP 8:289). For Hobbes, freedom from domination by others and
acquisition of dominion over them are chiefly means to safeguard one's own
life. The sovereign's compulsion – by means of the threat of death – merely
makes use of the individual's will to live in order to achieve a secure existence
for all. As Rousseau saw clearly, Hobbesian human beings undergo no basic
change in their nature when they pass from the natural to the civil condition.
Hobbes's theory aims merely to describe a mechanism through which the individual's will to live – originally the cause of war and insecurity – may be
employed to establish peace and secure the survival of all. Kant, too, insists
that the love of life is a powerful natural urge (VA 7:276). But since it is not
peculiar to human (or rational) beings, it plays no special role in Kant's theory of history or in the foundation of the state. The founding of civil society
is instead based on the rational-social passions for freedom and for superiority over others. For Kant (as for Rousseau) the transition from the natural
to the civil state involves a fundamental change in human nature – for Kant,
a taming of the original passion for freedom ("breaking of the individual's
self-will") – which is involved in people's becoming accustomed to civil rule.
In the civil condition, the passion for freedom is modified and transformed
under the guidance of reason, both into a set of new social passions and also
into a new kind of desire, arising solely out of reason itself. Social antagonism
is based on a desire to gain superiority over others, which is basic to our natural desires and lies at the foundation of our self-interest. Hobbes comes
closest to Kant when he attributes to human beings "ambition," a desire for
"glory" or "a desire of office or precedence" (Hobbes, Leviathan 1.6 (Works,
London: Bohn, 1839), 3:44). But this competitiveness between people is
not for Hobbes the fundamental cause of war between them, and it can be
overcome by rational appeal to their self-interest. For Kant, however, the
fundamental cause of social antagonism is a basic human desire to achieve
superior status in comparison with others. This fundamental conflict continues unabated in the civil state even when its scope is confined by coercive
laws, and the passions it inspires lead to imprudence as well as immorality, so
that mere appeals to rational self-interest cannot be guaranteed to curb
them. In this respect, social life for Kant is a "war of all against all" in an even
deeper sense than it is for Hobbes. Because Kant thinks people's natural self-
interest is founded on their unsociable sociability, a true state of peace between them can never rest on self-interest, but must involve an altogether different interest, generated by pure reason alone, independently of and even
opposed to natural desire.

   This difference between Hobbes and Kant is related to a basic difference in methodology. Hobbes is attempting to explain the existence of the state through the desires and actions of the individuals who compose it (to provide "microfoundations" for a social macro-structure). Kant addresses historical changes that the human race has undergone and seeks an account of these changes in terms of basic natural tendencies (natural purposes), which reside less in individuals as such than in the entire species and the situation in which it has been placed. The will to live for Hobbes triggers behavior that is predictable according to uniform mechanistic laws. The Kantian passion for freedom, however, is an organic propensity, capable of changing its nature in response to different environmental conditions and therefore linking a series of historical stages, each of which operates on the basis of a natural purposiveness systematizing the contingent, empirical laws specific to it. Hobbes's methodology points toward orthodox social and economic theories based on timeless, formalistic microfoundations. Kant's methodology points toward the organic theories of history found in German idealism and Marxism.

5. The Tunguses (or Olenni-Tungusi) were a hunting people of Siberia. For Kant, they are the stock example of a "savage" or "uncivilized" people (R 6: 176, MS 6:231).

6. This point is perceptively discussed in Howard Williams, *Kant's Political Philosophy* (New York: St. Martin's, 1983), pp. 114–121.

7. Kant appears to take it for granted that men are superior to women not only physically but also intellectually, which is why he thinks it is in the common interest – in the woman's interest as well as the man's – for the man to make decisions on behalf of the family in economic and other practical matters (MS 6:279). The result is that the man is the official governor of the household, but the woman rules over him subtly by manipulating his feelings (VA 7:309–310). Kant compares the relation of husband and wife to that of the minister to the monarch: "For inclination reigns, but understanding governs . . . [The husband] will be like a minister to his monarch, who thinks only of amusement" (VA 7:310). This exactly reverses Rousseau's use of the same analogy: "[A wife] should reign in the home as a minister reigns in the state, by contriving to be ordered to do what she wants" (Rousseau, *Emile* 4:534). But Rousseau and Kant may disagree more about how monarchies typically work than about how marriages typically work, since both agree that the woman's role is not to be in direct authority but to have her way by manipulating her husband, while the man's is to exercise real power but to be manipulated by his wife in the way he uses it.

8. See Allen W. Wood, "Exploitation," in E. Frankel-Paul, F. Miller, J. Paul (eds.), *The Just Society.* New York: Cambridge University Press, 1995; reprinted in Kai Nielsen and Robert Ware (eds.) *Exploitation.* (New York: Humanities Press, 1997).

9. This point is effaced by feminist critics who argue (in Sally Sedgwick's words) that "women are excluded by Kant's moral theory because he finds them lacking in that quality that constitutes human dignity" (Sally Sedgwick, "Can Kant's Ethics Survive the Feminist Critique?" in Robin May Schott (ed.), *Feminist Interpretations of Immanuel Kant,* p. 89). Sedgwick is here reporting the views of others rather than expressing her own views, but she does not al-

together distance herself from the quoted remark. Similar claims are made or insinuated by other writers in the same collection. Thus Hannelore Schröder says that Kant "classifies women as natural serfs or animals" (p. 296). See also Jean Rumsey, pp.130–132, Monique David-Ménard, pp. 342–345, 352–353. But Kant's false anthropological view that women are intellectually inferior to men must be distinguished from the equally false ethical view (which Kant *did not* hold) that rational beings who are inferior to others in intellect or temperament are nonpersons or second-class persons compared to their intellectual or temperamental superiors. One has to wonder whether the intellectually gifted feminist scholars who advance these criticisms of Kant actually think that their intellectual inferiors (male and female) should be regarded as nonpersons or second-class moral persons. Or are they gratuitously attributing to Kant this patently anti-Kantian ethical view even though they clearly perceive its falsity?

The usual form of these charges derives not from Kant's view that women are intellectually inferior but from his other view that their temperament is more emotional than that of men, and hence that Kant regards them as generally inferior to men considered as moral agents. But of course for Kant it is one thing to have a *temperament* that makes the moral life more difficult and quite a different thing to be *worse* as a moral agent. (For instance, the person with worse temperament who acts according to duty will perform actions of greater moral worth than the person of better temperament who is not so sorely tempted.) So the critics will not find Kant saying such things as that women are in general *morally worse people* than men, since given Kantian moral principles, no such conclusion would follow. On the distinction between Kant's (deplorable) views about women and his (much more progressive) ethical principles, see Marcia Baron, "Kantian Ethics and the Claims of Detachment," in Schott (ed.), *Feminist Interpretations of Immanuel Kant*, pp. 145–170.

10. For instance, see Hegel, *Elements of the Philosophy of Right*, tr. H. B. Nisbet (Cambridge: Cambridge University Press, 1991), §§ 75R, 161A.

11. Andrea Dworkin, *Intercourse* (New York: Free Press, 1987), pp. 120–150. Cf. Barbara Herman, "Could It Be Worth Thinking About Kant on Sex and Marriage?" in L. Antony and C. Witt (eds.), *A Mind of One's Own: Feminist Essays on Reason and Objectivity* (Boulder, CO: Westview, 1992). The Kantianism of Dworkin's views should not surprise us too much. There is little in Dworkin that was not anticipated by Simone de Beauvoir, who is quite often condescended to by contemporary feminists, though not nearly as often as they make use of her ideas without acknowledgment (Simone de Beauvoir, *The Second Sex*, tr. by H. M. Parshley (New York: Knopf, 1952)). Beauvoir's discussion of sex is in turn dependent on Jean-Paul Sartre, who took over Kant's view of sex with mainly terminological and stylistic modifications. Sexual desire, namely, seeks to objectify the other in order to capture the other's freedom (Jean-Paul Sartre, *Being and Nothingness*, tr. Hazel Barnes (New York: Philosophical Library, 1956), Part Three, Chapter 3, I–II, pp. 364–412). Beauvoir's variant of this view, later echoed by Dworkin, is to identify the act of objectification as essentially male and the condition of being objectified

as essentially female. As we have seen, even Beauvoir's emendation of Sartre was to some degree anticipated by Kant, who also recognizes that sexual objectification is a greater threat to the woman's humanity than the man's. These comparisons also shed light on the cogency of the condescending explanations usually offered for Kant's views on sex. For it would not naturally occur to us to attribute the views of Beauvoir or Sartre to their sexual inexperience, to the lingering effects of their excessively religious upbringing or to the puritanical attitudes characteristic of mid-century Parisian intellectuals.

12. See the sad history of Kant's correspondence with "*die kleine Schwärmerin*" Maria von Herbert, between 1791 and 1793 (especially Ak 11:273–274, 331–334, 400–402, and Kant's letter to Elizabeth Motherby, Ak 11:411–412). Maria von Herbert committed suicide ten years after the correspondence ended.

13. Kant distinguishes tyranny proper, the desire to rule others through one's strength and their fear (the way Kant thinks men usually rule over women and over one another), from the desire to rule over others by manipulating them through charm and desire (the way he thinks women rule over men) (VA 7:273).

14. The importance of this theme, free rational communication, for Kantian ethics and for the critical enterprise as a whole, has been effectively emphasized by Onora O'Neill, *Constructions of Reason* (Cambridge: Cambridge University Press, 1992), especially Chapters 1 and 2.

15. Shakespeare, *Hamlet*, Act III, Scene 4, line 162. The importance of the theme of "permissible deception" in Kant's moral philosophy has been discussed by Natalie Brender in her doctoral dissertation, *Precarious Positions: Aspects of Kantian Moral Agency* (Baltimore: Johns Hopkins, 1997).

16. For a sensitive and insightful consideration of Kant on sympathy and pity, see Marcia Baron, *Kantian Ethics (Almost) Without Apology*, Chapter 6. My thinking about Kant's reservations concerning feelings such as sympathy and love was stimulated by some e-mail exchanges with Wayne Waxman.

17. It might be questioned whether on Kant's account the lover seeks the beloved's happiness *for her sake.* Insofar as the ultimate ground of our desire for her happiness is a perfection in the beloved, we do benefit the beloved for the sake of that perfection. Plato's theory of love is sometimes objected to on the ground that genuine love must seek to benefit the beloved not for the sake of the form of Beauty in which she participates, but simply for *herself.* (See Gregory Vlastos, "The Individual as Object of Love in Plato," *Platonic Studies*, 2nd ed. (Princeton, NJ: Princeton University Press, 1981), pp. 3–42.) Kant's position would seem to be that only rational philanthropic love is capable of loving the person truly for *herself* (since for Kant this means "for her rational nature"). Love as an empirical inclination is necessarily of the Platonic kind; it loves the beloved only for her perfections. But if philanthropic love identifies the person herself with her rational nature, then it looks as if it does not love her as an individual but only as a member of a rational species. Kant's best account of caring about a person *as an individual* will be found in his discussion of friendship (see § 6.1 and especially Note 23). The implication seems to be that no form of (what Kant calls) 'love'

(whether empirical or philanthropic) counts as what *we* think of as *love for an individual* except insofar as it is an element in (what Kant calls) 'friendship'.

18. Marcia Baron criticizes this doctrine in "Love and Respect in the Doctrine of Virtue," in N. Potter and M. Timmons (eds.), Kant's *Metaphysics of Morals*, *Southern Journal of Philosophy* XXXVI, Supplement (1998), pp. 29–44. But I think Kant and Baron may be to some extent arguing at cross purposes. Baron is considering the relation of love and respect as *moral or rational* feelings, correlated with duties of virtue toward others, and she is right to do so insofar as this appears to be the context in which Kant makes this claim. So regarded, love and respect cannot be opposed, since philanthropic love for human beings should be grounded on respect for them and is possible only on the basis of respect, as Kant agrees (ED 8:337). But in the Doctrine of Virtue, Kant is also considering duties in relation to human nature, and he cannot fail to note that (according to his anthropological theory) love and respect in their *natural* form do not stand in this harmonious relation but are even antagonistic to one another. For on the natural–social system of evaluation built into our natural inclinations, to respect someone is to have one's self-conceit thwarted by their worth, which humiliates and displeases us, making it harder to love them. The two opposed relationships of love and respect are both part of Kant's theory: the harmonious relationship, in which love is grounded on respect, is part of the moral system of evaluation arising from our matured reason, whereas the antagonistic relationship, in which respect is an obstacle to love, is part of the natural-social system of evaluation built into our natural inclinations and the propensity to evil residing innately in our power of choice.

19. See Jerome B. Schneewind, "Autonomy, obligation and virtue," in Guyer (ed.), *The Cambridge Companion to Kant*, pp. 310–311.

20. One of the few who have appreciated this is Christine Korsgaard, *Creating the Kingdom of Ends* (New York: Cambridge, 1997), Chapter 7. That Kant has an interesting theory of friendship was recognized much earlier by H. J. Paton, "Kant on Friendship," *Proceedings of the British Academy*, Aristotelian Society Supplementary Volume xxii, pp. 197–219, reprinted in Neera Kapur Badhwar (ed.), *Friendship: A Philosophical Reader*, pp. 133–154. But Paton says that in expounding Kant's theory "we have been concerned not so much with the Critical philosopher as with the Sage of Königsberg – almost, one might say, with Kant in slippers" (p. 145). This reflects the quaint sense of embarrassment Anglophone moral philosophers felt in those bygone days when they found themselves discussing anything that seemed to smack of "empirical psychology."

21. Aristotle, *Nicomachean Ethics*, Book 8, Ch. 2–3.

22. Aristotle, *Nicomachean Ethics*, Book 8, Ch. 3–4, especially 1157a16–25.

23. The irreducible importance of intimacy and mutual communication in love has been recently emphasized by Deborah Brown, "The Right Method of Boy-Loving," in Roger E. Lamb (ed.), *Love Analyzed* (Boulder: Westview, 1997). Kant does not mention this theme as a factor in sexual love, but it is central and fundamental to his theory of friendship. Aristotle of course also empha-

sizes that friends must experience one another (*Nicomachean Ethics*, 1158a15) and be aware of their reciprocated good will (1155b34–1156a4), and that friendship involves living together (1155b27, 1157b14–20, 1166a7). For Aristotle it is not this mutual awareness that constitutes the purpose and value of friendship, but instead the extension of one's own excellent activity through benefiting the friend and through the activities of the friend, who is "another self" (1161b28, 1168a5–10, 1169b2–1170b19). A bit closer to Kant's view is a passage from the *Magna Moralia* (1213a10–26), in which it is argued that friendship is to be valued because knowledge of the "other self" affords *self*-knowledge, which is pleasant for the good man (the argument is discussed by John M. Cooper, in "Aristotle on Friendship," in A. O. Rorty (ed.), *Essays on Aristotle's Ethics* (Berkeley, CA: University of California Press, 1980), pp. 320–324). For Kant, however, self-knowledge for even the best of us is a duty, not a pleasure, and we do not stand to ourselves (cognitively or affectively) in a relation like that to which we stand to our friend. We can put Kant's position by saying that a being whose nature is beset by radical evil is not destined to be its own best friend (see my comparison of Kant and Aristotle on these matters, Allen Wood, "Self-Love, Self-Benevolence and Self-Conceit," in S. Engstrom and J. Whiting (eds.), *Aristotle, Kant and the Stoics*, pp. 141–161).

24. Aristotle, *Nicomachean Ethics*, 1155b27–28, 1157a17–25, 1157b29–38, 1159b3.
25. Compare Plato, *Lysis* 214e–215c and Aristotle, *Nicomachean Ethics*, 1155a32–1155b16, 1156b20–22, 1159b12–24).
26. Aristotle agrees with this (*Nicomachean Ethics*, 1155a17–22, 1167a8).
27. Aristotle expresses a surprising degree of agreement with Kant here. Though he allows that there can be friendship between unequals (*Nicomachean Ethics*, Book 8, Chapter 7), he regards such friendships as necessarily deficient and equality as necessary for perfect friendship (1157b29–38, 1158b1).
28. One might be an equally good Kantian on this point, but have a more up-to-date view of things, by interpreting what he says here contrapositively: Marriage – or indeed any relationship between men and women – *can* be a true friendship but only if it is grounded on the *complete equality* of the partners and the *complete mutuality* of their interdependence. But if we interpret Kant in this way, then we must surely concede *something* even to his view that marriage can never be true friendship, namely, that it will be very hard for any marriage to meet these criteria of friendship under present social conditions.
29. Aristotle holds that friends share pleasures and distresses (*Nicomachean Ethics*, 1166a6) and that "friendship is community" (1171b32).
30. This saying is attributed to Aristotle by Favorinus, according to Diogenes Laertius, *Lives and Opinions of Eminent Philosophers*, 5.1.21. At one further place in Kant's lectures on ethics, the saying is quoted again, this time attributed to Socrates (VE 27:424). Stephen Menn points out to me that Diogenes' version is likely based on a textual corruption, since with only a change in the breathing marks, it would mean:"He who has friends (i.e., more than one friend) has no friend." Cf. Eudemian Ethics, 1245b20.

CHAPTER 9: THE HISTORICAL
VOCATION OF MORALITY

1. First option (content): Kant's theory of our unsociable sociability provides a naturally purposive account of the way self-conceit works its way into the content of our natural desires. But since those desires are deemed to be "natural" only in this purposive sense, it is entirely consistent to regard their content as also something for which we as rational beings are responsible. Having desires is not an evil act, but it is an evil act to incorporate into a maxim a desire that presupposes that I am worth more than other rational beings or prefers natural or comparative standards of self-worth to the rational, noncomparative standard involved in human dignity. It may raise eyebrows to say that our freedom is responsible for the content of natural desires. But there is a strong tradition in post-Kantian philosophy (running from Fichte to Sartre), which holds that freedom must be understood in this way if it is to exist at all.

   Second option (motivational strength): From the mere fact that our natural desires are at odds with morality in their content it does not follow that we have a propensity to prefer the incentives they offer us to the (rationally stronger) incentive of morality. While driving my car, I may have a sudden desire to hit the gas and try to weave through oncoming traffic at 100 mph. But if I am rational, this desire presents no incentive to floor the throttle that can compete in motivational strength with my powerful prudential incentives to protect myself from the risk I would incur by giving into it. If I choose despite this to speed up to 100 mph, that choice would require some explanation, such as that I have an irrational propensity to engage in extremely risky behavior. If the incentives of inclination (whatever their content) are likewise much weaker rationally than those of morality, it requires some explanation, such as a radical propensity to evil in our power of choice, to account for the fact that we so often give in to them. This propensity, too, can be seen on the Kantian account to serve the ends of nature, for without it human beings at earlier stages of history would not have plunged themselves into the competitiveness and discontent that spurred them on to develop the predispositions of the species. Without this irrational propensity to evil they would never have acquired the capacity to recognize the rational predominance of moral over natural incentives.

   The text of the *Religion* does not choose between these two options, but they do not exclude each other. We may understand the doctrine of radical evil in either way, or in both ways together.

2. Kant's view is criticized here by John R. Silber, "The Ethical Significance of Kant's Religion," in Theodore M. Greene and Hoyt Hudson, *Kant: Religion Within the Limits of Reason Alone* (New York: Harper, 1960), pp. cxxv–cxxvii. Kant does not deny that we can have *ends* directly contrary to those of morality. We have seen this already in his account of the vices of failed ambition: envy, malice, spite, and ingratitude. The happiness of others is an end that is also a duty, but these vices dispose us to seek the unhappiness of others for its own sake. Kant does not disagree with those who insist that we do "evil for

evil's sake" in that sense. It is not a merely empirical question (as Silber contends) but a theoretical (or conceptual) one how we may intelligibly describe the most extreme cases of evil. Kant argues (quite cogently, in my view) that any "stronger" conception of evil than the one he offers would be incoherent, since it would remove the necessary conditions for moral accountability and therefore no longer count as *evil*. Views like Silber's are best explained as the projection of irrational hatred and *resentment*, which are not uncommon. See Chapter 4, § 7.3.

3. Kant thinks we can be charged with evil only for what we *do*. Thoughts, dispositions, or motivations, whatever their character, are not evil unless they are exhibited in acts that are in some way blamable. Hence all three degrees of evil are cases of evil displayed *in conduct*. Frailty and impurity are revealed in actions only when we probe beneath the surface of conduct we might have thought wholly good if we had not asked the right questions about it. To reveal frailty, we have to ask about the relation between our (apparently virtuous) resolve and *other* conduct which fails to follow through on this resolve. We discover impurity in dutiful conduct only when we ask counterfactual questions, about whether we would still have acted dutifully if nonmoral incentives had not been present. Impurity is something evil in our actual conduct, however, insofar as it shows our apparently virtuous conduct to display less virtue than it appears to. For Kant, however, there is no impurity simply in the fact that someone *does* a dutiful action from some motive other than duty (e.g., tells the truth from a desire not to ruin his reputation for honesty). The question about impurity is rather whether the nonmoral incentive was "required" (*nötig*). That can be brought out only if we ask the counterfactual question whether the agent still would have told the truth if the lie would not have endangered his reputation. If it is true of me in a given case that I would have lied if I had not feared for my reputation, then my dutiful action, which is not blameworthy, proceeds from my adoption of an evil maxim, which is blameworthy. The fact that concern about my reputation played a role in motivating me to tell the truth would reveal no impurity in my will if it were true of me that I would still have told the truth if the lie would not have harmed my good name. Thus we also see that the impurity Kant is discussing in the *Religion* is not the same as the absence of "moral worth" or "moral content," which he alludes to in the overemphasized discussion of the good will in the First Section of the *Groundwork*. For if both doing my duty and protecting my reputation give me incentives to tell the truth, then my truthfulness has no moral worth (or moral content) whether or not my will is impure. That is, my act of truthfulness would in this case deserve praise and encouragement but not esteem, whether or not I would have lied if concern about my reputation had not provided me with an incentive to tell the truth.

4. There could be a problem about Kant's description of radical evil as "innate" or "inborn." For as we saw in Chapter 2, §2.3, he applies these predicates to what is implanted in us and denies them to what arises from the exercise of our own faculties. But radical evil does arise from the exercise of our faculties; it is an act of freedom. However, since it seems to arise indirectly, as a by-product of the development of reason, and since it is to be accounted for

by natural purposiveness (in the same way we account for our animal instincts), it may not be illegitimate to extend the concept of innateness to cover it.

5. I am grateful to Rudolf Haller for pressing me to clarify the role of R 6:20 in Kant's defense of the doctrine of radical evil. From this standpoint the doctrine of radical evil might seem impossible to argue for. If I am to be charged with evil, it seems that this must be on account of something *I* have done. That I have done it could surely be determined only from an empirical examination of my conduct. How could anyone be entitled to infer *my* guilty conduct on the basis of general principles about human nature (whether *a priori* or empirical)? The only point that needs to be made in response to this objection is that the right standard of argument is one for supporting a reasonable conclusion about what people (past, present, and future) are disposed to do, not one for justifying a verdict of guilty for crimes still uncommitted.

6. See Allen Wood, *Kant's Moral Religion* (Ithaca, NY: Cornell Press, 1970), pp. 219–226.

7. Allison, Kant's *Theory of Freedom*, pp. 154–155. Allison's version of the argument seems especially unpromising. First, from the finitude of a will (or the presence to it of desires other than those prompted by pure reason) it simply does not follow that it is not holy (at most it follows that, for all we know, it *might* not be holy, because those desires *might* be contrary to reason and the will *might* prefer them as incentives over the incentives of reason). Even if we did know that the human will is not holy, this would tell us only that it does not *necessarily* follow the moral law, not that it displays a *propensity not* to follow the law. Still less could we infer from either the finitude or the nonholiness of the human will that there is in human nature a *universal, innate* propensity of this kind, which lies at the ground of all the evil deeds human beings do. Allison has more recently given a more complex and more satisfying account, influenced by Anderson-Gold, in a paper comparing Kant's and Arendt's theories of evil: "Reflections on the Banality of (Radical) Evil: A Kantian Analysis," in Allison, *Idealism and Freedom* (New York: Cambridge, 1996), Chapter 12.

8. Sharon Anderson-Gold, "God and Community: An Inquiry into the Religious Implications of the Highest Good," in P. Rossi and M. Wreen (eds.) *Kant's Philosophy of Religion Reconsidered* (Bloomington, IN: Indiana University Press, 1991).

9. Kant identifies three predispositions (*Anlagen*) in human nature: animality, humanity, and personality. Animality and humanity (but not personality) can, despite their natural goodness, have moral vices "grafted" onto them (R 6: 26–27). The vices of animality are "gluttony" (*Völlerei*), "lust" (*Wollust*), and "wild lawlessness" (*Wildheit*) (R 6:27). We should immediately recognize the last two animal vices as the natural passions (for sex and for freedom, respectively) which were discussed in Chapter 8, § 2. In this way, the anthropological reading of the doctrine of radical evil can also be confirmed in the case of the vices of animality. Gluttony is not a *passion* because it is not directed at other people; yet it is a vice because it gives priority to satisfying natural inclinations over our absolute worth as rational beings.

10. Goethe wrote: "Kant required a long lifetime to purify his philosophical mantle of many impurities and prejudices. And now he has wantonly tainted it with the shameful stain of radical evil, in order that Christians, too, might be attracted to kiss its hem" (quoted by Emil Fackenheim, "Kant and Radical Evil," *University of Toronto Quarterly* 23 (1954), p. 340). Perhaps in the mid-1790s, Goethe could not yet comprehend Kant's idea that humanity comes by its highest powers only through falling into evil, and that its destiny is to use those powers to struggle uncertainly against the evil through which they were acquired. However, Goethe did grasp this idea eventually, since his greatest poem, the product of his lifelong labor, was devoted to expressing it. More likely, Goethe simply failed to recognize that he and Kant were working with the same idea, since he was already working on *Ur–Faust* at the time he read Kant's *Religion*.

11. Note, however, that Kant tries also to establish the universality of the doctrine by finding intimations of it in classical Greek and Roman literature and religion, in the Hebrew scriptures, and in Hindu religion (R 6:19); later he finds the related idea of a divine judge also in Egyptian, Gothic, and Persian religions (R 6:140–141n). In his contemporaneous essay *The End of All Things*, he locates versions of the doctrine of a last judgment also in Persian, Arabic, Burmese, Tibetan, and other cultures (ED 8:329–331).

12. In *Emile*, Rousseau proposes an entire system of education based on the idea that there is a mode of life which is naturally suited to human beings, and that the avoidable ills of human life are mainly due to our foolish deviations from it. Rousseau thinks it is unnatural to use swaddling clothes on infants (Rousseau, *Emile* 4:43), or to bathe them in warm water (Rousseau, *Emile* 4:69). He recommends against taking steps to protect children from danger and disease: "Half the children born die before their eighth year. . . . This is nature's law; why contradict it?" (Rousseau, *Emile* 4:49).

13. Rousseau therefore proposes that in educating a child, we follow nature's path, letting the child use its natural powers but refusing it any powers beyond these. He recommends that we allow children the full use of their strength, and help them get what they want whenever it involves the satisfaction of a natural need, but never aid them in trying to satisfy a desire that springs from caprice (Rousseau, *Emile* 4:78). Rousseau is convinced that just because their rational faculties are not yet fully developed, children are closer to nature than adults. Thus he attacks Locke's recommendation that we educate children by reasoning with them (Rousseau, *Emile* 4:109). Since the natural condition of human life is presocial (hence premoral) Rousseau also thinks that we should not deal with children in moral terms: Give them no orders or commands, make no demands on them based on your own rights or needs, and inflict no punishment as such on them. Instead, simply let them find out the bad consequences of their behavior for themselves (Rousseau, *Emile* 4:109, 123, 230). Because he regards the "path of nature" as more real and fundamental than any social order we may impose upon it, Rousseau thinks that his pupil should be taught a trade, such as carpentry, which will be useful to him in any condition of society (Rousseau, *Emile* 4:256). He is firmly convinced that there is a natural difference between the sexes and that the

natural path in educating a boy is different from that in educating a girl. In fact, much of the advice Rousseau has given us in the first four books concerning the education of Emile is retracted when it comes to educating Sophie. In particular, Rousseau does not recommend that girls be kept so long innocent of reason, morality, and the tyrannies involved in social institutions: "Acquaint a girl earlier than a boy with good and evil, since woman is made to submit to man and to endure even injustice at his hands" (Rousseau, *Emile* 4:519–520).

14. One of the few expositions of Kantian ethics that has stressed this is Roger Sullivan, *Immanuel Kant's Moral Theory*, Chapters 15–18. See also Pauline Kleingeld, *Fortschritt und Vernunft: Zur Geschichtsphilosophie Kants*, Ch. VIII–XI.

15. See *The German Ideology, Marx Engels Collected Works* (New York: International Publishers, 1975) 5:80–81.

16. Marx, *Contribution to a Critique of Political Economy*: Preface, in A. Wood (ed.), *Karl Marx: Selections* (New York: Macmillan, 1988), p. 136.

17. A persuasive argument that "philosophy" in this sense, with its orientation to the highest good, lies behind the architectonic structure of the entire critical philosophy, is made by Richard L. Velkley, *Freedom and the End of Reason: On the Moral Foundation of Kant's Critical Philosophy* (Chicago: University of Chicago Press, 1989).

18. This point is well argued by Burkhard Tuschling, "*Rationis Societas*: Remarks on Kant and Hegel," in P. Rossi and M. Wreen (eds.), *Kant's Philosophy of Religion Reconsidered* (Bloomington, IN: Indiana University Press, 1991), pp. 191–205.

19.   The disposition to welcome anomaly as a means of extending our understanding amounts to a kind of xenophilia. That is, it amounts to a positive valuation of human difference as intrinsically interesting and therefore worthy of regard, and a disvaluation of conformity to one's honorific stereotypes as intrinsically uninteresting. It dismantles the assumption that there is any cause for self-congratulation or self-esteem in conforming to any stereotype at all, and represents anomalous others as opportunities for psychological growth rather than mere threats to psychological integrity. It implies an attitude of inquiry and curiosity rather than fear or suspicion, of receptivity rather than resistance toward others; and a belief that there is everything to be gained, and nothing to be protected, from exploration of another person's singularity. We often see this belief expressed in the behavior of very young children, who touch, poke, prod, probe, and question one another without inhibition, as though in knowledge of another there were nothing to fear. (Adrian Piper, "Xenophobia and Kantian Rationalism," in Robin Schott (ed.), *Feminist Interpretations of Immanuel Kant*, p. 66.)

Piper's sentiments here are fundamentally Kantian, but need to be supplemented or qualified in two respects. First, Kant's sober awareness of our unsociable sociability must qualify the childlike trustingness Piper seems to be recommending here. Kant is aware not only that a certain distance between ourselves and others is morally required by respect but that it is also necessitated by prudence. In our present social condition, xenophilia requires courage as well as curiosity and an absence of self-conceit. Second, if she had wanted to be clearer in repudiating some pernicious intellectual fashions, Piper could have emphasized that xenophilia does not love what is other or different merely in order to behold it in a sort of quietistic awe (exhibiting disrespect for our rational powers of comprehension). Kantian reason seeks out what is other in order to bring our own thoughts, feelings, and volitions into harmony with it under common principles having universal validity. The point of xenophilia is *not* to let each singularity overwhelm us with its sublime absurdity.

20. See Wilhelm Vossenkuhl, "Schönheit als Symbol der Sittlichkeit. Über die gemeinsame Wurzel von Ethik und Asthetik bei Kant," *Philosophisches Jahrbuch* 99 (1992) pp. 91–104; Paul Guyer, *Kant and the Experience of Freedom* (New York: Cambridge, 1992), especially Chapters 1 and 7.

21. For a good discussion of the social side of Kant's aesthetic theory, see Salim Kemal, *Kant and Fine Art: An Essay on Kant and the Philosophy of Fine Art and Culture* (Oxford: Clarendon, 1986), and Paul Guyer, *Kant and the Experience of Freedom*, Chapter 8.

22. Kant holds that a woman remains in a permanent condition of tutelage to her husband (or other male guardian) not as regards her capacity to think but as regards her capacity to represent her own rights and interests in the civil sphere (economically, legally, and politically). He does not deny that women have the natural capability to represent their own interests in public – he remarks (wryly and misogynistically) that they are perfectly *mündig* in the sense that they have quite enough *Mundwerk* to defend themselves (and even their husbands as well). But he argues that just as going to war is not a proper social role for a woman to assume, so it is also not fitting for women to engage in public transactions, go to court, or participate in politics (VA 7:209). He makes no attempt to determine how far the grounds for this judgment might be relative to (unjust, irrational, alterable, and reformable) social customs and prejudices.

23. Mill, *On Liberty*, ed. Elizabeth Rapaport (Indianapolis, IN: Hackett, 1978), p. 10. Unlike Mill, Kant *does* have an entirely nonconsequentialist theory of the innate individual right to freedom which is the ground of *other* kinds of individual rights, such as the rights to bodily integrity, property, civil equality and civil independence (TP 8:290–296, MS 6:237–238). Against that background, his treatment of freedom of communication is even more conspicuously consequentialist than Mill's.

24. Kant therefore prominently includes free use of the printed word not only among the forces that *promote* enlightenment but also among those that *resist* it. In 1786, immediately after the death of Frederick the Great, Kant warned the "enthusiastic" side of the famous "pantheism controversy" that if freedom of thought is misused – if enthusiasm is substituted for the self-regulation of rational thinking – then it surely would be forfeited (O 8:145). Probably the kind of forfeiture he had mainly in mind was forcible suppression by the authorities. But he also considered freedom of expression to be forfeited when its forms are retained but it is regularly used in such a way as to betray the hopes enlightened people place in it.

25. Kant does hold that it would be contrary to right to impose creeds or doctrines on people (as by binding a church forever to confess certain doctrines). But even here his thinking is consequentialist, for the argument is that it would be contradictory to suppose that an entire public would set policies preventing all future intellectual progress (TP 8:305; cf. WA 8:38).

26. J. G. Hamann, Letter to Christian Jacob Kraus, 18 December 1784. See James Schmidt (ed.), *What Is Enlightenment? Eighteenth Century Answers and Twentieth Century Questions* (Berkeley, CA: University of California Press, 1996), p. 148.

27. In the *Idea toward a Universal History*, Kant describes the problem of achieving a civil society which can administer justice universally – a problem whose solution itself depends on the peaceful external relation between states – as "both the most difficult and the last to be solved by the human species" (I 8:23). We might conclude from this that Kant sees "peace with justice", especially the achievement of a just political constitution, as the final end of humanity, the single focus of all reason's end-setting activity. Kant may have wanted to give that impression so as not to give the lie to Schultz's report that one of Kant's "favorite ideas" is that "the final end of the human race is the attainment of the most perfect political constitution" (Ak 8:468). But it would clearly be false to say of his philosophy of history as a whole that it represents any merely *political* goal as the final human end. Kant sees peace with justice as nothing more than the regulation of the "healthy hostility" between people, which is a necessary condition for the development of their species capacities during the epoch of nature (I 8:26). The ends of morality, however, are not limited to right or justice, which is the coercive protection of external freedom. Morality aims at the positive unification of all rational wills in a realm of ends. The importance of defining these ends explicitly accounts for Kant's preoccupation throughout his works with determining the idea of the highest good (*summum bonum*). More generally, it accounts for his emphasis on the vocation of philosophy as the doctrine of final human ends in an age of enlightenment.

28. The importance of this distinction was observed by Keith Ward, *The Development of Kant's View of Ethics* (Oxford: Clarendon Press, 1972), p. 139; it was argued for in detail by Yirmiyahu Yovel, *Kant and the Philosophy of History*, pp. 170–180.

29. It should not be supposed that Kant believes human beings are the only rational beings. Quite apart from supernatural beings (God, angels, or spirits, etc.), whose existence Kant thinks we can neither prove nor disprove on the basis of theoretical reason, there is also the distinct possibility of rational beings in other parts of nature, that is, intelligent life on heavenly bodies other than the earth. In *Universal Natural History and Theory of the Heavens*, Kant appears to think it highly probable that there are such beings on other bodies in our own solar system, and he even speculates about how they might differ from us (AN 2:351–368).

30. Compare Aristotle, *Nicomachean Ethics* I.7, 1097a27–1097b7, which develops the concept of a "final" (*teleion*) good. Thus the concept of a final end also differs from that of an "end in itself" as used in Kant's formula of humanity.

For you can treat a person as an end in itself while treating the person as a means, as long as you treat the person at the same time as an end (G 4:429).

31. See Christine Korsgaard, "Two Distinctions in Goodness," *Philosophical Review* 92 (1983), pp. 169–195, reprinted in *Creating the Kingdom of Ends*, Chapter 9.

32. This way of looking at the conditional value of happiness is really better suited to God than to human beings. For God might be in a position to know people's deserts and apportion suitable rewards or punishments, while we can know none of this, even about ourselves. From the human point of view, the conditional value of happiness means that happiness is good only insofar as its pursuit is morally permissible. The happiness I enjoy through the violation of another's rights or my duty is not a good. But any piece of my happiness that I make my end without violating any of my duties thereby becomes a good and has an objective claim on all rational beings. Kant never suggests that we ought to deprive ourselves (still less others) of some happiness, which is neither in itself impermissible nor requires the use of impermissible means, merely because the person in question is deemed unworthy of it. In one's own case, that would be the superstitious sacrifice of "self-torment" or penance, which Kant sees only as a false (and often all too easy) substitute for what morality really demands, namely the resolve to do better in the future (R 6:24, 172). In the case of another, it would directly violate the principle of our duties of love to others, which is always to make their (permissible) happiness our end. The principle under which Kant justifies the punishment of a person under criminal law is *not* that the worth of happiness is conditional on (inner) *moral* goodness of will, but rather that the imputability of an *external deed* makes its author liable to legal consequences under principles of *right* (MS 6:227).

33. Kant sometimes talks about the highest good as if each person were concerned only with her *own* morality and her own happiness (KpV 5:108–109, VpR 28:1072–1073). This may seem unattractively egoistic (or "individualistic"), as if Kant thinks I am interested in the highest good only insofar as it concerns me and nobody else. I suggest that we see it instead as an expression of the *noncomparative* character of self-worth in Kantian ethics. We should think exclusively about our own virtue and our own happiness because we should not be concerned to compare our virtue or our happiness with anyone else's. The formulation to which this note is appended deftly combines both the idea of the highest good as the good of a world and the idea of it as my worthiness and my happiness as a member of that world.

34. This misleading picture of the highest good was presented by John R. Silber, "The Copernican Revolution in Ethics: The Good Re-examined," in Wolff (ed.), *Kant: A Collection of Critical Essays* and "Kant's Conception of the Highest Good as Immanent and Transcendent," *Philosophical Review* 68 (1959). Thinking of the highest good in Silber's way leads naturally to Lewis White Beck's conclusions that the concept of the highest good has "no practical consequences" and the duty to seek it "does not exist" (Beck, *A Commentary on Kant's Critique of Practical Reason*, p. 245). Cf. Wood, *Kant's Moral Religion*, pp. 95–96. The most illuminating recent discussions of Kant's idea of the highest good are Stephen Engstrom, "The Concept of the Highest Good in

Kant's Moral Theory," *Philosophy and Phenomenological Research* 52 (1992), pp. 747–780; Engstrom, "Happiness and the Highest Good in Aristotle and Kant," in S. Engstrom and J. Whiting (eds.), *Aristotle, Kant and the Stoics*, pp.102–138; Paul Guyer, *Kant and the Experience of Freedom*, Chapter 9, § II, and Philip Rossi, "The Final End of All Things: The Highest Good as the Unity of Nature and Freedom," in P. Rossi and M. Wreen (eds.), *Kant's Philosophy of Religion Reconsidered* (Bloomington, IN: Indiana University Press, 1991), pp. 132–164. An extensive and insightful application of the idea of the highest good to many aspects of Kant's philosophy is found in Richard L. Velkley, *Freedom and the End of Reason*.

35. I have discussed these arguments at length in *Kant's Moral Religion* (Ithaca, NY: Cornell Press, 1970), Ch. 1–4; see also "Rational Theology, Moral Faith and Religion," in P. Guyer (ed.), *The Cambridge Companion to Kant*, pp. 401–405.

36. We have a wide duty to promote our own virtue, but Kant denies that we have a duty to promote the virtue of others according to *our* conception of virtue (MS 6:386). To the extent that we do promote the moral perfection of others, we should do it as a way of helping them promote ends that they themselves have set. Kant thus concludes that we should conceive this pursuit solely under the heading of their happiness (MS 6:388, 394). Kant's denial that the virtue of others is among the ends of morality prohibits moral paternalism, which would violate the respect we owe others by trying to coerce or manipulate them into acting as we think they should in cases where they have a right to direct their own lives. But this represents the pursuit of virtue only from the perspective of each person's *individual* ends. It is entirely consistent with it to hold that every human being has an ethical duty to join a *free and voluntary community* united by a *collective* moral end.

37. The following comments are presented as a Hegelian critique of Kantian morality, but they are actually quite a bit closer to Kant's position on the matter than Hegel's:

> Any universalistic morality is dependent upon a form of life that *meets it halfway*. There has to be a modicum of congruence between morality and the practices of socialization and education . . . In addition, there must be a modicum of fit between morality and sociopolitical institutions. Not just any institutions will do. Morality thrives only in an environment in which postconventional ideas about law and morality have already been institutionalized to a certain extent. (J. Habermas, "Morality and Ethical Life: Does Hegel's Critique of Kant Apply to Discourse Ethics?" in R. Beiner and J. Booth (eds.), *Kant and Political Philosophy*, p, 329.)

38. Kant obviously does not conceive this "family" after the legal model of "domestic right" he was to develop a few years later in the *Metaphysics of morals* (MS 6:276–285). For that was intended as an account of the family only insofar as it is an institution subject to coercive authority, but such authority is explicitly excluded from the ethical community.

39. We of course have a juridical duty, and consequently, an ethical duty, to leave the state of nature and join in a civil society under coercive laws of right (MS

6:311–313). Those who wish to enter into sexual relations have a juridical (hence an ethical) duty to belong to a family, and all of us as children should be born into families imposing juridical duties on us (MS 6:276–285). But these are ethical duties only consequent to juridical duties. And all membership in other societies or human relationships is entirely voluntary, not required by ethical duties. Friendship and religion are the only two kinds of social relationships into which we cannot rightfully be coerced but into which we have an ethical duty to enter.

40. Christianity is privileged in Kant's account in other ways, too. He even declares that Christianity is "grounded on an entirely new principle, effected a revolution in doctrines of faith" (R 6:127). Christianity is the only faith which is "represented as coming *from the mouth of its first teacher* not as a statutory but as a moral religion" (R 6:167, cf. 6:131). Although these assertions do accord Christianity a special place among ecclesiastical faiths, they are at the same time direct attacks on any privileged status which institutionalized Christianity may now try to claim. For they clearly allow that other faiths, though originally statutory rather than moral, might very well (subsequently) transform themselves into moral religion. They even more pointedly hint that since its founding Christianity has fallen away from the revolutionary principle which came "from the mouth of its first teacher." The ethical community is Christianity not only as it was idealized in the pietist tradition in which he was brought up but also as Kant would radically transform it under the ideals of Enlightenment rationalism. It is a church with no political constitution or ruling hierarchy (R 6:102, 152–153), no creeds or catechisms (R 6: 14, 102, 153), no statutory rites or service to God beyond morally good conduct (R 6:104–105, 149, 159–163, 170–175).

There is no reason to doubt that Kant's sincere conviction is being expressed in his statement that Christianity alone came into the world as a pure moral religion. But throughout the *Religion* he is also obviously writing for his Christian contemporaries, trying to persuade them that the transition he wants them to make from a "merely ecclesiastical faith" to a "religion of pure reason" will not be difficult and will be especially easy for Christians, preserving fundamental Christian doctrines and convictions. The *Religion* attempts to reinterpret many Christian doctrines by seeing them as ways of expressing the moral experiences of a rational agent. This intention is put misleadingly when it is said that Kant's aim is "to show that all statements of revealed religion, if they have any objective validity at all, are completely translatable – without remainder – into the concepts and expressions of rational ethics" (Denis Savage, "Kant's Rejection of Divine Revelation and his Theory of Radical Evil," in P. Rossi and M. Wreen (eds.), *Kant's Philosophy of Religion Reconsidered*, p. 74). The term "translation" suggests that Kant would expect believers in an ecclesiastical faith to retain nothing of their faith that could not be expressed ("without remainder") in the language of rational ethics. Still worse, it suggests also that he would prefer them to use the latter language in place of the more familiar language of the historical ecclesiastical faith. But Kant's intention (and even his practice in the *Religion* itself) are precisely the reverse of that. His aim is to show how doctrines of rational ethics, and even more the lived experience of rational agents working at their ethical vocation, do find felicitous expression in traditional religious doctrines and ways of speaking. There is also no attempt on Kant's part to deprive traditional believers even of the "remainder" of their doctrines that does not correspond to anything in rational ethics, as long as they acknowledge that it is ethically optional, something whose absence from other ecclesiastical faiths should not be condemned or viewed as a ground of superiority in one's own faith.

41. In fact, for religion it is not even necessary to believe in God's existence. "[For religion] no assertoric knowledge [even of God's existence] is required, . . . but only a *problematic* assumption (hypothesis) about the supreme cause of things as regards speculation." The only "assertoric faith" needed for religion is "merely the idea of God . . . only the minimum cognition (it is possible that there is a God) has to be subjectively sufficient" (R 6:153–154). Kant thinks moral arguments can show that belief in God harmonizes with a moral disposition that makes the highest good its end, but these arguments do not constitute theoretical proofs. The theoretical situation is simply that we can neither prove nor disprove the existence of God, and we should not exclude from the religion of reason anyone whose beliefs fall within the range of opinion compatible with the theoretical evidence. Consequently, he says that the "minimum of theology" needed for religion is not that God exists, but only that God is possible (VpR 28:998; R 6:153–154).

   Kant understands religion as a matter of moral disposition, not as theoretical cognition or even belief (KpV 5:129, KU 5:481, SF 7:36, VpR 28:998, 1078). The most we can say regarding duties as divine commands is that our concept of God is such that our doing our duties is something that accords with God's will and hence something God would command. We know that our concept of God has these features, because (Kant argues) the only rationally acceptable concept of God as a supremely perfect being is one that is based on our rational conception of the moral law. Any concept of God that contradicts a purely moral one (no matter what source it may have) is to be rejected.

   For further discussion of issues relating to reason and revelation in Kant, see Allen W. Wood, "Kant's Deism," in P. Rossi and M. Wreen (eds.), *Kant's Philosophy of Religion Reconsidered*, pp. 1–22, and Wood, "Rational Theology, Moral Faith and Religion," in P. Guyer (ed.), *The Cambridge Companion to Kant*, pp. 404–416. A contrasting view is extensively argued in John E. Hare, *The Moral Gap: Kantian Ethics, Human Limits and God's Assistance* (Oxford: Clarendon, 1996).

42. Regarding God as a moral legislator involves no retraction of Kant's position that the moral law obligates only because we impose it on ourselves through our reason (MS 6:227). It is not God's will, but only our own, which is conceived as the *author* of the moral law (the one whose will makes obedience to it obligatory). The divine will is rather the moral law's *legislator,* the one who makes a law *public* and (if punitive sanctions are associated with it), commands through the law by imposing the corresponding sanctions. Viewing moral duties as divine commands does not abrogate the principle of autonomy, but it does give the moral law a public status it could not otherwise have.

43. Kant's experience spreading his Enlightenment conception of religion among theology students is reported by his closest colleague in later years and his earliest biographer: "Many of these apostles went forth to teach the gospel of pure reason" (Reinhold Bernard Jachmann, *Immanuel Kant* (Königsberg: [No publisher listed], 1804), p. 34). When King Frederick William II, the religiously reactionary successor to Frederick the Great, attempted to turn back the clock by imposing censorship on teaching and preaching throughout Prussia (which included a letter reproving Kant for his religious teachings and forbidding him to write or lecture on religious topics), the attempt did not survive his death because the leaders of the established Lutheran church were more in sympathy with the King's targets than with the King, and the only people he could find to carry out his repression were marginal officials and clerics, generally regarded as ignorant fanatics. This is why J. C. Wöllner, Minister of Education in charge of administering the reactionary policies was soon out of office after Frederick William's death (he died in poverty). It is also why Kant was able to ignore (or slyly interpret away) the King's command, and his promise to obey it, almost as soon as Frederick William's corpse was cold. See my Introduction to Allen W. Wood and George di Giovanni (ed. and trans.) *Kant: Writings on Religion and Rational Theology* (New York: Cambridge, 1996), pp. xi–xxiv.

44. Iris Murdoch writes: "Stripped of the exiguous metaphysical background which Kant was prepared to allow [the moral agent], this man is with us still, free, independent, lonely, powerful, rational, responsible, brave, the hero of so many novels and books of moral philosophy" (*The Sovereignty of Good*, p. 80). By now it should be clear where Murdoch's picture goes wrong. Moral heroes as Kant views them are surely "free, rational, responsible and brave," but they are less "independent" than Murdoch thinks, and if they are "lonely," because "stripped" of the friendly support of a rational religious community, then they will surely not be "powerful" in the way Kant most cares about (namely, having the strength of moral virtue).

45. This idea is clearly expressed in Max Adler, *Das soziologische in Kants Erkenntniskritik* (Vienna: Volksbuchhandlung, 1924), especially pp. 342ff. Adler sees the community sought by working class socialism as fulfilling the role of the religious community in Kant's philosophy. Neo-Kantian socialists included some of the most famous names in the neo-Kantian movement, including Hermann Cohen, Karl Vorländer, and Paul Natorp. See Harry van der Linden, *Kantian Ethics and Socialism* (Indianapolis: Hackett, 1988), especially "Appendix: A Historical Note on Kantian Socialism," pp. 291–308. Van der Linden's own exposition of Kant, with its emphasis on the socialist implications of Kant's philosophy of history and the idea of the highest good, belongs to the same tradition.

CONCLUSION

1. This first announcement was in a letter to Herder of 9 May, 1768 :

> At present my vision is directed chiefly at recognizing the authentic determination and the limits of human capacities and inclinations, and I believe that I have succeeded in it as far as morals is concerned, so that I am now

working on a metaphysics of morals, where I imagine myself able to provide the evident and fruitful principles and also the method according to which the very wide ranging but for the most part still fruitless strivings of this species of cognition have to be directed, if they are ever to achieve anything of utility. (Ak 10:74)

Even earlier, in a letter to J. H. Lambert of 31st December, 1765, Kant wrote of his intention to write treatises on "the metaphysical first grounds of natural philosophy and metaphysical first grounds of practical philosophy" (Ak 10:57). The first part of the *Metaphysics of Morals*, The Doctrine of Right, was published in 1797, but the entire system did not appear until 1798.

2. The first scholar in recent times to give the *Metaphysics of Morals* its due was Mary Gregor, in her 1963 book *Laws of Freedom*. See also Bruce Aune, *Kant's Theory of Morals*, Chapters V–VI, and Alan Donagan, "The Structure of Kant's Metaphysics of Morals," *Topoi* 4 (1985), pp. 61–72.

3. In the phrase "right action" as it is used in Anglophone moral philosophy, "right" does not correspond to Kant's German term *recht* but probably corresponds most closely to his term *pflichtmäßig* ("in conformity with duty"). "Right" is really the only suitable translation for *Recht* (alternatives such as "justice" and "rights" (pl.) are no improvement, and these English words are needed to translate their more straightforward German equivalents *Gerechtigkeit* and *Rechte*, respectively). The basic problem is that English has no term corresponding to the Latin *ius*, which expresses the fundamental conception of all the Roman legal systems dominant on the continent of Europe. In any English translation of works dealing with this concept (such as the legal and political writings of Kant, Fichte, and Hegel), the reader must simply become accustomed to understanding the English word "right" in a sense equivalent to Latin *ius* = German *Recht* = French *droit* = Italian *diritto* = Spanish *derecho* = Polish *prawo*, Russian Pp6BbiH, Hungarian *jog*, etc. The defect, after all, is with us English speakers, since our poor language lacks any word designating this fundamental Western ethical and legal concept.

4. By a "system of right" we may think first of all of a political state or system of legal justice. The justification of a system of right (if the system is itself justly constituted) is what Kant thinks can be deduced from his theory of right, but in the first instance he regards the system of right as an "*a priori* construction" of the concept of equal external freedom under laws, which he regards as analogous to the construction of a mathematical concept in intuition (MS 6:232–233; cf. KrV A726–736/B754–764). The distinction between this *a priori* construction and an empirical legal system is fundamental to Kant's procedure in the Doctrine of Right, as well as his distinction between natural right and positive right (see Note 6).

5. Kant argues that it is an analytical proposition that an action that coercively prevents a violation of freedom under universal laws promotes freedom under universal laws and is therefore right (MS 6:231). If an act coerces someone, it may still be *right* because it may not violate a system protecting freedom according to universal law. This might happen, for example, if it lawfully prevents another from performing an act that is not right (and whose pre-

vention therefore increases rather than diminishes external freedom according to universal law).

6. The standard of right, though not an *ethical* standard, is still distinct from standards of positive law, and Kant therefore distinguishes *natural right* from *positive right* (MS 6:237). It is contrary to right for the state to use coercion in violation of natural right, even if that coercion is permitted by its positive laws. I am grateful to Sharon Byrd for pressing me to clarify this point.

7. I am grateful to Paul Guyer, Otfried Höffe, Georg Geismann, Bernd Ludwig, Thomas Pogge, and Robert Pippin for helping me to clarify my ideas about the independence of right and ethics. In conversation, Pippin has urged the following quotation as evidence against the thesis that for Kant right is independent of ethics:

> But why is the doctrine of morals usually called (especially by Cicero) a doctrine of *duties* and not a doctrine of *rights*, even though rights have reference to duties? – The reason is that we know our own freedom (from which all moral laws, and so all rights as well as duties proceed) only through the moral imperative, which is a proposition commanding duty, from which the capacity of putting others under obligation, that is, the concept of a right, can afterwards be explicated. (MS 6:239)

This remark, however, refers only to our knowledge of all duties through freedom and the derivability of the *concept* of a right from the *concept* of a duty (since every right correlates with some duty). The passage does say that the concept of a duty proceeds from the moral imperative, in the sense that it is from this imperative that we acquire the general concept of a duty (that general concept that is employed both in right and in ethics). It is obviously supposed to be consistent with this that even the *concept* of a juridical duty differs from the *concept* of an ethical duty in that the former abstracts from the incentive for fulfilling the duty, while the latter makes duty itself the incentive. If *this* is consistent with the passage, then it is surely also quite consistent with it that the *principle* of juridical duties should be distinct from and independent of the *principle* of ethical duties. Hence what is said in this passage neither asserts nor implies that the *principle* of right is *derived from* the *principle* of morality. Still less does it say (or imply) that juridical duties (even duties of natural right) are conceived only as a species of moral duty.

8. It is noteworthy that Kant does *not* say here that a nation of devils would be interested in solving the problem. Unlike Hobbes, Kant does not think that rational self-interest is a sufficient incentive to induce people to set up a just political order. The value we attach to right, therefore, is certainly dependent in his view on moral considerations. But this is independent of the principle of right, which tells us what right is, or the subsequent development of this principle that tells us what institutions need to be set up and which actions ought to be coercively sanctioned in the interests of right.

9. I owe the idea behind this formulation to Lara Denis.

10. This argument works only if Kant holds that the end of an action constitutes a determining ground or indispensable reason for doing it. Otherwise, it might be that the moral reason for doing an action is solely that it conforms

to some description (e.g., "keeping a promise" or "obeying God's command") that doesn't mention the end to be produced by the action. It might be that any such action has an end to be produced, but that end could be arbitrarily left up to us as long as our action otherwise conforms to the description under which it is morally required. From what Kant says in the *Groundwork*, and especially the second Critique, some readers may even think that this is his view. But clearly it is not. On the contrary, he thinks that if the moral principle itself does not determine the ends to be pursued in actions required by ethical duty, then those actions would not be sufficiently determined in the rational ground for performing them, because the end to be produced by an action is indispensable to that ground. Cf. Chapter 4, § 1.3.

11. Sidgwick, *Methods of Ethics*, p. 386.

12. Since "others" here means "other fully rational beings," the perfections we have a duty to promote in children must be regarded differently. Even with children Kant thinks we should not simply impose our concept of perfection (e.g., of what is morally right) on the child, but should instead develop the child's own powers to determine this, since those powers will be the sole source of the moral perfection the child will have as an adult (KpV 5:151–161, MS 6:477–484).

13. Sidgwick, *Methods of Ethics*, p. 386, Note 2.

14. The italicized phrase at the beginning of this sentence is an important qualification because the *fundamental principle* from which Kant derives ethical duties is by no means consequentialist. This underlines the importance of distinguishing the *basic principle* of an ethical theory from the *style of reasoning* it favors in deciding what to do. Kant's theory of ethical duties is consequentialist in its style of reasoning, but not in its fundamental principle. Consequentialist theories look much more plausible if we confuse these two things, for since the end always justifies the means (see Chapter 2, Note 1), in deciding what to do it is always reasonable to choose one's action with regard to its consequences for the ends one has set (and always unreasonable to proceed in any other way). But it is a separate question whether the fundamental principle we use in setting these ends ought itself to have a teleological or consequentialist form. In fact, for reasons presented in Chapter 5, § 1, to assume such a principle would be to make the very concept of categorical obligation unintelligible.

15. See Shelly Kagan, *Normative Ethics* (Boulder, CO: Westview, 1998), pp. 72–74.

16. The claim is not, of course, that this lie *fails to maximize* my perfection. The claim that lying is wrong because it involves an end contrary to my perfection can be true even if it turns out that I can maximize my perfection only by telling this lie. That would have to be a case in which we could maximize our achievement of an end only by acting against that end. This is a phenomenon familiar enough to consequentialists, since it is quite often brought against them as part of the charge that consequentialism is self-defeating. We will see presently that Kant's version of consequentialism does not involve certain maximizing or aggregative assumptions commonly assumed by the standard versions of consequentialism. His view is therefore not threatened by this kind of self-defeat.

17. Kant thinks about the ends that are at the same time duties in something like the way that Robert Adams thinks about goods when he maintains that "more of a good thing is not necessarily better." For example, children are good but a larger family is not necessarily better than a smaller one; it is good that people are happy, but it is not necessarily better to have more happy people than fewer (Adams, *Finite and Infinite Goods*, Chapter 4, § 4 and Chapter 5, § 1). For Kant, it is meritorious to make my end something (call it *X*) that will contribute to your happiness, even if I do not make my end (or even give the least thought to) what would make you even happier than getting just *X*.

18. Williams, *Moral Luck* (Cambridge: Cambridge University Press, 1981), p. 12. I am grateful to Lisa Rivera for thoughtful discussion of this issue.

19. See my article "The Final Form of Kant's Moral Philosophy," *Southern Journal of Philosophy*, Volume XXXVI Supplement (1997), pp. 9–10.

20. For an antidote to the common view, see Robert B. Louden, "Kant's Virtue Ethics," *Philosophy* 61 (1986).

21. See Lewis White Beck, *A Commentary on Kant's Critique of Practical Reason*, pp. 227–229.

22. It follows that the possession of virtue (in general) cannot itself be a duty. Like respect, love of human beings and the other feelings through which reason operates on us, virtue is a presupposition of moral agency. Virtue as strength can be measured only in relation to the moral obstacles (vices, contrary inclinations or defects of temperament) which it must overcome (MS 6:405).

23. Thus people are misled when, misreading and overemphasizing Kant's expository strategy in the First Section of the *Groundwork*, they conclude that Kantian ethical theory is grounded on the concept of the *good will*. On the contrary, the fundamental *value* recognized by Kantian ethics is that of *humanity as an end in itself*, it grounds the *authority* of the moral law on *autonomy of the will*, and it grounds its *theory of ethical duties* on the concept of *virtue*. All three of these grounding conceptions are distinct from that of the good will, which is on the contrary grounded in diverse ways on them. Virtue is not the same as goodness of will (MS 6:408). The good will is good on account of the *dutifulness* of its maxims (G 4:399) but virtuous on account of their *strength* in fulfilling duty (MS 6:394). A person who has virtue (as the moral *capacity* to overcome vices and inclinations) may not do so because they lack good will (this would be "depravity," the highest and most explicit degree of evil). Conversely, a person with a good will might be too (morally) weak to overcome affects or inclinations (this is the basis of the will's "frailty"). See Chapter 9, § 1.2.

24. On Kant's theory, then, there seem as many possible virtues as there are obligatory ends, and we can discriminate virtues as finely as we can discriminate such ends. Thus a virtue might consist in the strength of one's commitment to the happiness of other human beings in general or to a particular way of promoting the happiness of some human beings (one's devotion to a particular good cause) or to a particular person (as Long John Silver's respect and affection for Jim Hawkins was his one redeeming virtue).

25. MacIntyre, *After Virtue*, p. 149. Compare Leslie Mulholland, *Kant's System of Rights* (New York: Columbia University Press, 1990), pp. 165–166.

26. Virtue for Aristotle is a state (*hexis*) having to do with rational choice or decision (*prohairesis*) (*Nicomachean Ethics* II.6, 1106b37, cf. III.2, 1111b5–7). So it is not clear that he would agree with MacIntyre in regarding virtuous action as produced by inclination (*empirical* desire). For a convincing argument that Aristotle values acting for the sake of the fine (*kalon*) in something like the way Kant values acting from duty, see Jennifer Whiting, "Self-Love and Authoritative Virtue: Prolegomenon to a Kantian Reading of *Eudemian Ethics* viii 3" in S. Engstrom and J. Whiting (eds.), *Aristotle, Kant and the Stoics*, pp. 162–202. Of course, Aristotle does want virtues *also* to be dispositions to feeling (1105b26) perhaps even dispositions to *empirical* feeling and *empirical* desire. In that case, it is not clear that he can consistently have everything he wants, since empirical feelings and desires are not rationally chosen. See L. A. Kosman, "Being Properly Affected: Virtues and Feelings in Aristotle's Ethics" in Amélie O. Rorty (ed.), *Essays on Aristotle's Ethics* (Berkeley, CA: University of California Press, 1980), pp. 103–116. At best, Aristotle may be including under "virtue" a somewhat heterogeneous collection of morally desirable features of a person which Kant has good reasons to want to keep distinct: for example, traits of *character* (strong commitment of the will to rational ends) and of *temperament* (the presence of feelings and desires that make it easier to pursue those ends). To the extent that "cultivation of the virtues" refers to the latter, Kant thinks it is a misnomer to call it "virtue." It is to be sure something that virtuously disposed people will try to bring about in themselves. But to the extent that dutiful conduct is to be attributed to such a happy temperament (whether inborn or cultivated), Kant would not regard the conduct as *virtuous* (deserving of *esteem* or possessing *inner worth*) but only as *praiseworthy*, and grounds for *congratulating* the person on their good fortune or on their success in achieving that happy temperament (or perhaps, depending on the case, for praising and congratulating those who succeeded in cultivating it in them).

27. Aristotle, *Nicomachean Ethics* II.1–3.

28. Aristotle, *Nicomachean Ethics* II.3, 1104b3–1105a17.

29. Kant speaks in one place of cheerfulness and joyousness as "the *aesthetic* constitution, the *temperament*, as it were, of virtue" (R 6:24). Here Kant means only that a person whose commitment to good ends is strong will pursue them joyfully and cheerfully, not reluctantly and begrudgingly. In a virtuous person this commitment is due to reason, and these "aesthetic" effects of it are due to the effects of reason on sensibility. They are not merely the empirical effects of one's (innate or acquired) temperament.

30. A few representatives of "virtue ethics" are: G.E.M. Anscombe, "Modern Moral Philosophy," *Philosophical Review* 33 (1958), Bernard Mayo, *Ethics and the Moral Life* (London: Macmillan, 1958), Lawrence Becker, "The Neglect of Virtue," *Ethics* 85 (1975), James Wallace, *Virtues and Vices* (Ithaca, NY: Cornell Press, 1978), John McDowell, "Virtue and Reason," *Monist* 62 (1979), Lawrence Blum, *Friendship, Altruism and Morality* (London: Routledge and Kegan Paul, 1980), Alasdair MacIntyre, *After Virtue*, Bernard Williams, *Ethics and the Limits of Philosophy* (Cambridge, MA; Harvard University Press, 1985), Christina Hoff Sommers, *Vice and Virtues in Everyday Life* (New York: Harcourt

Brace Jovanovich, 1985). Such people often say that ethics should be concerned less with what people *do*, and its conformity or nonconformity to
moral principles, than with what people *are*, their traits and dispositions. In
this connection they often insist on the way good traits of character, trained
into agents not by the learning of rules but through the education of their
perceptions and feelings, provide them with the ability to make the right
judgments about individual situations. At the same time, advocates of 'virtue
ethics' often pride themselves on taking greater account of the *social* nature
of morality, in contrast to what they see as the individualistic orientation of
moral theories that concern themselves with the deliberation of individual
agents about particular actions. This is in part an attempt to ground morality in the empirical details of social traditions, but also a belief in the importance of the observer's and moral judge's standpoint on actions, as distinct
from the standpoint of the deliberating agent. The sentimental empiricism
of virtue ethics usually makes it critical of Kant's emphasis on the motive of
duty and his denial of moral worth to empirical motives such as sympathy.

31. The importance of the irreducibility of judgment for politics in particular,
and the Kantian sources of the idea of this irreducibility, are emphasized and
explored by Peter Steinberger, *The Concept of Political Judgment* (Chicago: University of Chicago Press, 1993). An adventurous attempt to build an entire
"Kantian" political philosophy on his theory of aesthetic judgment was of
course made by Hannah Arendt in her posthumously published *Lectures on
Kant's Political Philosophy*, edited by Ronald Beiner (Chicago: University of
Chicago Press, 1982).

32. Those who think the feelings and intuitions of women are necessarily more
reliable than those of men in such times of change show themselves to be unattractively bigoted and deeply deluded. For a good critical discussion of
feminist positions that are vulnerable to this charge, see Marcia Baron, "Kantian Ethics and the Claims of Detachment," in Schott (ed.), *Feminist Interpretations of Immanuel Kant*, pp. 145–170.

Julia Annas praises Plato's system of moral education in the *Republic*:

> Plato suggests that we develop in young children attitudes of attraction to
> what they will later learn to be morally good and repulsion to what they will
> later learn to be morally bad. [In this way], they will learn that it is ugly and
> that people who do it are horrible, and later appreciate that it is wrong. If
> this process is successful, then instead of having a baffled and resentful
> attitude toward morality, they will 'greet reason as a friend': morality will
> be to them a comprehensible extension and reinforcement of the attitudes
> that are familiar to them already. (Julia Annas, *Introduction to Plato's Repub-
> lic* (Oxford: Clarendon, 1981), p. 84.)

However, as Annas also later observes, such a moral education also makes it
more difficult to criticize and correct the moral principles one is taught. She
therefore thinks it consorts well with Plato's view that most members of the
state should never develop the habit of questioning their moral beliefs, and
with the fact that Plato apparently cares mainly about whether people's moral
convictions are true and well-established, placing no value at all in their

having been arrived at by their own choice and their own thinking, based on good reasons *they* have come to appreciate. Further, she points out that this method of moral education even creates internal problems for Plato regarding the philosopher-rulers. For it is part of their job to discover moral truth and know the reasons for moral rules, for which they need critical capacities of rational inquiry. Annas is right to wonder how Plato expects them to acquire these capacities if they are given the kind of moral education he recommends (see *Introduction to Plato's Republic,* pp. 85–92).

33. See Michael Hardimon, *The Project of Reconciliation: Hegel's Social Philosophy* (Cambridge: Cambridge University Press, 1995).

34. For a thoughtful discussion of this problem, see G.A. Cohen. "Are freedom and equality compatible?" in J. Elster and K.O. Moene (eds.), *Alternatives to Capitalism* (Cambridge: Cambridge University Press, 1993), pp. 113–126.

INDEX

Abbreviations: All abbreviations of works cited, notations, and the table of duties of virtue are summarized on pages xvi–xxiii.

a priori, xiv, 10–11 55–60, 240, 401–402
abortion, 370–371
Adam and Eve, 126, 132–133, 235–244
Adams, Robert M., 373–374, 375–376, 415
addiction (*Sucht*), 253, 284
Adler, Max, 411
affect (*Affekt*), 52, 251–252
affinity, law of, 216
Africans, 3, 299–300, 339
agricultural economy, 244–249, 392
Allison, Henry, 51, 171, 287, 344, 347, 355, 379, 383, 402
ambition (*Ehrsucht*), 253, 262–265, 394
    as root of all evil, 289–290
    failed, 264–265, 275, 400
American Dream, 267
amour-propre, 291; *see also* self-conceit
analytic procedure, 19
Anderson, Elizabeth, 369
Anderson-Gold, Sharon, 287, 402
anger, 252
animal rationale/rationabilis, 199

animality (*Tierheit*), predisposition, 118, 324, 402
animals, 117, 124, 140, 231, 236, 241, 243, 347, 391, 396
Annas, Julia, 345, 417–418
Anscombe, G. E. M., 373, 416
antagonism, social, 213–215, 244–249, 254, 274–275, 293, 296; *see also* unsociable sociability
anthropology, 8–11, 14, 36, 180–182, 193–207, 287–289, 291, 382–387
    practical, 193–196, 383–384, 387
    pragmatic, 202–207, 387
anthropophobia (*Anthropophobie, Leutescheuen*), 274, 282
Antigone, 385
anxiety (*Angst*), 235–236
apathy, 252
Apel, Karl-Otto, 381
approval, 27, 30–33, 239, 304
Arendt, Hannah, 389, 402, 417
Aristotle, 18–19, 151, 162, 310, 330–331, 338, 366, 390, 406–407
    on friendship, 275–282, 389–399
    on virtue, 330–331, 416

arrogance (*Übermut, arrogantia*), 21,
    241, 262, 324; *see also* ambition;
    haughtiness; self-conceit
asceticism, 251
Asians, 3, 299–300, 339
Augustine, 56
Aune, Bruce, 355, 360, 364, 412
authority, 130
autonomy, 37, 81, 156–165, 239,
    305, 316, 335, 373–376, 410;
    see also Formula of Autonomy
Auxter, Thomas, 350, 369, 388
avarice (*Geiz*), 140–141, 261–262,
    266, 324
Averroes (ibn Rushd), 232–233, 390

Baier, Annette, 341
Baron, Marcia, 33, 344, 345, 396,
    397, 398, 417
Baumgarten, Alexander Gottlieb,
    197, 386
Baumgartner, Hans-Michael, xv
beauty (*Schönheit*), 198, 303–305,
    393
    empirical and intellectual interest
    in, 304–305
Beauvoir, Simone, 396–397
Beck, Lewis White, 189, 347, 350,
    357, 361, 379, 382, 383, 393,
    407, 415
Becker, Lawrence, 416
Beethoven, Ludwig van, 386–387
Beiser, Frederick C., 388
beneficence (*Wohltun, Wohltätigkeit*),
    8, 28, 30–31, 35–40, 45–46,
    91–97, 100–102, 149–150, 168,
    273–274, 324, 357, 371; *see also*
    duty of beneficence
benevolence (*Wohlwollen*), 271, 278,
    334; *see also* beneficence; love;
    philanthropy
    mutual, 276
biology, 208, 215–225, 338

blade of grass (*Grashalm*), 222
Blum, Lawrence, 416
Borgia, Cesare, 233
Boyd, Richard, 374–375
Brandt, Reinhard, 339, 386, 387
Brandt, Richard, 388
Brender, Natalie, 397
Briest, Effi, 345
Brown, Deborah, 398–399
brutes, *see* animals
Burke, Edmund, 198
Byrd, Sharon B., 413

CC test, *see* universalizability, con-
    tradiction in conception (CC)
    test for
CI, xx, 78, 165
CW test, *see* universalizability, con-
    tradiction in volition (CW) test
    for
CI-procedure, 337, 374
Cain and Abel, 245–247
capitalism, xiv–xv, 37, 170, 273, 335,
    418; *see also* American Dream;
    injustice, general; market
Cassirer, Ernst, 342
casuistry, 151, 332–333; *see also* judg-
    ment, practical
categorical imperative, *see* impera-
    tives, categorical
categories of quantity, 185–186
Cato, 372
causality, 172–182, 215–216, 289
Cavallar, Georg, 341
Chalmers, David, 382
character (*Charakter*), 46, 203, 205,
    331–333, 416
charity (*Gütigkeit*), 269, 273–274,
    281, 334
children, 144, 151, 292–293, 305,
    332, 370, 403–404, 414
Christianity, 29, 145, 291, 317–318,
    368, 376, 390, 403, 409–410

church, *see* ecclesiastical faith; ethical community; religion

Cicero, 413

civil society, 246–249, 391; *see also* constitution, political; right; state, political

civilization, 9, 226–233, 244–249, 265–269, 291–309, 342

clockwork trains, 105–106, 360

clothing, 239, 262

coercion, *see* constraint; right

Cohen, G. A., 354, 391, 418

Cohen, Hermann, 411

Cold War, 385

colonialism, 7, 297, 299–300

commercial spirit, 297

common rational moral cognition (*gemeine sittliche Vernunfterkenntnis*), 17–20

common sense (*sensus communis*), 303–304

common sense, moral, *see* common rational moral cognition

communication, 277, 280, 282, 300–309, 336

freedom of, 302, 306–309, 405–406

communism, 139, 319–320

community (*Gemeinschaft, gemeine Wesen*), 335; *see also* ends, shared; ethical community; individualism; realm of ends

compatibilism, 174–182

competition, 169–170, 213–215; *see also* unsociable sociability

complete determination (*durchgängige Bestimmung*), 184–185

conscience (*Gewissen*), 38

consequentialism, 41–42, 91–92, 154–155, 306–309, 326–328, 357–358, 405–406, 414

consistency, 84, 107–108, 302–303, 374

Constant, Benjamin, 385

constitution
political, 208–209, 214, 231, 297–298, 315, 318, 406
republican, 6, 261, 297, 323, 392

constraint, 42–44, 57–58; *see also* right

constructive engagement, 385

contempt (*Verachtung*), 140, 324

continuity, law of, 216

contradiction in conception (CC) test, *see* universalizability, contradiction in conception (CC) test for

contradiction in volition (CW) test, *see* universalizability, contradiction in volition (CW) test for

convenience killing, 99–100

conversion, moral, 314–317, 320

Cooper, John, 399

Correspondence Thesis, 84, 97–100, 325, 358–360

cosmopolitanism, 199, 204, 208, 298, 302, 317, 336, 386–387

courage (*Mut*), 19, 21–22, 24, 252, 305

creed, religious, 315, 406

Creon, 385

cruelty (*Grausamkeit*), 265, 270

Crusius, Christian August, 160

Cudworth, Ralph, 353

culture (*Kultur*), 303–305, 309
of discipline, 310, 321; *see also* civilization
of skill, 310, 321

Curtius, 372

custom (*Sitte*), 119, 160, 239–240, 295, 314; *see also* decorum; fashion; habit; morality, origin of; propriety

Cynicism, 215

Dancy, Johathan, 151, 371–372

Darwall, Stephen, 156, 353, 373

Darwin, Charles, 86, 207, 222–
    225
Darwinism, social, 225
David-Menard, Monique, 396
Davidson, Donald, 173
death penalty, 2, 370
death, fear of, 236; *see also* fear
deception, 83, 182, 265–269, 334;
    see also delusion; lying; self-
    deception
  permissible, 268–269, 397
decorum (*Anständigkeit*), 240
defamation (*Afterreden*), 141, 324
definition, 386
deism, 410
delusion (*Wahn*), 261–262, 263,
    266–268
Denis, Lara, 338, 413
deontology, 114, 413–414
deposits, 89–90
depravity (*Bösartigkeit*), 285–286
Descartes, René, 56, 347
desire (*Begierde*), 29, 37, 50, 53,
    64–65, 73, 128, 142, 235–237,
    238, 239–240, 295, 348
  faculty of (*Begehrungsvermögen*),
    50–60
  natural, 250–253
despotism, 161
Dewey, John, 340–341
dictionaries, 362
Diderot, Denis, 393
Dietrichson, Paul, 344, 358
dignity (*Würde*), xiv, 37, 115–118,
    143–144, 195, 240–242, 263,
    301, 334, 353, 368–369, 389–
    390
Diogenes Laertius, 399
discontent, 212–213, 230, 237, 242–
    244, 254
disposition (*Gesinnung*), 314, 330
  friendship of, 275–282
  moral, 278, 410

dissent, political, 307–308
dissimulation, *see* deception; lying;
    self-deception
distrust, *see* trust
divine service, 315
domination, 267; *see also* power;
    tyranny
Donagan, Alan, 363, 366, 368–369,
    371, 378, 388, 412
drunkenness, 140, 324
duelling, 370
Dumarsais, César Chesneau, 393
Duncan, A. R. C., 343
Dupré, Louis, 389
duties, of virtue, 195, 323–329,
    353–354
  derivation of, 97–100, 139–141,
    194–195, 383–384
  ethical, 139–141, 317, 408–409
  juridical, 44, 99, 140, 322, 325,
    327, 408–409
  meritorious, 44; *see also* merit
  metaphysical/special, 196, 324–
    325, 328, 385–386
  of friendship, 280–281
  of love/of respect toward others,
    44, 324
  perfect/imperfect, 44, 82–100,
    324–325
  strict/wide, 44, 324–325
  taxonomy of, xxiii, 97–100, 193–
    196, 324–325
  to or toward (*gegen*) someone,
    144, 324–325
  to pursue the highest good,
    313
  to join the ethical community,
    313–320
  toward God, 317
  toward oneself/toward others,
    324–325
  toward oneself as animal being,
    140–147–148, 324

toward oneself as moral being,
140–141, 324
to pursue the highest good, 313
duty (*Pflicht*), 10–11, 45, 270
acting from (*aus Pflicht*), 26–40,
274, 277, 363
conformity with (*pflichtmäßig*), 27,
412
determination of, 34
of beneficence, 100, 140, 324,
326, 353–354, 358–359, 407;
see also beneficence
of self-perfection, 300, 324, 326,
353–354, 408, 414
Dworkin, Andrea, 259, 396

Ebbinghaus, Julius, 341
ecclesiastical faith, 409–410
education, 203, 233, 314, 403–404
moral, 151, 332–333, 416–418
egoism, 301–302, 374, 394, 407
Elohim, 228, 236, 389
emotion (*Rührung*), 3, 121–122,
243, 393; *see also* feeling
empiricism, 201, 250, 348, 387
end in itself, 85, 114–115, 117–118,
133–135, 142, 301, 353, 415;
see also dignity; Formula of
Humanity
end justifies the means, 346–347
end (*Zweck*), 51–55, 61–65, 111–
118, 127–128, 235
existent, 115–118, 124; 362–
363
final, 309–311, 313
ends
moral, 195, 214–215; 309–313,
325–329, 353–354, 383–384;
see also duties, of virtue
natural, 85, 214–215, 217–225,
254, 276, 282, 289, 357; *see also*
judgment, teleological; teleology, natural

realm of, *see* Formula of the Realm
of Ends; realm of ends
shared, 148–149, 153, 165–170,
279–282, 298, 313–320, 336,
408
system of, 310–311, 366–367; *see*
also realm of ends
to be effected, 115, 142
ultimate, 309–310, 366–367
Engels, Friedrich, 246, 391
Engstrom, Stephen, 19, 343, 407–408
Enlightenment (*Aufklärung*), the, xv,
1–5, 10, 14, 59–60, 151, 181,
208, 226–233, 291, 316, 317,
319, 342, 409, 411
enlightenment (*Aufklärung*), 10,
283, 298, 300–309, 331, 336,
390, 405, 406
enthusiasm (*Schwärmerei*), 201, 250,
387
envy (*Neid*), 264, 268, 275, 288–290,
324, 400
Epicurus, 160, 215
equality, xiv, 5–9, 121, 132–139, 241,
254, 273, 274, 279, 281, 335,
368–369, 396
eros, 121, 272
erotetic method, 151
esteem (*Hochschätzung*), 27, 30–33,
45, 272, 363; *see also* self-esteem
ethical community (*ethisches gemeinen*
Wesen), 283, 315–320, 332,
408–410
ethics (*Ethik*), 321–333; *see also*
morality
history of, 3–4
of disposition/of responsibility, 385
eudaemonism, 160, 162; *see also*
happiness
evil (*Böse*), xv, 211, 230, 237, 273,
314, 342
as social product, 286–292
degrees of, 285–286

evil (*Böse*) (*cont.*)
  for evil's sake, 400–41
  proof of, 286–289, 402
  radical, 283–293, 334, 400–403
  struggle against, 300, 309–320
evolution, 222–225
exceptions to moral rules, 151, 350;
  see also casuistry
existentialism, 373
exploitation, 257, 335, 395
Eze, Emmanuel Chukwudi, 339

FA, *see* Formula of Autonomy
FG, *see* moral law, universal formula of
FH, *see* Formula of Humanity as End
  in Itself
FK, *see* moral law, universal formula of
FLN, *see* Formula of the Law of
  Nature
FM, *see* moral law, universal formula of
FRE, *see* Formula of the Realm of
  Ends
FUL, *see* Formula of Universal Law
Fackenheim, Emil, 371, 389, 391,
  403
fact of reason (*Faktum der Vernunft*),
  171–172
faith, 376
  moral, 313, 410
Falk, W. D., 341–342, 348, 351
Falkenstein, Lorne, 349
Fall, myth of, 235–244
Falstaff, Sir John, 369
family, 154, 316, 391, 408–409; *see
  also* marriage
fashion, *see* vanity
fatalism, 177–180, 381
Faust, 403
Favorinus, 399
fear, 161, 236 252, 260–261, 290,
  322, 397
federation of nations (*Völkerbund*),
  214, 297–298

feeling (*Gefühl*), 121–122, 220, 237,
  243, 280–281, 393
  moral, 38, 46–48, 160, 252, 304,
  393
Feldman, Fred, 358, 360
fetishism of commodities, 262
Fichte, Johann Gottlieb, 337, 378,
  412
Fielding, Henry, 199
final cause, *see* ends, natural; judgment, teleological; teleology,
  natural
FitzPatrick, William, 355
flattery (*Schmeichelei*), 264–265, 268
Flitcraft, Hildreth Milton, 102–105
flood, biblical story of, 247–248, 391
Fontane, Theodor, 345
Fontenelle, Bertrand Jouvenel, 136
Foot, Philippa, 10, 324, 352
formal principle, 111–114, 361
formalism, 3, 47–49, 76–78, 250
Formula of Autonomy (FA), xx, 18,
  19, 75, 81–82, 156–190, 364,
  373–383
  application of, *see* Formula of the
  Realm of Ends (FRE)
  derivation of, 158–159
  distinguished from FUL, 164–165
Formula of Humanity as End In Itself (FH), xx, 18, 37, 72, 75,
  81–82, 111–155, 167, 183–190,
  288, 325, 353, 356, 360–373
  application of, 139–155
  derivation of, 124–132; *see also*
  dignity; end in itself; humanity
Formula of the Law of Nature (FLN)
  xix, 17, 76–110, 167, 325, 355–
  360, 383
  derivation, 78–82; *see also* universalizability
Formula of the Realm of Ends (FRE)
  xx, 18, 82, 110, 163, 165–170,
  288, 325, 364, 376–377

application of, 167–170
derivation of, 166–167; *see also*
    ends, shared; ends, system of;
    realm of ends
Formula of Universal Law (FUL);
    xiii–xiv, xix, 5, 17, 47–49, 74,
    76–110, 142, 164–165, 167,
    183–190, 288, 325, 333, 355–
    360, 383
    application of, 79–80
    derivation of, 74–75, 78–82
    distinguished from FA, 164–165
    distinguished from FLN, 79–80
    problems with, 97–107; *see also*
        universalizability
Forster, Georg, 338
Forster, Michael, 390
fortune, gifts of (*Glücksgaben*), 21–26
Foucault, Michel, 342
frailty (*Gebrechlichkeit*), 285–286, 401
Frankl, Viktor Emil, 371
Frederick the Great (King Friedrich
    II of Prussia), 308, 372, 405,
    411
Frederick William II (King Friedrich
    Wilhelm II of Prussia), 411
free riding, 108, 360
freedom (*Freiheit*), xxi, 3, 126, 171–
    182, 201–202, 206, 234–238,
    242, 251, 267, 335, 364–366,
    379–381, 387, 405
    as passion, 253–256, 402
    civil, 306–309; *see also* right
    epoch of, 296–298, 321, 325, 406
    innate right to, 140, 323
    negative sense, 119, 172, 235–236
    positive sense, 172
    practical, 172
    to communicate, 302, 306–309
    transcendental, 3, 132, 172; *see
        also* autonomy
French Revolution, 6, 385
Freud, Sigmund, 202, 380–381

friendship (*Freundschaft*), xiv, 14, 95,
    267, 269, 275–282, 316, 398–
    399, 408–409
    as ethical duty, 280
    limits of, 281–282
    of disposition or sentiment (*Gesin-
        nung, Sentiment*), 275–282
    of need, 275–276
    of taste, 275–276
    moral, 276–277, 281
Fukuyama, Francis, 391

Galston, William, 389
Garve, Christian, 11, 342–343
Gauthier, David, 388
Geismann, Georg, 413
Gellert, Christian Furchtegott, 201
gender, 205; *see also* homosexuality;
    men; sex; women
general will (*allgemeine Wille, volonté
    generale*), 249, 377
Genesis history, 126, 132–133, 227–
    249
geography, physical, 181, 387
germ (*Keim*), 211, 338
Gerresheim, Eduard, xv
Gewirth, Alan, 367–368, 388
Gibbard, Allan, 151, 346, 388
gloating (*Schadenfreude*), 141, 265,
    275, 288, 324
glory, 161, 394; *see also* self-conceit
gluttony (*Völlerei*), 140, 324, 402
God, 133, 160–163, 210, 215, 218,
    219, 227–228, 230, 232, 234,
    241, 247, 289, 291–292, 313,
    315, 317–320, 368, 389–390,
    406, 410, 414; *see also*
    providence
    voice of, 234, 242
Goethe, Johann Wolfgang, 403
good (*Gut*), 127–132, 343–344
    complete (*vollendete Gut*), 312; *see
        also* highest good

good (*Gut*) (*cont.*)
  conditional/unconditional, 21–26, 312
  final, 312, 406–407
  instrumental, 312
  intrinsic/extrinsic, 312
  limited/unlimited, 21–26
  ultimate, 114–116, 361–362
good will, 3, 20–40, 54–55, 120, 133, 274, 276, 311–312, 343–344, 415
Gould, Stephen Jay, 223, 388
gout-sufferer, *see* podagrist
grace, divine, 376
  realm of, 376–377
gratitude (*Dankbarkeit*), 140, 268, 282, 324; *see also* ingratitude
greed (*Habsucht*), 253, 261–262, 289–290
Green, Thomas Hill, 67, 352
Gregor, Mary, 194–195, 346, 383–384, 385, 412
grief, 252
ground project, 329
grudging help, 37
grudgingness (*Mißgunst*), 264
Guevara, Daniel, 345
guilt feelings, 390–391
Guyer, Paul, xvi, 383, 393, 405, 413

Habermas, Jürgen, 302, 372, 374, 375, 381, 408
habit (*Gewohnheit, habitus, assuetudo*), 50, 52, 199–200, 330–331
Haezrahi, Pepita, 353, 366, 367, 371
Haller, Rudolf, 402
Haller, Viktor Albrecht, 201
Hamann, Johann Georg, 226, 308, 387, 406
Hamlet, 268–269, 397
happiness (*Glückseligkeit*), xiv, 19, 21–22, 24, 28, 42, 54, 65–70,

76, 91, 128, 140, 168, 228–233, 243–244, 254, 260, 271, 279–280, 311–313, 369, 377–378, 389–390, 393, 407
Hardimon, Michael, 418
Hare, John E., 410
Hare, Richard M., 166, 375, 377
Harman, Gilbert, 355
Harrison, Jonathan, 355
hatred (*Haß*), 265, 272
  of the moral law, 29
  reactive (*Gegenhaß*), 265
haughtiness (*Hochmut, superbia*), 263–265
Hawkins, Jim, 415
Hegel, G. W. F., xiii, 82, 84, 89–90, 225, 232, 240, 246, 250, 334, 337, 342, 356, 357, 359, 360, 377, 379, 380, 390, 391–392, 396, 408, 412, 418
Helvetius, Claude-Adrien, 214
Henrich, Dieter, 379
Henson, Richard, 345
Herbert, Maria von, 397
Herder, Johann Gottfried, xix, 9, 14, 212, 226–233, 236–238, 254–255, 292, 299–300, 339, 387, 388–390, 411
Herman, Barbara, 99–101, 345, 355, 358, 360, 396
Herz, Marcus, 197, 386
heteronomy, 159–163
highest good (*höchste Gut, summum bonum*), 311–313, 406, 407
Hill, Thomas, Jr., 135, 350, 345, 369–370, 369, 373, 384, 385
Hinduism, 403
Hinske, Norbert, 351, 386
Hippel, Theodor Gottlieb, 340
historical materialism, 14, 337–338, 391–393
history, 8–11, 60, 139, 181, 207–215, 224–225, 226–233, 292–298,

311, 316, 333, 335, 342,
387–393, 406
idea of, 208–215
pragmatic, 204
Hobbes, Thomas, 255, 393–395,
413
Höffe, Otfried, 413
Hogan, Desmond, 359
Holmes, Stephen, 385
holy will, *see* will, holy
homogeneity, law of, 216
homosexuality, 2, 145, 338
honeste vive, 140
Honnefelder, Ludger, xvi, 371
honor (*Ehre*), 23, 24, 263, 266, 290
love of (*Ehrliebe*), 263; *see also* ambition; self-conceit
human nature, *see* anthropology
indefinability of, 198–200
humanity (*Humanität*), 233
humanity (*Menschheit*), 77, 140, 154
as predisposition, 118–122, 364–366
Hume, David, 32, 47, 57, 77, 199,
204, 215, 348, 355, 371, 387
humility (*Demut*), 133–135, 136,
265, 368
false, 265
hunter-gatherers, 244–246, 255,
392
Hutcheson, Francis, 12, 32, 47, 128,
160
hypocrisy (*Heuchelei*), 264–265, 268

idea (*Idee*), 157–158, 208–210, 230,
392, 406
idealism, transcendental, 173–182
idolatry, 363
imperatives, 61, 348–349
analytic, 62–63, 350–351
assertoric, 65
categorical, 61, 70–78, 156–163,
349–350, 384

deduction of, 171–182; *see also*
moral law
imperatives, hypothetical, xxi, 60–65, 78, 115, 350–351
pragmatic, 65
problematical, 351
synthetic, 71
technical, 63, 351
impulse (*Antrieb*), 48, 50
impurity (*Unlauterkeit*), 34, 285–286,
401
incentive (*Triebfeder*), 28, 31–35, 51,
111–113, 143, 201, 285, 361,
400
inclination (*Neigung*), xiii–xiv, 11,
44, 47, 123–124, 235, 250–275,
284–285, 295, 329–330, 393–397, 400
incompatibilism, 173–182
incontinence, 52, 66
Incorporation Thesis, 51–53, 73
India, 299
individual concepts, 184–185
individual nature (*Naturell*), 205,
387
individualism, xiv, 203–204, 281,
289, 292, 316, 319, 340–341,
411
rugged, 94–97
inequality, social, 293–295, 340; *see
also* equality; injustice, general
infanticide, 370
ingratitude (*Undankbarkeit*), 265,
272, 274, 288, 324, 400; *see also*
gratitude
injustice, general (*allgemeine Un-
gerechtheit*), 7–8, 138, 273–274
innate, 59–60, 286, 349, 401–402
inner worth, 21–22, 133–139
innocence (*Unschuld*), 20, 23, 44–47,
228–230, 237
instinct, 234–235; *see also* animality,
predisposition; God, voice of

intention, 173
interdependence, human, 94–97
interest, 53–54, 260–262, 290
    pathological/practical, 54; see also
        self-interest
internalism/externalism, 129
intimacy, 277–282, 316, 398–399
Irwin, Terence, 352
Islam, 390

Jachmann, Reinhold Bernhard, 411
Jacobs, Brian, xvi
Jauch, Ursula, 340
jealousy (Eifersucht), 264, 268, 275
Jones, Karen, 372
Judaism, 403
judgment (Urteil), political, 417
    practical, 151–152, 332–333, 343,
        417; see also casuistry
    reflective, 208
    teleological, xxii–xiii, 9, 85, 215,
        226–227, 289; see also ends,
        natural
    teleology, natural; theoretical,
        176
Julius Caesar, 372
justice (Gerechtigkeit), 412; see also
    right

Kagan, Shelly, 369, 372, 414
Kant, Immanuel
    development of his ethical thought,
        5–8, 9–13, 191–196, 321
    doubtful role regarding Hippel's
        treatise on the civil advance-
        ment of women, 340
    ethical theory, 321–336
    ethical writings, 10–13
    favorite idea, 208–215
    fundamental moral philosophy,
        17–192
    interest in natural teleology, 215–
        225
    lectures on anthropology, 202–203
    man of science, 11–12, 318
    never traveled outside East Prussia,
        386
    philosophy of history, 207–215,
        226–249, 300–320
    relation to Herder, 226–233
    representative of the Enlighten-
        ment, 1–11
    sad correspondence with Maria
        von Herbert, 397
    theory of human nature, 193–207,
        250–300
    views on various moral and politi-
        cal topics, 2–8
    works, xvi–xix.
Kemal, Salim, 405
Kersting, Wolfgang, 378
kindness, see charity
Kitcher, Philip, 388
Kleingeld, Pauline, 387, 404
Klemme, Heiner, 387
Köhl, Harald, 385, 388
Korsgaard, Christine, 87, 108, 127,
    141, 312, 346, 347–348, 354,
    355, 357, 358, 360, 361, 362–
    263, 367, 369, 373, 375, 384,
    398, 407
Kosman, L. A., 416
Kraus, Christian Jacob, 406
Kristinsson, Sigurdur, 345

La Mettrie, Julien Offray, 207
labor, 236, 244, 248
Lambert, Johann Heinrich, 412
lasciviousness (Lusternheit), 235
latitude (Spielraum, latitudo), 44, 94,
    324–325, 329, 344, 359
Lavater, Johann Kaspar, 201
law (Gesetz), 164–165, 348–349
    author/legislator of, 81, 130, 160,
        160, 315, 317, 410
    empirical, 217

natural, 59, 79–80, 172
normative, 79–80, 172–182, 379–
380
positive, 23
Roman, 412
Leibniz, Gottfried Wilhelm, 184,
376–377
Letztbegründung, 381
liberalism, 166, 308, 316
libertarianism, 378
liberty, *see* freedom
liberty equality fraternity, 335
Liddell, Brendan, 383
life, furthering of, 85–86
Limmer, Seth, 371
Lo, P. C., 362
Locke, John, 69–70, 248, 353, 403
London, Jack, 116
Longuenesse, Béatrice, 383
Louden, Robert B., 339, 343, 415
love (*Liebe*), 38–40, 95, 161, 256,
262; 265, 269, 271–273, 281,
282, 295, 334
aesthetic, 271
and respect, 272–273, 398
individual as object of, 397–398
mutual, 280
pathological, 38, 271
philanthropic, *see* philanthropy
practical, 38, 270
reciprocal, 278–279
Lucifer, 373
luck, moral, 138
Ludwig, Bernd, 413
Lust (*Wollust*), 140, 324, 402; *see also*
sex
luxury (*Luxus*), 235
lying, 2, 140, 167, 200, 267, 324,
332, 335, 350, 385, 414; *see also*
deception

M1, *see* suicide
M2, *see* promising

M3, *see* rusting talents
M4, *see* refusing to help
Ma, *see* clockwork trains
MacIntyre, Alasdair, 10, 26–28,
330–331, 342, 343, 344, 356,
415–417
Mackie, John L., 77, 129, 350–351,
355, 367
majority (*Mündigkeit*), 305–306, *see*
also enlightenment
malice (*Bosheit*), 265, 275, 400
Mandeville, Bernard, 9, 160, 341–
342, 391
market, 170
marriage (*Ehe*), 257–259, 279, 399
Marx, Karl, 14, 225, 232, 244–249,
262, 294, 298, 319, 342, 391,
404
materialism, historical, 244–249
maxim, xxi–xxii, 40–42, 51–55,
164–165, 348–349, 357
fundamental, 284
maxims of thinking, 302–303, 374
Mayo, Bernard, 416
Mb, 105–106, 108
Mb', 106
McDowell, John, 151, 372, 416
Mc, 105–196
Md, *see* deposits
meanness (*Niederträchtigkeit*), 265
means, 54, 61–65, 142–144, 262
Medicus, Fritz, 341
men, 256–257, 272, 279, 404
Mendus, Susan, 340
Menn, Stephen, 399
mental powers (*Gemütskräfte*), 205
merit (*Verdienst*), 136–139, 324, 329
metaphysics of morals, 17, 193–197,
321–333, 338, 383–384,
411–412
methodological individualism, 209,
395
Metz, Thaddeus, xvi

Mill, John Stuart, 41–42, 84, 123,
        132, 346, 348, 356, 357, 366,
        405
Milton, John, 373
misanthropy, 274–275, 282, 291
misology, 71, 236–237, 390
Mk, *see* convenience killing
Mnk, 101
modernity, 1, 226–229
modesty (*Beschiedenheit*), 268–269,
        295; *see also* decorum; propriety
Molière (Jean-Baptiste Poquelin),
        199
money, 42, 141, 253, 261–262, 266;
        see also avarice; greed
Montaigne, Michel Eyquem, 160,
        201
Moore, G. E., 388
moral ambiguity, 265–266
moral feeling, *see* feeling, moral
moral law, 17–19; *see also* Formula
        of Autonomy; Formula of Hu-
        manity; Formula of the Law of
        Nature; Formula of the Realm
        of Ends; Formula of Universal
        Law
    deduction of, 171–182
    formulation of, 182–190, 343
    universal formula of, 187–190
moral philosophy, 3–4, 10
moral realism, 129–130, 157–158,
        162–163, 374–375, 381
moral sense, *see* feeling, moral
moral worth, 27–42, 343, 396, 401
morality, fundamental principle of,
        see moral law
    not more than one, 349
    origin of, 238–240, 295, 316
    theological, *see* theological morality
Motherby, Elizabeth, 397
motivation, 30–35, 285, 348, 363
    overdetermination, 30–35,
        344–345; *see also* incentive

motive (*Bewegungsgrund*), 37, 72,
        111, 361, 363
Mulholland, Leslie, 379, 415
Munzel, Gisela Felicitas, 343
Murdoch, Iris, 373, 411
Musulmänner (so-called, in Nazi
        death camps), 144–145, 371
Mv, *see* vengeance

Nagel, Thomas, 367
naïveté, 268
nation of devils, 323, 413
nations, 205
Native Americans, 3, 299–300, 339
Natorp, Paul, 411
natural selection, 222–225
naturalism, 180–182, 207, 221–222,
        380
nature
    ends of, *see* ends, natural
    epoch of, 296–298, 321, 406
    gifts of, 21–22
    in Rousseau, 291–293
    live according to, 215, 403–404
    state of, 249, 255, 392–393
necessitation, practical, 42–44,
        57–58
necessity, 57–58
Nell, Onora, *see* O'Neill, Onora
neo-Kantian socialism, 319–320, 411
never only as a means, 142–144,
        369–370, 389–390, 406–407
Newton, Isaac, 9, 222
Nietzsche, Friedrich, 162, 201–202,
        239, 371, 373, 376, 387, 391
Nisbet, Hugh Barr, 389, 391
nomads, 392; *see also* pastoral
        economy
nonrational beings, 144, 324, 371;
        see also animals
nothing in vain, 218–221
noumenal self, 173–182, 201–202,
        250; *see also* freedom

NT, NT1, NT2, NT3, *see* teleological judgment, maxims of
nuclear weapons, 378
Nussbaum, Martha Craven, 151, 372

O'Neill, Onora, xvi, 84, 104, 337, 349, 356, 357, 359, 373, 375, 382, 397
obedience, political, 3
objective ground, *see* reasons, objective
objective principle, 76–78
objective value, *see* value, objective
obligation, ground of, 156–163; *see also* duty
Olenni-Tungusi, 255, 395
opinion (*Meinung*), 260, 262–266
organized being, 218–225, 377
original sin, 291
overdetermination, motivational, 33–35

pantheism controversy, 405
paradise, 242–244, 292
Parfit, Derek, 347–348, 367
participation, political, 3, 154
particularism, 150–152, 371–372
Pascal, Blaise, 201
passion (*Leidenschaft*), 252–265; 266–267, 304, 393–397
natural, 253–259
social, 259–265
passive intellect, 390
pastoral economy, 244–249, 255, 392
paternalism, 153, 255, 300, 305, 408
patience, 252
Paton, H. J., 142, 194–195, 343, 344, 356, 357, 369, 382, 383–384, 398
penance, 390–391, 407
perfectibility, 211, 237, 301

perfection, 161–163, 271
moral, 140, 324
natural, 140, 168, 324; *see also* talent
permanent revolution, 333
perpetual peace, 6, 297–298, 338
personal identity, 347–348
personality (*Persönlichkeit*), 115, 118–124, 134, 144
as predisposition, 118–122, 364–366
personification principle, 144
Philanthropin academy, 5
philanthropy (*Menschenliebe*), 35–40, 270, 276, 278
philosopher, 393
philosophy, 301, 304–305
pietism, 11, 250, 318–319
Piper, Adrian, 302, 404–405
Pippin, Robert, 355, 413
Platner, Ernst, 197, 206, 386, 387
Plato, 56, 121, 279, 366, 377, 390, 397–398, 399, 417–418
pleasure/displeasure (*Lust/Unlust*), 50, 54, 271
pluralism, 301–302
podagrist, incontinent, 30, 66
Pogge, Thomas, 376, 413
political correctness, 333
politics, 170
postulate, 132, 366
Potter, Nelson, 346
poverty, 289; *see also* injustice, general
power, 23, 24, 266, 272, 290; *see also* tyranny
power of choice (*Willkür, arbitrium*), 50–60, 235–238, 284, 347
brute/free, 51–52
Powerball Lottery, 96
predisposition (*Anlage*), 118–122, 210–212, 221, 223, 288–289, 293; *see also,* animality; germ; humanity (*Menschheit*); personality

presumption (*Übermut, Anmaßung*),
    21, 264–265, 301
pride (*Stolz*), 263
priestcraft, 237, 305, 315, 390–391
Prince Hal, 369
Prior, Arthur N., 350
progress, 139; *see also* history
Promise Keepers, 333
promising, 40–41, 43, 80, 87–89,
    105–107, 117, 148, 153, 350,
    358
propensity (*Hang*), 283–284, 366
property (*Eigentum*), 89–90
    in land, 245–249, 392–393
    labor theory of, 248–249
    provisional/peremptory, 248–249
propriety (*Sittsamkeit*), 239, 295
prostitution, 258
providence, 9, 210, 215, 218, 231,
    238, 273, 311, 389–390; *see also*
    God; history; theodicy
prudence (*Klugheit*), 28–30, 65–70,
    96, 119, 204–205, 237, 252, 260,
    268, 351, 364, 365, 367, 378
    counsels of, 68–69
psychology, empirical, 197–198; *see*
    also anthropology
public use of reason, 306–309
public, enlightened, 298, 306–309
punishment, 2, 134, 153, 407
purple cows, how not to think about
    them, 352
purposiveness (*Zweckmäßigkeit*), or-
    ganic, 218–225; *see also* ends,
    natural; teleology, natural

questions, casuistical, *see* casuistry

R, *see* right, principle of
races, 205–206
racism, 3, 5, 7, 145, 335, 338–339
rape, 2, 338, 356
rational beings on other planets, 406

rational impartial spectator, 24
rational nature, 118–122; *see also* hu-
    manity, as predisposition
Rawls, John, 2, 96, 337, 338,
    368–369, 374–375
realm of ends (*Reich der Zwecke*), 143,
    165–170, 185, 279, 376–377
reason (*Vernunft*), 198–200, 211–
    212, 227–228, 230–233, 292–
    293, 300–309, 348, 393
    development of, 234–244
    instrumental, xxi, 60–65, 71, 118–
        119, 173, 350–352
    moral, 12, 55–60, 70–75, 250–251
    practical, xxi, 12, 55–60, 65–71,
        119, 351–353
reasons
    agent-neutral/agent-relative, 128,
        355, 367
    expressive, 141–142
    objective, 76–78, 82, 111–114, 131
Reath, Andrews, xvi, 162, 376
Reciprocity Thesis, 171–172
refusing to help, 91–95, 149–150,
    357–358, 375
regulative principles, 216–217
Rehberg, August Wilhelm, 1, 342
relativism, 349
religion, xiv, 6, 281, 283, 316–320,
    408–411
    ethical duty of, 314–315; *see also*
        ethical community; God
religious statutes, 86
representation, political, 3, 154, 308,
    340
repression, 202, 380–381
republic, *see* constitution, republican
resentment, 146–147, 401
resources (*Vermögen*), 253
respect (*Achtung*), 38, 42–47, 53,
    135, 262, 282, 346, 368–369
    for humanity, 144–145; *see also*
        feeling, moral; self-respect

revelation, divine, 227, 230, 316
ridicule (*Verhöhnung, Spottsucht*), 141, 324
right (*Recht*), xx, 91–97, 99, 140, 213, 246–249, 260–261, 296, 300, 321–323, 378–379, 386, 405, 412–413
  concept of, 412
  principle of, xx, 99, 322
right action, in Anglophone moral philosophy, 412
Rissom, Ingrid, xvi
Rivera, Lisa, 372, 415
Rorty, Richard, 10, 342
Rosati, Connie S., 378
Rosen, Allen, 379
Ross, W. D. (Sir David), 342, 343–344, 360, 362, 388
Rossi, Philip, 408
Rousseau, Jean-Jacques, xix, 5–9, 211, 215, 237, 244, 246, 248, 291–293, 295, 332, 341, 342, 377, 393, 395, 403–404
Rovane, Carol, 363
Rumsey, Jean, 396
Russell, Paul, 371
rusting talents, 90–91, 149, 357, 359

Sartre, Jean-Paul, 396–397
Savage, Denis, 409
scandal, 140, 324
Scanlon, Thomas M., 358, 377
Scheffler, Samuel, 349, 371
Schiller, Friedrich, 11, 28–29, 33, 250, 343, 344
Schneewind, Jerome B., xvi, 156, 368, 373, 383, 398
scholar (*Gelehrte*), 137, 307
scholasticism, 18, 204
Schönecker, Dieter, xvi, 346, 379
Schopenhauer, Arthur, 72, 93, 354, 358
Schott, Robin May, 366

Schrader, George A., 375
Schröder, Hannelore, 340, 396
Schultz (or Schulze), Johann, 208, 387–388
Schulz, Johann Heinrich, 177
science, 197–198, 305, 382
scripture, 316
Sedgwick, Sally, 395–396
self-conceit (*Eigendünkel*), 8–9, 11, 47, 138–139, 256, 259, 262–265, 272, 274, 281, 288, 290, 300, 334, 366, 394–395
self-conception, 72–74, 354
self-control, 19, 21–22, 24
self-deception, 45, 243, 265–269 358, 390–391
self-esteem, 212, 241–242, 272; *see also* esteem
self-interest, 28, 93; *see also* interest
self-judge, 140, 324
self-knowledge, 196–202, 269, 399
self-love (*Eigenliebe, Selbstliebe, philautia*), 85, 119, 140, 143, 262, 271, 324, 338; *see also* self-conceit
self-observation, 200–201
self-preference, 108–110; *see also* self-conceit
self-preservation, 116, 394–395; *see also* suicide
self-respect, 263, 368–369; *see also* dignity; humility
self-worth, 73–74, 125–127, 135, 142, 241–242, 251, 265, 287, 369, 407
Seneca, 372
sentimentality, 121–122, 270; *see also* enthusiasm
Sermon on the Mount, 139
servility (*Kriecherei*), 140, 264–265, 324
sex, 2, 140, 238–240, 269, 272, 279, 294, 335, 391, 395–397, 402
  as passion, 256–259

Shaftesbury, Anthony Ashley Cooper, third Earl of, 353
Shakespeare, William, 199, 268–269, 369, 397
shame, 252
Shell, Susan Meld, 389
Sherman, Nancy, 109–110, 360
shopkeeper, 27–32
Sidgwick, Henry, 36, 174, 326–327, 350, 359, 380, 388, 414
Siep, Ludwig, 385
Silber, John R., 400–401, 407
Silver, Long John, 415
sincerity (*Aufrichtigkeit*), 268, 280
Singer, Marcus, 350, 360
Sittlichkeit/Moralität, 239–240
Smith, Adam, 261, 342
Smith, Michael, 352
social science, 341
society, wholly in (*gänzlich in Gesellschaft*), *see* intimacy
sociobiology, 225, 388
Socrates, 151
solipsism, *see* egoism
Sommers, Christina Hoff, 416–417
Sophocles, 385
Sorell, Tom, 345
specification, law of, 216
spite (*Abgunst*), 264, 275, 400
Stark, Werner, 387
state of nations (*Völkerstaat*), 297–298
state of nature (*Naturzustand*), *see* nature, state of
state, political (*Staat*), 228–229, 246–249, 315, 319, 391; *see also* civil society; constitution, political; right
Steinberger, Peter, 417
Stern, Paul, 389
Stevens, Wallace, 328
Stevenson, Robert Louis, 415
stoicism, 160, 162, 215, 250, 378, 393

Strawson, Peter F., 371
strength, moral, 330, 415, *see also* virtue
Sturgeon, Nicholas, 357
sublime (*Erhabene*), 198, 393
suicide (*Selbstmord, Selbstentleibung*), 28, 30, 82–86, 140, 147–148, 152–153, 168, 324, 356, 372
Sullivan, Roger, 343, 351–352, 404
superstition (*Aberglaube*), 262, 266, 302, 318
supreme good (*oberste Gut, bonum supremum*), 312–313
Swift, Jonathan, 215, 342
sympathy (*Mitleid, Mitfreude, Teilnehmung, Sympathie*), 8, 32, 35–37, 77, 121, 140, 269–270, 276, 281, 363, 397
  duty of, 324
synthetic procedure, 19

Tahiti, 231, 299–300
talent, 21, 90–91, 149, 387; *see also* duty, of self-perfection; individual nature; perfection; rusting talents
taste (*Geschmack*), 119, 256, 295, 303–304
Taylor, Charles, 354, 388–389
teleological judgment, 207, 209–225, 357
  maxims of, 218–225
teleology, 9, 26
  immanent/transcendent, 313
  intentional, 217–218
  moral, 309–313, 325–329
  natural, 207, 209–225, 357; *see also* ends, natural; judgment, teleological
temperament, 21, 40, 45, 94, 137, 205, 330–331, 396, 416
temperance, *see* self-control
terrorism, 385

Teuwsen, Rudolf, xvi
theodicy, 9, 311, 389–390; *see also*
    providence
theological morality, 72, 160–163,
    317–318
theology, minimum of, 410
thinking for oneself, 302, 305–306,
    374; *see also* enlightenment
Thomson, Judith Jarvis, 347
trust (*Vertrauen*), 90, 267, 269, 272,
    278
Turgot, Anne-Marie-Robert, 342
Tuschling, Burkhard, 404
tutelage (*Unmündigkeit*), 305–306,
    405
two standpoints, 109, 174–182, 204,
    250, 382–383; *see also* freedom;
    noumenal self; self-preference
tyranny (*Herrschsucht*), 253, 260–
    261, 266–267, 272, 289–290,
    397

Ulpian, 140
unconscious mind, 202, 380–381
universality, 57–58
universalizability, 79–111, 139, 355–
    360, 372
  contradiction in conception (CC)
    test for, 84–90, 113, 165, 357
  contradiction in volition (CW)
    test for, 84, 90–97, 106, 113,
    165
  false negatives, 105–107, 164
  false positives, 84, 102–105
  logical/practical interpretations
    of, 87–90
  problems with, 97–107
unsociable sociability (*ungesellige
    Geselligkeit*), 213–215, 247, 271,
    273, 274–275, 282, 289, 308,
    334, 404
utility, 204
utopianism, moral, 384–385

value, objective, 46, 111, 142, 147,
    162; *see also* end in itself; good;
    moral realism; perfection
van der Linden, Harry, 411
vanity (*Eitelkeit*), 262, 304
Velkley, Richard L., 390, 404, 408
vengeance (*Rache*), 99
vice (*Laster*), 324
virtue (*Tugend*), 266, 268, 268–269,
    277, 321, 329–333 344, 415–
    416
  collective pursuit of, 313–320
  duties of, 323–329, 344
  role in friendship, 277, 280–281
  value of, 40–42
virtue ethics, 331–333, 416–417
virtues, four cardinal, 21–22
Vlastos, Gregory, 397
Voltaire, 136–137
von Wright, Georg Henrik, 382
Vorländer, Karl, 388, 411
Vossenkuhl, Wilhelm, 405

Wallace, James, 416
war, 214, 228, 248, 255–256, 293,
    296–298, 378, 391–392, 394
Ward, Keith, 406
Waxman, Wayne, 397
way of thinking (*Denkungsart*), 205;
    see also character; disposition
wealth, 23, 24, 94–97, 266, 290; *see
    also* avarice; greed; money
weather, 209
Weber, Max, 385
Wedgwood, Ralph, 359
weeping, 252
welfare state, 378
well-being (*Wohl*), 311; *see also*
    happiness
whistleblowers, 307–308
Whiting, Jennifer, 372, 416
wickedness (*Bösartigkeit*), *see* deprav-
    ity; evil

wild lawlessness (*Wildheit*), 402
will (*Wille, Wollen*), 50–60, 83–85, 348, 355–356
  determining grounds of, 111–113
  holy, 60–61, 174, 287, 379, 348–349
  weakness of, 52, 66
Williams, Bernard, 10, 329, 342, 368, 374, 388, 415
Williams, Howard, 340, 395
Williams, T. C., 343
wisdom, 304
  practical, 343
wish (*Wunsch*), 50, 54, 83
Wolff, Christian, 160
Wolff, Robert Paul, 382, 348, 357, 362–363, 372, 380
Wöllner, J. C., 411

women, 3, 5, 256–257, 272, 279, 335, 339–340, 387, 395–397, 404, 405
Wood, Allen W., 87, 178, 287, 337–338, 345, 357, 377, 382, 383, 391, 393, 395, 399, 402, 407, 408, 410, 411, 415
Wood, R., xvi
Wood, S., xvi
worldly knowledge (*Weltkenntnis*), 204, 387

xenophilia, 302, 404–405

Yovel, Yirmiyahu, 387, 388, 406

Zammito, John, 389
Zwenger, Thomas, xv

Made in the USA
Lexington, KY
17 October 2010